Effective Personnel Management

THE WEST SERIES IN MANAGEMENT

Consulting Editors:
Don Hellriegel   *Texas A & M University*
John W. Slocum, Jr.   *Southern Methodist University*

Aldag & Brief	Managing Organizational Behavior
Burack	Personnel Management: Cases and Exercises
Costley and Todd	Human Relations in Organizations, 2d Ed.
Daft	Organization Theory and Design
Downey, Hellriegel, and Slocum	Organizational Behavior: A Reader
Hellriegel, Slocum, and Woodman	Organizational Behavior, 3rd Ed.
Hrebiniak	Complex Organizations
Huse	Organization Development and Change, 2d Ed.
Huse	Management, 2d Ed.
Kelley and Whatley	Personnel Management in Action: Skill Building Experiences, 2d Ed.
Mathis and Jackson	Personnel: Contemporary Perspectives and Applications, 3d Ed.
Morris and Sashkin	Organization Behavior in Action: Skill Building Experiences
Newport	Supervisory Management: Tools and Techniques
Ritchie and Thompson	Organization and People: Readings, Cases, and Exercises in Organizational Behavior, 2d Ed.
Schuler	Effective Personnel Management
Schuler	Personnel and Human Resource Management
Schuler, Dalton, and Huse	Case Problems in Management, 2d Ed.
Schuler, McFillen, and Dalton	Applied Readings in Personnel and Human Resource Management
Veiga and Yanouzas	The Dynamics of Organization Theory: Gaining a Macro Perspective

Randall S. Schuler
NEW YORK UNIVERSITY

Effective Personnel Management

WEST PUBLISHING COMPANY

St. Paul   New York   Los Angeles   San Francisco

To a lot of great people, especially Susan

A study guide has been developed to assist you in mastering concepts presented in this text. The study guide reinforces concepts by presenting them in condensed concise form. Additional illustrations and examples are also included. The study guide is available from your local bookstore under the title, *Study Guide to Accompany Effective Personnel Management,* prepared by Walter Bogumil.

Cover design: Peter Thiel

Production coordination: Cobb/Dunlop Publisher Services, Inc.

Copyright © 1983 by WEST PUBLISHING CO.
50 West Kellogg Boulevard
P.O. Box 3526
St. Paul, Minnesota 55165

Library of Congress Cataloging in Publication Data
Schuler, Randall S.
  Effective personnel management.

  (The West series in management)
  Includes indexes.
  1. Personnel management.   I. Title.   II. Series.
HF5549.S2489   1983   658.3   82-23680
ISBN 0-314-69676-8

Contents

Preface   xvii

**SECTION ONE: UNDERSTANDING EFFECTIVE PERSONNEL
MANAGEMENT**   3

Chapter 1   Effective Personnel Management in Action   5

Critical Issues in Effective Personnel Management   7

Effective Personnel Management   8
Purposes of Effective Personnel Management   8

The Importance of Effective Personnel Management   9
Determining the Effectiveness of Effective Personnel
   Management   11

Functions and Activities of Personnel Management   14
Planning for Human Resource Management   14
Staffing the Personnel Needs of the Organization   15
Establishing and Maintaining Effective Working Relationships   16
Appraising and Motivating Employee Behavior   16
Compensating Employee Behavior   17
Training and Developing Employees   17
Improving the Work Environment   18
Managing Effective Union-Management Relationships   18

Effective Personnel Management in the Organization   18
Personnel Roles   19

Organizing the Personnel Department   21
Personnel in the Organization   21
Centralization versus Decentralization   22
Who's Responsible for Effective Personnel Management?   24

Staffing the Personnel Department   25
Qualities of the Personnel Manager and Personnel Staff   25
Personnel Budgets   26

Effective Personnel Management Jobs For You 26
How Much Do They Pay? 26
Increasing Professionalism in Personnel Management 27
Professional Certification 28

Plan of Book 29
Purposes 29
Themes of This Book 29
For Whom Is This Book Written? 30

Facing the Critical Issues in Effective Personnel Management 30
Case: Setting up the Human Resource Function in a Small Organization 32

SECTION TWO: EFFECTIVE PERSONNEL MANAGEMENT PLANNING 39

Chapter 2 Planning for Personnel Needs 41

Critical Issues in Personnel Planning 43

Effective Personnel Planning 44
Importance and Purposes of EPP 44
Relationships with Other Personnel Activities 45

What Effective Personnel Planning Is About 45
Who's Responsible for EPP? 45
Developing Personnel Planning Strategies 46
Effective Personnel Planning Programs 52

Important Events and Trends in the 1980s Influencing EPP 56
The Population and the Labor Force Characteristics 57
Trends in the Economy 60
Changing Social Values 62
Legislation and Regulation and Governmental Activity 64

Evaluating EPP 65

Facing the Critical Issues in Personnel Planning 65
Case: Dumpitt Waste Disposal Expands 68

Chapter 3 Designing and Analyzing Jobs 73

Critical Issues in Designing and Analyzing Jobs 76

The Job Design and Job Analysis Activities 76
Purposes and Importance 77
Job Design and Job Analysis Relationships 78

Job Design 79
Job Design Qualities 80
Job Design Approaches 83

Time for Job Redesign   87
Selecting a Job Design—A Diagnostic Approach   87
Implementing Job Redesign—A Summary   89

Job Analysis   90
Job Analysis Information   90
Structured Procedures for Analyzing Jobs   91
Methods Analysis in Analyzing Jobs   94
Collecting Job Information for Job Analysis   96

Evaluating Job Design and Job Analysis Activities   98

**Facing the Critical Issues in Designing and Analyzing
   Jobs**   98
Case: Redesign or Relocate?   101

**SECTION THREE: STAFFING THE PERSONNEL NEEDS
OF THE ORGANIZATION**   **105**

Chapter 4   Effective Recruitment   **107**

Critical Issues in Effective Recruitment   110

The Recruitment Activity   110
The Personnel Department-Line Manager Relationship   111
The Organization-Job Applicant Relationship   111
Purposes and Importance of Recruitment   111
The Relationships of Recruitment   112
Legal Considerations in Recruitment   114

Sources and Methods of Obtaining Job Applicants   122
Internal Sources   122
Internal Methods   123
External Sources   125
External Methods   129

Increasing the Pool of Potentially Qualified Applicants   131
The Realistic Job Preview   131
Expanding Career and Job Opportunities   131
Alternative Work Arrangements   133

Evaluating Recruitment   138

Facing the Critical Issues in Effective Recruitment   139
Case: The Lafayette International Soccer Team (LIST)   141

**Chapter 5   Selection and Placement Procedures, Legal
Considerations, and Job Applicant Information**   **151**

Critical Issues in Selection and Placement   153

Selection and Placement   154
Purposes and Importance of Selection and Placement   154

Selection and Placement Relationships with Other Personnel
Activities   154

Legal Considerations   156
Laws and Guidelines Affecting Selection and Placement   157

Selection and Placement Information   162
Organizational Context   163
Job Qualities   163
The Job Applicant   163

Obtaining Job Applicant Information   164
The Selection and Placement Interview   165
Employment Tests   173
The Application Blank   177
Case: Qualified?   180

Chapter 6   Selection and Placement Decisions   **185**

Selection and Placement Decisions   187
The Single Predictor Approach   187
The Multiple Predictors Approach   188
The Assessment Center Approach   189

**Criteria for the Evaluation of Selection and Placement
Procedures**   190
Validity   191
Reliability   195
Base Rate versus Predictor Rate   196
Selection Ratio   197
Costs and Benefits   198

The Selection and Placement Decision   198
Promotion and Transfer Decisions   199

Evaluating Selection and Placement Procedures   202

Facing the Critical Issues in Selection and Placement   202
Case: Multiple Hurdles or Multiple Hindrances?   205

**SECTION FOUR: ESTABLISHING AND MAINTAINING EFFECTIVE
RELATIONSHIPS WITH EMPLOYEES**   **211**

Chapter 7   Communicating with Employees   **213**

Critical Issues in Communicating with Employees   215

Communicating with Employees   216
Purposes and Importance of Communicating with Employees   216
Relationships of Communicating with Employees   218

Issues in Communicating with Employees   219
Organizational Policies and Expectations   220

Content of Communicating with Employees   223
The Value of Effective Upward Communications   223

Skills in Communicating Effectively   225
Barriers to Upward Communication   225
Principles of Verbal Communication   227
Principles of Nonverbal Communication   227
Listening Efficiently   228
Providing Effective Feedback   229

Methods of Communicating with Employees   229
The Organizational Survey   229
Effective Supervisory Communications with Employees   232

Evaluating Communicating with Employees   235
Communications and Productivity   235
Communications and Quality of Work Life   235

**Facing the Critical Issues in Communicating with
   Employees**   236
Case: Not Everything Goes as We Think It Will   238

Chapter 8   Employee Rights   **243**

Critical Issues in Employee Rights   245

Employee Rights   246
Purposes and Importance of Employee Rights   246
Relationships of Employee Rights   248

Employee Rights to Job Security   250
Legal Considerations   250
Employer Strategies for Employee Job Security Rights   253

Employee Rights on the Job   254
Legal Considerations   254
Employer Strategies for Employee Rights on the Job   256

Evaluating Employee Rights Activities   260

Facing the Critical Issues in Employee Rights   261
Case: The Payback   264

**SECTION FIVE: APPRAISING AND MOTIVATING EMPLOYEE
BEHAVIOR**   **269**

Chapter 9   Appraising and Evaluating Employee Performance   **271**

**Critical Issues in Appraising and Evaluating Employee
   Performance**   274

Appraising the Performance of Employees   275
The Importance and Purposes of Performance Appraisal   275
Legal Considerations in Appraising Employee Performance   276

Performance Appraisal as a Set of Processes and Procedures 278
Criteria and Standards 279
Performance Appraisal Forms 279
Sources of Performance Data 284
The Performance Appraisal Interview and Feedback 285
Errors in Gathering Performance Data 287
Matching Purpose with Method 288

Monitoring Performance Processes and Procedures 290

Evaluating PAPPs 290

Facing the Critical Issues in Appraising and Evaluating Employee Performance 291
Case: The Pain of Performance Appraisal 294

Chapter 10   Motivating Employees   **299**

Critical Issues in Motivating Employees 302

Motivating Employees 302
Desired and Undesired Behaviors 302
Purposes and Importance of Motivating Employees 304
Legal Considerations in Motivating Employees 306

Understanding Employee Motivation and Behavior 307
An Expectancy Model of Employee Motivation 307
Motivation-Behavior-Satisfaction Relationships 309
Why Employees Are Not Motivated 309
A Model of the Determinants of Employee Behavior 310

Strategies to Motivate Employees 311
Ignore the Undesired Behavior 311
Recognize, Record, and Establish Rules and Policies 311
Diagnosis and Determination of Causes 314
Control Strategies 315
Preventive Strategies 316

Evaluating Strategies to Motivate Employees 318

Facing the Critical Issues in Motivating Employees 318
Case: Whether to Kick or to Pat 321

SECTION SIX: COMPENSATING EMPLOYEE BEHAVIOR   **327**

Chapter 11   Total Compensation   **329**

Critical Issues in Total Compensation 332

Total Compensation 332
Purposes and Importance of Total Compensation 333
Total Compensation's Relationships with Other Personnel Activities 334

Environmental Impact on Compensation 334
Federal and State Laws 334
Unions 337
The Market 337

The Basic Pay Structure 338
Job Evaluation 338
Determining Job Classes 345
Wage and Salary Surveys 345
Individual Wage Determination 346

Issues in Wage and Salary Administration 347
Participation Policies 348
Pay Secrecy 349
Satisfaction with Pay 349
All-Salaried Work Force 350

Evaluating Total Compensation 350

Facing the Critical Issues in Total Compensation 351
Case: What Motivates Employees? 353

Chapter 12   Performance-Based Pay   **359**

Critical Issues in Performance-Based Pay 361

Performance-Based Pay Systems 362
Conditions When Performance-Based Pay Plans Work Best 363
Importance of Performance-Based Pay 363
Prevalence of Performance-Based Pay Plans 364

Merit Pay Plans 365
Merit versus Cost-of-Living Increases 366

Types of Incentive Plans 367
Individual-Level Incentive Plans 367
Group-Level Incentive Plans 368
Organization-Level Incentive Plans 370

Administrative Issues in Performance-Based Pay 371
Lump Sum Salary Increases 371
Participation in Performance-Based Pay Plans 371

Evaluating Performance-Based Pay Systems 372

Facing the Critical Issues in Performance-Based Pay 374
Case: The Merit Award: A Pat on the Back or a Push Out
   the Door? 377

Chapter 13   Indirect Compensation   **383**

Critical Issues in Indirect Compensation 385

Indirect Compensation 386
The Purposes and Importance of Indirect Compensation 386

Legal and Environmental Impact on Indirect Compensation 387
Environmental Conditions 388
Legal Conditions 388

Protection Programs 389
Public Protection Programs 389
Private Protection Programs 392

Pay For Time Not Worked 395
Off the Job 395
On the Job 395

Employees Services and Perquisites 396

Administrative Issues in Indirect Compensation 396
Determining the Benefits Package 397
Providing Benefit Flexibility 398
Communicating the Benefits Package 398

Evaluating the Benefits of Indirect Compensation 400

Facing the Critical Issues in Indirect Compensation 401
Case: Flowers: Fiasco or Fringes? 405

SECTION SEVEN: TRAINING AND CAREER DEVELOPMENT   **411**

Chapter 14   Training and Developing Employees   **413**

Critical Issues in Training and Development 416

Training and Development 416
The Importance and Purposes of Training and Development 417
Training and Development Relationships with Other Personnel
   Activities 417
Legal Considerations in Training and Development 421

**Determining Training and Development Needs and
   Targets** 422
Organizational Needs Analysis 422
Job Needs Analysis 423
Person Needs Analysis 423
Type of Training Needs Identified 424
Targeting the Types of Training 425

Implementing Training and Development Programs 425
Training and Development Considerations 427
Training and Development Programs 431
Selecting a Program 435

Evaluating Training and Development Programs 437
Evaluating Designs 439

**Facing the Critical Issues in Training and
   Development** 441
Case: A Training Misdiagnosis or Mistake? 444

Chapter 15   Career Planning and Development **451**

  Critical Issues in Career Planning and Development 453

  Career Planning and Development 453
  The Purposes and Importance of Career Planning and
    Management 454
  Relationships of Career Planning and Development 455

  Organizational Career Development Programs 458
  Career Pathing 458
  Success without Promotion 459
  Career Stress Management 459

  Your Career Planning Activities 461
  Personal Appraisal and Career Thinking—Step 1 462
  Identify Types of Jobs, Organizations and Industries—Step 2 463
  Prepare for Organizational Life—Step 3 464
  Getting Job Offers—Step 4 465
  Choosing an Offer—Step 5 467
  Doing Well—Step 6 467

  Evaluating Career Planning and Management Activities 469
  The Individual Perspective 469
  The Organizational Perspective 469

  **Facing the Critical Issues in Career Planning and
    Development** 470
  Case: Retired on the Job: Career Burnout or the Nonmotivated
    Employee? 472

SECTION EIGHT: IMPROVING THE WORK ENVIRONMENT **479**

Chapter 16   Improving Productivity and Quality of Work Life **481**

  Critical Issues in Improving Productivity and QWL 484

  Productivity and Quality of Work Life 485
  The Importance and Purposes of QWL and Productivity 485
  Relationships of QWL and Productivity 488

  Programs for QWL Improvement 491
  Quality Circles 492
  Semiautonomous Work Groups 494
  Organizational Restyling 495
  The Tarrytown Project—A Case Example in QWL
    Improvement 498

  Programs for Productivity Improvements 499
  Task Changes 500
  Automation 504
  Office Design 505
  Delta: The World's Most Profitable Airline—A Case Example
    in Productivity Improvement 506

Evaluating QWL and Productivity Programs 507
QWL Programs 507
Productivity Programs 507

Facing the Critical Issues in Improving Productivity and QWL 508
Case: The 25% Solution: A Case in Organization Productivity 510

Chapter 17 Improving Safety and Health 517
Critical Issues in Improving Safety and Health 520

Occupational Safety and Health in Organizations 521
What Is Occupational Safety and Health? 521
Importance and Benefits of Improving Safety and Health 521
Model of Occupational Safety and Health 522
Safety and Health's Relationships with Other Personnel Activities 522

Legal Environment of Safety and Health 524
Occupational Safety and Health Act of 1970 524
Legal Responsibility for Safety and Health: Who Has It? 526

Sources of Safety and Health 526
Factors Affecting Occupational Accidents 527
Factors Affecting Occupational Diseases 528
Factors Causing a Low Quality of Work Life 531
Sources of Organizational Stress 532

Safety and Health Strategies for Improvement 534
Safety and Health Rates 534
Strategies for Improving Occupational Safety and Health in the Physical Work Environment 536
Strategies for Improving Occupational Safety and Health in the Sociopsychological Work Environment 539

Evaluating Safety and Health Activities 540
Evaluating the Occupational Safety and Health Administration 540
Evaluating Organizational Safety and Health Activities 541

Facing the Critical Issues in Improving Safety and Health 542
Case: The Reluctant Employee 544

SECTION NINE: UNION–MANAGEMENT RELATIONS 549

Chapter 18 Unionization of Employees 551
Critical Issues in the Unionization of Employees 554

Unionization of Employees 554
Importance and Purposes of Unionization 554
Relationships of Unionization with Other Personnel Activities 556

**The Legal Framework for Unionization and Collective
  Bargaining** 557
Railway Labor Act 557
National Labor Relations Act 558
Labor-Management Relations Act 558
Labor-Management Reporting and Disclosure Act 559
Federal Employee Regulations 559
State and Local Employee Regulations 561
Court Decisions 561

The Attraction of Unionization 562
The Decision to Join a Union 562
The Decision Not to Join a Union 565

The Development and State of Unionization 566
The Early Days: Tough Times 566
The Recent Days 567
Structure of Unionization in America 570
Operations of Unions 572

The Organizing Campaign 572
The Campaign to Solicit Employee Support 573
Determination of the Bargaining Unit 575
The Preelection Campaign 575
Election, Certification, and Decertification 577

Evaluating the Unionization of Employees 580

**Facing the Critical Issues in the Unionization of
  Employees** 580
Case: A Bad Place to Work 583

**Chapter 19 Collective Bargaining, Negotiating, Conflict
Resolution, and Contract Administration**   **589**

**Critical Issues in Collective Bargaining, Negotiating,
  Conflict Resolution, and Contract Administration** 592

The Collective Bargaining Process 593
Union-Management Relationships 593
A Model of the Bargaining Process 595
Management Strategies 598
Union Strategies 599
Joint Union-Management Strategies 600

Negotiating the Agreement 601
Negotiating Committees 601
The Negotiating Structure 601
Issues for Negotiation 602

Conflict Resolution 608
Strikes and Lockouts 608
Mediation 609
Arbitration 609

Contract Administration 609
Grievance Procedures 610
Grievance Issues 611
Management Procedures 613
Union Procedures 613

Public-Sector Collective Bargaining 614

Evaluating the Effectiveness of the Entire Union-Management Relationship 617
Effectiveness of Negotiations 617
Effectiveness of the Grievance Procedure 617

Facing the Critical Issues in Collective Bargaining, Negotiating, Conflict Resolution and Contract Administration 618
Case: Quality Circles or Quality Problems 622

SECTION TEN: TRENDS AND COMPARISONS 629

Chapter 20 Effective Personnel Management in the 1980s 631

Critical Issues for Personnel Management in the 1980s 633

Trends in Personnel Management 633
Planning for Personnel Management 633
Staffing 634
Establishing Relationships with Employees 635
Appraising and Motivating Employee Behavior 636
Compensating Employee Behavior 636
Training and Career Development 638
Improving the Work Environment 638
Union-Management Relations 639

Personnel Practices in Other Countries 641
Japan 641

Evaluating Personnel Management in the 1980s 643

Facing the Critical Issues of Personnel Management in the 1980s 643

Appendix A Legislation and Court Decisions Affecting Effective Personnel Management A-1

Appendix B Activities Handled by Personnel Departments A-10

Appendix C Journals in Personnel and Human Resource Management A-13

Appendix D How to Prepare a Resume A-16

Appendix E Measuring the Costs of Absenteeism A-19

Glossary G-1

Name Index I-1

Subject Index I-3

Preface

The challenge, importance, and excitement of personnel management have never been greater. Organizations today are facing a crisis in productivity and a level of international trade competition never before experienced. Together these are threatening the very survival of many organizations. At the same time, organizations are being asked to deliver an increased quality of work life to employees and comply with an extremely intricate and complex set of laws, regulations and court decisions. Although effectively dealing with the crisis in productivity is difficult enough, organizations also have to deal effectively with the demand for a high quality of work life and comply with an extensive network of laws, regulations, and court decisions. Thus what is facing most organizations is an almost impossible situation.

It is this almost impossible situation that is creating such an exciting time for personnel management. This is because "people" are at the heart of these three issues: productivity, quality of work life, and legal compliance. Organizations that do a better job in managing their people, their human resources, are more likely to be more effective in solving their productivity crisis, in creating a high quality of work life, and in complying with the network of laws, regulations, and court decisions.

Since the essence of personnel management is managing people, personnel management has the capacity to play a very significant role in the survival and operating effectiveness of organizations. The more effectively personnel management is done, the more likely the organization will survive and even flourish. Effective personnel management can mean effective organizations.

How can personnel management be effective? It can be effective by having the appropriate knowledge related to the three critical issues and by being able to implement this knowledge in an organization. Since this textbook is about effective personnel management, it attempts to provide you with both the appropriate knowledge and an awareness of how to implement this knowledge in organizations. It does this through a dynamic, real-life, hands-on, bottom-line, applications orientation. This is done through several features of this textbook. These features include:

Personnel in Action Inserts   Managing people is a dynamic, challenging process. To help capture this process many real life examples are provided in each chapter. These examples are taken from sources such as *The Wall Street Journal, Business Week,* and *The New York Times.* These examples illustrate how personnel activities are actually implemented in organizations. They also provide you with a great deal of knowledge of the current laws, regulations, and court decisions.

Cases   At the end of each chapter is a short case you can use to apply the material in the chapter. To further enhance the applicability of the material, a *For Your Career* feature is at the end of each chapter. This feature suggests how the material in the chapter relates or could relate to your career in organizations.

Appendixes   The material in the appendixes includes a summary of the most relevant laws, regulations, and court decisions in personnel; names and addresses of useful personnel journals, newsletters, and associations; an example of how to write a resume; a listing of the types of jobs in personnel; and an example of how to determine the cost of absenteeism for an organization.

To complement this bottom-line, applications orientation, a concern-for-the-reader orientation is used. This concern is reflected in several other features of this textbook:

Margin Notes   These notes are found in the margins in every chapter. They are used to summarize, outline, and philosophize about the material.

For Your Career   For Your Career inserts are a further way of summarizing material in the chapter, adding material to further clarify a concept in the chapter, and providing you with more career-relevant information.

Critical Issues   A feature which is used to support the applications orientation as well as the reader orientation is called Critical Issues. Based upon a survey of personnel managers, each chapter begins with what are the major or critical issues on that topic facing personnel managers. We return to these at the end of each chapter. By that point you should be comfortable responding to these issues. Short responses, however, are provided, based upon my discussions with the personnel managers.

Key Concepts and Discussion Questions   These are provided to help give further focus to what's critical in personnel and in each chapter specifically. If you know these well and are able to respond to the Critical Issues, you have mastered many of the essential points of the chapter.

Glossary   The glossary is meant to provide further clarification and uniformity to the key concepts being used throughout this textbook.

As you read through this textbook you will also note that the references used are very current, many since 1980. This is done because personnel is such a dynamic field. By doing this, such current issues as comparable worth, employee rights, quality circles, and court decisions such as *Gunther* can be discussed in depth. Consequently you'll have not just the knowledge about personnel management, but the most current, relevant, and critical knowledge possible.

Although I had a great deal of pleasure writing this book, it is written for you. I hope you enjoy it as well as learn from it.

Acknowledgments

This book was written with a great deal of cooperation and assistance of many individuals and organizations. Those who helped with their many good ideas include several personnel practitioners, namely, Gary Turner, Suzanne Forsyth, Jim Marsh, Wes Baynes, Jim Handlon, Jim Wilkins, Charles Theisen, Paul Schaller, Mary Schaller, and Mary Miner. In addition to these practitioners were many others at the Washington Personnel Association who provided tidbits of information along the way. Several academics who shared their invaluable ideas include Jan Muczyk at Cleveland

State; John Blair at Texas Tech; George Biles at American University; Craig Schneier at the University of Maryland; Susan Jackson at the University of Maryland; Bill Todor at Ohio State; Dan Dalton at Indiana University; Richie Freedman at New York University; Greg Oldham at the University of Illinois; Stuart Youngblood at Texas A&M; and Jerry Hurwitz at the University of Maryland.

The following individuals also provided many good ideas and suggestions in their roles as reviewers of the manuscript prior to publication:

Walter Bogumil   *University of Central Florida*

Stuart A. Youngblood   *Texas A & M University*

Anne Harper   *Humber College (Canada)*

Jan Muczyk   *Cleveland State University*

Ray Montagno   *Ball State University*

Douglas W. Naffziger   *Western Illinois University*

Kenneth Kovach   *George Mason University*

E. L. Roach   *Algonquin College (Canada)*

Cathy Rudolf   *The University of Texas at Arlington*

Paul Keaton   *University of Wisconsin-LaCrosse*

Special thanks go to the fine secretarial and support services staff at the University of Maryland. They made the preparation of this manuscript a great deal easier. Those who provided the majority of the help are Kate Smith, Ellen Horan, Bernadette Mills, Chien Hu, Nona Martin, Kathy McKinley, Susan Flynn, and Jeanne Fineran.

Special thanks also go to several individuals who contributed cases for each of the chapters. They are Cathy Rudolf at the University of Texas at Dallas; Bill Fitzpatrick at the University of Maryland; John Slocum at Southern Methodist University; Don Hellriegel at Texas A&M; George Biles at American University; Al Randolph at the University of South Carolina; Jerry Hurwitz at the University of Maryland; Dan Dalton at Indiana University; Charles Thomas; and Magid Mazen at Illinois State University.

Critical to adding all the realism and applications orientation to this book is obtaining permission to use the materials from so many publishers. Jeannie Williams endured this tedious but critical process so that the project could be completed on time. Also invaluable to the text and the total package were the contributions of Steve Fitch. He wrote the discussion questions for each chapter, the glossary, and aided in the preparation of the extremely thorough Instructor's Manual. He also provided several good ideas for the format of each chapter.

Finally I wish to thank those who have been with me on several projects with West. Again they have been outstanding. Without the dedication and professional competence of Richard T. Fenton, sponsoring editor, and Sherry H. James, production editor, this book would not have been possible.

Randall S. Schuler

Effective Personnel Management

Understanding Effective Personnel Management

Chapter One
Effective Personnel Management
In Action

Chapter Outline

Critical Issues in Effective Personnel Management

Effective Personnel Management
Purposes of Effective Personnel Management
Importance of Effective Personnel Management
Determining the Effectiveness of Effective Personnel Management

Functions and Activities of Effective Personnel Management
Planning for Human Resource Management Needs
Staffing the Personnel Needs of the Organization
Establishing and Maintaining Effective Working Relationships
Appraising and Motivating Employee Behavior
Compensating Employee Behavior
Training and Career Development
Improving the Work Environment
Managing Effective Union Management Relationships

Effective Personnel Management in the Organization
Personnel Roles

Organizing the Personnel Department
Personnel in the Organization
Centralization versus Decentralization
Who's Responsible for Effective Personnel Management?

CHAPTER **1**

Effective Personnel Management in Action

Staffing the Personnel Department
Qualities of the Personnel Manager and Personnel Staff
Personnel Budgets

Effective Personnel Management Jobs For You
How Much Do They Pay?
Increasing Professionalism in Personnel Management
Professional Certification

Plan of Book
Purposes
Themes of This Book
For Whom Is This Book Written?

Facing the Critical Issues in Effective Personnel Management

Summary

Key Concepts

Discussion Questions

Case

For Your Career

Endnotes

Personnel in the News

Quality Concern

Quietly, almost without notice, a new industrial relations system with a fundamentally different way of managing people is taking shape in the U.S. Its goal is to end the adversarial relationship that has grown between management and labor and that now threatens the competitiveness of many industries. (Reprinted from p. 85, May 11, 1981, issue of Business Week *by special permission,* © *McGraw-Hill, Inc., New York, N.Y. 10020. All rights reserved.)*

People Count

It assumes that people want to work together in common purpose, and it challenges the sharp distinction, inherent in classical Western industrial organization, between the actual work of producing goods or services and the planning and coordination of that work. Today's employees, it holds, are able and willing to participate more fully in management decisions at all levels, and the organization that does not let them do so not only turns them off but also wastes valuable intelligence.

No area of management has been more neglected than improving the way people work together. There have always been "people managers" with the gift of inspiring loyalty and outstanding performance (though many more executives only think themselves good people managers). And what Thomas J. Peters of McKinsey & Co. calls "obsessive attention to people in every aspect of the business" is a fundamental part of the culture at well-run companies as diverse as IBM, Delta Airlines, Hewlett-Packard, and Walt Disney Productions. (From Charles Burck, "Working Smarter," p. 70, June 15, 1981, in Fortune *Magazine* © *1981 Time, Inc. All rights reserved.)*

Productivity Matters

Trying to make up for lost time, American companies are making significant investments in new technology to improve productivity, according to a survey conducted by Productivity, *a monthly newsletter. The United States has lagged behind its most productive foreign competitors in capital investment for years. Now, as the responses from more than 500 of* Productivity's *subscribers reveal, companies plan on taking advantage of new technology that offers real promise for boosting productivity. The following statistics illustrate where money will be invested:*

(1) Computers. *More than 70% of the respondents said their organizations will spend more on computers. Fifty-five percent said they will invest more in computer systems that automate the design and manufacture of products.*

(2) Robots. *Thirty percent of the respondents said their companies will invest more in robots. Despite their productive potential, robots have made only a minor impact on the American workplace—but experts expect this to change over the next decade.*

(3) Other Equipment. *More than a third of the respondents said they will increase investment in new plants; 60% said they will put more money into new equipment in general.*

While it appears that American corporations are prepared to make major invest-ments in new technology, the majority of respondents to the survey believe that people are the most essential ingredient in any productivity improvement program.

The newsletter asked its subscribers to rank a variety of approaches according to their effectiveness in boosting productivity. Employee participation programs were ranked as the most powerful, followed by better communications, better labor-man-agement relations and increased training. More than 50% of the respondents said employee participation programs are in operation at their firms. Sixty-eight percent reported that their companies will invest more in such programs. (From p. 666, September 1981 issue of Personnel Journal. *Reprinted by permission of the publisher.)*

These few paragraphs reflect two very significant points: (1) Productivity is a dominant concern in organizations today. In fact, it is hard to find a manager in any organization who is not concerned with productivity. (2) People are vital resources who are the critical bridge in achieving productivity improvements. These two points are extremely significant for us because they make the effective management of people necessary in today's organizations, and this is what effective personnel man-agement is all about.[1] Consequently, personnel management is growing in impor-tance in many organizations because it is widely recognized by them as the way to get increased productivity. In addition it is seen as the way to meet the growing needs of people in organizations for a good quality of work life. This recognition of the impor-tance of personnel management makes this book vital to your career in organizations. This recognition also raises some very critical issues in the minds of personnel manag-ers today.

> Effective personnel management benefits organizations, people, and society.

CRITICAL ISSUES IN EFFECTIVE PERSONNEL MANAGEMENT

1. *How can personnel management demonstrate its worth to the rest of the organiza-tion; that is, really be "effective" personnel management (EPM)?*
2. *How can EPM benefit individuals in organizations?*
3. *What can be done to get organizations to recognize the importance of EPM?*
4. *What role are you going to play in EPM?*

In order to address these critical concerns, you need to know "what" personnel departments in organizations do and "how." Describing and examining in detail the "what" and the "how" are what this book is about. But first the essence of what effective personnel management departments do must be defined. After that, this chapter briefly examines the functions and activities of personnel management and the people who perform them. An example of the roles that personnel can play in organizations is also examined. The following section addresses the jobs that are available to you in the field of personnel. The chapter ends with a discussion of the Critical Issues, the book's plan, its themes and philosophy, and what it intends to accomplish.

EFFECTIVE PERSONNEL MANAGEMENT

Of great importance to organizations today is how to effectively utilize their human resources. As such, there is viability for effective personnel management.

Effective personnel management is the recognition of the importance of an organization's work force as vital human resources and the utilization of several functions and activities to ensure that they are used effectively and fairly for the benefit of the individual, the organization, and society.

Purposes of Effective Personnel Management

Three key
purposes:
▪ Productivity
▪ Quality of
   work life
▪ Legal
   compliance

In the definition of effective personnel management (EPM), three major purposes are identified. Although some organizations may value one purpose above the others, increasingly these purposes are becoming directly tied to the goals and purposes of the entire organization. The three purposes are:

Productivity.   Without doubt this purpose of EPM is one of the most important goals of organizations:

> Top management has given productivity the highest priority, declares Douglas D. Danforth, vice-chairman of Westinghouse Electric Corp.[2]

Although individual personnel managers and personnel specialists can do little to influence the capital, material, and energy aspects that contribute to productivity, they can uniquely influence the utilization of the work force, top management's human resource philosophy, and the personnel practices of the organization that also contribute to productivity. Thus personnel has a unique and timely opportunity for improving productivity.[3]

Quality of Work Life (QWL).   The dissatisfaction of industrial—or clerical—work is no longer disputed. Today's employees need and value a greater level of involvement in their jobs than was previously assumed by management. They also have a greater need to participate in decisions that affect them. In addition, they have a need to rise above routine tasks and face challenging tasks, tasks that allow for personal growth. Other needs and values of today's employees (the New Breed) include

- A need for rewards geared to accomplishments
- A need for organizational recognition of his or her contributions
- Decreasing concern for job security and stability
- A view of leisure as being more important than work

- A need to perform work that is challenging and worthwhile
- Stronger employee identification with his personal role than with his work role
- A need for communication from management regarding what's going on in the company[4]

These are the needs and values of today that are driving the demands of employees. It is the meeting of these needs and values that can create a high quality of work life and satisfaction for the "New Breed." Not meeting these needs and values produces a low quality of work life and dissatisfaction for the New Breed. Ignoring these needs and values also appears to be counter to an organization's productivity goal:

> Every significant poll or survey further underscores the likelihood of a payoff. A major survey of U.S. workers' attitudes toward productivity conducted by Gallup for the U.S. Chamber of Commerce in 1979 found "the overwhelming majority believe that if they are more involved in making decisions that affect their job, they would work harder and do better."[5]

Legal Compliance.   Organizations must comply with many laws, executive orders, guidelines, and court decisions in managing their employees. A summary listing of many of them is found in Appendix A. These laws and regulations affect almost all of the functions and activities utilized in EPM. EPM, however, must be constantly concerned not only in complying with the current laws and regulations and new ones that are promulgated frequently. If personnel fails to keep abreast of what's happening, and aware of what organizations must comply with, organizations may find themselves paying out large sums of money for lawsuits and fines.[6] Fortunately personnel can avoid these costs by constantly monitoring the legal environment for any changes, by complying with those changes, and by practicing effective personnel management. Many examples of costly lawsuits and effective personnel practices to avoid them are provided throughout the text. All of these examples highlight just one of the four reasons effective personnel management is so important in organizations today.

THE IMPORTANCE OF EFFECTIVE PERSONNEL MANAGEMENT

Although there are many reasons for practicing effective personnel management, four major ones are (1) the costs associated with human resources, (2) the productivity crisis, (3) the increasing pace and complexity of social, cultural, legal, and educational changes, and (4) the symptoms of dysfunction in the work place.

Human Resource Costs.   Today corporations realize that it pays to be concerned with how they manage their human resources.

> Top management has finally realized that the people costs are as important as other costs. Management realizes that its important assets are not simply financial resources but having the people on hand at the right time and the right place to make a thing go.[7]

(By the way, for those of you who can "make a thing go," the rewards are attractive. A recent study by Heidrick & Struggles, Inc., a Chicago-based executive search firm, indicates that the average salary of top-level, human-resource executives is approximately $80,000.)

The positive results from personnel activities designed to manage and develop human resources effectively are significant reductions in accidents, absenteeism, and error rates and significant increases in morale, quality of the product or service, and productivity and profits, their important byproducts.[8] For example:

> After running several surveys to measure employee attitudes and morale, Ruben Krigsman, manager of personnel research at Union Carbide Corporation, instituted several new training programs and reorganized the workplace which gave the blue-collar workers more responsibility. The result? In just three months, productivity soared by 25%; the amount of finished goods passing inspection jumped from 50% to 80% and absenteeism dropped from 5% to 3%.[9]

The three most productive nations are:
- United States
- USSR
- Japan

The Productivity Crisis.   During the 1960s, productivity in the United States increased at an annual rate of about 3 percent. By 1973 it was nearly zero. It fell sharply in 1974.[10] From 1973 to 1978, the increase in the annual rate of productivity in major industrial states averaged 3.1 percent in Japan, 3.2 percent in West Germany, and 0.4 percent in the United States. In addition, the average Japanese auto worker produces between forty and fifty cars a year, compared with twenty-five in the United States and eleven in West Germany. This productivity crisis is not only a real threat to the U.S. economy but also underlines the importance of effective personnel management.

> This is so, because to date the more effective management of human resources seems to be the best hope for stopping the slide in productivity. Human resource managers will have an unprecedented opportunity to have the ear of top management if they can propose concrete solutions to these real problems.[11]

The Pace and Complexity of Change.   Several ongoing changes in the cultural and educational levels and social order of the United States have contributed to the concerns of personnel management. For example, because midlife career changes are becoming more common and most occupations require increased knowledge, training and development programs for all employees have developed rapidly. Many organizations, however, claim that during the 1980s they will still face a shortage of well-qualified middle managers and a surplus of unskilled college graduates. Yet during the 1980s the group of workers in the eighteen to twenty-four age group will decline. This will result in too few needed young workers and too many middle-aged workers with frustrated career ambitions.

In 1940 the U.S. Department of Labor was enforcing 16 statutes and executive orders affecting personnel practices. By 1960 the number had grown to 40, and by 1980 there were no fewer than 130.[12]

In 1952 women made up less than 33 percent of the work force. Today they make up almost 50 percent. The change in the percentage of women in the work force is even more dramatic when 1920 is compared with 1980.

The current work force is generally becoming more knowledgeable and better informed. Whereas in 1970 only one of eight workers had a college degree, in 1980 one of every four workers who entered the labor force had one. These high-quality human resources are potentially more productive. However, this opportunity presents a real challenge to organizations: "As society becomes better informed, it also tends to become more critical, less accepting of authority and more cynical."[13] Young workers appear to be particularly cynical about decisions made by supervisors and correspondingly more resistant to authority. Older workers, however, still tend to "reflect earlier values of society and are, therefore, more inclined to be organization people, to accept authority and to seek primarily the satisfaction of lower level needs at work."[14] Thus the effective management of human resources requires not only knowing how to manage and channel the skills of the young workers but also knowing how to manage a work force with a mixed set of values.

Symptoms at the Work Place.   Rapid social change has been accompanied by changes in the relationship between the worker and the job. Some of the terms used to describe what is happening in the workplace include *worker alienation, boredom,* and *job dissatisfaction.*[15] These symptoms are often associated with decreasing motivation and increasing counterproductive behavior and worker demands on the workplace. Although these symptoms can certainly be found in most workplaces, whether they are factories or offices, public or private organizations, the extent to which these symptoms are reported to exist in the workplace varies greatly.[16]

Determining the Effectiveness of Personnel Management

Now that personnel can show that there are several reasons why it should be important, it must *show* that it can be important. It must show it can be *effective.*

> Perhaps the most damning criticism of the traditional personnel role is the lack of focus on performance. As a service function, the human resources department doesn't have a clear, direct link to the generation of profit—the bottom line. Sales vice-presidents or sales managers can track sales, which link directly to profits. Production vice-presidents or managers can track production cost and volume, both of which relate directly to profits. If you ask the traditional human resources manager how things are going, there is little he can say other than, "Things seem okay; people are smiling." Of course, some measureable aspects—turnover and absenteeism, for example—can be useful barometers, but they are lagging indicators of what's going on. In any event, managers often accept these measures as a cost of doing business instead of viewing them as a way of measuring a company's internal health.[17]

Since the effective management of personnel is vital to an organization, personnel must show how it can be effective.

In reading this statement it is important to realize what the consequence *was* to personnel management for not focusing on performance, for not showing it can be effective. It often brought statements like

> The image of personnel is zero, though some gripes are unjustified. Personnel is reluctant to get rid of its obvious nonperformers. The image of personnel in the community is poor.[18]

But in many organizations and communities today the image of the personnel department is changing. It is changing in large part because personnel is showing that it is effective, that it does have an impact on the "bottom line," that it does influence the profit level of the organization, and that it helps the nonprofit or government organization stay within its budget and/or get more done with less.

FOR YOUR CAREER

Thus effective personnel management means that the functions and activities being utilized by personnel in the management of human resources save money for the profit-oriented organization, resulting in a more profitable company or they help nonprofit-oriented organizations and government agencies to stay within their budgets resulting in a more satisfied public upon which it depends for support.

The questions *now* are *"How* can personnel management show it is effective?" and *"What* are the general indicators personnel can use that will result in EPM?" The answer to the first question: by showing that improvements occur as a direct result of a particular personnel function or activity.[19] For example:

> The Employment Manager has at least four functions which can be quantitatively assessed. The first and most obvious is cost of hiring. We have found that among organizations which do any measuring, this is usually the first one worked on. The manager's job is to set the strategy, train the recruiters and provide a support system. Judgement of a manager's degree of success can be seen in trend lines of cost per hire for different levels and job groups.[20]

In that example the effectiveness of the recruitment activity was demonstrated through its improvement on the costs of hiring. As dollars are saved by the organization's recruiting practice, the more effective is the recruiting activity. This type of analysis can be done with each personnel activity, and we will do this in each subsequent chapter. For now, however, we want to look at the three *general* indicators we will use to demonstrate the effectiveness of the entire personnel management area. Note that, in the recruitment example, the costs of hiring was used as a *specific* indicator to evaluate the effectiveness of just the recruitment activity.

Three measures to show how effective personnel is:
▪ Productivity
▪ QWL
▪ Legal compliance

Productivity Indicators. Productivity, the first general indicator, represents the efficiency with which an organization uses its work force, capital, material, and energy resources to produce its product. Other things being equal, reducing the work force but getting the same output improves productivity. Similarly, if each employee's performance increases, total output increases, and so does productivity. Reducing absenteeism is also a way to increase productivity, as is the reduction in turnover of good employees. Thus the productivity indicators used here to measure the effectiveness of personnel management are

■ Employee performance
■ Employee absenteeism
■ Employee turnover

Quality of Work Life (QWL) Indicators. Although improving the quality of work life may result in increased performance and reduced absenteeism and turnover, its results can also be measured in other ways.[21] For example, the more individual needs and values that are met by the organization, the more likely the work force will be more involved with their jobs, register higher satisfaction with their jobs, supervisors, and coworkers, suffer from less stress, and have fewer accidents and better health. Thus the QWL indicators that can be used to measure the effectiveness of the personnel department are

■ Employee job involvement
■ Employee satisfaction
■ Employee stress
■ Employee accidents and health

Legal Compliance Indicators.   As shown in Appendix A, there are many laws and regulations with which to comply. Failure to comply with them can result in significant settlement costs such as a recent $23 million settlement between Ford Motor Company and the Equal Employment Opportunity Commission (EEOC). Other effects include cancellation of future contracts with the federal government and state and local governments. In addition, individual employees can bring suit against the company for

Exhibit 1.1
Components of Personnel Management and Indicators of Effectiveness

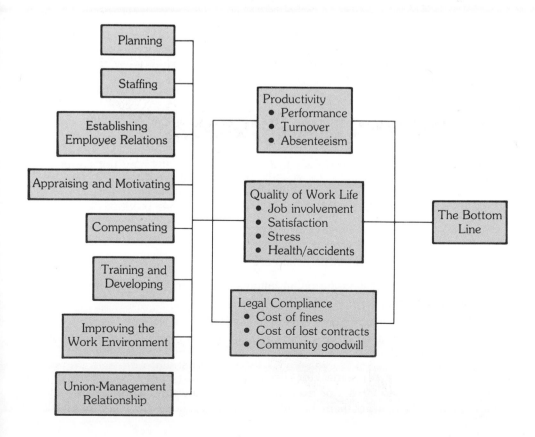

violations of some laws and regulations.[22] Goodwill with potential job applicants and the community can be significantly diminished if a company chooses not to comply with laws and regulations. Thus the legal compliance indicators that can be used to determine the effectiveness of personnel management include

- Cost of fines for law and regulation violation
- Cost of contracts lost for not adhering to laws and regulations
- Community goodwill and general reputation in the community

A summary of these indicators and the eight personnel functions used to influence these indicators is shown in Exhibit 1.1. Since these eight personnel functions are the essence of effective personnel management, it is useful to discuss them now along with the personnel activities in each function. Together, the functions and the activities are the essence of this book.

FUNCTIONS AND ACTIVITIES OF PERSONNEL MANAGEMENT

There are eight major personnel functions. Within each function are activities.

Eight personnel management functions and activities are described in this book. These eight generally include all of the functions and activities that personnel department actually do, as shown in Appendix B.

- Planning for human resource needs
- Staffing the personnel needs
- Establishing effective working relationships
- Appraising and motivating employee behavior
- Compensating employee behavior
- Training and career development
- Improving the work environment
- Managing effective union-management relationships

Although the personnel departments of many organizations may not currently be performing all these functions, the trend is clearly in that direction.

Planning for Human Resource Management

The two major activities in this function are

- Planning and forecasting the organization's short-term and long-term human resource requirements
- Analyzing the jobs in the organization to determine the skills and abilities that are needed and designing jobs to accommodate to the needs of the individual and organization

These two activities are essential for effectively performing many of the other personnel management activities. For example, they help indicate (1) what types of employees and how many of them the organization needs today as well as tomorrow; (2)

how the employees will be obtained (for example, from outside recruiting or by internal transfers and promotions); and (3) the training needs the organization will have. In fact, these two activities can be viewed as the major factors influencing the staffing and development functions of the entire organization.

Although these two activities are so vital in the management of human resources, most organizations have only recently incorporated them into personnel departments. Today, in almost all of the nation's 500 largest industrial companies, personnel managers have responsibility for human resource planning; this was true for only a handful of companies five years ago. Now organizations are increasingly relating human resource planning to corporate goals or strategies. Typical of the trend is Tenneco's requirement that vice presidents submit five-year "executive resources" plans along with five-year business plans:

> If a division, for example, is planning to shift from a marketing to a production orientation, the company vice-president of employee relations must make certain that it is planning not only to develop a large enough production staff to meet the new demands in that area but also to make a suitable reduction of marketing specialists.[23]

Staffing the Personnel Needs of the Organization

Once the organization's human resource needs have been determined, they have to be filled. Thus staffing activities become necessary. These include

- Recruiting job applicants (candidates)
- Selecting from among the job applicants those most appropriate for the available jobs

The organization must cast a wide net for potential employees in order to ensure a full and fair search for job candidates.

> Time was when the organization could rely on "walk-ins" to provide the major source of supply for nonexempt employees: it could choose exempt employees from traditional sources. If a comer was spotted, the organization might carefully tailor the job description so that the requisite experience fit *him*—and probably only *him*—to the job. Now, however, the organization must prepare job descriptions and specify requisite experience and training with care and publicize its openings.[24]

These recruiting procedures apply to external candidates (those not currently employed by the organization) as well as to internal candidates (those who are currently employed by the organization).

After the candidates have been identified, they must be selected. Common procedures used in selection include obtaining completed application forms or resumes; interviewing the candidates; checking education, background, experience, and references; and various forms of testing. Regardless of the exact procedures used, however,

Legal considerations are especially numerous in staffing.

> selection procedures must be based on job-related standards. In other words, any criteria a manager chooses to use—from candidate's experience or education to performance on any preemployment test—must be demonstrably related to job performance.[25]

In other words, selection procedures must result in a match between a candidate's ability and the abilities required by the job.

Establishing and Maintaining Effective Working Relationships

When the organization has obtained the employees it needs, it must take care to bring them into the organization and to provide conditions that will make it attractive for them to stay. A significant part of retaining good employees is communicating with them and respecting their rights. Thus the two major activities in this function are

- Employee communications
- Employee rights

A consequence of wanting to retain good employees is the establishment of a process to orient the employees to the organization's policies and procedures. Thus the organization will communicate these to the employees through formal orientation programs, supervisor communications and formal policies posted or available throughout the organization. In addition, the personnel manager will want to ensure that the employees have a way to communicate with the organization. One way to do this is through organizational surveys.

Increasingly, employees are gaining more rights as employees. Consequently employment decisions such as discharges, layoffs and demotions must be made with care and evidence. It is important that the managers of the organization be aware of all the rights employees have. The personnel manager is in an excellent position to inform other managers (line) of these rights.

It is critical for personnel to stay in touch with the employees in order to be effective.

Appraising and Motivating Employee Behavior

After employees are on the job, it becomes necessary to determine how well they are doing and to reward them if they are doing well. If they are not doing well, it becomes necessary to determine why. This determination may indicate that the reward structure needs to be changed. It may also indicate that employee training is necessary or that some type of motivation should be provided. To these ends this function incorporates these two activities:

- Appraising and evaluating employee behavior
- Analyzing and motivating employee behavior

Although performance appraisal can be painful to both supervisor and employee, it is a critical activity. It is especially critical since legal compliance dictates that employment decisions be made on the basis of performance. For example, if someone is to be selected for a promotion, it should be based on an evaluation of that employee's performance.

For most organizations, firing is not a practical way to deal with problem employees.

Not all employees are "good" ones. Some may be continuously absent, some may be alcoholics, or some may be late to work all the time. With the rise of employee rights, greater social responsibility, and the cost of replacing employees, however, organizations may find it preferable to assist employees in correcting their undesired behavior and motivate them to perform as well as possible rather than to terminate them.

Compensating Employee Behavior

Employees are generally rewarded on the basis of the value of the job, their personal contributions and their performance. Although providing rewards based on level of performance can increase an employee's motivation to perform, many rewards are more generally given on the basis of the value of the job, rather than on the employee's level of performance. However, rewards (namely, indirect benefits) provided just for being a member of the organization are rapidly increasing.

Which form of compensation is most fair? Which form is most effective for the organization? By what methods can jobs be evaulated fairly to determine their value? These questions and others are part of the compensating function which includes

- Administering direct compensation
- Providing performance based pay
- Administering indirect compensation benefits to employees of the organization

None of these activities is easy, but all must be done to ensure the effective use of human resources. They must be done not only to get employees to join the organization, to participate, and to perform but also to determine possible training and development needs.

Training and Developing Employees

Training and developing activities include training employees, developing management, and helping to develop careers. These activities are designed to increase the abilities of the employees of the organization in order to facilitate employee performance. The training and development function includes

- Determining, designing, and implementing employee training and development programs to increase employee ability and employee performance

Employee training and development programs may be seen as activities meant to increase employee performance in the short run, whereas career management can be seen as a way for the employee and the organization jointly to increase employee performance and long-run satisfaction.

Effective organizations provide career management opportunities.

> It is very true, though seemingly trite, to say that the continuity and success of any organization depend to a great extent on its ability to attract, evaluate, develop, utilize and retain well-qualified people at professional and managerial levels. Translated into fewer words, this merely means that a successful organization must have well organized and well administered human resource and *career planning programs?*[26]

Thus the second activity in the training and developing function is

- Designing and providing opportunities for managing careers

Making career information and alternatives available to employees can result in higher employee satisfaction and retention rates. In addition to the organization being concerned about employees' careers, the employees themselves must also be concerned with their careers. Because individual career planning and *self*-responsibility are so critical, aids will be provided for *you* to start this process *now*.

Improving the Work Environment

Two activities in which the employee-management relationship has been crucial for personnel management are

- Improving the physical work environment to maximize employee safety and health
- Improving the work environment, especially in regard to the quality of work life and productivity improvement programs

The federal regulations specified in the Occupational Safety and Health Act of 1970 have special influence in improving the work environment of employees. These improvements directly and positively influence the physical safety and security of employees and their sociopsychological well-being.

QWL is as important to organizations as it is to employees.

Remember that the primary purpose of the improvement activities is to improve organizational conditions to make the work environment better for the employee and the organization, whereas the primary purpose of the training and development activities is employee performance. In practice as well as theory, however, there is some overlap. For example, in many programs designed to improve the work environment, employee performance may increase along with satisfaction, responsibility, and self-control.[27] One of the programs that is aimed at improving both the QWL and productivity is the Quality Circle effort. This, however, is only one of many programs now being used to increase productivity and only one of several to be discussed in Chapter 16.

Managing Effective Union-Management Relations

This function is composed of two sets of activities that relate to how employees organize themselves in dealing with the organization and how the organization bargains and negotiates with its organized employees. Specifically, the activities are

- Understanding the reasons and methods used by employees in organizing
- Bargaining and settling grievances with employees and the organizations representing them

This function is particularly important for organizations that have unionized employees. On one hand, the formal union-management relationship can effectively define the extent to which other personnel functions can be applied to the work force. And on the other hand, the union-management relationship can be instrumental in developing new programs for the improvement of human resources.

Although all these functions and activities are important, not all organizations perform them. Whether or not they do, however, often reflects the importance of personnel in an organization.

EFFECTIVE PERSONNEL MANAGEMENT IN THE ORGANIZATION

Although personnel can be very important, not all organizations have viewed the personnel department as very important. This was, in part, due to the role the personnel department often played in the organization:

There was a time when the personnel director was primarily concerned with only blue-collar workers: he had little effect on company policy(s). He was viewed as little more than a record keeper and director of recreation, one chief duty being to preside at retirement parties.[28]

Today, however, the personnel department in many organizations is much more vital. It is not only performing all eight personnel functions and activities but is performing them at three distinct levels: The *strategic level* (long-term); the *managerial level* (medium-term); and the *operational level* (short-term).[29] Performing personnel activities at all three levels indicates that personnel is influencing what an organization does today as well as tomorrow and that every level of management from the bottom to the top is involved in effective personnel management. The number of personnel functions and activities performed by the personnel department and the levels at which they are performed are reflected in the role personnel plays. And the more roles it plays, the more important personnel is to the organization.

Personnel Roles

There are several roles personnel can play in an organization.[30] The more roles it plays, the more likely it will be effective in (1) improving the organization's productivity, (2) enhancing the quality of work life in the organization, and (3) complying with all the necessary laws and regulations related to human resource utilization.

The four personnel roles are
- Formulator
- Provider and Delegator
- Auditor
- Innovator

The Policy Formulator Role.   One role the personnel department can play is that of providing information to be used by top management (at the strategic level). The specific types of information can include the concerns of the employees and the impact of the external environment.

Personnel staff can also provide advice in the process of policy formulation. The chief executive may still make policy statements, but these could be regarded as drafts of policy. Formal adoption of a final policy can then take place after other executives, such as the personnel manager and line managers, have had a chance to provide their comments. At Honeywell there is an executive employee-relations committee, composed of five operating group vice presidents and five staff vice presidents, that is the senior policy board for employee-relations issues. This committee not only helps ensure extensive informational input into personnel policies but also increases their likelihood of being accepted.

The Provider and Delegator Role.   In reality, personnel programs succeed because line managers (at managerial and operational levels) make them succeed. The "bread-and-butter" job of the personnel department, therefore, is to enable line managers to make things happen. Thus in the more traditional personnel activities, such as selecting, interviewing, training, evaluating, rewarding, counseling, promoting, and firing, the personnel department is basically providing a service to line managers. In addition, the personnel department administers direct and indirect compensation programs. Since the line managers are ultimately responsible for their employees, many of them see these services as useful. The personnel department can also assist line managers by providing information on and interpretation of equal employment opportunity legislation and safety and health standards.

The responsibility of the personnel department is to provide the services needed by the line managers on a day-to-day basis, to keep them informed of regulations and legislation regarding human resource management, and to provide an adequate supply of job candidates for the line managers to select from. But to fulfill these responsibilities, the personnel department must be accessible. When the department is not accessible, the personnel manager loses touch with the needs of line managers. Consider this typical statement made by a line manager: "If only the personnel people would visit us sometime, they might better understand what it is we do."[31] The personnel staff should be as close to where the people and the problems are as possible. This is an organizing concern, so getting the personnel staff close to the action will be discussed in the section on organizing later in the chapter.

The Auditor Role. Although personnel may delegate much of the implementation of personnel activities to line managers, personnel must still be responsible for seeing that activities are implemented fairly and consistently. This is especially true today because of fair employment legislation. Various state and federal regulations are making increasingly sophisticated demands on organizations. Responses to these regulations can best be made by a central group supplied with accurate information, the needed expertise, and the blessing of top management.

Expertise is also needed for implementing many personnel activities, such as distributing employee benefits. And since having personnel experts is costly, organizations hire as few as possible and centralize them. Their expertise then filters to other areas of the organization.

In organizations that have several locations and several divisions or units, there is often tension between the need to implement policy at the point of action (decentralization) and the need to implement it fairly across several divisions of an organization. There is also tension between the need for decentralization and the need for having the expertise necessary to comply with complex regulations and for advising on the best methods for personnel activities.

The Innovator Role. A final important and ever-expanding role for the personnel department is that of providing up-to-date application of current techniques and of developing and exploring innovative approaches to personnel problems and concerns.

> Naturally, the innovative role must be in tune with the times and the set of issues confronting a particular company. In periods of rising inflation and escalating wage and salary demands, the emphasis may be on compensation issues. In times of retrenchment and falling profits, creative work sharing and lay-off plans may be needed.[32]

Today, the personnel-related issues demanding innovative approaches and solutions revolve around how to improve productivity and the quality of work life while complying with the law in an environment of high uncertainty, energy conservation, and intense international competition. How effective an organization is in addressing these issues depends upon how well it organizes and staffs the personnel department.

ORGANIZING THE PERSONNEL DEPARTMENT

For personnel to be effective, organizations must not only allow personnel to play all roles but also allow it to organize well. Several issues related to the organization of personnel include

- The need for the personnel staff to be where the action is and to identify with the organization they are a part of
- The need for a fair and consistent application of personnel policies in the organization, regardless of how small or large and diversified it is
- The need for the views of the personnel department to be an integral part of personnel policy
- The need for the personnel department to have sufficient power and authority to help ensure that personnel policies will be implemented without discrimination, legally and affirmatively
- The need for the personnel department not just to react to personnel crises but to be active and innovative in dealing with human resource management

These five issues, which are the essence of the roles that personnel departments can play, affect the *organization* of personnel and human resources. For example, the personnel department can be organized so that it effectively plays only one of the four roles. Or it can be organized so that it plays two or more roles. The number of roles played often depends on the way top management views personnel activities and what it is willing to let the personnel department do. A key indicator of how top management views personnel is the status it is given in the hierarchy.

Personnel in the Organization

The importance an organization assigns to personnel is reflected in its status in the hierarchy. This in turn helps determine the number of roles personnel plays and the levels at which they are played.

Personnel in the Hierarchy. For the effective fulfillment of the four personnel roles, the personnel department should have its top manager at the top of the organizational hierarchy. James Henderson, the top manager at Cummins Engine Company, Columbus, Indiana, agrees:

> The person who has explicit responsibility for human resource problems should be positioned at a high level in the organization's hierarchy and should not, because of disrespect for the function, be deprived of the status that will make him or her effective.[33]
>
> I have always viewed top management and the personnel function as a partnership. Management is, after all, people. At Cummins the personnel head has always reported to the senior operating officer and has been a part of all major decisions.[34]

Being at the top allows the personnel manager to play a part in personnel policy formulation and to have the power necessary for its fair and consistent implementation. Doubtless, when personnel has this much importance it is likely to be performing all three levels of personnel activity. Yet being at the top of the hierarchy does not address the need for personnel to be where the action is.

Centralization versus Decentralization

The organizing concept of centralization versus decentralization relates to the issue of the balance between getting personnel to where the action is and fairly and consistently applying personnel policies. It is also related to the balance between the benefits of having personnel generalists and of having personnel specialists. **Centralization** means that essential decision making and policy formulation is done at one location (at headquarters); **decentralization** means that the essential decision making and policy formulation is done at several locations (in the divisions or departments of the organization).

With the recent increases in regulatory requirements for use of human resources and the increased expertise necessary to deal with complex personnel functions, organizations are moving away from personnel generalists and toward personnel specialists. And at the same time, organizations, especially larger ones, are moving personnel staff into the organization's divisions. As a result, there are trends to centralize some aspects of personnel and to decentralize others. Paul Corballis, director of corporate employee relations at Pitney Bowes, Inc., describes these events at his company:

> We have been slowly divisionalizing, putting the day-to-day work [personnel] out into the operating divisions. And as we have divisionalized, at the corporate level we have created a group of individual specialties, a pension group, an insurance group, compensation and benefits, and so forth.[35]

For the personnel activities that require expertise, organizations generally hire specialists. But because of the expense, as few specialists as possible are hired. If an organization is large and has several plants or offices or divisions, the specialists are located in one place (at corporate headquarters) but serve all the divisions. The personnel activities requiring less-specialized expertise are staffed by people at the divisional level, thereby increasing the autonomy of the divisions. Thus in a large, multidivision organization (which describes most of the largest industrial, retailing, and financial organizations), there is generally a corporate personnel and human resource department staffed largely with specialists and several divisional personnel departments staffed largely with generalists. The personnel department at headquarters then has two purposes:

Organizations must balance the desire for decentralization with the need for centralization.

- ▪ To develop and coordinate personnel policy for the personnel staff in all locations, including headquarters
- ▪ To execute the personnel functions and activities for all the employees at headquarters

As the divisions grow, they begin to hire their own specialists and to administer almost all their own personnel functions and activities. The result is almost a complete personnel department, similar to what would be found in most organizations without divisions. An illustration of such a department is shown in Exhibit 1.2. The chart shows that a rather complete set of personnel activities is conducted in the Information Group division of Xerox; however, specialists in many of these activities may still be located at

Exhibit 1.2

Personnel Organization of Xerox Corporation's Information Group* (Reprinted, by permission of the publisher, from "Organizing and Staffing the Human Resources Function: A Personnel Symposium," *Personnel*, January/February 1978, p. 19, © 1978 by AMACOM, a division of American Management Associations. All rights reserved.)

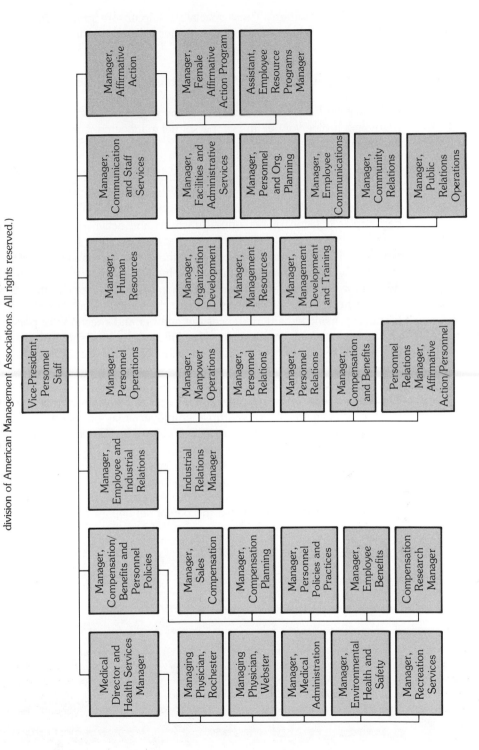

corporate headquarters. These specialists help ensure some fairness and consistency in the administration of personnel activities in all of the divisions.

Who's Responsible for Effective Personnel Management?

Utilizing fully the human resources of the organization is a responsibility shared by many, not just personnel. In fact, personnel management can be shared by all managers and employees.

The Managers. Personnel management is the task of individuals who have specialized in and who are primarily responsible for personnel management (personnel managers) and of individuals not specialized in but often responsible for the day-to-day implementation of personnel functions and activities (line supervisors and line managers). This is not meant to imply that the personnel manager never implements personnel functions and activities or that the personnel manager does not get involved in their development and administration. Indeed, these two managers are interdependent in the effective management of human resources. Nor can the effective management of human resources occur without the support and direction of top management. Top management influences the number and execution of personnel functions and activities in an organization. This influence is best shown by the role that top management allows the personnel manager and department to play in the organization.

> Really everyone is responsible for effective personnel management.

The Employees. Increasingly, employees are taking a role in personnel and human resource management. For example, employees may be asked to appraise their own performance or the performance of their colleagues. Employees may also help determine their own performance standards and goals. It is no longer uncommon for employees to write their own job descriptions. Perhaps most significantly, employees are taking a more active role in managing their own careers, assessing their own needs and values, and designing their own jobs. Nonetheless, personnel must help guide this process. Thus it is important that the personnel department be staffed with qualified individuals.

FOR YOUR CAREER

The term *personnel manager* (or executive) or *personnel and human resource manager* refers to the person or position heading the personnel department. In organizations, this position may also be labeled the vice president of personnel or the vice president of employee relations.

The term *personnel and human resource department* can be used interchangeably with the term *personnel department* or just *personnel*. These different names are used in different organizations. Neverthe-

less, all the functions and activities of personnel and human resource management relate to any of the terms. The term *staff* or *personnel staff* refers to the employees in the personnel department (either generalists or specialists) working for the personnel manager.

Line manager (or *supervisor*) refers to the person in charge of the employees who are working directly on the product that the organization produces. The terms *individual, person,* and *worker* or *workforce* refer to anyone in the organization. The term *employee* generally refers to the person who works for the line manager or the personnel manager; this person may also be called a nonmanagerial employee. Use of the term *subordinate* is avoided—except in Chapter 9, where the terms *subordinate* and *superior* are explained.

STAFFING THE PERSONNEL DEPARTMENT

Perhaps the most effective person who can head the personnel department is an outstanding performer, a superstar from the line organization. Since attracting the superstar means paying a higher salary than the person has been receiving, the effect of the superstar's acceptance of the position is to increase the personnel department's credibility and prestige in the organization. However, even if the person is not a superstar, line experience gives the personnel manager influence over the other line managers. To understand just how far some companies have gone in this area, consider IBM's policy of assigning line managers to work in the corporate personnel department for two or three years.

In addition, the well-trained personnel specialist often gains influence by becoming a personnel generalist through training and experience. The personnel specialist who wants to reach the top may benefit greatly by rotating through a line job in order to increase his or her ability to understand and deal with the entire organization.

Qualities of the Personnel Manager and Personnel Staff

For the personnel management department to be effective, high-quality people are needed. The exact qualities that are most useful differ for the personnel manager, the personnel generalist, the personnel specialist.

The Personnel Manager.   Now that you know where to look for the person to head the personnel department, you need to know what to look for. What qualities should personnel managers possess?

To begin with, personnel managers need to be effective managers. They must be able to identify problems, develop alternative solutions, and then select and implement the most effective one. In addition, they must develop and maintain an integrated and effective management information system for helping to identify problems and implement policy. They must be innovative and aggressive and be willing to take such risks as serving as the conscience of the organization. Furthermore, they must be effective at selecting, building, and developing an entire personnel staff to carry out the eight functions.

Personnel Generalists.   What qualities do the rest of the personnel staff need, and where do they come from? Line positions are one important source. A brief tour by a line supervisor in a personnel position, usually as a personnel generalist, can convey to the personnel department the knowledge, language, needs, and requirements of the line. As a result, the personnel department can more effectively fill its service role. Another source of personnel talent is current nonmanagerial employees. In many organizations personnel positions are staffed with former hourly employees. Like line

Personnel generalists are more effective if they have line management experience.

managers, these people bring with them information about the needs and attitudes of employees. In many cases they are particularly effective in their personnel positions.

Personnel generalists should possess many of the same qualities as personnel specialists, but it is apparent that the generalist's level of expertise in a personnel specialty generally need not be at the same depth as the specialist's. The generalist, however, needs to have a moderate level of expertise in many personnel activities and must be able to get more specialized knowledge when it is needed.

Personnel Specialists. Personnel staff specialists should have skills related to the specialty, an awarness of the relationship of that specialty to other personnel activities, and a knowledge of the organization and where the personnel department fits. Individuals joining an organization for the first time should also have an appreciation for the political realities of organizations. Another thing is for individuals in personnel to guard against the development of 'them' and 'us' situations and remember that they are not in business to promote the latest fads—and companies are not in business to perpetuate personnel departments. Universities are an important source of personnel specialists. Since specialists may work at almost any personnel activity, qualified applicants can come from specialized programs in law, personnel psychology, labor and industrial relations, personnel management, counseling, organizational development, and medical and health sciences.

Personnel Budgets

The money allocated by organizations to their personnel department continues to rise each year. For example, the per-employee personnel costs rose from $385 in 1980 to a median $433 in 1981 and rose again in 1982. Nonmanufacturing business organizations tend to spend the most per employee ($503 in 1981) and nonbusiness firms the least ($202 in 1981). Firms with up to 250 employees generally have the largest personnel budget as a percentage of the total company payroll (3.6 percent).[36]

EFFECTIVE PERSONNEL MANAGEMENT JOBS FOR YOU

Now that you have a good idea what personnel is and how important it is, you may want to consider a job in personnel.

How Much Do They Pay?

Of course, it is important to know how much money such jobs pay. A recent survey found the median pay for several different types of personnel jobs to be as follows:

Employment Interviewer (Clerical)	$15,122
Employment Interviewer (Professional/Managerial)	17,000
Employee Health Nurse/Plant Nurse	17,251
Recruiter (General)	19,042
Compensation Analyst (Salaried Personnel)	20,000
Recruiter (Professional/Managerial)	21,575

Training Specialist (Sales)	21,795
Safety Specialist	22,252
Employment Manager	23,100
Employee Benefits Manager	24,810
Training Manager (Plant)	26,936
EEO/Affirmative Action Manager	27,000
Compensation & Benefits Manager	28,000
Training & Organizational Development Manager	28,564
Labor Relations Manager	29,580
and Personnel Research Manager	29,940[37]

Salaries were generally higher for those individuals in larger organizations, for those with more experience, and for those with more education. In addition, salaries were higher in New York City, Los Angeles, and the states in the South and Southwest.

Although the opportunities in personnel are attractive and expanding, opportunities are better for you if you enter personnel after gaining experience in a line position.

> In fact, it may be that those persons with a few months or years of background and experience in line positions may be well ahead of those who do not have this perspective. In other words, while it may not be possible for graduating students to go directly into personnel administration, it also may not be wise for them to go directly into the field even if they have the opportunity.[38]

The background in a line position is helpful because it provides you with a better understanding of the organization. It also will give you more credibility with other line managers when you are in personnel trying to work with them. In addition, since there are many more line jobs than personnel jobs, it will be easier to get a line job and demonstrate your skills and abilities there. Then it will be much easier for you to transfer into personnel.

Increasing Professionalism in Personnel Management

If and when you do choose a personnel career, you'll be pleased to know that it is *now* a well respected profession.[39] And as with any profession, it follows a code of professional ethics, and has an accreditation institute and certification procedures. The code of ethics that personnel follows is shared by all professions. The code means that

1. The practitioner must regard the obligation to implement public objectives and protect the public interest as more important than blind loyalty to an employer's preferences.

2. In daily practice, the professional must thoroughly understand the problems assigned and must undertake whatever study and research are required to assure continuing competence and the best of professional attention and treatment.

3. The practitioner must maintain a high standard of personal honesty and integrity in every phase of daily practice.

4. The professional must give thoughtful consideration to the personal interests, welfare, and dignity of all employees who are affected by his or her prescriptions, recommendations, and actions.

5. Professionals must make very sure that the organizations that represent them maintain a high regard and respect for the public interest and that they never overlook the importance of the personal interests and dignity of employees.[40]

Professional Certification

In 1976, the American Society for Personnel Administration (ASPA) helped establish an independent group called the AAI (ASPA Accreditation Institute). Its purposes are

1. To provide colleges and universities with guidelines for curricular development
2. To help students select courses related to various career objectives
3. To help senior practitioners keep up to date and demonstrate competence in their field
4. To help young practitioners establish career goals and development plans
5. To help employers identify qualified practitioners.

The AAI has established two major categories of personnel practitioners, *generalists* and *specialists.* It accredits only active practitioners as generalists. Specialists include active practitioners, educators, and consultants, to name a few. One need not be a member of ASPA to be accredited, and about one in four of those accredited are not ASPA members.

Specialists may be accredited (certified) in six functional areas:

1. Employment, placement, and personnel planning
2. Training and development
3. Compensation and benefits
4. Health, safety, and security
5. Employee and labor relations
6. Personnel research.

For each of these areas there are "Functional Standards Committees" consisting of experts who define the knowledge required for each function and develop bibliographies and examination questions. The accreditation exams are conducted and evaluated by The Psychological Corporation.

Specialists are awarded two types of accreditation, *APS* (Accredited Personnel Specialist) and *APD* (Accredited Personnel Diplomate). The combination of education and experience must amount to six years for the APS and ten years for the APD. A bachelor's degree is counted as four years, and a master's degree counts as five years toward the total six-year (APS) and ten-year (APD) requirements.

Generalists are also awarded two types of accreditation, APM (Accredited Personnel Manager) and AEP (Accredited Executive in Personnel). The APM has a six-year requirement, and the AEP has a ten-year requirement.[41]

An addition to these aspects of the personnel profession, is the existence of a rather large number of specialized associations, such as the American Compensation Association, to which practitioners can belong. Also there are many research oriented and practitioner oriented journals and magazines of interest to the teacher as well as to the practitioner of personnel. The names and addresses for many of these journals are found in Appendix C.

PLAN OF BOOK

The overall plan of the book is to demonstrate the excitement, credibility, and importance of effective personnel management. Within this overall plan there are several critical purposes and themes.

Purposes

This book has several purposes. They include:

- Increasing your expertise in the functions and activities of personnel management
- Assisting you in being an effective manager of human resources
- Presenting the complexities, challenges, and trade-offs involved in being an effective manager of human resources
- Sharing with you a concern and an excitement for effective personnel management
- Helping you identify your personal qualities and the aspects of organizations that may assist you in choosing the right job

Themes of This Book

This book is written to be useful and accurate. In doing this, it combines both real-life illustrations of what effective personnel management is and explorations of why it is effective and how it can be made even more effective.

Applications and Practical Realities. A major theme of this book is the applications and practical realities of effective personnel management. Examples from organizations and personnel managers are used to illustrate the application, and the difficulties in that application, of the personnel activities being examined. Thus each chapter begins with several real-life scenarios or quotations. Then several more real-life short scenarios and quotations are provided throughout each chapter. In addition, there are two major types of inserts. One is called *Personnel In Action.* It illustrates personnel events really happening in actual organizations. The *For Your Career* inserts highlight issues particularly relevant to your career or to increase your understanding of the chapter. A *For Your Career* is also found at the end of each chapter.

To further reinforce this theme of applications orientation and practical realities, the feature on *Critical Issues* is used at the beginning of each chapter to help focus your reading. These Critical Issues came from a survey of several personnel vice presidents of public and private organizations (large and small) made especially for this book.[42] The Issues are presented as their concerns. Their comments also helped determine what personnel information to include in many of the chapters. At the end of each chapter, each of these Critical Issues is briefly addressed. You should be comfortable addressing them in more detail as if being asked to do so by a personnel manager seeking your advice.

Theory and Research. The other major theme is to provide the most current and useful information related to personnel management. Thus extensive use is also made of current research and theory related to the effective use and management of human resources. Consequently, you will receive not only an extensive description of all the current personnel functions and activities but also an understanding of *why* personnel functions and activities should work and how they *actually* work.

To further increase your understanding of the personnel applications, a case study is provided at the end of each chapter. After each case study are questions that you should be able to answer after reading the chapter. Remember in answering to draw on your knowledge of both why and how the personnel activity works.

For Whom Is This Book Written?

This book is written for you who will one day work in organizations or are already working in an organization. Knowledge of effective personnel functions and activities is vital for anyone working in organizations but particularly for managers and especially for personnel staff (specialists or generalists) and managers. This is true whether you work in a private or public organization, a large or small organization, a slow-growing or fast-growing organization. Although the type and size of the organization may influence the size of the personnel department, the functions and activities that are performed, and even the roles that are played, there is generally a personnel department in any organization—and effective management of human resources is always necessary.

FACING THE CRITICAL ISSUES IN EFFECTIVE PERSONNEL MANAGEMENT

Now that all the essential concepts of effective personnel management have been introduced and the purposes and importance of personnel discussed, it is useful to face the critical issues listed at the beginning of this chapter. In facing these issues, which personnel practitioners have indicated are important to them, only an outline of the complete answer will be provided. You should add much more to this outline.

Issue: *How can personnel management demonstrate its worth to the rest of the organization, that is, really be effective personnel management?*
You should be real comfortable in answering this one. This is the foundation for understanding how personnel departments in organizations can show they are important to the organization. Essentially, personnel can show its effectiveness by saving dollars or doing more for the same (or less) in managing the organization's human resources. Personnel can do this by improving the organization's productivity and the quality of work life for employees and by complying with the legal regulations. For each of these three ways, there are specific indicators to determine if (and how much) they are being improved or complied with.

Issue: *How can EPM benefit individuals in organizations?*
When personnel is performing effectively, as described in this chapter, individuals benefit because they (1) are allowed to be productive and perform meaningful jobs; (2) can enjoy a high quality of work life in which they can become involved in their work and experience comfortable levels of satisfaction yet only moderate levels of

stress and high levels of safety; and (3) are provided equal opportunities for promotion and training, are paid fairly and enjoy many employee rights.

Issue: *What can be done to get organizations to recognize the importance of EPM?*

By demonstrating the *E* in EPM. The personnel manager should take charge and begin to have his or her staff show, with hard eveidence, that each of the personnel activities results in either the improvement of productivity or the quality of work life and that it has been done in legal compliance. Thus personnel must be prepared to evaluate each of its activities as well as the total personnel department. (Ways to do this are discussed specifically at the end of each chapter and more generally in Chapters 7 and 14.) This can be done and must be done. It results in personnel playing many more roles in the organization.

Issue: *What role are you going to play in EPM?*

Effectively utilizing personnel resources is the responsibility of everyone in the organization, especially line managers and those in personnel—the personnel managers, the generalists, and the specialists. You may end up playing all of these roles. One thing for certain, whatever role you play will become even more critical to organizations in the 1980s. The value of human resources to organizations will continue to grow.

SUMMARY

This chapter examines the growing importance of the functions and activities of personnel management, defines what personnel management is, and lists its purposes. Because of the increasing complexity of personnel management, nearly all organizations have established a department for it. However, not all of these departments perform all of the personnel functions and activities discussed in this textbook. Which ones a department actually performs and the way it does so depend greatly on the roles that the department plays in the organization. There are four roles that a personnel department can play. Organizations that are most concerned with effective personnel management allow their personnel departments to play all four roles.

After determining the roles and hence the functions and activities that a personnel department will perform, the organization is in a position to organize and staff the department. The organization must decide whether to centralize or decentralize personnel functions and activities and what sources to tap in staffing the department.

This book is for everyone who is or will be working in an organization but especially for those who are responsible for the management and use of human resources—line managers and personnel managers and staff. And in order to make this book as useful (and enjoyable) as possible, it has been written around the major themes of why personnel functions and activities should work and how they work in practice.

The remaining chapters will expose you to a great deal of information about personnel management. You will also be asked to consider many questions, some of which are not answered in this book. That's because only you can provide the answers. Try to answer them all. By the end of the book, you will not only know a great deal about personnel management but also a great deal about yourself and your life in organizations.

KEY CONCEPTS

centralization

decentralization

functions and activities

effective personnel management

personnel roles
   personnel criteria (effectiveness
   indicators)

personnel generalist

personnel specialist

DISCUSSION QUESTIONS

1. Why are personnel departments becoming more important?
2. Identify and describe the three major purposes of EPM.
3. How can a personnel manager demonstrate that his or her personnel management programs are effective?
4. What is the relationship between the roles played by the personnel department and the functions and activities it performs?
5. What is the meaning of EPM?
6. What are the four QWL indicators that can be used to measure the effectiveness of the personnel department?
7. What is the difference between a personnel specialist and a personnel generalist?
8. Name three of the points established in the code of ethics for personnel management.
9. What are the two most dominant concerns in organizations today?
10. What are the critical issues facing effective personnel management?

CASE

Setting up the Human Resource Function in a Small Organization

Terry Van Eyck was hired to set up the HR function in a small, privately owned manufacturing concern. Just six years old, the firm had grown in this period from two brothers producing computer parts in their garage during their spare time to six production lines and more than 80 full-time employees. If the business continued to expand at its present rate, it would need more than 500 employees in the next six years.

Before Van Eyck was hired, the sales manager (one of the brothers who owned the firm) had handled some of the organization's personnel activities. With the help of a part-time secretary, he kept records on employees, maintained a very simple benefit plan, submitted necessary paperwork to governmental offices and issued payroll checks. In general, though, the personnel activities of the organization were decentralized and highly idiosyncratic: the six foremen of the production lines individually handled employee recruitment, selection, hiring, orientation, training, wages, promotions, discipline and terminations. They consulted the elder of the two brothers, who served as the firm's general operating manager, before making decisions on particularly important matters—especially those related to pay increases or terminations. The employees were not unionized.

During the first few weeks of his new job, Van Eyck devoted most of his time to examining current personnel practices in the organization, speaking with employees and foremen and looking through the personnel records. To his astonishment, he discovered that the employee personnel records were disorganized and lacked all uniformity, that the organization had no formal personnel policies of any kind and that the firm's managers had only a vague idea of personnel costs or of manpower needs. After all, there were no formal job descriptions, no job specifications, no performance appraisal system and no records on turnover or absenteeism. There was a formal pay plan, but many employees received wages well above prevailing rates as specified in the plan.

In discussions with employees, he found that they were quite bitter about what they perceived as the capricious and inconsistent practices of the foremen. Yet the foremen were pleased with the present arrangement, which they felt allowed them sufficient flexibility and power to reward or punish workers as they saw fit. They made it clear that they did not want a centralized personnel function, nor did they need staff advice about how to manage their lines. The owner-manager recognized the need for an HR function that the firm could grow into; however, at the same time he wished to avoid, as he put it, "stirring up trouble or interfering with the present work or duties of the foremen I hired and promoted."

As a first year budget, Van Eyck has $5,000 (excluding his salary). He has an office, a desk, a telephone, two filing cabinets, a wastebasket and a part-time secretary who works only two mornings per week.

Case Questions

1. What are the problems facing Terry and where should he begin?
2. How can Terry avoid the potential problems and successfully design and implement an HR function under these conditions?
3. What personal skills does Terry need to be successful here?
4. How could Terry have minimized some of the difficulties he now faces?

FOR YOUR CAREER

▪ Personnel managers gain the respect of others in the organization by producing programs that improve the bottom line of the organization.

- It is useful to have gained experience as a line manager before going into personnel.
- Since productivity and QWL are likely to be critical issues through the 1980s, personnel will increase in importance.
- Your effectiveness in an organization increases as you get to know all aspects of its operation.
- Your effectiveness as a line manager will be aided by your knowing about effective personnel management. After all, your success depends upon other people doing the work.
- Your career experiences are likely to be better if you are with a company where the personnel department plays all four roles and is perceived as important by top management.

ENDNOTES

1. Jac Fitz-enz, "Measuring Human Resources Effectiveness," *Personnel Administrator,* July 1980, pp. 33–36.

   Ross A. Hennigar, "People Management in the 1980's: A CEO's View," *Personnel Journal,* November 1980, pp. 898–903.

2. "More Jobs, And Better Productivity At Last," *Business Week,* June 1, 1981, p. 98.

3. Ellen Kelly Burton, "Productivity: A Plan for Personnel," *Personnel Administrator,* September 1981, pp. 85–92.

   James Day Hodgson, "An Impertinent Suggestion for Personnel Practitioners," *Personnel Administrator,* September 1981, pp. 85–92.

4. Lauren Hite Jackson and Mark G. Mindell, "Motivating the New Breed," *Personnel,* March/April 1980, p. 55.

5. Charles G. Burck, "Working Smarter," *Fortune,* June 15, 1981, p. 73. For more information, see these additional sources:

   Charles G. Burck, "What Happens When Workers Manage Themselves," *Fortune,* July 27, 1981, pp. 62–69.

   "Personnel Widens Its Franchise," *Business Week,* February 26, 1979, p. 116.

6. Joan S. Lublin, "Employers Act to Curb Sex Harassing on Job; Lawsuits, Fines Feared," *Wall Street Journal,* April 24, 1981, p. 1.

   F. E. Schuster, "Human Resources Management: Key to the Future," *Personnel Administrator,* December 1978, p. 68.

7. "Personnel Widens Its Franchise," p. 116. Reprinted from the February 26, 1979, issue of *Business Week,* by special permission, © 1979 by McGraw-Hill, Inc., 1221 Avenue of the Americas, New York, NY, 10020. All rights reserved.

8. T. Mills, "Human Resources: Why the New Concern?" *Howard Business Week Review,* March/April 1975, p. 133.

9. "Personnel Widens Its Franchise," p. 121.

10. Schuster, p. 68.

11. Schuster, p. 34. Reprinted with permission from the December 1978 issue of the *Personnel Administrator* copyright 1978, The American Society for Personnel Administration, 30 Park Dr., Berea, Ohio, 44017.

12. Fred K. Foulkes, "Organizing and Staffing the Personnel Function," *Harvard Business Review,* May–June 1977, p. 142.

13. Schuster, p. 34.

14. Schuster, p. 35.

15. U.S. Department of Health, Education and Welfare, *Work in America,* report of a special task force to the Secretary (Cambridge, Mass.: MIT Press, 1973).

16. Mills, 1975, and *Work in America.*

17. T. F. Cawsey, "Why Line Managers Don't Listen to Their Personnel Departments," *Personnel,* January–Feburary 1980, (New York: AMACOM, a division of American Management Associations, 1980) p. 14.

18. Reprinted by permission of the *Harvard Business Review.* Excerpt from "Organizing and Staffing the Personnel Function" by Fred K. Foulkes (May–June 1977), p. 142. Copyright © 1977 by the President and Fellows of Harvard College; all rights reserved.

19. Logan M. Cheek, "Cost Effectiveness Comes to the Personnel Function," *Harvard Business Review,* May–June 1973, pp. 96–105.

Jac Fitz-enz, "Quantifying the Human Resources Function," *Personnel,* March–April 1980, pp. 41–52.

Foulkes, 1977, p. 147.

20. Fitz-enz, p. 35. Reprinted with permission from the July 1980 issue of the *Personnel Administrator,* copyright 1980, The American Society for Personnel Administration, 30 Park Dr., Berea, Ohio, 44017.

21. "The New Industrial Relations," *Business Week,* May 11, 1981, pp. 85–98.

22. Bruce R. Ellig, "The Impact of Legislation on the Personnel Function," *Personnel,* September–October 1980, pp. 49–53.

R. C. Hodgson, "Where the Action Is: A Perspective on the Future of Personnel Management," *Business Quarterly,* Spring 1977, pp. 92–95.

23. "Personnel Widens Its Franchise," p. 116. Reprinted from the February 26, 1979, issue of *Business Week* by special permission, © 1979 by McGraw-Hill, Inc., 1221 Avenue of the Americas, New York, NY, 10020. All rights reserved.

24. Jennie Farley, *Affirmative Action and the Woman Worker: Guidelines for Personnel Management* (New York: AMACOM, a division of American Management Associations, 1979), p. 33.

25. Ibid.

26. "Toward a More Comprehensive Career Planning Program" by Stephen L. Cohen and Herbert H. Meyers, p. 611. Reprinted with permission of *Personnel Journal,* Costa Mesa, Calif. Copyright September 1979 by *Personnel Journal;* all rights reserved.

27. R. E. Walton, "Work Innovations in the United States," *Harvard Business Review,* July–August 1979, pp. 88–98.

28. Reprinted by permission of the *Harvard Business Review,* Excerpt from "The Expanding Role of the Personnel Function" by Fred K. Foulkes (March–April 1975), p. 73. Copyright © 1975 by the President and Fellows of Harvard College; all rights reserved.

29. Mary Anne Devanna, Charles Fombrun and Noel Tichy, "Human Resources Management: A Strategic Perspective," *Organizational Dynamics,* Winter 1981, pp. 51–67.

George S. Odiorne, *MBO II: A System of Managerial Leadership for the Eighties* (Belmont, Calif.: Fearon-Pitman, 1979).

30. Jack W. English, "The Road Ahead for the Human Resources Function," *Personnel,* March–April 1980, pp. 35–39.

Paul C. Gordon, " 'Magnetic' Management: The Real Role of Personnel," *Personnel Journal,* June 1980, pp. 485–487, 500.

Deborah R. Hugar, AEP, "The Personnel Professional in the Small Organization," *Personnel Administrator,* April 1981, p. 41.

James W. Peters and Edward A. Mabry, "The Personnel Officer as Internal Consultant," *Personnel Administrator,* April 1981, pp. 29–32.

Harold C. White, APD, and Michael N. Wolfe, "The Role Desired for Personnel Administration," *Personnel Administrator,* June 1980, pp. 87–97.

31. Foulkes, 1977, p. 146.

32. Reprinted by permission of the *Harvard Business Review.* Excerpt from "Organizing and Staffing the Personnel Function" by Fred K. Foulkes (May–June 1977), p. 147. Copyright © 1977 by the President and Fellows of Harvard College; all rights reserved.

33. Reprinted by permission of the *Harvard Business Review.* Excerpt from "The Expanding Role of the Personnel Function" by Fred K. Foulkes (March–April 1975), p. 77. Copyright © 1975 by the President and Fellows of Harvard College; all rights reserved.

34. J. A. Henderson, "What the Chief Executive Expects of the Personnel Function," p. 42. Reprinted with permission from the May 1977 issue of the *Personnel Administrator,* copyright 1977, The American Society for Personnel Administration, 30 Park Dr., Berea, Ohio, 44017.

35. Reprinted by permission of the publisher, from "Organizing and Staffing the Human Resources Function: A Personnel Symposium," *Personnel,* January–February 1978 (New York: AMACOM, a division of American Management Associations, 1978), p. 16.

36. Steven Langer, "Budgets and Staffing: A Survey, Part II," *Personnel Journal,* June 1981, pp. 464–468.

Steven Langer, "The Personnel/Industrial Relations Report—An Overview of Current Staffing and Budgeting Ratios," *Personnel Journal,* February 1980, pp. 95–98.

Mary Green Miner, "Personnel Budgets and Staffs: How Big Should They Be?," *Personnel Administrator,* July 1980, pp. 51–55.

37. Steven Langer, "Personnel Salaries: A Survey, Part 1," *Personnel Journal,* December 1980, p. 984. Reprinted with the permission of *Personnel Journal,* Costa Mesa, California; all rights reserved.

38. Duff A. Greenwell, "Starting A Career in Personnel Administration," p. 16. Reprinted with permission from the September 1981 issue of the *Personnel Administrator,* copyright 1981, The American Society for Personnel Administrations, 30 Park Dr., Berea, Ohio, 44017.

39. Steven H. Appelbaum, APD, "The Personnel Professional and Organization Development: Conflict and Synthesis," *Personnel Administrator,* July 1980, pp. 44–49.

Gene F. Brady, "Assessing the Personnel Manager's Power Base," *Personnel Administrator,* July 1980, pp. 57–61.

Fred R. Edney, "The Greening of the Profession," *Personnel Administrator,* July 1980, pp. 27–30, 42.

"Playing on the Team," *Personnel Journal,* August 1981, pp. 598–600.

40. Dale Yoder and Herbert Heneman, Jr., *PAIR Jobs, Qualifications, and Careers,* ASPA Handbook of Personnel and Industrial Relations, 1978, p. 18.

41. Ira R. Weiss and Anna D. Gowans Young, "Professional Certification Programs," *Personnel Administrator,* April 1981, pp. 63–68.

Yoder and Heneman, pp. 29–30.

42. Approximately one hundred vice-presidents of personnel were sent a brief questionnaire asking them to indicate what they thought were the critical issues relevant to each of the personnel functions and activities presented in this text. In addition, they were asked to suggest solutions to the issues. One-half of the questionnaires were returned in time to use them in this text. All four types of organizations—public and private and large and small—from the four major regions of the United States were represented in the set of usable questionnaires. Since the vice-presidents represented different types of organizations and geographical locations, their views on what are the critical issues varied. Consequently, for many of the personnel functions and activities there were more than four critical issues. When this occurred, I took only the four most frequently mentioned issues to use in the text. Only four issues were used because of space considerations and because four issues tended to reflect the most common concerns of our group of vice-presidents.

Effective Personnel Management Planning

Chapter Two
Planning for Personnel Needs

Chapter Three
Designing and Analyzing Jobs

Chapter Outline

Critical Issues in Personnel Planning

Effective Personnel Planning
Importance and Purposes of EPP
Relationships with Other Personnel Activities

What Personnel Planning is About
Who's Responsible for EPP?
Developing Personnel Planning Strategies
Effective Personnel Planning Programs

Important Changes in the 1980s Influencing EPP
The Population and the Labor Force Characteristics
Changes in the Economy
Changing Social Values
Legislation and Regulation and Government Activity

CHAPTER **2**

Planning for Personnel Needs

Evaluating EPP Activity

Facing the Critical Issues in Personnel Planning

Summary

Discussion Questions

Key Concepts

Case

For Your Career

Endnotes

Personnel in the News

Planning for Success

Society is moving into a period of labor shortages, continuing government interven-
tion, changing work values, increasing labor costs, and declining productivity.

In this environment, human resource planning can spell the difference between
the success or failure of an enterprise. It is an important job that managers must
shoulder, a complex job that can only be done properly if it has been simplified. The
solution to that paradox is to break the task down into small parts and to complete
them systematically—one step at a time.

If implemented correctly, however, the benefits of human resource planning are
substantial. (From Craig B. Mackey, *"Human Resource Planning: A Four-Phased*
Approach," Management Review, *May 1981* [New York: AMACOM, a division of
American Management Associations, 1981], p. 22.)

New Jobs, New Skills

The accelerating shift to automation in U.S. plants and offices promises to bring with it
a badly needed improvement in productivity and a new competitive strength in world
markets. At the same time, it will confront U.S. employers and educators with the
necessity for training and retraining workers on a scale never attempted in this country
or anywhere else.

Some 45 million jobs—almost half of the total—will eventually be affected by
office and factory automation. Though the process will be spread over a period of time
and attrition will take care of some of the turnover, new skills will be required, and in
many cases the new jobs will demand higher levels of technical training.

Individual companies can ease the shock of transition by giving ample notice, by
bringing workers in on the decisions about new technology, and by explaining the
long-run advantages of automation. It is important, however, for policymakers to
recognize that automated industry and business will provide few opportunities for the
uneducated, unskilled job applicant. Just as the switch from muscle power to ma-
chines closed the plant gate on the man with the broom and shovel, the shift to
automation will eliminate repetitive assembly-line jobs. Even if the economy goes into
a prolonged period of strong growth, it will not absorb the pool of unskilled workers
that has accumulated in major cities.

All employers and the U.S. educational establishment will have to come to grips
with the problem of training new workers and retraining older ones to qualify for the
new jobs. It has been a long time since U.S. employers could use a man "with a strong
back and a weak mind." In the future, there will not be many places for men or
women with well-trained hands and badly trained minds. (Reprinted from the August
3, 1981, issue of Business Week *by special permission,* © 1981 by McGraw-Hill, Inc.,
New York, NY 10020, p. 96. All rights reserved.)

Personnel Planning Pays

The case history of the Harris Corporation, a Cleveland based firm, demonstrates the importance of planned executive succession to the success of the company. The Harris Corporation, in 1964, as an important goal of its five year plan, planned to boost sales from $100 million to $250 million in 1969. During the company's growth, the firm realized that it had not been developing its future management team in necessary depth or detail. The existing junior management training program was revitalized and a senior executive program was initiated to develop the necessary managerial talent. A management-manpower planning program was formed which required the manager of each division to meet with corporate top management to discuss the progress of his or her organization.

The results of these programs were that the 1969 sales goal was reached one year ahead of schedule and that the Harris Corporation surpassed a half-billion dollars in sales by June 30, 1974. The president called the manpower planning and development programs "one of the most important uses of executive time." (From Guvene G. Aplander, "Human Resource Planning in U.S. Corporations," California Management Review, © 1980 by the Regents of the University of California. Reprinted from California Management Review, vol. 22, no. 3, pp. 28–29, by permission of the Regents.)

These three quotations point out several important aspects of personnel planning. One aspect is that personnel planning is becoming more vital to organizations every day. Second, personnel planning is becoming more vital because of the rapid changes in our society, especially the growing competitiveness of the world, the increased pressure for increased productivity, the rapid acceleration of technology and automation, and the changing nature of the U.S. work force. And a final aspect, nicely illustrated by the last quotation describing the use of executive personnel planning, is that personnel planning can save an organization big dollars and enable it to attain its strategic goals. These quotations also serve to highlight the critical issues in personnel planning today.

CRITICAL ISSUES IN PERSONNEL PLANNING

Of the many critical issues raised by our personnel managers, the four most critical are

1. *What are the aspects of our society that will be changing and increasing the need for organizations to engage in personnel planning?*
2. *How are the critical aspects of our society changing? In what directions are they going?*
3. *What are the implications of these changes for effective personnel planning?*
4. *Why is it often diffcult to establish a personnel planning program and how can the roadblocks to its establishment be removed?*

As we consider in this chapter what effective personnel planning is about, think how you would address each of these Critical Issues. Then at the end of this chapter you will be ready to expand on the responses provided for each of the four Critical Issues.

EFFECTIVE PERSONNEL PLANNING

Effective personnel planning (**EPP**) is the first step of any effective personnel program. It involves predicting human resource needs and planning the steps necessary to meet these needs. As such,

> Human resource planning is directly tied to strategic business planning. Strategic business plans define steps that the organization will take to meet the demands of the future. Human resource plans assure that the right number and the right kind of people become available at the right time and place so that organizational needs can be met. No doubt, human resource planning is one of the fastest growing areas of personnel administration.[1]

Importance and Purposes of EPP

EPP is important to an organization because it serves so many purposes. A major purpose of EPP is to help the organization use human talent effectively and in the interests of the individual employee and the organization. EPP can also reduce expenses associated with excessive turnover and absenteeism, low productivity, inefficient internal labor markets, and an unproductive training program.

Specific purposes of personnel planning are to

Planning helps prepare an organization for the future.

- Reduce personnel costs by helping management to anticipate shortages or surpluses of human resources and to correct these imbalances before they become unmanageable and expensive
- Provide a better basis for planning employee development that makes optimum use of workers' attitudes
- Improve the overall business planning process
- Provide more opportunities for women and minority groups in future growth plans and identify the specific skills available
- Promote greater awareness of the importance of sound human resource management throughout all levels of the organization
- Provide a tool for evaluating the effect of alternative human resource actions and policies[2]

All of these purposes are now more easily attained than ever thanks to the enormous amount of computer technology. This technology allows vast job-related records to be maintained on each employee, in essence creating a human resource information system. These records in the system, which include information on employee job preferences, work experiences, and performance evaluations, provide a job history of each employee in an organization and a complete set of information on the job and positions in the organization.

Exhibit 2.1
Relationships of Effective Personnel Planning with Other
Personnel Activities

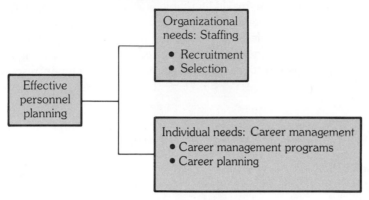

Relationships with Other Personnel Activities

EPP is important because it influences almost all of the other personnel activities. Although all these relationships are important, perhaps two are most critical as shown in Exhibit 2.1.

Staffing.   EPP helps determine the human resource staffing needs of an organization. In conjunction with job analysis, it indicates how many and what types of people need to be recruited. Recruitment influences the pool of available job applicants, which in turn influences the needs for selection and placement. Thus EPP can be viewed as a major input into an organization's staffing function.

Career Management.   EPP helps career management programs aid an organization in retaining valued employees and keeping them from becoming obsolete. Thus career management programs play an important role in determining an organization's supply of human resources and ultimately its needs. For example, if career management programs and career planning by employees help reduce employee turnover and absenteeism, the organization can plan on a larger supply of qualified human resources and, therefore, a smaller need for additional human resources.

WHAT EFFECTIVE PERSONNEL PLANNING IS ABOUT

While it is critical to know the purposes, importance, and relationships of EPP, it is also necessary to know what EPP is about. After examining in detail what EPP is about, the influence of the environment on EPP is discussed.

Who's Responsible for EPP?

The responsibility for EPP rests with top management, the personnel manager, and the line managers. Together they determine the success and effectiveness of EPP, but each plays a different role. Top management is responsible for encouraging EPP, aiding in its implementation, and ensuring its use. The personnel manager is responsible for developing EPP, gathering the necessary information, creating a human resource information system, making it usable and available, coordinating EPP with the other personnel activities, and evaluating the effectiveness of EPP. Line managers and supervisors are responsible for providing the necessary information for EPP and for working with the personnel manager to ensure that the organization's human resources are used as effectively as possible and that its human resource needs are provided.

Developing Personnel Planning Strategies

Although EPP is extremely critical to EPM, it has been a relatively neglected personnel activity in many organizations.[3] This is due to the extensive set of EPP roadblocks.

Oftentimes it seems easier to react than to plan.

EPP Roadblocks.   One of the key roadblocks to developing planning strategies has been the lack of top management support. This roadblock is also a key in preventing the personnel department from playing all the major personnel roles discussed in Chapter 1. Personnel must show with data and hard, bottom-line facts that EPP and EPM pay. Another roadblock is the difficulty in obtaining integration with other personnel activities, such as recruitment and career development, so necessary to make EPP work. A challenge for personnel is to create a personnel system in which all the functions and activities are integrated and coordinated. This will not only help remove a personnel planning roadblock, it will also enhance the effectiveness of all the personnel activities.

A third roadblock is the lack of involvement of line managers. Failure to involve line management in the design, development and implementation of a human resource planning system is a common oversight for first-time planners. Personnel managers are often tempted (by themselves) to develop or adopt highly quantitative approaches to planning. These approaches often have little pragmatic value to line managers in the problems they have such as reducing excessive turnover, identifying and training replacements for key positions, and forecasting staffing needs. Therefore, personnel planning, to be effective, must be useful. An integral part of being useful is serving the line managers' needs. With this important point in mind, personnel can go ahead and begin developing planning strategies.

Getting Started.   Personnel planning is generally accomplished in four phases:

A good plan starts with where you want to go.

1. Gathering and analyzing data through personnel inventories and forecasts (and creating a human resource information system)

2. Establishing human resource objectives and policies and gaining approval and support for them from top management

3. Designing and implementing plans and action programs, in such areas as recruitment, training, and promotion, that will enable the organization to achieve its human resource objectives

4. Controlling and evaluating personnel plans and programs to facilitate progress toward human resource objectives.[4]

Exhibit 2.2 shows the relationships among these phases as well as their relationships with corporate objectives, policies and plans, and with environmental components.

The *first phase* of EPP involves developing data that can be used in determining corporate objectives, policies, and plans as well as human resource objectives and

Exhibit 2.2

The Human Resource Planning and Programing Process (Adapted from E. W. Vetter, *Manpower Planning for High Talent Personnel* [Ann Arbor, Mich.: Bureau of Industrial Relations. Graduate School of Business, The University of Michigan, 1967], p. 29.)

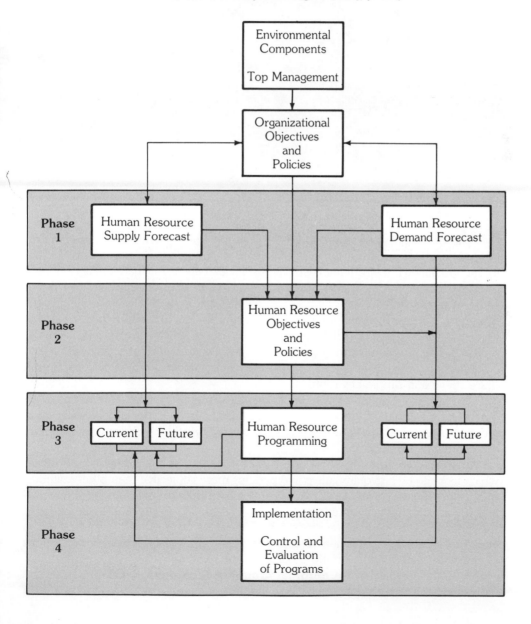

policies. As shown in Exhibit 2.2, the human resource supply and demand forecasts are both influenced in turn by the corporate objectives, policies, and plans. The interaction of these aspects of human resource planning helps to determine the current human resource situation and future human resource needs.

FOR YOUR CAREER

Forecasting techniques are used by personnel departments to tell them about the future supply and demand of human resources. Forecasts can be made by experts who give their opinions ("guesstimates") of what the future will be like. Forecasts can also be made by statistical techniques to predict the future from what has happened in the past. Sometimes organizations wish to do more than have experts predict the future or have the past forecast the future. They desire to do this because they think that either there are too many events affecting the future for a few people to guess what it will be like or that what happened in the past may not happen again. In response,

organizations develop models to represent all the events likely to affect the future. For example, events likely to affect an organization's demand for human resources include the rate at which its employees retire, the rate of demand for the company's product, and the rate of automation. Since these rates may vary, the organization derives different levels of human resource demand by plugging into the model different rates of these events and estimating what rates are most likely. Because this is mathematically complex to do, computers are used to help forecast (simulate) the future.

The data developed in phase 1 for the supply and demand forecasts represent information retrieved from the past, observed in the present, and forecast for the future. Obtaining data from the past may be difficult because of inadequate or nonexistent records, and forecasting data with reliability and accuracy may be difficult because of uncertainties. Nevertheless, they need to be provided, however tentatively. The more tentative the data, the more flexible and subject to revision they should be. Contingencies causing uncertainties in the forecasts should be incorporated into the forecasts, perhaps in the form of estimated ranges. Organizations in more unstable and complex environments are faced with many more contingencies than organizations in more stable and simple environments.

Three classes of forecasting techniques are frequently used to determine the organization's projected demand for human resources. In order of increasing complexity, these are *expert forecasts, conventional statistical projections,* and *computer simulations and modeling.*

The most common method of the *expert forecast* is the **Delphi technique,** which tends to be less quantitative and perhaps more subjective than other methods. In a Delphi forecast, a large number of experts take turns at presenting their forecasts and assumptions. An intermediary passes each expert's forecast and assumptions to the others, who then make revisions in their forecasts. This process continues until a final forecast emerges. This final forecast may represent specific projections or a range of projections, depending on the positions of the experts.

A related method is the **nominal grouping technique** (**NGT**). Here several individuals sit around a conference table and independently list their ideas on a sheet of paper. After ten to twenty minutes, they take turns expressing their ideas to the group. As these ideas are presented, they are recorded on larger sheets of paper so that everyone can see all the ideas and refer to them in later parts of the session.

Although the two techniques are similar in process, the Delphi technique is more frequently used to generate predictions, and the nominal grouping technique is used more for identifying current organizational problems and solutions to those problems. Only in the NGT, however, are the individuals generally in the same location or room.

The most common *statistical procedures* are simple linear regression analysis and multiple linear regression analysis. In **simple linear regression** analysis a projection of future demand is based on a past relationship between the organization's employment level and a variable related to employment, such as sales. If a relationship can be established between the level of sales and the level of employment, predictions of future sales can be used to make predictions of future employment.

Multiple linear regression analysis is an extension of simple linear regression analysis. Instead of relating employment to one other variable related to employment, several variables are used. For example, instead of using only sales to predict employment demand, productivity data and equipment-use data may also be used. Because it incorporates several variables related to employment, multiple regression analysis may produce more accurate demand forecasts than linear regression analysis. It appears, however, that only relatively large organizations use multiple regression analysis.

Computer simulations and *modeling techniques* are even less frequently used by organizations. However, they offer the advantage of being able to quickly revise forecasts based on changes in the determinants or assumptions. For example, the General Electric Company has developed a computer simulation called MANPLAN to determine labor forecasts. These forecasts may be used on a number of different product lines, the forecasted sales for each product line for the next year, the existing plant capacity, and the possibility of working the current work force overtime. Since each of these determinants of the labor forecast has its own relationship with the level of employment, the projected level of employment can be altered by changing estimates of the determinants or the assumed relationships between them and the level of employment. As with multiple linear regression analysis, the use of simulation and modeling is found only in extremely large organizations, such as the U.S. Defense Department, General Electric, IBM, and the U.S. State Department.

Estimating human resource needs is really a match of forecasted supply with forecasted demand. A forecast of the internal labor supply can be compared with projected trends in the external labor pool to paint a picture of the organization's overall human resource supply. This supply forecast can then be compared with the human resource demand forecast to help determine, among other things, action programing for identifying human resource talent and for balancing supply and demand forecasts. However, most current forecasting of labor supply and demand is short-range and for the purposes of budgeting and controlling costs. Forecasts for over a five-year period, when made, are used in planning corporate strategy, facilities, and identifying managerial replacements. A sample of a replacement chart is shown in Exhibit 2.3. Note that the chart depicts the current staffing of an organization and the individuals who are likely replacements for the current job incumbents. It also indicates the promotion potential of employees and what improvements may be necessary to make them promotable.

Data in the skills inventory can often be used in drawing up replacement charts, which generally are used to forecast the human resource supply. In the process of forecasting unit demand, managers also determine a supply forecast.

Managers often determine the productivity of their employees in relation to other employees in the unit as well as those in other units. On the basis of productivity data and adjustments for absenteeism and turnover, managers can begin to establish fore-

Exhibit 2.3

Sample Employee Replacement Chart* (From *The Expanded Personnel Function* Studies in Personnel Policy 203 [New York National Industrial Conference Board 1966])

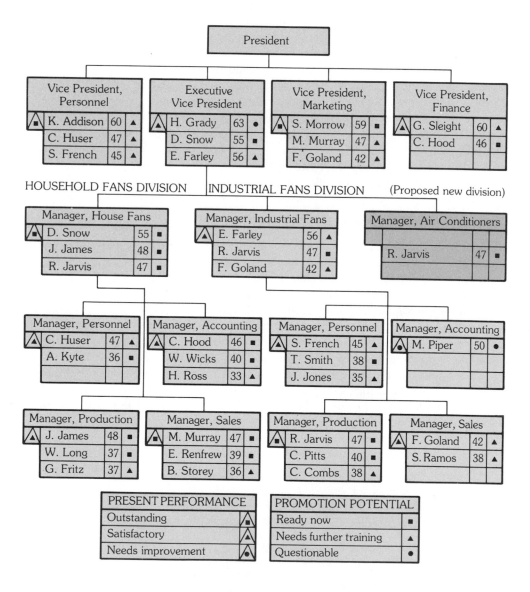

*The ages of potential replacements appear next to their names

casts for the supply of labor. However, evaluation of employees' promotion potential and dismissal potential is more directly related to the forecast. Although replacement charts have traditionally been devised only for managers, nonmanagerial employees are now being included as well.

As shown in Exhibit 2.2, the *second phase* in the personnel planning and programing process is setting human resource objectives and policies. The impact of the organization's objectives, policies, and plans on human resource planning would seem difficult to deny, yet many organizations do not link their organizational plans with their personnel plans.

The *third phase* in EPP is an extremely important extension of the second phase of personnel planning. After the assessment of an organization's human resource needs, action programing must be developed to serve those needs. Action programs may deal with recruitment policies and procedures (especially if more people need to be hired), training and development programs, policies and procedures for selecting applicants, and policies and procedures for dealing with redundant employees.

Planning is an important element in the design of action programs for three reasons: (1) it helps coordinate the activities of the programs and reduces duplication and inefficiencies; (2) it applies pressure for developing programs that might otherwise be neglected; and (3) it stimulates the development and use of individualized programs for an organization rather than programs that may be used because they are available or because other organizations are using them.

In developing action programs, care must be taken to specify in detail what each program contains and how it is to be done. Furthermore, each program should reflect an awareness of current problems and issues pertaining to personnel management. The range of action programs is too broad to cover them all here. Three action programs an organization can develop that are critical include (1) *new organizational designs;* (2) *preretirement counseling;* and (3) *dealing with the redundant worker.* Before we discuss these action programs, the last phase of EPP should be highlighted.

Action programs are critical to EPP.

The *fourth phase* of EPP is the control and evaluation of personnel plans and programs that are essential to the effective management of human resources. Therefore, Exhibit 2.2 shows program control and evaluation as the last phase of EPP. Efforts in this area are clearly aimed at quantifying the value of human resources. These efforts recognize human resources as an asset to the organization. Of course, the quality of work activities must also be evaluated.

An **HRIS** (human resource information system) facilitates program control and evaluation by allowing for more rapid and frequent collection of data to back up a forecast of personnel needs. This data collection is important not only as a means of control but also as a method for evaluating plans and programs and making adjustments.

The collection of data should be formalized to occur at the end of each year and at fixed intervals during the year. The evaluation should occur at the same time in order to hasten revisions of existing forecasts and programs. It is likely that revisions will influence short-run, intermediate, and long-run forecasts. The degree of formality present in the data-collection process varies with the activity or program:

> A written progress report by the college recruiter might be an adequate control device for that activity. In salary administration, however, statistical evaluation of the distribution of wages by salary grade, departments, and job classifications may be desired.[5]

Now that the four phases of personnel planning have been examined, let us present three examples of action programs that personnel can develop to deal with personnel planning needs.

Effective Personnel Planning Programs

Personnel programs help the organization fill its personnel needs.

EPP is essentially concerned with ensuring that an organization has the right people in the right place at the right time. In fulfilling this charge, the personnel manager must make sure that the organization is able to attract and retain employees. If the organization is unable to do these effectively, personnel planning will be more difficult and organizational effectiveness will suffer. Thus an organization will want to develop programs that will enable the organization to attract and retain employees. With these programs in place the organization will find it easier to recruit new job applicants when it needs them. Increasing organizational effectiveness, however, does not always depend upon attracting and retaining individuals. It sometimes depends upon reducing its work force, which can be even more difficult and painful than increasing the attractiveness of the organization to new individuals. But because both these activities, attraction and reduction, are critical to organizational effectiveness they must be done as well as possible.

Attraction: New Organizational Designs. In response to the current and anticipated shortages of key people, organizations are making radical changes in order to attract job applicants.

> Changes in our society, particularly in the values of the workforce, have seriously undermined the traditional relationship between organizations and their members. This has led to a crisis for organizations that may only be resolved by the evaluation of new organizational forms.[6]

FOR YOUR CAREER

The term *organizational form* is used to describe what an organization is like: what it values, how it treats its employees, whether its jobs are simple and routine or complex and variable, how much it controls its employees, how much it trusts its employees, and how it rewards its employees. Organizational forms are neither good nor bad, but some forms are more attractive and motivational to some people than are other forms. Thus it is useful for an organization to recruit and select people who are likely to be most attracted to the form of the organization. If the organization is unable to attract the people it needs with the form it has, it may need to change its form.

The most apparent results of this crisis have been the decline in productivity. Organizations have been losing their ability to effectively utilize the human resources available to them. What is becoming critical now is the growing inability of current organizational forms to adapt to the changing demands of society and values of employees discussed earlier in this chapter. For organizations once again to become viable and productive, they must become attractive places for individuals to work. The values of the "New Breed" need to be satisfied. This New Breed must once again become involved in their jobs and more committed to what they do. The work place must be able to recognize individual differences and afford opportunities for meeting various personal goals. Now as never before the organization must begin to be concerned with satisfying two matches—the job demands-individual ability match and the job rewards-individual value (needs) match.

Organizational shapes and designs need to be created to attract the "New Breed".

The match that organizations have been concerned with is making sure people get the job done (matching demands and ability—**Match 1**). In the past, because of this concern and the assumption that people really worked primarily for money, organizations designed jobs that were simple and routine and almost anyone could do. Employees were essentially replaceable. If people didn't have the necessary skills, they could be easily trained. The preoccupation with this match resulted in organizational reliance on close supervision, economic incentives, and the threat of loss of job security. These are characteristics of what we will refer to as the **traditional organization form.** Although this form used to result in high productivity, today it accomplishes less because of the New Breed.

The match that individuals (the New Breed type) are now concerned with is making sure that they can satisfy personal needs for involvement, growth, and responsibility. They want the organization to provide rewards that match their New Breed values (Match 2). This concern has come about through the increased affluence in our society and increased educational levels. In addition:

> Young people are beginning to claim the right to have an interesting, self-fulfilling, self-developing, individually-centered job.[7]

Organizations can satisfy both needs for productivity and QWL.

Thus the New Breed, which is becoming the majority of the work force, want jobs and job conditions that are the opposite of those of the traditional organizational form. They want a new flexible, adaptable organizational form that can satisfy their concern: **Match 2.** The organization in which Match 2 can be satisfied is called here the **contemporary organizational form.** This form can result in both productivity and QWL gains.

FOR YOUR CAREER

Two Critical Matches in Personnel Management

Match 1: Job Demands = Employee Ability
        Key Concern: Productivity
Match 2: Job Rewards   = Employee Needs
        Key Concern: Productivity and QWL

In the contemporary form, concern for both matches is shown.

In the traditional form, concern for only Match 1 is shown.

The contemporary organizational form reflects qualities in which employees exercise discretion. Supervisors don't closely supervise. They may inform and coordinate, if they are present at all. Jobs are designed to not only allow people to exercise more discretion but also to use more skills and to provide more identity and significance. Frequently individuals work as members of teams. Often these teams make central decisions involving work flows, job designs, and even personnel such as selecting, rewarding, and appraising each other. Because these qualities are becoming recognized as the way to make employees more productive as well as to make organizations more attractive, organizations are changing from the traditional form to the contemporary form. Many of the characteristics that organizations are changing are presented in detail in Chapter 16 on Productivity and QWL. It is important, however, to become comfortable with these two organizational forms and matches now because they will be used throughout the rest of the chapters. To help you, Exhibit 2.4 summarizes this information.

Exhibit 2.4
The Traditional and Contemporary Organizational Forms

Traditional Organizational Qualities/Characteristics	Contemporary Organizational Qualities/Characteristics
▪ Close Supervision; employees are controlled by the boss	▪ Loose Supervision; employees exercise self-control; employees participate
▪ Jobs tend to be repetitive and have low significance; narrow job descriptions exist	▪ Jobs tend to have variety and some importance to the employee and the organization; broad job descriptions exist
▪ Traditional ways of doing things are used to manage people	▪ Innovative approaches in managing people are tried
▪ Productivity is the major concern (Match 1)	▪ Productivity and QWL are of equal concern (Match 1 and Match 2)

Reduction: Dealing with Job Loss.   Although many organizations face the need to attract more people to the organization, some are faced with the opposite situation—how to eliminate some of the people they currently have. This situation is particularly true for companies in the basic industries, such as steel, rubber and, of course, automobiles.

> The plight of Chrysler will create a new demand for "redundance planning," that is, anticipating structural and technological changes in the economy and preparing to retrain and find new jobs for workers who will have to be laid off.
>
> During the next few years, this demand will be intensified by the almost predictable closing of a number of steel mills that will become technically obsolete beyond repair. Indeed, labor unions are already proposing that Congress impose redundancy planning on industry.[8]

Indeed, the discussion later in this chapter describes the increased pace of technological innovation, automation, and robots, and the resulting shifts in labor force levels and patterns. The story of the newspaper typographers (see Personnel in Action p. 61) will be written more and more frequently in the years ahead. What should employers do in the face of these massive changes in employment profiles? Should an employer just displace workers with machines in the name of productivity? What responsibility do you think an employer has to employees, especially those who have many years of loyal service? If employers do accept some responsibility for **redundancy planning,** what can they do?

> Since it is obvious that automation is here to stay, company and/or industry committees might be set up in all industries to discuss the problem of redundancy. These committees could each include, along with representatives from government and industry, several redundant workers, so that a better understanding of the more human effects of redundancy can be obtained. It is important that such committees not be limited to industries that are currently experiencing the impacts of automation. To be most effective, planning for redundancy must begin well before the problems occur.[9]

Unions, of course, can also play a central role in redundancy planning. For example, the New York Typographical Union offers a fairly complete training program for its out-of-work typesetters. The union, however, in no way guarantees that any of this training will facilitate their getting jobs. In Western Europe, trade unions are stepping up their efforts to win reductions in the number of hours worked per week in an effort to stem the swelling tide of displacement.[10]

Government can also provide some assistance to employers and the potentially displaced employees. In California, for example, short-time compensation (STC) is the new alternative to layoffs and the full costs (to the employer and state) of worker unemployment compensation benefits:

> California's STC program (called work sharing) reduces or eliminates the costs of layoffs and spares employees from the trauma of full unemployment. It can be used by employers who need to temporarily or permanently reduce labor costs. When employees are retained during a temporary slowdown, the employer can quickly and efficiently return to the former level of production. In the case of a permanent layoff, STC can be a transition to layoff: affected employees work reduced hours and have the opportunity to find other employment.[11]

In essence, STC allows employers to cut back the number of hours employees work per week as the alternative to layoff. The state then provides a portion of the unemployment compensation payment the employees would receive if they were totally unemployed. The STC program works so that the employees always take home more money with a combination of a reduced work week and partial unemployment compensation than with complete layoff and total unemployment compensation.

Preretirement Counseling.   Employee plans (or lack of plans) for retirement also play a role in employers' efforts at redundancy planning. Some employees may be unaware that they are able to retire early. Some may not retire because they are afraid of what their future will be like without work. They may think that they can't afford to retire. Consequently the organization may have people who would gladly retire if they knew how. A special type of counseling may be particularly beneficial to these workers and the organization is **preretirement counseling.**[12] This counseling can facilitate an employee's transition from work to nonwork and by doing so encourage employee retirement. Thus personnel may help an organization reduce the bottlenecks discussed earlier as well as avoid or reduce the number of redundant workers by making sure that preretirement counseling programs are provided and that employees who can retire are identified and made aware of their options to retire and are aided in their retirement plans.

Regardless of whether personnel *should* establish preretirement counseling programs, new organizational designs, or redundancy planning programs, there is little doubt that personnel *will need to* do these things and more. This is because of so many significant changes occurring in society. These changes are having and will continue to have a severe impact on the human resource needs and supplies of an organization. Since human resource needs and supplies are the responsibility of personnel, personnel must be aware of and knowledgeable about the important changes likely to influence effective personnel planning.

IMPORTANT EVENTS AND TRENDS IN THE 1980S INFLUENCING EPP

As the quotations at the start of this chapter illustrate, there are many events and trends occurring that are a dramatic influence on organizations. In turn, they are

Exhibit 2.5
Effective Personnel Planning Relationships with the External Environment

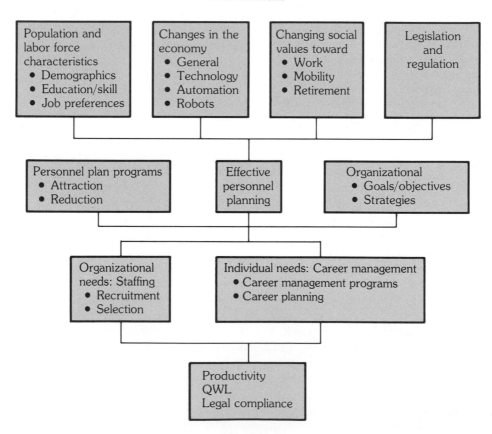

having a dramatic effect on personnel management and raising the importance of EPP to new highs. Because of the significance of these events and trends, it is important to discuss them and see their impacts on human resources.

The job of EPP encompasses the whole range of societal, demographic, economic, and government regulatory factors that influence changes in an organization's current and future work force. Just as personnel management is concerned with the "whole person," EPP must be increasingly aware of the total external environment that will shape the kind of work force, and its concerns, on hand tomorrow as well as the environment that is shaping the current work force. These relationships are shown in Exhibit 2.5.

The Population and the Labor Force Characteristics

A critical feature of the external environment for organizations is the people. Organizations need to know the characteristics of the population in general and of the labor force in particular.

Demographics.   The counter clerk handing you your Burger King sandwich next time may not be the usual teenager.[13] Rather, you may see some teenager's grandparent! The major reason is the shrinking supply of young workers. After more than two decades of growth, the nation's population between sixteen and twenty-four has now peaked. As shown in Exhibit 2.6, the sixteen to twenty-four age group will continue to decline as a percentage of the total labor force. In the meantime, the twenty-five to fifty-four age group (especially the twenty-five to forty-four segment) will continue to rise. These trends will help cause bottlenecks in the promotion paths for that age group for the next several years.

Exhibit 2.6
Percentage of Labor Force Distribution by Age (Source: H. N. Fullerton, "The 1995 Labor Force: A First Look," *Monthly Labor Review* 103 (December 1980): 15)

	Actual			Projected	
	1975	1979	1985	1990	1995
Total	100.0	100.0	100.0	100.00	100.00
Age					
16 to 24	24.1	24.5	21.3	18.8	17.2
16 to 19	9.4	5.1	7.5	6.9	6.7
20 to 24	14.5	14.8	13.8	11.7	10.5
25 to 54	60.7	61.6	65.8	70.2	72.4
25 to 34	24.1	26.1	28.4	28.5	25.9
35 to 44	18.2	28.9	22.5	25.7	27.7
45 to 54	18.3	16.3	14.8	15.9	18.9
55 and over	15.2	13.9	12.9	10.9	10.2
55 to 64	12.2	11.3	10.3	8.7	8.3
65 and over	3.2	2.4	2.7	2.4	1.9

Looking at the same age categories by sex and race, we can see several other interesting trends.[14] The total number of men in the labor force will continue to diminish while the number of blacks and women will continue to increase. These projections are illustrated in more detail in Exhibit 2.7.

Exhibit 2.7
Labor Force Distribution by Sex and Race (Source: H. N. Fullerton, "The 1995 Labor Force: A First Look," *Monthly Labor Review* 103 (December 1980): 16)

WHITE	1975	1979	1985	1990	1995
Total, age 16 and over	88.6	88.0	87.2	86.5	85.9
Men	53.8	51.5	49.4	47.8	46.6
16 to 24	11.6	11.3	9.7	8.2	7.4
25 to 54	33.4	32.1	32.8	33.8	34.0
55 and over	8.7	8.0	6.8	5.7	5.0
Women	34.7	36.4	37.7	38.7	39.3
16 to 24	9.5	9.7	8.9	7.9	7.4
25 to 54	20.0	21.7	24.3	26.7	28.0
55 and over	5.0	4.9	4.5	4.0	3.8
BLACK AND OTHER					
Total, age 16 and over	11.3	11.9	12.7	13.4	14.0
Men	6.1	6.2	6.4	6.5	6.7
16 to 24	1.4	1.5	1.3	1.1	1.1
25 to 54	3.8	3.9	4.3	4.6	4.9
55 and over	.8	.7	.7	.6	.6
Women	5.1	5.6	6.3	6.8	7.3
16 to 24	1.3	1.4	1.3	1.2	1.2
25 to 54	3.3	3.6	4.3	4.9	5.4

FOR YOUR CAREER

Some Terms Used in Government Labor Studies

- *Civilian labor force:* All people classified as employed or unemployed

- *Employed:* All those who worked for pay at any time during the survey week; worked fifteen hours or more as unpaid workers in the family business; or had a job but were not working due to illness, bad weather, or the like

- *Unemployed:* All those who were not working during the survey week, but made specific efforts to find a job in the preceding four weeks; were laid off and waiting to be recalled; or were waiting to report to a new job within thirty days

- *Not in civilian labor force:* All people not classified as employed or unemployed

- *Labor force participation rate:* The labor force as a percentage of the population
- *Unemployment rate:* The unemployed as a percentage of the labor force
- *Fulltime workers:* Those who usually work thirty-five hours or more per week
- *Parttime workers:* Those who usually work one to thirty-four hours per week

Education and Skills.   Although the number of people in the work force with high school diplomas and college degrees will continue to increase, the number of skilled jobs that go unfilled will also increase. What we are seeing is the formation of a **labor force dichotomy:** those with high education levels trained to be managers and professionals and those without sufficient education and generally able to fill only unskilled jobs.[15] The result is a skilled worker shortage that will probably only get worse. But even those with training do not always have the right training. Consequently, there will be (and are) job shortages in rather attractive job categories.[16]

Job Preferences.   Currently the occupational makeup of the civilian labor force reflects much higher percentages of women than males in clerical positions and higher percentages of males employed in managerial and administrative jobs and as craftworkers. The exact distribution of males and females in the nine major occupational categories maintained by the U.S. Department of Labor are shown in Exhibit 2.8. Although these data indicate that 16 percent of the females occupy professional and technical positions, most of those are in the nursing and teaching professions. Thus a majority of the female work force are in service, clerical (secretarial), nursing, and teaching jobs. The majority of males, on the other hand, are in semiskilled (operative), skilled (craftworkers), managerial and administrative, and professional and technical jobs. These distributions have resulted from the notion of **job sex-typing.** That is, a job takes on the image of being appropriate only for the sex that dominates the job.

Exhibit 2.8

Occupational Makeup of the Civilian Labor Force (Adapted from U.S. Department of Labor, Bureau of Labor Statistics, *Employment and Earnings,* vol. 27, no. 3 (Washington, D.C.: Government Printing Office, March 1980), p. 41.)

OCCUPATIONAL GROUP	PERCENTAGE OF TOTAL LABOR FORCE	PERCENTAGE OF MALE WORKERS	PERCENTAGE OF FEMALE WORKERS
Professional and technical	14	14	16
Managerial and administrative	11	14	7
Sales	6	6	7
Clerical	18	6	34
Craftworkers	14	21	2
Operatives	15	17	11
Laborers	6	9	1
Service workers	14	10	21
Farmworkers	2	3	1

Job and role typing restrict individual opportunity.

Consequently, once a job becomes sex-typed, it attracts only those of that sex. Job sex-typing combined with **sex-role stereotyping** has traditionally restricted perceived job choices and preferences of both males and females. There is evidence, however, that indicates that the range of perceived choices and preferences is expanding for both males and females. For example, as of the end of 1978 nearly 9,000 women were enrolled in skilled trades apprenticeship programs—a 52 percent increase over 1977. Also, between 1972 and 1978, the number of male secretaries increased 24 percent, telephone operators 38 percent, and nurses 94 percent.[17]

These trends have been facilitated in part by the gradual reduction of the strength of sex-role stereotyping in our society. In addition, some of the job sex-typing has been reduced through the desexing of job titles (as shown in the *Personnel in Action* insert) and legal mandates to encourage employers to hire females in previously male-dominated jobs and vice versa.

These job preference and choice changes will provide both challenges and opportunities for personnel planning practitioners. The challenges will center around the social impact felt when males or females enter nontraditional jobs, for example, women in the skilled trades. The opportunities are in developing well-planned programs that will help ensure that these employees are able to remain in those nontraditional jobs.[18]

FOR YOUR CAREER

Whereas *job sex-typing* refers to the labeling of jobs as being for males only (men's jobs) or females only (women's jobs) (as shown in the job desexing list), *sex-role stereotyping* refers to labels or characteristics or attributes that become attached to the sex categories and, consequently, to any individual who is a member of that sex *solely* because she or he is a member of that sex.

Trends in the Economy

Most major corporations devote substantial resources to economic forecasting, in addition to subscribing to the macroeconomic analyses of banks, insurance companies, private economists, and governmental agencies. Since economic conditions are certain to affect the future work force and conditions of employment, they should be considered in personnel planning.

General Economic Conditions. One trend that will certainly affect personnel planning is continuing inflation in the range of 5 to 9 percent.[19] At an inflation rate estimate of 7 percent, the cost of most goods sold will double by the end of the decade. Similarly, wages and salaries (to keep up with inflation) will also double. This will make it particularly imperative for organizations to increase productivity through better methods. Continued inflation will also influence the cost of employer-paid fringe benefits, further enhancing the need for productivity gains and better work-force utilization.

PERSONNEL IN ACTION

FIFTY TWO sex-stereotyped job titles have been changed by the Census Bureau's Occupational Classification System in order to help eliminate the idea of "men's jobs" and "women's jobs."

The suffix "men" has been dropped from most of the occupational titles, and replaced by "worker" or "operator." Government officials point out that it's unrealistic to expect that women will apply for jobs advertised for foremen, salesmen, or credit men, or that men will apply for jobs calling for laundresses, maids, or airline stewardesses.

Under the new system stewardesses, for example, will be called flight attendants and salesmen will become sales workers. Also, the title for the major group, craftsmen and kindred workers, has been changed to craft and kindred workers. Other changes:

FORMER TITLE	NEW TITLE
Cranemen	Crane operators
Forgemen and hammermen	Forge and hammer operators
Clergymen	Clergy
Public relations men	Public relations specialists
Credit men	Credit and collection managers
Newsboys	Newspaper carriers and vendors
Office boys	Office helpers
Foremen	Blue collar worker supervisors
Pressmen	Printing press operators
Dressmakers and seamstresses	Dressmakers
Boatmen and canalmen	Boat operators
Fishermen and oystermen	Fishers, hunters, and trappers
Longshoremen	Longshore workers
Chambermaids and maids (except private households)	Lodging quarters cleaners
Busboys	Waiters' assistants
Firemen	Fire fighters
Policemen	Police
Laundresses (private household)	Launderers
Maids (private household)	Private household cleaners

Reprinted by permission from *Fair Employment Practice Service*, copyright 1981 by The Bureau of National Affairs, Inc., Washington, D.C.

Faced with these general economic conditions, as well as the increased international competition, organizations are rapidly turning to advanced technologies, automation, and robots.

Technologies, Automation, and Robots.   Although many critics assert that the United States is losing its world leadership in the use and understanding of technology, automation, and robots, such an event does not appear likely in the 1980s.

> Fortunately, American technology is alive and well. Despite the alarmed outcries in recent years that the U.S. is losing its technological vigor, there is growing evidence to the contrary. If anything, the pace of innovation is accelerating.[20]

The technologies in which the United States is advancing most rapidly and that have the most potential for enhancing productivity and work-force utilization are microelectronics, artificial intelligence, materials research, material surfaces, biotechnology, and geology.

A significant application of microelectronics will result in increased automation (and computerization) and the use of robots. Even though the utilization of these products increases productivity dramatically, it increases the size of the needed work force and the pride and self-esteem of employees. These effects are poignantly illustrated in the printing/newspaper industry described in the *Personnel in Action* insert. Similar occurrences, however, are also taking place in the white-collar industries (with office technology), such as banking and insurance. For example,

> In the letter-of-credit department of Citibank's Wall Street Office, Richard Matteis, a Citibank vice president, describes how the company automated the handling of letters of credit using a variety of computer-controlled equipment and record storage: "Where it once took days, 30-odd separate processing steps, 14 people, and a variety of forms, tickets, and file folders to process a single letter of credit, it now requires one individual less than a day to receive, issue, and mail out a letter of credit—all via a terminal that is fully online to a minicomputer-based system."[21]

Thus, though the rise of these advances such as robots can help people by eliminating dull and dangerous jobs, their use also eliminates the pride, self-respect, and earnings of those displaced. Robots also eliminate jobs. Thus the personnel planning needs of the organization must be altered when robots are considered. Where robots are likely, redundancy planning may be especially useful.

Changing Social Values

Closely linked with the changes in the population and labor force and the changes in the economy are those in the social values held by the population and the labor force. The areas in which these values are particularly important for personnel planning are *work itself, mobility,* and *retirement.*

PERSONNEL IN ACTION

The Impact of Computers on Employment

By Bruce Gilchrist and Arliaana Shenkin

The very rapid development of the electronic computer over the past 30 years has spawned thousands of new companies, created many new jobs, made possible new industrial and consumer products, enabled man to reach the moon and probe the universe—the list of benefits seems endless. However, the computer has also caused some jobs to disappear, made others less interesting, and made some people feel more like numbers than individuals.

Economists add up the pluses and minuses, and usually conclude that the computer has been good for the economy. We agree with this overall conclusion, but want to point out that there are individuals who have not experienced this "overall good." In particular, the 44 skilled craftsmen discussed below found that the computer mainly brought them trouble.

In 1978, the owner of two small New York-based trade newspapers decided that he could reduce his expenses significantly if he automated his composing room. In fact, by moving to a newly automated plant he was able to decrease his typesetting staff from 61 to 3.

We attempted to contact all the displaced workers and were successful in locating 44 of them. Although our sample is small and was not randomly selected, we believe that it is reasonably representative of what is happening in the printing industry.

Over the four-year period 1974–78, three major New York City newspapers reduced their employment of typesetters by 31%, 39%, and 43%. This decrease was achieved through attrition and early incentive retirement plans. Similarly, at a large newspaper in Washington, D.C., in the early part of 1979, 80 typesetters "volunteered" to leave with $40,000 in severence pay under threat by the owners to declare bankruptcy and put all 1,800 employees out of work.

All of the workers in our sample received some severance pay. At one of the papers, there was an 11-year contract with an automation clause requiring the employer to provide each permanent employee $35,000 severance pay in the event of a layoff. At the other paper, the contract had run out. The owner, however, voluntarily decided to give long-term employees $8,000 each.

Both Income and Pride Are Lost

One 58-year-old man had spent 30 years as a typesetter, working on the now antiquated linotype machine. Because he had worked for his current employer for less than one year and was not protected by any contract, he received only half of the regular $8,000 severance pay given to 31 of the typesetters.

With a wife and son to support and a sizable mortgage to pay, the $4,000 helped him financially, but it did nothing for his sinking morale. "I was afraid to go to work and leave my husband alone. He was starting to fall apart," his wife explained. A few months later, his wife was in a mental institution.

For the next year, he tried to obtain another printing job, but what little self-esteem he had left dropped further when he found that the only jobs being offered were for salaries of $150 per week, about one-third of what he had been earning. The family saw no income for six months after his unemployment insurance ran out. His wife believes the tremendous financial and mental support their friends and neighbors gave them during this difficult period helped the family to pull through. Today, he works as a telephone operator, earning less than half his former salary. His wife is too sick to work.

One typesetter's wife never had a job before her husband was laid off. Now the couple is living on her paycheck. She explained that her husband feels quite frustrated because he cannot get a job and, at 48, he is too young to do nothing and too old to start something new.

From Bruce Gilchrist and Arliaana Shenkin, "The Impact on Employment,"*Futurist* (published by the World Future Society, 4916 St. Elmo Avenue, Washington, D.C. 20014), February 1981, p. 44.

Values toward Work. It is often said that people do not work as hard today as people used to, that people don't have the work ethic. This, however, is not necessarily the case.

> The work ethic has not disappeared. People today are willing to work hard on "good" jobs, providing they have the freedom to influence the nature of their jobs and to pursue their own lifestyles.[22]

Thus people still value work, it's just that the type of work they value has changed. The New Breed want jobs with challenge, and they want jobs in which they are provided

QWL will become more important throughout the 1980s.

the freedom to make some decisions. These desires are entirely consistent with the list of values in Chapter 1. Those values and these desires constitute the essence of the quality of work life movement. *What QWL represents then is personal control, self-respect, and power to influence what is going on.* It also represents a belief in and demand for participation in the work place, a voice in the way things are run (Match 2 concerns). Underlying this belief is the slogan:

> All people can think and
> Nowhere is it chiseled in
> Stone that those in management
> Think best.

Economic and demographic changes are making promotional opportunities less likely.

Values against Mobility. Employee values toward work are having a significant effect on employee feelings about moving around from job to job when it entails moving from one region of the country to another.[23] As with the new employee values toward work, the new employee value against mobility will have (and is having) a significant impact on personnel management especially in recruiting, training, promoting, and motivating managers and professionals. Thus large companies like Boeing, General Electric, Norton, Georgia-Pacific, Bell Telephone, and IBM are having a difficult time getting their employees to move. This growing reluctance, however, may not be all that bad a trend for companies. In the past five years, according to the Employee Relocation Council in Washington, D.C., the average cost to a company of moving a home-owning employee has tripled. It is now $30,000!

Values toward Retirement. "Many fear golden years might become just brass." The American predilection for early retirement appears to be waning, slowing a trend of the 1970s that many once predicted would put the nation's average retirement age below fifty-five by the year 2000.[24] Thus many workers are bypassing provisions for early retirement (such as at fifty-five or sixty) and even staying past the traditional retirement age of sixty-five. This is largely in response to inflation rates, concerns over the stability of the social security system, and federal and state legislation protecting the older employee, such as the Age Discrimination in Employment Act.

EPM will depend upon effectively dealing with bottlenecks.

One significant consequence of this change in value toward retirement is the bottleneck it creates in the promotion paths for younger employees, particularly minorities and women. Note that this bottleneck resulting from later retirement adds to the bottleneck problem for personnel managers due to the changing demographics of the larger twenty-four to fifty-four age work-force population discussed earlier. Thus, personnel managers will need to play the innovative role very astutely to accommodate the older work force yet retain and motivate the younger work force.

Legislation and Regulation and Governmental Activity

Perhaps at no time in history has governmental activity so greatly impinged on the human resource function in organizations. In some respects, the modern corporate personnel department has been shaped by the requirements of federal and state legislation. See Appendix A for evidence of the many laws and regulations that impose requirements on the managment of human resources. As we proceed it will be apparent how all of personnel functions and activities are influenced and will continue to be influenced by legislation and regulation.

In summary, the changes in these four major areas—demographics, the economy, social values, and government regulation—are likely to have significant impact on the management of human resources. Knowing what these changes will be will aid a personnel manager in more effectively managing an organization's work force. For this knowledge to really help, however, the personnel manager must use this knowledge in developing and implementing effective personnel planning strategies. Once implemented, these strategies need to be evaluated and revised, then implemented and evaluated again. Only by doing this continuously will personnel planning and all of personnel management be effective.

EVALUATING EPP ACTIVITY

Personnel planning can really make or break an organization. Without effective personnel planning an organization may find itself with a plant or an office without the people to run it. Organizations can no longer assume that the right number of appropriately qualified people will be ready where and when the organization wants them. So on a broad level, the EPP activity can be evaluated on the basis of whether or not the organization has the people it needs, that is, the right people at the right place, at the right time, and at the right price (salary).

At more specific levels, EPP activities can be evaluated by how effectively they (along with recruitment) attract new employees, deal with job loss, and adapt to the changing characteristics of the environment. Since an important part of EPP is forecasting, EPP can be evaluated by how well its forecasts (whether of specific personnel needs or of specific environmental trends) compare with reality. Accuracy here can be very critical since it is unlikely that EPP can do well on a broad level if it fails to do well in forecasting.

FACING THE CRITICAL ISSUES IN PERSONNEL PLANNING

Now that the essence of effective personnel planning has been described and the dynamic forces of the environment have been illustrated, it is useful to briefly discuss the critical issues faced by personnel practitioners.

Issue: *What are the aspects of our society that will be changing and increasing the need for organizations to engage in personnel planning?*

The major aspects of our society that are changing that influence EPM include: (1) The population and labor force characteristics such as the age, sex, and race composition; education and skill levels; and job preferences; (2) changes in the economy including general economic conditions and the increased use of automation and robots; (3) the changing social values, especially those toward work, mobility, and retirement; and (4) the changing legislation and level of government activity. Changes in any of these areas make personnel planning even more important.

Issue: *How are the critical aspects of our society changing? In what directions are they going?*

The critical aspects in the first question are changing at a more rapid pace than ever before. Each of the components of these aspects is changing in a unique way. You should be familiar with each of them. For example, the shrinkage of the eighteen to twenty-four age group implies that it will be harder for organizations to get younger workers. Recruiting efforts may have to be modified. At the same time, the increase of the twenty-four to fifty-four age group will cause bottlenecks in the promotion paths that used to be open. Now organizations will need to develop strategic and operational plans in how to deal with career aspirations of employees who want to be promoted when no openings are available.

Personnel departments must also develop strategic and operational plans for all phases associated with human resource utilization. These strategic plans of personnel describe the broad-range, long-term goals of personnel. These should be tied into the strategic plans of the rest of the organization. The operational plans specify how the strategic goals are to be attained. By moving the personnel department into a more vital position in the management of the total organization, it can begin to play several roles described in Chapter 1, one of which is of policy formulation. This can help ensure that personnel is seen as a vital and useful department in the organization. It can also ensure that the organization's human resources are utilized as effectively as possible.

Issue: *What are the implications of these changes for effective personal planning?*

Organizations can no longer assume that the right number of the right people will be available at the time when they are needed. Because the right people at the right place and in sufficient numbers may not happen, organizations must be proactive. Personnel must take charge of an organization's personnel planning. It must assess what the organization will need and who will be available. Action programs must then be developed to eliminate the possibility of any discrepancy between the demand and supply of needed human resources. In summary, the expected changes will cause effective personnel planning to be more proactive which may result in the development of very innovative action programs to ensure organizations of needed human resources.

Issue: *Why is it often difficult to establish a personnel planning program (PPP) and how can the roadblocks to its establishment be removed?*

It is often difficult to establish a PPP because top management sometimes fails to see the need for it. Most of us are too busy with things that are happening today to worry about things that may never happen. This is the same with managers in organizations. In addition, top management is just not used to thinking that the personnel department can influence the bottom line. This is due to the past image and practice of the personnel department. Much of the roadblock to PPPs can be removed by getting top management support. This support can be obtained by showing that the PPP can be effective. This can also be aided by showing that the personnel department can be effective. The personnel manager should also show the organization all of the events and trends that are occurring and how they are influencing the use and supply of human resources.

SUMMARY

The environment of organizations is exceedingly complex, as shown in Exhibit 2.1. In addition, it is changing rapidly. These changes are having and will have severe implications for the effective management of human resources. Unless the impact of these changes is planned for, organizations will find themselves without the necessary people to operate effectively. Planning for these changes, however, is difficult. Nevertheless, the personnel manager should take charge in this planning process. The entire organization should be enlisted in projecting its human resource needs. It should also be used in evaluating the current and future supply of its human resources.

With this information, personnel should then develop programs to ensure that what the organization needs, it has when appropriate. To develop personnel planning programs that will actually help the organization, personnel must get top management support. It can get this support by showing the impact of the changing environment, its impact on the organization, how personnel can help meet the impact, and how specific programs can get done what is needed, thus be effective.

KEY CONCEPTS

labor force dichotomy

job sex-typing

sex-role stereotyping

Delphi technique

nominal grouping technique

simple linear regression

multiple regression

Match 1

Match 2

redundancy planning

preretirement counseling

effective personnel planning (EPP)

traditional organizational form

contemporary organizational form

human resource information
  system (HRIS)

DISCUSSION QUESTIONS

1. What are the purposes of effective personnel planning?
2. In what ways are EPP related to other personnel activities?
3. What are the techniques used to forecast the demand for human resource needs? Which are used most?
4. List the four phases of EPP.
5. What types of characteristics are associated with the traditional organizational form and the contemporary organizational form?
6. What three reasons can be listed to demonstrate that planning is an important element in the design of action programs?
7. What external factors are becoming increasingly important in EPP? Give some specific examples.
8. Why is it that we are likely to see more women filling so-called men's jobs in the future?

9. If you were a personnel manager of an organization relying on computers to increase its productivity, what effects would you predict for the future of the organization and its employees?

10. EPP is essentially concerned with ensuring that the organizations can fulfill what function?

CASE

Dumpitt Waste Disposal Expands

Horace Dumpitt, Jr., chairman of the board of Dumpitt Waste Disposal (DWD) has decided to increase the scope of the firm's operations by developing a new division devoted to the collection and disposal of hazardous industrial wastes. DWD was founded in 1929 by Horace Dumpitt, Sr., to collect and bury household wastes. Through hard work and astute business decisions, DWD has grown into a large full-service organization dealing with all aspects of household and light commercial waste collection and disposal. Disposal and recycling of chemical waste, therefore, would represent a logical avenue for corporate expansion. Dumpitt has entrusted the crucial task of developing a plan for the expansion to his granddaughter, Eula Dammwelle Dumpitt, a recent MBA graduate.

Conscious of the recent declaration by the president of the United States of hazardous waste treatment and disposal as the major environmental issue facing the United States in the 1980s, Eula recognizes the field as presenting an opportunity to capitalize upon a government commitment significantly greater than that accorded to clean air or clean water issues. Two major acts of the United States Congress have mandated cradle to grave monitoring of hazardous waste. As a result of the regulations implementing these acts, the price of disposal of a ton of hazardous waste has increased from approximately $25 per ton in 1975 to $400 per ton in 1982 (constant 1980 dollars are quoted).

The Dumpitt Waste Disposal Corporate Planning Division has concluded that the company could derive 35–40 percent profit after taxes if a new chemical waste treatment and disposal division could be developed and placed in operation in the near future. Market entry is not anticipated to present a problem as the company has been in the disposal business in excess of fifty years and is fully cognizant of the political, economic, and practical ramifications of market entry. Further, the company's considerable size and prestige are sufficient to prevent competitors from blocking entry.

Eula has concluded, therefore, that her major problem is to determine the staff requisite for rapid and efficient implementation of the new division. Fortunately, due to a speculative building boom, considerable new office space is available, and Eula has leased a large amount of office space adjacent to the main DWD parking lot, thereby eliminating any potential relocation expense with respect to employees selected for transfer to the new division. Nevertheless, Eula realizes that the transfer of existing employees may create gaps in the existing DWD organizational structure, and that a whole cadre of new employees will have to be hired. Eula has concluded that DWD must, therefore, make provisions to assemble the staff to carry out this new effort.

Case Questions

1. Is Eula right? Will a whole cadre of new employees have to be hired?
2. When should Eula have developed personnel plans to meet potential expansion needs?
3. What steps should Eula take to ensure that Dumpitt will be able to staff the new division?
4. Who should be involved with Eula in developing the personnel plans for Dumpitt?

FOR YOUR CAREER

- The environment in which we live is changing rapidly. Consequently it is as critical for you as it is for organizations to plan ahead. It pays to plan.
- Without planning, you are likely to get stuck in a situation where you don't have the necessary skills to do well.
- Without planning, you are likely to get stuck in a situation where you aren't being challenged or where your skills and abilities are not being fully utilized.
- You should look closely at the traditional and contemporary forms of organizations and decide which one you prefer and why.
- To what extent do you think organizations should replace workers with robots and automated equipment?
- In your career planning, consider nontraditional jobs.

ENDNOTES

1. Guvene G. Aplander, "Human Resource Planning in U.S. Corporations," *California Management Review,* © 1980 by the Regents of the University of California. Reprinted from *California Management Review,* vol. 22, no. 3, p. 29.

2. E. W. Vetter, *Manpower Planning for High Talent Personnel,* (Ann Arbor, Mich.: Bureau of Industrial Relations, Graduate School of Business, The University of Michigan, 1967), p. 15.

3. Craig B. Mackey, "Human Resource Planning: A Four-Phased Approach," *Management Review,* May 1981, pp. 17–22.

4. John J. Leach, "Merging the Two Faces of Personnel: A Challenge for the 1980's," *Personnel,* January–February 1980, pp. 52–57.

   "Manpower Planning and Corporate Objectives: Two Points of View," *Management Review,* August 1981, pp. 55–61.

   Edwin L. Miller and Elmer H. Burack, "A Status Report on Human Resource Planning from the Perspective of Human Resource Planners," *Human Resource Planning,* 1981, pp. 33–40.

   Stella M. Nkomo, "Stage Three in Personnel Administration: Strategic Human Resources Management," *Personnel,* July–August 1980, pp. 69–77.

George S. Odiorne, "Developing a Human Resource Strategy," *Personnel Journal,* July 1981, pp. 534–536.

James A. Sheridan, "The Relatedness of Change: A Comprehensive Approach to Human Resource Planning for the Eighties," *Human Resource Planning,* 1979, pp. 123–133.

James W. Walker and Robert Armes, "Implementing Management Succession Planning in Diversified Companies," *Human Resource Planning,* 1979, pp. 123–133.

Jan P. Muczyk, "Comprehensive Manpower Planning," *Managerial Planning,* November–December 1981, pp. 36–41.

5. Vetter, p. 67.

6. Louis E. Davis, "Individuals and the Organization," *California Management Review,* © 1980 by the Regents of the University of California. Reprinted from *California Management Review,* vol. 22, no. 3, p. 5.

7. Lauren Hite Jackson and Mark G. Mindell, "Motivating the New Breed," *Personnel,* March–April 1980, p. 54.

8. Peter F. Drucker, "Planning for Redundant Workers," *Personnel Administrator,* January 1980, p. 32.

9. Bruce Gilchrist and Arliaana Shenkin, "The Impact of Computers on Employment," *Futurist* (published by the World Future Society, 4916 St. Elmo Avenue, Washington, D.C. 20014), February 1981, p. 49.

10. "The Unions Press to Cut the Work Week," *Business Week,* August 31, 1981, pp. 60–61.

11. Alan H. Locher, "Short-Time Compensation: A Viable Alternative to Layoffs," *Personnel Journal,* March 1981, p. 213. Reprinted with the permission of *Personnel Journal,* Costa Mesa, California; all rights reserved.

12. "Helping Employees Through a Major Life Transition," *Behavioral Sciences Newsletter,* February 26, 1981, Chapter 13.

13. Joann S. Lublin, "Effects of 'Baby Bust' Are Shrinking Ranks of Younger Workers," *Wall Street Journal,* September 10, 1981, pp. 1, 16.

14. Vincent P. Barabba, "Demographic Change and the Public Work Force," *Proceedings of the 2nd Public Management Research Conference, November 17–18, 1980,* pp. 29–41.

Elizabeth Hartzell and Roger Lewis, "Soothsayers and Parables: The Workforce Now and Tomorrow," *Personnel Journal,* June 1981, pp. 444–448.

Donald L. Luda, AEP, "Personnel Management; What's Ahead?" *Personnel Administrator,* April 1981, pp. 51–60.

Donald E. Pursell, "Planning For Tomorrow's Personnel Problems," *Personnel Journal,* July 1981, pp. 559–561.

Raymond R. Wingard, "Our Real Corporate Responsibility," *Personnel Journal,* August 1980, p. 620.

15. P. Zollman, "There's Jobs in Abundance for Americans with Skills," *Columbus Dispatch,* 20 May 1979, UPI Business Writer, sec. C., pp. 1, 8.

16. Zollman, p. 8.

17. Carol Hymowitz, "More Men Infiltrating Professions Historically Dominated by Women," *Wall Street Journal,* February 25, 1981, p. 25.

18. Peter F. Drucker, "Working Women: Unmaking the 19th Century," *Wall Street Journal,* July 6, 1981, p. 12.

Nancy R. Brumer, "Blue Collar Women," *Personnel Journal,* April 1981, pp. 279–282.

Amitai Etzioni, "The Blue Collar Renaissance," *Washington Post,* Section D, pp. 1, 3, 1981.

Amitai Etzioni, "The Lasting Changes Brought by Women Workers," *Business Week,* March 15, 1982, pp. 59, 62, 67.

Howard N. Fullerton, Jr., "The 1995 Work Force: A First Look," *Monthly Labor Review,* December 1980, pp. 11–21.

"A Look at the Workers You'll Boss in the 80's," *Industry Week,* June 26, 1978, pp. 24–26.

Kenneth A. Kovach, "Women in the Labor Force: A Socio-Economic Analysis," *Public Personnel Management Journal,* Volume 9, Number 4, 1980, pp. 318–326.

Patricia Somers, Charles Poulton-Callahan, and Robin Bartlett, "Women in the Work-force: A Structural Approach to Equality," *Personnel Administrator,* October 1981, pp. 61–64.

19. Christopher Conte, "Analysts are Confident of Economic Health as the Decade Pro-ceeds," *Wall Street Journal,* September 14, 1981, pp. 21, 23.

20. "Technologies for the '80s." Reprinted from the July 6, 1981, issue of *Business Week* by special permission, © 1981 by McGraw-Hill, Inc., New York, NY 10020, p. 48.

21. Colin Norman, "How Microelectronics May Change the Workplace," *Futurist,* (published by the World Future Society, 4916 St. Elmo Avenue, Washington, D.C. 20014) February 1981, p. 38.

22 "Expectations That Can No Longer Be Met." Reprinted from page 84 of the June 30, 1980, issue of *Business Week* by special permission, © 1980 by McGraw-Hill, Inc., New York, NY 10020. All rights reserved.

John Andrew, "In High School Today, Youths are Absorbed With Material Goals," *Wall Street Journal,* June 3, 1981, pp. 1, 22.

Albert Cherns, "Work and Values: Shifting Patterns in Industrial Society," *International Social Science Journal,* Vol. 32, No. 3 (1980); 427–441.

Rosabeth Moss Kanter, "Work in a New America," *Daedalus,* Journal of the American Academy of Arts and Sciences, Vol. 107 (1978):47–77.

Rosemary J. Erickson, "The Changing Workplace and Workforce," *Training and Develop-ment Journal,* January 1980, pp. 62–65.

Phil Parrish, "PAIR Potpourri," *Personnel Administrator,* July 1981, pp. 15–16.

John Holt, "Growing Up Engaged," *Psychology Today,* July 1980, pp. 14–16, 23–24.

Marsha Sinetar, "Management in the New Age: An Exploration of Changing Work Value," *Personnel Journal,* September 1980, pp. 749–755.

23. "America's New Immobile Society," *Business Week,* July 27, 1981, pp. 58–62.

24. Lawrence J. Holt, "Retirement: A Time to Enjoy or Endure?," *Personnel Administrator,* November 1979, pp. 69–74.

"Working for Life: The New Reality," *Plain Dealer,* July 15, 1979, Section 2, p. 2.

Jerome M. Rosow and Robert Zagar, "Work in America Institute's Recommendations Grapple With the Future of the Older Worker," *Personnel Administrator,* October 1981, pp. 47–53, 80.

Kenneth P. Shapiro, "The Reversing Early Retirement Trend," *Personnel Administrator,* April 1980, pp. 77–79.

Chapter Outline

Critical Issues in Designing and Analyzing Jobs

The Job Design and Job Analysis Activities
Purposes and Importance
Job Design and Job Analysis Relationships

Job Design
Job Design Qualities
Job Design Approaches
Time for Job Redesign
Selecting a Job Design—A Diagnostic Approach
Implementing Job Redesign—A Summary

Job Analysis
Job Analysis Information
Structured Procedures for Analyzing Jobs
Methods Analysis in Analyzing Jobs
Collecting Job Information for Job Analysis

CHAPTER 3

Designing and Analyzing Jobs

Evaluating Job Design and Job Analysis Activities

Facing the Critical Issues in Designing and Analyzing Jobs

Summary

Key Concepts

Discussion Questions

Case

For Your Career

Endnotes

Personnel in the News

The Job Is Critical

Since the Industrial Revolution, the development and introduction of new technology in the work place has been America's leading tool for increased productivity, economic growth and higher standards of living.

However, in 1979, productivity in the United States began to fall, and for the first quarter of 1980, this trend continued as productivity in the private sector fell at an annual rate of 0.6%. While there are more machines on the market with great capabilities and potential uses than ever before, new technology is falling short of its full potential.

The primary reason for this failure is that management has too often thrown new and expensive production technologies into the work place without adequate consideration of the human element in the productivity equation.

Greater consideration must be given to the needs of those workers who operate new machinery and equipment. The lessons learned from behavioral science in the past 20 years should be applied when new technology is introduced into the work place. The cost of applying the behavioral sciences for greater productivity is much less than that of making additional and unwarranted capital investments; and the results can be beneficial for both employees and the company.

A widely held tenet about job satisfaction, motivation and worker performance states that a job, to be completely satisfying, must provide a worker three experiences: meaningfulness, responsibility and knowledge of results. Given these factors and the technical knowledge of how machines operate, how can management make the worker-machine interface more compatible for greater productivity and improved quality of goods?

To reap the full benefits of advanced technology, management must recognize that the majority of workers are capable of doing far more than their jobs require or allow. Management recognition and acceptance of this fact is especially critical today when one considers that signs of lagging productivity are everywhere.

In addition, we see coming into our work force a new generation of workers with value systems and expectations about work which are completely different from those held by previous generations. These new workers are willing and motivated to work hard; however, they want their work to be meaningful as they define it, not as the organization defines it. Today's workers will neither tolerate nor be completely productive in jobs where their work activities are controlled by machines.

All organizations should seriously consider how the machine operator's job can be redesigned to effect increases in productivity. New technology presents management with the opportunity to eliminate or significantly reduce the segmented nature of most jobs.

Most jobs involving worker-machine interface are comprised of assignments that are too functional in nature. For example, companies hire and train "specialists" to perform even the simplest production and maintenance tasks when in many instances these tasks can logically be combined with operators' jobs for greater productivity and job satisfaction.

Many workers perceive their jobs to be meaningless and boring because there is little skill variety to the work. This is detrimental to both productivity and quality of output. Too often when a machine breaks down, production stops while a maintenance worker is called to the scene, causing production costs to increase unnecessarily because management does not permit production workers to make certain repairs to their equipment. While this example does not suggest that all maintenance work should be done by production workers, common sense should dictate combining certain tasks in the maintenance/production areas and in numerous work areas throughout the plant or office.

When evaluating the impact of worker-machine interface on productivity, management must also consider the importance of performance feedback. All of us want and need to know how we are doing at our work. In most cases, management fails to provide workers with meaningful and timely feedback, and so productivity declines further because it can be weeks or months before workers learn that they have not been doing their jobs correctly. (Roy W. Walters, Personnel Journal, *September 1980, p. 707. Reprinted with the permission of* Personnel Journal, *Costa Mesa, California; all rights reserved.)*

The Law and Job Analysis

A company may be selecting employees in violation of Title VII of the Civil Rights Act of 1964 if it uses a test which has not been shown to relate to the nature of the job. Thus job analysis is necessary. (Albermarle Paper Company v. Moody [1975].)

The performance appraisal system of an organization is a selection procedure and therefore must be validated. That is, it must be anchored in job analysis. (Brito v. Zia Company [1973].)

To prevent discriminatory practices in promotion decisions, a company should have written objective standards for promotion. These objective standards can be determined by job analysis. (Rowe v. General Motors [1972].)

In addition to having objective standards for promotion, the standards should describe the job to which the person is being considered for promotion. These standards can be determined through job analysis. (U.S.A. v. City of Chicago [1978].)

The analysis of the **worker-job interface** by Roy W. Walters, an eminent figure in job design, indicates that our productivity and quality of work-life problems are due to the way jobs are designed. Further, he cautions organizations from installing new technologies to increase productivity without consideration of the human element in the productivity equation. His fear is that organizations will install these technologies the same way that they installed the old technologies. When old technologies were installed the result was specialized and repetitive jobs for the workers. And although workers *then* performed those jobs, it is apparent that workers *now* do not want to perform them. In essence, we are facing the potential for a real worker-job crisis. This, in turn, raises several critical issues for job design.

In addition to these job design issues, organizations are facing several critical issues in describing the jobs that are designed. The court decisions cited show how important job analysis is and reflect that organizations must do job analysis if they are to avoid illegal discrimination in their employment practices.[1] And, as discussed in the first two chapters, illegal discrimination can lead to costly legal settlements. Furthermore, selection decisions not based on a sound job analysis can lead to low productivity and low QWL. Consequently, there are several *very* critical issues in job design and job analysis.

CRITICAL ISSUES IN DESIGNING AND ANALYZING JOBS

The four most critical issues identified by our personnel managers are

1. *Why is the worker-job crisis really so important?*
2. *What can be done to avert this crisis?*
3. *Is it really possible for organizations to design jobs so that both productivity and QWL are high?*
4. *How can jobs best be analyzed so that the resulting job descriptions meet legal requirements?*

In large part, many of the functions and activities of personnel management and the behaviors and attitudes of employees have their roots at the interface of employees and their jobs. As indicated in Exhibit 3.1, job analysis influences staffing (recruitment and selection), compensation, training and development and performance appraisal.

THE JOB DESIGN AND JOB ANALYSIS ACTIVITIES

In turn, job analysis is a consequence of the way jobs are designed. And job design is influenced by several organizational and personnel qualities. Thus **job design** results in a set of purposes, task characteristics, and task duties in a given organizational setting based on a set of unique organizational and personnel qualities. **Job analysis** is the process of describing and recording the purposes, task characteristics, and task duties in a given organizational setting and of determining the appropriate match of individual skills, knowledge, abilities, and needs. Thus job analysis generally has two components: a **job description** and a **job specification,** as shown in Exhibit 3.1.

This definition of job analysis suggests that job descriptions should contain more than the traditional set of duties, conditions, and purposes (though even these are not always clearly stated in some job descriptions). They should also contain a description of the characteristics of the job (although this generally is not done now). This definition also suggests that job specifications should contain more than the traditional set of needed skills, knowledge, and abilities to successfully perform the job duties under the given conditions. Rather, job specifications should also contain a description of individual needs that might best be served by the job.

These two modifications of the traditional job description and the traditional job specification are in keeping with our concern for attaining two of the three major

Exhibit 3.1
Job Design and Job Analysis Relationships

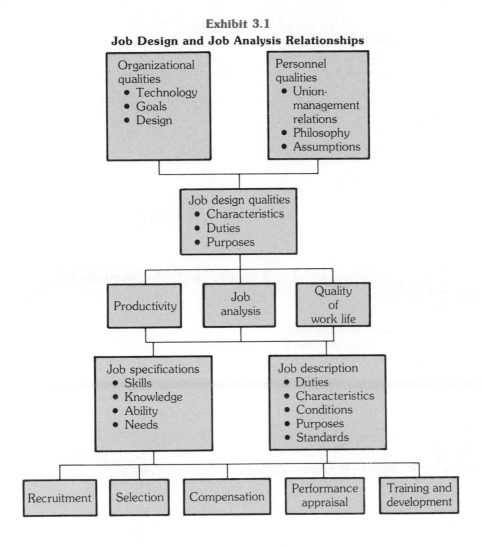

purposes of EPM: high productivity and a low QWL. The other major purpose of EPM, complying with legal regulations, begins to be served just by doing the job analysis. The way these modifications help attain our two purposes and why they are becoming necessary will be discussed in the next major section, Job Design.

Purposes and Importance

As shown in Exhibit 3.1, the job-related information obtained through job analysis can be used to influence several personnel functions and activities. A more specific enumeration of the personnel functions and activities influenced by job analysis is presented in Exhibit 3.2. An organization rarely uses job analysis for all these purposes, but the expanse of the list suggests the importance of job analysis in an organization. The legal necessity for job analysis, as shown in the beginning quotations, now adds considerably to this importance. Thus legal compliance is another major reason for job analysis.

Exhibit 3.2

Purposes of Job Analysis Adapted from E. J. McCormick, "Job and Task Analysis," in Marvin D. Dunnette (ed.), *Handbook of Industrial and Organizational Psychology,* Chicago: Rand McNally, 1976), p. 683. (By permission of the editor)

Individual
Vocational guidance
Vocational preparation

Organization
Human resource planning
Job design
Job evaluation
Recruiting
Selection and placement
Training
Personnel appraisal

Labor Relations
Management-union relations

Public Policy and Administration
Legal aspects (standards, licensing, certification, etc.)
Public employment services
Public training and education programs
Social security administration
Safety programs

Research
Population analysis (economic, social, etc.)
Behavioral research related to job or occupational characteristics
Validation of selection test and performance appraisal form

The design of jobs can make or break a QWL program.

The purposes of job design reflected in Exhibit 3.1 are to (1) serve as a basis for forming a job for job analysis; (2) result in a set of task activities (characteristics, duties, and purposes) that will lead to high productivity; and (3) form a set of task activities that will lead to a high QWL. It is becoming more apparent that job design really does serve these purposes, which is making job design more important than ever. Much of the work currently being done in organizations to improve productivity and QWL is aimed at changing the workers' jobs, either enriching individual jobs or creating teams (this is discussed further in Chapter 16). The assembly line technology is being attacked, whether it is used in offices or plants, as the culprit of worker boredom, alienation, turnover, absenteeism, and lower productivity. Though many workers may still prefer assembly line jobs, job design knowledge is critical for EPM. And because job design (of whatever form) does relate to productivity and QWL, we refer to it again in Chapter 16 on productivity and QWL programs.

Job Design and Job Analysis Relationships

Because job analysis serves so many purposes, it has extensive relationships with several other personnel activities. For example, on the basis of job analysis and in conjunction with EPP, the organization knows whom to recruit. Only with job analysis information can an organization show that its selection procedures are job-related. To effectively evaluate employee performance, the appraisal method that is used must reflect the duties of the job (this relationship is discussed again in Chapter 9) and only by examining the skills required for a job (as defined in the job specifications) can the organization train and promote employees.

Job analysis underlies almost all other personnel activities.

Job analysis also plays a vital role in one of the most important concerns of individuals in organizations—pay. It is on the basis of the job analysis that jobs are evaluated. Since job evaluation determines the worth or value of a job to the organization, it often determines how much an employee gets paid for doing that job. Job analysis is also important in ensuring that the level of pay for a job is fair in relation to other jobs. That is, job analysis helps ensure that employees in jobs of equal worth receive the same pay. The type of technology being used by and available for an organization is also critical because it determines what types of job designs are possible and what types of jobs are appropriate for various organizational designs. For example, U.S. automobile manufacturers, with huge investments in plants and machinery to make cars on assembly lines, find it almost impossible to convert their car-making technology so that groups of workers make the cars. The result is that most assembly jobs are fairly segmented and repetitive and remain that way. Furthermore, assembly line technology helps determine the structure or design of the organization and in turn the most appropriate types of job designs.

The design of jobs not only reflects the design and technology of the organization but also its goals. Because organizations create them, jobs are in fact very explicit statements by organizations of what they have determined to be the most appropriate means for accomplishing their goals. Furthermore, if the concepts that workers have of their organization help determine their behavior, then the stated goals and the subsequent standards of excellence that an organization establishes give very clear cues to employees about what is important and where their efforts are required. In addition, since goals also help determine the products and environments of organizations, they help determine the criteria against which workers will be evaluated—hence their behaviors. The criteria and goals, in turn, also determine the kinds of individuals who will be attracted to the organization, evaluated highly, and promoted.

Thus organizational goals can help establish the reasons for jobs, the nature of the organization's expectations from the workers performing the jobs, and even the legitimacy of the job demands. Goals have several other consequences through their relationship with the structure of the organization, which is in turn related to the design of jobs.[2]

JOB DESIGN

Although job design is only concerned with job characteristics, duties, and purposes, the results of job design have a profound influence on employee productivity and QWL. Unfortunately, this influence can be very negative, for example, when it results in employee boredom, absenteeism, and sabotage. On the other hand, this influence can be very positive because it can lead to feelings of greater responsibility, challenge, and meaningfulness. Do you think you could design a job so an employee in an organization could experience responsibility, challenge, and meaningfulness? How would you do it? This is a critical design question, and one you should be able to begin to answer by the end of this chapter. A step in the direction of assisting you in answering this question (if you haven't already done so) is to briefly explain the job design qualities. By the way, Chapter 16 provides additional information to help explain how certain job characteristics can have beneficial effects.

Job Design Qualities

As shown in Exhibit 3.1, there are three job design qualities: **characteristics, duties,** and **purposes.**

Characteristics. There are seven critical job design characteristics. These seven and their definitions are

The three job design qualities are
- Character-istics
- Duties
- Purposes

1. **Skill variety:** The degree to which a job requires a variety of different activities in carrying out the work, involving the use of a number of different skills and talents of the person

2. **Task significance:** The degree to which the job has a substantial impact on the lives of other people, whether those people are in the immediate organization or in the world at large

3. **Task identity:** The degree to which a job requires completion of a "whole" and identifiable piece of work, that is, doing a job from beginning to end with a visible outcome

4. **Autonomy:** The degree to which the job provides substantial freedom, independence, and discretion to the individual in scheduling the work and in determining the procedures to be used in carrying it out

5. **Job feedback:** The degree to which carrying out the work activities required by the job provides the individual with direct and clear information about the effectiveness of his or her performance[3]

6. **Task overload:** There are two types of overload. The first is having more duties to do than there is time to do. This is **quantitative overload.** The second is having to do duties which require more skill and abilities than the employee has. This is **qualitative overload**

7. **Task underload:** This is essentially the reverse of task overload. **Quantitative underload** is having too few duties to do in the time allotted. **Qualitative underload** is having more skills and abilities than necessary to perform the job duties

Duties. The specific activities that comprise the job are called duties. The job description of an animal keeper in a zoo shown in Exhibit 3.3 illustrates the specific duties or activities that together form the essence of the animal keeper's job.

Purposes. A critical aspect of a job is the reason for its creation and its existence. Why does the job exist? How does it relate to the final product or goal of the organization?

Exhibit 3.3
Position Description—Animal Keeper—WG–9 (National Zoological
Park, Washington, D.C.) (Used by permission of the Smithsonian
Institution, National Zoological Park, Washington, D.C.)

Introduction

This position is located in the Office of Animal Management, National Zoological Park, and is directly supervised by the Curator of the assigned unit.

The function of the keeper is to perform the described duties, most of which require specialized skills that result in the proper care, feeding, exhibition and propagation of a collection of wild and exotic animals many of whom are rare and endangered. The keeper is also responsible for maintaining a presentable exhibit so that the animal may be shown to the public in an attractive setting. At this level, one is considered a journeyman in the craft of animal care.

All duties are performed in accordance with established policies and procedures of the Office of Animal Management. The incumbent is informed of any changes governing policies and procedures by the Animal Manager and/or Curator who are available for consultation when new or unusual problems arise. Assignment areas will normally include any or all cages and enclosures in the assigned unit. The keeper receives technical supervision and daily work assignments from the Animal Manager of an assigned section of the unit.

Duties

a. Cleaning of animal enclosures, including hosing, sweeping, scrubbing, raking, and removal and disposal of manure, unconsumed food, and other refuse.

b. Maintenance of enclosure materials, such as trimming and watering of plants, and cleaning and maintenance of perches, nest boxes, feed containers, and decorative materials, and provision of nesting and bedding material.

c. Feeding and watering of all animals, including measurement and preparation of feed items and prepared diets, placement in feed pans or other containers, and timely distribution and placement in animal enclosures.

d. Cleaning of service areas and of public areas adjacent to the animal enclosures.

e. Inspection of all animals at specific times to insure security of animals in proper enclosures and to assure prompt reporting of illness or abnormal behavior.

For these routine duties, the incumbent will adhere to standard operating procedures including lists of mandatory daily duties and the normal order and time in which they should be completed. Incumbent confers at all times with the Animal Manager of the assigned section when problem situations arise.

Prepares reports on daily or periodic basis, as instructed, to be presented to the Animal Manager while working on an assigned line. May be asked to note and record relevant observations on animals and record these on the daily report. Examples, such as breeding encounters, nesting activity, courtship rituals, aggression between cage mates, feeding by offspring would be considered relevant. The keeper may be expected to learn and be familiar with the terminology used in keeping the records such as common names or scientific names of animals.

Maintains a close watch over the animals in the collection for symptoms of sickness, injury or other unusual conditions and reports information to the Animal Manager and/or Curator, in their absence, to the Veterinarian. When it is necessary, the keeper will capture, handle, crate, uncrate, transport, mark, force feed or restrain any animal in the assigned area. This will involve aiding the Veterinarian in administering treatment to animals, or under instructions from the

Animal Manager independently giving prescribed medicines to an animal, administering first aid, and feeding and hand rearing newborn or abnormal animals.

The keeper will, in accordance with specifications, prepare the animal diets for all the animals in the assigned area when called upon to do so. The keeper will increase or decrease the diets as instructed by the Animal Manager and/or Curator and may recommend changes in feed and feeding sites from observations to the Animal Manager and/or Curator. All animals must be given water as required.

At this journeyman level, the keeper will use proper nest boxes, nest materials and nest sites in attempting to get animals to breed and raise young. Uses proper techniques of young animal care including correct methods of collecting and incubating eggs with special regard to preventing injury to the animals. The keeper may be asked to aid or participate in projects carried out by other NZP offices that involve the scientific study of the collection. The keeper may either under the supervision of the Curator, Animal Manager or others actively carry out an independent study project on the collection animals.

Incumbent assists Animal Manager in the development and construction of new exhibits. May be asked to collect exhibit materials such as logs, rocks, sand, dirt and gravel. The keeper also monitors conditions of all exhibits in an assigned section, including plants and foliage, perches, logs, nesting boxes and substrate materials. Maintains the exhibits in an assigned section in a clean and orderly condition.

The incumbent may be asked to train and instruct lower grade employees in any or all of the above duties assigned to the WG-9 animal keeper. Examples, such as animal husbandry techniques, understanding of the animals in an assigned section, and the zoological principles involved as well as operating procedures.

Must be familiar with all safety, first aid and emergency equipment and procedures in the unit. The keeper must be familiar with security procedures for all areas of the section, to prevent animal escapes, injury to visitors, and malicious damage to the animals.

Makes recommendations to supervisors regarding establishment or modification of procedures that will make the unit more effective in reaching its objectives.

The keeper may be required to drive an automobile, scooter or small truck to do incidental driving such as transporting animals to other zoos, to depots of public transportation or to the Conservation Center.

May be required to work any assigned eight-hour shift during the 24-hours of operation and is subject to call at any time. Must be available for duty on weekends and holidays.

May be asked to pass the SI scuba diving certification test, so that aquatic vertebrate pools can be cleaned. On a routine basis are required to mix and add chemicals to the filter systems for these pools.

Performs other related duties as assigned.

Physical Requirements and Conditions:

This position requires considerable walking, standing, heavy lifting up to 100 pounds, stooping, and other types of physical effort and dexterity in moving and distributing animals, animal feed, cage materials, equipment, and in opening and closing cage doors and gates. Although safety measures are taken, there is always a hazard of injury in working with exotic and unpredictable animals.

Incumbent will be required to work both indoors and outdoors during all types of weather, and may be required to work in areas which are hot, cold, dusty, odorous, or with high humidity, as well as in closed areas and cramped spaces.

Job Design Approaches

Jobs can be designed in many different ways. We will, however, consider only four major ways. The other ways of designing jobs are essentially combinations of the four major ones. Regardless, jobs designed differently differ primarily on the three job design qualities. This will become more clear as the four major job design approaches are discussed: *scientific* (traditional), *individual contemporary, team contemporary,* and *ergonomics.*

Job design
approaches
- Scientific
- Individual
contempo-
rary
- Team
contempo-
rary
- Ergonomics

Scientific. Traditionally, job analysis has been used to describe the dimensions of the job to be performed and the required worker specifications. And as illustrated in Exhibit 3.1, the dimensions of the job described in the analysis are largely determined by *job design.* Under the **scientific approach,** job analysts took special pains to design jobs so that the tasks performed by employees did not exceed their abilities. In fact, the jobs designed by scientific management often resulted in work being partitioned into small, simple segments. These tasks lent themselves well to motion and time studies and to incentive pay systems, both for the purpose of obtaining high productivity.[4] The scientific approach to job design was an important part of the traditional organization. It reflected the assumption that workers generally disliked work and were motivated by economic rewards. Generally, the result was a job with minimal levels of variety, significance, autonomy, feedback, and identity. Since the jobs were so small, as a result of a high division of labor, they often had a qualitative underload and a narrow purpose.

> It turned out, however, that many workers did not like jobs designed according to the dictates of scientific management. In effect, the person-job relationship had been arranged so that achieving the goals of the organization (high productivity) often meant sacrificing important personal goals (the opportunity for interesting, personally challenging work).[5]

The only reward that employees received under scientific job design was monetary. Yet many employees had needs not served by monetary rewards, such as the need for responsibility and autonomy. Yet organizations continued to treat the design of the job as inviolate, something not to be changed. Methods were developed to select people who would be satisfied with economic rewards and job with simple segments.

It is not hard to understand why the success of this strategy has been limited. Many employees, though by no means all, want jobs that give them responsibility and autonomy, as well as good pay. Organizations have responded by designing jobs in other ways.

Individual Contemporary. This approach and the team contemporary are job designs to work in a way that achieves high productivity without incurring the human costs that are sometimes associated with the scientific approach.[6] There are three **individual contemporary approaches** that you should be aware of: job rotation, job enlargement, and job enrichment.

Job rotation really does not change the nature of a specific job. It does, however, often increase the number of duties an employee performs over a period of time. This is because the employee moves from one job to another after a specified period of time. As you can see, the nature of each of the separate job's task characteristics may or may not be varied. But because the employee is now performing several jobs,

Horizontal
Loading means
adding more of
the same
characteristics.

it is reasonable to assume that an employee's sense of identity and scope of purpose with what she or he does increase.

Job enlargement differs from rotation by adding more duties to a specific job rather than moving an employee around to experience the duties of several jobs. Job enlargement is the opposite of the scientific approach, which seeks to reduce the number of duties.

Job enrichment differs from job enlargement by seeking to load a job vertically rather than horizontally. **Horizontal loading** means adding more duties with the same types of characteristics. **Vertical loading** in job enrichment means creating a job with duties with many different characteristics, for example, making a job more significant and requiring more skills to perform it. The impact of job enrichment is further discussed in Chapter 16.

Vertical
Loading means
adding
different
characteristics.

Team Contemporary. Whereas the individual contemporary and scientific approaches design jobs for *individuals*, the **team contemporary** approach designs jobs for *teams of individuals*.[7] The final designs generally show a concern for the social needs of individuals as well as the constraints of the technology. In the team contemporary approach, teams of workers often rotate jobs and may follow the product they are working on through to the last step in the process. If the product is large, for example, an automobile, teams may be designed around sections of the final car. Each group then completes only a section and passes its subproduct to the next team. In the team contemporary design, each worker learns to handle several duties, many requiring different skills. Thus they can satisfy worker needs for achievement and task accomplishment and some needs for social interaction. The Volvo car example of this approach is discussed in Chapter 16.

Two other aspects often associated with the team contemporary design are *group gain sharing* and *participation in decision making*. When faced with decisions, teams generally try to involve all members. If their decisions and behaviors result in greater output, all team members share in the dollar benefits. Although increased participation can also be given to employees working individually, it is less a part of the design of those employees' jobs than it is under a team contemporary job design approach.[8]

Ergonomics. This approach is concerned with trying to design and shape jobs to fit the physical abilities and characteristics of individuals so they can perform the jobs. The **ergonomic approach** is critical to organizations. It is helping organizations redesign jobs to accommodate women and handicapped individuals generally (to serve legal equal employment and affirmative action objectives). In addition to helping aid organizations in serving their legal objectives, this accommodation helps organizations better utilize their work force. It has been shown that when jobs are designed along ergonomic principles, worker productivity is greater. In a recent study done by the National Institute for Occupational Safety and Health (NIOSH), two groups of employees working under an incentive pay system were compared. The group working on jobs designed according to ergonomic principles was 25 percent more productive than the group working on the jobs designed without these principles.

Ergonomics, however, is not a panacea for an organization's legal employment obligations as shown in the *Personnel in Action* insert, "Blue-Collar Women." A summary of the advantages and disadvantages of these four job approaches is shown in Exhibit 3.4.

Exhibit 3.4
A Summary of the Advantages and Disadvantages of the Four
Job Design Approaches

APPROACH	ADVANTAGES	DISADVANTAGES
Scientific	Ensures predictability Provides clarity Fits ability of many people Can be efficient and productive	May be boring May result in absenteeism, sabotage, and turnover
Individual contemporary	Satisfies needs for responsibility, growth and knowledge of results Provides growth opportunity Reduces boredom Increases quality and morale Lower turnover	Some people prefer routine and predictability May need to pay more since more skills needed Hard to enrich some jobs Not everyone wants to rotate
Team contemporary	Provides social interaction Provides variety Facilitates social support Reduces absenteeism problem	People may not want interaction Requires training in interpersonal skills Group no better than weakest member
Ergonomics	Accommodates jobs to people Breaks down physical barriers Makes more jobs accessible to more people	May be costly to redesign some jobs Structural characteristics of the organization may make job change impossible

PERSONNEL IN ACTION

Manager's Journal

by Liz Roman Gallese

Blue-Collar Women

As women increasingly break down barriers in high-paying craft, trade and assembly-line jobs, some employers have expressed grave reservations about women's ability to handle the work.

American Telephone & Telegraph Co., for example, which had been under a court order to hire wom-

en into these jobs, says women have three times as many accidents in all outdoor jobs and six times as many accidents in the tough, physically demanding job of pole-climbing. As recently as two years ago, more than 15 times as many women as men called it quits in the semi-skilled outdoor jobs.

And when Ford Motor Co. announced in April the closing of its big plant in Mahwah, N.J., the company cited poor quality as a major reason. At least one reason for the quality problems, some managers privately say, was the influx of women into blue collar jobs previously held primarily by men.

Officially, John Manoogian, Ford's executive director of product assurance, says that the company hasn't investigated possible differences between men and women in their ability to stay on the job and do the work.

However, some plant managers, union officials and workers say that many women hadn't been up to assembly line work and had to quit, adding to the high turnover that was bedeviling quality at Mahwah. There is also criticism of the women who stayed. A worker recalls that women couldn't handle the heavy instruments used to pound windshields into place on trucks. "They kept cracking the windshields," he says.

Ergonomists—the physicians, psychologists and other scientists who try to fit job requirements with people's abilities to do tasks—declare almost unanimously that physical differences between men and women are significant when it comes to certain kinds of work.

"Are there differences? Absolutely!" says Christian Stiehl, senior industrial engineer at Polaroid Corp., the Cambridge, Mass. camera-and-film maker.

Specifically, ergonomists say the differences boil down to just two: size and strength. An average woman is 85% the size of an average man and has two-thirds his strength, explains Stover Snook, a psychologist and ergonomist at the Liberty Mutual Research Center, an arm of Liberty Mutual Insurance Co., the big worker's compensation insurer. An average woman has about half a man's strength in her arms, about three-fourths his strength in her legs.

Ergonomists caution, however, that some attributes thought to make a difference probably don't. A different in hormones thought to make men more "aggressive" probably amounts to nothing more than a difference in the way boys and girls are reared, says Mr. Stiehl, the Polaroid engineer. The belief that women's menstrual cycle renders them less capable on those days of the month "is a lot of bunk," he says.

Ergonomists insist, furthermore, that physical differences between the sexes do not justify companies' excluding or limiting women from jobs on the line.

Ergonomists explain, for example, that just because the *average* woman differs in size and strength from the average man doesn't mean that there aren't women out there who can do the job. Just as in any other line of work, companies must seek out people who can fill the requirements of the job.

"Companies must search for above-average wom-

en. After all, they don't hire economists with I.Q.'s of 100," says Mr. Stiehl.

Even more critically, ergonomists say that companies must redesign equipment so that it accommodates not only women but also a broader range of men. At Polaroid, for example, a greater number of women than men had accidents driving big trucks that lift and carry boxes. But the force required to hit the brakes was "excessive," it was found. Since the brakes were adjusted, neither men nor women have had accidents.

Likewise, General Motors Corp. began buying air-operated tools in three sizes rather than one. Previously, the one size the company bought had been too big for the average woman's hands. "Equipment is like bowling balls. Be it a hit with 10-lb. or 16-lb. ball, the strike is the same," says Dr. Robert Wiencek, GM's director of health services.

Skilled blue-collar work, moreover, has been pitched directly at men only. Even work clothes, such as safety shoes, often come only in men's sizes. "So everything from her safety shoes on up gives a woman this message: You have a right to do it, but gee, we wish you wouldn't," says Mr. Stiehl.

Consultants to companies hiring women on the line cite lack of acceptance and outright hostility to women as a key problem. A vice president of Goodmeasure Inc., a Cambridge, Mass., consulting firm, says that at AT&T, male workers had figured out how to do one job better than the way they were taught, but wouldn't pass tips along to their female co-workers.

For its part, AT&T acknowledges that acceptance of women by peers and superiors, as well as improper screening and equipment, have been problems.

But two years ago, the company began requiring a test for physical aptitude to better screen both male and female applicants. Likewise, the company modified some equipment. It began using lighter fiberglass ladders, for example.

But despite the changes, AT&T says the accident rate improved only slightly. The improvement in turnover also leaves a lot to be desired. Accordingly, the company lowered its goal for women in outdoor jobs to 9% from 19%. (Currently, women comprise 3% of skilled and 6% of semi-skilled outdoor jobs.) "The previous goal was ridiculous," says Donald Liebers, director of equal opportunity and affirmative action. "Physical demands are the chief deterrent" to women in these jobs.

Time for Job Redesign

In Chapters 1 and 2, we considered the concern many people have (some call it a crisis) for what they see as a decline in the productivity and QWL of American companies. In trying to explain why, many people point to the nature (design) of the jobs in organizations combined with the changing work-force values. They say most jobs are too simple and repetitive. Furthermore, many workers could do a lot more than they are doing. They could be performing more duties and using more skills and abilities. In essence many jobs are designed along the principles of the scientific approach. Consequently, many people are calling for a change. They say it's a time for job redesign. They say job redesign will serve several purposes including

- Increasing employee motivation
- Increasing productivity and QWL
- Serving as an alternative to promotion in career development
- Accommodating more women into traditionally male jobs
- Making work more possible for older individuals and handicapped individuals

These are the five purposes of job redesign.

Since jobs in most organizations have been designed under the scientific approach, the demands for change generally focus on change by either the contemporary individual or contemporary team approach. It is not entirely certain, however, that these two contemporary approaches will work well for everyone under all conditions. In fact, it is certain that some people prefer the scientific approach to jobs and that conditions may only permit the scientific approach. The question then you have to ask is how to select a job design approach.

Selecting a Job Design—A Diagnostic Approach

In selecting an approach to job design, the personnel manager should examine three major areas.[9] The results of this examination will help determine which job design approach is most appropriate for the organization. Note that this examination in selecting a job design approach can be used either when an organization is just starting and all jobs are new or after it has existed for awhile and there is a determined need for a job design change (or job redesign). Thus all of the following discussion is useful for you, whether you join an already existing company or start your own.

Employee Knowledge, Skills, Needs, and Satisfaction. Knowing all of these qualities is critical in determining the appropriate and feasible job design. If jobs are to be enriched, employees must have the knowledge relevant to doing the new job. If the contemporary team approach is selected, employees will need interpersonal skills and problem-solving skills in order to work effectively as a group. Without these interpersonal and problem-solving skills, the scientific approach may be more feasible and appropriate. The ergonomics approach may be more feasible and appropriate if employees lack the physical strength or size to do a particular job.

Working on enriching jobs or working in teams is not for everybody, just as working on specialized, repetitive jobs is not boring and dull to everyone. Enriched jobs usually help satisfy individual needs for challenge, responsibility, and a sense of meaningfulness. Jobs designed around a group approach may satisfy some of those needs *and* satisfy individual needs for social interaction and support.

In job redesign it is important to remember that not all workers want enriched jobs.

Critical Questions for Determining the Need for Job Redesign

1. Is there a problem in the organization that can be solved by changing the design of jobs?

2. Are there legal pressures to accommodate individuals that could be reduced by redesign?

3. Is the organization ready for a change? Will the personnel system, the technological system, and control system accommodate a change?

4. Are the employees ready for a change? Do they have the appropriate skills, abilities, needs, and satisfaction levels?

5. Are the labor-management relations favorable to job redesign?

6. Is the organization prepared to support and maintain the job changes?

As you know, it's pointless to be concerned about the design of a job if you don't have one. Many employees are by necessity more concerned about their job security, such as the employees in the typographical industry we considered in Chapter 2. It also appears that if employees are not satisfied with their pay, coworkers, or supervisor, they are less concerned with the design of their jobs.

Organizational Technological Systems, Personnel Practices, and Control Systems. The **technological system** of an organization refers to the machines, methods, and materials that are used to produce the organization's product. The type of technology can strongly influence the job design approach used. The assembly line is often used as an example of a technology in which the jobs are extremely repetitive and very simple. Jobs that skilled workers perform and that some managers perform are generally the opposite of assembly-line jobs. Both skilled workers and managers can control the pace of their work and often can use a variety of skills.

Although technology can strongly influence the design of jobs, organizations can sometimes choose the type of technology they want to use in making the same product. For example, in the manufacture of automobiles, GM, Ford, and Chrysler have traditionally chosen to use the assembly line. This, however, is not the only way to make cars. Volvo in Sweden is an example where a nonassembly method was adopted.[10] This switch in technologies represented a very significant change. It had a major impact on the rest of the organization. The switch represented more than a change in technology, however; it also represented a way of thinking about people as human resources. No longer were people thought of as replaceable parts but rather as irreplaceable components of the organization. Thus in diagnosing the technological system, it is important to realize its impact on job design and also the variety of technologies that can actually be used in making a product.

Personnel practices in organizations are generally used with the good intention of providing for the fair and consistent treatment of workers. To help ensure this, fixed job descriptions are written. They often specify what a worker should do as well as the methods the worker should use. These descriptions also specify the skills and abilities needed by workers. In turn these descriptions and specifications are used in picking selection tests, in choosing the performance appraisal devices, in designing training programs, and in the all-important area of determining pay levels for jobs. This really represents a lot of areas that *have to be* changed when jobs are redesigned. Since these areas are usually under the control of different personnel specialists and generalists, they all have to be convinced of the need for the job design change. Once they are convinced, their efforts have to be coordinated. Without their support and coordination, any job design effort will be unlikely to be adopted or to succeed.[11]

Control systems are also likely to prevent the organization from adopting a new job design or a particular type of design. Control systems include such things as production and quality control reports, scrap reports, supervisors, attendance reports, and time sheets (cards). Because it is important to locate who is responsible for problems or errors, control systems often specify who is accountable, how things should be done, and from whom to get approval for doing something differently. Although this helps reduce the complexity of each job and the responsibility of each worker, the effect is to set up "impersonal" boundaries. The boundaries then become critical in the way people behave and what they will not do. Have you ever heard someone say, "I'm not responsible for that"?

Changing control systems is just as difficult as changing personnel practices. Yet both of them need to be changed to facilitate job design changes. Furthermore, particular types of job designs are unlikely to be adopted given the philosophies of key decision makers. For example, if the top management or owners want to retain close control or if they really don't think employees can act responsibly, it is likely that they will choose the scientific approach to job design rather than one of the contemporary approaches.

Union-Management Relationships.   Although less than 25 percent of the work force is unionized, union influence and leadership are critical for almost all employees. Without union support, organizations find it almost impossible to change the design of jobs. This is because job redesign can influence job classification, often a critical concern of unions because it influences the pay scale for the jobs redesigned. In Chapters 16 and 19 we will consider the benefits that result when union and management do work together in changing jobs to improve the QWL and productivity. These joint union-management efforts in turn become examples for other nonunion organizations. Many nonunion organizations, however, engage in job design changes without union assistance or union-management example.

Some unions are very much behind job enrichment programs.

Implementing Job Redesign—A Summary

Successful implementation of a job redesign project begins with the diagnosis of

- Individual needs, skills, and abilities
- Organizational technological systems, personnel and practices control systems
- Union-management relationships

In addition, top management must be in complete support of the project. Although it is inappropriate to prescribe what approach to job design an organization should select, many organizations are considering one of the contemporary forms. Examples of some current job enrichment programs are described in Chapter 16. It is important, however, to remember that the scientific approach to job design still has many appropriate uses. In addition, the use of ergonomics is critical to many people in our work force. Also keep in mind that there are many other ways that personnel can improve organizations without changing the design of the job itself, such as new spatial arrangements and new furniture, new compensation programs, and different selection and training programs. These are also examined in Chapter 16. Nevertheless, if the jobs are redesigned they must be reanalyzed, a process, though costly, that is extremely critical.

JOB ANALYSIS

As shown in Exhibit 3.1, job analysis is the basis of job descriptions and job specifications. While job analysis is necessary for legal purposes to validate methods used in making employment decisions such as selection, promotion, and performance appraisal determinations, it is also critical for several other reasons (that help attain the purposes shown in Exhibit 3.2):

Here are several reasons for the importance of job analysis.

- It helps determine the relative worth of jobs, which is necessary in maintaining external and internal pay equity.
- It helps ensure that companies do not violate the "equal pay for equal work" provision of the Equal Pay Act of 1963.
- It aids the supervisor and employee in defining the duties and responsibilities each has.
- It provides a justification for the existence of the job and where it fits into the rest of the organization.
- It helps determine the recruitment needs (when used together with the personnel planning needs discussed in Chapter 2) and the information necessary to obtain in making employment decisions.
- It serves as the basis for establishing career development programs and paths for employees.
- It serves as a vehicle by which to convey to potential job applicants what will be expected of them, the general working conditions, and the types of individual needs the job may fill.

Job Analysis Information

In order for job analysis to be useful, two major pieces of information need to be gathered: job descriptions and job specifications.

Job Descriptions. In writing or preparing job descriptions it should be kept in mind that the job should be described in enough detail so that the reader can understand: (1) what is to be done (the duties); (2) what products are to be generated (the purposes of the job); (3) what work standards are applied (standards such as quality and quantity); (4) under what conditions the job is performed; and (5) the task characteristics of the job.[12] In addition to these general categories included on the job description, there are the

- Job or payroll title
- Job number and job group the job belongs to (as a result of job evaluation for compensation purposes)
- Department and/or division where the job is located
- Name of the job analyst (optional)
- Primary function or summary of the job
- Summary description of the major duties and responsibilities of the job, sometimes with a percentage of time for each duty

An example of a typical job description containing many of these features is shown in that of the animal keeper (Exhibit 3.3). Note that this job description does not provide information regarding performance standards, task characteristics, purposes of the job, or job conditions. Purposes, however, are implied in the introductory section. Job standards are typically not specified in job descriptions. Increasingly, however, these are being included. Organizations sometimes prefer to retain the flexibility and include standards in the performance appraisal form. Information on task characteristics, such as the amount of skill variety and identity, is rarely included in job descriptions. On the basis of our job design discussion, however, you may see it as reasonable and useful to explicitly include standards, purposes, and even task characteristics in job descriptions.

Job Specifications. This presentation of job descriptions does not include a discussion of what skills the worker should have to perform the job because they are not always a part of or are not shown on a job description. Nevertheless, for effective personnel management, the required skills, knowledge, and abilities and the appropriate needs (or preferences) should be stated for each job. Although specifying the required skills, knowledge, and abilities is legally necessary for selecting employees, specifying the appropriate needs is not. Again, you should see the usefulness of determining what individual needs are filled by the jobs and trying to match those with the needs of individuals. Specifying information about needs as well as skills, knowledge, and ability, however, should more likely lead to effective personnel management. This is in keeping with our desire to satisfy both Match 1 and Match 2.

Structured Procedures for Analyzing Jobs

There are many ways organizations can choose to analyze jobs. That is, there are many ways or procedures that can be used to determine what job information to collect and how to organize and present it in job descriptions and specifications. Most of the procedures, however, are structured.

Structured job analysis is the use of a standard format for job descriptions so that all organizations or all units of an organization can use the same job categories. The most common approaches for structured job analysis are *functional job analysis,* the *position analysis questionnaire,* the *management position description questionnaire,* and the *Hay plan.* When organizations use similar methods to analyze jobs, they can (among other things) exchange compensation information and develop more valid methods of recruitment, selection, and performance appraisal.[13]

Structural job analysis includes
- FJA
- PAQ
- MPDQ
- Hay plan

Functional Job Analysis (FJA). The U.S. Training and Employment Service (USTES) in the U.S. Department of Labor developed **functional job analysis** to describe the nature of jobs in terms of people, data, and things and to develop job summaries, job descriptions, and employee specifications. FJA was designed to improve job placement and counseling for workers registering for employment at local state employment offices. This was part of an intensive research program directed toward producing the 1965 edition of the **Dictionary of Occupational Titles (DOT).** Today, many aspects of FJA are used by a number of private and public organizations.[14]

A personnel manager who has to prepare job descriptions and job specifications may start with the *Dictionary of Occupational Titles* to determine the general job analysis information and use the *Handbook for Analyzing Jobs* for more specific resource planning, recruitment, selection, placement, performance evaluation, training, and job design.

McCormick's Position Analysis Questionnaire (PAQ). Although the *FJA* approach is complete, it requires considerable training to use well and is quite narrative in nature. The narrative portions tend to be less reliable than more quantitative approaches, such as the **position analysis questionnaire,** which describes jobs in terms of worker activities. The six activities analyzed in the *PAQ* are

■ *Information input:* Where and how does the worker get the information used in performing the job? Examples are the use of written materials and near-visual differentiation.

■ *Mental processes:* What reasoning, decision-making, planning, and information-processing activities are involved in performing the job? Examples are the level of reasoning in problem solving and coding/decoding.

■ *Work output:* What physical activities does the worker perform, and what tools or devices are used? Examples are the use of keyboard devices and assembling/disassembling.

■ *Job context:* In what physical or social contexts is the work performed? Examples are high temperature and interpersonal conflict situations.

■ *Relationships with other people:* What relationships with other people are required in performing the job? Examples are "instructing employees" and "contacts with the public or customers."

■ *Other job characteristics:* What other activities, conditions, or characteristics are relevant to the job?[15]

The *PAQ* uses a checklist to rate each job (numerically) on the basis of 194 descriptors related to these six activities. Then using these six activities, jobs can be analyzed, compared, and clustered. The job clusters can then be used for, among other things, staffing decisions and the development of job descriptions and specifications.

The *PAQ*'s reliance on only these six activities allows it to be applied across a variety of jobs and organizations without modification. This, of course, allows organizations to more easily compare their job analyses with those of other organizations. The major drawback in adopting the *PAQ* is its sheer length (194 descriptors), even though its checklist format helps speed up the analysis approach.

Management Position Description Questionnaire (MPDQ). The *MPDQ* is another method of job analysis that relies upon the checklist method to analyze jobs. It contains 208 items related to the concerns and responsibilities of managers, their demands and restrictions, and miscellaneous characteristics.[16] These 208 items have been condensed into thirteen job factors:

- Product, market, and financial planning
- Coordination of other organizational units and personnel
- Internal business control
- Products and services responsibility
- Public and customer relations
- Advanced consulting
- Autonomy of action
- Approval of financial commitments
- Staff service
- Supervision
- Complexity and stress
- Advanced financial responsibility
- Broad personnel responsibility

With each factor there is a description guide used by the job analyst to "measure" each job on each factor. The *MPDQ* is designed for managerial positions, but responses to the items vary by managerial level in any organization and also in different organizations. The *MPDQ* is appropriate for determining the training needs of employees moving into managerial jobs; evaluating managerial jobs; creating job families and placing new managerial jobs into the right job family; and compensating managerial jobs.

The Hay Plan. Another method of analyzing managerial jobs is the **Hay plan,** which is used in a large number of organizations. Although much less structured than the *MPDQ* and *PAQ,* it is systematically tied into a job evaluation and compensation system. Thus use of the Hay plan allows an organization to maintain consistency not only in how it describes managerial jobs but also in how it rewards them. The purposes of the Hay plan are management development, placement, and recruitment; job evaluation; measurement of the execution of a job against specific standards of accountability; and organization analysis.

The real heart of the Hay job description is the information about the nature and scope of the position, which covers five crucial aspects:

- How the position fits into the organization, including reference to significant organizational and outside relationships
- The general composition of supporting staff. This includes a thumbnail sketch of each major function of any staff under the incumbent's position—size, type, and the reason for its existence.
- The general nature of the technical, managerial, and human relations know-how required

Exhibit 3.5
Summary of Characteristic Strengths and Weaknesses of Four
Structured Approaches to Job Analysis

	FJA	HAY PLAN	PAQ	MPDQ
Strengths	Helps improve job placement Tied into the *DOT* and the *Handbook for Analyzing Jobs* Useful for a wide variety of jobs	Comparative data on jobs in other organizations exist Highly systemitized Immediate use for job evaluation	Applicable to many jobs and functions Highly researched Produces reliable results	Helps spot training needs Reliably classifies new jobs Immediate use for job evaluation
Weaknesses	Limited to analyzing jobs by only three factors Omits factors for many jobs	Limited to managerial jobs Encompasses only three major factors Requires extensive training to use accurately	Large number of items Rates/Analyst may resist filling out form Requires a great deal of time to complete accurately	Applicable only to managerial jobs Raters may resist filling out form Does not specify skills needed for job

- The nature of the problem solving required: What are the key problems that must be solved by this job, and how variable are they?
- The nature and source of control on the freedom to solve problems and act, whether supervisory, procedural, or vocational or professional

Information related to the accountability objectives tells what end results the job exists to achieve and the incumbent is held accountable for. There are four areas of accountability; organization (including staffing, developing, and maintaining the organization); strategic planning; tactical planning, execution, and directing the attainment of objectives; and review and control.

A summary of the strengths and weaknesses of these four approaches is shown in Exhibit 3.5.

Methods Analysis in Analyzing Jobs

Two forms of methods analysis are
- Work measurement
- Work sampling

Structured procedures generally focus on describing the job and its general duties, the conditions under which the duties are performed, and the levels of authority, accountability, and know-how required. Equally important, however, is a description of how to do the job as efficiently and effectively as possible. This is the purpose of **methods analysis.** Although methods analysis could be used for many jobs, it is more frequently applied to nonmanagerial jobs. In these jobs, individual activity units can often be identified more readily. Methods analysis can be especially critical in designing jobs using the scientific approach or the ergonomic approach.

Methods analysis, or motion study, had its origins in industrial engineering. Some of the principles it is based on include

- The movements of the two hands should be balanced, and the two hands should begin and end their motions simultaneously.
- The hands should be doing productive work and should not be idle at the same time except during rest periods.
- Motions of the hands should be made in opposite and symmetrical directions and at the same time.
- The work should be arranged to permit it to be performed with an easy and natural rhythm.
- Momentum and ballistic-type movements should be employed wherever possible to reduce muscular effort.
- There should be a definite location for all tools and materials, and they should be located in front of and close to the worker.
- Bins or other devices should be used to deliver the materials close to the point of use.
- The work place should be designed to ensure adequate illumination, proper work-place height, and provision for alternated standing and sitting by the operator.
- Wherever possible, jigs, fixtures, or other mechanical devices should be used to relieve the hands of unnecessary work.
- Tools should be prepositioned wherever possible in order to facilitate grasping them.[17]

Proper application of these principles results, according to the industrial engineers, in greater motion economy and working efficiency. There are two major types of methods analysis: *Work Measurement* and *Work Sampling*.

Work Measurement. One form of methods analysis is **work measurement** or **time study.** In essence, work measurement determines standard times for all units of work activity in a given task or job. Combining these times gives a standard time for the entire job. These standard times can be used as a basis for wage-incentive plans (incentives generally are given for work performance that takes less than the standard time), cost determination, cost estimates for new products, and balancing production lines and work crews.[18] Establishing standard times is a challenge of some consequence, since the time it takes to do a job can be influenced as much by the individual doing the job as by the nature of the job itself. Consequently, determining standard times often requires measurement of the "actual effort" the individual is exerting and the "real effort" required. This process, as you can imagine, often means trying to outguess someone.

Common methods of collecting time data and determining standard times include the stopwatch time studies, standard data, predetermined time systems, and work sampling for determining standard time.

Work Sampling. **Work sampling** is not only a technique for determining standard times but also another form of methods analysis. "Work sampling is the process of taking instantaneous samples of the work activities of individuals or groups of individuals."[19] The activities from these observations are timed and classified into predetermined categories. The result is a description of the activities by classification of a job and the percentage of time for each activity.

Work sampling can be done in several ways: The job analyst can observe the incumbent at predetermined times; a camera can be set to take photographs at predetermined times; or at a given signal, all incumbents can record their activity at that moment.

Work sampling lends itself to use in many types of jobs. Exhibit 3.6 shows its use with two different types of managerial jobs.

Exhibit 3.6

Results of a Work Sampling Study (Adapted from C. L. Brisley, "Tips to Help You Save Time," *Factory Management and Maintenance* (December, 1958), p. 60.)

	PERCENTAGE OF TIME IN ACTIVITY	
ACTIVITY	Top managers*	Operating managers†
Talking (oral communication)		
Consulting with colleagues	10.5	3.6
Deciding on course of action	9.4	6.3
Discussing with colleagues	6.2	4.0
Interviewing visitors	3.0	3.5
Telephoning	8.8	8.2
Dictating	3.7	1.9
Meeting	3.7	1.9
Regularly scheduled	1.4	4.0
Special	8.0	6.0
Discussing at lunch	14.3	11.0
Visiting other offices	14.7	36.1
Writing	4.1	3.8
Reading	13.2	9.2
Miscellaneous	2.7	2.4

*General manager, plant manager, director of industrial and public relations, and so on.

†Managers of operations, quality control, industrial engineering, and so on.

Collecting Job Information for Job Analysis

Regardless of the actual procedure or method used to analyze jobs, there are several ways to obtain the information necessary to write the job descriptions and specifications. These ways, often used in conjunction with methods analysis or one of the structured ways to analyze jobs, are shown in Exhibit 3.7. There are also several people who can gather the information.[20]

For What Jobs Is the Information Collected? Job information is usually gathered for at least four major categories of jobs or positions:

- Nonsupervisory, not office workers: Hourly rated, **nonexempt** from not being paid overtime (the employer pays for any overtime work)
- Nonsupervisory office workers: Salaried, **nonexempt**
- Supervisory, technical, and office employees: Salaried, **exempt** from not being paid overtime (the employer does not pay for overtime work)
- Managerial, executive, and professional employees: Salaried, **exempt**

However, not all organizations have job descriptions for all four groups of employees. Job descriptions have traditionally been used only for hourly rated employees. But as it becomes necessary for organizations to demonstrate that their selection procedures (measures to predict performance) are related to the skills required to perform the job, more are writing job descriptions for all four groups of employees.

Exhibit 3.7
Methods for Collecting Job Information (Adapted from E. J.
McCormick, "Job and Task Analysis," in Marvin D. Dunnette (ed.),
Handbook of Industrial and Organizational Psychology, copyright © 1976
by Rand McNally College Publishing Company, p. 683.
[By permission of the editor])

Observation

Interview with job incumbent

Interview with several job incumbents as a group

Technical conference with experienced personnel

Structured questionnaire

Open-ended questionnaire

Diary

Critical incidents (records of worker behaviors that are "critical" for very good or very poor job performance)

Equipment design information (blueprints and other design data of equipment being developed)

Recordings of job activities (films, mechanical recordings of certain job activities, etc.)

Available records (maintenance records, etc.)

Who Collects the Information?   Traditionally someone in personnel, along with a supervisor, collects the job information. Increasingly, it is becoming more common for the incumbent, or the person in the job, to provide information also. Often a combination of these three is used. The exact combination—the information each provides, how it is used, and who has the final responsibility—often depends upon whether the jobs and individuals are exempt or nonexempt.

The procedure at Bunker Ramo Corporation (Oak Brook, Illinois) usually involves the incumbent, the supervisor, and an analyst, says Manager of Compensation Donald C. Kraft. He sent in two position responsibility questionnaires—one for exempt employees and one for nonexempt employees.

Another procedure that involves incumbents is the one from W. R. Sturgeon, senior vice-president and director of Personnel, Indian Head Bank (Nashua, New Hampshire): "A questionnaire is completed by employees. The analyst writes the position description and the supervisor and employee agree (the supervisor has the last word). The job analysis committee reviews it and decides on level."[21]

Joseph Springer, personnel manager at Cook Electric Division, Northern Telecom, Inc., Morton Grove, Illinois, describes the process at his company.

For hourly production and maintenance jobs, the information is collected and the writing-up done by a personnel representative with review by two levels of line management; the top line manager has veto power concerning content while the personnel manager has veto power in matters of job analysis. For exempt salaried positions, the incumbent writes up the information in coordination with Personnel; veto power is held by the line function director or vice-president.[22]

EVALUATING JOB DESIGN AND JOB ANALYSIS ACTIVITIES

Both job design and job analysis are critical in EPM. Their effectiveness can be shown quite readily. The effectiveness of job design activities can be demonstrated with productivity measures such as employee performance, turnover, and absenteeism. If jobs are redesigned using the individual contemporary approach, turnover and absenteeism can be expected to decline. Whether they actually do can be measured. Redesign effectiveness can also be evaluated by QWL indicators such as satisfaction and involvement.

Job analysis is critical to an effective recruitment, selection and training program. Without job descriptions and worker specifications, potentially qualified job applicants cannot be identified, and valid section measures cannot be developed. The result may be rather expensive recruiting efforts and noncompliance with equal employment regulations. As such, these two measures can be used to evaluate the effectiveness of job analysis. More specifically, the ratio of qualified applicants to total applicants can be determined and the cost of equal employment violations can be calculated.

FACING THE CRITICAL ISSUES IN DESIGNING AND ANALYZING JOBS

Now that the vital elements of job design and job analysis have been discussed, it is good to turn to the Critical Issues listed at the beginning of this chapter. The responses offered here are only meant to provide a start for you. You should be able to greatly expand upon each of the responses.

Issue: *Why is the worker-job crisis really so important?*

This crisis is so important because the worker-job interface is a key element in the productivity crisis facing our nation. Solving the crisis in the worker-job relationship will go a long way in helping solve the productivity crisis. It will also help in improving the quality of work life.

Issue: *What can be done to avert this crisis?*

While it may not be possible to be completely successful in averting this crisis, a critical starting point in trying to is to think in terms of job redesign possibilities. The worker-job crisis basically stems from a mismatch between worker skills and needs and job duties and characteristics. There are some legal issues in job design that can also be addressed by job redesign. Thinking in job-redesign terms leads to using a diagnostic approach to determine the exact nature of the crisis. Based upon this diagnosis and an awareness of the organizational systems affected by job redesign, specific redesign efforts can be implemented.

Issue: *Is it really possible for organizations to design jobs so that productivity and QWL are high?*

Yes. There are several worker-job design combinations where both productivity and QWL are high. Although this is not frequently attained, the steps suggested in the answer to the second question can help attain this condition.

Issue: *How can jobs best be analyzed so that resulting job descriptions and job specifications meet legal requirements?*

By gathering as much objective information as possible from several different sources who know something about one or both of these components of job analysis. There is no single way that is best or that is agreed upon. Certainly, however, some ways are better than others in given situations.

SUMMARY

The worker-job interface is of vital importance to organizations today. This interface helps determine employee performance, satisfaction, and job involvement. Since the trend in these factors is downward, the worker-job interface is seen as a crisis—a crisis in both productivity and QWL. Fortunately, job redesign efforts may solve these two crises. The challenge to personnel is to determine if and which job redesign can solve the crisis and then to implement the job redesign program.

Once jobs are designed, they must be analyzed, job descriptions and worker specifications must be written. Job analysis has a significant impact on the rest of the personnel activities and on the organization's equal employment considerations. Although there is no magical way to do job analysis perfectly, it can be done and, furthermore, must be done. Without a sound job analysis, effective personnel management is impossible.

KEY CONCEPTS

Dictionary of Occupational Titles (DOT)

functional job analysis

Hay plan

job analysis

individual contemporary

team contemporary

characteristics

duties

purposes

job description

job design

job specifications

Position Analysis Questionnaire (PAQ)

skill variety

significance

identity

autonomy

feedback

overload

underload

structured job analysis

time study/work measurement

work sampling

methods analysis

job rotation

job enlargement

job enrichment

exempt

nonexempt

worker-job interface

ergonomic approach

scientific approach

technological system

personnel practices

control systems

DISCUSSION QUESTIONS

1. Compare and contrast job design and job analysis.
2. What are the purposes of job design?
3. Identify and describe four of the seven critical job design qualities.
4. List the four major job design approaches. Identify which approach has been used extensively in the past; which approaches are basically concerned with the individual; which approach is basically concerned with social interaction of individuals; and which approach is best suited to the needs of the elderly and the handicapped.
5. What is the difference between structured job analysis and methods analysis in collecting job information? Give examples of each.
6. Regardless of the actual procedure or method used to analyze jobs, what are some of the means used to obtain that information and from whom it is obtained?
7. Why is evaluation of job design and job analysis activity important? What indicators might be used for each?
8. Why does job analysis play a vital role in the interface between the employee and the organization?
9. What is the primary reason for job redesign?
10. What are the three major areas in selecting a job design using a diagnostic approach?

CASE

Redesign or Relocate?

During the past five years productivity and worker satisfaction at the Jackson Toy Company have been declining. Productivity is now so low that Dr. Jackson, the company's founder and president, is seriously considering closing the plant and moving south.

When Dr. Jackson, a mechanical engineer, originally founded the toy company in 1965, she installed an assembly line so that workers could become specialized at their jobs and, hence, very productive. Although the employees were very productive during the first ten years of operation, several of the younger, newly hired employees began complaining about the repetitive, boring nature of the work. It was about that time that Dr. Jackson began to notice a decline in productivity. Her critical response was to assume that pay was too low. Whereas many of the original employees were essentially "second income earners," the newly hired employees were sole income earners. Since pay was only minimum wage, Jackson assumed that the younger employees were moonlighting in order to earn more money. Then when they came to work they were too tired to work efficiently. Consequently she increased everyone's salary by 20 percent. Since there were seventy-five employees, this represented a substantial increase in payroll expenses. Nevertheless, she was concerned about productivity as well as the "plight" of the workers.

About two months after the salary increase, Jackson noted that the level of productivity had not increased. In fact, productivity actually declined slightly. Disappointed, but resolved to do something, Jackson called the local university. Professor Brief, a specialist in job redesign, suggested that Dr. Jackson needed to redesign the jobs for the employees or implement a job rotation program. Although it would be more costly to redesign the jobs than to implement a rotation program, Professor Brief said that it would be worth it. Dr. Jackson, however, wondered if it would be more trouble than it's worth.

CASE QUESTIONS

1. How do you explain why the original workers were productive and the younger, newly hired ones were not? Do you agree with Dr. Jackson's income-earner status assumption?
2. Why didn't increased pay lead to increased productivity? Can it ever?
3. How could the assembly-line tasks be redesigned? Would job rotation really be less effective than job redesign?
4. Should Dr. Jackson relocate or redesign? What are the costs and benefits of each?

FOR YOUR CAREER

■ Write a job description of a job you would really like to have as your first one. Include the characteristics, duties, and purposes of the job.

∎ Managers often say that they can't redesign the jobs of their employees because of the technological constraints or the goals of the organization. How would you respond to these managers?

∎ Job design and job analysis underlie almost all of the other personnel activities. They are critical to productivity, quality of work life, and legal compliance. You should know how and why they are so critical.

∎ It is likely that you will be given the chance to write your own job description someday.

∎ Being skilled in the principles and techniques of job redesign may make you an especially valuable employee to any organization.

∎ Like skinning cats, there are really several ways to design jobs. Take a job of your choice and design it in three different ways.

ENDNOTES

1. Donald W. Myers, "The Impact of a Selected Provision in the Federal Guidelines on Job Analysis and Training," *Personnel Administrator*, July 1981, pp. 41–45.

Wayne F. Cascio and H. John Bernardin, "Implications of Performance Appraisal Litigation for Personnel Decisions," *Personnel Psychology* 34 (1981):211–226.

Gerald A. Kesselman and Felix E. Lopez, "The Impact of Job Analysis on Employment Test Validity for Minority and Non Minority Accounting Personnel," *Personnel Psychology* 32, no. 1 (Spring 1979):91–108.

Lawrence S. Kleiman and Robert H. Faley, "Assessing Content Validity: Standards Set by the Court," *Personnel Psychology* 31 (1978):701–713.

2. Susan R. Rhodes, Michael Schuster, and Mildred Doering, "The Implications of an Aging Workforce," *Personnel Administrator*, October 1981, pp. 19–22.

3. R. J. Aldag and A. P. Brief, *Task Design* (Scott Foresman & Company, 1979).

J. Richard Hackman and Greg R. Oldham, *Work Redesign* (Reading, Mass.: Addison-Wesley Publishing Company, 1980), pp. 78–81.

4. Jon L. Pierce, "Job Design in Perspective," *Personnel Administrator*, December 1980, pp. 67–74.

5. J. R. Hackman, "Work Design," in J. R. Hackman and J. L. Suttle, *Improving Life and Work*, p. 101, copyright 1977. Reprinted by permission of Goodyear Publishing Company, Inc., Santa Monica, Calif.

6. Antone F. Alber, "How (and How Not) to Approach Job Enrichment," *Personnel Journal*, December 1979, pp. 837–841, 867.

"Moving Beyond Assembly Lines," *Business Week*, July 27, 1981, pp. 87–90.

7. M. Scott Fisher, "Work Teams;: A Case Study," *Personnel Journal*, January 1981, pp. 42–45.

8. Antone Alber and Melvin Blumberg, "Team vs. Individual Approaches to Job Enrichment Programs," *Personnel*, January–February 1981.

9. Hackman and Oldham, *Work Redesign*.

10. Peter G. Gyllenhammar, "How Volvo Adapts Work to People," *Harvard Business Review*, July–August 1977, pp. 102–113.

11. "Stonewalling Plant Democracy," *Business Week,* March 28, 1977, pp. 78–82.

12. "Job Analysis," *Employee Relations in Law Journal* 6, no. 4 (1981):586–587.

13. Ronald A. Ash and Edward L. Levine, "A Framework for Evaluating Job Analysis Methods," *Personnel,* November–December, 1980, pp. 53–59.

Paul van Rijn, *Job Analysis for Selection: An Overview,* U.S. Office of Personnel Management, Examination Services Branch, Office of Personnel Management, August 1979.

14. E. J. McCormick, "Job and Task Analysis," in Marvin D. Dunnette (ed.), *Handbook of Industrial and Organizational Psychology,* copyright 1976 by Rand McNally College Publishing Company, p. 111.

Dictionary of Occupational Titles, 3 vols., 3rd ed. (Washington: U.S. Government Printing Office, 1965).

Handbook for Analyzing Jobs. U.S. Department of Labor (Washington: U.S. Government Printing Office, 1972).

15. B. Schneider, *Staffing Organizations* (Santa Monica, Calif.: Goodyear Publishing Company, 1976), p. 23.

E. J. McCormick and J. Tiffin, *Industrial Psychology,* 6th ed. (Englewood Cliffs, N.J.: Prentice-Hall, Inc., 1974).

16. W. W. Tornow and P. R. Pinto, "The Development of a Managerial Job Taxonomy: A System for Describing, Classifying and Evaluating Executive Positions," *Journal of Applied Psychology,* no. 11 (1976), pp. 410–418.

17. H. T. Amrine, J. Ritchey, and D. S. Hulley, *Manufacturing Organization and Management,* 3rd ed., 1975, p. 130. Reprinted by permission of Prentice-Hall, Inc., Englewood Cliffs, New Jersey.

18. E. J. McCormick, *Job Analysis: Methods and Applications* (New York: AMACOM, a division of the American Management Associations, 1979), pp. 77, 79.

19. Ibid., p. 83.

20. Thomasine Rendero, "Job Analysis Practices," *Personnel,* January–February 1981, pp. 4–12.

21. Thomasine Rendero, "Consensus," *Personnel,* January–February 1981 (New York: AMACOM, a division of American Management Associations, 1981), p. 8.

22. Ibid., p. 7.

Staffing the Personnel Needs of the Organization

Chapter Four
Effective Recruitment

Chapter Five
Selection and Placement Procedures,
Legal Considerations, and Job Applicant Information

Chapter Six
Selection and Placement Decisions

Chapter Outline

Critical Issues in Effective Recruitment

The Recruitment Activity
The Personnel Department-Line Manager Relationship
The Organization-Job Applicant Relationship
Purposes and Importance of Recruitment
The Relationships of Recruitment
Legal Considerations in Recruitment

Sources and Methods of Obtaining Job Applicants
Internal Sources
Internal Methods
External Sources
External Methods

Increasing the Pool of Potentially Qualified Applicants
The Realistic Job Preview
Expanding Career and Job Opportunities
Alternative Work Arrangements

CHAPTER **4**

Effective Recruitment

Evaluating Recruitment

Facing the Critical Issues in Effective Recruitment

Summary

Key Concepts

Discussion Questions

Case

For Your Career

Endnotes

Personnel in the News

Wanted: Secretaries

If there is one condition that links personnel managers, personnel directors, and vice presidents of personnel into one big unhappy family, it is the current shortage of secretaries.

The dimensions of the problem are staggering: the Department of Labor reports that more jobs are opening up in the secretarial work field than in any of the other 299 work classifications. Although there are a record 3.6 million secretaries on public and private payrolls, new positions are being created at a rate of 440,000 a year. Today, almost 20% of the new jobs go begging. The Labor Department predicts that by 1985, we will be short 250,000 secretaries. (Personnel Journal, *June 1980, p. 482. Reprinted with the permission of* Personnel Journal, *Costa Mesa, Calif.; all rights reserved.*)

Wanted: More Skilled Workers

To meet the competitive economic challenge that is now coming from abroad, the United States is going to have to repair some of its major structural weaknesses. Nowhere are the repairs more urgent than in the institutions, or lack of institutions, for training skilled blue collar workers—the tool and die makers, machinists, pipefitters and the like.

During recessions America's inability to train enough skilled blue collar workers is hidden, but shortages break out whenever unemployment falls. What do employers complain about in tight labor markets? Certainly not an inability to hire unskilled workers, or college-educated labor. Complaints almost always focus on shortages of skilled blue collar workers.

As the economy expands, it runs into bottlenecks created by shortages of skilled labor. Production cannot expand. Standards of living stagnate and Americans cannot build the products that would allow them to compete with the rest of the world.

As rising demand presses in on limited supply, prices rise and inflation breaks out. In an ultimately self-defeating effort to get the skilled blue collar workers they need, employers begin to raid one another for labor. As the bids fly, wages soar.

Our national defense suffers. Employers raid the military services for skilled technicians. The Armed Forces find that they cannot maintain their equipment because they have lost their skilled blue collar workers. Military equipment sits unrepaired because there is a shortage of people to use an abundance of parts and equipment. When the defense industries expand, as they are poised to do now, they raid civilian industries.

Paradoxically, the shortage of blue collar workers creates unemployment for the rest of the population. (Lester C. Thurow, The New York Times, *Sunday, May 3, 1981, Sec. F, p. 2, © 1981 by The New York Times Company. Reprinted by permission.*)

Recruiting and the Law

Federal contractors are required to "take affirmative action to employ and advance in employment qualified handicapped individuals at all levels of employment." (Section 503 of the 1973 Rehabilitation Act.) This includes, of course, the executive level. A "handicap" is nebulously defined in the rules set by the enforcing agency—the Office of Federal Contract Compliance Programs (OFCCP)—as any "impairment which substantially limits one or more of a person's major life activities." Whatever else this definition may mean, one thing is certain: A "major life activity" is employment. Under the OFCCP rules, a "qualified handicapped" is one who is "capable of performing a particular job." (OFCCP has proposed to change this definition to one who is able to perform a job's "essential functions.")

The rules further provide that employers with 50 or more employees who hold federal contracts totaling $50,000 or more must prepare written affirmative action programs for handicapped workers in each of their establishments—for example, each plant or field office. This condition must be met within 120 days after the contractor receives the federal contract. Those who hold contracts or subcontracts of less than $2,500 aren't covered by this Act. Those with federal contracts that range from $2,500 to $50,000 are required to include an affirmative action clause in their contracts, but they don't have to have a written affirmative action plan. (Donald J. Petersen, "Paving the Way for Hiring the Handicapped," Personnel, March–April 1981 [New York: AMACOM, a division of American Management Associations, 1981], pp. 43–44.)

Problems to Consider in Recruiting

As companies attempt to recruit qualified labor from the ranks of American women, compensation benefits regarding childcare will increase, regardless of the particular form of assistance. These benefits will undoubtedly range from the actual provision of childcare facilities at the plant site to additional time off when school-age children are ill. Specifically, we need to be responsive to the needs of the many divorced (especially single heads of households) as well as married women whose financial contribution is necessary to the well-being of their children. Corporate policies should promote more flexible and family-conscious work practices: flexible scheduling, part-time work, child-rearing leaves and childcare assistance.

Corporations that are developing effective policies and programs regarding childcare have been applauded for a social responsibility that goes beyond a concern for corporate image and public relations. They reap the financial benefits of decreased turnover rates and lowered training costs. Companies can increase their workforce stability by attracting hard-to-recruit office workers for whom daycare availability or assistance is a real incentive. (Personnel Journal, June 1981, p. 436. Reprinted with the permission of Personnel Journal, Costa Mesa, Calif.; all rights reserved.)

Together these scenarios illustrate some of the concerns organizations face in recruitment today. Organizations are facing shortages of skilled workers at the same time that between 7 and 10 million people are unemployed in the United States. Organizations are also confronted with legal constraints that require many of them to adopt hiring goals and quotas that can only be filled by aggressive, innovative, and attractive recruiting practices. Such practices include offering job applicants a choice in job schedules, in time and place, and offering more extensive provisions for childcare assistance. Such practices are also becoming essential due to the changes in the labor force discussed in Chapter 2. These recruiting concerns underlie the critical issues that confront organizations now.

CRITICAL ISSUES IN EFFECTIVE RECRUITMENT

1. *How are employers going to get the skilled workers they need?*
2. *What are the legal obligations employers have to fulfill?*
3. *How can employers make their organizations more attractive so they can recruit the people they really need and want?*
4. *Do realistic job previews really pay off?*

Recruitment is generally defined as searching for and obtaining potential job candidates in sufficient number and quality so that the organization can select the most appropriate people to fill its job needs.[1] In addition to filling job needs, the recruitment activity should also be concerned with filling the needs of job candidates. Consequently, recruitment not only attracts individuals to the organization but also increases the chance of retaining the individuals once they are hired. Of course, the recruitment activity must be done in compliance with an extensive set of rules and legal regulations. Thus **recruitment** is specifically the set of activities and processes used to legally obtain a sufficient number of the right people at the right place and time so that the people and the organization can select each other in their own best short-run and long-run interests.

THE RECRUITMENT ACTIVITY

Effective recruitment results when the needs of the organization and the needs of the individual are served.

Behind this definition of recruitment is an important philosophy. You, however, are by now familiar with it. The philosophy is one of being concerned with the needs of the organization as well as with the needs of the individual—our two matches discussed in Chapter 2. Applying it here results in seeing recruitment as a two-way street, a process of **mutual recruitment** and attraction.

Mutual recruitment refers to the reciprocal relationships among parties to the recruitment process. Two particular relationships are (1) the relationship between the personnel staff and the line managers; and (2) the relationship between the organization and the job applicant.

The Personnel Department-Line Manager Relationship

The personnel department and the line managers can often work together to get the right person on the right job. Line managers often initiate a request for additional employees. They can help by specifying the nature of the job and necessary employee qualifications (particularly if it's a new job or one that has changed since the last job analysis). They often play an important role in interviewing and decision making, and they can help evaluate the effectiveness of the recruitment process.

Effective recruitment depends on good line manager-personnel manager relationships.

The Organization-Job Applicant Relationship

The traditional approach to recruiting is concerned with matching the abilities of the job applicant with the skills required by the job (Match 1 only). The more recent approach to recruiting, although still concerned with matching skills and abilities, is also concerned with matching the needs of the job applicant and the rewards supplied by the job (Match 1 and 2). Getting job applicants to stay is as important as recruiting job applicants who can do the job for effective personnel management.

Two components of the newer approach to recruiting (concern for Match 1 and Match 2) are *job matching programs* and the *realistic job interview*. (The realistic interview is discussed in a separate section near the end of this chapter.) **Job matching** is a systematic effort to fit and identify the abilities and preferences of people to the job openings. Increasing pressure on organizations to maintain effective recruitment, selection, and placement of new and current employees may make an automated job matching system worthwhile. For example, Citibank's job matching system for non-professional employees evolved from an automated system designed to monitor job requisition and internal placement processes. The system is currently used to identify suitable positions for staff members who wish to transfer or who are seeking another job due to technological displacement or reorganization and to ensure that suitable internal candidates haven't been overlooked before recruiting begins outside the organization. Thus the system appears not only to help recruit people and ensure that they stay but also to provide a firm basis for job-related recruitment and selection procedures. (Job-relatedness is an important part of legal compliance and is discussed in Chapter 5).

Job matching helps ensure that more people will know about job openings.

There are two major components in a job matching system—**job profiles** and **candidate profiles.** The job profiles at Citibank were developed from prior job-family studies conducted at Citibank using the U.S. Department of Labor's *Handbook for Analyzing Jobs*, and such job analysis instruments as the *PAQ* (see Chapter 3). Thus the job profiles are elaborate job descriptions and job specifications. The candidate profiles contain information regarding the candidate's experience or skills related to specific jobs. These jobs are the same ones described in the job profiles. It also lists their job preferences, reflecting their needs. With these profiles, the organization can identify many more potentially qualified job applicants for specific jobs than ever before.

Purposes and Importance of Recruitment

The general purpose of recruitment is to provide a pool of potentially qualified job candidates to select from. More specifically, the purposes of recruitment are to

- Determine the present and future recruitment needs of the organization in conjunction with the personnel planning and the job analysis activity
- Increase the pool of job applicants with minimum cost
- Help increase the success rate of the selection process by reducing the number of obviously underqualified or overqualified job applicants
- Help reduce the probability that job applicants, once recruited and selected, will leave the organization after only a short period of time
- Meet the organization's responsibility for affirmative action programs and other legal and social obligations regarding the composition of its work force
- Start identifying and preparing potential job applicants who will be appropriate candidates
- Increase organizational and individual effectiveness in the short and long term
- Evaluate the effectiveness of various techniques and locations of recruiting for all types of job applicants.

Several important activities are a part of effective recruitment, including: (1) determining the organization's long- and short-range needs by job title and level in the organization; (2) staying informed of job market conditions; (3) developing effective recruiting materials; (4) developing a systematic and integrated program of recruitment in conjunction with other personnel activities and with the cooperation of the line managers; (5) obtaining a pool of qualified job applicants; (6) recording the number and quality of job applicants produced by the various sources and methods of recruiting; and (7) following up on applicants, those hired and not hired, in order to evaluate the effectiveness of the recruiting effort.

Meeting all these purposes effectively for the organization enables the organization to avoid costly legal battles and settlements, and it enables the organization to select only those applicants who are indeed qualified and thus will be productive. And because the recruiting activity is as concerned with getting job applicants to stay once selected as it is with getting an initial pool of potentially qualified job applicants, it should also lead to a higher QWL. In essence, effective recruiting helps an organization attain the three general purposes of EPM discussed in Chapter 1.

The Relationships of Recruitment

As shown in Exhibit 4.1, the recruitment activity has several critical relationships. On the one hand it results in a pool of potentially qualified job applicants and on the other it results from the personnel activities discussed in Chapters 2 and 3, personnel planning and job analysis.

Personnel Planning. Personnel planning determines what types of jobs the organization needs to and will need to fill and thus the skills and abilities needed by job applicants. As part of the personnel planning, programs are established in close coordination with recruiting to indicate where and how the individuals with the needed skills and abilities will be found. Results of past recruiting efforts can be used in determining where particular types of individuals may be located again. Caution must be used here, however, because use of past sources may result in an organization's

Exhibit 4.1
The Recruitment Activity

```
┌──────────────┐  ┌──────────────┐  ┌──────────────────────┐
│  Personnel   │  │ Job Analysis │  │ Legal Considerations │
│   Planning   │  │     and      │  │                      │
│              │  │  Job Design  │  │                      │
└──────────────┘  └──────────────┘  └──────────────────────┘
              │         │                    │
              └─────────┼────────────────────┘
                        │
              ┌──────────────────────┐
              │  Recruitment         │
              │   • How many         │
              │   • Where            │
              │   • What             │
              └──────────────────────┘
              ┌──────────┴──────────┐
              │                     │
┌─────────────────────────┐  ┌──────────────────────────┐
│ Internal                │  │ External                 │
│  • Sources              │  │  • Sources               │
│    ▪ Promotion          │  │    ▪ Agencies            │
│    ▪ Transfer           │  │    ▪ Schools             │
│                         │  │    ▪ Trade Association    │
│  • Methods              │  │        Unions            │
│    ▪ Posting            │  │  • Methods               │
│    ▪ Career management  │  │    ▪ Radio               │
│    ▪ Referrals          │  │    ▪ TV                  │
│                         │  │    ▪ Newspaper           │
│                         │  │    ▪ Trade Journal       │
└─────────────────────────┘  └──────────────────────────┘
              └──────────┬──────────┘
                         │
          ┌──────────────┐   ┌──────────────────────────┐
          │ Pool of      │   │ Recruitment Activities   │
          │ Potentially  │◄──│  • Realistic interview   │
          │ Qualified    │   │  • Expanding career and  │
          │ Applicants   │   │    job opportunities     │
          │              │   │  • Alternative work      │
          └──────────────┘   │    arrangements          │
                             └──────────────────────────┘
```

inability to fulfill its legal considerations, such as its affirmative action programs for minorities, women, and the handicapped.

Job Analysis and Job Design.   Although personnel planning identifies the organization's needs for jobs, it is the job analysis activity that is responsible for identifying the necessary skills, knowledge, and abilities and the appropriate individual needs for each job type. Because jobs can change and be changed, job analysis must be viewed as a dynamic, ongoing activity. Thus jobs may need to be reanalyzed from time to time. This is particularly so when jobs need to be redesigned. Jobs may need to be redesigned to accommodate the needs of the handicapped or they may need to be altered to allow women to perform them with the same facility as men.

Job redesign possibilities make it easier to recruit job applicants.

    This flexible, dynamic approach to job design and job analysis should also be applied to other personnel activities. It is often beneficial and essential for organizations to be flexible and dynamic so that they are capable of meeting federal and state laws. For example,

- AT&T has developed a program to train managers who supervise disabled people. "A lot of employees have never known people with a disability," says Jay Rochlin, an AT&T district manager of EEO and AA programs. The company's awareness training program, he notes, is "crucial" to its affirmative action efforts.

- Sears, Roebuck & Co. has been running an affirmative action program for the disabled since 1947, according to Paul Scher, corporate manager of the company's handicapped program. The company has employed handicapped people successfully in all job categories, Scher says. The firm uses a series of tests to screen applicants and to assess employees' progress, says Scher, adding that the performance and progress of disabled employees are monitored to ensure equitable treatment.

- Levi Strauss & Co. developed an architectural survey in 1976 to measure the accessibility of its facilities to disabled people. The study's findings prompted the company to install ramps and other aids to make its buildings more accessible. In addition to special efforts to make its personnel offices accessible, the company also makes special accommodations, where necessary, to provide easy access for disabled individuals, notes Gaylene Pearson, an affirmation action specialist.

- In 1972, IBM began a program to train and place severely physically handicapped people in entry-level computer jobs. The program has expanded to 16 training centers throughout the country, and additional centers are being developed. The company provides disabled employees with special equipment, such as display screens with a synthesized voice for blind computer professionals, battery rechargers for wheelchair users, and telephones with printouts for deaf employees.

- Control Data Corporation initiated a program in 1978 to provide suddenly disabled employees with computer training that would help them get back on the job. "Programming was chosen because it can be done remotely and allows you to track performances," says Kenneth Anderson, the company's home employment marketing manager. So far, he notes, 10 trainees have returned to work and 40 more are participating in the program.[2]

Legal Considerations in Recruitment

Recruitment is critical in an organization's attempt to serve its objective of legal compliance.

Legal considerations, obligations, and requirements play a critical role in the recruitment of most companies in America. Although much of the legal initiative is directed at employment decisions such as hiring, firing, health and safety, and compensation, it essentially begins with the organization's search for job applicants, whether the search is inside the organization or outside.

Although it is important for an organization to make certain that its present employment practices do not discriminate on the basis of race, color, religion, or sex, many organizations must do more. Organizations may also need to demonstrate that they employ these groups in proportions that are representative of their availability in the area of recruitment. Programs designed to ensure proportional representation are referred to as **Affirmative Action Programs (AAPs)**.[3] In general, when a company writes an AAP it is specifying its hiring and promotion goals, quotas, and timetables necessary in order to integrate its work force.

AAPs generally arise from three different conditions, each of which is described in detail below:

1. If a company has a federal contract greater than $50,000 it is required to file with the Office of Federal Contract Compliance Programs an affirmative action plan outlining steps to be taken for correcting "underutilization" in places where it has been identified. Goals and quotas are a critical part of these plans.

2. A federal court may require an AAP if a discrimination suit brought against the organization through the Equal Employment Opportunity Commission (EEOC) has found evidence of past discrimination. An AAP under these conditions is generally part of a **consent decree,** a statement indicating the specific affirmative action steps an organization will take.

3. The organization may voluntarily decide to establish certain goals for hiring and promoting women, members of minority groups, and handicapped individuals. The exact content of AAPs depends on the organization, the area it is located in, and the extent to which various minorities are underrepresented.

Here are three types of AAPs. They are discussed more in the next three pages.

Goals and Quotas.   The specific components of AAPs are specified by the Department of Labor in the Office of Contract Compliance Programs (OFCCP). One important component is **goal setting.** AAPs attack employment discrimination by relying on goals to provide relief:

> An acceptable affirmative action program must include an analysis of areas within which the contractor is deficient in the utilization of minority groups and women, and further, goals and timetables to which the contract's good faith efforts must be directed to correct the deficiencies.[4]

The AAPs are currently enforced by the OFCCP and EEOC through Executive Order (EO) 11246. It is suggested by some, however, that this enforcement be done by the Justice Department.

The other component of AAPs is the establishment of **quotas** as a form of relief. Use of quotas was imposed by the courts under Title VII of the Civil Rights Act of 1964 and has been upheld by the U.S. Constitution, the post-Civil War Civil Rights Act (1866), and EO 11246 (1965). An example of the impact of imposing quotas on an organization, particularly its recruitment program, is provided in the Kansas City *Personnel in Action* insert.

Goals refer to desired targets or end points. For example, a company sets as its goal increasing the representation of females and minorities by 10 percent per year for three years. Goals do not have to be stated numerically. They can be statements such as "Our company wants to improve the attitude of our supervisors towards acceptance of handicapped employees." But whether qualitative or quantitative, goals are established steps, and timetables specify how they will be attained are usually indicated. These goals, steps, and timetables, however, are not ironclad and do not constrict a company's immediate employment practices as much as quotas do.

Quotas essentially specify how many of a specified group of individuals (for example, women and minorities) are to be hired out of all of those who are hired. Or as in the Kansas City *Personnel in Action* insert in this chapter, quotas may be used to establish what the percentage of women and minorities must be in certain job categories. On the basis of quotas for job categories, a company may establish hiring goals and timetables in order to fulfill those quotas.

PERSONNEL IN ACTION

Kansas City Company Ordered to Maintain 25% Quota of Women

U.S. District Court Judge Howard Sachs ordered a Kansas City company May 18 to establish and maintain a work force of 25% women in its technical and production departments.

The order, considered a sweeping one in the district, also included the hiring with seniority and granting of back pay to women discriminated against by the Cook Paint & Varnish Co. between October 1973 and June 1975.

The suit was brought in June 1975 by the Equal Employment Opportunity Commission as a class action. EEOC had received a complaint the year before from Joyce Chamberlain, who had applied for a job in the technical department but was hired as a clerical worker. Later she applied for a transfer to the department but was denied. The judge found the company had discriminated against women seeking jobs in the technical and production departments and held Cook liable for damages.

Sachs found that about 25% of the company's 24 technicians were women, about the same percentage of women applying for the jobs since 1975. The judge found that only 12% of about 200 production workers were women, though as high as 31% of those applying for jobs in the department were women.

Sachs ordered the company to advertise weekly for a month in three area newspapers in an effort to locate women whose applications were denied because of sexual discrimination, since the company contends its personnel records for October 1973 to June 1975 were destroyed. If they accept a job, the women are to be hired with seniority dating to their original application, and will become eligible for back pay.

"The assumption that a 25% level of women technicians is normal . . . will be reconsidered if the applicant ratio changes during the [five-year] course of remedial proceedings," Sachs wrote, adding that the company should be careful to avoid using the 25% figure as a cap on female employment.

Fair Employment Report, June 8, 1981.

How are goals and quotas established for an organization? First, the exact numbers of minorities and women available are calculated and then related to these factors:

- The minority and female population of the labor area surrounding the organization
- The proportion of minority and female workers in the total work force in the immediate labor area

Here are the guidelines to help determine the goals and quotas for an organization.

- The availability of promotable and transferable minorities and women within the operating location
- The availability of minorities and women with the requisite skills in the immediate area
- The existence of training institutions capable of training them in the requisite skills

- The degree of training that the operating location is reasonably able to undertake as a means of making all job classes available
- The availability of minorities and women seeking employment in the labor recruitment area of operating location
- The availability of minorities and women with the requisite skills in an area in which the operating location can reasonably recruit (this refers primarily to nationwide recruitment of managers, professionals, and salespeople).[5]

The establishment of goals and quotas has a significant impact on the organization's selection and placement activities: It determines the types of individuals who will be hired. However, goals and quotas relate only to future hiring decisions. That is, current employees cannot be laid off in order to hire minorities or women to accommodate goals and quotas.

FOR YOUR CAREER

A consent decree is a ruling or decree of action handed down by a judge, such as increasing its hiring rates of women and minorities. The mandate becomes a *consent* decree when the company agrees to (consents to) the decree. Note that when a company accepts a consent decree it is not admitting past wrong or guilt. As such, consent decrees are directed to what the company will do in the future.

Consent Decrees. One of the most famous AAPs resulting from a consent decree involved AT&T, which the EEOC found to be discriminating against women. Although AT&T did not admit nor was it required to admit any act of discrimination, it entered into a consent decree after the EEOC opposed its application for a rate increase. The first five-year cost of this settlement (1973–1978) is estimated to have been more than $75 million. The Ford Motor Company more recently agreed to spend $23 million on training and back pay to settle its case with the EEOC. As you read the following story, it becomes evident how consent decrees can influence an organization's recruitment efforts.

PERSONNEL IN ACTION

Ford Agrees to $23 Million Settlement Of Sex, Race Discrimination Complaint

The Ford Motor Co. and the Equal Employment Opportunity Commission announced yesterday that the company has agreed to spend $23 million on training and back pay to settle a race and sex discrimination complaint against it.

The agreement, signed last week, is one of the

largest monetary awards ever won by the EEOC, and settles a complaint that goes back seven years.

The agency's largest settlement, $52 million in back pay and other adjustments, came in 1973 in an action against the American Telephone and Telegraph Co.

Ford, the nation's second largest automaker, denied race and sex discrimination charges in resolving the dispute. Instead, Ford's labor relations vice president, Peter J. Pestillo, said yesterday that the company accepted the settlement because it "provides an opportunity to eliminate longstanding areas of disagreement between Ford and government agencies charged with administering federal equal employment opportunity laws."

The settlement also "avoids the possibility of prolonged litigation," Pestillo said. He added that the "EEOC acted very professionally" in handling the case and that both the company and the federal agency now recognize that "each . . . is committed to equal employment opportunity."

These are the highlights of the Ford-EEOC agreement, implementation of which will begin no later than January 1982:

▪ About $13 million of the settlement money will go to individuals claiming race or sex discrimination at the company. Of that amount, $8 million will go to about 5,000 women who had applied but were rejected for employment at Ford in the early 1970s.

▪ Ford must hire the women who were rejected in the period cited in the settlement. In order to qualify for the settlement money, the women must reapply and remain on the Ford payroll for at least a year. (Company spokesmen say 80 percent of the women in the affected class are expected to reapply.)

▪ About $3.5 million of the $13 million in individual award money will go to salaried minority and female employees—mostly clerical workers—who began working for the company before 1975. Approximately $1.5 million of the individual award sum will go to women in hourly jobs—mostly lower skilled—who were employed before 1972.

▪ Ford will spend $10 million of the total settlement amount "for special training and affirmative action programs to help employees develop job skills and enhance their qualifications for promotional opportunities," according to a company statement on the agreement.

Nothing in the agreement will affect the "recall rights" of the 50,000 Ford employees currently on indefinite layoff and the 1,050 who have been laid off temporarily because of a downturn in the auto market, according to Pestillo.

"We can't do anything that will hurt the interests of those people. . . . They have the right to return" to their jobs if and when circumstances permit, Pestillo said of the laid-off workers.

(From Warren Brown, *Washington Post,* November 26, 1980, p. A5.)

Voluntary AAPS. Organizations may establish their own affirmative action programs without pressure from the EEOC or OFCCP. By doing so, however, they may run the risk of being charged with reverse discrimination, although the risk seems to have lessened since the *Bakke* and *Weber* cases (see Appendix A). In both cases, the courts supported the qualified use of quotas.

The *Weber* case is clearer in its support of voluntary AAPs and illustrates the issues involved when unions and seniority concerns are at stake. In brief, the United Steelworkers and Kaiser Aluminum set up a training program that reserved 50 percent of its openings for blacks. A white worker, Brian Weber, charged that the program was discriminatory.

The Supreme Court, however, ruled that Title VII of the 1964 Civil Rights Act does not condemn *all* private, voluntary affirmative action programs. As such, the program between Kaiser and the United Steelworkers is lawful, particularly because it does not unnecessarily trammel the interest of the white employees.

The key considerations now in an organization's establishment of a legal voluntary AAP are that it be

1. Remedial in purpose
2. Limited in its duration
3. Restricted in its reverse discrimination impact
4. Flexible in implementation
5. Minimal in its harm to innocent parties

One aspect above all that the voluntary AAP must have is that it be *formal and structured:*

Informal Affirmative Action Reversed

An employer that selected a black job applicant over a more experienced white applicant in accordance with an informal affirmative action program violated Title VII, the U.S. Court of Appeals at Chicago decides.

In 1972, an interstate trucking firm hired a white and a black worker as temporary employees. When a permanent position came open, the black worker was selected over the white employee, who had more experience. The hiring manager acknowledged that he had chosen the black employee because of his race, in accordance with the employer's informal affirmative action plan that specified certain "attainment levels" for workforce composition. The white worker filed Title VII discrimination charges, arguing that the company's racial hiring preference amounted to an impermissible quota under the U.S. Supreme Court's *Bakke* decision (421:946). The employer argued that the hiring decision was not the result of a quota system, but was designed only to conform to one of the "attainment levels" set forth in its voluntary affirmative action plan. Such race-conscious hiring decisions, the employer insisted, were permitted under the Supreme Court's *Weber* decision (421:945).

The appeals court stresses that the manager's hiring decision was not made in conformance with "an actual affirmative action program." The manager's "ad hoc informal affirmative action decision" to hire the black worker, the court declares, violated Title VII. Asserting that *Weber* attempted "to strike a balance between the societal interest in affirmative action and the right of individuals to be free from race discrimination," the court says that the employer's affirmative action plan was not so "organized" as to meet *Weber's* "procedural and substantive commands" that all employees be "treated fairly" under an employer's AAP efforts.

The court stresses that the manager who made the hiring decision was only "vaguely aware" of the employer's need for hiring minority workers and did not have any ascertainable hiring goal in mind when he selected the black applicant. Such a system "is fraught with dangers," the court concludes, because, in such situations, a hiring manager "may unfairly discriminate against non-minority employees beyond a reasonable goal." (*Lehman v. Yellow Freight System*, CA 7, 1981, 26 FEP Cases 75)[6]

AAPS and the Handicapped Worker. The Vocational Rehabilitation Act of 1973 prohibits discrimination against handicapped individuals in hiring and promotion, but it applies primarily to affirmative action programs of federal contractors. Thus organizations that must submit AAPs for women and minorities to the OFCC must also submit AAPs for the handicapped. Organizations that have federal contracts in excess of $2,500 also must

1. Take positive steps to attract qualified handicapped persons not currently in the work force

2. Modify their personnel practices to meet the needs of the handicapped applicant or worker

3. Make reasonable accommodation to the physical and/or mental limitations of an employee or applicant

4. Conduct regular meetings with *all* employees to discuss the company's policy and individual responsibility in implementing the Vocational Rehabilitation Act of 1973.[7]

Compliance with employment laws is often in the hands of the manager.

A Matter of Commitment. Although equal employment guidelines, goals, and quotas are usually established for the organization by the EEOC, the OFCCP, or the courts, the actual implementation of these efforts is in the hands of the managers in organizations. As with many other personnel techniques, having them is one thing and using or abiding by them is another. If organizations are really to fulfill the spirit as well as the letter of the law, managers must be committed to implementing goals and quotas. Six important characteristics of EEO (equal employment opportunity) efforts that increase managerial commitment are

1. Government influence on goals, policies, and practices

2. The clarity of goals

3. Top management support for implementing goals

4. Managerial accountability for implementing goals

5. Managerial participation in setting goals and policies

6. The amount of training managers receive for implementing goals[8]

The government not only establishes goals, policies, and practices for EEO but also furnishes technical assistance to organizations trying to comply.

Knowledge of these laws and regulations is an important first step in developing an effective EEO program and an AAP. A summary of all these steps in writing an AAP are shown in Exhibit 4.2.

Exhibit 4.2
Basic Steps to Develop an Effective Affirmative Action Program
(Adapted from the EEOC *Affirmative Action Guidelines, Technical Amendments to the Procedural Regulations,* Federal Register, Friday, June 19, 1979, part xi.)

---

1. Issue Written Equal Employment Policy and Affirmative Action Commitment.

2. Appoint a Top Official with Responsibility and Authority to Direct and Implement Your Program.
   a. specify responsibilities of program manager
   b. specify responsibilities and accountability of *all* managers and supervisors.

3. Publicize your policy and affirmative action commitment.
   a. internally
   b. externally

3. Survey present minority and female employment by department and job classification.
   a. identify present areas and levels of employment

b. identify areas of concentration and underutilization

c. determine extent of underutilization.

4. Develop goals and timetables to improve utilization of minorities, males and females in each area where underutilization has been shown.

5. Develop and implement specific programs to achieve goals.

a. review entire employment system to identify barriers to equal employment opportunity, areas needed to review and initiate action:

—recruitment (all personnel procedures)

—selection process (job requirements; job descriptions; standards and procedures; pre-employment inquiries; application forms; testing; interviewing)

—upward mobility system (transfers; promotions; training; etc.)

—wage and salary structure

—benefits and conditions of employment

6. Establish internal audit and reporting system

7. Develop supportive in-house and community programs.

The EEO goal for personnel managers is to stay aware of and on top of the most recent court decisions about hiring practices. But as you have seen, even a personnel manager who does so cannot be guaranteed an easy job or be certain of legal compliance. The lack of certainty and the apparent conflict between legislation and the Constitution may be tempting reasons for a personnel manager to address the issue less than enthusiastically but, as one personnel specialist suggests,

> EEO is a concept that will invariably step on someone's toes. The EEO professional must continually say to him or herself "ever so gently." The efforts of these people must be deliberate, well thought-out approaches toward meeting an established goal or objective. It takes guts, savvy, communication and, most of all, understanding—understanding not only of the many and different individuals involved but of the subject matter itself.[9]

PERSONNEL IN ACTION

AAA to Pay Women $3.5-Million in Job Bias Case

About 7,000 women employees and applicants for jobs at the Automobile Club of Michigan are to get between $3.5-million and $3.75-million under a proposed settlement of a class action sex discrimination suit.

The agreement says that the women will receive seven of the first 15 openings in 1981 in commissioned sales; 12 of the first 25 openings in 1982 and 1983; and 42% of all jobs in sales thereafter.

U.S. District Judge John Feikens ruled in February

1980 that the Auto Club had discriminated against women employees by paying them less than men for doing the same work and hindering their chances for advancement. The settlement affects women who left the Auto Club after 1974 and women whose work applications were allegedly rejected because of Auto Club policies. The unsuccessful job applicants will be paid out of a $300,000 pool set aside for them. The settlement also provides for back pregnancy benefits and sets quotas for women managers and executives.

Fair Employment Report, July 18, 1981, p. 7.

The personnel department, however, is in the best position in the organization to address this issue, and it must.

SOURCES AND METHODS OF OBTAINING JOB APPLICANTS

Now that we are aware of the legal considerations of organizations, we can go ahead and examine the sources where job applicants can be found and methods used to recruit them.

Internal
sources:
▪ Promotions
▪ Transfers

Internal Sources

Internal sources include present employees, friends of employees, former employees, and former applicants. Promotions, demotions, and transfers can also provide applicants for departments or divisions within the organization.

Current employees are a source of job applicants in two respects: They can refer friends to the organization, and they can also become applicants themselves by potential promotion transfer.

Promotions. The case for promotion from within rests on several sound arguments. One is that internal employees are better qualified. "Even jobs that do not seem unique require familiarity with the people, procedures, policies and special characteristics of the organization in which they are performed."[10] Another is that employees are likely to feel more secure and to identify their long-term interests with the organization that provides them the first choice of job opportunities. Availability of promotions within an organization can also motivate employees to perform. Internal promotion can also be much less expensive to the organization in terms of time and money.

Promotion
from within
may prevent
creativity and
"new blood."

Disadvantages of a *promotion-from-within* policy may include an inability to find the best qualified person. Also, infighting, inbreeding, and lack of varied perspectives and interests may result. If an organization has a policy of promotion from within, it must identify, select, and prepare candidates for the promotion. The initial step in the process may very well be determining whether affirmative action dictates selection.

It is not surprising to find organizations doing some internal promoting while obtaining some applicants from external sources. Organizations tend to obtain particular types of employees from particular sources. For example, many organizations are more likely to hire highly trained professionals and high-level managers from the outside than to promote from within.[11]

Transfers. Another critical way to recruit internally is by transferring current employees without promotion. Transfers are often important in providing employees with a more broad-based view of the organization that is necessary for future promotions. Consequently providing transfers can be a way of getting job applicants from outside the organization as well as inside. Recent trends, however, suggest that transfers or promotions that involve relocation may not be as attractive as they once were.

> "I may not take a transfer," she mused then. "I really like Nashville, and I am beginning to have strong nesting urges or whatever you call them . . . Moving is emotionally trying. I am not terribly gregarious. I don't frequent the singles bars, and it is not that easy for a single woman to meet people . . . I am trying to weigh all my options. My job accounts for 75% of my emotional involvement. I am probably overinvested and would like to be able to back off and not take it so seriously."[12]

Nevertheless, women appear to be the exception to the growing reluctance to relocate. This is particularly true when a promotion or near-term promotion is involved:

> Career-minded single women apparently almost never turn down promotions that involve transfers. But some who gamely pack up and move live to regret it, or at least to feel that they are paying a heavy price for their upward mobility.[13]

As a consequence of their mobility desire, companies are increasingly giving women foreign assignments as well as domestic assignments involving relocation:

> Previously, companies simply assumed that foreign businessmen, accustomed to more patriarchal cultures, would shy away from doing business with U.S. women and that these women would decline to make the sacrifices involved in spending time in strange lands once they discovered the reality of those sacrifices. But when companies responded to the social pressures that have moved women into almost all aspects of corporate life and acceded to the growing number of requests for overseas assignments, they discovered that they had been wrong on both counts.[14]

Thus, it appears that organizations will continue to transfer and promote employees, although the dominant composition may shift from men to women in the relocation move. Transfers and promotions are likely to continue despite some of the disadvantages, because of the many advantages to organizations summarized in Exhibit 4.3. The question now remains how to identify internal job candidates and which methods work best in doing so.

Internal Methods

The next step is the identification of candidates. As Exhibit 4.4 indicates, there are many methods for internally advertising job vacancies. Candidates can also be identified by (1) word of mouth; (2) company personnel records; (3) promotion lists based on performance; (4) potential ratings obtained from assessment activities; (5) seniority lists; and (6) lists generated by the skills inventory in an organization's personnel files. Since the "Notice on the Bulletin Board" (**Job Posting**) is the most frequently used method, it is examined here along with a method rapidly growing in use—**Employee Referral Programs.**

Transfers help broaden an employee's organizational perspective.

Exhibit 4.3

Sources of Job Applicants (Robert L. Mathis and John H. Jackson, *Personnel: Contemporary Perspectives and Applications*, 3rd ed. [St. Paul, Minn.: West Publishing Co., © 1976, 1979, 1982], p. 184. Reproduced by permission. All rights reserved.)

INTERNAL

Advantages	Disadvantages
Morale of promotee	Inbreeding
Better assessment of abilities	Possible morale problems of those not
Lower cost for some jobs	promoted
Motivator for good performance	"Political" infighting for promotions
Have to hire only at entry level	Need strong management development
	program

Job Posting. This method refers to the prominent display, for all current employees to see, announcing one or several job openings currently available. In essence job posting is extending an open invitation to all employees in an organization to apply for a job vacancy.[15] This serves four purposes:

1. To provide opportunity for employee growth and development
2. To provide equal opportunity for advancement to all employees
3. To increase staff awareness regarding salary grades, job descriptions, general pro-

Exhibit 4.4

Methods for Advertising Job Openings Internally (Adapted from "Employee Promotion & Transfer Policies," *PPF Survey No. 120* [Washington, D.C.: The Bureau of National Affairs, Inc., January 1978], p. 2.)

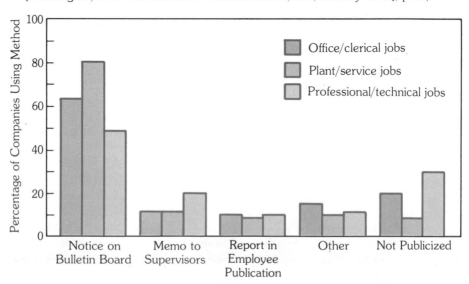

motion and transfer procedures, and what comprises effective to outstanding job performance

4. To communicate organization goals and objectives while allowing each individual the opportunity to self-select the best possible "fit" for himself/herself in the organization job structure[16]

Although job postings are usually found on bulletin boards, they are also frequently in company newsletters and circulated in employee lounges and announced at staff meetings. Generally all openings, except for management positions, are posted. Sometimes salary information is posted, but job grade and pay range are more typical. Job posting is quite beneficial for organizations. It improves morale because it's a fair way of providing opportunities; it provides employees opportunity for job variety; it facilitates an even better matching of employee skills as well as needs; and it provides a good way to fill positions at a low cost. These benefits, of course, are not always attained. The posting may attract too many unqualified applicants and then provide disappointment to many who "got their hopes up." Furthermore, it may not be seen as an honest search, especially if it is suspected that the real applicant has already been identified and the company is just going through the motions.

> Job posting is the internal advertisement of a job opening.

Employee Referral Programs (ERPs).   These are essentially word-of-mouth advertisements. ERPs generally involve rewarding employees for referring skilled employment applicants to organizations.[17] This method has proved to be a low-cost-per-hire way of recruiting applicants, even though the applicants do not necessarily come from just inside the organization. This method is especially useful for finding skilled applicants who are in very short supply and also managerial applicants. For successful referrals, employees may receive as much as $500, especially if they refer someone with a very critical skill or in an occupation high in demand, such as nursing. A major concern with ERP is that types of individuals similar to those who are currently in the organization are likely to be referred. While this may not necessarily produce difficulties in fulfilling AAP obligations, it has in the past demonstrated the potential to do so.

External Sources

Recruiting internally does not always produce enough qualified job applicants. This is especially true for organizations that are growing rapidly or that have a large demand for high-talent professional, skilled, and managerial employees. Thus organizations need to recruit from **external sources.** Recruiting from the outside has a number of advantages, including bringing in people with new ideas. It is often cheaper and easier to hire an already professional or skilled employee, particularly when the organization has an immediate demand for scarce labor skills and talents. External sources can also supply temporary employees, who provide the organization with much more flexibility than permanent employees. External sources, however, have disadvantages, as summarized in Exhibit 4.5.

> External sources:
> ● Employment agencies
> ● Temporary help agencies
> ◀ Trade associations and unions
> ▪ Schools
> ▪ Aliens

Employment Agencies.   Employment agencies (especially private ones) are a good source of temporary employees and an excellent source of permanent employees. Employment agencies may be public or private. **The public employment agencies** in the United States are under the umbrella of the U.S. Training and

Exhibit 4.5
Sources of Job Applicants (Robert L. Mathis and John H. Jackson,
Personnel: Contemporary Perspectives and Applications, 3rd ed.
[St. Paul, Minn.: West Publishing Co., © 1976, 1979, 1982], p. 184.
Reproduced by permission. All rights reserved.)

EXTERNAL

Advantages	Disadvantages
"New blood," new perspectives	May not select someone who will "fit"
Cheaper than training a professional	May cause morale problems for those internal candidates
No group of political supporters in organization already	Longer "adjustment" or orientation time
May bring competitors' secrets, new insights	May bring in an attitude of "This is the way we used to do it at XYZ Company."

Employment Service (USTES). The USTES sets national policies and oversees the operations of the state employment services, which have branch offices in many cities. The Social Security Act in general provides that any worker who has been laid off from a job must register with the state employment agency in order to be eligible for unemployment benefits. The agencies then have a roster of potential applicants to assist organizations looking for job applicants.

State employment agencies provide a wide range of services. Most of these services are supported by employer contributions to the state unemployment funds. The agencies offer counseling, testing, and placement services to everyone. They provide special services to individuals, military veterans, minority groups, and college, technical, and professional people. The state agencies also make up a nationwide network of job information and applicant information in the form of **job banks.** These job banks have one drawback, however: USTES and its state agencies do not actually recruit people but passively assist those who come to them and often those who do come in are untrained or only marginally qualified for most jobs.

In your career you may use a private employment agency.

Private employment agencies tend to serve two groups of job applicants—professional and managerial workers and unskilled workers. The agencies dealing with the unskilled group often provide job applicants that employers would have a difficult time finding otherwise. Many of the employers looking for unskilled workers do not have the resources to do their own recruiting or have only temporary or seasonal demands for unskilled labor.

The cost of using private agencies is rather high.

Private agencies play a major role in recruiting professional and managerial applicants. These agencies supply services for job applicants of all ages; many, however, have had some work experience beyond college. During the past ten years, the executive recruiting industry has grown phenomenally. Some estimates suggest that the search firm industry now generates more than $150 million in fee billings. The fees charged by these agencies range up to 33⅓ percent of the first year's total salary and bonus package of the job to be filled. Yes, the search firm gets this money whether or not they are successful in finding someone who is eventually selected for the job![18]

The *Personnel in Action* insert describes other important aspects of executive recruiters, who are sometimes called *head hunters*. Note that these agencies often identify job applicants who are already working with other organizations. Consequently this method of dealing with a potential candidate is very secretive. This also means that it is likely that an agency is talking to people where you are working.

Temporary Help Agencies.   Whereas the private recruiting agencies provide applicants for full-time positions, temporary help agencies provide applicants for part-time positions. Today, the temporary help agencies represent a $3 *billion* business. There are over 3,000 temporary help offices that annually employ over 2,500,000 people.[19] Their use is growing as skilled and semiskilled individuals find it preferable to work less than a 40-hour week or at least on a schedule of their own choice. If you worked for a temporary help agency you would work in any sort of company that may call in for temporary help to cover vacations, sicknesses, or other employee shortages. You probably would get paid more per hour from the agency than you would if you worked full-time for the company itself. This results because you receive only direct compensation—no indirect compensation, the worth of which is discussed in Chapter 13.

Organizations are using temporary help agencies more than ever because some hard-to-get skills can be obtained only through them. (This is especially true for small companies that aren't too visible or can't spend the time to recruit themselves). In addition, there are many times when organizations need people only for a short time.

PERSONNEL IN ACTION

Executive Recruiters Start Raising Fees, Prompting Some Companies to Go It Alone

The search for good executives is often tough. And now, it's getting more expensive.

Some of the nation's largest executive recruiting concerns are raising their fees. Several say the move is needed to counter declining profit margins. But the fee increases are encouraging some companies to bypass recruiters and hunt for executives on their own.

"Recruiters are raking in so much money it is ridiculous," complains K. R. Kiddoo, Lockheed Corp.'s personnel director. He calls the new rates "obscene." Many recruiters have raised their fees from 30% to 33.3% of the executive's first-year salary and expected bonus. Until the mid-1970s, 25% was standard.

Fees are still in flux. Many firms are staying with 30% until they assess resistance to higher rates. Ward Howell International proposed some searches to clients at 33.3%, but encountered such strong resistance

that it stuck with 30%, says Max Ulrich, president. But Korn-Ferry International, a huge concern that raised rates to 33.3% from 30%, expects to charge 35% within two years, says Lester B. Korn, chairman.

No Thanks

Some companies plan to resist the recent increases. Paul W. Kayser, vice president for human resources at American Standard Inc., says that if recruiters asked him for 33.3%, "I wouldn't pay it, nor would I use them." The New York-based diversified manufacturer finds "there are still a large number" of good recruiters who charge 30%.

Alan F. Lafley, executive vice president of Chase Manhattan Bank, says rising fees "reinforce" the bank's decision to use outside recruiting less than in the past. Four or five years ago, the New York bank used search concerns for practically all of its outside hiring for middle management and above, but it has reduced the figure to about 50%, Mr. Lafley says.

The change has saved "well into six figures a year," he adds. When seeking people with rare skills, it often pays to hire a search firm, he says. But for many jobs, "you don't generally need search firms."

Lockheed's Mr. Kiddoo says the aircraft maker uses search companies only about half as often as five years ago. "When recruiters went to 30%, we started cutting back, and I expect the latest raise will accelerate this."

Mr. Kiddoo says some recruiters quoting high fees are willing to negotiate, "though most of them wouldn't admit it." He says a recruiter recently quoted a fixed fee which worked out to more than 30% of salary and bonus. "I said, 'no way,' and they went down to 30%," he recalls.

Competition in the field, he says, opens the way to negotiation. "You have never seen so many search firms. They're pounding on our door. I don't think they can make this 33.3% stick."

Recruiters who have raised prices, however, generally don't believe that fees are the main reason for gaining or losing business. "The main reason recruiters think they can raise fees is that they believe there is no price sensitivity in this market," says James H. Kennedy, publisher of the newsletter Executive Recruiter News. Richard S. Lannamann, vice president of Russell Reynolds Associates, adds: "We have lost an insignificant amount of business because of the increase" to 33.3% last year.

Getting the Best

At W. R. Grace & Co., a diversified New York industrial concern, a personnel executive says he deals with a recruiter who charges a 30% fee and with another charging 33.3%. "If a firm is especially good in a given area, it may be worth the extra 3.3%," he says. "What you're looking for is results; the fee isn't the primary consideration."

At first glance, the higher fees would seem to mean more Gucci shoes and silk shirts for recruiters. Most established recruiters at major firms earn between $75,000 and $150,000 a year, says Mr. Kennedy of Executive Recruiter News.

But one reason some companies are eager to raise fees is that their profit margins are dropping. "Before I knew too much about this business, I thought it was pie in the sky, but recruiters are always falling out of bed," Mr. Kennedy says. "There's a lot of handholding. Companies change their minds, or the chairman says, 'I don't like guys with mustaches. I should have told you.'"

At Boyden Associates, revenue rose to $14 million last year from $8 million in 1977, but earnings increased "nowhere near" as much, says Carl W. Menk, president. "We have to go to twice as much work per search" as several years ago, he adds. He blames this largely on the growing resistance to relocate and on the shortage of capable, experienced executives stemming from the low birth rate in the 1930s.

Familiar Faces

Recruiters say that as client companies become more familiar with search firms, they are demanding more service, and that brings increases in overhead costs. The big search firms have opened dozens of fancy offices in the last few years. These are designed partly to generate additional business through local contracts. But they are also a competitive necessity to bolster the firm's claim that it can conduct a nationwide—or even world-wide—search.

The pressure to claim branch offices is so strong that some recruiters simply cheat. Executive Recruiter News frequently exposes search firm "branch offices" that turn out to be nothing more than mail drops. Some recruiters list nebulous foreign "affiliations" on their letterheads. And a Chicago recruiter used a friend's Manhattan apartment as a New York address.

Trade Associations and Unions. In some industries, such as the building trades and the maritime, unions often assume responsibility for supplying employers with skilled workers. This practice removes the company from many labor decisions, such as job assignment. However, the Taft-Hartley Act restricts these "hiring hall" practices to a limited number of industries.

Trade and professional associations are also important sources for recruiting. They often have newsletters and annual meetings, which can be used to provide notice of employment opportunities. Annual meetings can also provide employers and potential job applicants an opportunity to meet. Some communities and schools have picked up this idea and now bring together large numbers of employers and job seekers at "*job fairs.*" Of course, these fairs provide only a limited time for interviews and thus serve only as an initial step in the recruitment process, but they do provide an efficient way of recruiting for both employers and individuals.

Schools.   Schools can be categorized into three types—high schools, vocational and technical schools, and colleges and universities. All are important sources of recruits for most organizations, although their importance varies depending on the type of applicant sought. For example, if an organization is recruiting for managerial, technical, or professional applicants, then colleges and universities are the most important source. But they become less important when an organization is seeking blue-collar and clerical employees.

Recruiting at colleges and universities is often an expensive process, even if the recruiting visit eventually produces job offers and acceptances. Approximately 30 percent of the applicants hired from college leave the organization within the first five years after initial employment. This rate of turnover is even higher for graduate management students (MBAs).[20] Some people attribute this high rate of turnover to the lack of job challenge provided by organizations. Organizations claim, however, that people just out of college have unreasonable expectations (this is discussed in Chapter 15). Partly because of the expense, organizations are questioning the necessity of hiring college graduates for some of their jobs. Another reason for reevaluation of a policy of hiring only college graduates is the legal guidelines requiring an organization to show that a college degree is related to performance of the job. If it cannot, it may want to question the policy of recruiting and hiring only college graduates. Nevertheless, college placement services are helpful to an organization in recruiting for particular types of jobs, such as engineering and microelectronics and in locating highly talented and qualified minorities and women. Note, however, that college placement offices are not legally allowed to screen students for sex or race unless they can show that sex or race is a **Bona Fide Occupational Qualification (BFOQ).** In addition, organizations are using campus recruiting visits to obtain foreign graduate students in engineering, physical sciences, and mathematics.

College recruiting is expensive because of the high turnover rates of new recruits.

Aliens.   As indicated in one of the scenarios at the start of this chapter, obtaining skilled workers is very difficult. There is a real shortage of these workers, particularly chemical engineers, nurses, and geologists. However, many of these recruits can be obtained from abroad. In response to this "skills crisis" the paperwork process necessary to bring these aliens into the United States has been made easier and faster. Where it used to take up to one year for an organization to get the necessary paperwork processed by the U.S. Labor Department, the Immigration and Naturalization Service, and the Department of State, it can now take as little as three months.[21]

External Methods

Many organizations looking for applicants engage in extensive advertising on radio and television, in the local paper, in the *Wall Street Journal* or *New York Times.*

Organizations
must be
concerned
about the costs
of recruitment.

Radio and Television. Of the approximately $2 billion spent annually on recruitment advertising, only a tiny percentage is spent on radio and television.[22] Companies are reluctant to use these media because of fear that

- They are too expensive
- They will make the company look desperate
- They will damage the firm's conservative image

Yet organizations *are desperate* to reach certain types of job applicants such as skilled workers. In reality there is nothing desperate about using radio or television. Rather it depends upon *what is said* and *how it is delivered* that implies some level of desperation. Recognizing this, organizations are increasing their recruitment expenditures for radio and television advertisements with very favorable results. For example, Infonet, a division of Computer Sciences Corporation in El Segundo, California, placed sixteen 30-second spots on a local newsradio station. The result: Infonet received over 120 responses, two of whom were hired. The cost of the ads was $2,000.

Newspapers and Trade Journals. Newspapers have traditionally been the most common method of external recruiting.[23] They reach a large number of potential applicants at a relatively low cost per hire. Newspaper ads are used to recruit for all types of positions, from the most unskilled to the most highly skilled and top managerial positions. The ads range from the most matter-of-fact type fo the most creative type.

Trade journals enable organizations to aim at a much more specific group of potential applicants than the newspapers. Ads in trade journals are often more creative and of a higher quality, and the paper stock quality is better than newsprint. Unfortunately long lead times are required, and thus the ads can become dated.

By the way, preparing ads to be placed in newspapers and trade journals or on radio and television requires considerable skill.[24] Many organizations hire advertising firms to do this rather than spending the time and money to do this themselves. Selecting an advertising agency must be done with care equal to the care used in selecting a private recruiting agency.

FOR YOUR CAREER

Recruiting can result in obtaining potentially qualified applicants who can be

- Hired and put on the job immediately
- Hired and trained
- Hired for part-time work
- Hired for full-time work
- Hired for temporary or permanent work

Although recruiting helps prevent labor shortages, organizations can also prevent labor shortages by

- Transferring current employees
- Training current employees
- Having the current employees work overtime
- Increasing employee productivity

INCREASING THE POOL OF POTENTIALLY QUALIFIED APPLICANTS

Although organizations may use both external and internal sources of recruitment, they may not always obtain the applicants they want. This is especially true in highly competitive markets and for highly skilled individuals. But the organization can enhance recruitment through the enticements it offers, such as relocation assistance or through its efforts to establish programs such as career development or childcare, to facilitate working in the organization. Here it is important to discuss several things organizations are doing to increase their pools of potentially qualified job applicants. As an added benefit, the things that companies are doing also increase the probability that, once hired, the applicant-employee will stay.

The Realistic Job Preview

A vital aspect of the recruitment process is the interview. A good interview is a good way to provide the applicant with a realistic preview of what the job will be like. A **realistic job preview** can definitely be an enticement for an applicant to join an organization, just as a bad one can turn away many applicants.

The realistic interview means telling it like it is.

The quality of the interview is just one aspect of the recruitment process. Other things being equal, the chances of a person's accepting a job offer increase when interviewers show interest and concern for the applicant. In addition, it has been found that college students feel most positive toward the recruitment interview when they can take at least half of the interview time to ask questions of the interviewer and when they are not embarrassed or put on the spot by the interviewer.[25]

The content of the recruitment interview is also important. Organizations often assume that it is in their best interests to tell a job applicant only the positive aspects of the organization. But it has been reported in studies by the life insurance industry that providing realistic (positive and negative) information actually increases the number of eventual recruits! In addition, those who receive realistic job information are less likely to quit once they accept the job.[26]

An organization is better off having an applicant refuse a job than having the applicant accept a job and soon quit.

Assuming that job applicants pass an initial screening, they should be given the opportunity to interview a potential supervisor and even coworkers. The interview with the potential supervisor is crucial, for this is the person who often makes the final decision.

Expanding Career and Job Opportunities

Organizations can enhance the attractiveness of the organization and increase its applicant pool at the same time by providing new career opportunities, by breaking down some job sex-typing, aiding in job relocation and providing childcare assistance. The importance and even the necessity of providing these reflects the changing nature of the work force discussed in Chapter 2.

Career Opportunities. The decision to provide career opportunities involves several choices for the organization. First, should the organization have an active policy of promotion from within? Second, should the organization be committed to a training and development program to provide sufficient candidates for internal promotion? If answers to these questions are yes, then the organization must identify career ladders consistent with organizational and job requirements and employee skills and preferences such as done at Citibank with its job-matching program.[27]

An organization may identify several career paths for different groups or types of employees. This concept is based on the premise that an organization cannot afford to recruit applicants for jobs at the lower rungs of the ladder when applicants already possess those skills necessary for jobs at the higher rungs of the ladder. This actually occurs, however, with many people recruited from college. Although they are essentially overqualified for their first jobs, the organization hires them for more difficult future jobs. This approach is partially to blame for the high turnover rate of new college graduates. It is also a cause for concern regarding legal compliance. Employers may claim that a college degree is necessary for an entry-level managerial job when they may actually consider the degree necessary for the second or third job. Such a policy can lead to discriminatory barriers for recruitment and promotion.

One way to reduce this possibility is for an organization to establish career ladders and career paths. When organizations have career ladders and paths with clearly specified requirements anchored in sound job analysis, the organization can present a better defense (legal) for its recruitment policy. Organizations with clearly defined career ladders may also have an easier time attracting and recruiting qualified job applicants and a better chance of keeping the employee. (Career paths are also discussed in Chapter 15.)

An attractive way to begin recruitment is to offer temporary career opportunities to individuals, especially those who are less apt to be familiar with organizational life. Two of the most popular temporary opportunities are summer internships for college students and internships for middle-aged women looking for careers.[28]

The existence of sex job-typing makes effective recruitment more difficult.

Reducing Job Sex-Stereotyping. In Chapter 2 sex job-typing and sex-role stereotyping are discussed to explain why females and males traditionally occupy the jobs they do. To open up job opportunities organizations can desex job titles as shown in Chapter 3, and they can avoid using the "old boy network" for recruitment and requests for "male only applicants." Although these changes will help increase pools of applicants for many more jobs, especially the top jobs, based upon the progress of the 1970s, the increases will likely be only gradual.[29]

The costs of moving are both monetarily and psychologically high.

Relocation Assistance. As organizations find employees more reluctant to relocate, they find it more necessary to provide relocation assistance.[30] This assistance can be made available for employees who are promoted or transferred. With high interest rates and high inflation rates, the costs of relocation have soared, for both the individual and the organization. Consequently, the cost and extent of relocation assistance have soared.

For example, companies like Union Carbide are assisting the spouse of the employee in finding a job in the new city or town.

> Union Carbide, for one, found it had to do much more, however, when it set about moving Brenda Steenland's husband, Donald, from New York City to its new headquarters in Danbury, Conn., 18 months ago. Forced to leave her job as a management-procedures analyst with International Telephone and Telegraph in

New Jersey, Mrs. Steenland received job counseling and was given personal referrals to companies in the Danbury area.

Then, Union Carbide itself offered her a job as an administrative assistant—an offer that was kept active even though she had to take an interim job elsewhere while she looked for something more suitable. In the end, she accepted the Union Carbide offer and says of its help in the job search: "It was far more than just paying lip service to an idea."[31]

Providing low-interest mortgages to employees who have to sell their houses in one town and buy (often with mortgages at much higher interest rates) houses in the new town is also becoming more common.

Childcare Assistance. There is a wide spectrum of childcare services available for meeting the needs of working parents that organizations can provide. The possibilities include

1. *Supporting existing facilities.* Employers can help lower program costs for participants and, at the same time, improve the delivery of child-care services by contributing funds or products or donating "in-kind" assistance.

2. *Setting up information and referral systems.* To help eliminate some of the worries of being a working parent, the personnel department can keep a current list, fee schedules, and eligibility requirements of child-care centers.

3. *Subsidizing employees' child-care costs.* Providing vouchers and "subletting" center slots are the two most common ways of underwriting child-care expenses. In the former, the employer issues a voucher for use at any participating center, which then bills the company for the amount of the subsidy. Under the latter arrangement, management reserves a number of slots in a center and then passes along to employees the savings associated with the group rate.

4. *Establishing a child-care center.* Where community services are deficient, management can set up its own child-care program for workers or even join with other area employers to form a community center.[32]

Although providing these types of programs is expensive, it is probably less so than the expenses due to less effective recruitment, absenteeism, and turnover from not having these programs. However, to help keep costs in line and to provide the most appropriate assistance, a careful analysis of the organization's needs for this type of service and a careful review of what's available in the community should be the responsibility of the personnel department.

Alternative Work Arrangements

This may be the decade in which Americans free themselves from the tyranny of the time clock. Already 7.6 million workers have done so by working under one of several types of alternative (flexible) work arrangements. Reinforcing the prediction of even more workers under alternative work arrangements are the growing number of single-parent families, the high costs of commuting, the desire for larger blocks of personal time, and the desire of older workers to reduce their hours yet still continue to work. Far from contributing to or representing a decline in the work ethic, alternative work arrangements strengthen it by reducing the stresses caused by the conflict between job

Alternative work arrangements include
- Standard schedules
- Flextime
- Compressed work weeks
- Permanent part-time
- Job sharing

demands, family needs, leisure values, and educational needs. Thus organizations can only enhance their recruiting attractiveness by offering alternative work arrangements along with offering their standard work arrangements.[33]

Standard Work Schedules. These include the standard daytime, evening, and night work sessions and forty-hour-per-week schedules. (In the 1860s the average work week was seventy-two hours—twelve hours a day, six days a week. It was fifty-eight hours in 1900 and is approximately forty hours a week today). Standard work schedules also include overtime work, part-time work, and shift work over a forty-hour week.

Someone who does shift work might work from 7 A.M. to 4 P.M. one week and from 4 P.M. to midnight the next. Since the end of World War I, shift work systems have become more prevalent in industrialized countries. Currently about 20 percent of all industrial workers in Europe and the United States are on shift work schedules.[34]

The percentage of employees on part-time schedules has also increased steadily—from approximately 15 percent in 1954 to 23 percent today.

All of these standard work schedules have advantages and disadvantages, as shown in Exhibit 4.6, but traditionally they provide little choice to employees. Initially employees may have some choice in the schedules they choose, but after that the days of the week (generally five) and the hours of the day (generally eight) are fixed. Because employee needs and values change, what may have been at one time an appropriate work schedule becomes inappropriate. If alternative arrangements are not provided, the employee may leave the organization. Furthermore, the organization may have a difficult time attracting similar types of employees. Thus provisions for

Exhibit 4.6

Advantages and Disadvantages of Standard Work Schedules

(From ''Part-time and Temporary Employees,'' ASPA-BNA Survey 25,
Bulletin to Management, December 5, 1974, p. 5. Reprinted by
permission from *Bulletin to Management,* copyright 1974 by The Bureau
of National Affairs, Inc., Washington, D.C.)

TYPE OF SCHEDULE	ADVANTAGES	DISADVANTAGES
Regular	Allows for standardization, predictability, and ease of administration; consistent application for all employees	Does fit needs of all employees; not always consistent with preferences of customers
Shift	More effective use of plant and equipment; allows continuous operation and weekend work	Can be stressful, especially if rotating shifts; lower satisfaction and performance
Overtime	Permits more efficient utilization of existing work force; cheaper than alternatives; allows flexibility	Job performance may decline; may not be satisfying and may contribute to employee fatigue
Parttime	Allows scheduling flexibility to the organization, enabling it to staff at peak and unusual times; cheaper than fulltime employees	Applicable to only a limited number of jobs; increased costs of training; no promotion opportunities

nonstandard work schedules become more necessary.[35] Employees are often given a choice between a nonstandard schedule and a standard schedule, as well as a choice of hours, days, and total number of hours to work per week.

Flextime Schedules.   This is the most popular nonstandard work schedule. It is popular with organizations because it decreases absenteeism, increases employee morale, induces better labor-management relations, and encourages a high level of employee participation in decision making, self-control, and discretion.[36]

Simply stated, **flextime** is a work schedule that gives employees choice in the timing of work and nonwork activities. Consideration is given to **band width,** maximum length of the work day. This band (often ranging between ten and sixteen hours) is divided into core time and flexible time. **Core time** is when the employee has to work; **flexible time** allows the employee the freedom to choose the remaining

Exhibit 4.7.
Sample of Flextime Scheduling (Adapted from A. Cohen and H. Gadon, *Alternative Work Schedules: Integrating Individual and Organizational Needs* [Reading, Mass.: Addison-Wesley, 1978], p. 35. Reprinted with permission.)

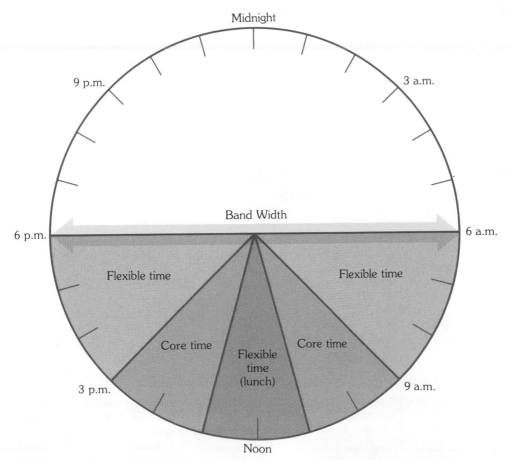

time to work. Exhibit 4.7 shows how a twelve-hour band width can be divided into blocks of flexible time and core time.

Among the advantages of flextime are its ability to increase employee productivity, although it does not do so on all occasions. The disadvantages are that it forces the supervisor to do more planning, sometimes makes communications between employees (especially with different schedules) difficult, and requires more records of employees' hours. Furthermore, most flextime schedules still require employees to work five days per week.

Compressed Work Weeks.　　Provisions for employees who want to work fewer than five days per week have led to **compressed work weeks.** By extending the workday beyond the standard eight hours, employees generally need to work only three to four days per week for a standard forty-hour work week. At two General Tire & Rubber plants, some employees work only two twelve-hour shifts each weekend and yet are considered full-time employees.[37] Compressed work weeks are becoming especially popular for certain occupations such as nursing.

Compressed work weeks are also becoming popular with organizations. Organizations can make better use of their equipment and can decrease their turnover and absenteeism. Scheduling and legal problems, however, can accompany compressed work week arrangements, but legal exceptions can be made, and scheduling can become a joint process between supervisor and employees. The impact of a compressed work schedule at Fluorcarbon in Anaheim, California, is described in the *Personnel in Action* insert.

PERSONNEL IN ACTION

For Nine Straight Years This Company Has Worked Four-Day Week

Jack Tilley likes to spend Fridays playing basketball or raquetball. Gayle Griffithe prefers to study. Carol Gust, Sandy Herman and Audrey Lee just try to catch up with everyday living chores. Gene Price packs up the family on Thursday night and heads out for a weekend of camping, water skiing or desert motorcycling.

Who are they? They're all employed by the Fluorocarbon Company in Anaheim, Calif., and they work only four days a week.

That's because they're on the 4/40 plan—40 hours of work in four days. One of the first in the nation to start the program on a regular and continuing basis, Fluorocarbon has been working four days since 1971.

The company employs over 1,150 people in 22 divisions throughout the nation. A majority of the facilities are able to be on the four-day program. A major

manufacturer of high-performance plastic and rubber components, Fluorocarbon has annual sales of $62 million. How can this firm work "four tens" when companies larger, smaller and even the same size wouldn't dare try it? Because Fluorocarbon knows that without good employees a company cannot grow. And the way to get and keep good employees is to provide benefits that are different and better than other companies that are trying to attract the same employees.

Working conditions are of primary importance: comfortably dressed employees in air-conditioned plants, incentive and recognition programs and wages generally above the community scale. But the four-day week is the icing on the cake.

Working hours are Monday through Thursday, 7 a.m., to 5:30 p.m., with half an hour for lunch and two

10-minute coffee breaks. If overtime is necessary, it is usually worked on Friday instead of Saturday. The schedule applies to all employees except inside and outside salesmen who work a straight five-day week.

Longtime employees still recall the time when a four-day week was coupled with a national holiday and a record-setting month. The result was a five-day break which was not charged to vacation time.

Peter Churm, president, is one of those who likes to remember how it started. He had read a book about it, was impressed, and suggested that the plant managers talk about it.

"The seed was planted," he recalls, "even though the managers didn't think much of the idea at the time." The more Churm researched the idea, however, the more it sounded like an ideal work schedule. It was a more efficient way to operate. Who wouldn't like three days off a week? What a recruiting tool!

Churm's enthusiasm for the schedule rubbed off on the managers.

Looking at its present industry position, Fluorocarbon is now convinced the plan works. Increased productivity, lower absenteeism, higher employee morale, stronger recruiting and lower turnover are facts. Direct costs have decreased five percent. The short week has also proved valuable in acquiring new companies, an activity which is high on the list of Fluorocarbon priorities. "Both salaried and hourly personnel in new acquisitions are usually eager to make the change," says Churm.

Another benefit that has been discovered is reduced commuting time. Most Fluorocarbon employees start for work early, leave late and avoid peak, rush-hour traffic.

There obviously are other benefits, and it may be that the most important of all in today's world is energy conservation.

When the company went on the schedule nine years ago, energy conservation was not even a consideration. But with the fuel crisis now a major topic, the company estimates that the 20 percent savings in gasoline for 500 company employees who commute one day less per week saves between 8,000 and 9,000 gallons per month. The savings in natural gas, fuel oil and electricity is estimated at 5 percent per month with some plants averaging as much as 8 percent.

Recently, the California issue of an influential newsletter (the Kiplinger California Letter) ran a brief paragraph about Fluorocarbon's 4/40 plan. For the next month, the company was so besieged with inquiries it has put together a packet of written information to respond to questions such as: Does it really work? How will it do in my industry (business)? Are there legal problems with overtime? What about laws concerning a woman's workday? How do you start a four-day program? What if you want to discontinue it?

The questions were many, so Fluorocarbon conducted a survey among workers at one of its plants. The outcome revealed that employees were overwhelmingly in favor of the four-day workweek.

From "Supervision Briefs" in *Supervision*, September 1981, p. 15. Reprinted by permission of *Supervision* magazine © 1981 by The National Research Bureau, 424 N. Third St., Burlington, Iowa 52601.

Permanent Part-time Work and Job Sharing. Sometimes productive employees cannot maintain a full-time commitment to the organization.

> We realized several years ago it was stupid to cut off relations with good employees. Full-time Equitable employees can switch to part-time work after five years and enjoy a full range of fringe benefits . . . Most so far have been women, mostly in the child-rearing years. (E. James Young, Vice-President, Equitable Life Insurance): I think that job sharing is fantastic. If I had to work full time I just couldn't give enough time to my year-old baby. This way I am a real part of the organization and have a chance for a full-time job when I'm ready. (Receptionist, Alza Corporation).[38]

Traditionally, part-time work has meant filling positions that only lasted for a short time, such as those in retail stores during holiday periods. Now some organizations have designated **permanent part-time** (**PPT**) positions. A PPT work schedule may be a shortened daily schedule (say, from 1 to 5 P.M.) or an odd-hour shift (say, between 5 and 9 P.M.). Organizations can also use PPT schedules to fill in the remainder of a day composed of two ten-hour shifts (representing a compressed work week).

Job Sharing. It is a particular type of part-time work. In job sharing, two people divide the responsibility for a regular full-time job. Both may work half the job, or one may work more hours than the other.

Part-time workers generally receive little or no indirect compensation, but workers on PPT and job-sharing schedules often do. The benefits to these workers are not equal to those of full-time workers but are prorated on the amount of time they work.

Both PPT and job sharing provide the organization and individuals with opportunities that might not otherwise be available. They provide organizations the flexibility in staffing to meet actual demands and do so with employees who are at least as productive, if not more so, than regular full-time employees. Individuals benefit from being able to enjoy permanent work with less than a full-time commitment to the organization.

EVALUATING RECRUITMENT

Remember, at the base of effective recruitment is the two-way matching process.

The recruitment activity is supposed to attract the right people at the right time within legal limits so that people and organizations can select each other in their best short-run and long-run interests. Since this is what recruitment is supposed to do, this is how it should be evaluated. More specific criteria for evaluating recruitment are shown in Exhibit 4.8. The criteria in Exhibit 4.8 are grouped by the stage of the recruitment processes in which they are most applicable.

Recruitment is not concerned just with attracting people but rather with attracting those whose needs will most likely be served by the organization and who have the

Exhibit 4.8
Some Criteria for Evaluating Recruitment (From J. P. Wanous,
Organizational Entry, © 1980, Addison-Wesley Publishing Company, Inc.,
Reading, Mass., Table 3.3, p. 62. Reprinted with permission.)

STAGE OF ENTRY	TYPE OF CRITERIA
Preentry	Ability of the organization to recruit newcomers
Entry	Initial expectations of newcomers
	Choice of organization by the individual (needs being matched with climate)
Postentry	Initial job attitudes, such as
	▪ satisfaction with one's job
	▪ commitment to the organization
	▪ descriptive statements about the job (to be compared with the expectations held as an outsider)
	▪ thoughts about quitting
	Job performance
	Job survival and voluntary turnover rates

abilities to perform adequately. It is only by matching needs and abilities that the recruitment activity will result in productive, satisfied, and committed employees. Furthermore, these employees will be less likely to leave the organization.

As shown in Exhibit 4.8, an organization's recruitment activity at the preentry and entry stages can be evaluated by the number of qualified job applicants it attracts and by whether the applicants have a realistic picture of what the organization is like and whether it fits their needs. Postentry criteria measure how well the long-run interests of the individual and the organization are being served. Organizations prefer employees who perform well and prefer that good performers stay. Individuals prefer to be satisfied, to have a job that fits their needs and abilities, and to work in an organization they like. In essence, the longer the better-performing employees stay and the more satisfied they are, the more effective the recruitment activity is.

One criterion of recruiting effectiveness that covers all stages is legal compliance. Job applicants must be recruited fairly and without discrimination. During the entry and postentry stages, they must also receive fair and affirmative opportunities to be matched to appropriate jobs and to perform to their maximum abilities. (Legal compliance is more fully discussed in Chapters 5 and 6.)

In addition to evaluating each stage of the recruitment process, each method or source of recruitment can be evaluated ("costed-out"). For example, for each method, such as radio advertising or employee referrals, the cost per applicant and cost per hire can be determined. Then benefits can be determined for each method, such as the average length of time the newly hired employee stays and the average level of performance of each employee. All these costs and benefits of each method can then be compared. On the basis of this comparison, some methods may be used more, some dropped, or some just modified to reduce their costs.

FACING THE CRITICAL ISSUES IN EFFECTIVE RECRUITMENT

Now that the recruitment activity has been described in detail, it is appropriate to respond briefly to the Critical Issues listed at the start of this chapter.

Issue: *How are employers going to get the skilled workers they need?*

Many organizations are really concerned about this issue. The Personnel in Action inserts in this chapter illustrate this concern. Organizations may need to step up their training efforts. In fact, recruitment activity is being added to personnel departments faster than almost any other personnel activity. This concern can also be addressed by job redesign efforts and by intensified or novel recruiting approaches. Our nation as a whole has to become concerned with the issue too. It may require a national training policy aimed specifically at increasing the number of skilled workers.

Issue: *What are the legal obligations employers have to fulfill?*

Technically, there are no legal guidelines on recruitment as there are on selection. We have taken the approach in this chapter, however, that recruitment is strongly influenced by an organization's affirmative action programs, some of which may be legally imposed and others voluntary. Nevertheless, they indicate who the organization needs to select, thus who it needs to recruit.

Issue: *How can employers make their organizations more attractive so they can recruit the people they really need and want?*

There are several ways including (1) Provide realistic interviews (recruitment should be evaluated by the candidates whom it attracts *and* by the number of applicants hired who stay); (2) Provide extensive, yet appropriate career opportunities; (3) Reduce and eliminate sex job typing and sex stereotyping; (4) Provide relocation assistance and childcare assistance; and (5) Make available alternative work arrangements applicants can choose from.

Issue: *Do realistic job previews really pay off?*

It is tempting to make the organization look as appealing as possible so the candidates are impressed. But if negative aspects are not discussed, the applicants once hired will soon discover them. They will then become dissatisfied and/or leave. Since both of these actions are indicators of ineffectiveness, it hardly pays to be less than honest. Being honest means telling as much as possible about the job situation the applicant is likely to experience. It means giving a realistic interview. Do you think that it even pays a job applicant not to be honest with the interviewer?

SUMMARY

Recruitment is a major activity in an organization's program to manage its human resources. After human resource needs have been established and job requirements have been identified through job analysis, a program of recruitment can be established to produce a pool of job applicants. These applicants can be obtained from internal or external sources.

For recruitment to be effective, it must not only consider the needs of the organization but those of society and the individual as well. Society's needs are most explicitly defined by various federal and state regulations in the name of equal opportunity. The needs of individuals figure prominently in two aspects of recruiting—attracting candidates and retaining desirable employees. An effective way organizations can serve the needs of individuals in these two aspects of recruiting is by conducting realistic job previews. Another way is by offering more alternative work schedules and by giving applicants a choice of schedules. As the work force continues to change, methods of attracting individuals will also. Thus the personnel manager must continually be aware of work-force changes. Assuming she or he is and, assuming potentially qualified job applicants are attracted to the organization, the next major step in effective personnel management is selection and placement of the applicants.

KEY CONCEPTS

external source	candidate profiles
internal source	goals and quotas
Affirmative Action Programs	job matching
job profiles	private employment agency

job banks	flextime
public employment agency	flexible time
recruitment	compressed work weeks
mutual recruitment	permanent part-time
realistic job preview	job sharing
consent decree	band width
job posting	core time
Employee Referral Programs (ERPs)	handicap

DISCUSSION QUESTIONS

1. What relationship does the personnel department have with line managers in recruiting qualified applicants?
2. What is an AAP, and how does it affect the organization?
3. List five purposes associated with recruitment in effective personnel management.
4. Identify the advantages and disadvantages of using internal sources for obtaining job applicants.
5. What are the internal and external sources of recruitment?
6. What is a realistic interview, and why is it important in recruitment?
7. What are some of the services and opportunities organizations are currently using to increase their pool of potentially qualified applicants and to retain valued employees?
8. What is meant by "a matter of commitment" when referring to an organization's compliance with legal requirements (for example, EEO) in recruitment?
9. List and describe the internal and external methods for obtaining job applicants.
10. Why should organizations offer childcare assistance for potentially qualified applicants and current employees of an organization?

CASE

The Lafayette International Soccer Team (LIST)

The grass on which she was lying was as green as it was on the other side. Excited by the confidence and challenged by the responsibility, Donna was anxiously waiting for his arrival. Two days earlier she was voted assistant to the coach, Joe, who himself was selected the team's coach the week before.

LIST is only a three-year-old team, but it is growing steadily. It is not the Cosmos, the Sting, or anything like that. However, it takes advantage of American and international students and citizens at Purdue University and the surrounding community.

"The word 'International' was added to the team's name because it sounded attractive; but that was that, nothing really fancy," said Joe.

Upon his arrival at the field for his meeting with Donna, one hour before the team's first practice under the new leadership, Joe reviewed the primary, and somewhat difficult to implement, general objectives of his coachmanship: (1) maintaining the same or better record than last year's; (2) encouraging people of both sexes to join the team, either to play or to learn and then play for the team; and (3) having a good time and keeping everybody happy.

While these three objectives may seem reasonable, Joe and Donna, who know the team's background and personality mix, realized how difficult a task it was. To begin on solid ground they agreed to come to the meeting prepared to compare notes. "Where shall we start, Coach?" said Donna. "Well," replied Joe, while reaching for his handbag, "let us begin by coming up with a unified evaluation of the team inventory, assistant Coach." "Boy, are we disciplined already," said Donna.

A half hour later, Joe and Donna had the following evaluation of players presently on the team. Additional personnel can be attracted from the University and its vicinity. However, this is not an easy task because of the motivational mix of players currently on the team. In their evaluation, the coach and his assistant agreed to rate the present skill of each player on a scale from zero to ten, the latter describing a very skillful player while the former describes a totally new person to the game:

The Defense Line

1. Mark: goalie, 7–8, undisciplined, moody and uncontrollable. He is the only goalkeeper available, and he knows it.
2. Mickey: 3–4, can be improved. Plays very physical to compensate for lack of skills. Willing to listen.
3. Jack: 8–9, dedicated, excellent physical shape, performs both defensive and offensive duties. Joined the team two months earlier.
4. Leo: 2–4, one of the four team founders. Willing to learn but his abilities are extremely limited. Extremely hungry for personal power. Now he is the team manager. Does not mind being powerful and playing any dirty tricks (for example, bad mouthing). Very physical on the field and has not improved appreciably in the last two years.
5. Mike: 7–8, as good as Jack but does not perform offensively. Disciplined, pleasant, and a joy to watch.
6. Sam: 5, fairly inconsistent performer despite his good abilities. Plays summer only when he comes to town from his college.

The Half Line

7. Jim: 6–7, a team founder, low-key. His technical soccer skills have been growing very fast; improves everyday. His personality is respected by everyone. However, he lacks knowledge of the rules of the game and different strategies.

8. Tod: 7–8, a Ph.D. student in the University, low key, has been the team captain for several games. Tod does not participate on the offense line as he should, needs to get in better physical shape.

9. Jose: 3–4, a little weak body- and skill-wise, lack of stamina, a good friend of Jim and he was the one who brought him to the team in the first place. Is not available for traveling games.

The Offensive Line

10. Alvaro: 8–9, may be considered the best available player on the team. His skills and physique are almost perfect. The only drawback on his style is that he dribbles excessively, but he listens.

11. Juan: 7–8, not physically fit, shouts all the time at anybody around him, dribbles everybody and everything nearby. Loves to score, and never listens.

12. Bill: 5, runs like a horse, argues with everybody: his colleagues, opponents, the referee, linemen, and sometimes members of the audience. Never makes mistakes and always wants it his way.

13. Che: 6–7, small, fast, appears to listen carefully but never acts upon what he attentively listens to. He is a pleasant person during the team parties, however.

14. Jane: 3–4, lacks stamina, has put herself on a program to lose weight, carries out position duties up to her physical limitation.

15. Marla: 6–7, fast, trouble shooter, play maker. Whenever her husband is casually practicing with the team, she loves to incapacitate him (soccer-wise).

16. Karen: 7–8, strong, trouble shooter, and best used on one-to-one duties.

17. Rick: 1–2, team founder, physically unfit (knee injury). Willing to learn. His part as a team founder is fading, however, because of his business involvement.

18. Paul: 5–6, team founder, physically less fit. Seems that he was a better player fifteen years ago, he is now forty-two. Willing to use his seniority only to get himself to play, no more personal power.

Joe and Donna agreed that they are short on good players. Donna's comment was true: "While it is easy to get to town or the University and possibly find ten more players, it won't be easy forcing them on the team." "You're right," said Joe, "the better the players we recruit the less the chances that people like our founders who have to vote on accepting new players, will get to play. Tough isn't it?" Faced with this dilemma, Joe and Donna agreed to operationalize the situation into specific questions:

Case Questions

1. Shall we recruit summer students to play for the team until we train those who are on the team? What is our prospective pool for such potential, temporary players?

2. What recruiting techniques can be used by LIST to attract good temporary players?

3. If the LIST decides to train players before the season starts, should it attempt to train all of them now on the team or just the semigood players?

4. For the longer term, what else can LIST do to help ensure it has a large pool of potentially qualified players from which to recruit and select?

FOR YOUR CAREER

- You can be a valuable aid to a manager or organization if you can interpret the complexities of laws and regulations facing an organization's use of human resources.

- The image of a personnel manager is greatly enhanced if she or he can help the line managers in dealing with equal employment laws.

- With respect to compliance with equal employment laws, the personnel manager can serve as the conscience as well as the advisor of the organization.

- You should be prepared to interview the interviewer. Only in this way will you really learn about the organization.

- What are your preferences for work arrangements? What hours and when would you like to work?

- You may learn about your next job on the radio, so stay tuned.

ENDNOTES

1. J. P. Wanous, *Organizational Entry* (Reading, Mass.: Addison-Wesley, 1980).

2. BNA *Bulletin to Management,* September 24, 1981, p. 3. Reprinted by permission from *Bulletin to Management,* copyright 1981 by The Bureau of National Affairs, Inc., Washington, D.C.

3. Alfred W. Blumrosen, "Equal Employment Opportunity in the Eighties: The Bottom Line," *Employee Relations Law Journal* 6, no. 4 (1981):535–543.

David A. Brookmire, "Designing and Implementing Your Company's Affirmative Action Program" *Personnel Journal,* April 1979, pp. 232–237.

Bob Gatty, "Business Finds Profit in Hiring the Disabled," *Nation's Business,* August 1981, pp. 30–35.

"Fair Employment Digest," Employee and Labor Relations Committee, American Society for Personnel Administration, Berea, Ohio, June 1981.

William J. Kilberg and Stephen E. Tallent, "From 'Bakke' to 'Fullilove': The Use of Racial and Ethnic Preferences in Employment," *Employee Relations Law Journal* 6, no. 3 (1981): pp. 364–379.

Neil D. McFeeley, "Weber Versus Affirmative Action?" *Personnel,* January–February, 1980, pp. 38–51.

Donald J. Petersen, "Paving the Way for Hiring the Handicapped," *Personnel,* March–April 1981, pp. 43–52.

Andrew J. Ruzicho, "The Weber Case—It's Impact on Affirmative Action," *Personnel Administrator,* June 1980, pp. 69–72.

4. D. A. Brookmire and A. A. Burton, "A Format for Packaging Your Affirmative Action Program," *Personnel Journal,* June 1978, p. 295. Reprinted with the permission of *Personnel Journal,* Costa Mesa, Calif.; all rights reserved.

5. Howard R. Bloch and Robert L. Pennington, "Measuring Discrimination: What Is a Relevant Labor Market," *Personnel,* July–August 1980, pp. 21–29.

Kenneth E. Marino, "Conducting an Internal Compliance Review of Affirmative Action," *Personnel,* March–April 1980, pp. 24–34.

Howard R. Bloch and Robert L. Pennington, "Labor Market Analysis as a Test of Discrimination," *Personnel Journal,* August 1980, pp. 649–652.

6. BNA, *Fair Employment Practices,* July 16, 1981, pp. 1–2. Reprinted by permission from Fair Employment Practice Service, copyright 1981 by The Bureau of National Affairs, Inc., Washington, D.C.

7. Petersen, pp. 43–52.

8. F. S. Hall and S. A. Meier, "Developing Managerial Commitment to EEO," *Personnel Administrator,* May 1977, pp. 36–39.

9. S. A. McCollister, "EEO: An Approach for the 70's," p. 39. Reprinted with permission from the January 1978 issue of the *Personnel Administrator* copyright 1978, The American Society for Personnel Administration, 30 Park Drive, Berea, Ohio 44017.

10. L. R. Sayles and G. Strauss, *Managing Human Resources* (Englewood Cliffs, N.J.: Prentice-Hall, 1977), p. 147.

11. J. P. Campbell, M. D. Dunnette, E. E. Lawler III, and K. E. Weick, Jr., *Managerial Behavior, Performance and Effectiveness* (New York: McGraw-Hill, 1970).

12. "Corporate Women—Now Eager to Accept Transfers." Reprinted from the May 26, 1980, issue of *Business Week,* pp. 153, 156, by special permission, © 1980 by McGraw-Hill, Inc., New York, N.Y. 10020. All rights reserved.

13. Ibid., p. 156.

14. Corporate Women—A Rush of Recruits for Overseas Duty." Reprinted from the April 20, 1981, issue of *Business Week,* p. 120, by special permission, © 1981 by McGraw-Hill, Inc., New York, N.Y. 10020. All rights reserved.

15. J. Robert Garcia, "Job Posting for Professional Staff," *Personnel Journal,* March 1981, pp. 189–192.

16. Thomasine Rendero, "Consensus," *Personnel,* September–October 1980. New York: AMACOM, a division of American Management Associations, 1980, p. 5.

17. Rick Stoops, "Employee Referral Programs: Part 1," *Personnel Journal,* February 1981, p. 98, Part 2, pp. 172–173.

18. Wayne J. Bjerregaard and Mark E. Gold, "Employment Agencies and Executive Recruiters: A Practical Approach," *Personnel Administrator,* May 1981, pp. 127–131, 135.

Wayne J. Bjerregaard and Mark E. Gold, "Executive Utilization of Search Consultants," *Personnel Administrator,* December 1980, pp. 35–39.

Richard J. Cronin, "Executive Recruiters: Are They Necessary?," *Personnel Administrator,* February 1980, pp. 31–34.

Bruce Horovitz, "Where Headhunters Hunt," *Industry Week,* February 9, 1981, pp. 43–47.

C. Edward Kur and Philip G. Stone, "An Untapped Source of Consulting Help," *Personnel Administrator,* December 1980, pp. 29–33.

Ronald V. Raine, "Selecting the Consultant," *Personnel Administration,* December 1980, pp. 41–43.

19. Charles W. L. Deale, "How to Choose a Temporary Help Service: A Guide to Quality Supplemental Staffing," *Personnel Administrator,* December 1980, pp. 55–57.

David Diamond, "For Rent: Nomadic Engineer (Expensive)," *New York Times,* September 27, 1981, section F, p. 6.

Teresia R. Ostrach, "A Second Look at Temporaries," *Personnel Journal,* June 1981, pp. 440–442.

20. David L. Chicci and Carl L. Krapp, "College Recruitment From Start to Finish," *Personnel Journal,* August 1980, pp. 653–657.

Thomasine Rendero, "Consensus," *Personnel,* May–June 1980, pp. 4–10.

P. Zollman, "There's Jobs in Abundance for Americans With Skills," *Columbus Dispatch,* May 20, 1979, UPI Business Writer, p. C 1, 8.

21. "A Warmer Welcome for Foreign Technicians," *Business Week,* August 17, 1981, pp. 31–32.

Thomas M. Chesser, "Foreigners Snap Up The High-Tech Jobs," *New York Times,* July 5, 1981, sec. F, p. 13.

Lester C. Thurow, "Wanted: More Skilled Workers," *New York Times,* May 3, 1981, sec. F, p. 2.

Joanne G. Minarcini, "Illegal Aliens: Employment Restrictions and Responses," *Personnel Administrator,* March 1980, pp. 71–78.

22. Jo Bredwell, "The Use of Broadcast Advertising for Recruitment," *Personnel Administrator,* February 1981, pp. 45–49.

Rick Stoops, "Radio Advertising as an Effective Recruitment Device," *Personnel Journal,* January 1981, p. 21.

Rick Stoops, "Radio Recruitment Advertising: Part II," *Personnel Journal,* July 1981, p. 532.

"Affirmative Action in the 1980's: What Can We Expect?" *Management Review,* May 1981, pp. 4–5.

23. Rick Stoops, "Advertising in Trade Journals," *Personnel Journal,* September 1981, p. 678.

Rick Stoops, "A Marketing Approach to Recruitment," *Personnel Journal,* August 1981, p. 608.

24. Murray J. Lubliner, "Developing Recruiting Literature That Pays Off," *Personnel Administrator,* February 1981, pp. 51–55.

Margaret M. Nemec, "Recruitment Advertising—It's More Than Just 'Help Wanted,'" *Personnel Administrator,* February 1981, pp. 57–60.

Rick Stoops, "Recruitment Advertising," *Personnel Journal,* October 1980, p. 806.

25. G. S. Odiorne and A. S. Hann, *Effective College Recruiting* (Ann Arbor, Mich.: Bureau of Industrial Relations, Graduate School of Business, University of Michigan, 1961).

26. Schneider, p. 102.

27. R. M. Coffina, "Management Recruitment Is a Two-Way Street," *Personnel Journal,* February 1979, p. 88.

28. "Summer Internships Receive High Marks From College Students," *Wall Street Journal,* August 27, 1981, pp. 1, 20.

"Firms Providing Business Internships Lure Middle-Aged Women Looking for Careers," *Wall Street Journal,* September 2, 1981, p. 23.

Robert L. Lattimer, "Developing Career Awareness Among Minority Youths: A Case Example," *Personnel Journal,* January 1981, p. 17.

29. Robert S. Greenberger, "Many Black Managers Hope to Enter Ranks of Top Management," *Wall Street Journal,* June 15, 1981, pp. 1, 16.

Carol Hymowitz, "More Men Infiltrating Professions Historically Dominated by Women," *Wall Street Journal,* February 25, 1981, p. 25.

Carol Hymowitz, "Women Coal Miners Fight for Their Rights to Lift, Shovel, Lug," *Wall Street Journal,* September 10, 1981, pp. 1, 18.

Ann Hughey, "Minority Journalists Are in Meager Supply in Nation's Newsrooms," *Wall Street Journal,* June 11, 1981, pp. 1, 21.

Kenneth A. Kovach, "Implicit Stereotyping in Personnel Decisions," *Personnel Journal,* September 1981, pp. 716–722.

30. Margaret Magnus and John Dodd, "Relocation: Changing Attitudes and Company Policies," *Personnel Journal,* July 1981, pp. 538–548.

Gaylord F. Milbrandt, "Relocation Strategies: Part 1," *Personnel Journal,* July 1981, pp. 551–554.

31. Andree Brooks, "Job Help for Wives," *New York Times,* August 30, 1981, Sec. F, p. 8.

32. Deborah Rankin, "When Uncle Sam Is the Baby Sitter," *New York Times,* September 13, 1981, Sec. F, p. 14.

Rosalyn Weinman Schram, "Parents, Kids and Companies: New Rules for Business," *Personnel Journal,* June 1981, pp. 436–437.

33. Sally A. Coltrin and Barbara Barendse, "Is Your Organization a Good Candidate for Flextime," *Personnel Journal,* September 1981, pp. 712–715.

Lois F. Copperman, Fred D. Keast and Douglas G. Montgomery, "Older Workers and Part-Time Work Schedules," *Personnel Administrator,* October 1981, pp. 35–38.

Talmer E. Curry, Jr. and Deane N. Haerer, "The Positive Impact of Flextime on Employee Relations," *Personnel Administrator,* February 1981, pp. 62–66.

Phil Farish, "PAIR Potpourri," *Personnel Administrator,* June 1981, p. 10.

Donald J. Petersen, "Flextime in the United States: The Lessons of Experience," *Personnel,* January–February 1980, pp. 21–31.

Damon Stetson, "Work Innovation Improving Morale," *New York Times,* September 20, 1981, p. 53.

"Why Flextime Is Spreading," *Business Week,* February 23, 1981, pp. 455–460.

34. T. A. Mahoney, "The Rearranged Workweek: Evaluations of Different Work Schedules," *California Management Review,* Summer 1978, pp. 31–39.

M. Maurice, *Shift Work* (Geneva, Switzerland: Internal Labor Office, 1975).

D. L. Tasto and M. J. Collegan, Shift Work Practices in the United States (Washington, D.C.: National Institute for Occupational Safety and Health, 1977).

35. R. T. Golembiewski, and R. J. Hills, "Drug Company Workers Like New Schedules," *Monthly Labor Review* 100 (1977):65–69.

R. T. Golembiewski, R. Hills, and M. S. Kagna, "A Longitudal Study of Flextime Effects: Some Consequences of an OD Structural Intervention," *Journal of Applied Behavioral Sciences* 4 (1974):503–532.

36. S. D. Nollen, "Does Flextime Improve Productivity?" *Harvard Business Review,* 57 (1979):16–18, 76, 80.

37. "A Full-Time Job—Weekends Only," *Business Week*, October 15, 1979, pp. 151–152.

R. B. Dunham and D. L. Hawk, "The Four-Day/Forty-Hour Week: Who Wants It?" *Academy of Management Journal* 20 (1977):644–655.

M. D. Fottler, "Employee Acceptance of the Four-Day Workweek," *Academy of Management Journal* 20 (1977):656–668.

J. S. Kim and A. F. Campagna, "Effects of Flextime on Productivity: A Field Experiment in a Public Sector Setting," paper presented at the *National Academy of Management*, Detroit, Mich., 1980.

V. Schein, E. Maurer, and J. Novak, "Impact of Flexible Working Hours on Productivity," *Journal of Applied Psychology* 62 (1977):463–465.

38. A. R. Cohen and H. Gadon, *Alternative Work Schedules: Integrating Individual and Organizational Needs* (Reading, Mass.: Addison-Wesley, 1978), p. 66.

Chapter Outline

Critical Issues in Selection and Placement

Selection and Placement
Purposes and Importance of Selection and Placement
Selection and Placement Relationships with Other Personnel Activities

Legal Considerations
Laws and Guidelines Affecting Selection and Placement

Selection and Placement Information
Organizational Context
Job Qualities
The Job Applicant
Obtaining Job Applicant Information

Selection and Placement Procedures, Legal Considerations, and Job Applicant Information

Obtaining Job Applicant Information
The Selection and Placement Interview
Employment Tests
The Application Blank

Summary

Key Concepts

Discussion Questions

Case

For Your Career

Endnotes

Personnel in the News

"More Fat People Are Going to Court, Charging Employers with Job Bias"

Joyce English has a college degree in law enforcement and social work, but since graduation she has worked as an adult-bookstore cashier, plantation field hand, babysitter and tomato peeler at a canning factory.

When she applied for a job as a customer service representative at Philadelphia Electric Co., she was assured that the job was hers as soon as she passed a physical exam. But Miss English weighs 350 pounds, and the examiners ruled her "unfit" because of "morbid obesity." She said she was discriminated against because of her weight, and sued. The Pennsylvania Human Relations Commission agreed and awarded her the job and $20,000 in back pay.

Her battle is one campaign in a revolt by fat Americans. Once too embarrassed to complain about alleged discrimination in employment, many are fighting and winning. (M. Langley, Wall Street Journal, *August 14, 1981, p. 25. Reprinted by permission of the* Wall Street Journal, © *Dow Jones & Company, Inc., 1981. All rights reserved.*)

Consider Equal Employment in Promotion

The effects of EEO (equal employment opportunity) on promotion decisions deserve special comment. Assuring equal employment opportunity is a major consideration in most organizations today. Like other personnel practices, such as hiring, transfers and layoffs, management promotion decisions are subject to EEO regulations. Discrimination barring women and minorities from higher level jobs is illegal, and the courts have not been lax in imposing remedies or obtaining stringent settlements. Often, the first step in a promotion process is to determine whether affirmative action obligations will influence the choice of candidates. ("What Every Personnel Director Should Know About Management Promotion Decisions," *by M. London,* Personnel Journal, *October 1978, p. 555. Reprinted with permission of* Personnel Journal, *Costa Mesa, Calif., copyright 1978. All rights reserved.*)

Job Placement Violates Title VII

Against his wishes a black personnel specialist was assigned to work in minority recruitment. The employer, extremely anxious for its minority recruitment program to succeed, felt that a black person would be able to develop a better rapport with minority applicants than a white person. But the employee thought the assignment was racial and sued the employer. The U.S. Court of Appeals in New York said that "no matter how laudable" the employer's affirmative action intentions were, assigning this employee to the minority recruitment program against his will was race discrimination in violation of Title VII. In the court's opinion, the job assignment was based on the "racial stereotype that blacks work better with blacks." The employer was saying that the employee's race was directly related to his ability to do the job and was therefore making race a qualification for the job, which is discriminatory and illegal. (Knight *v.* Nassau County Civil Service Commission, *649 F2d 157. From FEP Guidelines 192 [7]).*

Together these quotations highlight the legal considerations that organizations face in making selection and placement decisions. The quotations also illustrate the cost to the organization of failing to consider the legal regulations and court decisions. Finally, they show the several bases upon which job applicants and current employees can sue organizations for violating employment laws.

Although the legal impact on most organizations' selection and placement decisions is very considerable, personnel managers also face other issues in making these decisions. The issues include: (1) how to collect information on job applicants; (2) how to make selection and placement decisions; (3) how to validate tests used in making selection decisions; and (4) how to make the entire set of selection and placement procedures more useful.

CRITICAL ISSUES IN SELECTION AND PLACEMENT

Of the many issues identified by our group of personnel managers the four most critical ones are

1. *What are all of the laws that organizations must consider in making selection and placement decisions?*
2. *What are the best ways (and most legal ways) to get the information needed in making selection and placement decisions so organizations can still select the best candidate?*
3. *How do organizations know when they are violating the law?*
4. *How can organizations improve their selection and placement procedures to make them more effective?*

In order for you to effectively address these and other issues in selection and placement, extensive discussions are necessary on (1) obtaining selection and placement information; (2) observing the legal regulations; (3) using selection and placement information; and (4) making the selection and placement operation more effective. Since each of these discussions is complex, they are presented in two chapters. First, we consider the relevant legal regulations and how to obtain selection and placement information. In the next chapter, we consider the use of the selection and placement information obtained and how selection and placement decisions can be made more effectively. Because all this information is so interrelated, it is summarized at the end of Chapter 6 when the Critical Issues are addressed.

The process of gathering information for the purposes of evaluating and deciding who should be hired, under legal guidelines, for the short- and long-term interests of the individual and the organization is called **Selection. Placement** is concerned with ensuring that job demands are filled and that individual needs and preferences are met. Traditionally, selection and placement have primarily been concerned with matching employee skills and abilities with the demands of the job.[1] Now, however, there is an additional emphasis on matching employee needs and preferences with job rewards.[2]

SELECTION AND PLACEMENT

Recruitment and selection and placement need to be closely coordinated to fulfill Match 1 and Match 2.

The concern for the two-way matching in selection and placement is consistent with our emphasis in recruitment and job analysis and job design. In fact, although these two activities are treated separately in this book, they share many qualities. For example, both use information on the characteristics and qualities of the organization, the job, and the individual. Both seek to serve the short- and long-term interests of the organization and the individual. They also share many of the same purposes and goals.

Purposes and Importance of Selection and Placement

Selection and placement procedures provide the very essence of organizations—their human resources. And it is largely by effective selection and placement that organizations can obtain the human resources most likely to serve the needs of the organization. Effective selection and placement is thus critical to any organization. Serving the needs of the organizations and being effective with selection and placement means attaining several purposes including

- To fairly, legally, and in a nondiscriminatory manner evaluate and hire the potentially qualified job applicants
- To evaluate, hire, and place job applicants in the best interests of the organization and the individual
- To engage in selection and placement activities that are useful for initial hiring as well as future selection and placement decisions for the individual (for example, in promotions or transfers)
- To make selection and placement decisions with consideration for the uniqueness of the individual, the job, the organization and the environment, even to the extent of adapting the job or organization to the individual[3]

In order to serve these purposes effectively, personnel must integrate selection and placement with several other personnel activities.

Selection and Placement Relationships with Other Personnel Activities

The success of an organization's selection and placement procedures depends on several other personnel activities. As Exhibit 5.1 illustrates, selection and placement

Exhibit 5.1
Selection and Placement Procedures

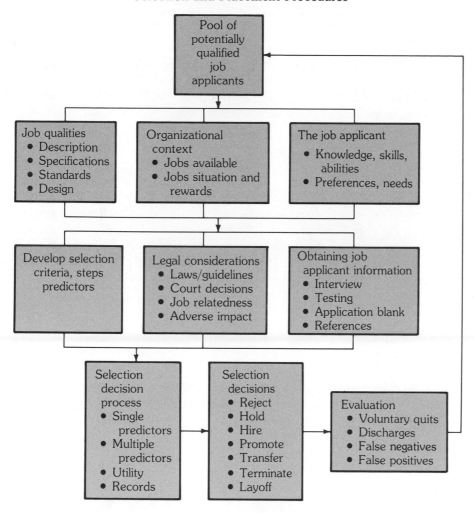

decisions begin with a pool of potentially qualified job applicants, an analysis of the qualities of the jobs that are open, and a description of the organizational context. The first two of these steps are directly related to recruitment and job analysis activities.

Job Analysis.   Selection and placement (S and P) decisions should be made to benefit the individual and the organization. In order to do this, the qualities of the jobs to be filled must clearly be identified. When the essential job dimensions and worker qualifications are known, selection devices can be developed. Selection devices developed on the basis of a job analysis are more likely to be job-related—thus more effective and more likely to serve legal considerations.

However, selection devices based on job analysis tend to focus on the worker's ability to do the job (Match 1). It is also necessary to use information about job rewards

S and P decisions should be made on the basis of job demands and job applicant abilities.

S and P decisions should be made on the basis of job rewards and job applicant preferences or needs.

so that job applicants can be placed in jobs that match their needs (Match 2). As noted in Chapters 3 and 4, these two matches help ensure that the short-run and long-run interests of both individuals and organizations are served.[4]

Recruitment.   The success of selection and placement activities depends on the effectiveness of the recruiting activity. If recruiting does not provide a large pool of potentially qualified, ready job applicants, it is difficult for the organization to select and place individuals who will perform well and not quit. And even if recruitment does provide some applicants, if the pool is small the effectiveness of the selection and placement activities is limited.

Performance Appraisal.   Selection and placement also depend on performance appraisals as a source of feedback to show that the selection devices do, indeed, predict performance. If performance appraisal is done poorly, it is difficult for the organization to develop and use selection devices to predict meaningful employee performance. As a result, selection and placement are unable to serve their purposes.

While recognizing all these relationships that selection and placement have is critical, personnel must also recognize an extensive set of legal considerations. Without this recognition, effective selection and placement are impossible.

LEGAL CONSIDERATIONS

The legal environment for most organizations is growing so complex that equal employment legislation is increasingly becoming a first consideration in making employment decisions. Knowing how the legislation impacts on the selection and placement decision process is a second consideration. Both of these considerations finally rest upon the personnel manager.[5]

FOR YOUR CAREER

Who's Protected by What (Major Federal Laws and Acts)

Title VII of the Civil Rights Act of 1964, as amended in 1972, prohibits discrimination in employment on the basis of race, color, national origin, sex, or religion.
Age Discrimination in Employment Act of 1967, as amended in 1978, prohibits discrimination against employees and applicants for employment who are at least forty but less than seventy years of age.

Equal Pay Act of 1963 prohibits discrimination between employees on the basis of sex by paying a wage rate higher for one sex than another on the jobs that are equal in skill, effort, responsibility, and working conditions.
The Rehabilitation Act of 1973 prohibits discrimination against persons with physical or mental handicaps

that substantially limit one or more major life activities or who have a history of an impairment that is visible to others.

Vietnam Era Veterans Readjustment Act of 1974 protects disabled veterans and veterans of the Vietnam era in seeking employment opportunities.

Note: These are only the major federal laws and acts. State and local governments also have their own laws and acts. See Appendix A for the details of other laws and acts, such as the extent of coverage of the act and the minimum size of the organization, and other laws and court decisions.

Laws and Guidelines Affecting Selection and Placement

Determining exactly what an organization's equal employment obligations are is made complex by an extensive web of federal laws, federal and state constitutions, state and local legislation, court decisions, executive orders, guidelines, quasi-judicial bodies such as EEOC and OFCCP and state EEO agencies. Before the 1960s, this web of laws and guidelines that required equal opportunity in the field of employment was much less extensive. Appendix A lists the large number of equal employment laws that have been enacted since 1960.

It's important for you to become familiar with all these equal employment laws.

The most significant federal laws related to selection and placement decisions are the Title VII of the *Civil Rights Act of 1964*, the *Age Discrimination Act of 1967* and the 1978 amendment, the *Equal Employment Act of 1972* (an amendment to the 1964 Civil Rights Act), the *Equal Pay Act of 1963*, and the *Rehabilitation Act of 1973*.[6] Three important executive orders (EOs) in this area are EO 10925 (signed by President Kennedy in 1961), EO 11246 (signed by President Johnson in 1965) and EO 11375 (signed by President Ford in 1975). The Fifth and Fourteenth Amendments to the U.S. Constitution are also critical.

In addition to these laws, executive orders, related court decisions and the constitutional amendments, two sets of guidelines on equal employment procedures have had a major impact. The first set was issued in 1970 by the Equal Employment Opportunity Commission; the second set was initially formulated in 1976 by three other agencies charged with equal employment responsibility: the Office of Federal Contract Compliance Programs (OFCCP), the Department of Labor, and the Justice Department. In 1978 the second set was issued when the EEOC joined these three agencies to adopt what is known as the *Uniform Guidelines on Employee Selection Procedures* (often referred to as the *Uniform Guidelines*), a 14,000-word catalog of do's and don'ts for hiring and promotion. Today these Uniform Guidelines and several court decisions constitute the legal constraints on selection and placement activities.[7] They can be divided into four basic categories: (1) adverse impact; (2) job relatedness; (3) bona fide occupational qualification procedures; and (4) the affirmative action programs (discussed in Chapter 4).

Two sets of guidelines, in addition to those of 1970 and 1978, have recently been published by the Equal Employment Opportunity Commission. In November 10, 1980, the EEOC issued Guidelines on Discrimination Because of Sex (sexual harassment), and on December 29, 1980, it issued the Guidelines on Discrimination Because of National Origin. The national origin guidelines extended earlier versions of this protection by defining national origin as a *place* rather than a *country* of origin. It also established the "speak-English-only rules." This means that employers require

English to be spoken if they can show this is job-related. Sexual harassment is discussed in Chapter 8.

Adverse Impact. Shortly after the EEOC established the 1970 Guidelines, the Supreme Court established in *Griggs* v. *Duke Power* (1971) the legal framework for employment testing and approved the procedures in the 1970 EEOC guidelines. One provision of the guidelines was that tests used for selection be *job-related.* The only way job relatedness could be proven was by validation procedures, a comparison of test scores with job performance.

Validation procedures show if a selection decision is job-related.

Now, however, according to the courts, validation is no longer required in *all* cases:

> It is essential only in instances where the test or other selection device produces an *adverse impact* on a minority group. Under the new guidelines, adverse impact has been defined in terms of selection rates, the selection rate being the number of applicants hired or promoted, divided by the total number of applicants.[8]

There are several ways to demonstrate adverse impact.

A selection rate for any minority group of less than 80 percent of the rate for the group with the highest rate is generally regarded as evidence of **adverse impact.**[9] This aspect of the 1978 Uniform Guidelines is called the **80 percent rule or the bottom-line criterion.** This is also referred to as the 4/5 rule. If, for example, a company hires 50 percent of all white male applicants who apply in a particular job category, then it must hire at least 40 percent (80 percent × 50 percent) of all blacks who apply and 40 percent of all women and other protected groups. It need not meet the 80 percent rule, however, if it can show that the selection procedures being used are job-related.

In addition to this statistical 80/20 (4/5) rule there are other statistical percentage rules that can be used as proof of adverse impact. They and the *prima facie* evidence rule for showing adverse impact are listed in the *For Your Career* insert. As a consequence of these rules, the organization has to keep records of the number of applicants and those hired by sex and racial and ethnic group, including separate figures for black, Indian, Hispanic-surname, and Caucasian people.

Some Methods Used to Demonstrate Adverse Impact, Thus Causing Need to Defend Selection or Employment Practices

1. Prima facie evidence (*McDonnell Douglas Corporation* v. *Green* [1973] by showing (by the plaintiff):
   a. she or he belongs to a racial minority;

   b. she or he applied for job for which employer was seeking applicants;

   c. that despite her or his qualifications, she or he was rejected; and

d. after her or his rejection, employer kept looking for people with applicants' qualifications.

2. Statistical proof includes one of these four:

  a. whether members of protected class as a whole (or in given area) are disqualified at a disproportionately high rate by the employment practice;

b. comparison of the percentage of minority applicants with the percentage of other job applicants excluded by the practice; and

c. examination of whether the percentage of the protected class employed by defendant is equivalent to that in relevant geographic area.

d. violation of 80 percent rule.

Requiring organizations to keep these records necessitates their obtaining this information. Thus the Uniform Guidelines now allow organizations to obtain this information on the application blank or in the job interview. Previously organizations were not allowed to ask this information.

But any of these methods, if adverse impact is charged and demonstrated by the *plaintiff* (generally by the employee or job applicant or his or her representative, such as EEOC or a state civil rights commission), the burden of proof to show job relatedness shifts to the *defendant* (generally the organization). The organization can successfully dispute the adverse impact evidence by showing job relatedness, by showing a BFOQ, or in the absence of showing either of these, by showing a business necessity exists. The organization's defense, however, need only consist of a legitimate, nondiscriminatory explanation. This is further explained in the *Personnel in Action* insert. The plaintiff must then show that the organization's defense is really a pretext for discrimination or that alternative procedures exist that would yield less adverse impact. So just because an organization can demonstrate it is abiding by the 4/5 rule, does not mean it is justified in using the selection procedure.

PERSONNEL IN ACTION

Proof of Bias Rests with Employee or Applicant, Supreme Court Declares

A defendant in a job discrimination case need only provide a legitimate, nondiscriminatory explanation for not hiring or promoting a woman or minority, and need not prove that the white or man hired was better qualified, the Supreme Court ruled March 4.

The Civil Rights Act of 1964 "does not demand that an employer provide preferential treatment to minorities or women" if white male applicants are equally qualified for a job. Nor must an employer restruc-

ture his employment practices to maximize the number of minorities and women hired, the justices ruled in the unanimous decision.

Spelling out what steps an employer must take to defend himself or herself against job discrimination suits, the high court ruled that all an employer must do is to declare that there was a valid reason for choosing one employe or applicant over another. Once an employer has stated the reason, it is up to the complaining employe to persuade the court that the reason given was ficticious, and the actual basis for the choice was discrimination.

The case, *Texas Department of Community Affairs v. Joyce Ann Burdine* (79–1764), lightens the burden employers facing in defending themselves. Burdine worked as a field service coordinator for the public service careers division of the community affairs department. Her supervisor, the project director, resigned and she was given additional duties. After a department reorganization, one man was brought in to become project director, another man was promoted to Burdine's old spot and the plaintiff and two others were fired. Burdine filed suit in U.S. District Court for the Western District of Texas charging sex discrimination, although she was later rehired by the department in another capacity. After a trial, the court in December 1976 ruled that the department did not act with discriminatory intent.

Three years later, the U.S. Court of Appeals for the Fifth Circuit ruled that while there has not been discrimination in the decision to hire a new project director, the Texas department had failed to provide a preponderance of evidence that it had relied on nondiscriminatory reasons to retain the male employe but fire Burdine.

From *Fair Employment Report,* March 16, 1981.

In other words, an organization may do well by continuing to seek better selection procedures. Furthermore, just because a selection procedure may be shown to be job-related does not mean other procedures *more* job-related do not exist. Thus an organization should keep looking for better (alternative) selection procedures, procedures that have less adverse impact and are more job-related. But what is job relatedness anyway?

Job Relatedness. **Job relatedness** means that the company must show that its selection and placement procedures (predictors) are related to being successful on the job. This can be done by showing that the predictors have empirical, content, construct, or face validity (discussed in detail in the next chapter). It is important to note here, however, that of these validities the 1970 Guidelines gave more importance to empirical validity. The 1978 Uniform Guidelines gave equal importance to empirical, content, and construct validity. The courts have accepted these validities as well as face validity. In addition, there is the necessity of providing differential validity.

FOR YOUR CAREER

The essence of job relatedness is that if a predictor is used as a basis for selection and placement decisions and if those decisions result in adverse impact, then the predictors must be shown to be related to doing the job successfully. Job relatedness encompasses the concept of bona fide occupational qualification (BFOQ), which generally refers to the idea that if selection is made on the basis of sex or race, it must be job-related. For example, it is legitimate to audition only men for the part of a man in a play.

To ensure fairness, tests must also be *differentially validated.* The 1970 Guidelines contained a provision for the differential validation of tests. It was thought that a test may be a valid predictor of performance for one group but not another. Therefore, a separate validation was required for each group to determine if a test may be valid for one group and not another (this is the essence of differential validity). Many psychologists and much research suggest, however, that differential validity is a specious concept and that carefully constructed tests are equally valid for all groups. But the 1978 Uniform Guidelines not only continue to suggest differential validity but also describe the procedures for making such studies in substantial detail in the name of special studies of fairness.

Although showing the job relatedness of a selection procedure or device is desirable, it may not always be possible. In fact, it may be dangerous to do so. Some courts recognizing this situation have allowed companies to defend their selection procedures by showing business necessity.

Business Necessity.   Business necessity, along with job relatedness, can be used as a basis for defending adverse impact. Whereas job relatedness requires a demonstration of actual predictor-criterion relationships, business necessity does not.

> For example, in Diaz vs. Pan American World Airways, Inc., Pan Am had demonstrated that selection of female flight attendants and exclusion of male flight attendants was based on evidence that females were better at attending to the unique "psychological needs of its passengers." Further, while the company did not make the case that males could never perform this task successfully, it did demonstrate that very few males had the requisite abilities and that it was too costly to search for those few males. Hence, the company relied on sex as a hiring criterion for flight attendants. The court struck down this criterion on the grounds that "the primary function of an airline is to transport passengers safely from one point to another . . . No one has suggested that having male stewards will so seriously affect the operation of an airline as to jeopardize or even minimize its ability to provide safe transportation from one place to another."
>
> The court went on to note that "discrimination based on sex is valid only when the 'essence' of the business operation would be undermined by not hiring members of one sex exclusively." In short, while the job relatedness of sex was demonstrated, the job in question was not the heart of the business, and therefore the criterion of sex could not be used. What the Diaz case seems to suggest is that job relatedness and business necessity are not identical concepts. It also plainly suggests that job relatedness may be necessary evidence for defending oneself against adverse impact, but it is clearly not sufficient, at least not in this case.[10]

Business necessity is a much broader concept than job relatedness.

Thus, in many cases **business necessity** can modify adverse impact. However, in cases where business necessity clearly is high, it is not even necessary to demonstrate that the selection procedure is job-related (see *Spurlock* v. *United Airlines* and *Hodgson* v. *Greyhound Lines, Inc.* in Appendix A).

Alternative Procedures.   Even when business necessity or job relatedness can be shown to exist, a company could be required to show that there are no other procedures that would have been as effective in screening out unsuitable candidates and yet not have as much adverse impact. This is called the **alternative procedures requirement.** This requirement was contained in the 1970 Uniform Guidelines, but in the 1978 Uniform Guidelines the burden of meeting these requirements shifted from the individual to the organization. The courts, however, have indicated that the burden may be on the individual rather than the organization. Nevertheless, finding a "better" predictor could almost be a never-ending process. It has been referred to by some as a **cosmic search.**

Bona Fide Occupational Qualifications. Another defense for adverse impact is **bona fide occupational qualifications** *(BFOQ)*. For example, requiring that labor and delivery nurses in the obstetrics and gynecology department in a hospital be female is a BFOQ according to the U.S. District Court for the Eastern District of Arkansas (*Backus* v. *Baptist Medical Center,* 1981). Requiring males to play the roles of males in plays and theater productions is a BFOQ also.

Closely related to BFOQs are *bona fide seniority systems.* As shown in the *For Your Career* insert about the *Teamsters* ruling, certain types of seniority systems can legally influence employment decisions. According to the insert in the *Teamster* decision, the Supreme Court created a "grandfather clause," a clause indicating that only those seniority systems established before 1965 are bona fide and may continue to exist even though they may perpetuate discriminatory practices. Note that the insert reports on the Fourth Circuit Court's interpretation of *Teamsters* v. *United States* and is not that of the Supreme Court. The Supreme Court hearing this case on appeal (*American Tobacco* v. *Patterson,* 1982), reversed the decision of the Fourth Circuit Court.

FOR YOUR CAREER

Ever since the Supreme Court's 1977 ruling in *Teamsters* v. *United States,* the Title VII exception for bona fide seniority systems has been interpreted in various ways. Many courts have allowed systems that "perpetuate the effects of past discrimination," as long as seniority provisions are now applied neutrally. But the Fourth Circuit Court of Appeals has voiced a different view—one shared by EEOC. The Fourth Circuit says that what the Supreme Court meant to do in *Teamsters* was create a "grandfather clause," rather than make an exception. According to this court, only se-

niority systems established before the date Title VII went into effect (1965) qualify under the *Teamsters* rule. The seniority system examined by the Fourth Circuit locked women and minorities into certain jobs because of past discriminatory practices. Although the practices had been discontinued long ago, the discriminatory effects still lingered. But since the seniority system dated only from 1968, it was a post-act system, which the court said did not qualify for the Title VII exception. (*Patterson* v. *American Tobacco,* November 18, 1980. From *FEP Guidelines* 187[2]).

Now that we have examined the legal considerations necessary for effective selection and placement, it is necessary to discuss the types of information an organization actually needs to make selection and placement decisions. After discussing the types of informations and how to act on them, we turn to the statistical considerations necessary for effective selection and placement.

SELECTION AND PLACEMENT INFORMATION

As shown in Exhibit 5.1, there are three major sets of information needed for selection and placement: *organizational context; job qualities;* and *individual qualities.*

Organizational Context

To determine who is to select and place, we first need to identify job vacancies. This identification can be initiated through the organization's personnel planning or through direct requisitions from supervisors. Because many organizations do not effectively plan human resource needs, supervisor requisitions often become the major source of information about job openings. However, with forecasts of managerial shortages by the mid-1980s, more organizations are beginning to program systematically for their human resource needs. Managerial succession programs are evidence of this systematic effort. Organizations such as Nationwide Insurance Company, Detroit Edison, and Owens-Illinois also have department and division managers forecast job openings and human resource needs for one- and five-year periods. Without effective personnel planning, job availability is often not determined until there are job vacancies. Consequently, recruitment, selection, and placement may be undertaken without awareness of all the jobs that are open or be done so quickly that a thorough recruitment and selection process is not possible.

An employee's job performance may be determined only in part by the employee. Such characteristics of the organization as compensation policies, group pressures, philosophy of management, and quality of supervision also determine an employee's level of performance. In fact, there are many job situations in which employee performance is really determined by the pace of the machines more than any qualities of the employee. Because these aspects of the organization and job situation are so important, they must be accounted for in selection and placement procedures. For example, two jobs may require the same technical skills. But if one is isolated and the other is part of a larger group, the selection process for the job in the larger group may need to include a measure of interpersonal competence or need for affiliation; selection for the isolated job would not. The job situation not only influences employee performance but also determines job rewards. This information helps since the two matches are necessary for effective selection and placement.

Effective personnel planning and job analysis are the basis of effective selection and placement.

Job Qualities

Information about job requirements or demands and specifications is obtained from the job analysis. This information is needed to match individual ability with job demands. In addition to obtaining job analysis information, job design information should also be provided even though most organizations currently do not provide this. This is critical in helping job applicants determine if their preferences and needs would be satisfied by the job. As we observed in Chapter 3, the job design and individual preference information can also be used in redesigning jobs and in placing applicants in the more appropriate jobs. To further aid the applicants in choosing jobs and in performing well once hired, *standards* of performance should be obtained (from the job analysis) and conveyed to the applicants.

The Job Applicant

Information about the organizational context and job qualities are only about half of the information needed to match ability to demand and need to reward. The remaining half comes from the job applicant. The specific types of information obtained on an individual are aptitude, achievement or experience, and motivation (particularly personality, interest, and preferences). This information is the basis for predicting how well (successfully) a job applicant will perform. Procedures used to gather this information are often called **predictors** (when they are used to make selection decisions, they are called *tests*). The standards used to determine the level of "success" or at what level the applicant will perform are called **criteria.**

Predictors forecast what the future is likely to be, how well someone will perform on the job (criteria).

Predictors for Selection and Placement Decisions. What the organization wants is a predictor or set of predictors that will enable it to tell (predict) how a job applicant will perform according to the criteria established for the job. Remember, the essence of job relatedness of a predictor is that it indicates how successfully the applicant will be rated on the performance criteria if hired.

The most commonly used predictors are *interviews, application blanks,* and *employment tests.* Since selection and placement decisions are made on the basis of the information obtained by these predictors, each is discussed in more detail after the discussion of criteria for and steps in selection and placement decisions.

Criteria for Selection and Placement Decisions. Based on our discussion of job relatedness you should now recognize how important it is that the criteria that are selected are really critical to the job the organization wants to fill. For example, in the zoo keeper's job (Chapter 3), making sure that cages are cleaned every day and the animals are fed properly are probably more critical than ensuring that the zoo keeper dresses nicely and smiles. According to the job description of the zoo keeper shown in Chapter 3, there are certainly other criteria or standards of performance critical to the job. The exact ones and their relative importance are critical to developing valid predictors and having a valid performance appraisal system.

Selection decisions that are job-related are in the best interests of the organization.

After the important criteria are identified, the predictors must be chosen that will best obtain the information that will correctly predict an applicant's chances of performing well on those criteria. This process is neither easy nor is it inexpensive. If done correctly, however, it results in selection and placement decisions which are effective and serve the legal considerations. Since this process is rather complex, it is done in a series of steps.

Steps in Selection and Placement Decisions. Selection and placement decisions are very important to the organization. As such, personnel managers often use several predictors to make them.[11] Because managers can handle only so much information at one time, the information is generally gathered in steps or stages. An example of the typical steps in selection taken by personnel is shown in Exhibit 5.2, which also shows the major ways by which job applicant information is obtained. Since this information is important for selection and placement decisions, it is worthwhile to examine the major ways of obtaining it.

OBTAINING JOB APPLICANT INFORMATION

The major information-gathering procedures for selection and placement decisions are interviews, tests, and background information supplied by the applicant.

It is important to note that using information on the individual to predict perfor-

Exhibit 5.2
Steps in Selection

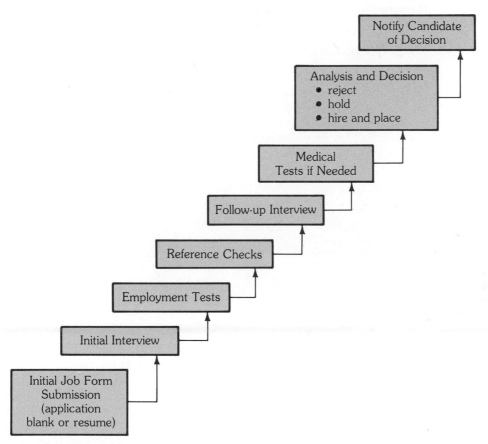

Notify Candidate of Decision

Analysis and Decision
• reject
• hold
• hire and place

Medical Tests if Needed

Follow-up Interview

Reference Checks

Employment Tests

Initial Interview

Initial Job Form Submission (application blank or resume)

mance represents concern for only one match—the match between ability and job demands (Match 1). This is the match that is subject to legal constraints and traditionally of major interest to organizations. However, individual information should also be gathered to predict employee satisfaction, absenteeism, and voluntary turnover. These predictions reflect a concern for the match between needs and rewards (Match 2). Many organizations have not focused on needs and rewards, but with the high cost of absenteeism, turnover, and dissatisfaction, they may begin to find that it pays to do so.

Since all the selection and placement information can be used for both matches, both will be discussed. But the ability-demand match is the primary concern for many organizations and is subject to legal constraints, so it is highlighted in this chapter and the next.

Only job-related information should be obtained from the job applicant.

The Selection and Placement Interview

Although aptitude, achievement, personality interests, and preferences are more reliably assessed by paper-and-pencil or carefully developed situational tests, the interview

Exhibit 5.3
Sources of Information about Job Applicants (Adapted from
Personnel Management Policies and Practices, Report No. 22 [Englewood
Cliffs, N.J.: Prentice-Hall, April 2, 1975]).

"Our most important source is . . ."

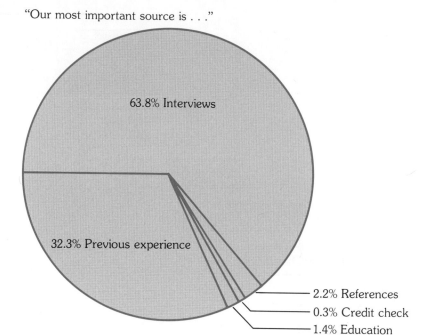

63.8% Interviews

32.3% Previous experience

2.2% References
0.3% Credit check
1.4% Education

remains the most important method of obtaining information (see Exhibit 5.3). It is a good procedure for gathering factual background information, although it is not a particularly good procedure for making assessments, because it is too subjective.[12]

Paradoxically (because the EEOC questions its job relatedness) the use of interviews as the means of gathering and assessing information has increased, not decreased, with pressures for more objective methods of selection. This is partially due to the rules and regulations of several equal opportunity agencies as illustrated in the *Personnel in Action* insert on interviews and tests. Thus the interview continues to be a much-used procedure for gathering selection and placement information.

PERSONNEL IN ACTION

Interviews and Tests Counting More As Past Employers Clam Up

Getting information about job applicants from former employers has become a bit like interrogating prisoners of war: The only data they offer is name, rank, dates of employment and final salary.

The missing intelligence, which was once routinely given, is an assessment of the individual's work, perhaps even of his or her character.

Rather than risk lawsuits from disgruntled workers,

an increasing number of Twin Cities firms, including Honeywell, Control Data and Northwestern National Bank, have adopted policies of not providing evaluations of former employees.

As a result, employers say, hiring decisions rely more than in the past on interviews, tests of skills and psychological health, friendships with people in other firms who can give them the straight skinny, even a sort of code language.

David Nelson, Honeywell's manager of selection and placement, noted that many employers will comment when a worker's performance has been excellent. If he or she has been a poor worker, nothing will be said.

The major reason employers stay mum is their fear of lawsuits. According to lawyers who advise executives on personnel matters, an employer who is critical of a former employee could be sued for libel and slander. If the employer's comments are shown to be malicious and untrue, he or she may have to pay damages.

Moreover, the Fair Credit Reporting Act sometimes requires that the prospective employer disclose to the applicant the name of an employer who has given a bad reference. And equal employment laws might apply if the recommendation can be shown to be discriminatory.

Courts have recognized that such laws discourage employers from honestly evaluating former employees. Because of this, court decisions have granted employers a qualified privilege, that is, limited protection from libel and slander suits.

But as Dale Beihoffer, a lawyer with the Faegre and Benson firm in Minneapolis, explained, "The boundaries (of the qualified privilege) aren't very clear and court decisions in this area have presented a moving target.

"Institutions want certainty . . . So if there's a question about it (whether to offer an assessment), the employer is going to say 'Why should I spend the time and money protecting myself against a possible lawsuit?'

"The prudent thing is not to do anything."

In a case decided last summer, the Minnesota Supreme Court upheld a lower court's finding that Parke, Davis and Co. defamed Neil Stuempges, a salesman, when his supervisor gave a false and malicious job reference. The court awarded Stuempges $37,750 in damages and reimbursement for lost income.

In its decision, the supreme court focused on the supervisor's malicious intent in giving the bad refer-

ence. It also criticized the supervisor for lying—promising Stuempges to provide a good reference and instead providing a carping one.

At the same time, the court wrote, "It is certainly in the public interest that this kind of information be readily available to prospective employers, and we are concerned that, unless a significant privilege is recognized by the courts, employers will decline to evaluate honestly their former employees' work records."

Judging from no-evaluation policies of many local employers, that concern is justified. Tom Vogt, attorney with the Felhaber, Larson, Fenlon and Vogt firm in St. Paul, believes employers often are excessively concerned with laws that might constrain them from evaluating former employees.

But he also sympathizes with their feeling that "It's not our fight so why should we get involved?"

Given the greater difficulty it has obtaining candid assessments of job applicants from former employers, Honeywell is relying more than in the past on skill, aptitude and other sorts of tests, especially when filling sales, engineering and production supervisors' jobs.

Meanwhile, Northwestern Bell tests management trainee applicants for basic intelligence and prefers people graduating in the top half of their college class.

The company does not check many references because they usually are a tad too glowing, explained Howie Tucker, district manager of management employment and college relations. "They all say this is the greatest individual the world has ever seen, the next president, at least," he explained, adding wryly, "It isn't always accurate."

Tucker noted that despite the restriction of information, trainees hired in recent years stay longer and have been more successful than ones hired a decade ago, when recommendations were easier to come by.

"I think we're getting smarter at probing and finding out information" in interviews, he said.

Nationally, many other firms also are shifting emphasis to the interview. A recent survey of personnel executives by the recruiting firm Robert Half, Inc., found that a candidate's personality and demeanor during the interview was the single most important factor in the hiring decision. Specific skills and qualifications ranked second in importance.

Last on the list was the detailed, glowing resume. As Half himself observed, "Resumes are often balance sheets—without any liabilities."

(By Linda McDonnell, *Minneapolis Tribune*, May 3, 1981. Reprinted by permission of the *Minneapolis Tribune*.)

As shown in Exhibit 5.2 the interview process is important at two points—at the beginning and end of the selection procedure. The way the interview is conducted depends on the type of job being filled. In the case of middle- and upper-level managerial and executive jobs, individuals often submit resumes to organizations (by mail or through a placement or job search firm). An initial interview is made over the phone if the organization wants to gather more information from the applicant. For lower-level management and nonmanagement jobs, an individual may see a job advertised in the newspaper or posted on the organization's bulletin board and fill out an application. Then the initial interview may follow. Because of the increased legal necessity for organizations to keep records of the people who have applied for jobs and have been hired, it makes good sense for an organization to document that information before beginning the interview.

Frequently several individuals interview the applicant, especially if the job is a middle-level or upper-level managerial or executive one. Often these interviews ask for in-depth information about motivation, attitudes, and experience. These interviews are for the purpose of making assessments, not just gathering information. However, even the initial interview has an assessment aspect, because a reject or pass decision could be made at that stage. Therefore, both interview stages are crucial.

Types of Interviews. Interviews can be categorized according to the techniques and format used. One common interview is the *depth interview*. The interviewer has only a general outline of topics to be covered and often pursues them in a rather unstructured way. You as the interviewee may be allowed to expand greatly on any question asked. Because the quality of this interview often depends on the skill of the interviewer, organizations often use a *patterned or structured interview*. This interview, in order to ensure consistency, actually seems like an oral questionnaire because the exact questions asked in the interview have already been written down in a fixed order. Then, regardless of who the interviewer is, the same questions are asked in the same order (discussed in Chapter 7). Because the questions and the order are fixed, validation studies indicate that the patterned interview can be quite useful in predicting job success.

When several individuals interview one applicant, it is called a *panel interview*. Because of its cost, it is usually reserved for managerial job applicants. Another type of interview that may be used for certain types of managerial job applicants is called the *stress interview*. The types of managerial or nonmanagerial jobs for which applicants would be subjected to a stress interview are those where it is important to remain calm and composed under pressure. In the stress interview, the applicant may be annoyed, embarrassed, or frustrated by the interviewer to see how the applicant reacts. Although this may be a particularly good format for certain types of jobs, such as found in law enforcement and the military, it appears to be less useful for most organizational jobs.

Regardless of the interview format and technique used, there are several problems that afflict interviews. An awareness of them can help reduce their likelihood of occurrence. Personnel can play a key role here by making sure that the people doing the interviewing are aware of the problems, are trained in how to avoid them, and are reinforced for conducting interviews correctly.

Common Interview Problems. There are several problems that interviewers often encounter.[13] They relate to the interview as a procedure for gathering information as well as for assessing that information.

- Managers (as interviewers) do not seek applicant information on all the important dimensions needed for successful job performance. Often the interviewers do not have a complete description of the job being filled or an accurate appraisal of its critical requirements. In addition, the interviewer often does not know the conditions under which the job is performed. Nevertheless, for performance and legal reasons, it is important that all the information obtained be job-related.

  Although interviews are filled with problems, you must do well in them.

- Especially with several interviewers, managers overlap in their coverage of some job-related questions and miss others entirely. It may happen that an applicant has not four interviews but one interview four times. All managers ask the same questions and are provided the same information.

- Managers may make "snap" judgments early in the interview. Consequently they block out further potentially useful information.

- Managers permit one trait or job-related attribute to influence their evaluation of the remaining qualities of an applicant. This process, called the **halo effect,** occurs when an interviewer judges an applicant's entire potential for job performance on the basis of one characteristic, such as how well the applicant dresses or talks. The halo effect may lead to poor and discriminatory choices by the interviewer; it may also affect the choices made by the job applicant:

  > The interviewer becomes the symbol for the company, and yet he represents a sample size of only one. Nevertheless, the applicant often places more importance on his estimate of the representative of the company than on his judgments based on the company literature.[14]

- Managers have not organized the various selection elements into a system. Exhibit 5.2 depicts an order in the selection activities, but often these activities are really not done so orderly. Key references may not be checked before the intensive interviews, resulting in interviews with unqualified applicants. Occasionally, applicants are treated differently, some given certain tests and others not. This may be a result of forgetfulness or lack of clarity on who was to do what. Regardless, the result is unfair and discriminatory selection practices.

  Remember you only get one chance to make a good first impression.

- Information from interviews with an applicant is not integrated and discussed in a systematic manner.
  If several interviewers share information on an applicant, they may do so in a very haphazard manner. They may not identify job-related information or seek to examine any conflicting information. This casual approach to decision making may save time and confrontation—but only in the short run. In the long run, everyone in the organization will pay for poor hiring decisions.

- Managers' judgments are often affected by the pressure (or price) to fill the position. With pressure to fill a position, managers lower their standards. If this leads to a bad decision, the manager who made the decision can always claim an excuse. Managers may also hire an applicant because of the price (salary demands). Personnel managers can reduce this possibility by not revealing salary demands to the line managers responsible for hiring. The best philosophy is first to select the best person for the job and then to be concerned with the cost.

▪ Managers' judgments regarding an applicant are often affected by the available applicants.

Two important concepts—**contrast and order effects**—are important here. First, a good person looks better in contrast to a group of average or below-average people (**contrast effect**). An average person looks below-average or poor in contrast to a group of good or excellent people. Second, there are two important **order effects**— first impression and last impression. At times a first impression (*primacy effect*) is important and lasting; the first person may become the standard used to evaluate the quality of all the other people. But an interviewer, especially at the end of a long day of interviewing, may be more likely to remember the last person better than many of the other people (*recency effect*). As an applicant, you should be aware of these effects. Try to get an interview in the middle of an interviewer's schedule and try to be interviewed around the time that applicants less qualified than you are being interviewed.

Overcoming Potential Interview Problems. There are several ways to over-come the above problems. The methods suggested here are essentially ways to in-crease the validity and reliability of the interview (increase its job-relatedness, the scope of qualifications measured, and the consistency and objectivity of the informa-tion gathered).

▪ *Gather only job-related information:* That is, be sure to use only information from job-related questions as predictors of future performance. This requires that a job analysis be done on the jobs to be filled and, if possible, validation results be obtained for the predictors being used (these issues are examined in more detail in Chapter 6).
  Although it is not always easy to know what is job-related or what will predict future performance, a job analysis will make it easier.

▪ *Use past behavior to predict future behavior:* Essentially, concentrate on getting information about the applicant's job-related behavior. This background informa-tion can be obtained conveniently in the initial interview. It is best to get specific examples of performance-related experiences and events surrounding those exam-ples. Care must be taken, however, in using these examples because past perfor-mance may not always be a good predictor of what a person will do in the future. Consequently, a potentially qualified applicant could be rejected if past perfor-mance were the only basis for the selection decision.

▪ *Coordinate the initial interview and succeeding interviews with each other and with the other information-gathering procedures:* The information should be combined in an objective, systematic, job-related manner.
  The coordination and combination of information can aid in reducing quick deci-sions, bias, and the use of sterotypes in selection. Also assisting in this reduction is the final step.

▪ *Getting several managers involved in interviewing and in the final decision:* This can be done as a group or individually.
  Although the final decision may be made by only one person, several should be involved in gathering the information and assessing its merits.

Interview Tips for Your Next Interview

- Take advantage of order effects
  - Primacy
  - Recency
  - Contrast
- Use the halo effect to your benefit

- Know the company
- Organize your thoughts
- Think through before the interview why you want a job with that company and why that job
- Exhibit good eye contact and firm handshake

Nonverbal Cues in Interviews. Another important aspect of the interview is the nonverbal component, the part not conveyed with words. Things like body movements, gestures, firmness of handshake, eye contact, and physical appearance are all **nonverbal cues.** Often interviewers put more importance on the nonverbal than on the verbal.

> It has been estimated that, at most, only 30 to 35 percent of the meaning conveyed in a message is verbal: the remainder is nonverbal. Similarly, in terms of attitudes or feelings, one estimate is that merely seven percent of what is communicated is verbal, while nonverbal factors account for the remaining 93 percent.[15]

Therefore, it is important to be aware of nonverbal cues. "In fact, one of the reasons that nonverbal cues are so powerful is that, in most cases interviewers are not aware of them as possible causal agents of impression formation."[16]

What to Ask. Interviewers may ask anything that, when combined with other information about the job applicant, can be a useful predictor of how well the applicant will perform once hired. Useful questions include:

- Has the applicant performed in a similar capacity before?
- How does the applicant feel about present job qualities and organizational context?
- If the applicant is changing jobs, why is a change being made?
- Is the applicant likeable?
- What are the applicant's career objectives?
- Does the applicant like working closely with other people?
- How has the applicant performed considering the environment of that performance?[17]

What Not to Ask. A list of inappropriate (but not necessarily illegal) questions to ask in the selection interview is shown in Exhibit 5.4, along with recommended

Employers can ask almost anything; what's legally protected is how they use the information; however, only job related information should be asked.

substitutes that are more job-related. What makes any of these questions illegal is if they are used as a basis for selection decisions that result in adverse impact against protected groups that can not be defended by the organization.

Exhibit 5.4
What Not to Ask and What to Ask in a Selection Interview (From E. C. Miller, "An EEO Examination of Employment Applications," p. 68. Reprinted with permission from the March 1980 issue of the *Personnel Administrator*, copyright 1980. The American Society for Personnel Administration, 30 Park Drive. Berea. OH 44017.)

Inappropriate Question	More Appropriate Question
Do you have any physical defects?	Do you have any physical defects or impediments that might hinder your ability to perform the job you have applied for?
Have you had any recent or past illness or operations?	Have you had any recent or past illness or operations that might hinder your ability to perform the job you have applied for?
What was the date of your last physical exam?	Are you willing to take a physical exam at our expense if the nature of the job requires one?
Are you a U.S. citizen?	Do you have the legal right to live and work in the U.S.?
What is your date of birth?	Are you over eighteen and less than seventy?
What is your age?	Are you over eighteen and less than seventy?
Who should we contact in an emergency? What is the relationship?	Who should we contact in an emergency?
Do you possess a legal driver's license?	Do you possess a legal and current driver's license? (only for applicants who want a job driving a company vehicle)
What are your hobbies? Interests?	Do you have any hobbies or interests that have a direct bearing on the job you are seeking?
Have you ever been convicted of a misdemeanor or felony?	Have you, since the age of eighteen, ever been convicted of a misdemeanor or felony? (Note: A conviction will not necessarily bar you from employment. Each conviction will be judged on its own merits with respect to time, circumstances, and seriousness.)
When did you attend high school? Grammar school?	Did you complete grammar school? High school?
When did you graduate or last attend high school? Grammar school?	Did you complete grammar school? High school?
In what extracurricular activities did you participate? Clubs?	While in school, did you participate in any activities or belong to any clubs that have a direct bearing on the job you are applying for?
What subjects interested you in college?	While in college, did you take any courses that directly relate to the job you are applying for?

Inappropriate Question	More Appropriate Question
What salary or earnings do you expect?	If you are employed, are you willing to accept the prevailing wage for the job you are seeking?
What organizations do you belong to? (with or without EEO disclaimer)	Have you ever belonged to a club, organization, society, or professional group that has a direct bearing on your qualification for the job you are seeking?

Employment Tests

Testing is another important procedure for gathering, transmitting, and assessing information about an applicant's aptitudes, experiences, and motivations. Employment tests include any paper-and-pencil or performance measures used as a basis for an employment decision. The three most common types of tests measure aptitude, achievement, and motivation.

The validity and reliability of these approaches are of utmost importance for both the organization and the job applicant. Validity and reliability help ensure that an applicant will perform at a certain level. They also help provide the job applicant with a sense of fairness and legality in the selection procedure.

Employment tests:
- Aptitude
- Achievement
- Motivation
- Lie detector

It is recommended that organizations inform job applicants of the procedures used in gathering information, particularly from paper-and-pencil tests. The Life Insurance Marketing and Research Association also recommends that organizations using tests inform those taking tests

- That the test is only one step in the hiring process
- What the test measures and that it does so with validity and reliability
- Why it is being used
- What passing or failing means to them and about them[18]

Aptitude Tests. **Aptitude tests** measure the potential of individuals to perform. Measures of general aptitude, often referred to as general intelligence tests, include the Wechsler Adult Intelligence Scale and the Stanford-Binet test. These tests are primarily used to predict academic success in a traditional setting. Thus several multidimensional job-related aptitude tests were developed, including: Differential Aptitude Tests, the Flanagan Aptitude Classification Test, the General Aptitude Test Battery, and the Employee Aptitude Survey. Exhibit 5.5 shows what these tests measure. Because they are standardized, they are not specific to any particular job. But they are reliable and general enough to be used in job situations, especially for indicating the contribution that more specific tests can make.[19]

Another group of aptitude tests, called **psychomotor tests,** combines the mental and the physical. Two of the more widely used psychomotor tests are the Mac-Quarrie Test for Mechanical Ability and the O'Connor Finger and Tweezer Dexterity Tests. The MacQuarrie test measures skills in tracing, tapping, dotting, copying, locating, arranging blocks, and pursuing. This test seems to be a valid predictor for such

Exhibit 5.5

Some Multidimensional Aptitude Tests for Use in Selection

(From *Staffing Organizations* by B. Schneider, p. 153. Copyright © 1976
by Scott, Foresman and Company. Reprinted by permission.)

Differential Aptitude Tests (DAT)	Flanagan Aptitude Classification Test (FACT)	General Aptitude Test Battery (GATB)*	Employee Aptitude Survey (EAS)†
Verbal reasoning	Inspection	Verbal	Verbal comprehension
Numerical ability	Coding	Numerical	Numerical ability
Abstract reasoning	Memory	Spatial	Visual pursuit
Space relations	Precision	Form perception	Visual speed and accuracy
Mechanical reasoning	Assembly	Clerical perception	Space visualization
Clerical speed and	Scales	Motor coordination	Numerical reasoning
accuracy	Coordination	Finger dexterity	Verbal reasoning
Language usage (spelling)	Judgment and	Manual dexterity	Word fluency
Language usage	comprehension	General intelligence	Manual speed and
(sentences)	Arithmetic		accuracy
	Patterns		Symbolic reasoning
	Components		
	Tables		
	Mechanics		
	Expression		

*General intelligence is a combination of spatial, verbal, and numerical scores.
†Designed specifically for industrial situations.

occupations as aviation mechanic and stenographer. The O'Connor test is a valid predictor for power sewing machine operators, dental students, and other workers requiring manipulative skills.[20]

A final group of aptitude tests relates to personal and interpersonal competence. One test of **personal competence**, called the Career Maturity Inventory, measures whether individuals know how to make appropriate and timely decisions for themselves and whether they really put forth the effort to do so. It includes five competence tests related to problems, planning, occupational information, self-knowledge, and goal selection. The better the score on these five competency tests, the more likely an individual is to make career decisions resulting in higher satisfaction and performance.[21]

Interpersonal competence tests have been designed to measure social intelligence. These include aspects of intelligence related to

information, non-verbal, which is involved in human interactions where awareness of attention, perceptions, thoughts, desires, feelings, moods, emotions, intentions and actions of other persons and of ourselves is important.[22]

Achievement Tests. **Achievement tests** predict an individual's performance on the basis of what he or she knows. Validation is required of any test used by an organization, but validating achievement tests is a rather straightforward process. The achievement tests almost become samples of the job to be performed. However, hiring on the basis of achievement tests may exclude applicants who have not had equal access to the opportunities to acquire the skills. It should also be noted that not all achievement tests are samples of the job, some are less job-related than others.

Paper-and-pencil achievement tests tend to be less job-related because they measure facts and principles—not the actual use of them. For example, you could take a paper-and-pencil test measuring your knowledge of tennis and pass with flying colors and yet play very poorly. Although this is a serious deficiency, paper-and-pencil achievement tests continue to be used in many areas. For example, admission to the legal profession is through the bar exam, and the medical profession is entered through medical boards.

The **recognition test** is often used in advertising and modeling to select applicants. The applicants bring to the job interview portfolios of their work, samples of the work they have done. However, portfolios contain no clues to the conditions or circumstances under which they were done. Some organizations may insist on seeing written samples from school work for jobs where written expression may be important.

Recognition tests are really examples of past behavior; **simulation tests** are used to see how applicants perform now. Only the task itself—not the situation in which the task is performed—is recreated. Even so, simulation can be extremely useful as a training and practice device. You may recall from good crime movies, that the crime is rehearsed many times before actually being committed. Simulations are especially good preparation for events that happen only once, like the first moon landing.

Some achievement tests overcome the artificiality of simulations by using the actual task and working conditions. These are called **work sample tests.** Work sample tests are frequently given to applicants for secretarial jobs. Applicants may be asked to type a letter in the office where they would be working. There still tends to be some artificiality in work sample tests, however, because the selection process itself tends to promote some anxiety and tension.

Anxiety and tension may not be artificial for some jobs, such as a managerial job under time pressure. In fact, a work sample test referred to as the **in-basket exercise** has been created for that type of job. Its objective is to create a realistic situation that will elicit typical on-the-job behaviors. Situations and problems encountered in the job are written on individual sheets of paper and set in the in-basket. The applicant is asked to arrange the papers by priority. Occasionally the applicant may need to write an action response on the piece of paper. The problems or situations described to the applicant involve different groups of people—peers, subordinates, and those outside the organization. The applicant is usually given a set time limit to take the test but is often interrupted by phone calls meant to create more tension and pressure.

Motivation Tests. Designed to measure an individual's motivation to perform, **motivation tests** may focus on personality, interests, or preferences for certain types of jobs. Tests of the individual's traits or characteristics are sometimes referred to as **personality inventories.** Several common multidimensional tests of personality are the Edwards Personal Preference Schedule; the California Psychological Inventory; the Gordon Personal Profile; the Thurstone Temperament Survey; the Guilford-Zimmerman Temperament Survey; and the Minnesota Multiphasic Personality Inventory. These personality inventories have limited validity for organizations but may be useful for predicting the performance of salesclerks, clerical workers, and the like.[23] At present, the utility of personality tests for selection appears limited. Once a selection decision is made, however, they may be useful for placement and career counseling.

Interest tests can be used to help serve the job reward—individual needs match.

Placement and career counseling decisions can also be facilitated by **interest tests.** Two major interest tests are the Strong Vocational Interest Blank and the Kuder Preference Records. Both are essentially inventories of interests. Although generally not predictive of performance on the job, they can predict which occupation will be more in tune with an individual's interests. Many people take the Kuder Preference Records in high school to find out what jobs or occupations might match their interests. Records are grouped into ten vocational categories—outdoor, computational, scientific, persuasive, artistic, literary, musical, social service, and clerical. Specific jobs can be identified within each of the ten groupings. Both of these interest tests should be used with caution. It is unlikely that either could predict performance in a job, nor are they always valid for predicting the specific type of job one will choose within a vocational or occupational grouping.

Preference tests are especially useful in matching employee needs with rewards of the job. One scale that may be used to infer an individual's preferences for a specific job design is the Job Diagnostic Survey, a sample of which appears in Exhibit 5.6.

Exhibit 5.6

Sample Preference Test from the Job Diagnostic Survey (From J. R. Hackman and G. R. Oldham, *Task Design* [Reading, Mass.: Addison-Wesley, 1980]. p. 136. Reprinted by permission of the authors.)

Listed below are a number of characteristics that could be present on any job. People differ about how much they would like to have each one present in their own jobs. We are interested in learning *how much you personally would like* to have each one present in your job.

Using the scale below, please indicate the *degree* to which you would like to have each characteristic present in your job.

Would mildly like having this		Would strongly like having this		Would very strongly like having this		
1	2	3	4	5	6	7

_____ 1. High respect and fair treatment from my supervisor
_____ 2. Stimulating and challenging work
_____ 3. Chances to exercise independent thought and action in my job
_____ 4. Great job security
_____ 5. Very friendly co-workers
_____ 6. Opportunities to learn new things from my work
_____ 7. High salary and good fringe benefits
_____ 8. Opportunities to be creative and imaginative in my work
_____ 9. Quick promotions
_____ 10. Opportunities for personal growth and development in my job
_____ 11. A sense of worthwhile accomplishment in my work

Lie Detector Tests. Increasing numbers of organizations routinely ask job applicants to submit to a polygraph test as part of the selection procedures.[24] This is particularly true in situations where the applicant is being considered for a fiduciary position or has access to pharmaceuticals or any small consumer item that has resale value. A 1978 survey showed that approximately 20 percent of the country's largest organizations use lie detector tests to check on applicants' backgrounds and honesty. It has been estimated that as many as one-third of all job applicants lie in some way to prospective employers![25]

Although you cannot be forced to take a polygraph test in order to be hired or promoted in most states (there is no federal law in this regard), many companies may ask you to sign a release indicating you are taking the test voluntarily. Generally you should be prepared, as any job applicant should be, to answer questions honestly, especially as they pertain to what is on your application blank. Refusal to answer questions about your religion, sexual activity, politics and other nonjob issues is appropriate. You may, however, want to take this up with the employer after the exam. Typically organizations hire polygraph examiners, and they are in an office away from the company with which you are seeking employment. Because of the costs and hassles in using polygraph tests, companies are beginning to use paper-and-pencil tests to predict individuals who are likely to lie or steal.

The Application Blank

Many of the interviewing and testing procedures used in the selection process are only moderately valid or not valid at all. Therefore, organizations typically gather additional information a third way—directly from the applicant through an application blank. The **application blank** is a form seeking information about the job applicant's background and present conditions (including current address and telephone number). Although application blanks used to request a great deal of information, often including a photograph, legal constraints have reduced the requests substantially. As mentioned earlier, there are many topics the organization may not and should not inquire about. This is true whether the organization tries to obtain the information through the selection interview, the application blank, or the polygraph test.[26]

Application blanks often ask for a great deal of information. In order to use this information in the most job-related way possible, organizations weight the information. That is, some information on the application is given more importance as a predictor of performance than is other information. In essence this procedure describes what is called a *weighted application blank.*

What is asked on the application blank, for example, an applicant's mental health history, should help predict how well a job applicant will perform once on the job. Because the job situation can influence an employee's performance, information about an employee's past performance record is especially helpful in predicting future performance when job situations are similar. When they are not similar, accurate prediction is more difficult, and incorrect decisions may be made. Furthermore, the decisions may violate the law, as shown in the *For Your Career* insert. You might be saying to yourself, "To prevent that from happening, all you need to do is call the previous employer and find out what happened." Easier said than done. Today, many organizations are reluctant to provide more data than the fact that the person in question did work there at one time for a certain number of years.

The reluctance to provide additional data, shown in the earlier Personnel in Action insert, is explained by recent events surrounding **reference verification,** which is a method of measuring individual differences among job applicants by acquiring personal information about them. The more common approaches include checking an applicant's record with a previous employer, creditor, high school or college office, and teachers.

However, reference verification involves conflicting values—*liberty and privacy.* On the one hand, employers should be free (have the liberty) to discriminate among job applicants, especially when seeking performance-related information about them. On the other hand, liberty for the organization often leads to infringement of an individual's privacy.[27] Currently, this conflict has led to several lawsuits. The result has been several state and federal laws regarding the use of personal information for employee decision. The conflict between liberty and privacy promises to remain a central issue in personnel management for the next several years.

FOR YOUR CAREER

Does your application form ask applicants if they have ever been treated for mental illness? According to the U.S. District Court for Northern New York, such questions may violate the Rehabilitation Act of 1973, which prohibits discrimination against disabled people. A school board refused to hire a certified teacher who admitted to having been treated for a nervous breakdown. The court said the inquiry was not job related, since a history of treatment for mental or emotional problems is no indication of a job applicant's "present fitness" for a position. If the board "sincerely wanted to employ persons that were capable of performing their jobs," said the court, "all it had to ask was whether the applicant was capable of dealing with various emotionally demanding situations" (*Doe* v. *Syracuse School District,* 2/26/81. From *FEP Guidelines* 192 [7].)

SUMMARY

This chapter examines what selection and placement procedures are and how they relate to other personnel activities. It also examines in detail the legal considerations, such as BFOQs, business necessity, job-relatedness, and adverse impact, in making selection and placement decisions. Organizations want to ensure that they hire job applicants with the abilities to meet job demands. Increasingly, they also want to ensure that job applicants will not only perform well but also stay. Thus organizations want to attain a match between the needs of the job applicants and the rewards offered by the job qualities and organizational context.

In order to match individual ability to job demands and individual needs to job rewards, organizations need to gather information about job applicants. The three most common methods for doing so—interviewing, testing, and application blanks— must operate within legal regulations. These legal regulations are not intended to discourage the use of these methods but rather to ensure that information is collected, retained, and used with recognition of an individual's rights to privacy and equal opportunity and an organization's right to select individuals on the basis of job-related qualifications.

KEY CONCEPTS

halo effect

selection

placement

job relatedness

order effect

business necessity

adverse impact

bona fide occupational
   qualifications

alternative procedures requirement

achievement test

application blank

aptitude test

in-basket exercise

interest test

interpersonal competence

psychomotor test

recognition test

reference verification

simulation tests

work sample test

bottom-line criterion

predictors

criteria

motivation test

nonverbal cue

paper-and-pencil achievement test

personal competence

personality inventory

preference tests

cosmic search

contrast effect

DISCUSSION QUESTIONS

1. What is the major difference between selection and placement in effective personnel management?
2. Why should selection and placement activities be thought of as a two-way street?
3. Identify and describe the three major sets of information needed for selection and placement.
4. What is the "80% rule" or "bottom-line criterion"?
5. List three ways organizations can avoid adverse impact charges.
6. What is the difference between predictors and criteria for selection and placement decisions? Give examples of each.
7. What is the most important method for obtaining information from the applicant and what are some disadvantages associated with this method?
8. What is the major difference between aptitude tests and achievement tests?
9. What topical areas are organizations forbidden to use to obtain information for selection and placement?
10. What role does nonverbal behavior play in an interview setting? Why is this important?

CASE

Qualified?

John Blair, the personnel manager at Aztec Industries, a medium-sized electronics company, was told by the company president, Martha Klein, that Aztec had just received a very large contract from the United States Defense Department. Since the contract was for $15 million, and it was Aztec's first federal contract, Blair realized that an affirmative action program had to be written. Fortunately, he had recently hired a personnel assistant with experience in writing affirmative action programs. Thus, Blair's real concern dealt with finding and hiring two hundred new employees qualified to work on the Defense Department contract.

In the past, Aztec's growth rate required adding only twenty-five new employees per year. With Dallas nearby, Blair never found it difficult to find enough people to fill the job openings, even if some of the new employees quit or failed to perform adequately. Blair knew, however, that things were different now. Never had the company needed to hire so many people so quickly and never had the company been concerned with meeting affirmative action goals and timetables. In addition, a majority of the new jobs had to be filled with semiskilled and skilled workers. Previously, the majority of new hires filled unskilled jobs. Consequently, when he needed job applicants before, he just advertised in the Dallas newspaper and filled most of the openings on a "first come, first served" basis.

Blair realizes now that he must largely abandon his previous selection policy of hiring the first person who walked through the door. He knows that it will be necessary to find out the skills of the new job applicants. Furthermore, as his new assistant has informed him, his selection efforts must recognize and embrace affirmative action. Frankly, Blair has serious doubts about being able to identify qualified people and also fulfill the company's affirmative action requirements.

Case Questions

1. How should Blair go about identifying qualified, or at least, potentially qualifiable job applicants?
2. How will his efforts to hire qualified job applicants affect the company's new affirmative action requirements?
3. Will Aztec be forced to hire job applicants who are not qualified?
4. Should Blair have serious doubts about being able to identify qualified people and to fulfill affirmative action requirements?

FOR YOUR CAREER

- It's as important for you to select an organization carefully as it is for an organization to select you carefully.

- In selecting an organization you should find out the job rewards as well as the job demands.

- In selecting an organization, know how the job and organization will benefit you in the long run as well as the short run.

- Sometimes organizations fail to follow up after a selection interview as soon as they promise (if at all). If you're anxious to know, call them.

- You have many legal protections against your not being selected for nonjob-related reasons. It pays to become familiar with these legal protections.

- You can often learn more about yourself by taking motivation and preference tests. Career counseling centers often have these tests.

ENDNOTES

1. R. D. Arvey, *Fairness in Selecting Employees* (Reading, Mass.: Addison-Wesley, 1979).

   Marvin D. Dunnette and Walter C. Borman, "Personnel Selection and Classification Systems," *Annual Review Psychology* 30 (1979):477–525.

   J. P. Wanous, *Organizational Entry* (Reading, Mass.: Addison-Wesley, 1980).

2. T. F. Cawsey, "Why Line Managers Don't Listen to Their Personnel Department" *Personnel*, January/February 1980, pp. 11–20.

3. Scott T. Rickard, "Effective Staff Selection," *Personnel Journal*, June 1981, pp. 475–478.

4. Frank A. Malinowski, "Job Selection Using Task Analysis," *Personnel Journal*, April 1981, pp. 288–291.

5. Barry J. Baroni, "Age Discrimination in Employment: Some Guidelines for Employers," *Personnel Administrator*, May 1981, pp. 97–101.

   Richard Marr and Joseph Schneider, "Self-Assessment Test for the 1978 Uniform Guidelines on Employee Selection Procedures," *Personnel Administrator*, May 1981, pp. 103–108.

   Charles F. Schanie and William L. Holley, "An Interpretive Review of the Federal Uniform Guidelines on Employee Selection Procedures," *Personnel Administrator*, June 1980, pp. 44–48.

   Jerry L. Wall and H. M. Shatshat, "Controversy Over the Issue of Mandatory Retirement," *Personnel Administrator*, October 1981, pp. 25–30, 46.

6. R. D. Arvey, Fairness in Selecting Employees, © 1979 Addison-Wesley Publishing Company, Inc., pp. 35–37.

   F. S. Hills, "Job Relatedness vs. Adverse Impact in Personnel Decision Making," *Personnel Journal*, March 1980, pp. 211–215, 229.

7. For an excellent discussion of the impact and interpretation of the Uniform Guidelines and many other issues related to selection and testing, see the special issue of the *American Psychologist*, October 1981.

8. "New Directions in EEO Guidelines," by D. E. Robertson, p. 361. Reprinted with permission of *Personnel Journal*, Costa Mesa, CA., copyright July 1978; all rights reserved.

9. Robertson, "New Directions in EEO Guidelines."

10. F. S. Hills, "Job Relatedness vs. Adverse Impact in Personnel Decision Making," p. 212.

Reprinted with permission of *Personnel Journal,* Costa Mesa, Calif., March 1980, p. 212; all rights reserved.

11. Rickard, "Effective Staff Selection."

    Frank L. Schmidt and John E. Hunter, "New Research Findings in Personnel Selection: Myths Meet Realities in the 1980's." *Public Personnel Administration: Policies and Procedures for Personnel* (Englewood Cliffs, N.J.: Prentice-Hall, 1980.)

12. B. Schneider, *Staffing Organizations* (Santa Monica, Calif.,: Goodyear, 1976).

    "Interview Guide for Supervisors," *College and University Personnel Association,* Wash., D.C., 1981.

    Sigmund G. Ginsburg, "Preparing for Executive Position Interviews: Questions the Interviewer Might Ask—or Be Asked," *Personnel,* July–August 1980, pp. 31–36.

    "Editor to Reader," *Personnel Journal,* February 1981, pp. 82–87.

    "Reader to Editor," *Personnel Journal,* August 1980, p. 618.

    Jeffrey D. Latterell, "Planning for the Selection Interview," *Personnel Journal,* July 1979, pp. 466–467, 480.

    Thomas J. Neff, "How to Interview Candidates for Top Management Positions," *Business Horizons,* October 1980, pp. 47–52.

    Elliott D. Pursell, Michael A. Campion, and Sarah R. Gaylord, "Structures Interviewing: Avoiding Selection Problems," *Personnel Journal,* November 1980, pp. 907–912.

    William T. Wolz, "How to Interview Supervisory Candidates from the Ranks," *Personnel,* September–October 1980, pp. 31–39.

13. W. C. Byham, "Common Selection Problems Can Be Overcome," *Personnel Administrator,* August 1978, pp. 42–47.

14. C. W. Downs, "What Does the Selection Interview Accomplish," *Personnel Administrator,* 31(1968), p. 100.

15. J. D. Hatfield and R. D. Gatewood, "Nonverbal Cues in the Selection Inverview," p. 35. Reprinted with permission from the January 1978 issue of the *Personnel Administrator,* copyright 1978.

16. Ibid., p. 37.

17. D. T. Michaels, "Seven Questions That Will Improve Your Managerial Hiring Decisions," *Personnel Journal,* March 1980, pp. 199–200, 224.

18. Life Insurance Marketing and Research Association, *Recruitment, Selection, Training, and Supervision in Life Insurance,* (Hartford, Conn.: Life Insurance Marketing and Research Association, 1966).

19. Schneider, *Staffing Organizations.*

20. J. B. Miner and M. G. Miner, *Personnel and Industrial Relations,* 3rd ed. (New York: Macmillan, 1977), p. 315.

21. Daniel Goleman, "The New Competency Tests: Matching the Right Jobs," *Psychology Today,* January 1981, pp. 35–46.

22. J. P. Guilford, *The Nature of Human Intelligence,* (New York: McGraw-Hill, 1967), p. 77.

23. E. E. Ghiselli, *The Validity of Occupational Aptitude Tests.* (New York: Wiley, 1966).

24. "Personal Business," *Business Week,* July 27, 1981, pp. 85–86.

25. Christine Hudgins, "Lying to get job? Beware Maloney," *The Minneapolis Star,* Tuesday, Dec. 15, 1981, p. 6B.

26. Clifford M. Koen, Jr., "The Pre-Employment Inquiry Guide," *Personnel Journal,* October 1980, pp. 825–829.

Ernest C. Miller, "An EEO Examination of Employment Applications," *Personnel Administrator,* March 1980, pp. 63–69, 81.

Carole Sewell, "Pre-Employment Investigations: The Key to Security in Hiring," *Personnel Journal,* May 1981, pp. 376–379.

27. E. L. Levine, "Legal Aspects of Reference Checking for Personnel Selection," *Personnel Administrator,* November 1977, pp. 14–16, 28.

Chapter Outline

Selection and Placement Decisions
The Single Predictor Approach
The Multiple Predictors Approach
The Assessment Center Approach

Criteria for the Evaluation of Selection and Placement Procedures
Validity
Reliability
Base Rate versus Predictor Rate
Selection Ratio
Costs and Benefits

The Selection and Placement Decision
Promotion and Transfer Decisions

CHAPTER **6**

Selection and Placement Decisions

The Selection and Placement Decisions

Facing The Critical Issues in Selection and Placement

Summary

Key Concepts

Discussion Questions

Case

For Your Career

Endnotes

Personnel in the News

New York City Adopts Lottery to Hire Police Officers

New York City officials and black and Hispanic groups signed an agreement August 6 creating a lottery system, instead of set racial quotas, by which to hire police officers over the next two years.

The groups had charged that a test used in 1979 was discriminatory because many of the questions had little or no bearing on whether a proper answer would make a person a good police officer. In addition, the high score was selected at random, based on the number of eligibles needed. The suit led to findings by U.S. District Judge Robert Carter that the city had discriminated against minorities. He ordered the city to hire one black, Hispanic or Asian officer for every two white officers it hires.

The lottery system, which must first be approved by Carter, provides for a random selection of officers from among the 16,000 applicants who passed a department examination given last June. The top 12,000 scorers will be put into one group from which the first random selections will be made. Some of those selected, if they pass further examinations, could be among the class of 2,000 recruits scheduled to enter the Police Academy next January. In the past, applicants who passed were ranked according to their scores, with those scoring the highest to be the first hired.

"This lottery guarantees that the city will have qualified police officers including blacks and Hispanics, without committing the city to a racial quota," said Mayor Edward Koch, a staunch opponent of numerical goals.

Corporation Counsel Allen Schwartz said the city intends to return to rank-order hiring after developing a test that will avoid allegations of racial discrimination. (From Fair Employment Report, *August 17, 1981, p. 132.)*

Experience Required

When a woman was turned down for a job in a truck yard, she sued the employer, claiming a two-year experience requirement had a disproportionate adverse impact on women, who only make up a small percentage of the national truck driving work force. She further argued that to escape Title VII sex discrimination liability the employer had to prove it could have used no alternative standard for hire that would have had a more favorable effect on the employment of women seeking entry into the work force. But the Court of Appeals in Cincinnati ruled that the employer need only show that the experience requirement was job related, not that the safe and efficient operation of its business could have been achieved in a less discriminatory manner. That was for the job applicant herself to prove. Since the employer could show that two years of driving experience was a reasonable, if potentially discriminatory, requirement for the job, and since the applicant couldn't come up with an alternative more favorable to women, the court dismissed her case (Chrisner v. Complete Auto Transit, 3/19/1981). *(From* FEP Guidelines *191 [6])*

These two decisions point out several factors that are important to organizations in making selection and placement decisions. In the *Chrisner* decision, although there was adverse impact in the selection process, the predictor of success used to make the hiring decision (two-years work experience) was a **valid predictor** of job performance. In other words, the two-years experience requirement was job-related or a valid predictor.

In the ruling by Judge Carter, New York City was required, in essence, to set hiring quotas. But an alternative method, the use of a lottery, was developed as an acceptable selection alternative. Note, however, the steps still agreed to and used in making the final selection decisions. First, the applicants must pass an entrance examination, a hurdle they must jump successfully before continuing. If they do jump it successfully they are put into a pool from which they are randomly selected. After this second step, further tests are given to those randomly selected, not necessarily the top third scores on the first exam. Finally, 2,000 from the original 12,000 are selected to enter the Police Academy. Note in this situation the number of decision steps used in making the selection and placement decisions. This is only one set of steps that an organization can use. In this chapter we examine several major ways selection and placement decisions can be made. In addition, we discuss the issues surrounding and methods related to increasing the usefulness (utility) of those decisions. By the time we finish, you will be able to answer with ease the Critical Issues presented in Chapter 5.

T he methods for collecting selection and placement information—interviews, tests, and application blanks—are outlined in Chapter 5. The question now becomes how can they be used in making selection and placement decisions? Generally, one method can be used alone in making the decision (the single predictor approach) or several methods can be combined (the multiple predictor approach).

SELECTION AND PLACEMENT DECISIONS

The Single Predictor Approach

When personnel managers use only one piece of information or one method for selecting an applicant, they are taking the **single predictor approach.** In the *Chrisner* case, Complete Auto Transit's use of the two-year experience requirement as the sole predictor in its selection decisions is an example of using the single predictor approach. A single predictor is used by many organizations to select employees, especially when it can readily be validated. This occurs most frequently when a single predictor captures the essence or the major dimension of the job, thus making it easy to validate:

> A few hiring tests are easy enough to validate, especially those in which the candidate actually performs a task he will have to perform on the job. It makes obvious good sense, for example, to require a candidate for a secretarial job to pass a typing test, and generally the equal-opportunity establishment accepts such tests.[1]

But for many jobs, a single predictor (test) cannot be used, nor can a single dimension (duty), such as typing, really be used to explain the essence of the job. Many jobs can be explained only with several job dimensions (duties), as illustrated in the job description shown in Chapter 3. Thus several predictors are used in making the selection and placement decisions.

The Multiple Predictors Approach

When information from several sources or methods is combined, selection and placement decisions are made with a **multiple predictors approach.** As you might guess, there are several ways to combine information. The type of job often influences how and what information is combined.

Multiple Hurdles. This method of combining information is based on the idea that every job to be performed has several dimensions and thus several predictors (hurdles). A job applicant must be able to get over every selection hurdle in order to perform adequately on the job. Failing on one predictor cannot be compensated for by doing extremely well on another one. For example, an applicant for an air traffic controller job cannot compensate for failure on a visual recognition test.

The use of multiple hurdles excludes many job applicants who may fail only one hurdle. Unless the organization has a large number of applicants, it may not fill all job openings. Note that the bottom-line criterion described in Chapter 5 allows an organization to use several predictors (multiple hurdles) without having to validate each predictor. However, if the bottom-line effect of the multiple hurdles is adverse impact, the organization may need to validate each hurdle. It may need to also even without adverse impact (*Connecticut v. Teal,* 1982).

But even if the organization does have a sufficient number of applicants, this approach may unnecessarily exclude people who, except for one deficiency, could do well. In an effort to accommodate applicants, some organizations are making multiple hurdles unnecessary through physical changes in buildings and floor arrangements, more alternative work arrangements, and job design changes as illustrated in the *Personnel in Action* insert featuring AT&T in Chapter 3.

Compensatory Approach to Multiple Predictors. You know from your own experience that what people lack in ability they can make up for in drive and motivation. In classes, there are always students who do well by working harder than other students. The same is true in organizations. If a job applicant scores low on motivation, he or she can make up for it by scoring well on the ability test.

The compensatory approach is applied when one quality can compensate for another quality. It is also applied when not doing well on one dimension of a job can be compensated for by doing well on all the other dimensions.

Combined Approach to Multiple Predictors. Many organizations use the combined approach, often beginning with recruitment. The combined approach uses aspects of both the multiple hurdles and compensatory approaches. Generally, the multiple hurdle component is used first: "You have to get through the door before we'll consider you." Once in, the compensatory approach applies. For example, an organization may establish minimum requirements—an undergraduate major in accounting or a high grade-point average—for students who want an interview. After that requirement has been met, strong areas can offset weak areas. One multiple predictor method of selection in which strong areas can offset weak areas is the assessment center.

The Assessment Center Approach

In the assessment center approach, job applicants or current employees are evaluated as to how well they might perform in a managerial or higher-level position.[2] Over 20,000 companies use this method, and its use grows each year because of its validity in predicting the job applicants who will turn out to be successful and those who will turn out to be unsuccessful.

An **assessment center** is usually composed of a half dozen to a dozen people who have been chosen or have chosen to attend the center. The center is usually run by the organization, for one to three days, but off the premises. The performance of attendees is usually determined by managers in the organization who are trained accessors. An excellent example of the use of an assessment center is the General Motors *Manufacturing Supervisors Assessment Program*. The purpose of the Assessment Program and the exercises and tests is to help determine potential promotability of applicants to the first-line supervisor's job as described in the *Personnel in Action* insert. Note that the composite performance in the exercises and tests is often used to determine an assessment center attendee's future promotability and the organization's personnel planning requirements and training needs, as well as to make current selection and placement decisions.

Assessment centers are becoming an important way to select managers.

Manufacturing Supervisors' Assessment Program

The Manufacturing Supervisors' Assessment Program was developed to assist all GM divisions in evaluating the qualifications of candidates for positions as first-line supervisors of hourly employes (foremen). It provides evaluations on a number of key areas of performance necessary for success as a manufacturing supervisor. These evaluations are intended to supplement other information on candidates, such as on their experience, work record, education, and technical knowledge. This will provide a comprehensive picture of each candidate's qualifications and make possible the most effective selection of persons for manufacturing supervisory positions.

The Manufacturing Supervisors' Assessment Pro-

gram was developed on the basis of accumulated experience and research results from its predecessor, the one-day supervisory selection assessment program introduced in 1972 and used by approximately ninety GM units since then. In addition, suggestions from all units using the former program were considered in developing the Manufacturing Supervisors' Assessment Program, and recent technical and professional developments in the assessment field were incorporated into it. The result is a considerably improved version of an already proven and widely used program. The Manufacturing Supervisors' Assessment Program may be used to evaluate the qualifications of candidates for first-line supervisory positions in any manufacturing area, such as production, quality, materials, maintenance, and skilled trades. It has been designed to measure areas of performance found in all of these positions and that commonly appear as candidate qualifications on requisitions prepared for them.

This program measures eight areas of qualifications identified through job analyses and other research as essential to good performance on manufacturing supervision. These are

- Organizing and planning
- Analyzing
- Decision making
- Controlling
- Oral communications
- Interpersonal relations
- Influencing
- Flexibility

The program also provides an overall evaluation of each candidate's qualifications.

The program content includes a wide range of evaluation techniques, such as group problems, interviews, in-baskets, tests, videotape exercises, and questionnaires. These were designed to simulate the situations and problems which manufacturing supervisors regularly encounter on their jobs. As candidates go through these exercises, their performance in them is observed by a specially trained team of observers/evaluators ("assessors") drawn from the local management group. After the candidates have finished the program the assessors then meet to discuss the candidates and prepare evaluations, based on the combined judgments of all of the assessors, of the candidates in the areas of performance listed above.

The program is operated locally by the division's or plant's manufacturing management and a few members of the Personnel Department. These people are trained in the administration of the program by the corporate Human Resources Management Activity. The program covers twelve candidates in one day, using a four-person assessor team and a coordinator, plus the better part of the following day for the assessors and coordinator to discuss and evaluate the candidates. The program is available in two equivalent forms, so that an initially unselected candidate can later be reassessed on different, but comparable, content.

In summary, the general characteristics of the Manufacturing Supervisors' Assessment Program are

- Applicability to supervisor selection in all areas of manufacturing in all GM divisions and plants
- Reliable, accurate, and objective measurement of eight areas of qualifications essential to good performance on manufacturing supervision, plus an overall evaluation
- Evaluations based on the combined judgments of a specially trained team of assessors, observing candidates' performance in a wide range of exercises simulating situations which manufacturing supervisors actually encounter in their jobs
- Local control and operation of the program
- Alternate forms of the program to facilitate re-assessment of candidates
- An improvement of an already proven program, incorporating research results, divisional and plant suggestions, accumulated experience, and current technical and professional advances, able to meet all technical, professional, and legal requirements
- Corporate assistance and training in adoption of the program and corporate support in its continued use
- A program known to be able to provide the selection advantages it is designed to produce and to be favorably accepted by candidates and management alike. (Courtesy of General Motors Corporation. Used with permission.)

CRITERIA FOR THE EVALUATION OF SELECTION AND PLACEMENT PROCEDURES

Utility of selection decisions is influenced by
- Validity
- Base rates

Organizations use selection and placement procedures (for example, predictors such as tests, interviews, and references) to make hiring job applicants more efficient and effective. If anyone could do a particular job, it would be completely unnecessary to administer any test of ability to select job applicants. The use of a predictor would not increase the chance of hiring people who would do well. And after all that's what selection and placement procedures are all about: *increasing the chances that the job applicants hired will actually perform well.* Thus when an organization uses selection and placement procedures to hire job applicants, *it is assuming that not all applicants can perform as well as others; in fact some can perform much better than others.*

If the organization can select and place the applicants who do in fact turn out to perform well, organizational productivity will benefit. In addition, if the organization fails to select and place applicants who would have performed poorly, organizational productivity will also benefit. Now note this critical point: *when an organization makes selection and placement decisions based on activities that benefit organizational productivity it is making decisions using predictors that are valid and serve its legal considerations.* Using predictors that do not result in selection and placement decisions that benefit productivity are counterproductive. Furthermore, a predictor that is unrelated to job performance has no validity and could result in illegal discriminatory hiring practices if it results in adverse impact.[3]

Thus it pays an organization to use job-performance-related predictors in making selection and placement decisions. Easier said than done, however! It is not always easy to find performance-related predictors. After all, to do this requires, at minimum, that job performance for all the different jobs in the organization be defined and individual specifications (qualifications) identified (remember, you get this information largely from the job analysis, as shown in Exhibit 6.1). But then the next big step is to demonstrate that the predictors you are using are actually job-performance-related. That is, you need to show that they are *valid* or that they have *validity*.

- Predictor rates
- Selection ratios

Validity

When a test (or any other predictor) is said to exhibit **validity** or to be a valid predictor, it statistically predicts what it is supposed to predict. A job applicant who passes a welding test, for example, should be able to perform well as a welder if the test is valid.

It is important to note that there is a **range of validity.** The degree of validity for a particular test is indicated by the magnitude of the **correlation coefficient,** which ranges from -1 to $+1$ (most valid) to 0 (least valid). In fact, -1 and $+1$ show perfect validity (perfectly correlated), and 0 shows the absence of validity (perfectly uncorrelated). Perfect validity comes in two forms: **Perfectly positive validity** $(+1)$ means the two variables move in the same direction; **perfectly negative validity** (-1) means they move in the opposite direction.

But what do these values of validity mean in the real world? Perfect validity means that a job applicant who scores high on a test will score exactly that high on what the test predicts. An applicant who scores twice as well on the test as another applicant will perform twice as well on the job. If the test lacked validity, it would be impossible to predict on the basis of test scores whether one job applicant would be a better performer than the other. Generally, most tests used by organizations have less than perfect validity. Under these general conditions, an applicant who scores twice as well on the test as another applicant would be likely to perform better on the job but not by twice as much. Nevertheless, most organizations would still hire the higher scoring applicant.

The term *validity* is extremely important for you to know. It is the heart of many personnel decisions. In fact, the more valid (job-related) the test, the more efficient

You are as likely to find a perfectly valid test as a perfect person.

Exhibit 6.1
Role of Job Analysis in Validation Studies (Adapted from M. L.
Blurn and J. C. Naylor, *Industrial Psychology Its Theoretical and Social
Foundations* [New York, Harper & Row, 1968]. p. 27)

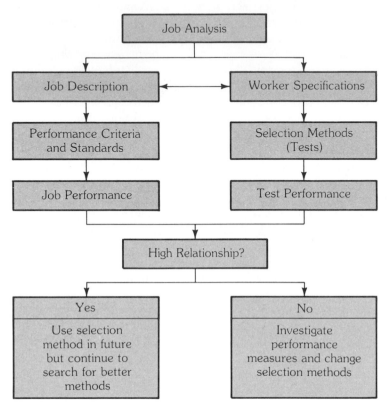

selection and placement decisions can be. And the more efficient these decisions, the better the hired workers will likely perform—thus the more efficient the organization.

Note that while the Uniform Guidelines require organizations to demonstrate the job relatedness of a test, they do not specify the actual degree of job relatedness. Thus an organization can claim its tests are job-related or valid even though the correlation coefficient between the tests and performance is +0.3 rather than +0.8 or +0.9. While the Guidelines do not specify the size of the correlation necessary to claim job relatedness, they do indicate that the correlation be statistically significant.

There are several types of validity, five of which are particularly relevant in selection and placement decisions: *empirical, content, construct, face,* and *differential validity.* Although all are determined to be critical, the strategies used to collect the information to correlate them are substantially different. You need to know them so that you can show or demonstrate the validity of a predictor. These are necessary in defense of an **adverse impact charge.**[4]

Validity:
▪ Empirical
▪ Content
▪ Construct
▪ Differential
▪ Face

Empirical Validation. **Empirical validity,** or **criterion validity,** is a measure of how well a test predicts performance. There are two types of empirical validation strategies—*concurrent* and *predictive*—shown in Exhibit 6.2.

Exhibit 6.2
Empirical Validity

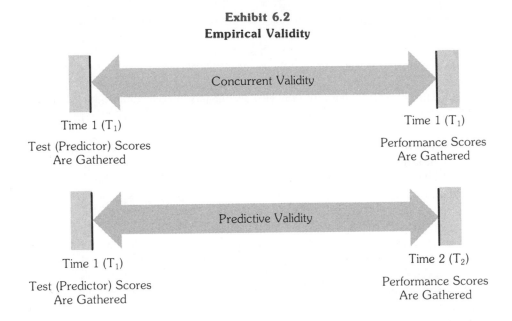

Time 1 (T$_1$)

Test (Predictor) Scores
Are Gathered

Time 1 (T$_1$)

Performance Scores
Are Gathered

Time 1 (T$_1$)

Test (Predictor) Scores
Are Gathered

Time 2 (T$_2$)

Performance Scores
Are Gathered

Concurrent validation determines the relationship between a predictor and a performance score for all employees in the study at the same time. For example, to determine the concurrent validity of the correlation between years of experience and job performance, personnel would collect from each person in the study (by the way, they all would have to be working in similar jobs generally in the same job family or classification) information about years of experience and performance scores. Then a correlation would be computed.

The steps in determining **predictive validity** are similar, except that the predictor is measured some time before performance is measured, as shown in Exhibit 6.2. Thus the predictive validity of a predictor could be determined by measuring an existing group of employees on a predictor and waiting to gather their performance measures later or by hiring a group of job applicants regardless of their scores on the predictor, measuring them on their performance later.

For either type of empirical validation, it is also important to demonstrate that the performance criteria are related to the duties of the job.

Content Validity.   **Content validity** differs from empirical validity in that it *estimates or judges* the relevance of a predictor as an indicator of being able to do the job without actually collecting the actual performance information. This is done by showing that the predictor is related to the duties of the job described in the job description. The administration of a typing test (actually a **job sample test** if used for typists) as a selection device for hiring typists is a classic example of a predictor *judged* to have content validity.[5] Notice that in this case the predictor is a skill related to a task that is actually part of the job. Content validity thus refers to predictors that measure skills, knowledge, or behaviors related to those required of the actual job. Thus to demonstrate content validity, it is necessary to know the duties of the actual job and the individual qualities needed to perform those duties. As discussed in Chapter 3, information about job tasks and responsibilities can be obtained using several standardized

Once again job analysis is critical for effective personnel management.

forms, and then it can be used to develop job descriptions. These descriptions can be used in turn to determine the individual qualities assumed necessary to perform the tasks and to determine the criteria for job success.

Although job analysis is discussed here as a critical element in content validation, it should be regarded as the starting point and the thread that ties together any basic validation study (see Exhibit 6.1). It is also a critical activity in determining construct validity.

Construct validity. Instead of showing a direct relationship between a test or other selection information (for example, education or experience levels) and job performance, selection methods often seek to measure (often by tests) the degree to which an applicant possesses traits and aptitudes ("psychological traits") that are *deemed necessary* for job performance. These underlying "psychological traits" are called **constructs** and include, among many others, intelligence, leadership ability, verbal ability, interpersonal sensitivity, and analytical ability. Constructs deemed necessary for the performance of jobs are *inferred* from job behaviors and activities (duties) as indicated in the job analysis.

Construct validity thus requires demonstrating that a relationship exists between a selection procedure or test (a measure of the construct) and the psychological trait (construct) it seeks to measure derived from the job duties. For example, does a reading comprehension test really measure how well people can read and understand what they read? In order to demonstrate construct validity, one would need data showing that high scorers on the test actually read more difficult material and are better readers than low scorers on the test and that reading ability is related to the duties shown in the job description.

An illustration of these three types of validities is shown in the insert, *For Your Career.* This illustration uses some of the information contained in the job description of the animal keeper in Chapter 3, Exhibit 3.3.

Another type of validity that courts have used is **face validity.** Though not described in the Uniform Guidelines of 1978 as an acceptable validation technique, it simply refers to whether the test (predictor) questions seem to or appear to relate to the job. In other words, if the test seems to logically relate to the job (without showing that it really does), then it has face validity.

Differential Validity. So far, validity has been discussed as the extent to which a predictor really predicts. That is, if an individual scores well on a valid predictor, that person is likely to do well in the future. But there may be situations in which the predictor is valid for some people and not valid or less valid for others. For example, a person with high ability may perform well on a job regardless of his or her score on a manual dexterity test. But for a person with low ability, high scores on the manual dexterity test may be necessary for him or her to perform well. Thus the manual dexterity test is a valid predictor of performance for only the person with low ability. It is not valid for the person with high ability. Thus the manual dexterity test has **differential validity.** Since any test may have differential validity, it is important for a personnel department to conduct several validity studies for any test being used. Legally, differential validity studies must be done for protected employees in relationship to the majority group.[6]

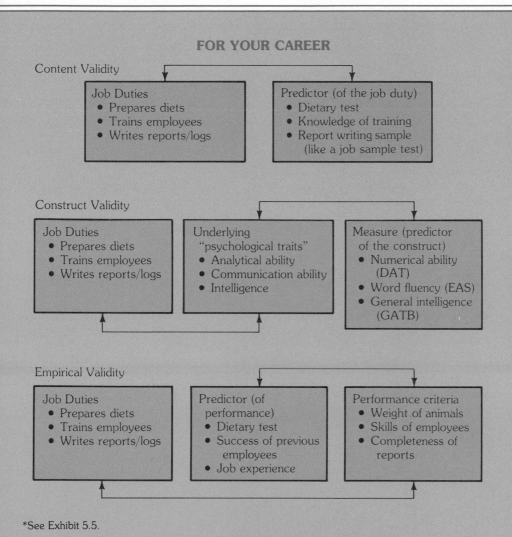

FOR YOUR CAREER

Content Validity

Job Duties
- Prepares diets
- Trains employees
- Writes reports/logs

Predictor (of the job duty)
- Dietary test
- Knowledge of training
- Report writing sample
  (like a job sample test)

Construct Validity

Job Duties
- Prepares diets
- Trains employees
- Writes reports/logs

Underlying "psychological traits"
- Analytical ability
- Communication ability
- Intelligence

Measure (predictor of the construct)
- Numerical ability (DAT)
- Word fluency (EAS)
- General intelligence (GATB)

Empirical Validity

Job Duties
- Prepares diets
- Trains employees
- Writes reports/logs

Predictor (of performance)
- Dietary test
- Success of previous employees
- Job experience

Performance criteria
- Weight of animals
- Skills of employees
- Completeness of reports

*See Exhibit 5.5.

Reliability

An important component in the use of selection procedures such as tests is **reliability.** If a test (predictor) is administered time after time under identical conditions, the results should be the same; if the results are not the same the test is unreliable. Actually, reliability is like validity in that it has a range. That is, the reliability of a test can range anywhere from completely unreliable to completely reliable.

Because reliability can influence validity, the Uniform Guidelines asks that the estimates of reliability be reported for all selection procedures if available. Furthermore, these estimates should be made for relevant race, sex, and ethnic subgroups.

Base Rate versus Predictor Rate

Another big step in finding, developing and using job-related predictors is in showing how beneficial they are if, indeed, they are helpful. Remember we said that in using predictors an organization assumes: (1) that some job applicants will perform better than others; (2) that they can be spotted (by using predictors) and selected; and (3) that a greater percentage (**predictor rate**) of those selected using the predictors will turn out good than if they had been selected at random, the base rate (or on a first-come-first-served basis). In other words, the organization is assuming (betting on) the predictor rate to exceed the base rate. The more it exceeds the base rate, the more useful the predictor.

The importance of having a higher predictor rate than base rate can be illustrated by introducing the concepts of *false negatives, false positives* and *true positives, true negatives.* What an organization wants in selecting employees is to make as many *true* decisions as possible and to minimize the number of *false* decisions. Using a test with a predictor rate higher than the base rate results does this. For example, if the base rate is 0.5 (half the applicants hired turn out to be good performers) and the predictor rate is 0.8 (80% of the applicants hired turn out to be good performers), many more true decisions will be made using the predictor. This can be illustrated using two scatter-grams, each with one hundred applicants hired, one showing a 0.5 base rate and the other a 0.8 predictor rate. Note that *cut-off scores* are used to categorize the employees as being good performers and poor performers and those who would be hired using the predictor and those would be rejected:

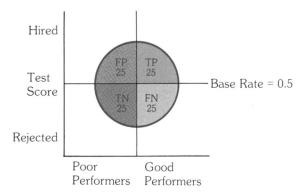

In the above scattergram there is essentially no relationship between test score (if one had been used) and performance. Note that an equal number of applicants turned out to be true positive (TP), false positive (FP), true negative (TN), and false negative (FN).

If a test with a 0.8 predictor rate (degree of correlation coefficient) were used to select the applicants, the results would be substantially different:

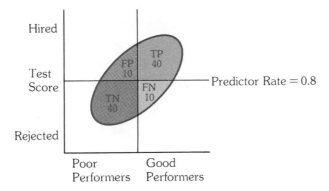

In this second scattergram the number of individuals in the four categories is not equal. In fact FP and FN are each 10 and TP and TN are each 40. Thus 80 correct decisions were made. In the first example, the base rate (with just random selection or using another predictor) is 0.5 and the number of correct decisions is 50. So the comparison is rather dramatic: 80 correct decisions as opposed to only 50!

True decisions are better than false decisions even if they are negative.

Selection Ratio

A further concept that is important in evaluating selection and placement procedures is the notion of the **selection ratio.** The selection ratio is defined as the proportion of individuals hired to those who applied. For example, there may be 200 applicants but only 10 individuals are hired. This would represent a selection ratio of 10/200 or 5 percent. Generally speaking, a selection system has greater value when the selection ratio is small—that is, when there are many more applicants than jobs.[7]

Smaller selection ratios are better than large selection ratios. Why?

The fewer applicants an organization has, the less assured it is that it has the best possible applicant. With few applicants, it must be more careful in matching them to the jobs available. If an organization must hire all the applicants because there are so few, the validity of the selection and placement devices becomes irrelevant. This is especially true when there is only one type of job available.

When everyone who applies is hired, the chance that all will have the ability to do well is low. Consequently, the organization may need to establish extensive training programs, but this may be rather costly. The organization can also try to attract more job applicants by raising wages, but that may only lead to more trouble. For example, raising the wages of new employees may be unfair to the rest of the employees. This in turn may cause many of the current employees to be unhappy (these ideas are discussed again in Chapter 11). Thus it pays an organization to attract as many *potentially qualified* applicants as possible and to reduce its selection ratio. It also pays an applicant to do the same. In general then, it is in the best interests of organizations and individuals to have a choice—of applicants and of jobs. Without choice, the utility of selection devices is minimal; with choice, their utility is high. The more choice, the greater the chances the applicant chosen will do well and be satisfied.

To summarize thus far, the value of selection and placement procedures varies as a function of three basic criteria:

1. The magnitude of the validity coefficient—*As validity increases, so does the value of the procedures.* The same is true for the reliability coefficient.
2. The base rate—*As the differential between the base rate and predictor rate increases, the selection procedures demonstrate greater value.*
3. The selection ratio—*As selection ratios become smaller, the value of the selection procedures increases.*[8]

Costs and Benefits

A final criterion influencing the evaluation of selection and placement procedures is the cost of the increase in actual job performance versus the cost of getting the same increase using other techniques, such as job design or supervisory training programs. There are two major types of costs in selection and placement.

1. Actual costs (*costs actually incurred in hiring applicants*).
   a. *Recruiting and assessment costs—salaries of personnel staff, advertising expenses, travel expenses, and testing personnel evaluation costs.*
   b. *Induction and orientation costs—administrative costs of adding the employee to the payroll, and salaries of the new employee and of those responsible for orienting him to his new job.*
   c. *Training costs—salaries of training and development staff, salary of the new employee during training, and costs of any special materials, instruments, or facilities for training.*

2. Potential costs (*costs that might be incurred if a wrong selection decision is made*).
   a. *Costs associated with hiring a person who subsequently fails—record-keeping costs, termination costs, costs of undesireable job behavior such as materials or equipment damaged; loss of customers, clients, or patients; loss of good will, etc.; and costs incurred in replacing a failing employee.*
   b. *Costs associated with rejecting a person who would have been successful on the job—competitive disadvantage if he is hired by another firm (for example, loss of a top sports star to a competing team), and costs of recruiting and assessing an additional applicant to replace the rejectee.*[9]

Knowing all these criteria for the evaluation of selection and placement procedures allows an organization to select the procedures that are most likely to result in effective decisions. Let's see what those decisions are likely to be.

Selection decisions include:
▪ Hire
▪ Hold
▪ Fire
▪ Lay off
▪ Promote
▪ Demote
▪ Transfer

THE SELECTION AND PLACEMENT DECISION

Selection and placement seek to put the right person in the right job. The right person may be found outside or inside the organization. Whether a person is right depends on the match between the person's abilities and job skill demands and between the person's needs and job rewards. An organization may want job applicants to fill newly created jobs or jobs that have become vacant as a result of retirement, transfer, or voluntary quitting (turnover). Vacancies may also be created by demotions and discharges. Because demotions and discharges are an important part of personnel management, they are discussed further in Chapters 8 and 10.

The final selection and placement decision may be one to hire a new job applicant or hire (or transfer) one from within the organization. The decision may also be to not hire a particular applicant or set of applicants, but rather go out and do more recruiting. The decision could also be to "put on hold" some applicants who are qualified but for whom no jobs are currently open. Although generally not thought of as such, the final selection and placement decisions could be to demote or terminate an employee. Though these decisions do not seem like a part of selection and placement, you should think of them as such since they are subject to the same legal considerations as hiring, transfer, or promotion. Consequently all of these are shown in Exhibit 5.1.

Transfers will increase in use while promotions will decrease in use.

Except for the selection and placement decisions for entry-level jobs and those involving termination or layoff, the selection and placement decision is generally related to a transfer or promotion or at least a potential promotion. Don't forget, applicants from outside the organization can be selected to fill higher level jobs. This decision, however, often has a negative impact on employee morale. Thus organizations would rather try to promote from within. And as the twenty-five to fifty-four age group increases in the 1980s and 1990s, transfers will become the alternative to promotions, at least in providing challenge and variety to valued employees. Because promotions and transfer decisions are critical, let's look at them in more detail.

Promotion and Transfer Decisions

"Going outside is the exception rather than the rule, and promotion from within is a standard practice in most organizations."[10] Some job vacancies, however, are filled by outside sources, particularly for highly skilled jobs or when the organization has been caught by surprise and has no employee ready to take the job. To help prevent surprises, organizations like BancOhio National Bank, XEROX, IBM, Nationwide Insurance Company, and AMAX have managerial succession programs. In these programs, which are really part of the organization's personnel planning and programing, current managers identify employees who may one day be able to take over their managerial jobs.

It doesn't always pay to be the best.

FOR YOUR CAREER

In times when organizations must reduce their work forces, promotions and transfers still continue, but organizations will often

- Reduce the rate of new hires, promotions, and transfers
- Train employees so they can fill job openings instead of having to lay them off and hire new people
- Reduce the number of hours employees work (per day or per week)
- Engage in indefinite layoffs
- Engage in temporary layoffs
- Close plants or offices
- Make early retirement attractive
- Establish job-sharing programs

Types of Promotion and Transfer. Promotions can occur within a department, a division, or an entire organization.[11] They also can occur between two nonmanagerial positions (for example, from Typist I to Typist II), between two managerial positions, and between a nonmanagerial and a managerial (or supervisory) position.

Although promotions generally refer to vertical moves in the organization, promotions may occur when an employee moves to another job at the same level but with more pay or status. However, this type of promotion may violate federal wage guidelines and equal pay regulations, and so it should be made advisedly. Although such a move could be regarded as a transfer, a transfer generally refers to a move at the same level and at the same pay.

Making Promotion and Transfer Decisions. Immediate supervisors have a major role in deciding who to promote or transfer.

> In many cases, the immediate supervisor must search for qualified candidates and make a choice when a vacancy arises. This process may be carried out in close consultation with one or more higher level supervisors who ultimately have to approve the choice. On the other hand, the immediate supervisor may have almost total control over the decisions.[12]

Immediate supervisors may have most control when a new job is being created. They may be able to determine exactly who will be promoted by writing the job description to fit only one person. This is not necessarily a fair practice, but it's a common one. It is important to remember, however, that promotion decisions are just like other selection decisions and as such must be done without illegal discrimination. Several court decisions have been handed down indicating that promotion decisions by the immediate supervisor can violate Title VII, especially when they are made without objective standards of performance (See *Rowe* v. *General Motors Corp.; Robinson* v. *Union Carbide Corp.;* and *United States* v. *City of Chicago* as described in Appendix A).

Identifying Candidates for Promotion and Transfer. Candidates may be identified by word of mouth, inspection of the organization's personnel records (this is easy if the organization has a computerized human resource information system such as the one in Citibank's job-matching program), promotion lists based on performance or managerial ratings, and formal programs for identifying potential candidates for promotion, such as assessment centers. The human resource information system is also valuable here because it can store information on employee preferences and needs.[13] This will help ensure that candidate identification can then be made with consideration for both matches. This will help reduce the number of employees turning down promotions or soon leaving a job to which they were only recently promoted or transferred.

Comparing Candidates. Methods for identifying candidates can also be used to evaluate and compare candidates. Although many companies administer a battery of tests to assess mental ability, personality, and interests, one study concluded that tests are ignored more often than not as decision-making aids for internal promotions. Behavioral tests; however, are used extensively by Standard Oil of Ohio, General Electric, Sears, Wickes, and J. C. Penney.

Job experience and performance history are also used to evaluate candidates. Interviews are used as well, although they are used more widely for candidates from external sources. A powerful sponsor (often a manager at a higher level in the organization who "adopts" and looks out for an employee at a lower level) can help ensure that an individual's strengths are noted by others. A final basis for comparing candidates is seniority.

Making the Final Choice.   Making a decision is difficult if different types of information are available for competing job applicants. Even if this is the case, however, all of the candidates can be screened quickly, and only those with an obvious potential to do well are retained. Those remaining can be sequentially evaluated. Although this may not result in selection of the best candidate, at least the one who is chosen should perform adequately.

A strategy used by managers who favor a particular candidate, the inside candidate, is the **confirmation approach.** To make the selection process appear legitimate, a manager may select several candidates, in addition to the favorite, for others to evaluate. The catch is that the other candidates are far less qualified than the favorite. Although there is a choice, it is more apparent than real.

Why Not the Best?   All too often, the best people are not the ones who are promoted or transferred.[14] There are several reasons for this.

First, staff people are often not considered for line jobs. Many organizations promote only line managers to upper management. Exceptions to this tradition are occurring, however. IBM has a company policy of promoting managers in and out of line and staff jobs.

Second, decentralized departments and divisions operate like independent organizations. Thus when vacancies occur, that department or division tends to select only from its own employees and not from the total organization. Decentralization can also result in a separate performance appraisal system for each division; even if divisions did obtain candidates from other divisions, they could be hard to evaluate. This issue is discussed again in Chapter 9.

A third reason that the most qualified person may be overlooked is related to sex discrimination.

> Probably one of the more overlooked banks of promotable talent is the huge reservoir of women in the work force. Except in service industries such as banks, insurance companies, and advertising firms, women have been largely ignored in management promotions.[15]

Ignoring women (and minorities) means selecting managers (often illegally) from a small percentage of the employees.

Fourth, the best person may not be promoted because subjective, personal criteria are used in selection rather than objective criteria. Subjective criteria include how well they are liked by the manager, how they dress, and how popular they are.

Finally, many competent managers are refusing promotion because it often means moving to another location. Increasingly members of dual-career families are refusing promotions involving a geographic change because the change may require a career sacrifice on the part of the other person. In addition, some managers refuse promotions because they are more interested in pursuing leisure rather than work.

EVALUATING SELECTION AND PLACEMENT PROCEDURES

Selection and placement procedures are meant to determine which job applicants should be selected and what jobs they should be placed in. As with the recruitment activity, selection and placement must serve the interests of both the individual and the organization. In addition, these activities must take place within a specified set of legal constraints, as shown in Exhibit 5.1.

Selection and placement procedures can be evaluated by measuring employees' satisfaction with work, the extent to which they feel their skills and abilities are being used and their needs satisfied, and their level of involvement with the job and the organization. Since employee satisfaction, involvement, and skill levels can change, personnel managers must continually monitor these activities. Regular, periodic organizational surveys are one method (see Chapter 7).

The organization's interests are often closely related to the individual's. If the best person is selected and placed in a job, the organization will gain from having a productive employee who is satisfied, who attends work regularly, and who stays with the organization. Thus selection and placement procedures can be measured from the organization's viewpoint by employee satisfaction, performance, absenteeism, and turnover. These, too, can be monitored.

An important aspect of the evaluation of selection and placement procedures is the calculation of percentages: How many employees of each race, sex, religion, national origin, and age are at various levels in the organization? What proportion do they bear to protected groups in the community? This aspect of evaluation not only complies with legal constraints but also helps put the right person in the right job. As a way of monitoring progress in meeting legal constraints, the personnel department can gather figures on the rates of promotion for various groups, the numbers of minorities hired from the number recruited, and even the number of actionable charges filed by employees for violation of equal employment opportunity guidelines.

FACING THE CRITICAL ISSUES IN SELECTION AND PLACEMENT

Now that we have discussed the essential aspects of the selection and placement procedures available to the personnel manager, it is useful to once again address the Critical Issues listed at the beginning of Chapter 5.

Issue: *What are all of the laws that organizations must consider in making selection and placement decisions?*

As shown in Appendix A, there are many laws, court decisions, and guidelines that almost any personnel manager must consider in making selection and placement decisions. Foremost among the legal considerations are Title VII of the Civil Rights Act of 1964; the Age Discrimination in Employment Act (ADEA) of 1967 as amended in 1978; the Rehabilitation Act of 1973, and the Equal Pay Act of 1963.

Because new laws and court decisions at all levels are being determined almost daily, a personnel manager should read the biweekly newsletters like the Bureau of

National Affairs' *Bulletin to Management* and *Fair Employment Reports,* the Commerce Clearing House, and various ASPA newsletters, and the *FEP Guidelines* and *Fair Employment Practices.*

Issue: *What are the best ways (and most legal ways) to get the information needed in making selection and placement decisions so organizations can still select the best candidate?*

Most organizations collect selection and placement information from (1) Interviews, often at least two; (2) Application blanks; (3) References; and (4) Employment tests.

Generally, using these legally is the best way to use them. Using the legally means that the information gathered must be job-performance-related. Note that, when used in making selection and placement decisions, all four ways to gather information are also called predictors or tests. When used as predictors or tests they are being used to indicate who among the job applicants will perform well if hired and who will not perform well. The predictors that most frequently make these determinations correctly represent the best ways to collect information for selection and placement decisions.

Issue: *How do organizations know when they are violating the law?*

Notification from the EEOC or any one of several state or local civil or human rights commissions or agencies may indicate organizations are violating the law. Short of this they can tell if they are violating the law by determining if their selection and placement procedures are resulting in adverse impact without a legal defense. Adverse impact can be determined in several ways. There are several bases for a legal defense. The ways to determine adverse impact and show a legal defense are shown in the inserts in Chapter 5. A personnel manager should realize that all the bases of defense are not equally useful. Their usefulness, at minimum, varies with the type of adverse impact and the court/judge hearing the case if it reaches that level. The same can be said about the ways of determining adverse impact. This uncertainty in part is what makes the personnel manager's job so challenging and so vital to the organization. Nevertheless personnel should take a proactive stance and conduct self-analyses to identify potential liabilities in the organization's selection and placement procedures and to remove those liabilities. Doing this will help personnel be much more effective in many of its activities besides selection and placement.

Issue: *How can organizations improve their selection and placement procedures to make them more effective?*

An organization's selection and placement procedures can be made more useful (effective) in several ways. One way is to search for, develop, and use predictors that have high degrees of validity. Another is to make sure that, because searching for the developing predictors is so expensive, using predictors is really necessary. The determination of need can be made by calculating and comparing the base rate and predictor rate. Selection and placement procedures are most useful when the base rate is much less than the predictor rate. By improving the selection ratio, the activities can also be made more useful. Thus an organization should have an effective recruiting activity that produces as many potentially qualified job applicants as possible. Finally, the usefulness of an organization's selection and placement procedures can be improved by constantly evaluating the benefits and costs of the activities used. Sometimes procedures can produce equal benefits at very dissimilar costs.

SUMMARY

The last two chapters have assumed that an essential goal of selection and placement is to get the right person for the right job in order to serve the short- and long-run interests of both the organization and the individual. This means that organizations should make selection and placement decisions based on information about an individual's needs and the rewards of the job and organization as well as about an individual's abilities and the demands of the job. Only by considering both matches can the major purposes of selection and placement be attained.

Selection and placement decisions, therefore, require a great deal of information. Fortunately, there are many ways by which organizations can gather information for selection and placement decisions. In the process of gathering information, however, the organization must be aware of several legal considerations. Failure to do so may not only result in expensive lawsuits but also in decisions to hire less than the best-qualified job applicant.

Legal considerations are also important when the organization actually combines the information gathered to make the final selection and placement decision. The personnel manager must consider these legal regulations as well as the methods by which to combine information in making the final employment decision.

Once the final decision has been made to hire a job applicant, care must be taken to bring that person on board. The organization must take steps to orient and socialize the new employees and continue to monitor how well they are doing and what they are thinking and feeling. Because these are critical for an organization to know, they are discussed in Chapter 7.

KEY CONCEPTS

adverse impact charge	perfectly positive validity
base rate	perfectly negative validity
construct validity	predictor rate
range of validity	valid predictor
selection ratio	assessment center
single predictor approach	predictive validity
validity	concurrent validity
content validity	confirmation approach
differential validity	reliability
empirical validity	face validity
multiple predictor approach	correlation coefficient
job sample test	

DISCUSSION QUESTIONS

1. What is the major difference between single and multiple predictor approaches?
2. List the three kinds of multiple predictor approaches and the philosophy behind using them.

3. What is the basic reason for or essence of selection and placement activities?

4. What is meant by the concept of validity and why is it important to selection and placement activities? Give an example.

5. Define the selection ratio and explain when it is of more value to a selection system.

6. What are the three variables that influence the value of a prediction system and in what ways do they affect the value of that system?

7. What are the two "potential costs" related to selection and placement procedures?

8. List some of the results when the final selection decision is "not to hire."

9. What are three indicators that can be used to evaluate selection and placement procedures vis-à-vis the individual and the organization?

10. Why is it that the best people are often not the ones hired for the job?

11. What are the most important laws not to overlook when making selection and placement decisions? How can you stay abreast of changes in legislation?

CASE

Multiple Hurdles or Multiple Hindrances?

Over the past fifty years, Acme Auto Parts had built a reputation in the industry as being a quality parts supplier to automobile dealers, local automobile mechanics and retail stores in a five-state area in the Midwest. With the trend of people holding on to their cars longer, the demand for parts to repair and maintain cars is expected to increase ten percent a year during the 1980s. Consequently Bill Dalton, Acme's president, sees great things for Acme Auto in the 1980s. He realizes, however, that greatness largely depends upon getting good people. Currently Acme has five hundred employees across fifteen locations in the five-state area. With half of these employees in their fifties and a desire to open five new locations, Bill estimates that Acme will need to hire three hundred new employees in the next seven years.

Since Bill Dalton has many things to do, he hires you as his personnel director. Currently, two of Bill's assistants and a secretary do the necessary personnel activities, particularly selection and payroll. Since Acme has grown gradually over the past fifty years, the number of employees selected each year has recently averaged fewer than fifteen. Because hiring fifteen people didn't take much time, the two assistants could do this, in addition to a number of other things they did for Bill. But now Acme needs to hire forty to forty-five people each year for the next seven years. As personnel director, your primary job is to select what Bill calls "the best people we can."

After a few weeks on the job, you learn that Acme has no trouble getting job applicants; in fact, there are almost too many applicants. However, you also learn that almost everyone hired in the past ten years has been referred by a current employee.

In addition, all but the clerical staff is male. The result is essentially a work force without women and minorities. Since you and Bill recognize and are firmly committed to the importance and reality of equal opportunity, you know that past hiring practices will have to be altered. You also believe that providing equal opportunity works best when the people hired do well. Since previous applicants had to clear two hurdles that did not provide equal opportunity, you know that new hurdles are needed. These new hurdles will have to provide equal opportunity and ensure that Acme hires "the best people we can."

Case Questions

1. Where do you start? Do you think you can do the job?
2. What do you think Bill means by the phrase "the best people we can"?
3. What hurdles are you likely to use to select applicants to provide equal opportunity and to provide the best employees?
4. What is likely to be the reaction of the current employees to your new hiring practices? How will you deal with them?

FOR YOUR CAREER

- One important test you are likely to encounter in your career is the assessment center. Be ready to volunteer to participate in one if you are offered the chance.
- You can be a critical employee (especially in personnel) if you can conduct validity studies.
- The test validation process not only helps an organization in making legally fair selection decisions; it also helps the organization to make economically sound selection decisions.
- Remember to use selection devices only when you know some applicants will perform better than others, that those people can be spotted, and that using predictors will produce better decisions on the applicants than will pure chance.
- Although you may be the best performer, you may not be the one promoted. Why?
- It will get harder and harder to get promoted. Transfers or job enrichment are likely to be more widely used.

ENDNOTES

1. L. Smith, "Equal Opportunity Rules Are Getting Tougher," *Fortune*, June 19, 1978, p. 152. Courtesy of *Fortune* Magazine, © 1978 Time, Inc. For more information, see:

Dennis J. Kravetz, "Selection Systems for Clerical Positions," *Personnel Administrator,* February 1981, pp. 35–42.

Harry Levinson, "Criteria for Choosing Chief Executives," *Harvard Business Review,* July–August 1980, pp. 112–120.

Edward M. Miller, "Personnel Selection in the Presence of Uncertainty," *Personnel,* September-October 1980, pp. 67–76.

Thomas A. Petit and Terry W. Mullins, "Decisions, Decisions: How to Make Good Ones on Employee Selection," *Personnel,* March–April 1981, pp. 71–77.

Thomasine Rendero, "Consensus," *Personnel,* March–April 1980, pp. 4–10.

2. Stephen L. Cohen, "Pre-Packaged vs. Tailor-Made: The Assessment Center Debate," *Personnel Journal,* December 1980, pp. 989–995.

L. A. Digman, "How Well-Managed Organizations Develop Their Executives," *Organizational Dynamics,* Autumn 1978, pp. 65–66.

Leland C. Nichols and Joseph Hudson, "Dual-Role Assessment Center: Selection and Development," *Personnel Journal,* May 1981, pp. 350–386.

Treadway C. Parker, "Assessment Centers: A Statistical Study," *Personnel Administrator,* February 1980, pp. 65–67.

James C. Quick, William A. Fisher, Lawrence L. Schkade, and George W. Ayers, "Developing Administrative Personnel Through the Assessment Center Technique," *Personnel Administrator,* February 1980, pp. 44–46, 62.

Joyce D. Ross, "A Current Review of Public Sector Assessment Centers: Cause for Concern," *Public Personnel Management,* January–February 1979, pp. 41–46.

3. Theodore H. Curry II, "A Common-Sense Management Approach to Employee Selection and EEO Compliance for the Smaller Employer," *Personnel Administrator,* April 1981, pp. 35–38.

L. Smith, "Equal Opportunity Rules Are Getting Tougher," *Fortune,* June 19, 1978, p. 156.

4. Richard S. Barrett, "Is the Test Content-Valid: Or, Who Killed Cock Robin?" *Employee Relations Law Journal* 6, No. 4 (1981), pp. 584–600.

Richard S. Barrett, "Is the Test Content-Valid: or, Does it Really Measure A Construct," *Employee Relations Law Journal* 6, No. 3(1981), pp. 459–475.

S. Wollack, "Content Validity: Its Legal and Psychometric Basis," *Public Personnel Management,* November–December 1976, pp. 397–408.

E. P. Prien, "The Function of Job Analysis in Content Validation," *Personnel Psychology* 30 (1977), pp. 167–174.

L. S. Kleiman and R. H. Faley, "Assessing Content Validity: Standards Set by the Court," *Personnel Psychology* 31(1978), pp. 701–713.

W. Cascio, *Applied Psychology in Personnel Management* (Reston, Va.: Reston Publishing Company, Inc., 1982 (2nd ed.).

5. L. Smith, p. 154.

6. Although differential studies are required by the Uniform Guidelines, there is evidence suggesting that good tests are not differentially valid. See F. L. Schmidt and J. E. Hunter, "Employment Testing: Old Theories and New Research Findings," *American Psychologist,* October 1981, 93940 pp. 1128–1137.

7. R. D. Arvey, *Fairness in Selecting Employees,* © 1979, Addison–Wesley Publishing Company, Inc., pp. 35–37. Reprinted with permission. Arvey provides an excellent in-depth discussion of these issues.

8. Ibid.

9. *Personnel Selection and Placement,* by M. D. Dunnette. Copyright © 1966 by Wadsworth Publishing Company, Inc. Reprinted by permission of Brooks/Cole Publishing Company, Monterey, California, pp. 174–175.

10. H. J. Sweeney and K. S. Teel, "A New Look at Promotion from Within," *Personnel Journal,* August 1979, p. 532.

11. M. London, "What Every Personnel Director Should Know About Management Promotion Decisions," *Personnel Journal,* October 1978, p. 550. Sweeney and Teel, pp. 532–533.

12. "What Every Personnel Director Should Know About Management Promotion Decisions," by M. London. p. 551. Reprinted with permission *Personnel Journal,* Costa Mesa, Calif., copyright October 1978.

13. Alfred J. Walker, "Management Selection Systems that Meet the Challenge of the 80's," *Personnel Journal,* October 1981, pp. 775–780.

14. D. D. McConkey, "Why the Best Managers Don't Get Promoted," *Business Quarterly,* Summer 1979, pp. 39–43. *Business Quarterly* published by the School of Business, The University of Western Ontario, Canada.

15. Ibid., p. 40.

Establishing and Maintaining Effective Relationships with Employees

Chapter Seven
Communicating with Employees

Chapter Eight
Employee Rights

Chapter Outline

Critical Issues in Communicating with Employees

Communicating with Employees
Purposes and Importance of Communicating with Employees
Relationships of Communicating with Employees

Issues in Communicating with Employees
Organizational Policies and Expectations
Content of Communicating with Employees
The Value of Effective Upward Communications

Skills in Communicating Effectively
Barriers to Upward Communication
Principles of Verbal Communications
Principles of Nonverbal Communications
Listening Efficiently
Providing Effective Feedback

CHAPTER **7**

Communicating With Employees

Methods of Communicating with Employees
The Organizational Survey
Effective Supervisory Communications with Employees

Evaluating Communicating with Employees
Communications and Productivity
Communications and Quality of Work Life

Facing the Critical Issues in Communicating with Employees

Summary

Key Concepts

Discussion Questions

Case

For Your Career

Endnotes

Personnel in the News

Productivity and Communications

One of the problems in many organizations, hard as it may be to believe, is to overcome the view held by a considerable number of managers that employees "couldn't care less about productivity." From the data we have gathered over the years, it is clear employees not only believe people are important to productivity, but also that productivity is important to people. What has been needed to translate those beliefs into productivity improvement is a way to mesh employee and management perceptions and expectations of productivity and the quality of working life.

So, enter communications.

Effective, two-way communications is certainly the catalyst which can help bring it off. It's been the case in Japan, where open communications—up, down, lateral and diagonal—is a staple of business life. Communications is viewed in exactly the same manner and with the same order of priority as product quality, in fact, the two are inseparable. As one Japanese businessman said to an associate of mine who led a study tour to Japan last year: "We could never achieve our high standards of quality or reach our current levels of production without good employee communications." Employee communications is the glue that holds the industrial machine together. (Roy G. Foltz, Personnel Administrator, July, 1981, p. 12.)

Communication

Often, supervisors fail to recognize three important characteristics of human communication. First, communication can be a process of influence through which people try to exert some control over one another. When a supervisor tells an employee to perform some duty, for example, he or she is trying to have some impact upon that employee's behavior. Similarly, in virtually every communication encounter the participants seek to have an impact upon the thoughts, attitudes and/or behaviors of the people to whom they are speaking. Second, communication should be viewed as a means, not an end. It is not something that should be done for its own sake; rather, it is a tool to be used to achieve specific results. Too many meetings occur simply because a supervisor or manager feels that a meeting should be held and not because that supervisor or manager wants the meeting to achieve something. Lastly, the best communication is that which is prepared systematically. An effective supervisor or manager does not rely upon his or her spontaneous, gut reactions to communicate with employees. Rather, he or she carefully thinks through the things which employees ought to be thinking, feeling and/or doing and then prepares messages designed specifically to produce those results. (John E. Baird, Jr., Personnel Administrator, July 1981, p. 28.)

What Management Can Expect from an Employee Attitude Survey

It's an unending management dilemma. How do you find out what employees are really thinking about the company? Are you motivating employees to increase pro-

ductivity while maintaining quality? The most effective way of tackling these problems is to begin with an employee attitude survey.

Employee attitude surveys have become increasingly popular during the past few years. Even small organizations use surveys to find out what employees really think about the organization and its policies. The prime objective of an employee attitude survey is to seek out ways to increase employee motivation by soliciting the opinions and ideas of the employees themselves. It identifies weak and strong areas within the organization. It can strengthen internal communications, initiate feedback on employee relations policies, pinpoint reasons for excessive turnover, identify wage or benefit concerns and identify promotion and discipline problems. (Wallace Martin, Personnel Administrator, *July 1981, p. 75.*)

Together these three quotations illustrate how important communicating with employees is for productivity, morale, and motivation and in understanding the needs and feelings of the employees. Yet these three also illustrate the difficulties in communicating with employees effectively. Sometimes it's a lack of skill in how to do it, for example, how to conduct a survey; sometimes it's a belief that rank-and-file employees are different from managers and less concerned with productivity, and at other times it is just a lack of recognition of the role of communication and the most effective techniques to use in communicating.

Most line managers and personnel managers now recognize the growing importance of effectively communicating with employees. This is in large part due to the current "productivity crisis" in America and demand by workers for an improved quality of work life. Since personnel managers are concerned about productivity and quality of work life, they want to help their organizations and line managers communicate with their employees as well as possible.

CRITICAL ISSUES IN COMMUNICATING WITH EMPLOYEES

Of the many issues they identified, the four of most concern to the personnel managers are:

1. *If organizations are going to communicate more with their employees, what topics do they communicate? What do employees want to know?*
2. *Is it really important to have two-way communications? Do employees really want to tell what they think?*
3. *How can organizations get their supervisors and managers to be better communicators? What and how should they communicate?*
4. *More and more is being said about organizational surveys. How can they be done? Are they good to do?*

Having the right information at the right time in the right place is of vital importance to an organization. **Information** is the knowledge or data that are useful and desireable for employees, managers, and the entire organization to have. It is impossible to conduct personnel activities effectively without accurate and timely information. Thus the personnel manager must be involved with, as well as concerned in, the transmission of information in the organization, namely in the process and procedures in communicating with employees.

COMMUNICATING WITH EMPLOYEES

Communicating is the process by which information is exchanged and understood between two or more people, for example, between the supervisor and his or her employees, between two or more employees or managers, and between the organization and the employees. *Communicating with employees* here refers primarily to the *communications* between the organization and its employees or the supervisors (managers) and his or her employees. In this framework, communicating with employees is **formal communications**: it follows the lines of authority prescribed by the organization, and it is the communication that the organization must be responsible for and in control of. This is in contrast to **informal communications** that do not necessarily follow the lines of authority of the organization. Although the organization is not responsible for informal communications, the organization should realize that the less effective it is communicating (formally) with employees, the more extensive informal communications are likely to be. In turn, ineffectiveness in communicating with employees reduces the organization's opportunities for serving its goals and those of its employees. This follows from our definition of **communicating with employees** as the processes by which information is formally exchanged and understood between the organization or supervisors and the employees to the benefit of the employees as well as the organization or supervisors. Thus greater effectiveness in communicating with employees results in increased benefits for the organization, supervisors, and the employees.[1] As such there is less need for informal communications in the organization.

Purposes and Importance of Communicating with Employees

Communi-
cating
effectively
means finding
out what
people want
and
responding to
them. It also
means "telling
it like it is."

The overall purposes in communicating with employees should be to serve the needs of the employees as well as those of the organization. By communicating effectively everybody wins. Communicating effectively with employees produces this result because it

- Finds out what employees want and think about the organization, supervisors, and all of the organization's policies and practices;
- Conveys to the employees the state of the organization including the realities of its constraints (for example, economic problems) and opportunities; and
- Conveys to the employees what the organization and supervisor expect, what the performance standards and goals are, and what opportunities exist for career development and improvement.

Still, to produce the situation where everyone wins three conditions have to be met: (1) the employees must respond positively and work for the ends of the organization; (2) the organization and supervisor must have the ability and skill to find out what employees are thinking and to convey the state of the organization, expectations, standards, goals, and opportunities; and (3) the organization must respond and adapt to what the employees want.[2]

As the first quotation of this chapter indicates, employees are likely to respond positively when the organization communicates effectively with them. Many personnel programs to improve organizational productivity and profitability are enthusiastically supported by employees once management conveys to them the urgency of the situation and asks for their involvement and support. Examples of this are presented in detail in Chapter 16 "Improving Productivity and Quality of Work Life." Also presented in Chapter 16 are examples of organizations responding and adapting to what employees want by increasing the quality of their work life. The *results* of all the programs for improving the quality of work life and productivity initially based on communicating effectively with employees are *increased* performance, cohesion, satisfaction, job involvement, safety and *decreased* absenteeism, turnover, and accidents. Thus when everybody wins from communicating effectively with employees: organizations benefit from improved productivity, and employees benefit from improved quality of work life. A summary of these relationships is shown in Exhibit 7.1.

> The beneficial results from effective communications are extensive.

Now all that remains is to have Exhibit 7.1 come to life. Since the personnel manager is in the best position to do this by helping the supervisors and organization, we need to ensure that organizations and supervisors as well as personnel managers know: (1) How to find out what their employees need and think; (2) How to best convey to the employee expectations, performance standards, goals, and opportunities; and (3) What to convey about the state of the organization and its policies and practices. The main purpose of this chapter is to help ensure that personnel managers, supervisors, and organizations know how to do these things. These are discussed under the three major headings of *Methods in Communicating, Skills in Communicating* and *Issues in Communicating*. These are examined after looking at the relationships of communicating with employees.

> It takes real skills to communicate effectively. They can be learned, however.

Exhibit 7.1

Communicating Effectively with Employees by the Organization, Supervisors, and Personnel Managers

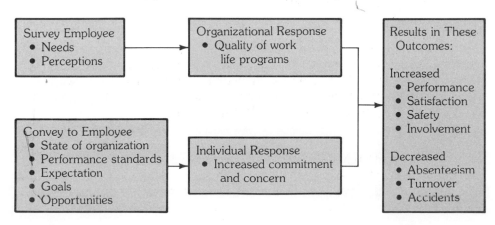

Exhibit 7.2
Relationships and Three Major Components of Communicating
with Employees

	Legal Considerations		
Employee Rights	Issues in Communicating • Policies • Content • Direction	Purposes • Expectations • Understanding • Cohesion (pride) • Motivation • Quality of performance • Satisfaction • Involvement • Less absenteeism	
Performance Appraisal			
Training and Development	Skills in Communicating • Talking • Listening • Feedback • Nonverbal		
Compensation			
Safety and Health			
Union-Management Relations	Methods of Communicating • Supervisor styles • Surveys • Quality circles		
Productivity and QWL			

Relationships of Communicating with Employees

As shown in Exhibit 7.2 there are many other personnel activities related to communicating with employees.

Productivity and Quality of Work Life (QWL). In Chapter 16 many personnel programs to improve QWL and productivity are discussed. But in order for any of these programs to be effective, there must be effective communications with employees. In fact employee communications is the core of some of these programs such as quality circles and semiautonomous work groups.[3]

Safety and Health. Communicating with employees is also effective in improving the safety and health in an organization. The more communications with employees, the greater awareness of safety and health hazards. Safety committees in which labor and management communicate openly in an atmosphere of trust are central in the efforts of many organizations to improve safety and health.

Union-Management Relations. Unions thrive on management mistakes. "The biggest mistake is an insensitive management—one that doesn't listen at all or one that listens and doesn't act. Unions are often sought out by disgruntled employees who have grievances that have been ignored or handled poorly by the supervisors."[4]

Consequently many managers should use organizational surveys to ask their employees what they are thinking and feeling and what their perceptions are.[5] When survey work is done by personnel specifically to find out the attitudes of employees toward unions, it must be reported to the Department of Labor under the *Labor-Management Reporting and Disclosure Act* (1959), Section 203 (b).

Compensation. Two aspects of total compensation related directly to communicating with employees are pay secrecy and indirect benefits. While many organizations practice pay secrecy, a few, however, practice openness and communicate salary information in one form or another to their employees.[6] Although indirect benefits cost a great deal of money, their benefit is often lost because they haven't been communicated to the employees. These notions are discussed more thoroughly in Chapters 11–13.

Training and Development. Supervisors in organizations are often the critical link between the employees and the rest of management. How well supervisors communicate with their employees—for example, in interviews or counseling sessions—can literally make or break an organization. Since skills for communicating effectively with employees are often lacking in supervisors, it is important that these skills are part of a supervisory training program.

Performance Appraisal. A roadblock to productivity improvement in organizations is employees not knowing what's expected of them and not knowing how well they are doing. Consequently employees are unable to perform as well as they might. Communicating performance expectations, standards, and goals to employees thus may be a critical first step in improving productivity in organizations. It is also a critical step in meeting legal requirements since this information must be communicated to employees if performance evaluations are to be used in rewarding and punishing employees (See *Donaldson* v. *Pillsbury Co.* [1977] and *Weahkee* v. *Perry* [1978] and other court decisions in Appendix A). Communicating skills are also essential in doing an effective performance appraisal interview (Chapter 9).

Employees perform well when they know what's expected, have goals, and are rewarded for performance.

Employee Rights. Essentially what is happening in organizations is that employees are demanding the right to know about many work-related topics. Such topics include knowing about safety and health hazards, how promotion and salary decisions are made and why management is doing what it is doing, for example, closing a plant. The whole area of employee rights is expanding rapidly. Some of it is supported by law and some is not. Since employee rights is an important area for personnel, the next chapter is devoted to it.

ISSUES IN COMMUNICATING WITH EMPLOYEES

Three issues important in communicating with employees are: (1) What are the most effective ways organizations can communicate organizational policies and expectations? (2) What should be the content of the communications? and (3) In what directions should the communication flow?

Organizational Policies and Expectations

Policies set by top management, sometimes with the assistance of the personnel manager, set the tone and tempo for the entire organization. Though not always, the policies of top management convey to the employees what's expected and how to behave. As an example, the top management may establish a communications policy with the following aspects:

Here are components of a good communications policy.

- Always keep employees informed on company matters
- Set up clear channels of communication between employees and top management
- Always define a person's job and the expected results
- Encourage employee creativity, and try to keep jobs as challenging as possible
- Encourage self-improvement and point out opportunities for advancement
- Finally, never oversell a candidate in the employment interview.[7]

Organizational policies also often communicate to employees what's rewarded and what the organization thinks of the employee. The time when the organization can have the greatest impact communicating these messages is when the employee joins the organization.

Orientation Programs. Orientation programs are frequently used to brief new employees on benefit programs and options, to advise them of rules and regulations, and to provide them with a folder or handbook of the policies and practices of the organization. The table of contents from a large organization's orientation handbook is shown in Exhibit 7.3.

Use orientation programs to learn as much as you can about the benefits and policies of the organization.

Orientation programs also usually contain information about EEO practices, safety regulations, work times, coffee breaks, the structure and history of the organization, and perhaps the products or services of the organization. Typically, however, the orientation program does not tell employees about the real politics of the organization—for example, the fact that the organization may soon be going out of business or be merging with another company or even that there may soon be an extensive layoff.

The orientation program conveys some information about the norms, values, attitudes, and behaviors appropriate for new employees, but much of the socialization is left to informal day-to-day interactions among employees. Nevertheless, orientation programs are useful for factual information, and the handbook can be used to tell employees where to get additional information after orientation is over.

Orientation programs are almost always coordinated by the personnel director of the organization. The program is often run by a staff member of the personnel department, with some participation by line managers or representatives from other departments or divisions in the organization.

When organizations are large, orientation programs are often conducted every week. Some organizations even have two orientation sessions one week apart. Typically these programs are run for groups of new employees. Although this is an efficient method, it tends to negate each employee's sense of identity and consequence.[8] Therefore, each employee is often assigned to a trainer or buddy (sometimes the immediate supervisor) who can answer further questions and introduce him or her to the other employees in the work unit or department.

Orientation programs are usually conducted within a week of an employee's initial employment date. For maximum effectiveness, the earlier the better. Organiza-

Exhibit 7.3
Sample Orientation Handbook Table of Contents

CONTENTS

	Page
Getting Started	1
Orientation	1
About the Company	2
Principles and Objectives	4
Philosophy	5
Where We Operate	7
What We Do	8
What You Earn	9
Your Salary	9
Salary Grades	9
Salary Review	10
Cost-of-Living Adjustment	10
Paydays	11
Payroll Deduction Services	11
Federal Tax Exemptions	11
Social Security Changes	11
Paycheck Stub	12
Benefits and Services	14
Vacations	14
Holidays	14
Permission Absences	15
Maternity Provisions	15
Military Procedures	15
Worker's Compensation	16
Educational Assistance	16
Credit Union	16
Suggestion Awards	16
When You Are on the Job	17
Personal Appearance	17
Personal Business—Phones	18
Protection of Records	18
Change in Status	18
Attendance	18
Probationary Period	19
Overtime	19
Job Problems	19
Resignation	20
Career Opportunities	21
Promotion from Within	21
Equal Opportunity	21
Training for the Future	21
Progress and Development Reviews	21
Appendix—Working in the Home Office or Regional Office	22

tions that put off orientation programs run the risk of letting the new employees gain critical information about the company from current employees. This may not be in the best interests of the organization or the new employees.[9]

Orientation programs are effective if they transmit appropriate and timely information to new employees regarding values, norms, attitudes, and behaviors and if they benefit the organization as well as the employee. Reduced turnover and increased employee motivation and commitment to the organization have all been shown to be related to effective, realistic orientation activities.

Although orientation programs are an important part of the "joining-up process," they are only one part. Most orientation programs last for only a few hours and are done within the first week or two of employment. Occasionally there is an orientation follow-up a year or so later. But most employees take longer than just one or two weeks to acquire all the information contained in the orientation program. In addition, orientation programs do only part of the job of socialization. Therefore, other methods are also used.

Job Assignments. The important communicating aspects of job assignments are the characteristics of the initial job, the nature of early experiences on the job, and the first supervisor. As already indicated, the initial job often determines the new employee's future success. The more challenge and responsibility the job offers, the more likely it is that an employee will be successful with the organization.[10] A challenging (but not overwhelming) job assignment communicates that the organization believes the employee can do well and that the organization values him or her. Many times organizations give new employees simple jobs or rotate them through departments to get a feel for different jobs. But employees may interpret these practices to mean that the organization does not yet trust their abilities or loyalties.[11]

The supervisor is critical in the first job assignment.

Closely related to the first job are employees' initial experiences, which are often provided by supervisors. Here's an example of how a supervisor can communicate to an employee in order to get him or her to play a more humble role.

> . . . from an engineering company where a supervisor had a conscious and deliberate strategy for dealing with what he considered to be unwarranted arrogance on the part of engineers whom they hired. He asked each new man to examine and diagnose a particular complex circuit, which happened to violate a number of textbook principles, but actually worked very well. The new man would usually announce with confidence, even after an invitation to doublecheck, that the circuit could not possibly work. At this point the manager would demonstrate the circuit, tell the new man that they had been selling it for several years without customer complaint and demand that the new man figure out why it did work. None of the men so far tested were able to do it, but all of them were thoroughly chastened and came to the manager anxious to learn where their knowledge was inadequate and needed supplementing. According to this manager, it was much easier from this point on to establish a good give-and-take relationship with his new man.[12]

These types of experiences help prepare (socialize) new employees for the acquisition of the appropriate values, norms, attitudes, and behaviors. If new employees are appropriately socialized (brought in) to the organization, it will have fewer motivational concerns later on (see Chapter 10). Note that an important part of this process begins with the realistic job preview.

People tend to behave as they are expected to behave.

Supervisors of new employees can also serve as role models and set expectations. The positive influence that the supervisor's expectations can have on the new employee is referred to as the **Pygmalion effect.** If the supervisor believes that the new employee will do well, this belief will be conveyed to the employee, who will be apt to live up to those expectations. [13]

Content of Communicating with Employees

In addition to communicating with employees at the time they join the organization, it is necessary to communicate on a regular and consistent basis. The questions that many supervisors ask at this point are (1) "What should we tell our employees?" and (2) "What do employees want to hear?" Since answering the second question often provides an answer to the first, it is appropriate to first look at what employees want to know about.

What Do Employees Want to Know? In a recent study among forty companies in the United States and Canada the topic that emerged as being of greatest importance to know was the "organization's future plans." [14] The topic of least importance was "personal news of other employees such as their birthdays and anniversaries." A breakdown and ranking of the top ten topics indicated are shown in Exhibit 7.4.

Exhibit 7.4
Top Ten Topics and Percentage of Employees Very Interested or Interested in Hearing about Them. (Adapted from "What to Tell Employees," *Personnel Administrator,* August 1981, p. 9.)

Topic	Percentage Very Interested or Interested
1. Organization's future plans	95.0
2. Personnel practices and policies	90.3
3. Productivity improvement	89.7
4. Job-related information	89.4
5. Job advancement opportunities	88.4
6. Effects on external events	87.6
7. Organization's competitive position	87.1
8. News of other departments	85.9
9. How my job fits in	85.6
10. How organization uses its profits	83.2

Although orientation programs and job assignments are critical in communicating effectively with employees, they are essentially forms of downward communication. While **downward communication** is certainly necessary in conveying expectations, performance standards, goals and opportunities to employees, it is only one-half of the communicating process. As organizations are beginning to recognize the value of **upward communication,** they are writing corporate policy statements to the effect of encouraging "open communications". Besides being the other half of the communicating process, effective upward communication has many values to supervisors as well as employees.

Organizations must work hard to get good upward communications.

Personnel must train managers in communication skills.

Value to Supervisors. Many of management's best ideas are sown on cold and sour soil, not tilled and prepared in advance for the information. Where attitudes and feelings are transmitted freely upward, however, management is forewarned of possible failure and can better prepare the seed bed before its own ideas are broadcast. Upward communications tell us not only when employees are ready to hear messages, but also how well they are likely to accept our message when it is told. There is no better means of knowing whether downward communications have been received and believed than upward communications.

Finally, effective upward communication encourages employees to offer ideas of value to themselves and the organization. The need here is for supervisors and organizations to devise and use every form of upward communication that will draw these ideas from all employees likely to know about and be affected by a communication.

Listening is hard but the rewards make it all worthwhile.

Value to Employees. Upward communication helps satisfy many basic human needs. Most employees look upon themselves as having inherent worth at least as great as the personal worth of their supervisors. This is true even if they feel their own inferiority in managerial ability or in some other skill. They often think, just as you and I do, that because they are individual human beings they have certain values and rights. The extent of these rights and management's reaction are discussed in the next chapter. This sense of personal worth is always injured when people do not get a chance to express their ideas—when they are merely told, without opportunity to comment or reply. This principle applies even if the *telling* (the downward communication) is very well done. Supervisors respect their employees' dignity when they allow, or better still invite, employees to express their reactions to what is told—preferably before action is taken.

FOR YOUR CAREER

A mechanism that many organizations attempt to use to encourage upward communication is the suggestion system. Although these systems are not always successful, the characteristics of those that are include:

1. All suggestions are responded to with reasons for acceptance or rejection within a reasonable time.
2. Useful suggestions are rewarded. Employees receive rewards of money and recognition.
3. Ideas from the suggestion system are not stolen by management.
4. The suggestion system is made known to all and is respected.
5. Management and employees have a history of mutual trust and respect.

Now that we have established what should be communicated and the desirability of downward as well as upward communications, it is useful to examine several skills that make the process of communicating—that is, getting the information from one person to another—more effective. This is the second major component of communicating with employees shown in Exhibit 7.2.

SKILLS IN COMMUNICATING EFFECTIVELY

Since most managers spend so much time communicating with employees it is advantageous to do it as effectively as possible.[15] In attaining this objective, it is necessary to

- Remove barriers to upward communication
- Engage in several talking principles, both verbal and nonverbal
- Listen more efficiently
- Provide effective feedback

Barriers to Upward Communication

Even though supervisors may appreciate the need for effective upward communication, they may not translate this need into action. It becomes apparent at once that to swim up the stream of communication is a much harder task than to float downstream. The currents of resistance, inherent in the temperament and habits of supervisors and employees and in the complexity and structure of modern organizations, are persistent and strong. Let us examine some of these deterrents to upward communication.

Barriers Involving Characteristics of the Organization. The *physical distance* between supervisors and employees impedes upward communications in several ways. Communication becomes difficult and infrequent when supervisors are isolated so as to be seldom seen. In large organizations executives are located in headquarters or divisional centers, at points not easily reached by their employees. In smaller organizations their offices are sometimes remotely placed, or they hold themselves needlessly inaccessible.

Movement of information through *many levels* dilutes or distorts it. Since supervisors consciously or unconsciously select and edit the information they pass up, the more levels of supervision, or filter stations, it passes through before it reaches the top, the less accurate it becomes. Also, in a large company with hierarchy of management, contacts become fewer and more hurried as one ascends in the organization. A group leader contacts his or her workers more often than a president contacts his or her vice presidents.

Barriers Involving Characteristics of Supervisors. Supervisors' attitudes and behaviors in listening play a vital role in either encouraging or discouraging communications. If the supervisor seems anxious to get the interview over with or appears to be impatient with the employees, or annoyed or distressed by the subject being discussed, this attitude will place an insurmountable communications barrier between them in the future.

Supervisors may fall into the familiar error of thinking that *no news is good news,* whereas lack of complaint or criticism is often a symptom that upward communication is working in very low gear; or they may assume, often wrongly, that they know what employees think or feel; or they may have such an exaggerated sense of duty that they feel it disloyal to listen to complaints, especially if made intemperately. This attitude tends to discourage employees with justifiable complaints from approaching their supervisors.

Barriers must be removed if communications are to be effective.

No news isn't good news, it's no news.

Supervisors often *resist becoming involved with the personal problems of their employees*. This resistance to listening may affect the employees' willingness to communicate up on other matters more directly related to the job. Moreover, job problems and personal problems are often closely linked, and it is difficult to discuss the one without the other.

One of the strongest deterrents to communication up is the *failure of management to act* on undesirable conditions previously brought to its attention. The result is that the workers lose faith both in the sincerity of management and in the value of communication.

Failure to follow up on ideas reduces the chances of getting more ideas.

By communicating we convey the message: "We care."

Barriers Involving Employees.   Communications down may run more freely than communications up because supervisors are free to call in employees and talk to them at will. The employees do not have the same freedom to intrude upon their supervisors' time. There are exceptions to this, however, as described in the *Personnel in Action* inserts on "Big Jim." In communicating up, employees must explain themselves and get acceptance from one who has greater status and authority. The employees' difficulties are greater also because they likely to be less fluent and persuasive than the supervisors who communicate down to them.

PERSONNEL IN ACTION

'Big Jim' Is Watching at RMI Co., And Its Workers Like It Just Fine

NILES, Ohio—When James Daniell arrived here nearly four years ago to take over as president of RMI Co., the gloom was knee-deep and rising.

RMI, an integrated titanium producer and a unit of U.S. Steel Corp. and National Distillers & Chemical Corp., had suffered big losses. The company was about to be convicted of price fixing. Management was lackluster, and employe morale was in the dumps.

Since then, RMI has done a flip-flop. Unit sales last year were up 500% from 1976, and productivity has soared. In late 1978, the company reported its first quarterly profit in four years. It's tempting to search for a sophisticated answer for the turnaround: an expensive consulting study, perhaps, or a couple of super-smart MBAs.

Big Jim Speaks

Well, the titanium market has improved, but forget the rest. Mr. Daniell credits most of the improvement to an employe relations program that is pure corn—a mixture of schmaltzy sloganeering, communication, and a smile at every turn.

"If You See a Man Without a Smile, Give Him One of Yours," says a big sign hanging on a factory wall. "People Rarely Succeed at Anything Unless They Enjoy Doing It," says another. The slogans are signed: "Big Jim."

Mr. Daniell was captain of the Cleveland Browns professional football team in 1945, which probably accounts for the rah-rah style and such homilies as: "I'm the quarterback, I make the calls, the union is the line, and my management team, the backfield, will get through the holes they open."

"Believe it or not, for a big, dumb football player I have a philosophy," Mr. Daniell adds. "Do unto others as you would have them do unto you."

Union in the Know

This new low in cliches has helped produce a new high in morale. "He calls us into meetings and lets us know what's going on, which is unheard of in other industries," says Charles Corman, president of the Clerical and Technical Union local.

Robert Paul, a Lockheed Corp. vice president and an RMI customer, calls the Daniell method, "A management approach this whole country needs to get production up."

The company's logo, a yellow smile face, grins from stationery, from the front of the factory and from workers' hard hats. Mr. Daniell has renamed the Niles headquarters Smiles, Ohio.

Riding through the factory in a golf cart, Mr. Daniell, 62 years old, waves and jokes with workers. He says he knows all 700 Niles employes by name. "If I don't wave to these people, they pout," he says.

Cindy Ris, *Wall Street Journal*, August 4, 1980. Reprinted by permission of the *Wall Street Journal*, © Dow Jones & Company, 1981. All Rights Reserved.

Principles of Verbal Communication

For a person, such as the supervisor or you in your day-to-day communications, communicating should follow several principles and, if adhered to make communicating much more effective.

1. *Seek to clarify ideas before communicating.* The more systematically the problem or idea to be communicated is analyzed the clearer it becomes. This is the first step toward effective communication. Many communications fail because of inadequate planning.

2. *Follow up on communication.* The best efforts at communication may be wasted, if follow-up is not done to see how well the message was put across. It is often useful to have the listener repeat the message just sent.

3. *Be sure actions support communications.* In the final analysis, the most persuasive kind of communication is not what is said but what is done. When a person's actions or attitudes contradict the words, we tend to discount what has been said.

4. *Last, but by no means least: Seek not only to be understood but to understand— be a good listener.* Listening is one of the most important, most difficult, and most neglected skills in communication. It demands that we concentrate not only on the explicit meanings another person is expressing, but on the implicit meanings, unspoken words, and undertones that may be far more significant.

Principles of Nonverbal Communication

We talk a great deal about sending wordless messages. Since these messages are without words, we seldom respond with words. If someone gives us a message with tone of voice, we usually respond, with tone of voice; if someone communicates something to us with body position, we may respond in like manner, unless we are uncertain of the meaning of the message being sent. Then we might respond with a "What's wrong?" or "What are you trying to tell me?" But our willingness to risk asking would depend a lot on our relationship to the other person.

Actions do speak louder than words.

Greater Awareness. Consequently, we need to develop more than an intellectual understanding of nonverbal communication. Intellectual understanding needs to be combined with the emotional, the "feeling" that constitutes a human response to another human. When people do not speak the same language, they have to rely on nonverbal communication, and some people do remarkably well.

Increased Sensitivity. Some persons seem to possess a natural understanding and sensitivity. They communicate genuine interest in the other person, and a warmth and acceptance that transcends cultural boundaries. In a group of people who do not speak your language, you find yourself liking some people more than others, feeling closer to some than to others, and feeling that you can categorize many of them in categories you use in your own culture. All of this is based on nonverbal cues. What are these cues? Do you send them to others? How do you know or not know if they are received?

Listening Efficiently

Just as often as we forget to pay attention to nonverbal cues in communications, we forget to listen efficiently. This is because most people are not trained to listen.

What We Communicate by Listening. By constantly listening to a speaker you are conveying the idea that "I'm interested in you as a person, and I think that what you feel is important. I respect your thoughts, and even if I don't agree with them, I know that they are valid for you."

It's amazing how poorly we listen.

But We Usually Listen Inefficiently. The average person has only about 30 percent listening efficiency. This means we hear only 30 percent of what we listen to. We spend about 40 percent of our day listening. Put these two things together and we find that the average person is only 30 percent efficient for 40 percent of the typical day. From a business and personal standpoint this could be disastrous.

Efficient Listening. Since it is necessary to become more efficient in our listening skills, here are four ways to do that.

1. *Active Listening.* Among his or her essential responsibilities, the manager has to develop employee potential, delegate responsibility, and achieve cooperation. To do so, the manager must have, among other abilities, the ability to listen intelligently and carefully to others. This kind of listening is called **"active listening"** because the listener has a very definite responsibility. The listener does not passively absorb the words that are spoken, but actively tries to grasp the facts and feelings in what is said.

2. *What To Do?* Just what does active listening entail, then? Basically, it requires that we get inside the speaker, that we grasp, from his or her point of view, just what he or she is communicating to us. More than that, we must convey to the speaker that we are seeing things from his or her point of view.

These effective listening skills should be taught in personnel training programs.

3. *Listen For Total Meaning.* Any message a person tries to get across usually has two components: the *content* of the message and the *feeling* or attitude underlying this content. Both are important; both give the message meaning.

4. *Respond To Feelings.* In some instances the content is far less important than the feeling that underlies it. To catch the full flavor or meaning of the message one must respond particularly to the feeling component.

Providing Effective Feedback

If we wish to reduce misunderstanding and conflict, it is important that our perception of reality be tested against another. One way is through the *effective use of feedback,* something that is seldom accomplished except through a particular kind of experience with other people achieved in a training situation. **Feedback** is communication to a person (or group) regarding the effect that that person's or group's behavior has on another person's perceptions, feelings, and reactions. *It is not criticism; criticism is evaluative, feedback is descriptive.* Evaluation is difficult to accept, and more difficult to work with constructively. Feedback provides the individual with information, data she or he can use in performing his or her own evaluation. If the person is not being evaluated, she or he is not as likely to react so defensively.

Feedback helps, criticism hurts.

Characteristics of Effective Feedback.   There are many things that make feedback effective, here are ten:

1. It is *specific* rather than general.
2. It is *focused on behavior* rather than on the person.
3. It takes into account the *needs of the receiver* of the feedback.
4. It is directed toward behavior that the *receiver can do something about.*
5. It is *solicited,* rather than imposed.
6. It involves *sharing of information* rather than giving advice.
7. It is *well-timed.* In general, immediate feedback is most useful (depending, of course, on the person's readiness to hear it, support available from others, and so forth).
8. It involves the *amount of information the receiver can use* rather than the amount the giver would like to give.
9. It concerns what is said or done, or how—not why.
10. It is *checked* to ensure clear communication.

Practice these in your own personal relationships.

METHODS OF COMMUNICATING WITH EMPLOYEES

Although there are many methods of communicating with employees—for example, company bulletin boards, memos, company newspapers, loudspeakers, and regular meetings—three are especially important to discuss in more detail: the first because it involves the majority of companies' communication with employees, the second because it is the major way to find out what the employees are thinking, and the third because it is a newer method. Since this third method, **quality circles,** is also a popular method for improving quality of work life and productivity, it is discussed in Chapter 16 rather than here. First we start with the major way of finding out what "the troops" are thinking, doing, and perceiving.[16]

Methods of communicating:
• Survey
• Supervisor
• Quality circles

The Organizational Survey

More and more personnel managers are becoming aware of the potential value of conducting an organizational survey. The task is not easy, however, since there are many things to survey and many steps in conducting the survey.

Survey work is critical to doing personnel management effectively.

What Do We Measure? In each of the applications of personnel data discussed so far, the data gathered have been either measures of job performance itself or predictors of job performance, such as tests and background characteristics. But the personnel manager often has need of other types of data. For example, in order to develop ways to improve employee performance, the personnel manager needs to measure how the employees perceive their environment, including the consequences of job performance, qualities of feedback, task interference characteristics, and aspects of goal setting. It is equally necessary to gather data on the employee's perceptions of the quality of work life and employee stress. This is not to say, however, that the objective qualities of the job are not important. Only with at least these two pieces of data can the personnel manager begin to make useful changes in job design.

It is also important to know how employees react to the environment and job qualities. Many of these reactions are symptoms of employee stress, which include such physical measures as blood pressure and heart rate. Since one of our criteria for the effectiveness of personnel management is employee health, additional measures of employee reactions may become more common.

These need to be measured in order to take steps to improve an organization and demonstrate personnel effectiveness.

Thus organizational surveys can measure the following:

- *Employee perceptions:* role awareness, job involvement, satisfaction, role conflict, qualities of the job, interpersonal qualities such as supervision and organizational characteristics
- *Employee reactions:* feelings such as satisfaction and physiological responses such as heart rate and blood pressure
- *Behaviors:* employee performance, absenteeism, and turnover

Purposes of an Organizational Survey. An organizational survey serves several purposes. First, it helps determine the effectiveness of personnel functions and activities. Second, it measures the quality of the organization's internal environment and, therefore, helps to locate elements that require improvement. Finally, the survey aids in the development of programs to make the necessary changes, and then it helps in evaluating the effectiveness of these programs.

Steps in an Organizational Survey. There are several important steps and issues for the personnel manager—or an outside consultant—to consider when conducting an organizational survey.[17] These become necessary, however, only after top management has given its support for the survey.

As the first step, the personnel manager must consider the following:

- The specific employee perceptions and responses that should be measured
- The methods that will be used to collect the data, including observations, questionnaires, interviews, and personnel records
- The reliability and validity of the measures to be used
- The people from whom the data will be collected—all employees, managerial employees only, a sample of employees, or only certain departments within the organization
- The timing of the survey and the way to make the survey part of a longer-term effort
- The types of analyses that will be made with the data
- The specific purposes of the data—to determine reasons for the organization's turnover problem, for example

This last consideration is important, because by identifying the problem, the personnel manager can determine which models or theories will be relevant to the survey. Knowing which model or theory to use tells the personnel manager what data are needed and what statistical techniques will be necessary to analyze the data. The next step is the actual collection of data. Three things are important here. It must be decided who will administer the questionnaire—the line manager, someone from the personnel department, or someone from outside the organization. It must also be decided where, when, and in what size groups the data will be collected. Both these considerations are influenced by the method used to gather the data. For example, if a questionnaire is used, larger groups are more feasible than if interviews are conducted. Finally, employee participation in the survey must be ensured. This can be done by gathering the data during company time and by providing feedback—for instance, by promising employees that the results of the survey will be made known to them.

The actual feedback process is the third step in the survey. As part of this process, the data are analyzed according to the purposes and problems for which they were collected. The results of the analysis can then be presented by the personnel department to the line managers, who in turn discuss the results with their employees. The feedback sessions can be used to develop solutions to any problems that are identified and to evaluate the effectiveness of programs that may already have been implemented on the basis of results of an earlier survey.

The extent to which employees actually participate in the development of solutions during the feedback process depends on the philosophy of top management. Organizations that are willing to survey their employees to ask how things are going are also usually willing to invite employee participation in deciding to make things better. It is this willingness that allows organizational surveys to be used most effectively.

A Sample Questionnaire. "The paper-and-pencil questionnaire is the most common method of obtaining survey data."[18] Exhibit 7.5 is a questionnaire asking students to describe the degree to which they know what's expected of them (role awareness) and how much conflict they face in doing what's expected (role conflict). Measures of role awareness and role conflict have been used extensively in organizational surveys; typical items have been reworded here to apply to a classroom situation. To use this questionnaire, circle the appropriate numbers before reading further.

Once you have completed the questionnaire, add the numbers you circled in items 1, 6, 7, 9, 10, and 12. This is your *role awareness* score. Now add the remaining numbers you circled to determine your *role conflict* score. Next, circle the response below that you think best describes your overall level of satisfaction with the class:

Questionnaire surveys are an efficient way to collect a lot of information.

	Strongly Disagree	Disagree	Neutral	Agree	Strongly Agree
All in all, I am very satisfied with this class	1	2	3	4	5

How does your score on satisfaction compare with your scores on role conflict and role awareness? Are you high on all three or low on all three, or do you have a mixed pattern?

Exhibit 7.5
Role Awareness and Role Conflict Questionnaire (Adapted from J. R. Rizzo, R. J. House, and S. I. Lirtzman, "Role Conflict and Ambiguity in Complex Organizations," *Administrative Science Quarterly*, no. 15 (1970) p. 156.)

Read each classroom characteristic, and select the scale number that best reflects your opinion.

				Definitely characteristic of this class
Definitely not characteristic of this class				
1	2	3	4	5

1. I know what my responsibilities are.	1 2 3 4 5
2. I receive assignments without the time to complete them.	1 2 3 4 5
3. Part of my grade depends on a group project.	1 2 3 4 5
4. I have to go through all sorts of hassles to find out what's expected of me.	1 2 3 4 5
5. Good work or a good idea is not really recognized by the instructor.	1 2 3 4 5
6. I have been given clearly planned goals and objectives for this class.	1 2 3 4 5
7. I know how to study for this class to do well.	1 2 3 4 5
8. I do things that are apt to be accepted by the instructor at one time but not accepted at another time.	1 2 3 4 5
9. I feel certain about how much I am responsible for.	1 2 3 4 5
10. I know exactly what is expected of me.	1 2 3 4 5
11. I have to do things that can be done in different ways.	1 2 3 4 5
12. Explanations of what has to be done are clear.	1 2 3 4 5
13. I work on unnecessary things.	1 2 3 4 5
14. The amount of work I am expected to do is fair.	1 2 3 4 5

What is the importance of these scores? In most organizational surveys, employees are asked for their perceptions of and attitudes toward many aspects of the organization. These surveys generally reveal very definite patterns. Satisfaction, for instance, tends to have a negative relationship with role conflict but a positive relationship with role awareness. Role conflict and role awareness are also frequently related to employee performance and stress. Therefore, an employee's role conflict and role awareness scores reveal a great deal more about the employee. Other variables—for example, the employee's supervisor, the job, and the extent of the employee's perceived participation in decision making—also tell a lot about the employee.

Effective Supervisory Communications with Employees

Supervisors are the critical communications link. Training programs should be provided for them.

One of the most important opportunities for effective communications to occur is between the supervisor and the employees.

Well-informed and communications-conscious supervisors are the key to the establishment and maintenance of a good employee relations climate. The most expensive multimedia productions extolling the excellent policies and programs of good old XYZ Company won't buy happiness or contentment. In fact, in an atmosphere of hostility, apathy, and distrust, such efforts can easily be counter-productive.

Survey after survey after survey shows conclusively that immediate supervisors are by far the most important influence on employees' attitudes toward their work and their employers. That influence can be positive, negative, or neutral.[19]

In this section we will see how supervisors, through the style of their communications behaviors, can produce a positive influence on their employees. Knowing this, personnel can train supervisors in these styles of communications. Note that while we have already considered the communication *skills* needed by supervisors and any other people communicating, we have not examined the *style* the supervisor should use in communicating with employees.

Style of supervisory communication refers to *what, how,* and *when* the supervisor communicates to employees that influences their level of role awareness, satisfaction, and performance. Although there are many styles (or communication behaviors) supervisors can use in passing along information to their employees, only seven are described here. Examples of each are given to help illustrate each style.

There are many styles of supervisory communication; some are more effective than others.

Achievement Communication Behavior. By this behavior the supervisor conveys statements of goals, challenge, confidence, and high expectations to the employee. Such a statement may be "You know, Sam, that I really feel you can do this job, even though it is especially complex and difficult." Achievement communication behavior builds the self-worth of the employee and gives him or her confidence that he or she has the ability to do the job. Knowing one has the *ability* to do the job can reduce or eliminate a potentially stressful situation.

Ego Deflation Communication Behavior. This is the reverse of achievement communication behavior. As suggested by the title, this supervisory behavior reduces the employee's feeling of self-worth, reduces the employee's self-confidence, and makes the employee feel incapable of doing anything. Ego deflation communication is captured in this statement of a supervisor to an employee: "You know, I can never trust you to do it right!" A nonverbal communication of ego deflation would be closely watching or checking up on the employee. The phrase "he's always on my back" is a classic description of ego deflation communication by a supervisor.

Contingent Approval Communication Behavior. This aids the employee in knowing what is expected and how well he or she is doing. The supervisor communicates a *contingent* approval by praising or otherwise rewarding the employee when performance is good. The approval or reward given by the supervisor is called contingent because whether or not it is given depends upon the employee's performance. The phrase "That's really a good job, Mary" is an example of contingent approval communication. That phrase lets Mary know how well she is doing and also that she is performing as expected. This communication behavior tends, however, to be historically oriented, not future oriented. If jobs are constantly changing, the employee who receives only contingent approval may be in a state of uncertainty about future expectations, since past behaviors and rewards may not continue.

Contingent Disapproval Communication Behavior. This communication style lets the employee know what is *not* rewarded, or more specifically what results in punishment or disapproval. A supervisor engaging in this communication behavior may tell an employee "You really screwed up that job" or "I could have done *that* better myself." The employee suffers from negative or embarrassing information or feedback from the supervisor because the performance level wasn't up to par. In order to get the most benefit from this communication behavior, the supervisor should specify the *exact* behavior or performance of the employee that was below par. Frequently, because the supervisor wasn't specific enough, the employee doesn't know why he or she was reprimanded. In addition to being related to specific behavior, the contingent disapproval should be aimed only at the behavior or performance of the employee, not at the employee—such as "You're really a crummy worker."

Since both contingent behaviors are useful for improving poor performance, they are discussed again in Chapter 10.

Participative Communication Behavior. This communication style of the supervisor can be helpful in establishing future goals for the employee and/or deciding how best to do a job. This communication behavior usually refers to decisions that should be made and can refer to how and when to do things and to what can and should be done. This behavior is especially useful when the employee is faced with a difficult job or when the job changes without new performance levels and goals being established. Used in these conditions, participative communication behavior can clarify what is expected and what is rewarded and even can reduce some conflicts because the supervisor and employee discuss and iron out inconsistencies or conflicts. Participation could be extended to include more than two supervisors of an employee and is then perhaps the most useful tool in reducing conflict.

There are occasions, however, when an employee, regardless of the situation, would prefer just to be told what to do. There are also organizational conditions making participation less effective. These are discussed in Chapter 16.

Directive Communication Behavior. This is especially appropriate when the employee wants directions and guidance or when circumstances warrant it, such as when the employee is joining the organization, when changes are being made by others and need to be communicated to the employee, and when time may preclude participation. Directive communication also may prove appropriate when the employee is not performing well because he or she doesn't really know the desired performance. When directive communication is used with contingent disapproval, the combination is sometimes called *constructive criticism*. This behavior is used frequently by sports coaches to get the best performances from their players in a short period of time.

Directive communication behavior sounds like "Here's what I want you to do today." Directive behavior may refer to both what to do and what the goals are, as well as to how to get to them. For example, "Here's what I want you to do today (goals), and here's how I want you to do it (how to)." If the employee doesn't want or have the information to determine what to do or how to do something, directive communication behavior is appropriate. The end result is an employee who knows better what is expected and how to do it.

Supportive Communication Behavior. This one indicates concern for the employee as a person, not as an instrument of production. This quality helps increase the trust level between the supervisor and the employee. Supportive communication is really necessary for the preceding six supervisory communication behaviors to be effective. For a supervisor it's necessary to be good, to be supportive. A supportive supervisor may say to an employee: "Good morning, Ruth. How are you feeling today?" Nonverbal supportive communication includes keeping commitments, being on time, and removing some barriers of distinction between supervisor and employee.

Supportive communication has nothing *directly* to do with an employee knowing what is expected, how to do something, or what is rewarded. Its impact on employee performance is indirect through increasing trust between supervisor and employee to facilitate other supervisory communication behaviors.

EVALUATING COMMUNICATING WITH EMPLOYEES

As shown in Exhibit 7.1, when organizations and supervisors are communicating effectively with employees, several favorable outcomes are likely to occur. Looking at Exhibit 7.1, we see both quality of work life and productivity outcomes. Although the legal considerations must be served, these two categories are generally used in evaluating communications. Those related to productivity include performance, safety, accidents, absenteeism, and turnover. Satisfaction and job involvement are related to quality of work life.

Communications and Productivity

When organizations and supervisors start communicating effectively with employees, they convey expectations, goals, and opportunities to the employees. They also find out what their employees are thinking and what they want. When this is done with proper communication skills, supervisory communication styles, and survey techniques, employees are likely to respond with increased performance and decreased absenteeism and turnover.

Because it is difficult and costly for an organization to launch several programs aimed at improving communications with employees, it is useful to first conduct an organizational survey to find out the current state of affairs. Perhaps the employees are really unsure of what is expected. But further analysis shows the uncertainty is isolated to only those employees who have the same supervisor. Without knowing that second piece of information, the organization could have gone ahead and changed its orientation program. But with the added information, that one supervisor can be put in a supervisory training program designed for supervisory communication styles.

This diagnosis through the organizational survey makes it more likely that more effective orientation and training programs can be designed and that the productivity indicators will increase. After the first survey step is taken, the relative effectiveness of different programs can be measured.

Communications and Quality of Work Life

Just as diagnosis is critical in the development of programs to improve communications to enhance productivity, so it is also when an enhanced quality of work life is desired. Thus the organizational survey should be used here as a first step in determining what really needs to be done (if anything) to improve communications. Remember that the survey may indicate that other things besides those related to communication skills and supervisory styles need to be improved.

If properly diagnosed, however, improved communications can get employees more involved in their jobs and much more satisfied with the organization and their supervisors. Although these outcomes are more difficult to quantify in dollars and cents than the productivity outcomes can be, their level of change can be determined by comparing before and after measures. For example, a measure of satisfaction with supervisor before and after supervisors are trained in supervisory communication styles can be used to measure and compare the change due to the supervisory communication styles. Methods of evaluating training program effectiveness are also discussed in Chapter 14.

FACING THE CRITICAL ISSUES IN COMMUNICATING WITH EMPLOYEES

Now that we have examined many aspects associated with communicating with employees, you should be able to tell a personnel manager how to communicate effectively. You should also be able to respond in detail to the Critical Issues presented at the beginning of this chapter. To get you started, brief responses are offered here.

Issue: *If organizations are going to communicate more with their employees, what topics do they communicate? What do employees want to know?*

What organizations should communicate are those topics that employees want to hear about most. These topics include the future plans of the organization, the personnel policies of the organization, the plans for productivity improvements, and other job-related information. In general, they want to know about important task-related topics much more than they do about social topics such as whose birthday it is.

Issue: *Is it really important to have two-way communications? Do employees really want to tell what they think?*

Yes to both questions. It appears that many employees do want to tell management what they think, often in a constructive rather than a destructive vein. The success of some quality circle programs and semiautonomous work group programs (described in Chapter 16) suggest that employees not only want to participate but that they have good ideas. Thus two-way communications should be encouraged, unless management prefers not to hear what the employees have to say or will not act on employee ideas when they do hear them. If this is not the case and employees trust management, two-way communication can benefit everyone.[20]

Issue: *How can organizations get their supervisors and managers to be better communicators? What and how should they communicate?*

Of course no one changes unless they are dissatisfied with the current situation or the rewards for making the changes are irresistible. Assuming the existence of one or both of these conditions, supervisors should be trained in seven supervisor communication behaviors. These behaviors or styles communicate information to employees that influence their levels of what's expected, their satisfaction, and their performance. These seven behaviors include achievement communication, contingent disapproval and approval, ego deflation, participation in decision making, directiveness, and supportiveness.

Issue: *More and more is being said about organizational surveys. How can they be done? Are they good to do?*

Organizational surveys are vital to an organization. As a physical exam is to an individual, surveys tell organizations what is going on, where problem areas exist. They are also helpful in evaluating the success of programs done by organizations to improve upon the problem areas aimed at ultimately improving productivity or quality of work life. There are many aspects of doing surveys. They range from deciding what should be measured to the types of analysis that will be used on the data that are collected. For an organization conducting a survey for the first time, it is useful to get some expert help unless someone on the staff is well trained in survey work.

SUMMARY

Communicating effectively with employees is critical to organizations. It not only helps improve productivity and the quality of work life directly but improves it indirectly by establishing (through diagnosis) what else can be done. For example, a diagnosis through an organizational survey may reveal that employees are dissatisfied with the career opportunities. Such being the case, the personnel manager can work on career opportunities. Communicating with employees is also critical because it involves collecting data essential in justifying the importance of the other personnel activities to the organization.

In essence, communicating with employees is almost a foundation personnel activity necessary in order *to do* the other ones as effectively as possible and *to show* how effective they really are.

KEY CONCEPTS

information	downward communication
communicating	upward communication
formal communications	feedback
informal communications	active listening
orientation programs	style of communication
Pygmalion effect	quality circles

DISCUSSION QUESTIONS

1. What is the overall purpose in communicating effectively with employees? In what way does communicating effectively benefit the organization and the employees?

2. What three conditions must exist before communications benefit the organization and the individual?

3. What is the biggest mistake management can make in regard to labor-management relations?

4. Discuss two common ways organizations convey messages about organizational policies and practices?

5. What type of communication should be most valued by the superior? By the employee? Why?

6. What are the objectives in having skills to communicate effectively?

7. List the four principles of verbal communication.

8. What is meant by listening with greater awareness?

9. What is meant by providing effective feedback, and what are the characteristics of effective feedback?

10. What is measured by organizational surveys in determining whether communications have been effective in the organization?

CASE

Not Everything Goes as We Think It Will

In December 1982, the Executive Management Committee of the Foolproof Wood Stove Company made a recommendation to the President that the employee cafeteria be air-conditioned. The Committee's recommendation was based on the fact that the temperature in the foundry and other production areas was often over 100 degrees Fahrenheit, and, because company profits for the fiscal year had been good, the Committee felt that the employees were entitled to share in the profits. The air-conditioned cafeteria would represent management's appreciation of the employees' good work.

At the end of the following year, the Executive Management Committee held a meeting and reviewed the company's operation for the past year. Again, profits were high, labor productivity had been good, and labor turnover had been low. The Committee unanimously agreed that the employees deserved additional recognition for their work, and the group considered how to show management's appreciation. Since the company cafeteria had been air conditioned during the past year on the recommendation of the Committee, the Chairman and other members wondered if this sort of action was appreciated by the employees. In the course of discussion, the Chairman asked the Personnel Director to send a questionnaire to a sample of fifty employees and obtain their reaction to the air-conditioned cafeteria. The Committee agreed to meet again in two weeks and hear a report from the Personnel Director.

The Personnel Director mailed a simple form to fifty employees and asked for the following information: "Please state your reaction to the air-conditioned cafeteria." Of the fifty forms mailed, forty-six were returned. The answers could be classified generally as follows:

Reaction	Total Number
■"I didn't know it was air-conditioned."	16
■"I never eat there."	8
■"I wish the entire plant were air-conditioned."	8
■"If management could spend money like that, they should pay us more."	6
■"That is a cafeteria for management people."	4
■"It's O.K."	2
■Miscellaneous comments	2

Case Questions

1. Do the results of the survey indicate that the employees are ungrateful about the air conditioning in the cafeteria?
2. When should the survey of employee attitudes have been done?
3. Were the reasons management wanted to air-condition the cafeteria very good ones?
4. Based upon the survey results, what should have been done by management?

FOR YOUR CAREER

■ *You* are not communicating effectively until the *other* person understands you.
■ Remember that most people only *hear* 30 percent of what they are told.
■ You communicate as much verbally as nonverbally, and remember "action speaks louder than words."
■ Managers spend a majority of their days communicating with others. Their productivity and QWL can increase significantly with more effective communicating skills.
■ To be an *effective* manager and communicator, you need to empathize with your listener.
■ One of the most critical types of communication a manager can give an employee is *feedback,* positive as well as negative.

ENDNOTES

1. Gene Milbourn and Richard Cuba, "OD Techniques and the Bottom Line," *Personnel,* May–June 1981, pp. 34–42.

2. Roy G. Foltz, "Productivity and Communications," *Personnel Administrator,* July 1981, p. 12.

   Robert E. Kushell, "How to Reduce Turnover by Creating a Positive Work Climate," *Personnel Journal,* August 1979, pp. 551–552.

   Harold C. White, "Personnel Administration and Organizational Productivity: An Employee View," *Personnel Administrator,* August 1981, pp. 37–48.

3. "Quality Circles," *Personnel Journal,* June 1981, pp. 424–426.

4. Roy G. Foltz, "Labor Relations Communications," *Personnel Administrator,* March 1980, p. 20.

5. Fred K. Foulkes, "How Top Non-Union Companies Manage Employees," *Harvard Business Review,* September–October 1981, pp. 90–96.

6. "More Communication," *Personnel Journal,* September 8, 1981, p. 668.

7. Kushell, p. 552.

8. M. Lubliner, "Employee Orientation," *Personnel Journal,* April 1978, pp. 207–208.

9. Ibid.

   E. H. Schein, "Organizational Socialization and the Profession of Management," *Sloan Management Review,* 9, No. 2, (Winter 1968), p. 5.

10. D. Berlew and D. T. Hall, "The Socialization of Managers: Effects of Expectations on Performance," *Administrative Science Quarterly,* September 1966, pp. 207–233.

11. Schein, p. 5.

12. Schein, p. 3.

13. J. S. Livingston, "Pygmalion in Management," *Harvard Business Review,* July–August 1969, pp. 81–89.

14. Jeffrey P. Davidson, "Communicating Company Objectives," *Personnel Journal,* April 1981, pp. 292–293.

    Roy G. Foltz, "Communique," *Personnel Administrator,* July 1981, pp. 13, 86.

    "What to Tell Employees," *Personnel Administrator,* August 1981, p. 9.

15. John E. Baird, Jr., "Supervisory and Management Training Through Communication by Objectives," *Personnel Administrator,* July 1981, pp. 28–29.

    Richard I. Lester, "Leadership: Some Principles and Concepts," *Personnel Journal,* November 1981, pp. 868–870.

    John T. Samaras, "Two Way Communication Practices for Managers," *Personnel Journal,* August 1980, pp. 645–648.

16. Ellen Joy Berstein, "Employee Attitude Surveys: Perception vs. Reality," *Personnel Journal,* April 1981, pp. 300–305.

    Wallace Martin, "What Management Can Expect From An Employee Attitude Survey," *Personnel Administrator,* July 1981, pp. 75–79, 87.

    John F. Runge, "Dynamic Systems and the Quality of Work Life," *Personnel,* November–December 1980, pp. 13–24.

    Walter St. John, "In House Communications Guidelines," *Personnel Journal,* November 1981, pp. 872–878.

17. R. B. Dunham and F. J. Smith, *Organization Surveys*, (Glenview, Ill.: Scott, Foresman, 1979), Chapter 5, pp. 91–97.

18. Dunham and Smith, p. 13.

19. Foltz, "Labor Relations Communications."

20. Steven Briggs, "The Grievance Procedure and Organizational Health," *Personnel Journal*, June 1981, pp. 471–474.

Fred A. Olsen, "Corporations Who Succeed Through Communication—Three Case Studies," *Personnel Journal*, December 1979, pp. 858–864, 874.

Marsha Sinetar, "Mergers, Morale and Productivity," *Personnel Journal*, November 1981, pp. 863–867.

James P. Swann, Jr., "Formal Grievance Procedures in Non-Union Plants," *Personnel Administrator*, August 1981, pp. 66–70.

Chapter Outline

Critical Issues in Employee Rights

Employee Rights
Purposes and Importance of Employee Rights
Relationships of Employee Rights

Employee Rights to Job Security
Legal Considerations
Employer Strategies for Employee Job Security Rights

Employee Rights on the Job
Legal Considerations
Employer Strategies for Employee Rights on the Job

CHAPTER **8**

Employee Rights

Evaluating Employee Rights Activities

Facing the Critical Issues in Employee Rights

Summary

Key Concepts

Discussion Questions

Case

For Your Career

Endnotes

Personnel in the News

Firing

It used to be that employers could fire employees anytime, for any reason at all. That has changed. Now there are laws, unions, court orders, and public policies that limit an employer's prerogative to fire its employees, whether discharge comes as the result of discipline or a necessary reduction in the work force. What do these constraints mean in practical terms? For instance, can you still fire a high-salaried employee who is nearing retirement age because you can get a younger replacement for much less money? Can you fire the female employee who causes a row and files charges over alleged sex harassment when you don't think there's been any discrimination? Do you escape a discrimination charge if you fire minority employees because other employees or customers don't want to work with them? And what about the disabled employee who isn't making it on the job, or the recovered cancer patient who wants to come back to work? Can you fire them without risking liability for employment discrimination?

The answer to all of the above is no. Each of these employees is protected from discriminatory discharge by federal laws like Title VII, the Age Discrimination Act, the Rehabilitation Act, and a variety of state antidiscrimination laws that in many cases impose standards even stricter than the federal ones.

In addition, you must consider the powerful impact of union contracts, which usually spell out "just cause" for disciplinary discharge and define the order in which employees can be laid off.

Then there are the courts to contend with. Judicial interpretation of firings may include concepts like "public policy" (what is generally believed to be the best for the labor market as a whole), "equity" (what's commonly held to be fair), or "implied" contractual relations based on promises employers have made to employees, either orally or in written form—an employee handbook, for example. Some courts are also beginning to recognize a "wrongful discharge" when an employee is fired for challenging an employer's business practices, ethically or legally. And most courts accept the notion of "constructive discharge," in which the employer is said to pressure an employee into quitting voluntarily, thus escaping an accusation of firing. Courts find constructive discharge when the employer makes the job or work environment so unbearable that the employee has no reasonable choice but to quit. (From FEP Guidelines 192 (7) July 1981).

Fight for Rights

Employee rights long looked upon with suspicion by management are shaping up as the hottest personnel topic since affirmative action.

No longer just a catch phrase of radical workers, employee rights in recent years have gained respectability in a few board rooms and have been bolstered in the courts. A handful of pioneering companies already have laid down new corporate rules that safeguard worker privacy, guarantee a fair hearing for unhappy workers and protect dissenters inside the company from reprisals by vengeful bosses.

Union employees, of course have won many such rights through collective bargaining. But only about one-fourth of the nation's private work force is unionized.

(Many government workers also enjoy civil-service-type protection). By and large, all other jobholders serve at the whim of their employers.

So far, there has been more talk about these jobholders rights than action. "Of 20,000 companies in the U.S. with 500 or more employees, a few hundred are doing something," says Alan Westin, a Columbia University law professor and management consultant on employee rights. "Its just beginning to hit home that something is going on here. It will be common in the mid-1980s to address these issues."

Staunch opposition to employee rights persists at many companies, especially from middle managers. To them, employee rights sanctions second-guessing of management decisions. "Managers are very paranoid of anything they see as usurping their authority," says Frederica Dunn, who was the first ombudsman appointed to hear white-collar workers' complaints at General Electric Co.'s aircraft-engine group back in 1973. "Some managers were very uptight at first and let it be known subtly that they didn't want anyone in their departments to see me." (By Lawrence Ingrassis Wall Street Journal, *July 24, 1980, pp. 42–43. Reprinted by permission of* Wall Street Journal, *copyright Dow Jones and Company, 1980. All rights reserved).*

These two quotations briefly describe what is becoming a very prominent issue in effective personnel management: **employee rights.** As viewed by some managers, it means employees can "run the place." As viewed by some other managers and many employees, employee rights help ensure that management decisions are made on sound, justifiable basis and that employees are protected from arbitrary and vindictive actions by management.

Obviously, these views are in sharp contrast. Although it is unlikely the differences will be resolved soon, effective personnel management requires an appreciation of them. It also requires the personnel manager to be current on what the law says regarding employee rights and to develop strategies his organization can use in addressing employee rights.

What these two quotations do not do is to show the broad range of issues discussed under employee rights. Although there are numerous issues, the major ones affecting many employees are (1) protection against arbitrary dismissal, (2) privacy of personal records, (3) the right to a job, (4) prevention of plant closings without due process, and (5) the right to work environments that respect the individual. Since these are the issues that for today and through the 1980s are most likely to be the focus of employee rights, they are the essence of this chapter. The day-to-day challenges and headaches that the entire area of employee rights presents to an organization are illustrated in the Critical Issues identified by our personnel managers.

CRITICAL ISSUES IN EMPLOYEE RIGHTS

Of the many issues raised regarding employee rights, the four that emerged as most critical are

1. *Organizations seem to exist in a time when the employee can do no wrong; everything is the fault of the employer. Is there any way organizations can fire employees without being called on the carpet for it?*

2. *What can organizations do about sexual harassment? Many supervisors claim that what they used to regard as good-natured fun is now treated as a criminal offense.*

3. *If organizations have to close a plant or an office, how can it be done most effectively?*

4. *What rights of employees do organizations have to observe regarding their personnel files? Do they even have to keep employee records?*

Although much of the current discussion of employee rights addresses the right of employers to "terminate at will," employee rights cover much more. They cover, not only the employee's right to a job under almost any conditions, but also the employee's right to fair, just, and respectable treatment while on the job. Within these two broad areas of employee rights are several more specific issues including freedom from sexual harassment; the right of plant closing notification; due process treatment in discharge cases; freedom from discriminatory treatment based on sex, race, religion, or national origin; and the right to have personal records remain confidential. While some of these rights are protected by law or collective bargaining agreements, others are not. But if some rights are covered by only collective bargaining agreements, this leaves the 80 percent of the nonunionized work force unprotected.[1]

EMPLOYEE RIGHTS

Employee rights are regarded here as:

Those rights desired by employees regarding the security of their jobs and the treatment administered by their employer while on the job irrespective of whether or not those rights are currently protected by law or collective bargaining agreements.

Two Major Employee Rights:

- Job Security
- On the Job

In this chapter our discussion of employee rights regarding job security covers the topics of termination at will, the job as a property right, and unjustifiable and justifiable dismissals. Employee rights "on the job" that are discussed include privacy and confidentiality of personal information, cooperative acceptance and the right to notification of plant/office closings.

Purposes and Importance of Employee Rights

Respecting employee rights helps retain good employees.

While discussion on recruitment and selection focused on getting job applicants into organizations, we must now turn our attention to treating the job applicants who are hired. In the previous chapter, we considered the importance of making sure employees (new and old) are informed what's expected of them and what opportunities are available in the organization. Now we want to be sure that employees are treated fairly and with respect while on the job and in the case of terminating their employment. This, after all is the thrust behind employee rights.

Treating employees fairly and with respect is important to organizations. Where there is legal protection of employee rights—for example, the right to not be discriminated against in employment decision—violation can result in severe penalties and fines. The *Personnel in Action* insert is an example of such a use. Had their employee not been fired, Hunter Associates would have saved $35,000.

Some employee rights are legally protected and others are not.

FOR YOUR CAREER

In general, the thrust of the two-way match that underlies much of our discussion of the personnel activities is expanded by the concern for employee rights. Whereas the two-way match focused on matching (1) job demands and employee abilities and (2) job rewards and employee needs/values, concern for employee rights focuses on also matching (really balancing) on (3) management rights and employee rights.

PERSONNEL IN ACTION

Hunter Associates Settles Sex Bias/ Harassment Case for $35,000

Hunter Associates Laboratory, engineering supply firm in Reston, Va., agreed to pay $35,000 to a former employe who charged she had been sexually harassed and discriminated against on basis of sex.

Fairfax County Human Rights Commission said this was its largest negotiated settlement of discrimination charges.

Hildie Carney, a marketing coordinator, charged the company denied her a promotion because of her sex and that she was fired for insubordination when she refused to perform perfunctory secretarial duties. Carney also charged that during her six years with the company, a supervisor made continuous attempts to fondle her and had propositioned her. Hunter officials denied both charges and said the settlement was based on expediency rather than validity.

Fairfax human rights director Patricia Horton called the settlement a victory for local discrimination agencies and women who cannot afford to hire a private attorney to prosecute sexual complaints. Most of the agency's sexual harassment settlements have been for about $3,000 each, she said.

"This settlement represents the growing realization by both victims and employers in the workplace that sexual harassment is, indeed, a very important problem and that the only way this problem can be successfully addressed is if victims like Carney have the courage to bring these complaints to the attention of investigative agencies . . . and if employers like Hunter Lab are willing to give credibility to these complaints and take appropriate remedial action," Horton said.

The man charged with harassing Carney is no longer an employe of the company but works as a consultant to the firm.

(From *Fair Employment Guidelines*, October 26, 1981, p. 171.)

Becoming as costly to organizations is the violation of employee rights that do not have explicit legal protection. This means that no acts have been passed and no court decisions rendered that explicitly cover the employee right that is being violated. Thus, in many cases of employee rights, violation by the employer may be because she or he was naive or at best uncertain since there may be some law or court decision or an arbitrator's decision that only *could be* interpreted to apply. Nevertheless, you can't avoid a speeding ticket by saying you didn't know what the speed limit was. Similarly, organizations must pay the price for violating employee rights even though the employee may not have explicit legal protection.[2] For example, in June 1980, the Michigan Supreme Court ruled that Blue Cross/Blue Shield and MASCO Corporation each unfairly dismissed one employee because they had made oral assurances that the employees would not be fired as long as they performed their jobs. As a consequence, the Blue Cross/Blue Shield employee was awarded a $72,000 settlement, and the employee from MASCO was awarded $300,000. Although the companies said they were merely following the traditionally accepted **termination-at-will** practice, the court said that that practice cannot be used where employment contracts (explicit or implied) exist.[3] (See the *Personnel in Action* insert for a description of the termination-at-will doctrine.)

The price for not respecting employee rights can be high.

Relationships of Employee Rights

As shown in Exhibit 8.1 the topic of employee rights has extensive relationships with other personnel activities. Although these are not the only relationships it has, these are some of the most important.

Union-Management Relations.   Where unions exist, employee job security rights are generally protected by the union-management contract. Since less than 25 percent of the labor force is unionized, many workers are left without this protection. However, as more cases similar to those in the Blue Cross/Blue Shield and MASCO Corporation cases are settled, the protection afforded the union-management contract becomes less attractive. Nevertheless, if job security becomes a major issue, it may stimulate organizing activity.

Exhibit 8.1
Relationships and Aspects of Employee Rights

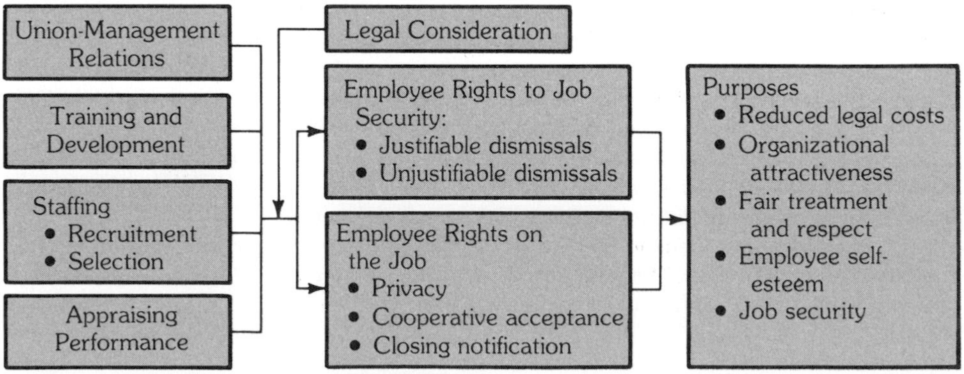

Training and Development. Supervisors are more likely to unjustifiably dismiss employees and commit sexual harassment offenses if they have not received effective training on these issues than if they have received such training. Consequently, a frequently suggested approach to the issue of sexual harassment is to develop an organizational policy on it and train all the supervisors and managers in avoiding it.

Staffing. Organizations that treat their employees fairly and with respect should be much more attractive places to work. If so, qualified job applicants should be easier to recruit and current employees more likely to stay, resulting in reduced recruiting costs and needs. Since these staffing activities are rather costly, observing employee rights can save organizations big dollars.

PERSONNEL IN ACTION

History of the Termination-at-Will Rule

The termination-at-will rule, which was developed in the United States nearly 100 years ago, was explained by one Tennessee court in 1884 in this way: "All may dismiss their employee(s) at will, be they many or few, for good cause, for no cause, or even for cause morally wrong without being thereby guilty of legal wrong [*Payne v. Western & A.R.R. Co.,* 81 Tenn. 507 (1884)]. Thereafter, the common law rule became so well established that, in the absence of some explicit contractual provision, every employment was considered to be an employment at will; employers could dismiss employees for any reason or for no reason at all. A century of court rulings provided a variety of justifications for the termination-at-will rule: If an employee can quit for any reason, an employer can discharge for any reason. The employment relationship should not be forced upon either the employer or the employee; seldom do both parties expect an employment relationship to be permanent. Some experts traced the rationale for the termination-at-will rule to those sections of the *Restatement of Agency* that provide that the employee be viewed as an agent of the employer and thus legally bound to obedience and loyalty to the employer. Hence the common law protection of the employer's right to discharge has traditionally been viewed as a protection of the organization's economic activity.

Early in this century many courts were adamant in their strict application of this common law rule. For example, the termination-at-will rule was used in a 1903 case, *Boyer v. Western Union Tel. Co.* [124 F 246, CCED Mo. (1903)], in which the court upheld the company's right to discharge its employees for union activities and indicated that the results would be the same if the company's employees had been discharged for being Presbyterians. Later on, in *Lewis v. Minnesota Mutual Life Ins. Co.* [37 NW 2d 316 (1949)], the termination-at-will rule was used to uphold the dismissal of the life insurance company's best salesman—even though no apparent cause for dismissal was given and the company had promised the employee lifetime employment in return for his agreement to remain with the company.

Only recently have court decisions and legislative enactments moved the pendulum of protection away from the employer and toward the rights of the individual employee through limitations on the termination-at-will rule.

(From S. A. Youngblood and Gary L. Tidwell, "Termination at Will: Some Changes in the Wind," *Personnel*, May–June 1981, p. 24.)

Appraising Performance.   A frequent ground for dismissal (in addition to using the termination-at-will doctrine) that supervisors often use is poor employee performance. When asked by the court to show evidence of such, supervisors and personnel managers are often unable to produce it. Often records of employee performance are never maintained. Sometimes employees are never made aware that they are performing inadequately or never given a chance to respond to charges of poor performance nor to improve (lack of due process). As a consequence of more suits against unjustifiable dismissal being won by the employees, organizations are likely to intensify efforts to train supervisors and managers in good appraisal practices, to maintain effective personnel records, and to establish grievance procedures to ensure due-process protection.

EMPLOYEE RIGHTS TO JOB SECURITY

Whereas once employers could dismiss employees at will, employers find it almost impossible to dismiss employees except under very restricted conditions. These conditions are being established, by and large, in the courts, by the National Labor Relations Board, and in contracts between unions and managements. Together these represent the legal considerations that organizations face in dealing with employee rights to job security.

Legal Considerations

The insert describing the history of the termination-at-will rule presents several historical and legal considerations that are used to justify termination of an employee at the will of the employer without cause. Although employers have relied on the termination-at-will doctrine over the years, using it today as a justifiable defense is proving to be less effective. This is because of several recent legal considerations.[4] These considerations include:

- Title VII of the Civil Rights Act of 1964, which prohibits discharge due to sex, race, religion, or national origin;
- The National Labor Relations Act of 1935 (NLRA), which prohibits discharge due to *union organizing activities* or for the assertion of rights under a union contract. Note that the NLRA, which established the National Labor Relations Board (NLRB), created a special situation in relation to discharge by the employer where employees are represented by a union. In this situation the termination-at-will doctrine essentially does not apply. What replaces this doctrine is the union-management contract. Although the contract provisions cannot violate statutory law, they can specify (either very explicitly or more generally) the conditions under which employers can be fired. One provision of most contracts is that, regardless of the charge against an employee as grounds for discharge, due process must be followed. This due process provision is reflected in contracts by a formal grievance procedure (this is discussed in detail in Chapter 19). Often the final step in the grievance process is the calling in of an outside arbitrator who ultimately decides if a discharge is justifiable.
- The Occupational Safety and Health Act of 1970, which prohibits discharge for resistance to work under unsafe conditions (*Whirlpool Corp.* v. *Marshall* [1980]);

- Court decisions like *Petermann v. International Brotherhood of Teamsters* (1959) and *Ness v. Hocks* (1975), which protect employees against discharge for failing to do what the employer ordered; note, however, that this protection may not be afforded to employees in states whose laws stipulate that (because of the termination-at-will or employment-at-will doctrine) employees can be fired for any or no reason;

- Court decisions like those handed down by the Michigan Supreme Court (*Toussaint v. Blue Cross/Blue Shield* [1980] and *Ebling v. Masco Corporation* [1980]) protecting against discharge if there is a *written or implied contractual agreement* between employer and employee;

- Court decisions like *Morge v. Beeke Rubber Co.* (1974) that protect employees from discharge for retaliation or malice that is not in the best interests of our economic system or the public good; and

- Court decisions like the *Board of Regents of State Colleges v. Roth* (1972) and *Perry v. Sindermann* (1972) that protect workers from discharge when *due process* protection has not been given by the employer.

As indicated in the discussion of legal consideration, there are a significant number of laws and acts that support an employee's right to job security from being terminated at will (or without cause). Yet, after all is said and done the employer still retains the right to termination without cause. Granted, however, this right is shrinking and is gradually being taken in the direction of **termination for good cause.** This would be similar to **termination for just cause** found in union-management agreements where workers are unionized. See the *Personnel in Action* insert "Good-Cause Compromise" for a description.

Although termination for good cause has not been an explicitly accepted doctrine for nonunion organizations, the decisions that courts are rendering suggest that the safest grounds for discharge include

Termination for:
- No cause (at will)
- Good cause
- Just cause

- Incompetence in performance that does not respond to training
- Gross or repeated insubordination
- Too many unexcused absences
- Repeated lateness
- Verbal abuse
- Physical violence
- Falsification of records
- Drunkenness on the job
- Theft

Although many discharge situations are far from clearcut, it may be said with certainty that employers cannot fire employees for

- Engaging in union activity, as long as it's peaceful and lawful, or taking concerted action (union or nonunion) to protest wages, working conditions, or safety hazards
- Filing unfair labor practices charges with NLRB
- Filing discrimination charges with EEOC or a state or municipal fair employment agency
- Cooperating in the investigation of a charge

PERSONNEL IN ACTION

Manager's Journal

Good-Cause Compromise

Neither employes nor managers are happy today with the discharge provisions of American labor law.

Employes, particularly in non-unionized industries, complain that they have little protection against being arbitrarily fired. Under almost all union contracts, workers can resort to formal grievance procedures if they think they have been dismissed without good cause. Now agitation is growing for some kind of "good-cause" statutory job protection for all employes.

The Bullard bill, being actively pushed in the Michigan legislature, would provide protections in the non-union sector similar to those available to unionized employes under grievance arbitration. Drawing on a variety of theories, recent court cases in Connecticut, California and New York have given increased job protection to experienced employes. At the national level, a provision restricting the right to discharge is contained in the so-called Corporate Democracy Act supported by Ralph Nader and various union groups. The desirability of statutory job protection was the principal topic during the labor law section of the most recent annual meeting of the American Association of Law Schools.

Businessmen, in contrast, complain that it has become difficult enough as is to discharge an unsatisfactory employe. In the absence of a contract, managers used to have absolute power to fire employes—for good cause, no cause or even bad cause. Today, firing decisions are restricted by a maze of often overlapping statutes and executive orders.

The National Labor Relations Act prevents companies from arbitrarily dismissing employes engaged in union activity. The Equal Employment Opportunity Act, state status and executive orders protect employes against decisions based on race, age, sex or national origin. Veterans and handicapped workers are protected by special legislation of their own, as are those who complain to OSHA that working conditions are unsafe or unhealthy. In some jurisdictions, special statutes prohibit discharge based on sexual preference or marital status.

Each of these statutes and orders typically establishes its own enforcement machinery, and, in general, an employe who loses a claim in one forum is not precluded from bringing his case in another. It is, therefore, with some justification that employers complain of being subject to multiple jeopardy. A politically active, elderly, handicapped black woman might bring charges against a company in four or five different forums under eight or nine different theories. An employer who wins in one forum might lose in the next.

Given this background, it is not surprising that businessmen are resisting the movement for "good-cause" statutory job protection. Most employers think their traditional power has been limited enough, and they fear a new statute which would set up new opportunities for costly litigation, and possibly yet another administrative agency.

Yet it will probably be futile to resist the establishment of a good-cause standard. The proposal is gaining momentum. It is supported by the laws and practices of other countries such as Britain, France, Sweden, Germany and Japan, all of which limit discharges, as well as by the example of the American unionized sector, where the just-cause standard is routine and well accepted by management. If employers limit themselves to opposing any further loss of management's right to fire, they can delay but not stop the evolution of generalized protection against unfair discharge.

A more sensible strategy for managers would be to work out a compromise. In return for accepting the good-cause standard, employers could ask for a limit on the number of agencies that can sit in judgment on management attempts to discipline or fire unsatisfactory employes. All or nearly all current restrictions on firing could be incorporated into a single standard, enforced through a single agency similar to the National Labor Relations Board.

Such a consolidation would pose some tricky political and legal problems. Interest groups might resist the loss of their special status. And if would be necessary to resolve such questions as whether statutory remedies should be available to employes who already have contractual grievance procedures under their union contracts. Nevertheless, consolidation would have many advantages.

It would eliminate the possibility of multiple lawsuits growing out of a single incident, and thereby make it easier for an employer to be sustained in a legitimate discharge.

Consolidation would elevate the level of debate. In my experience, employes often don't mean it when they charge they are the victims of racial or sexual discrimination. What they really mean is that they think that they have been let go unfairly, but since that's not illegal, they feel compelled to accuse their employers of bias—an emotional charge that usually provokes outrage among managers. If debate focused instead on whether the employer had good cause to fire an employe, grievance proceedings would be much less likely to create permanent hard feelings.

Should the employe be ordered reinstated, the parties could then return more easily to a mutually satisfactory relationship.

Finally, an agency with broad jurisdiction is likely to recruit competent personnel and develop a generally neutral approach, rather than view itself as the advocate for any single interest group.

This quasi-bargain would address the legitimate grievances of both employes and managers. Though it might be rejected by some employers and some spokesmen for groups currently entitled to special protection, it would command a wide acceptance because it is fair and sensible.

(Julius G. Getman, *Wall Street Journal*, August 4, 1980. Reprinted by permission of *The Wall Street Journal*, © Dow Jones & Company, Inc. 1980. All rights reserved.)

Employer Strategies for Employee Job Security Rights

In addition to adhering to all the various legal considerations applying to job security rights, employers should do several things to ensure just dismissals.

Communicate Expectations and Prohibitions. Although ignorance is generally no excuse in nonemployment settings, it is in employment settings. In these settings employees may be disciplined only for conduct she or he knows or reasonably understands is prohibited.

There are many ways to respect the job security rights of employees.

Treat Employees Equally. If the employer discharges one employee for five unexcused absences, then another employee with five unexcused absences must also be discharged. Periodic training for supervisors can help ensure that discharge policies are communicated and administered the same way by all supervisors.

Grievance Procedures and Due Process. Not only should grievance procedures be established to ensure due process for employees, they should also be administered consistently and fairly. For example, evidence should be available to employee and employer, and both parties should have the right to call witnesses and refuse to testify against oneself.

Establish and Maintain Objective and Orderly Personnel Files. Having that kind of objective information at your fingertips is equally important when a discharge is disciplinary. Unfortunately, it's just the information needed that is often missing from the file. The biggest deficiencies in employment records often surface only after an employee challenges the legality of a discharge. Personnel files can be the best defense against discrimination charges when firing is the issue, but only if they've been properly kept.[5]

Establish Progressive Discipline Procedures. For most violations of company rules, firing is the last step in a carefully regulated system of escalating discipline, often called **progressive discipline.** Here are the steps possible in progressive discipline procedures:

▪ *Warning* may be oral at first, but should be written, signed by the employee, and a copy filed before you move on to the next step.

▪ *Reprimand* is official, in writing, and placed in the employee's file.

▪ *Suspension* can be for as short as part of a day or as long as several months without pay, depending on the seriousness of the employee's offense and the circumstances.

▪ *Disciplinary Transfer* may take the pressure off a situation that might explode into violence, or one in which personality conflict is a part of the disciplinary problem.

▪ *Demotion* can be a reasonable answer to problems of incompetence, or an alternative to layoff for economic reasons.

▪ *Discharge* is the last resort, used only when all else has failed, although it might be a reasonable immediate response to violence, theft, or falsification of records.

But firing can be exceedingly painful, even though it is well organized and planned. And many individuals are capable of effective performance but only in certain types of situations. Thus some organizations reassign employees to different parts of the organization and trade top-level managers to other organizations.[6]

Another form of progressive discipline is the **last chance agreement.** Before firing, an employer may be willing to grant an employee one more chance to prove himself or herself, but only with several stipulations. For example, instead of suspending or terminating an employee for excessive absenteeism, the employer may grant the employee one last chance.[7]

EMPLOYEE RIGHTS ON THE JOB

In addition to being concerned with the right to have a job, employees are also concerned with their rights once they have a job. As with employee rights to job security, employee rights on the job have expanded greatly over the past twenty years.

Legal Considerations

The rights on the job that many employees are concerned about include privacy rights, cooperative acceptance, and plant closing notification. Each of these rights has some legal protection.

Rights on the Job:

- Privacy
- Acceptance
- Notification

Privacy Rights. There are several legal considerations applicable in the various categories of employee rights on the job shown in Exhibit 8.1. There has been substantial activity in **privacy rights.** Recently there have been several lawsuits brought on behalf of individuals against organizations for invasion of privacy rights. These lawsuits have been related to or responsible for four federal laws. The encompassing law is the *Privacy Act of 1974*, which applies only to federal agencies. It pertains to the verification of references in selection and employment decisions. This act allows individuals to determine what records pertaining to them are collected, used, and maintained; to review and amend such records; and to bring civil suit for damages against those intentionally violating the rights specified in the act.

The second federal privacy law is the *Fair Credit and Reporting Act,* which permits job applicants to know the nature and content of the credit file on them that is obtained by the organization. The third law is the *Family Education Rights and Privacy Act,* or the *Buckley Amendment.* This allows students to inspect their educational records, and prevents educational institutions from supplying information without students' consent. If the students do not provide this consent, potential employers are prevented from learning of their educational record. The fourth law is the *Freedom of Information Act,* which also pertains only to federal agencies. This act allows individuals to see all the material an agency uses in its decision-making processes.

Although these four laws apply primarily to federal agencies, private organizations will most likely face similar federal or state laws in the near future. These laws will probably establish the right of all individuals to have access to their personnel (personal) files and to be notified of the pending release of information to third parties. Several states have already enacted privacy legislation affecting the privacy of job applicants as well as that of current employees. These laws influence the use of the personnel file, access to it and its contents, and implicitly the information collected for it.

Cooperative Acceptance. The category of **cooperative acceptance** refers to the right of employees to be treated fairly and with respect regardless of race, sex, national origin, physical disability, age, or religion while *on the job* (as well as in obtaining a job and maintaining job security). Although these rights are generally protected under Title VII, the Age Discrimination in Employment Act, the Rehabilitation Act, and the Vietnam Era Veteran's Readjustment Assistance Act, these acts are unable to create in organizations an atmosphere of *willing and supportive as well as cooperative acceptance.* This atmosphere must be created by the employer since laws cannot do this. This notion especially applies to the right of employees to be free of sexual harassment. It is in this area, where the law is inconclusive (despite the EEOC guidelines of 1980 indicating that sexual harassment is a form of sex discrimination under Title VII), that it is tempting for employers to not be concerned. Nonetheless, freedom from harassment is an important component of the employee's right to cooperative acceptance.

Plant Closing Notification. A final issue here of employee rights on the job relates to plant/office closing and relocation. The **right of employees to be notified of plant or office closings or relocation** is an important one.[8] The suicide rate among displaced workers is almost thirty times the national average. The right of employers to move production facilities is greatly affected by federal labor law under the NLRA, Section 8(a). It has been clearly established that employers must bargain over the *effects* of a plant closing/relocation. Although the employers must also bargain (where it is specified in the contract) over the issue of relocation itself, the U.S. Courts of Appeal have generally disagreed about the need to bargain when not specified in the contract. The Supreme Court recently ruled against the NLRB saying that a corporate decision to close out a particular location or even a product line is not a subject that must be negotiated in advance with the union as long as it is for solely economic reasons (*First National Maintenance* v. *NLRB* [1981]).

Note that the Supreme Court did not rule on whether a company must negotiate

If companies fail to give notification to their employees about closings or relocations, federal and state laws are likely to be made.

(bargain over) a decision to move a plant. Where a labor–management contract does not contain specific language on plant relocation, the right of management may still be restricted. Arbitrators, however, have generally ruled in these circumstances in favor of management's right.

Several states have now recognized the importance of plant or office closings. Many are considering legislation to control plant closings and relocations. Maine and Wisconsin require prenotification and have some penalties for employers who move plants (thus closing other plants); however, the laws are sometimes ignored.

At the federal level, legislation is still in the formulation stage. Possible legislation may require employers to give prenotification in decisions of plant closings and relocations and the payment of severance pay to those employees displaced.

Employer Strategies for Employee Rights on the Job

There are several things that employers can do in the area of employee rights on the job. They are presented here in the order shown in Exhibit 8.1.

Employee Privacy Rights.   A totally new element in personnel practice appearing since the 1960s is the concern for the privacy of personnel records and employee access to personnel files.[9]

As described in the section on legal considerations, privacy legislation generally does not cover private employer-employee relationships. Nevertheless, many companies are moving ahead on their own to establish policies and rules governing employee privacy and access rights. While a few years ago employers were only attempting to define employee privacy, today almost 50 percent of the major companies have written policies regarding the privacy of personnel records. In addition, over 85 percent provide employees access to records containing information about themselves.

Employer concerns about employee privacy rights is also influencing preemployment screening and the use of polygraph tests. Prehiring practices are being examined to ensure that only job-related information is collected, thinking that collecting nonjob information is an unnecessary intrusion into the private lives of job applicants. Similar comments are being echoed on the use of polygraph tests.

Sexual harassment is a violation of an employee's right to cooperative acceptance.

Employee Rights to Cooperative Acceptance.   While there are many issues associated with employee rights to cooperative acceptance, two of considerable concern to many employees and employers that have recently surfaced are sexual harassment and retaliation. Our focus on these two issues in no way, however, diminishes the issues related to the rights to cooperative acceptance on the basis of race, age, disability, national origin, or religion. In fact, a review of Chapters 4 and 5 indicates the contrary.

> "This entire subject [**sexual harassment**] is a perfect example of a minor special interest group's ability to blow up any 'issue' to a level of importance which in no way relates to the reality of the world in which we live and work."—A 38-year-old plant manager (male) for a large manufacturer of industrial goods.

> "In my own circumstances, sexual harassment included jokes about my anatomy, off-color remarks, sly innuendo in front of customers—in short, turning everything and anything into a sexual reference was an almost daily occurrence. I

have just left this company (a big chemical manufacturer) partially for this reason."—A 34-year-old first-level manager in environmental engineering (female) for a large producer of industrial goods.

"I'm baffled by this issue. I used to believe it was a subject that was being exaggerated by paranoid women and sensational journalists. Now I think the problem is real but somewhat overdrawn. My impression is that my own company is relatively free of sexual harassment. But I don't know the facts."—A 53-year-old senior vice president (male) of a medium-sized financial institution.[10]

Together these quotations demonstrate the impact of sexual harassment in the work place. Where once certain activities between supervisors (or managers) and employees may have been regarded as good-natured fun, today these same activities may constitute sexual harassment. They do, according to the 1980 EEOC guidelines on harassment, if they are verbal and physical conduct of a sexual nature such that

1. Submission to such conduct is made either explicitly or implicitly a term or condition of an individual's employment.
2. Submission to or rejection of such conduct by an individual is used as the basis for employment decisions affecting such individuals, or
3. Such conduct has the purpose or effect of substantially interfering with an individual's work performance or creating an intimidating, hostile or offensive working environment.

In a recent survey on sexual harassment the findings indicated that

- Sexual harassment is seen as an issue of power, thus it is more serious when it involves a supervisor than when it involves a coworker;
- The EEOC 1980 guidelines are reasonable and necessary and may not be difficult to follow; however, it may be hard to prove that innuendos and dirty jokes are in fact harassment;
- Many employees favor company policies against harassment, but few companies have them. This, despite the fact that employers are responsible for the sexual harassment violations committed by their employees (*Barnes* v. *Castle* [1972]). This is illustrated in the *Personnel in Action* insert, "Supervisory Suitor."
- Many people think sexual harassment can be a serious matter. It certainly has financial implications for companies such as Hunter Associates, and it has significant impact on the lives of such people as those quoted above.

PERSONNEL IN ACTION
Supervisory Suitor

The black bank employee found herself in a difficult position. She was successful at her work as a business machine operator. She had attained a superior job performance rating and had been granted a raise.

Then things went sour. She claimed that her white male supervisor had made a pass at her. He offered to get her a better job if she would be sexually "cooperative" with him. He supposedly told her that he wanted to get it on with a "black chick." The black woman said she refused her supervisor's advances. She was subsequently fired.

The woman took her story to the Equal Employment Opportunity Commission (EEOC). She stated that she had been fired because she had refused her supervisor's demand for sexual favors. EEOC gave the woman a "right to sue" letter. She leveled charges against the bank. She claimed that the bank had violated her rights under Title VII and the 1964 Civil Rights Act by firing her because of her race, color, and sex.

Blamed Bank

The bank immediately cried "foul!" It admitted that the discharge would be illegal if the bank was responsible for the black woman's discriminatory firing, but the bank claimed that only the supervisor himself could be held responsible. The bank pointed out that it had an express policy prohibiting supervisors from making such sexual advances to subordinates and providing for affirmative disciplinary action should the policy be violated.

The bank questioned why the woman hadn't made use of the bank's internal grievance procedures to seek reinstatement or some other remedy for the harm caused by her supervisor's improper actions. She didn't even try to get the bank to redress the wrong allegedly done to her, but ran directly to EEOC. Surely the bank should at least have been given an opportunity to right any wrong before being dragged into court?

Who Should Have Done What?

But the bank was dragged into court. And the judge said that the woman who claimed to be a victim of discriminatory discharge was not obliged to complain to her employer about her supervisor's behavior. She could go directly to EEOC. That agency, once it had concluded that the woman had grounds for complaint, could then approach the bank on behalf of the woman and attempt to resolve the dispute through "informal methods of conference, conciliation, and persuasion." At that point the bank would have an opportunity to employ its internal grievance procedures to redress any wrongs done to the woman by her supervisor.

The bank protested that it couldn't be held liable for the supervisor's actions because, if he did demand sexual favors from his female subordinate, the supervisor was violating bank policy. The judge wouldn't accept this reasoning. The supervisor was acting in the "course of his employment" with the bank when he fired the woman. The bank had invested the supervisor with the authority to fire employees (or at least to participate in a decision to fire). Therefore the bank must accept liability, if the supervisor had abused this authority, as the female employee claimed.

([*Miller v. Bank of America*, 600 F2d 211], *FEP Guidelines* 192. 1981, p. 3)

Many employers are ready to develop a program guide for preventing sexual harassment. The EEOC states that prevention is the best tool for elimination of sexual harassment. There are five steps for prevention of harassment that an organization should take.[11]

Step 1: The personnel manager should affirmatively raise the issue of harassment, and the fact that it exists, to the rest of the organization. Get top management to make it a rule that all discharges must be reviewed by a senior corporate officer or a review board.

Step 2: Since the employer is liable for sexual harassment, except where it can be shown the organization took immediate and appropriate corrective action, it pays to set up reporting (grievance) procedures for those who have been harassed. In addition,

▪ Publicize your internal grievance procedures. Make sure all employees know

that they exist and how to set them into motion.

▪ Administer internal grievance procedures equitably. No employee is going to complain about a supervisor unless sure of getting a fair shake and not jeopardizing the job by pointing a finger at a superior.

▪ Make it perfectly clear to all supervisors that you will not tolerate discrimination or other abuses of authority on their part.

▪ Keep an ear to the ground. If it comes to your attention that a supervisor may be stirring up trouble, investigate immediately. Let it be known that you want to know about any instances of discrimination, constructive discharge, supervisory harassment, and that you will keep all statements confidential.[12]

Step 3: Establish procedures for corroborating a sexual harassment charge. That is, the personnel manager should make sure that the person charged with sexual harassment has a right to respond immediately after charges are made by the alleged victim. Due process must be provided the alleged victim as well as the alleged perpetrator.

Step 4: Specify a set of steps in a framework of progressive discipline for perpetuators of sexual harassment. These could be the same steps used by the organization as a way of treating any violation of organizational roles and policies (See the progressive discipline procedures discussed earlier).

Step 5: Make all employees aware of the company's position on sexual harassment. Provide support such as training programs for managers and supervisors. Be available for questions and problems.

Title VII of the Civil Rights Act calls *getting even* with an employee for opposing an unlawful employment practice or participating in a discrimination proceeding **retaliation,** and it is a separate violation of that act and of almost every other fair employment law.[13] Retaliation carries the same penalties as a violation for actual discrimination. That means back pay awards, reinstatement, injunctions, bad publicity, morale problems, and costly legal fees. Obviously companies want to prevent their supervisors or managers from engaging in retaliation behavior.[14] Here's what companies can say to them:

- Maintain a "hands off" attitude toward employees who file discrimination charges until the matter is completely resolved. Consider it a legal matter to be handled primarily by your attorneys. Remember that employees who file charges are told by fair employment agencies that retaliation is illegal. They are also told to notify the agency immediately if "any attempt" at retaliation is made by their employer.

- Listen to employees who stop short of filing but nevertheless complain of discrimination. Set up a routine procedure that allows these employees to air their grievances. Make sure there is a flow of information from supervisors to top management, and vice versa. Make sure, too, that employees get responses, however ill-founded their complaints may be.

- Keep complete and objective employment records for all employees—not only the complainers—and keep these records on a routine basis. That way, in the extreme cases when you must discipline, you'll have the proof to back up your action.

- Avoid eleventh-hour attempts to document your case against employees. Don't place the employee in question under special surveillance, or whip up a folder full of reprimands and bad evaluations, or take any other action that could be interpreted as harassment.

- Inform supervisors that retaliation is against the law.[15]

Employee Rights to Plant/Office Closing Notification. Basically employees have few legal rights to notification by employers of a facility to be closed down and/or relocated. As in resisting the right of employees to a job, employers resist this notification right because they say it limits their flexibility to manage. They claim that it violates their management rights and rights of ownership. But as important to employees, employers argue that it really is better for management to have its rights because this leads to the survival of the company and more jobs.[16]

Plant closing notification may leave a company without employees to help close the plant.

These arguments, however, are beyond the immediate interest of the employees involved in a potential or actual plant closing. And despite their resistance, employers are recognizing the "humane" right of employees to be helped out when facilities are closed. Since this help starts before the facilities are closed, employees are notified in advance of the closing. While some of this help was initiated by the pressure of unions on management, many nonunion companies are now providing help. The most common form of help is *outplacement assistance*.

While outplacement assistance (discussed further in Chapters 13 and 20) is offered to individuals who are discharged or displaced, its major benefits are for entire work forces displaced because of plant/office closings. Outplacement assistance programs typically represent a large number of single components for employees. Since personnel managers should be in the forefront in putting together these programs, it is useful to present one program and its results.

The American Hospital Supply Corporation, Chicago, needed to close a division. As part of that closing it designed a six-month outplacement program. The single components were

- Severance pay
- Enhanced benefits
- Four-week termination notification period
- Training and development programs to help develop new skills and find other jobs
- Double pay for overtime work needed to get the facility ready to close down
- Retention bonus to encourage employees to stay until the time of actual closing

Results of this six-month, wind-down outplacement assistance included

- Zero exempt employee unplanned turnover and less than 5 percent nonexempt employee unplanned turnover during the wind-down period. This compares to 14 percent exempt and 22 percent nonexempt turnover during this six-month period in 1979.
- Approximately 23 percent of the employees were placed in other divisions of the corporation.
- Almost 90 percent of the outplaced employees received similar or superior compensation packages in their position.
- The six-month program was completed two weeks ahead of schedule.
- The outplacement assistance program enhanced the image of American Hospital Supply Corp. as a humane, people-oriented company.[17]

EVALUATING EMPLOYEE RIGHTS ACTIVITIES

When organizations recognize employee rights and establish programs to ensure they are observed, they can fulfill a third match: the match between employee rights and obligations and employer rights and obligation. In serving this third match both organizations and employees benefit. Organizations benefit from reduced legal costs, since not observing many employee rights is illegal, and their images as good employers increases resulting in enhanced organizational attractiveness. This in turn makes it easier for the organization to recruit a pool of potentially qualified applicants. And although it is suggested that expanded employee rights, especially job security, may reduce needed management flexibility, and thus profitability, it may be an impetus for better planning and resulting in increased profitability.

Increased profitability may also result from the benefits employees receive when their rights are observed: employees may experience a feeling of being treated fairly and with respect, increased self-esteem, and a heightened sense of job security. Employees who have job security may be more productive and committed to the organization than those without job security. As employees are beginning to see the guarantees of job security as a benefit, organizations are also gaining through reduced wage increase demands and greater flexibility in job assignments. This is happening in many of the traditionally unionized manufacturing industries. In those industries, how employee rights are addressed, especially job security, is more than a matter of profitability now, it's a matter of survival. As discussed in Chapter 18 and 19, it's also a matter of a new era of union-management relations.

An organization's employee rights activities can, therefore, be evaluated many ways. Some ways are more appropriate than others, depending upon the activity and right in question. For example, evaluating employee rights activities by the size of legal costs is certainly appropriate in the areas of cooperative acceptance and unjustifiable dismissal. Where employee rights are not legally protected, using legal costs to evaluate activities is much less appropriate. However, if organizations fail to recognize and observe those "humane" rights not now legally protected, they may soon find themselves using legal costs to evaluate all their employee rights activities. Many organizations recognize this and are moving to recognize and observe many "humane" rights. This seems particularly true in employee privacy rights recognition and facility closing notification.

FACING THE CRITICAL ISSUES IN EMPLOYEE RIGHTS

Now that several aspects regarding employee rights have been examined it is appropriate to return to the Critical Issues presented at the start of this chapter. As you will see, the responses to the issues presented here are brief. You should be able to expand significantly on each response.

Issue: *Organizations seem to exist in a time when the employee can do no wrong; everything is the fault of the employer. Is there any way organizations can fire employees without being called on the carpet for it?*

Compared to twenty or more years ago, it does appear as if employees have all the rights. Although they have many more rights now, you the employer still retain many rights, one of which is that of firing employees. Essentially you can terminate workers for poor performance, excessive absenteeism, unsafe conduct, and generally poor organizational citizenship. It is critical, however, that you maintain accurate records of these events for your employees and that the employees are informed how they stand. To be safe, it is also advisable to have a grievance process for employees if you are nonunion. This helps ensure that due process is respected. Doing all of these things is particularly useful in discharge situations that involve members of groups protected by Title VII, ADEA, the Rehabilitation Act, or the Vietnam Era Veterans Act. Though taking all of the above steps won't guarantee that you will not be called on the carpet, it will help ensure your right to discharge.

Issue: *What can organizations do about sexual harassment? Many supervisors claim that what they used to regard as good-natured fun is now treated as a criminal offense.*

Times do change, but what your supervisors called good-natured fun probably was only so for them. Those on the receiving end of their "fun" may have been just as offended as employees today are although now it may be treated as "criminal offense."

Nonetheless there are many situations of good-natured fun that are just that for everyone. It is important that supervisors be trained so that the fine line between what is really fun and what is harassment can be drawn, seen, and respected. To motivate supervisors to do these accurately, they should be evaluated on them and rewarded or punished accordingly. Top management should also be strongly behind the effort, in word and deed.

Issue: *If organizations have to close a plant or an office how can it be done most effectively?*

Although you have the right to just close down the facility without any notification, many employers are notifying their employees in advance of the closing. This is true even in nonunion companies. In addition to giving notification, employers are implementing outplacement assistance programs. These offer employees retraining for new jobs, counseling and aid in finding new jobs or in getting transfers, provisions for severance pay, and even retention bonuses for those who stay until closing time.

Closing a facility with notification and with outplacement assistance seems to produce positive results for the organization and minimizes the negative effects for the employees. This is probably the most effective way to go.[18]

Issue: *What rights of employees do organizations have to observe regarding their personnel files? Do they even have to keep employee records?*

It is now more important than ever to keep objective and orderly personnel files. They are critical evidence that you have treated your employees fairly and with respect and have not violated any laws. Without these, even if you are the model employer, you may get caught on the short end of a law suit.

Although there are several federal laws that influence record keeping, they are primarily directed at public employers. However, many private employers are (on their own initiatives) moving to give their employees the right to access to their personnel files and to prohibit the file information from being given to others without the employee's consent. In addition, employers are casting out of their personnel files any nonjob-related information and ending hiring practices that solicit that type of information.

SUMMARY

The entire area of employee rights is gaining considerable attention in our society. Though employees have won many legal rights over the years, the rights of most controversy are those not legally protected or those that may or may not be legally protected. Thus the courts and the state and federal legislative and executive bodies have a potentially very significant role in the future of employee rights. Whether the courts and the legislative and executive bodies move to increase the number of legally protected rights of employees depends to some extent on how employers behave in the area of unprotected employee rights. If they take a proactive position of recognizing many of the unprotected rights as "humane" rights that employees do have, the courts and the legislative bodies may be less inclined to legislate employee rights, both for job security and for on the job. At this time, however, a great deal of momentum has already gathered to provide some type of legal protection for job security rights. Nevertheless, personnel managers and employers can still have an impact in shaping the form of such legal protection.

Personnel managers also have an impact in how their organizations do in treating their employees in relation to the legally protected rights. To help ensure that managers and supervisors treat employees fairly and with respect, personnel managers must actively make the organization aware of the law and provide training opportunities so its managers and supervisors can implement the law.

KEY CONCEPTS

employee rights	termination for just cause
termination at will	good cause compromise
privacy rights	last chance agreement
cooperative acceptance	sexual harassment
right to plant notification	retaliation
termination for good cause	progressive discipline

DISCUSSION QUESTIONS

1. What types of considerations are necessary before an employer terminates an employee?
2. On what grounds is it unwarranted to fire an employee?
3. What are the four activities of personnel management that are most related to employee rights and in what way are they related?
4. What is meant by the concept of termination at will and how valid is it for today's employment decisions?
5. Define the concept of cooperative acceptance. Who is responsible for seeing that organizations practice cooperative acceptance?
6. Outline the steps in a progressive disciplinary procedure program.
7. Under what conditions does so-called good-natured fun constitute sexual harassment?
8. What employee rights upset an employer if she or he is going to close or relocate a facility? Is this always the best action to take? Why or why not?

9. List the types of measures that can be used to evaluate the emphasis and importance an organization places on employee rights.

10. What role can a personnel manager play in establishing and maintaining effective employee rights programs?

CASE

The Payback

Lucy Pascal was hired by ABC Jobbers, Inc, two months ago. She had considerable prior sales experience. ABC had wooed Lucy away from her previous employer because of an outstanding sales record. Enticed by a substantial boost in pay, commissions, and perks, Lucy was looking forward to widened professional contacts and increased income. Also, she was thrilled at having been one of the first women to be directly hired for sales work at ABC.

Lucy liked working for her new company even though she was certainly a rarity there. Virtually all of the other professionals and salespeople were male. Most were macho types, often joking and talking about their latest exploits with "a little number" met while on the road. When Lucy was around, they enjoyed teasing her to see what her reaction would be. She would change the subject pleasantly, but their conversations bothered her somewhat. Additionally, Lucy tried to ignore all the centerfold pictures prominently displayed in a lot of the offices. Yet, even with all this, she was still very pleased she had made the job move because of its growth potential.

On one of her initial sales calls in her newly assigned district, Lucy visited Frank Grumman, a major client who was responsible for signing off on all sales contracts for his company. Lucy gave Frank Grumman a sales pitch in her typically persuasive and professional manner. Frank responded that he was most impressed not only with the product but also with Lucy herself. He cajoled her to go out with him so they "could get to know each other better." Lucy began feeling increasingly uncomfortable with Frank's comments. It was obvious he was more interested in her as a woman rather than as ABC's sales representative.

Finally, in response to his insistent urgings that they take off together for the evening, Lucy, as nicely as she could, gave him a firm no. She, with a forced smile, advised him she had to catch an early flight.

Frank, feeling rejected, testily replied that Lucy really must not want the contract very much if she wasn't going to "entertain" him. Angered, Lucy told him in no uncertain terms what he could do with the contract if "entertaining" was part of the price she had to pay in order to get it. She stormed out of Frank's office.

Upon returning to her district office, Lucy related to James Roberts, her first-line supervisor and the District Sales Manager, what had happened on her sales call. James reacted with laughter. He said to Lucy, "There are certain things we all have to do to keep our clients happy. If you knew all the rounds of golf I've played with some real creeps for business purposes, then you'd realize what I was talking about." Lucy said "James, I'm not talking about playing golf. That's not the type of game he wanted me to play." James grew chilly. He told Lucy "By God, you better not lose that contract. You do, and you'll lose your district and all its fat commissions!"

Lucy had been placed in a no-win situation by both her client and her boss. As she pondered over her dilemma, the Chief Executive Officer of ABC saw her in the hall. "Lucy," said Donald Stubbs, "what's my favorite new sales gal looking so worried about? Come on into my office and tell me how things are going." The grandfatherly Mr. Stubbs gently ushered Lucy into his office. After only a few moments, Lucy blurted out her situation. Losing control, and to her great embarassment, she broke into tears. Concerned, Mr. Stubbs placed his arms around Lucy to console her. Lucy soon calmed down enough to apologize for her behavior. Mr. Stubbs advised her he would place some phone calls and try to smooth things over. As he lead her to the door, he admonished her: "You have to realize, Lucy, that men will be men. You'll just have to get used to these things in this business."

Lucy wandered down the hall wondering what was going to happen to her now. Samuel Kindel, a fellow salesperson, spotted Lucy and asked her if she'd like to have some coffee. Lucy replied she needed to talk to someone about the things that were happening to her. In the cafeteria, she told Samuel the entire story and the frustration she felt. Samuel became furious. He told her that "those guys are all no-good skunks." Lucy was relieved to have such a sympathetic ear to bend. As they continued their talk, Samuel said, "You know, I've been wanting to get to know you better ever since you got here, Lucy. What do you say we take in a movie tonight and forget this place."

Case Questions

1. Is Lucy being sexually harassed because of her office environment?
2. Samuel Kindel asked Lucy for a date. Was she being sexually harassed by him? How do you think she should have responded?
3. Could Lucy have dealt with the situation differently?
4. What type of company policies would you recommend that ABC Jobbers, Inc., institute for its employees to forestall sexually harassing behaviors?

FOR YOUR CAREER

- It pays to be aware of your rights on the job, both those legally protected and ethically justifiable (humane).
- Protect yourself against unjustifiable dismissal by keeping your own personnel file on your performance accomplishments and any other recognitions that reflect favorably on your behavior.
- You can gain a great deal more control over your work environment when you participate in the decisions made affecting you and your work.
- Although an employer can still fire you without cause (at will), it is becoming more difficult for an employer to legally get away with this.

- Employers use references less and less because most references provide only safe or positive information.
- Sexual harassment is an issue that will gain increasing attention in the 1980s. You should be thoroughly familiar with it.

ENDNOTES

1. Lawrence Ingrassia, "Non-Union Workers Are Gaining Status, But So Far the Talk Outweighs the Action," *Wall Street Journal,* July 24, 1980, p. 42.

   "The Growing Costs of Filing Non-Union Workers," *Business Week,* April 6, 1981, pp. 95–98.

2. *Fair Employment Guidelines,* No. 192, July 1981, pp. 1–8.

   James R. Madison, "The Employee's Emerging Right to Sue for Arbitrary or Unfair Discharge," *Employee Relations Law Journal* 6, No. 3, pp. 422–436.

   Stuart A. Youngblood and Gary L. Tidwell, "Termination at Will: Some Changes in the Wind," *Personnel,* May–June 1981, pp. 22–33

3. Clyde W. Summers, "Protecting All Employees Against Unjust Dismissal," *Harvard Business Review,* January–February 1980, pp. 132–139, 204–210.

4. Youngblood and Tidwell, p. 26.

5. *Fair Employment Guidelines,* No. 194, September 1981, pp. 1–8.

6. Daniel N. Adams, Jr., "When Laying Off Employees, the Word Is 'Out-Training'," *Personnel Journal,* September 1980, pp. 719–721.

   Tom Bailey, "Industrial Outplacement at Goodyear Part 1: The Company's Position," *Personnel Administrator,* March 1980, pp. 42–48.

   William J. Broussard and Robert J. Delargey, "The Dynamics of the Group Outplacement Workshop," *Personnel Journal,* December 1979, pp. 855–857, 873.

   Thomasine Rendero, "Consensus," *Personnel,* July–August 1980, pp. 4–11.

7. *Fair Employment Guidelines,* No. 192, August 1981, p. 3.

   Phil Farish, "Pair Potpourri," *Personnel Administrator,* August 1981, p. 8.

   Hermine Zagat Levine, "Consensus," *Personnel,* May–June 1981, pp. 4–11.

8. Gary L. Felsten, "Current Considerations in Plant Shutdowns and Relocations," *Personnel Journal,* May 1981, pp. 369–372.

9. David F. Linowes, "Update on Privacy Protection Safeguards," *Personnel Administrator,* June 1980, pp. 39–42.

   David F. Linowes, "Is Business Giving Employees Privacy?" *Business and Society Review,* Winter, 1979–80, pp. 47–49.

   Alan F. Westin, "What Should Be Done about Employee Privacy?" *Personnel Administrator,* March 1980, pp. 27–30.

10. Eliza G. C. Collins and Timothy B. Blodgett, "Sexual Harassment . . . Some See It . . . Some Won't," *Harvard Business Review,* March–April 1981, pp. 77–78.

    Kathryn A. Thurston, "Sexual Harassment: An Organizational Perspective," *Personnel Administrator,* December 1980, pp. 59–64.

11. George E. Biles, "A Program Guide for Preventing Sexual Harassment in the Workplace," *Personnel Administrator,* June 1981, pp. 49–56.

12. *Fair Employment Guidelines,* No. 194, 1981, p. 6.

13. *Fair Employment Guidelines,* No. 188, March 1981, p. 1–8.

14. Bette Bardeen Durling, "Retaliation: A Misunderstood Form of Employment Discrimination," *Personnel Journal,* July 1981, pp. 555–558.

15. *Fair Employment Guidelines,* No. 188, 1981, p. 3.

16. Phillip D. Johnston, "Personnel Planning for a Plant Shutdown," *Personnel Administrator,* August 1981, pp. 53–57.

17. Johnston, p. 53.

18. Bruce H. Millen, "Providing Assistance to Displaced Workers," *Monthly Labor Review,* May 1979, pp. 17–22.

"Outplacement Assistance," *Personnel Journal,* April 1981, p. 250.

Appraising and Motivating Employee Behavior

Chapter Nine
Appraising and Evaluating Employee
Performance

Chapter Ten
Motivating Employees

Chapter Outline

Critical Issues in Appraising and Evaluating Employee Performance

Appraising the Performance of Employees
The Importance and Purposes of Performance Appraisal
Legal Considerations in Appraising Employee Performance

Performance Appraisal as a Set of Processes and Procedures
Criteria and Standards
Performance Appraisal Forms
Sources of Performance Data
The Performance Appraisal Interview and Feedback
Errors in Gathering Performance Data
Matching Purpose with Method

Monitoring Performance Processes and Procedures

Appraising and Evaluating Employee Performance

Evaluating PAPPs

Facing the Critical Issues in Appraising and Evaluating Employee Performance

Summary

Key Concepts

Discussion Questions

Case

For Your Career

Endnotes

Personnel in the News

Taking the Pain Out of Performance Appraisal

"You know, Jimmy, these damn appraisal interviews are a pain in the neck. Doing the damn things not only takes time away from the job but I feel extremely uncomfortable when I have to tell my people they're doing a bad job. Besides, when I tell them they're doing poorly I never know how they'll react. Sometimes they even get worse after I tell them."

Supervisor to Personnel Manager

"I understand, Bob, but it's really important to tell people how they're doing. How are they ever going to improve if they don't know they're doing poorly? People want to know where they stand. And since your own evaluation is partly based on how well your people do, it seems like you have little choice but to tell them."

Personnel Manager to Supervisor

"Okay Jimmy, if I have to tell them how poorly they're doing, tell me how to do it without the pain. You got a training program on 'Appraisals without Pain'?"

Supervisor to Personnel Manager

"Sorry Bob. But good luck with your interviews." (From Randall S. Schuler, "Taking the Pain Out of Performance Appraisal Interviews," Supervisory Management, August 1981. [New York: AMACON, a division of American Management Associations, 1981], p. 8.)

The Ratings Game At Work

A good appraisal system "is fairly fundamental to improving performance," says former Harvard Business School Professor Sterling Livingston, who heads Sterling Institute, a Washington management consulting firm.

"If a person doesn't know what's expected of him or her, or if he or she doesn't get feedback, you're not likely to have the person doing well."

"Despite the emphasis in recent years on performance evaluation," adds the Work in America Institute, "a survey of 360 managers in 190 organizations reveals that more than two-thirds of this group have no idea what their standing is in their organization."

These managers, according to a report cited by the institute, "also feel that their accomplishments are not recognized and that their organizations do not have enough data to make sound decisions about compensation, promotions and other matters that require evaluative information."

"Most everyone in industry," says Livingston, "has recognized the desirability of performance appraisals, but very few are terribly happy with their system. They don't achieve their objectives."

When University Research Corporation, a Bethesda (Maryland) human-services consulting firm, surveyed its staff a few years ago, it heard a lot of these same complaints. Because employees felt the appraisal procedure was "arbitrary and capricious," says president Gary Jonas, "we made it a high priority to come up with a new system."

After extensive research, the firm developed a plan aimed at meeting these criticisms. It incorporates much of the new thinking that is going into new government and industry programs.

A basic feature is that the burden is put first on the employees. They write an initial self-assessment in which they judge themselves—in detail—against expectations established in advance for their particular tasks.

"We found," says Jonas, in determining job responsibilities, "the staff usually knows the subtleties better."

To make the appraisal a useful tool in upgrading productivity, supervisors are instructed to suggest ways employees might improve their effectiveness. In a turn-about, the subordinates then let their bosses know what help they need from them to do a better job. In a final segment, employee career objectives—"where they want to go"—are reviewed.

Underlying the plan is an effort to increase worker-boss communication, getting them to talk over problems and goals regularly. Says Jonas: "It's part of effective management. Talking about performance is difficult. But once the groundwork is laid, it becomes easier to do on a day-to-day basis." (From The Washington Post, March 25, 1981, B–5.)

Look Before Leaping

A case in which the plaintiffs were victorious was Mistretta v. Sandia Corp. The defendant in Mistretta was a federally funded private research laboratory. Thus, its work force was subject to changing federal appropriations.

Due to a budget cut, the defendant was forced to reduce its payroll by several hundred employees [the plaintiffs]. The reduction was carried out using, among other methods, an early retirement program for those eligible. Many employees were forced to take early retirement or face involuntary termination with subsequent loss of certain benefits.

The evaluation process used by the defendant in determining who would be asked to leave was found defective by the court. The Mistretta court criticized the evaluation system used because the ". . . evaluations were based only on the best judgment and opinions of the evaluators, and were not founded on any definite, identifiable criteria based on quality or quantity of work or specific performances that were supported by some kind of record." The court in Mistretta noted that other courts have condemned subjective standards as fostering discrimination, therefore declining to give much weight to a defendant's testimony when the justification of its decision or policy is based upon subjective criteria. Also, the defendant's contention that performance necessarily declines with age, and thus the lower performance ratings for older employees, was a clear indication that the defendant's evaluation policy was age-biased. The defendant failed to justify its evaluation policy with any business-related arguments.

In view of the language of Stringfellow and Mastie, the Mistretta decision is clearly not an aberration. The need for objective and identifiable criteria received equal emphasis in all three decisions. Both the Mistretta and Oshiver decisions show that an employer will not be able to leap first and look for a net later. Just as preparation for contingencies is a foundation of sound business management, so is it an invaluable aid in personnel matters. Just as performance appraisal evidence contrived just prior to trial will be viewed suspiciously, so will such appraisal evidence that is based on *arbitrary and biased factors. (From Michael H. Schuster and Christopher S. Miller, "Performance Evaluations as Evidence in ADEA Cases," Employee Relations Law Journal 6, No. 4 (Spring 1981): 572–573.)*

Together these three sets of quotations illustrate several important aspects of employee performance in organizations. One is that the way employee performance is appraised and evaluated has many legal implications. Courts emphasize that objectivity in appraising and evaluating employee performance is generally preferred over subjectivity. Another aspect is that performance appraisal and evaluation are fundamental to improving employee performance and to also letting employees know where they stand. Unfortunately letting employees know where they stand is often a difficult and painful process if the news is bad. Yet the quality of the superior-subordinate relationship is the real crux of the process of appraising and evaluating employee performance. As such, that relationship must be worked on in any performance appraisal program to understand what happens when employee performance is appraised and evaluated in organizations.

These three quotations bring out several other important aspects of employee performance that we will discuss in this chapter. These quotations also underlie the four critical issues identified by our group of personnel managers.

CRITICAL ISSUES IN APPRAISING AND EVALUATING EMPLOYEE PERFORMANCE

The four critical issues are

1. *What is the best way to appraise employee performance?*
2. *Do organizations have to validate performance appraisal forms? If so, how? What other legal considerations must organizations be aware of?*
3. *There are so many problems every time organizations appraise someone's performance that it's almost more trouble than it's worth. Really, why should it be done at all?*
4. *Should employees be allowed to appraise themselves? Should they evaluate the performances of their supervisors?*

These issues are critical indeed! Ask anyone in an organization to tell you about performance appraisal. Most likely the comments won't be pleasant. Fortunately, you can provide them with a great deal of insight into their concerns by the time you finish reading and studying this chapter.

In addition to knowing how to respond to the critical issues, you'll be able to describe for them the entire set of processes and procedures related to appraising and evaluating employee performance. Before we get into the set of processes and procedures, it is useful to develop a common meaning of appraising and evaluating performance, its importance in organizations, and its relationships with other personnel activities.

Appraising the performance of employees is an activity that organizations find necessary and that supervisors find uncomfortable. Although performance appraisal is often done informally, we are interested in it as a formal activity.

APPRAISING THE PERFORMANCE OF EMPLOYEES

Performance appraisal is a formal, structured system of measuring and evaluating an employee's job-related behaviors and outcomes to discover how and why the employee is presently performing on the job and how the employee can perform more effectively in the future so that the employee, the organization, and society all benefit. Note that this definition identifies employee performance in terms of the results or outcomes that people accomplish on the job and what they do (their job-related behaviors) that affects those results.

The Importance and Purposes of Performance Appraisal

Appraising employee performance is important because it provides information about how well jobs are being performed. It also identifies who is responsible for doing those jobs and how well they are performing them.

Performance appraisal serves many specific purposes in addition to identifying how well an employee is doing. The most frequent uses of appraisal are:

- *Management development:* It provides a framework for future employee development by identifying and preparing individuals for increased responsibilities.

- *Performance measurement:* It establishes the relative value of an individual's contribution to the company and helps evaluate individual accomplishments.

- *Performance improvement:* It encourages continued successful performance and strengthens individual weaknesses to make employees more effective and productive.

- *Compensation:* It helps determine appropriate pay for performance and equitable salary and bonus incentives based on merit or results.

Performance appraisal is so critical because it serves so many purposes.

■ *Identification of potential:* It identifies candidates for promotion.

■ *Feedback:* It outlines what is expected from employees against actual performance levels.

■ *Personnel planning:* It audits management talent to evaluate present supply of human resources for replacement planning.

■ *Legal Compliance:* It establishes the validity of employment decisions made on the basis of performance-based information. It, in turn, can minimize the financial losses due to unsuccessful courtroom defenses such as described in *Mistretta* at the start of this chapter.

■ *Communications:* It provides a format for dialogue between superior and subordinate and improves understanding of personal goals and concerns.

Other purposes of performance appraisal are demotions, terminations, internal recruitment, and research.[1]

A summary of these purposes is shown in Exhibit 9.1.

All these uses of performance appraisal indicate not only how important the activity is but also how extensive its relationships are with other personnel activities.[2] Note that since all the purposes of performance appraisal affect the "terms and conditions of employment" for employees, performance appraisal is viewed as an "employee selection procedure" and must follow the same validation procedures as those used for selection tests; and as with the other selection procedures, appraisal faces many legal considerations.[3]

Legal Considerations in Appraising Employee Performance

As illustrated in Exhibit 9.1, there are at least three general points in the processes and procedures of appraising employee performance where the organization must pay attention to legal considerations. Of course none of these considerations needs to become of legal concern to an organization if it does not make employment decisions that result in adverse impact.

Establishing Valid Performance Criteria and Standards. Developing performance appraisals that reflect critical job requirements are necessary if the appraisals are to be considered valid. The U.S. Circuit Court in *Brito* v. *Zia Company* (1973) found that Zia Company was in violation of Title VII when a disproportionate number of employees of a protected group were laid off on the basis of low performance scores. The critical point here is that performance scores were really not related to the job being done by the employees. Essentially what Zia did was to lay off employees using performance information not based on identifiable criteria. When companies do make performance-based decisions on the basis of appraisals that use definite, identifiable criteria based on the employee's job, the courts are happy (*Stringfellow* v. *Monsanto Corp.* [1970]; *United States* v. *City of Chicago* [1978]).[4]

Using Valid Performance Appraisal Forms. Once the critical job components are established, it is necessary to use forms that measure or relate to those job components. For example, if *quantity of output* is a critical job component, having a supervisor mark his or her general impressions of how personable and valuable the employee is on an appraisal form may lead to discrimination. Appraisal forms on

Exhibit 9.1
Processes and Procedures of Appraising Employee Performance

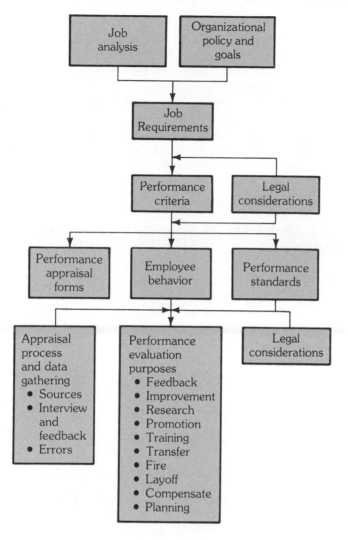

which the rater indicates by a check mark (√) his or her evaluation of an employee on things like level of responsibility, degree of initiative, friendliness are referred to as **subjective forms.** They are in contrast to appraisals where the evaluation is done against specifically defined behaviors, levels of output, level of specific goal attainment, or number of days absent. These appraisals are called **objective forms.** Although the courts will allow a company to use a subjective form (*Roger* v. *International Paper Co.* [1975]), they generally frown upon their use (*Albemarle Paper Company* v. *Moody* [1975]; *Oshiver* v. *Court of Common Pleas* [1979]; *Baxter* v. *Savannah Sugar Refining Corp.* [1974]; and *Rowe* v. *General Motors* [1972]) since they do not produce fair or accurate evaluations. You should, however, keep in mind two important points: (1) The courts have suggested that a company can make subjective forms more like objective forms by demonstrating that the company performs and relies on a thorough appraisal process that is intended to and is used fairly and accurately (*Mastie* v. *Great Lakes Steel Corp.* [1976]); and (2) Many companies still use subjective forms, and it is very likely your performance will be appraised by one some day soon.[5]

It's important to let employees know how they will be evaluated.

Communicating Performance Criteria and Standards. It is only fair, once job components, performance criteria and standards have been identified, that the employee be told what they are. Can you imagine being in a class and not knowing how your grade will be determined? Many employees, unfortunately, indicate that they *do not know* on what basis they are being evaluated. The courts, however, have clearly stated that if performance evaluation is used for any of the purposes shown in Exhibit 9.1, performance criteria and standards must be communicated to the employee (*Patterson* v. *American Tobacco Co.* [1976, 1978]; *Sledge* v. *J. P. Stevens and Co.* [1978]; and *Donaldson* v. *Pillsbury Co.* [1977]).[6] A summary of the characteristics that help make a performance appraisal system is shown in the *For Your Career* insert.

PERFORMANCE APPRAISAL AS A SET OF PROCESSES AND PROCEDURES

You may be getting the impression that performance appraisal and evaluation is really rather complex. Indeed, it is! Exhibit 9.1 shows many processes and procedures that are essential for an organization to do well in order to attain evaluation purposes and serve the many legal considerations. Let's consider some of the more important processes and procedures.

FOR YOUR CAREER

Summary of Characteristics of Legally Defensible Appraisal Systems

Formal and standardized with written instructions for users

Performance standards or criteria based on a thorough job analysis for each job type

Performance standards or criteria are based on work actually done by those being rated and are defined specifically

Decisions based on results do not "adversely impact" or discriminate against minorities, women, other groups

Users are oriented and trained

Intended uses of appraisal results are known and communicated to those affected

Supervisors, subjective evaluations are not relied upon exclusively

Appeal/review procedures are established

Raters have ample opportunity to observe ratees

(From *Performance Appraisal and Review (PAR) Systems* by Steve Carroll and Craig Schneier Copyright © 1982 Scott, Foresman and Company. Reprinted by permission.)

Criteria and Standards

To serve the organization's purposes and meet legal challenges, a performance appraisal system must appraise current employee performance. If the appraisal system is to uncover employees' potential for greater responsibilities and promotion, it must also provide accurate data about such potential. And the system must yield consistent data (be reliable) about what it is supposed to be concerned with (be valid).[7]

A valid performance appraisal system must specify **performance criteria** that are job-related and important, criteria that can most easily be determined through job analysis. Then employees' contributions to the organization can be evaluated based on the degree to which they perform those behaviors and attain those results specified in the job analysis. For example, if selling 100 units per month is the only important result of an employee's job, then the appraisal system should only measure the number of units sold. In this case, there is only one performance criterion.

Generally, job analysis identifies several performance criteria that determine employees' contributions.[8] Thus selling 100 units per month may be accompanied by such criteria as "effects of remarks to customers," "consistency in attendance," and even "effects on coworkers." If all of these performance criteria are found in the job analysis to be important, they all should be measured by the performance appraisal.

If the form used to appraise employee performance lacks the job behaviors and results important and relevant to the job, the form is said to be **deficient.** If the form includes appraisal of anything neither important nor relevant to the job, it is **contaminated.** Many performance appraisal forms actually used in organizations measure some characteristics and behaviors of employees unrelated to the employee's job. These forms are contaminated and in many cases also deficient.

In addition to performance criteria, **standards** are necessary to measure how well employees are performing. By using standards, performance criteria take on a range of values. For example, selling 100 units per month may be defined as excellent performance, and selling 80 units may be defined as average. Organizations often use **historical records** of how well employees have done previously (essentially to determine what is really possible) to establish what is only average performance or is, indeed, excellent performance. Standards can also be established by time and motion studies and work sampling described in Chapter 3. Whereas these methods are often used for blue-collar, nonmanagerial-type jobs, different methods are used for managers. Many organizations evaluate how well their managers do by how well or how many **goals** are attained. Often these goals are part of an entire performance appraisal method called *management by objectives* (to be discussed in a few pages). Increasingly, managers are also being evaluated against standards of profitability, revenues, or costs, which is necessary for effective personnel management.

Job analysis is critical for establishing performance criteria.

Performance Appraisal Forms

There are four major forms or approaches to performance appraisal: **comparative, absolute standards** (quantitative and qualitative), **management by objectives** or goals, and **direct or objective indexes.**[9]

The Comparative Approach. There are several **comparative methods** of evaluation, all comparing one subordinate to the others. The first is the **straight ranking,**

The four major appraisal approaches are:
- *Comparative*
- *Absolute*
- *Management by objectives*
- *Direct indexes*

in which a superior lists the subordinates in order from best to worst, usually on the basis of overall performance. The second method is the **alternative ranking,** which takes place in several steps. The first step is to put the best subordinate at the head of the list and the worst subordinate at the bottom. In the second round, the superior selects the best and worst from the remaining subordinates. Of these two, the best is placed second on the list and the worst is placed next to last. The superior chooses the best and worst until all subordinates are ranked. As you can see, the middle position on the list is the last to be filled by this method.

The remaining two comparative methods are more time-consuming but may provide better information. One is the **paired comparison method,** in which each subordinate is compared to every other subordinate, one at a time, on a single standard or criterion, such as overall performance. The subordinate with the second-greatest number of favorable comparisons is ranked second, and so on.

The three comparative methods discussed so far give each person a unique rank. This suggests that no two subordinates perform exactly alike. Although this may be true, many superiors say that subordinates' performances are too close to differentiate. The fourth method—the **forced distribution method**—was designed to overcome this complaint and to incorporate several factors or dimensions (rather than a single factor) into the ranking of subordinates. The term *forced distribution* is used because the superior must assign only a certain proportion of subordinates to each of several categories on each factor. A common forced distribution scale may be divided into five categories. A fixed percentage of all subordinates in the group fall within each of these categories. A problem with this method is, of course, that a group of subordinates may not conform to the fixed percentage. In fact, all four comparative methods assume that there are good and bad performers in all groups. You may know from experience, however, of situations where all the people in a group actually perform identically. If you encountered such a situation, how would you evaluate these people?

Absolute Standards.   In the comparative approach to performance evaluation, the superior is forced to evaluate each subordinate in relationship to the other subordinates, often based on a single overall dimension. In contrast, the absolute standard approach allows superiors to evaluate each subordinate's performance independent of the other subordinates and often on several dimensions of performance. However, there is still an element of force in the absolute standard approach, particularly in the qualitative category (the other major category is the quantitative).

When the qualitative method of evaluation is used, the superior simply indicates whether the selected performance dimensions do or do not apply to a particular subordinate. This method of evaluation does not reflect the extent to which a given dimension applies—just whether it exists. There are three general methods of qualitative evaluation: critical incidents, weighted checklist, and forced choice.

In the **critical incidents** format, superiors must indicate which of a number of incidents of performance (successful and unsuccessful) were exhibited by each subordinate. Usually these incidents—regarded as critical by the organization, subordinates, and superiors—are grouped into several categories representing separate dimensions of performance. Initially, the concept of critical incidents implied that some incidents were unique and relatively important. Superiors kept "little black books" of good, bad, and typical incidents for each subordinate. All of these incidents generally took on the same level of importance. Needless to say, however, some incidents are more important than others.

The **weighted check list** method was, therefore, designed to improve upon the traditional critical incidents method. To the traditional incidents were added weights (reflecting degrees of importance). Weighted check lists are developed by individuals familiar with the jobs of the subordinates to be evaluated, such as the personnel manager. The weighted check list thus represents the relative (weighted) importance of good and bad aspects of performance. The check list (without the weights) are given to the superiors, who check the incidents that each employee exhibits.

The **forced choice** method is also developed by someone who is familiar with the jobs of the subordinates, such as the personnel manager—but not by the superiors. The forced choice method differs from the weighted check list because it forces superiors to evaluate each subordinate by choosing which of two items in a set (of which there are several) better describes the subordinate.

Quantitative methods are different from the qualitative methods in that they do not force the superiors to make yes-or-no choices. There are two quantitative methods: the conventional or graphic rating and the behavior anchored rating scale.

The **conventional rating** is the most widely used method of performance evaluation (see Exhibit 9.2). Conventional forms vary in the number of dimensions of performance they measure. However, the term performance is used advisedly, because many conventional forms use personality characteristics rather than actual behaviors as indicators of performance. Frequently used traits are *aggressiveness, independence, maturity,* and *sense of responsibility.* Many conventional forms also vary on the range or degree of each dimension used. Some forms may have only four levels of performance, whereas others may have as many as twenty-five. Conventional forms are easy and quick and very popular, but the results are sometimes difficult to convey to subordinates, especially if the results are unfavorable. In addition, the results fail to indicate how subordinates could do better.

> The conventional rating form is the most common in organizations.

A conventional rating form used by a large company for **nonexempt** salaried employees is shown in Exhibit 9.2. When using it for **exempt** employees, who are generally supervisors and managers, the traits of administrative ability and technical ability are added.

The **behavior anchored rating scale (BARS)** was developed to provide results that subordinates could use to improve performance. They were also designed so superiors would be more comfortable giving feedback. The development of a BARS generally corresponds to the first steps in the critical incidents method. Then individuals familiar with the jobs of the subordinates evaluate the incidents in terms (degrees) of goodness and badness. Incidents that the individuals agree on are formally arranged in order of goodness and placed in clusters.[10] An example of one such cluster, organizational ability, is shown in Exhibit 9.3.

Management by Objectives.   Whereas the other approaches to performance appraisal often measure a subordinate's behavior or personality, the management by objectives approach measures performance by comparing the goals attained by the subordinate with those goals initially established. The **management by objectives** (MBO) or goal-setting form has four steps.[11] The first step is to establish the goals each subordinate is to attain. In some organizations, superiors and subordinates work together to establish goals; in others, superiors establish goals for subordinates. The goals can refer to desired outcomes to be achieved, means (activities) for achieving the outcomes, or both.

> MBO is a popular way by which to evaluate the performance of managers.

The second step involves the subordinates' performance in a previously arranged time period. As subordinates perform, they know fairly well what there is to do, what has been done, and what remains to be done.

Exhibit 9.2
Conventional Rating Form

Name of Employee_____ Department_____
Job Title_____ Date Hired_____
Division_____

INSTRUCTIONS

Evaluate the employee on the job now being performed. For each factor, place a check mark in the block that most clearly expresses your overall judgment. The care and accuracy with which this appraisal is made will determine its value to you, the employee, and the organization.

JOB KNOWLEDGE Knowledge of required duties as outlined in the position description	☐ Understands and is capable of performing all phases of job	☐ Understands and is capable of performing almost all phases of job	☐ Has adequate grasp of essential duties of job; can proceed without special instructions on all regular work	☐ Fair knowledge but lacks knowledge of some important aspects of job content	☐ Poor job knowledge; does not understand job duties
SUPERVISION NEEDED Degree of supervision required to perform job functions	☐ Requires very close supervision	☐ Requires regular checking to be sure work will be done on time and in accordance with instructions	☐ On only a few tasks is it necessary to check up to be sure of deadlines or following of instructions	☐ Regularly follows instructions; requires little followup	☐ Always follows instructions; you can be absolutely sure you will get just what you want when you want it
QUANTITY Ability to meet performance quota required to maintain department standards under normal conditions	☐ Seldom gets work done in required time	☐ Work output is below established requirements	☐ Turns out normal amount of work but seldom more output than is satisfactory	☐ Output of work exceeds amount deemed necessary for normal departmental operations	☐ Output of work is ordinarily high; regularly produces above and beyond the established requirements of position
QUALITY Neatness and accuracy of the individual's work	☐ Mistakes are extremely rare	☐ Very few errors, usually minor in nature; work seldom has to be done over	☐ Most work done well, usually acceptable in both accuracy and neatness	☐ Work often unacceptable; frequent errors or rejections	☐ Work constantly rejected because of inaccuracies and mistakes
ADAPTABILITY Speed with which the employee masters new methods or duties and grasps explanations	☐ Exceptionally fast to learn and adjust to changed conditions	☐ Learns easily; adjusts to changes rapidly	☐ Adjusts to changes in methods or duties on request, with average amount of instructions	☐ Adjusts to changes in methods or duties, but adjustment is slow and requires detailed instructions	☐ Unable or unwilling to adjust to new methods or duties
DEDICATION TO WORK Ability of the employee to effectively use available work time	☐ Spends much time away from desk, often interrupts work for idle talk	☐ Spends more time than necessary in talk or away from desk; sometimes causes delays in work output	☐ Spends no more time than necessary in talk or away from desk; shows fair planning to avoid delays	☐ Usually on job at all times; very little idle time; industrious	☐ Energetic; loses no time in starting and works right to last minute; plans work in advance so as to avoid delays

Comments

Exhibit 9.3
Sample Behavior Anchored Rating Scale for Nurses (From "Measurement of Job Performance in Nursing Homes," final report submitted to Health Resources Administration under grant No. 5R01 NU00612-02. Provided by John Sheridan, March 1980)

ORGANIZATIONAL ABILITY

Nurse demonstrates an effective use of time, equipment, and staff personnel to maintain high standards of nursing care.

My observations of this nurse's organizational ability include:

_____

_____

_____

Selects nursing activities and delegates responsibilities to make the most efficient use of time and personnel available

— 10

Checks orders for medication to be given during the day and attempts to maintain a daily schedule for distributing medication

— 9 If notified by telephone that family member was coming to take patient outside for a trip, would notify patient and aide so patient would be ready to leave

— 8

Requests early trays for patients who may take longer to eat

— 7

When short of linen, rearranges work assignments to accommodate bedridden patients first

Customarily makes and carries out a satisfactory work plan to handle daily assignments

— 6 Keeps a log of patient's personal articles so that there is a record in the event of death or discharge

— 5 If aides had completed their normal work assignments during night shift, would have them help clean equipment during remaining time on shift

— 4 Makes a routine check for paper supplies (for example, paper cups, medicine cups, nursing notes) available on unit

Fails to establish a daily work routine, and nursing activities are not completed according to any particular schedule

Approaches daily work assignments without foresight or systematic planning

— 3 Spends most time charting and very little time with patients and aides

— 2 Frequently leaves important work undone so that he or she can leave on time

— 1 Might make several trips to supply room to get a footboard for patient

— 0

The third step is comparison of the actual level of goal attainment against the agreed-on goals. The evaluator explores reasons for the goals not being met and for goals being exceeded. This step helps determine possible training needs. It also alerts the superior to conditions in the organization that may affect a subordinate's performance but over which the subordinate has no control.

The final step is to decide on new goals and possible new strategies for goals not previously attained. At this point, subordinate and superior involvement in goal setting may change. Subordinates who successfully reach the established goals may be allowed to participate more in the goal-setting process the next time.[12]

An approach similar to MBO, the **work standards approach,** uses more direct measures of performance and is usually applied to nonmanagerial employees. Instead of asking subordinates to set their own performance goals, as in MBO, organizations determine the goals.

Direct Index Approach. This approach differs from the first three (absolute, comparative, and management by objectives) primarily in how performance is measured. The first three approaches, except the work standards approach, depend on a superior evaluating a subordinate's performance. Thus there is a certain amount of subjective evaluation in these cases. However, the **direct index** approach measures subordinate performance by objective, impersonal criteria, such as productivity, absenteeism, and turnover. For example, a manager's performance may be evaluated by the number of employees working for that manager who quit or by the absenteeism rate of that manager's employees. For nonmanagers, measures of productivity may be more appropriate. Measures of productivity can be broken into measures of quality and measures of quantity. Quality measures include scrap rates, customer complaints, and number of defective units or parts produced. Quantity measures include units of output per hour, new customer orders, and sales volume.

Other Approaches. The four major approaches to performance evaluation reviewed thus far represent some of those most frequently used in organizations. The conventional evaluation or rating scale still appears to be the most widely used of these methods for both managers and nonmanagers. But when it is used, it is often supplemented with the **essay method,** which requires the evaluator to describe, generally in summary form, the strengths and weaknesses of a particular subordinate. Martin Marietta Corporation, for example, requires supervisors in its Aero Space Division to write broad essays describing an individual's strengths and weaknesses. This often can be done in conjunction with one of the four forms already described.

The preceding approaches appraise *current* performance. Occasionally it is necessary and useful to be able to appraise how employees would perform on a future job (generally one they would be promoted to). The **assessment center method,** which is used to determine the performance potential of managers, evaluates individuals on a large number of activities. The GM assessment center is described in Chapter 6.

Sources of data:
- Superiors
- Peers
- Self
- Subordinates

Sources of Performance Data

The appraisal process is primarily a matter of gathering data. Its major elements are (1) someone to gather data, and (2) a situation for gathering data. Appraisals can come from several different sources, each with its own advantages and disadvantages.

Appraisal by Superiors.   The superior is the immediate boss of the subordinate being evaluated. It is assumed that the superior is the one who knows best the job of the subordinate and the performance of the subordinate. But there are drawbacks to appraisal by the superior:

- Since the superior may have reward and punishment power, the subordinate may feel threatened.
- The evaluation process often is a one-way process that makes the subordinate feel defensive. Thus little coaching takes place; rather justification of actions prevails.
- The superior may not have the necessary interpersonal skills to give good feedback.
- The superior may have an ethical bias against "playing God."
- The superior, by giving punishments, may alienate the subordinate.

Because of the potential liabilities, organizations may invite other people to share in the appraisal process, even giving the subordinate greater input.

Self-appraisal.   The use of self-appraisal, particularly through subordinate participation in setting goals, was made popular as an important component of MBO. Subordinates who participate in the evaluation process may become more involved and committed to the goals.[13] It appears that subordinate participation may also help clarify employees' roles and reduce role conflict.[14]

Peer Appraisal.   Peer appraisals appear to be useful indicators of subordinate performance.[15] They are particularly useful when superiors lack access to some aspects of subordinates performance. However, the validity of peer appraisals is reduced somewhat if the organizational reward system is based on performance and is highly competitive, and if there is a low level of trust among subordinates.[16]

Appraisal by Subordinates.   Perhaps many of you, particularly as students, have had the chance to evaluate an instructor. How useful do you think this evaluation process is? A significant advantage of appraisal by students is that many instructors are unaware of how they are being perceived by their students. They may not realize that students fail to understand some of their instructions. It is the same in a work setting: Subordinates' appraisals can make superiors more aware of their impact on their subordinates.[17]

> Generally, the more performance information the better.

The Performance Appraisal Interview and Feedback

Feedback is an integral part of any learning experience.[18] **Feedback** in the appraisal process means suggesting to subordinates how to improve performance through an objective assessment of their present positions. Performance feedback is most effective when given immediately after the performance (behavior or result) itself. Thus the appraisal interview represents an excellent opportunity to summarize the past year's performance by citing incidents of success and failure. But this is easier said than done, particularly when discussing failures.

Negative Feedback.   Superiors often face two problems in giving negative feedback. First, performance appraisals, if communicated to the subordinate, can boomerang. Negative feedback can lead to poorer performance rather than better.

Many superiors fear that negative appraisals or even negative portions of otherwise favorable appraisals will discourage rather than motivate subordinates. Their uncertainties appear quite justified. A study at General Electric found that:

- Criticism had a negative effect on achievement of goals.
- Praise had little effect one way or the other.
- The average subordinate reacted defensively to criticism during the appraisal interview.
- Defensiveness resulting from critical appraisal produced inferior performance.
- The disruptive effect of repeated criticism on subsequent performance was greater among those already low in self-esteem.
- The average G.E. employee's self-estimate of performance before appraisal placed him at the 77th percentile.
- Only 2 out of 92 participants in the study estimated their performance to be below average.[19]

Useful feedback can be used to improve performance.

The second problem with negative feedback is that superiors often fail to distinguish between criticism and feedback. If they provide either, they usually provide criticism. But **criticism** is evaluative, implying "goodness" or "badness"; feedback is descriptive. Feedback provides the subordinate with information, data to be used in performing self-evaluations. If subordinates are not being evaluated or criticized, they are not so likely to react defensively. Nevertheless, employees like to know what their supervisors think and expect of them.[20]

Give and take feedback graciously.

How and What to Tell an Employee. Some managers tell their employees they are doing poorly by depersonalizing the interview process. Have you ever been on the receiving end of a poor evaluation and felt you never saw the eyes of the giver (most likely your boss)? Have you ever tried to give someone negative feedback by describing a hypothetical example, all the while hoping the person would pick up the analogy? If you've experienced either of these situations perhaps you've also shared in their dissatisfaction and ineffectiveness.[21]

Even if feedback is very constructive, employees still feel badly; but they will accept it.

What is the alternative? Present factual data on poor performance, not "Your performance wasn't quite up to par, Frank," or "your level of initiative was below average, Betty." Have specific examples of poor performance and even provide dates of the examples. Having this type of information on hand may require the manager to keep logs on all his or her employees' behavior since the typical performance appraisal form usually contains only the rather vague personality dimensions such as initiative, independence, assertiveness, and so on.

The presentation of this factual, nonpersonality, performance information should be presented in a problem-solving, participative manner. This involves active listening as well as active talking (described in Chapter 7). Nevertheless, employees often react unfavorably when first hearing the "bad news." Fortunately they often cool off as they go through five predictable stages in their reaction:

- Denial (shock)
- Anger
- Bargaining
- Depression
- Acceptance

Knowing these five stages that reaction to negative feedback may have is important. It not only cues the manager on what to expect from the employee but also suggests how the manager might most effectively choreograph the entire performance appraisal interview *process.* Managers are generally used to dealing with an employee's poor performance in one interview. After all, if the process is painful, why prolong it? But remember the reason for telling an employee about poor performance is so that improvement (a change in performance) will take place. With this objective in mind, a manager may want to think of the process of giving negative feedback as a *series of interviews,* not just one interview.

When Is the Best Time?   The best time to give an employee information on poor performance is immediately when the performance occurs. When does a child learn how hot the stove is? How many times does the child continue to touch the hot stove after the first time? So the hot stove principle is, *give the employee specific perfor-mance-related information immediately.* Yes, the employee, as with the child touching the stove, will get some immediate pain but it disappears quickly. How many people do you know who hate hot stoves?

Does It Do Any Good?   By giving negative feedback along the guidelines suggested above, the answer is yes. Of course, there are exceptions, and a manager may want to adapt the guidelines to his or her situations, personal style, and special needs and preferences of each employee. A manager may, for example, not have enough time to go through the five stages of performance interviews. Depending upon the employee, some stages could be dealt with in just one interview. Experience and judgment are probably the best guides in determining how these guidelines can most effectively be used.

Errors in Gathering Performance Data

Regardless of the form used and how valid and reliable it is, organizational influences may reduce the effectiveness of even the finest performance appraisal system.[22] A major aspect of this problem involves the characteristics of the superior and subordinate.

Problems with the Superior.   There are basically four problems with the superior that may arise. The first is that superiors may not know what employees are doing or may not understand their work well enough to appraise it fairly.[23] This particular problem occurs more frequently when a manager has a large span of control, a large number of responsibilities, and possibly a large number of employees working in different areas.[24] This problem also occurs when the tasks of the employees are varied and technically complex or changing.

The second problem is that even when superiors understand and know how much work subordinates do, they may not have performance standards for evaluating that work. As a result, subordinates may receive unfair (invalid) evaluations because of variability in standards and ratings.

The third problem is that superiors may use inappropriate standards or may allow personal values, needs, or biases to replace organizational values and standards. The general result is any one of several errors in evaluation. The most common errors occur when superiors rate an employee or group of subordinates on several dimen-

Common
Errors in
Evaluation:

- Halo
- Leniency
- Strictness
- Central
  tendency
- Recency

sions of performance. Frequently a superior will evaluate a subordinate similarly on all dimensions of performance just on the basis of the evaluation of one dimension, the one perhaps perceived as most important. This effect is the **halo error.** When superiors tend to give all their subordinates favorable ratings, they are said to be committing an **error of leniency.** An **error of strictness** is just the opposite. An **error of central tendency** represents a tendency to evaluate all subordinates as average. A **recency-of-events error** is a tendency to evaluate total performance on the last or most recent part of the subordinate's performance. This error can have serious consequences for a subordinate who performs very well for six months or a year but then makes a serious or costly error in the last week or two before evaluations are made.[25] Recall that many of these errors are also likely to occur in interviews (see Chapter 5).

Even the most valid and reliable appraisal forms cannot be effective when superiors commit these all-too-common errors.[26] But many of these errors can be minimized if

- Each performance dimension addresses a single job activity rather than a group of activities.
- The rater on a regular basis can observe the behavior of the ratee while the job is being accomplished.
- Terms like "average" are not used on a rating scale, since different raters have various reactions to such a term.
- The rater does not have to evaluate large groups of employees.
- Raters are trained to avoid such errors as leniency, strictness, halo, central tendency, and recency of events.
- The dimensions being evaluated are meaningful, clearly stated, and important.

Problems with the Subordinate. The problems for superiors in performance appraisal are difficult indeed. However, subordinates also present problems. For one thing, they may not know what's expected of them. This may be true regardless of the level of difficulty of their jobs and whether they work in hospitals, government agencies, or private organizations.

The second problem is that subordinates may not be able to do what's expected. It's not that they don't have the ability; they just don't know how to apply it.[27] The personnel manager can play an important role in these cases, working with superiors to spot reasons for performance deficiencies. Other problems that are likely to be determining a subordinate's performance are the nature of the job, goal characteristics, task interference, feedback and consequences. Since these are more a part of the environment and prevent people from performing, they are discussed in Chapter 10.

Matching Purpose with Method

The final step in the performance appraisal processes and procedures is personnel action, which includes the developmental and evaluative decisions that are made on the basis of the performance appraisal results. As indicated in Exhibit 9.1, the purposes that the organization wants to serve by its performance appraisal system determine which method it uses.[28] For ease of discussion, all of the purposes discussed at the beginning of the chapter can be condensed into five broad categories:

- Motivating subordinates to perform well
- Providing data for management decisions, such as compensation, promotion, and transfer
- Helping in human resource planning, training, and development
- Encouraging superiors to observe and coach their subordinates and
- Providing reference and research data

Only the methods and approaches that best match a given purpose are discussed here. Other methods of appraisal may also help achieve a particular purpose, although they may be less effective.

These purposes of performance appraisal can be served by one or several of the performance appraisal methods.

Motivation. Management by objectives and the work standards method appear to be quite useful in motivating subordinates to do well. Both clarify the goals and roles of subordinates and provide the opportunity for feedback in the form of knowledge of results. There is an important difference, however; MBO allows participation in the goal-setting process, which may lead to an inner commitment to improve performance. Work standards allow no participation.

Presumably, an important element in motivation is feedback. MBO and critical incidents are the two most effective methods for directly involving superiors in the feedback process, in either the written or oral form. These methods focus on performance or goals attained. This approach makes it easier for subordinates to accept feedback and improves future performance as well, because it avoids feedback based on traits or ranking of overall performance.

Data. Many personnel decisions—for example, on salary, promotion, and job assignments—require comparison of people doing different kinds of work. Techniques like MBO or work objectives, which apply to specific jobs, are, therefore, not appropriate for this purpose. They must at least be supplemented by more global methods that equally include all subordinates, regardless of their jobs. The most realistic method might be a conventional form combined with an essay form and supplemented with evaluations of a given subordinate by several levels of superiors. This is called the **field review** technique. Then the superiors could rank all of the subordinates, thus producing an order-of-merit list. The superiors could even rank the subordinates by category, as in the forced distribution method.

Training. MBO, critical incidents, and the essay method of performance evaluation are useful for identifying short- and long-range training and development needs and for helping to spot reasons for performance deficiencies. They also link the deficiencies to organizational action, such as recruitment, training, or job-matching programs. This is especially true if the organization has a good job-analysis system.

Coaching. The critical incidents, weighted check list, and behavior anchored rating scales are especially useful here, because they require superiors to observe subordinate behaviors and provide a log of evaluated behaviors by the time of the performance review session. However, the evaluation of the subordinates' behaviors should also be provided to the subordinates as soon as each behavior has been exhibited. This provides more meaningful and useful information to the subordinates, which they may then use to improve performance before the review session.

These methods also help superiors organize their approach to performance appraisals, because they provide a record of specific incidents and give superiors a basis for giving a high or low performance rating. More importantly, subordinates can learn which activities are valued by the organization. Overall, this process removes some of the pressures that superiors often experience when judging subordinates. It also provides them an opportunity to coach subordinates who have performance deficiencies in some areas. They can at the same time give praise for the strong points of subordinates' performances.

Research. For reference purposes, a simple essay and conventional rating form should be effective. Order-of-merit rankings are also useful in developing criteria for good and poor performance. This means defining a standard against which performance can be measured. In order for the measures to be useful, valid appraisal methods must be used when determining the order-of-merit rankings.

MONITORING PERFORMANCE PROCESSES AND PROCEDURES

Only by monitoring the appraisal system can its integrity and purposes be fulfilled.

In actuality, the **performance appraisal processes and procedures** (PAPPs) in many organizations are not always as elaborate as those presented in this chapter, although the trend is toward being as extensive as necessary to serve several purposes of performance appraisal. Because the design and installation of totally new PAPPs is extremely complex, costly, and challenging, it pays to monitor the consistency of its application, its health, and its legality.

As discussed previously, some superiors commit errors in their appraisals of subordinates. There's little problem if all superiors commit the same error, but superiors usually commit different errors. For example, two employees may perform identically, but if one superior commits a strictness error and one superior commits a leniency error, one of the employees will appear to be far less competent than the other. These errors are common in organizations using rating forms. If the organization is to treat all its employees fairly, it must try to reduce these errors, perhaps by monitoring the lack of consistency in the way superiors complete appraisal forms.[29]

EVALUATING PAPPs

If the personnel manager does an effective job of monitoring the performance appraisal processes and procedures, it is likely the PAPP will be effective.[30] That is, it is likely that the purposes for which performance appraisal and evaluation was designed will be attained. In addition, it is likely that the best performers will be correctly identified—the ones to get the highest raises and promotion opportunities—and that the worst performers will be correctly identified—the ones to get the lowest raises and the first to be laid off or demoted if needed. Nevertheless, the personnel manager must be sure that bias or favoritism does not influence the correct development or use of performance appraisal. Comparing the employment decisions made against the performance appraisal results can help reduce bias as well as evaluate the PAPPs. A closely related way to evaluate an organization's PAPPs is by the number of legal cases brought against the company and the number of cases lost and the amount of money expended to defend against and settle these cases. As with selection decisions that are not made on a valid basis, performance-appraisal-based employment decisions made on the basis of invalid appraisals can result in the violation of many laws and previous court decisions. And as you know by now, losing legal cases is very expensive. Thus the fewer cases brought that are due to performance appraisal, the more effective the PAPPs is likely to be.

FACING THE CRITICAL ISSUES IN APPRAISING AND EVALUATING EMPLOYEE PERFORMANCE

Now that we have rather extensively examined many aspects of appraising and evaluating employee performance in organizations, it is appropriate to return to the Critical Issues identified by personnel managers. Again, these issues are addressed only briefly. You should now be comfortable adding much more detail for each issue.

Issue: *What is the best way to appraise employee performance?*

In the discussion of matching method with purpose, a major point was that many methods of performance appraisal are appropriate. Which appraisal method is best (really, most appropriate) depends on the purpose the organization wants appraisal to serve, for example, making promotion decisions, spotting development needs, making salary decisions, or planning personnel needs.[31] As a consequence of there being no one best way, if an organization wants to attain all the purposes listed in Exhibit 9.1, it may want to use more than one performance appraisal method.

Issue: *Do organizations have to validate performance appraisal forms? If so, how do they do it? What other legal considerations must organizations be aware of?*

An organization's performance appraisal form is generally used to make many important employment decisions such as salary, layoff, terminations, and admission to training programs. These decisions greatly help or hinder employees. In essence, performance appraisal forms are just like any other selection test. As such, they come under equal opportunity legal consideration.

Validation of an appraisal form is done by comparing what's measured by the form such as traits, behaviors, or goals attained, with the components of the jobs of the employees being appraised. The components of the jobs should be identified through job analysis. Other legal considerations in appraising employee performance focus on the nature of the data gathering process and the criteria or standards used. The criteria against which to evaluate employees should also be job-related the same as the performance appraisal form. In the data gathering process, care must be taken to ensure that the superior doing the appraising is objective and correctly uses a standardized and formalized performance appraisal form.

Issue: *There are so many problems every time organizations appraise someone's performance that it is almost more trouble than it's worth. Really, why should it be done at all?*

This is a concern of many managers in organizations. Many feel that it is just impossible to have much influence on employee performance.[32] Most managers think that only monetary rewards can really motivate employees to change their behaviors and that they just don't have much money to do that. Yet, with the concern for more productivity, people should be considered a vital way to meet this concern. Indeed, many employees can perform much better than they do. And they do, when given the appropriate rewards such as more participation in decision making. They also perform better when goals are established, task interference reduced, and useful feedback is provided.

Getting employees to perform better is not only worth it, but is it very possible to do. Appraising employee performance is really not more trouble than it's worth, just the opposite.

Issue: *Should employees be allowed to appraise themselves? Should they appraise the performances of their supervisors?*

Why not? Unless the climate in the work group is very hostile, experience shows that employees are capable of appraising each other and of appraising the boss responsibly. Perhaps it is most appropriate, however, to provide the employees a choice in doing it or not rather than forcing your idea on them. If they choose to do so, they should also be allowed to participate in the design of the form to be used in the appraisal process. Since performance data from this source are only one of several sources, the employees should be told at the outset how their appraisal information will be used. Frequently, peer appraisal data and subordinate appraisal data are used in conjunction with performance data from the supervisor and other supervisors as input for salary decisions, as information to help improve performance, and as feedback to let everyone (including the boss) know where she or he stands.

SUMMARY

Appraising employee performance is a critical personnel activity. This chapter examined performance appraisal as a set of processes and procedures consisting of criteria, standards, forms, data collection results, personnel action, and feedback. To ensure the effectiveness of performance appraisal, personnel managers must be concerned with the implementation and monitoring of all these aspects of the performance appraisal system with awareness of legal considerations.

Because of information presented in this chapter, you should now be in a position to analyze the effectiveness of an organization's PAPPs within the constraints of organizational realities. You should also be able to understand more thoroughly the events and processes surrounding the performance appraisals you will be receiving.

Now we have an understanding of how to appraise and evaluate employee performance. Now it is critical to understand what determines it and to use this understanding in correcting shortcomings or deficiencies in performance. This is the topic of Chapter 10.

KEY CONCEPTS

supervisor   superior
manager   subordinate

performance appraisal   weighted checklist
subjective forms   forced choice
objective forms   conventional rating
performance criteria   nonexempt
deficient form   exempt
contaminated form   behavior anchored rating scale
performance standards   work standards
historical records   essay method
goals   assessment center method
comparative approach   criticism
absolute standards   feedback
management by objectives   halo error
direct indexes   error of leniency
straight ranking   error of strictness
alternative ranking   central tendency
paired comparison   recency of events error
forced distribution   field review
critical incidents format   PAPPs

DISCUSSION QUESTIONS

1. Why should performance appraisal be carried out in the first place?

2. What are some of the purposes that performance evaluation systems serve?

3. What are the three major areas the courts can hold organizations responsible for on performance appraisals?

4. Identify and discuss four forms used to obtain performance criteria and standards?

5. What are the four sources of obtaining performance data and what are their respective drawbacks?

6. What are the two most common problems faced by superiors when having to provide negative feedback to employees?

7. What are the four major potential errors in gathering performance data by the supervisor?

8. What purposes are best served by which of the four types of performance appraisal discussed in this chapter?

9. Why should an organization be concerned with monitoring performance processes and procedures?

10. What are some ways an organization can evaluate its performance appraisal system?

CASE

The Pain of Performance Appraisal

Joe Miller sat at his desk, looking over the performance appraisal form he had just completed on Bill Cox, one of his insurance underwriters. Bill was on his way to Joe's office for their annual review session. Joe dreaded these appraisal meetings, even when he did not have to confront employees with negative feedback.

A couple of years before, Essex Insurance Company, which had experienced very rapid growth, had decided to implement a formal appraisal system. All supervisors had been presented with the new appraisal form, which included five different subcategories, in addition to an overall rating. Supervisors were asked to rate employees on each dimension using a scale from 1 (unacceptable) to 5 (exceptional). They were also advised to maintain a file on each employee into which they could drop notes on specific incidents of good or poor performance during the year to use as "documentation" when completing the appraisal form. They were told they could only give an overall rating of 1 or 5 if they had "substantial" documentation to back it up. Joe had never given one of these ratings because he wasn't diligent about recording specific incidents in employee files and he believed it was just too time-consuming to write up all of the documentation necessary to justify such a rating. There were a couple of employees in his department who deserved a 5 rating in Joe's opinion, but so far no one had complained about the appraisals they received from Joe.

Bill was one of Joe's "exceptional" workers. Joe had three or four specific examples of exceptional performance in Bill's file, but looking over the form could not clearly identify the category in which they belonged. "Oh, well," Joe said to himself, "I'll just give him 3s and 4s. I don't have to justify those, and Bill has never complained before." One of the categories was "Analyzing Work Materials." Joe had never understood what that meant or whether it was relevant for the job of insurance underwriter. He had checked 3 (satisfactory) for Bill, as he did on all the evaluations he did. He understood the meaning of the other categories—Quality of Work, Quantity of Work, Improving Work Methods and Relationships with Coworkers—although he was confused as to what a 3 or a 4 indicated about each category.

Bill knocked on Joe's door and came in. Joe looked up and smiled. "Hi, Bill. Sit down. Let's get through this thing so we can get back to work, OK?"

Case Questions

1. Does Joe feel very comfortable giving Bill his performance appraisal?
2. What problems do you see with the appraisal system Joe is using?
3. What are Bill's likely reactions to being told by Joe that he scored 3s and 4s even though he is one of Joe's exceptional workers?
4. What suggestions do you have for improving the performance appraisal system?

FOR YOUR CAREER

- Nothing may be more important to you in your career than how your performance is evaluated by others.

- Organizations are devoting more attention to performance appraisal because of the potential legal consequences of making employment decisions without adequate performance information.

- Your performance in an organization will most likely be appraised on a subjective performance form. Consequently, you should know its strengths and weaknesses.

- Although the conventional rating is the one most commonly used, MBO is being used increasingly, especially for managers.

- It really pays to perform well even though you may not believe in an organization's performance appraisal system.

- You must learn to accept negative feedback and not take it personally. See it as a way to improve not as a reason to feel badly.

ENDNOTES

1. Thomasine Rendero, "Consensus," *Personnel,* November–December 1980, pp. 4–12.

   Kenneth S. Teel, "Performance Appraisals: Current Trends, Persistent Progress," *Personnel Journal,* April 1980, pp. 296–301, 316.

2. Ralph F. Catalenello and John A. Hooper, "Managerial Appraisal," *Personnel Administrator,* September 1981, pp. 75–81.

   R. Bruce McAgee, "Performance Appraisal: Whose Function?" *Personnel Journal,* April 1981, pp. 298–299.

3. C. O. Colvin, "Everything You Always Wanted to Know about Appraisal Discrimination," *Personnel Journal,* October 1981, pp. 758–759.

4. Patricia Linenberger and Timothy J. Keaveny, "Performance Appraisal Standards Used by the Courts," *Personnel Administrator,* May 1981, pp. 89–94.

5. Wayne F. Cascio and H. John Bernardin, "Implications of Performance Appraisal Litigation for Personnel Decisions," *Personnel Psychology* 34 (1981):211–226.

   Michael H. Schuster and Christopher S. Miller, "Performance Evaluations as Evidence in ADEA Cases," *Employee Relations Law Journal* 6, no. 4 (1981): 561–583.

6. William L. Kandel, "Current Developments in EEO," *Employee Relations Law Journal* 6, no. 3 (1981): 476–483.

   Steve Carroll and Craig Schneier, *Performance Appraisal and Review (PAR) Systems* (Glenview, Ill.: Scott, Foresman, 1982).

   Charles R. Klasson, Duane E. Thompson, and Gary L. Luben, "How Defensible Is Your Performance Appraisal System?" *Personnel Administrator,* December 1980, pp. 77–83.

7. R. I. Lazer and W. S. Wikstrom, *Appraising Managerial Performance: Current Practice and*

Future Directions (New York: Conference Board, Inc., 1977). The reliability should be obtained with the same rates across time and at the same time across raters.

8. For an excellent discussion of the criteria issue, see S. Zedeck and M. R. Blood, *Foundations of Behavioral Science Research in Organizations* (Monterey, Calif.: Brooks-Cole, 1974), pp. 75–94.

   For an excellent discussion of the criteria used to evaluate the entire performance appraisal system (in contrast to the criteria used to evaluate employee performance discussed by Zedeck and Blood), see J. S. Kane and E. E. Lawler III, "Performance Appraisal Effectiveness: HS Assessment and Determinants," in B. M. Staw (ed.) *Research in Organizational Behavior*, vol. 1 (Greenwich, Conn.: JAI Press, 1979), pp. 425–478.

   P. C. Smith, "Behavior, Results and Organizational Effectiveness," in M. Donnette, ed., *Handbook of Industrial and Organizational Psychology* (Chicago: Rand McNally, 1976), pp. 745–776.

9. L. L. Cummings and D. Schwab, *Performance in Organizations* (Glenview, Ill.: Scott, Foresman, 1973).

10. J. Goodale and R. Burke, "BARS Need Not Be Job Specific," *Journal of Applied Psychology* 60 (1975):389–391.

11. For argument for and against MBO, see S. J. Carroll and H. L. Tosi, "Goal Characteristics and Personality Factors in a Management by Objectives Program," *Administrative Science Quarterly* 15 (1970):295–305.

    J. P. Muczyk, "A Controlled Field Experiment Measuring the Impact of MBO on Performance Data," *Journal of Management Studies* 15 (1978):318–339.

    A. P. Raia, *Managing by Objectives* (Glenview, Ill.: Scott, Foresman, 1974).

    H. L. Tosi, J. R. Rizzo and S. J. Carroll, "Setting Goals in Management by Objectives," *California Management Review* 12 (1970): pp. 20–78.

12. Louis Olivas, "Adding a Different Dimension to Goal Setting Processes," *Personnel Administrator*, October 1981, pp. 75–78.

13. R. S. Schuler, "A Role and Expectancy Perception Model of Participation in Decision Making," *Academy of Management Journal*, June 1980, p. 338.

14. Cummings and Schwab, 1973, p. 106.

15. J. S. Kane and E. E. Lawler III, "Methods of Peer Assessment," *Psychological Bulletin* 3 (1978): pp. 555–586.

16. Angelo S. DeNisi and George E. Stevens, "Profiles of Performance, Performance Evaluations, and Personnel Decisions," *Academy of Management Journal*, September 1981, pp. 592–602.

17. Gerald W. Bush and John W. Stinson, "A Different Use of Performance Appraisal: Evaluating the Boss," *Management Review*, November 1980, pp. 14–17.

18. C. Cammon, D. A. Nadler, and P. H. Mirvis, *The Ongoing Feedback System: A Tool for Improving Organizational Management* (Ann Arbor: Survey Research Center, University of Michigan, 1975).

19. For a more thorough discussion of the conflicts between appraisals for developmental and evaluational purposes, see H. H. Meyer, E. Kay and J. R. P. French, Jr., "Split Roles in Performance Appraisal," *Harvard Business Review*, January-February 1965, pp. 123–129.

20. This section on interviewing is taken in part from R. S. Schuler, "Taking the Pain Out of the Performance Appraisal Interview," *Supervisory Management*, August 1981, pp. 8–13.

21. "Training Managers to Rate Their Employers," *Business Week*, March 17, 1980, pp. 178–179.

22. K. N. Wexley, "Performance Appraisal and Feedback," in S. Kerr, ed., *Organizational Behavior* (Columbus, Ohio: Grid, 1979), pp. 241–262.

23. For a more complete review of research in sex differences in performance appraisal, see F. S. Landy and J. L. Farr, "Performance Rating," *Psychological Bulletin,* January 1980, pp. 72–107.

24. Peter J. McGuire, "Why Performance Appraisals Fail," *Personnel Journal,* September 1980, pp. 744–746, 762.

25. W. Oberg, "Make Performance Appraisal Relevant" (working paper, Michigan State University, 1970), p. 10.

26. R. S. Schuler, "Male and Female Routes to Managerial Success," *Personnel Administrator,* May 1979, pp. 35–46.

27. Wexley, p. 256.

28. Many thoughts in this section are taken from two major and useful sources:

G. P. Latham and K. N. Wexley, *Increasing Productivity Through Performance Appraisal* (Reading, Mass.: Addison:Wesley, 1981).

B. McAfee and B. Green, "Selecting a Performance Appraisal Method," *Personnel Administrator,* June 1977, pp. 61–64.

29. M. E. Schick, "The Refined Performance Evaluation Monitoring System: Best of Both Worlds," *Personnel Journal,* January 1980, pp. 47–50.

30. "Appraising the Performance Appraisal," *Business Week,* May 19, 1980, pp. 153–154.

Phillip C. Grant, "How to Manage Employee Job Performance," *Personnel Administrator,* August 1981, pp. 59–65.

31. William J. Birch, "Performance Appraisal: One Company's Experience," *Personnel Journal,* June 1981, pp. 456–460.

Ed Yager, "A Critique of Performance Appraisal Systems," *Personnel Journal,* February 1981, pp. 129–133.

32. Robert I. Lazer, "Performance Appraisal: What Does the Future Hold?" *Personnel Administrator,* July 1980, pp. 69–73.

Ann M. Morrison and Mary Ellen Kranz, "The Shape of Performance Appraisal in the Coming Decade," *Personnel,* July–August 1981, pp. 12–22.

Chapter Outline

Critical Issues in Motivating Employees

Motivating Employees
Desired and Undesired Behaviors
Purposes and Importance of Motivating Employees
Legal Considerations in Motivating Employees

Understanding Employee Motivation and Behavior
An Expectancy Model of Employee Motivation
Motivation-Behavior-Satisfaction Relationships
Why Employees Are Not Motivated
A Model of the Determinants of Employee Behavior

Strategies to Motivate Employees
Ignore the Undesired Behavior
Recognize, Record, and Establish Rules and Policies
Diagnosis and Determination of Causes
Control Strategies
Preventive Strategies

CHAPTER 10

Motivating Employees

Evaluating Strategies to Motivate Employees

Facing the Critical Issues in Motivating Employees

Summary

Key Concepts

Discussion Questions

Case

For Your Career

Endnotes

Personnel in the News

The Most Difficult Variable to Control

In the whole production matrix, people are probably the most frustrating for managers since they constitute the most difficult variable to control and predict. No matter how predictable society tries to make its members through its various socializing mechanisms, people continue to give managers the most trouble. Managers are always complaining about "those workers." "If only they would do what we tell them or learn to follow instructions, we would surpass all our quotas." It is this obsession with the product and the consequent neglect of human needs that could fill case-history books with stories of management's insensitivity to workers. This insensitivity is often turned around and explained as a "lack of worker motivation." Workers become strangers to many managers and are seen only as an extension of a piece of machinery in which a capital investment has been made. This leads to the engineering dream of eliminating the "human element" in production. (From Robert Schrank, Ten Thousand Working Days *[Cambridge, Mass.: The MIT Press], copyright © 1978 by the Massachusetts Institute of Technology, p. 141. Reprinted with the permission of the publisher.)*

The Costs of Absenteeism

General Motors Corporation and the United Automobile Workers contractually authorize a 5 percent absenteeism rate. This rate has been negotiated in the form of paid holidays, paid personal absences, paid vacations, and paid personal holidays. The cost of contractually authorized time away from work has presumably been accepted by management and labor as a form of employee compensation. However, the rate of casual absenteeism, resulting from the failure of employees to report to work as scheduled, is equal to that of contractually authorized time off—5 percent. Casual absences constitute the heart of the absenteeism problem.

General Motors Corporation normally employs approximately 500,000 members of the United Automobile Workers Union. The average union member employed by General Motors earns $10 per hour. Fringe benefits, pro-rated over a standard forty-hour work week, amount to an additional $5 per hour. The fringe benefit component of the compensation package is paid regardless of whether or not an employee reports for work.

The 5 percent casual absenteeism rate translates into 25,000 employee absences each scheduled work day. Given 250 scheduled work days annually, absenteeism claims 6,250,000 work days or 50 million hours each year. Each hour lost to absenteeism costs General Motors $20—$5 in contractually guaranteed fringe benefits paid to the absent worker and $15 in compensation paid to the absent worker's replacement. The total annual cost of casual absenteeism amounts to $1 billion. (From C. R. Deitsch and D. A. Dilts, "Getting Absent Workers Back on the Job: The Case of General Motors," Business Horizons, *Fall 1981, pp. 52–53. Copyright 1981 by the Foundation for the School of Business at Indiana University. Reprinted by permission.)*

Is the Policy Fair?

"We're not going to put up with employees calling in sick all the time," manager Tom Hiltenbrand exclaimed. "You may think our absenteeism control program is strict, but we have a right to demand that employees regularly show up for work."

"The policy is not only strict, it's outrageous," Joe Rockman maintained. "Disciplining employees who are chronically absent is one thing, but requiring people who are legitimately sick to submit to counseling is going way too far."

"Sorry, the policy stands," Hiltenbrand said, "We've made our position clear, so let's just get on with the show."

Was the employer's policy fair?

Facts: An employer established an attendance control program that allowed workers three medically excused absences within 90 days. Employees who were absent for more than three days, or whose overall absenteeism rate exceeded 5 percent, were required to attend a counseling program designed to "bring the problem to the employee's attention" and "motivate" the worker to improve his attendance record.

A group of employees complained about the employer's application of the attendance program's provisions, charging that management was improperly including medically excused absences in computing a worker's overall absenteeism rate. Any absences that were medically excused should not count toward the 5 percent standard that triggered counseling, the employees contended, arguing that counseling was unwarranted for workers "whose absenteeism rate exceeds 5 percent but who would have a below 5 percent absenteeism rate if medically excused absences were excluded." Defending its policy, the employer claimed that it had a right to expect its employees to maintain a 95 percent attendance rate. Stressing that absenteeism had been "significantly reduced" since the program's inception, the employer insisted that it should be allowed to continue with its attendance "guidelines" since they had been very effective in curbing its attendance problems.

Award: The arbiter orders the employer to change its policy. (76 LA 1228) (the reasons for this are presented later in this chapter). (From Bulletin to Management, *September 10, 1981, p. 3. Reprinted by permission from* Bulletin to Management *copyright 1981 by the Bureau of National Affairs, Inc., Washington, D.C.)*

Together these three quotations represent only the tip of the iceberg in motivating employees. Although all of the other chapters in this text describe personnel activities most personnel managers must do, *together* they present fewer problems and challenges than the *single issue of motivating employees!* As indicated in the first quotation, trying to understand, predict, and correct employee behavior (these three are the essence of motivating employees) is extremely difficult at best. This is because human behavior is so uncertain. Consequently many managers are tempted to give up and not even try to motivate employees. What they do instead is to automate, to engineer the employee out of the job, to install complex computer systems, to move plants/offices to where people are "already motivated" or to just go out of business or close a facility.

Since many line managers often may not have the time to become concerned with the complexity of human motivation, the personnel manager can play a critical role in aiding the line manager in motivating employees. The personnel manager can

Managers often lament—"If only people were more predictable."

do this by gaining an understanding of employee motivation, developing and imple-menting strategies to motivate, and training line managers in motivating employees. Together these can make personnel management more effective. Thus this chapter is designed specifically to address these issues. First, however, let us identify the Critical Issues in motivating employees.

CRITICAL ISSUES IN MOTIVATING EMPLOYEES

The four issues most critical to our group of personnel managers are

1. *How can managers motivate their people? It seems as if people aren't motivated any more or the way they used to be.*
2. *Can organizations reduce absenteeism and turnover? How?*
3. *Organizations are having trouble with the growing number of employees with drinking and other drug problems. How can these be solved?*
4. *It's getting harder and harder to get employees to do even the smallest things. Employers are supposed to be lucky if the employee just comes to work! What happened to the good employees?*

In all of the four Critial Issues our personnel managers are concerned with *em-ployee behavior.* Specifically they are worried about whether they can get employees to exhibit the behaviors the organization desires.

MOTIVATING EMPLOYEES

The personnel managers really aren't sure whether they can do this, but they generally rest any hopes they might have on "motivating employees." That is, they think the key to getting desired behaviors is motivating employees. Since this is a reasonable thought, we use this same relationship in this chapter. Consequently, **motivating employees** means getting employees to continuously engage in behaviors that are desired by the organization and getting employees to continuously disengage in behaviors that are not desired by the organization.

Desired and Undesired Behaviors

There are four major categories of desired and undesired behaviors in organization. These four represent the behaviors of most concern to a majority of managers in

Exhibit 10.1
Determinants of Desirable and Undesirable Behaviors and
Strategies to Motivate

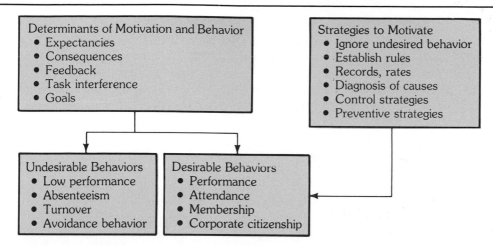

organizations. By and large the undesired behavior is the opposite of the desired behavior. Nevertheless both types of behavior are discussed since ways to motivate employees to engage in a desired behavior are often quite different from the ways to motivate employees to disengage (or never begin) in an undesired behavior. Ways to motivate these behaviors are shown in Exhibit 10.1.

High Performance/Marginal Performance. In Chapter 9, methods of measuring employee performance are discussed in detail. Each of the methods is important because each represents a different way to *measure* performance. Nevertheless, a measure of **high performance** indicates that an employee is in reality a high performer, regardless of method used. **Marginal performance** indicates that an employee is in reality less than an average performer. Notice that the average performer is generally not of sufficient concern for corrective action to be taken, even though high performance is preferred. In other words, we often correct only below average performance and fail to motivate average performers to be above average.

Desired
Behaviors:

- High performance
- Attendance
- Membership
- Citizenship

Attendance/Absenteeism. Organizations really desire employees at work *every day.* If employees must be absent, it is most desirable that the absence be scheduled. **Scheduled absenteeism** exists when it is planned for. Scheduled absenteeism can often be accommodated by an organization. It is the **unscheduled** (unplanned) **absenteeism** that is extremely undesirable. As such, discussions of absenteeism generally refer to the unscheduled type. Organizations often refer to their **rates of absenteeism.**[1] This rate is usually expressed as a percentage. One common method used to compute this percentage rate is

Undesired
Behaviors:

- Marginal performance
- Absenteeism
- Turnover
- Avoidance

$$\frac{\text{Number of worker days lost through absence during month (or year)}}{(\text{Average number of employees}) \times (\text{number of workdays})} \times 100$$

For example, if a company has an average of 300 employees who lost 36 days during the past 60 workdays, its rate of absenteeism would be 2%.

or

$$\frac{36 \text{ worker days lost}}{300 \text{ employees} \times 60 \text{ workdays}} \times 100 = 2\%$$

Membership/Turnover. **Turnover** is the permanent departure (voluntary or involuntary) of individuals from an organization. Because it is an expense to recruit and select new employees, organizations sometimes may seek to retain their current work force or membership. Thus turnover is often undesired. Turnover may be desirable, however, if ineffective employees are leaving, especially when the organization needs to reduce the size of its work force. Turnover also provides opportunities for new employees who may bring new perspectives to old problems. Nevertheless, when turnover is discussed it is generally regarded as undesirable. Remember, however, that it can be beneficial at times.

Organizations (personnel managers) keep track of how effective they are by measuring their **rate of turnover.**[2] Generally the rate covers only permanent separations, voluntary and involuntary. It usually does not include employees placed on temporary or indefinite layoff or furlough. One way the rate is computed is

$$\frac{\begin{array}{c}\text{Number of total separations}\\\text{during month (or year)}\end{array}}{\begin{array}{c}\text{average number of employees on payroll}\\\text{during month (or year)}\end{array}} \times 100$$

For example, if a company has 60 employees quit (separate) and the average number of employees is 300, the turnover rate is 20%
or

$$\frac{60 \text{ separations}}{300 \text{ employees}} \times 100 = 20\%$$

Corporate Citizenship/Avoidance Behavior. These two concepts are not always a part of the standard performance appraisal form. They are, however, certainly important to organizations and often influence how well an employee performs his or her job. **Corporate citizenship** (a desired behavior) means abiding by the spirit as well as the letter of work rules. It means helping out other employees, including managers, when they need assistance, whether or not it is required or solicited.

Avoidance behavior is undesirable in organizations. This behavior describes the "goof-offs," those who go to lunch early and come back late and those who play practical jokes. More importantly for our concern, avoidance behavior describes alcohol and other drug abuse. Since alcoholism is such a serious problem, it is the main focus of our discussion of avoidance behavior.

Purposes and Importance of Motivating Employees

The purpose for motivating employees is to increase desirable behaviors and to reduce undesirable behaviors, that is:

Increase	*Decrease*
High performance	Marginal performance
Attendance	Absenteeism
Membership	Turnover
Corporate citizenship	Avoidance behavior

Attaining these purposes is critical, in terms of both dollars and sense. As discussed in Chapter 1, employee performance in part accounts for an organization's productivity. Recent quality circle and QWL programs at many large corporations such as Ford, General Motors, General Electric, Motorola, and Westinghouse are aimed at increasing productivity through improving the quantity and quality of employee performance. Increasing productivity can save organizations millions of dollars and make the United States much more competitive internationally.

Costs of Absenteeism.   The savings from reduced absenteeism are potentially quite large. Recent surveys estimate that approximately 500 *million* workdays are lost each year to absenteeism in the United States. The estimated cost of this is between $10 and $25 *billion* dollars.[3] In the opening quotation about General Motors' absenteeism rate, excessive absences at GM are estimated to cost $1 billion dollars. This is due in large part to the need to have a much larger work force than actually necessary because of absenteeism. Interestingly enough, the damage done by absenteeism is largely due to only a few employees. Generally, less than 20 percent of an organization's work force account for more than 80 percent of its absences.[4]

The costs of undesirable behaviors are enormous. Fortunately these can be reduced.

Costs of Turnover.   The costs due to employee turnover are similar to those due to absenteeism. In addition, the rate of each is similar (about 2 percent per month for turnover and 3 percent per month for absenteeism). To get the yearly rates of absenteeism and turnover just multiply by 12. Organizations often determine the cost of turnover per employee and multiply this by the number who turned over to get total costs. In a recent survey, the costs of turnover per employee were determined for exempt (managers and supervisors) and nonexempt (the workers who do not manage or supervise) employees. The results are shown in Exhibit 10.2.

It becomes apparent from these data how much money an organization can save by increasing its rates of attendance and membership or by reducing its rates of absenteeism and turnover. If General Motors could reduce its rate of absenteeism by 20 percent (from 5 percent to 4 percent) it could save $200 million (20 percent × $1 billion).

Costs of Alcoholism.   The cost data on alcoholism (chemical dependency) are just as dramatic. Perhaps even more dramatic than with examples of absenteeism, turnover, and marginal performance are the *sense data* associated with reducing alcoholism. It makes good sense for an organization to reduce employee alcoholism because of its positive influence for the individual, his or her family and community, as well as for the organization. Here are some critical numbers on alcoholism in the United States:

- 1 in every 10 employee is an alcoholic.
- Among federal civil employees the estimated annual cost for alcoholism runs between $275 million and $550 million.

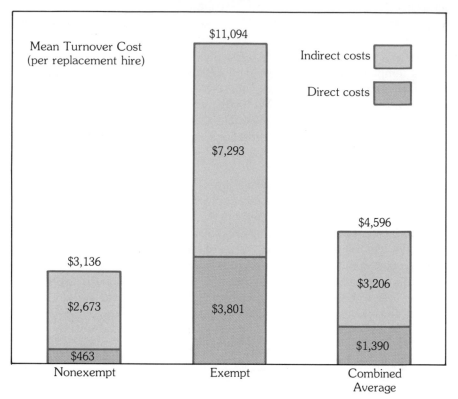

Exhibit 10.2
Average Turnover Costs for Surveyed Companies (*Personnel,*
July–August 1981, p. 51)

- 90% of industry's alcoholic employees range from 30 to 55 years of age and have been on their jobs for 12 to 20 years.
- Studies show that chemically dependent personnel at all levels of responsibility evidence an absenteeism rate 2 and ½ times greater than nonchemically dependent employees. They tend to have six to ten times higher incidence of accidents.
- 25% of each alcoholic's salary is the average cost to the employer in absenteeism, reduced productivity, accidents in the work place, and use of medical plan.
- It is estimated that 65%–80% of those who have received treatment for chemical dependency return to the work force and do a satisfactory job in the opinion of their supervisors.[5]

Legal Considerations in Motivating Employees

The primary legal considerations in motivating employees involve the *use* of rewards and punishments and the *determination* of who gets the rewards and punishments. As indicated in Chapter 9, employee performance must be determined as objectively as possible. Biases of the supervisor in making the evaluation of an employee's performance must be avoided since they can result in discriminatory and unfair conclusions. Remember that these conclusions become illegal when they are used in making employment decisions such as promotions, demotions, layoffs, and firings that result in adverse impact. Therefore, when these decisions are used as rewards and punishments to motivate employees, they become subject to legal considerations.

UNDERSTANDING EMPLOYEE MOTIVATION AND BEHAVIOR

Before looking at some strategies to motivate employees, it is useful to gain a better understanding of employee motivation and its relationship with behavior and satisfaction. This discussion is also quite useful for understanding Chapter 11.

An Expectancy Model of Employee Motivation

In understanding why people do what they do, it is important to keep in mind that an individual behaves because of his or her level of motivation to do so and his or her level of ability.[6] Assuming ability does not pose a problem (if it does, then training is needed), the personnel manager can encourage desired behaviors and discourage undesired behaviors by working on employee motivations.

According to the **expectancy model of motivation,** an individual's motivation to attempt to behave in a certain way is greatest when

Key Components of the Expectancy Model:

- Expectancy 2
- Outcome attractiveness
- Expectancy 1

1. The individual believes that the behavior will lead to certain outcomes (behavior-outcome expectancy). (Expectancy 2)
2. The individual feels that these outcomes are attractive. (Outcome attractiveness)
3. The individual believes that behavior at a desired level is possible (effort-behavior expectancy). (Expectancy)

Each of these three points represents the building blocks of the expectancy model of motivation:

1. **Behavior-Outcome Expectancy.** Every behavior has associated with it, in an individual's mind, certain outcomes (rewards or punishments). In other words, individuals believe or expect that if they behave in a certain way, they will get certain things. Examples of expectancies can easily be described. Individuals may have an expectancy that if they produce ten units, they will receive their normal hourly rate, while if they produce fifteen units, they will receive their hourly pay rate plus a bonus.
2. **Outcome Attractiveness.** Each outcome has an attractiveness to a specific individual. For example, some individuals may value an opportunity for promotion or advancement because of their needs for achievement or power, while others may not want to be promoted and leave their current work group because of needs for affiliation with others.
3. **Effort-Behavior Expectancy.** Each behavior also has associated with it, in an individual's mind, a certain expectancy or probability of success. This expectancy represents the individual's perception of how hard it will be to achieve such behavior

and the probability of his or her successful achievement of that behavior. For example, employees may have a strong expectancy that if they put forth the effort, they can produce ten units an hour.

Putting these building blocks together results in the arrangement shown in Exhibit 10.3.

Performance results from ability and effort.

Working from left to right in the model, motivation is seen as the force on an individual to expend effort. Motivation leads to an observed level of effort by the individual. Effort alone, however, is not enough. Performance results from a combination of the effort that an individual puts forth and the level of that individual's ability. *Ability* in turn reflects the individual's skills, training, information, and talents. *Effort* thus combines with ability to produce a given level of behavior. As a result of behavior, the individual attains certain outcomes. The model indicates this relationship in a dotted line, reflecting the fact that sometimes people perform but do not get outcomes. As this process of behavior-reward occurs, time after time, the actual events serve to provide information that influences an individual's perceptions (particularly expectancies) and thus influences motivation in the future. This is shown in the model by the line connecting the behavior outcome link with motivation.

Employees can reward themselves and get rewards from others.

Outcomes, or rewards, fall into two major categories. First, the individual obtains outcomes from the environment. These are called **extrinsic outcomes.** When individuals perform at a given level, they can receive positive or negative outcomes from supervisors, coworkers, the organization's reward system, or other sources. A second type of outcome occurs purely from the performance of the task itself (for example, feelings of accomplishment, personal worth, achievement, and so on). These are called **intrinsic outcomes.** In a sense, individuals give these rewards to themselves when they feel they are deserved. The environment cannot give them or take them away directly; it can only make them possible.

Exhibit 10.3
The Expectancy Model of Motivation and Behavior (Adapted from E. E. Lawler, *Pay Systems and Organization Development,* Copyright 1951, Addison-Wesley, Reading, Mass., p. 21. Reprinted with permission.)

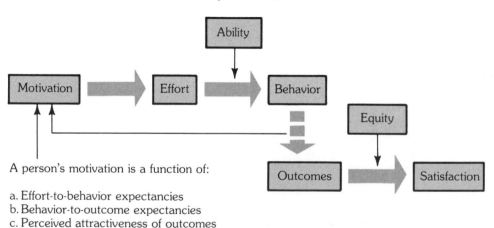

A person's motivation is a function of:

a. Effort-to-behavior expectancies
b. Behavior-to-outcome expectancies
c. Perceived attractiveness of outcomes

Motivation-Behavior-Satisfaction Relationships

The model suggests that satisfaction is best thought of as a result of behavior performance rather than as a cause of it. Strictly speaking, it does influence motivation in some ways. For instance, when satisfaction is perceived to come about as a result of behavior, satisfaction can increase motivation because it strengthens an employee's belief about the consequences of behavior. Also, it can lead to a decrease in the importance of certain outcomes and, as a result, decrease the motivation for those performances that are seen to lead to whatever reward becomes less important.

Note also the concept of equity in Exhibit 10.3. This essence of **equity** here is that an employee's satisfaction is influenced by his or her perception of outcomes received in relationship to those received by others. Even if an employee receives a high level of outcomes she or he may not be satisfied if another employee receives the same for doing less or more for doing the same. Since equity is an important influence in compensation systems, it is discussed further in the next chapter.

Equity or fairness is critical in employee satisfaction.

Why Employees Are Not Motivated

Technically, this subheading is nonsense. It implies that there are times when employees are motivated and times when they are not. Remember, however, that employees are always motivated, it's really a question of "motivated to do what?" or "how motivated are they?" This is illustrated in the insert about John Jayoo.

Thus an organization's concerns are (1) why employees are not motivated to engage in desired behaviors; and (2) why are they motivated to engage in undesired behaviors. These concerns can best be understood by using a framework for the determinants of performance. Such a framework can be used for helping us to understand the determinants of desired and undesired employee behavior.

PERSONNEL IN ACTION

John Jayoo, a cost accountant for the Macdee Company, had an assignment to complete a report for the controller by 5:00 P.M. Thursday, February 26. On Tuesday morning, February 24, Mr. Smithers, the controller, stopped by Jayoo's office to see how the report was going. Jayoo indicated that it was going slowly. In response to Smithers' inquiry as to why, Jayoo answered: "I'm just not motivated." Smithers sympathized but reminded Jayoo that the report was needed by Thursday as Smithers had a meeting Friday morning to discuss a project related to the report and he wanted to review the report before the meeting. On his way out of the building Tuesday evening, Smithers met Jayoo on the elevator and asked about the report. Jayoo indicated that he still hadn't been motivated.

Thursday morning Smithers dropped by Jayoo's office again to check on the progress of the report, and Jayoo indicated that he was still having difficulty getting motivated to do the report. Smithers stressed the importance of the report and his need for the information at the scheduled Friday morning meeting. As he left, Smithers suggested that, if Jayoo couldn't meet the 5:00 P.M. deadline, he should consider looking for a job elsewhere.

At 3:45 P.M. Thursday afternoon Jayoo handed the completed report to Smithers' secretary, who expressed surprise and asked how Jayoo managed to meet the deadline. Jayoo replied, "I got motivated."

A Model of the Determinants of Employee Behavior

There are six major determinants of employee behavior in organizations.[7] An understanding of them enables the personnel manager to diagnose any performance deficiencies and help correct them in a systematic way. Notice how these determinants influence an individual's motivation in terms of the expectancy model of motivation.

The Nature of the Job. On many jobs, the quality or quantity of performance may be outside the subordinate's control. This is particularly true on very routine jobs and where the pace of the jobs is controlled by machines. And when jobs are highly interdependent, it is difficult to separate the individual's performance from that of the group.

Ability of the Employee. If the selection process fails to identify and match an individual's skills, knowledge, and ability with the job requirements, a performance deficiency is likely to occur. At this point, training and development are the best methods by which to influence employee performance.

Consequences to the Employee. Is there anything you do without getting a reward for it? What is it? Perhaps you do it to avoid receiving a punishment. You may study to get an A (reward) on the exam or to avoid an F (punishment). You may also study in order to graduate (or avoid not graduating) someday and get a good job. This highlights the difference between short-term and long-term rewards and punishments (both outcomes). Many employees react the same way you do.

Feedback to the Employee. In Chapter 9 the benefits of giving feedback, whether positive or negative, are discussed. For the feedback to work effectively, however, it must have several important characteristics. It must tell the employee exactly what is right and wrong with his or her performance, it must be timely, and it must be understandable to the employee.

Task Interference. Although there may be plenty of short- and long-term positive consequences for some desired behaviors and the employee may receive adequate feedback she or he still may not perform all of those desired behaviors. This may be the result of task interference. There are two types of task interference: task conflict and task uncertainty. **Task conflict** occurs when the employee does not have enough time to do the job, or does not have enough materials or assistance from others to do the job. **Task uncertainty** occurs when the employee does not know what's expected and does not know his or her level of authority and responsibility.

Goal Characteristics. The final determinants of employee behavior are the characteristics of goals that exist for an employee. A critical goal characteristic is whether or not an employee has goals. Employees generally perform better with goals than without goals. They also perform better as their goals become more specific and clear and when they are moderately difficult.

Now that we have an understanding of employee motivation and behavior and their determinants, let's look at some strategies to reduce undesired behaviors and those to elicit desired behaviors. You may come up with more strategies in addition to those listed. Note that strategies are more likely to be effective if they are based on our understanding of motivation and the determinants.

Summary of Determinants of Employee Behavior

- Nature of the job
- Abilities, skills and knowledge
- Consequences to the employee
- Feedback to the employee
- Task interference
- Goal characteristics

STRATEGIES TO MOTIVATE EMPLOYEES

Because the lack of a desired behavior by an employee or the presence of an undesired behavior by an employee can be so costly, organizations develop strategies to motivate employees to exhibit behaviors they desire.

Strategies:
- Ignore
- Establish rules
- Record rates
- Diagnose
- Positive control
- Negative control

Ignore the Undesired Behavior

A typical response to undesired behavior is to ignore it. Managers and supervisors generally find it difficult to tell employees that they are ineffective and then take action to correct the problem. This is particularly true for new managers. In fact, managers may find it more trouble than it is worth to even evaluate an employee as an ineffective performer. Another reason for managers to avoid evaluating employees as ineffective is the possibility that the managers' competency will be questioned. For example, if an instructor gives out many low grades, the department chairperson or college dean might blame the instructor—not the students.

A related organizational reality is that organizations may refuse to fire employees because doing so is an admission of incompetence at selecting good employees. As a result, many organizations create conditions to encourage undesirable employees to resign, such as attractive retirement programs.

Recognize, Record, and Establish Rules and Policies

Because the cost and importance of undesirable behavior is so high, organizations cannot really afford to ignore it. The alternative is to recognize it, and start dealing with it. This involves collecting data on the undesirable behaviors, such as their rates of occurrence, establishing policies and rules, and then enforcing the rules.

Records and Rates. It is important for an organization to find out the frequency of undesirable behaviors. For example, performance evaluation records can be used to

Exhibit 10.4

Recording and Measuring Job Absence (From *Job Absence and Turnover*, Bureau of National Affairs Quarterly Report, 2nd Quarter 1981.)

	Percent of Companies					
		By Industry			By Size	
	All Companies	Mfg.	Nonmfg.	Nonbus.	Large	Small
Supervisors keep daily employee attendance records	82	71	90	96	91	75
Absence data are collected and reported through a company-wide system	68	70	66	64	71	65
Absence rates are computed for at least one employee group on a regular basis	59	72	49	43	55	62
Rates are computed*—						
■ Monthly	51	63	30	42	50	52
■ Annually	40	29	55	58	43	38
■ Quarterly	31	29	40	25	37	28
■ Weekly	16	27	—	—	7	22
■ Daily	15	17	10	17	17	14
■ Other	6	6	10	—	10	4
Absence rates are computed for all regular employees*	57	49	60	83	68	50

*Percentages are based on companies that compute absence rates on a regular basis.
Note: Percentages add to more than 100 percent because of multiple responses.

find out the number and location of marginal performers. Rates of absenteeism and turnover should be established along with ways to collect the data in the first place. Shown in Exhibit 10.4 are several ways by which and how frequently absenteeism data are collected by organizations. Note that the larger, nonmanufacturing companies rely upon their supervisors more than other types of companies to collect absenteeism data. Also shown in Exhibit 10.4 are the types of companies that compute absence rates for all their regular employees. It is often useful for an organization to be aware of these rates for other companies in order to help determine how effective it is.

The next step after recording and establishing rates of undesirable behaviors is to look at each category of behavior in terms of dollars and cents. What is shown in Exhibit 10.4 should be done for avoidance behaviors and marginal performance.

Establish Rules and Policy and Be Consistent.   No business can operate smoothly, safely, or effectively without work rules. Employers make the rules, supervisors enforce them, and employees follow them. That's the general scenario. But no employer has a completely free hand to establish any rules she or he wishes. Work rules are really part of your internal discipline system, because rule infractions only sometimes result in some form of discipline.

Your work rules must first be reasonably related to necessary management goals to be effective. They should also be effectively communicated (Chapter 7). You may also have to consider the constraints imposed by a labor contract. And there is another very important requirement: The rules you promulgate and enforce cannot unfairly discriminate if they result in adverse impact against any group of employees protected by fair employment laws. In other words,

- Your rules must apply equally to all employees, regardless of race, religion, national origin, sex, age, or disability.
- Your rules must be enforced objectively.
- Your records should reflect the information necessary to prove equal application and enforcement of work rules.[8]

An excellent example of a company's absenteeism policy is shown in Exhibit 10.5. But for even such a clearly stated policy to be effective and prevent the development of undesirable practices, the policy must be fairly and consistently enforced.

Exhibit 10.5
A "Point System" Absenteeism Control Policy (From Frank E. Kuzmits, "The Impact of Legalistic Control Policy Upon Selected Measures of Absenteeism Behavior," Appendix: Paper presented at Academy of Management Meeting, Eastern Division, May 1981. Used by permission of Frank Kuzmits.)

Absentee Policy

As a result of excessive absenteeism and/or tardiness, disciplinary action may be required and will be based on frequency of occurrences in accordance with the following:

Absenteeism is defined as being absent from work on any scheduled work day, even though the employee has reported off.

Each period of consecutive absence will be recorded as "one occurrence" regardless of the number of days' duration.

Tardiness will be considered reporting to work within ten (10) minutes of the scheduled starting time. One occasion of tardiness will be charged as one quarter ($\frac{1}{4}$) occurrence of absenteeism.

Employees who report to work late, as provided for in the reporting regulations, or who leave before the end of the shift (with management's permission) will be charged with one-half ($\frac{1}{2}$) of an absence occurrence for either of these occurrences.

Employees who are absent without call-in will be charged with two occurrences of absence for that occasion.

Absence due to Funeral Leave, Military Obligation, Jury Duty, or Union Business, (each as defined by the Contract), and further including hospital confinement and work-incurred injury will not be recorded as an occurrence of absence for purposes of disciplinary action.

For each calendar month of perfect attendance, an employee with an absentee record will have one occurrence deducted from his absentee record.

Absence records will be maintained for a consecutive twelve-month period, starting with the employee's first occurrence of absence. All absence records and warning slips which are one year old, or older, shall not be considered for purposes of disciplinary action under this policy.

Correction discipline will be administered according to the following: Three occurrences, or "points" within a twelve-month period—verbal warning; five occurrences, or "points," within a twelve-month period—written warning; seven occurrences, or "points," within a twelve-month period—second written warning; and twelve occurrences, or "points," within a twelve-month period—discharge.

The above policy is in addition to action which may be taken: when cumulative time lost from work for any reasons substantially reduces the employees services to the company; or as may be related to provisions of the contract.

It was the lack of consistency that caused the arbitrator in the quotation at the start of this chapter to order the employer to change its policy. According to the arbitrator in the opening quotation from "Is the Policy Fair?"

> The employer was "taking inconsistent positions." On the one hand, management treated absences for which a doctor's certificate was produced as "excused" for purposes of its 3-in-90 days provision. On the other hand, the employer refused to exclude medically excused absences from the 5 percent absenteeism calculation used to trigger the counseling program requirements.

> "An absence which is excused under one aspect of the attendance program," the arbiter emphasizes, "should also be excused under other aspects of it." "No useful purpose can be served by counseling an employee who has an overall absence record in excess of 5 percent when some of those absences were medically unavoidable and recognized as such by the employer," the arbiter stresses. "The general purpose of attendance counseling," the arbiter explains, "is to improve attendance in those cases where poor attendance can be reasonably avoided by the employee." "An absence excused for medical reasons," the arbiter decides, "is a legitimate reason to excuse an employee from counseling."[9]

Diagnosis and Determination of Causes

Diagnose:
- Nature of Job
- Employee Ability
- Consequences
- Task interference
- Feedback characteristics
- Goal characteristics

Even though rules and policies are established and clearly understood, desirable behavior is not ensured. As we saw in the section entitled "A Model of the Determinants of Employee Behavior," the six major determinants are

- Nature of Job
- Employee Ability
- Consequences
- Feedback characteristics
- Task interference qualities
- Goal characteristics

Since these six determinants are so critical for employee behavior and motivation, they should be used by the organization in diagnosing any behavioral problems. An understanding of these six determinants of employee behavior is not only useful in spotting reasons for behavioral deficiencies but is also useful for controlling and preventing the future occurrence of undesirable behavior but also eliciting the occurrence of desirable behaviors.

Control Strategies

Control strategies that organizations can use draw directly from the six determinants of employee behavior.

Positive Behavioral Control Strategy.   The positive approach to control involves efforts to encourage desirable behavior by establishing behavior standards and setting up reward systems that are contingent upon successful (desired) behaviors.[10]

A positive behavioral control strategy being used specifically to reduce absenteeism is called **earned time.** Rather than divide benefits into specific numbers of days for vacation and personal leave, sick leave, or short-term disability, earned time lumps these days into one package. These days can be used for a variety of purposes, including a cash payment at the time of voluntary termination. Earned time is available for use as soon as it is "earned" on the job. Earned time, in essence is "no-fault absence." | Earned time helps reduce unplanned absenteeism and false excuses.

The program's bottom line is that the number of earned time days for which an employee may receive a cash payment is less than the previous total of sick, vacation, jury, and all other benefit days combined. For example, the previous total combined may be divided by 2, 3 or 4 to get the earned time. And earned times are available to use without having to meet a plethora of special requirements. The program's prime advantages are (1) reduction in unplanned absences; (2) reduction in employee-supervisory conflict over legitimacy of absences and individual responsibility; and (3) flexibility for use of time to suit individual priorities.

Negative Behavioral Control Strategy.   Unlike positive controls, which seek to encourage desirable behavior patterns through systems of reward, negative controls seek to discourage unwanted behavior by either punishing it or ignoring it. Negative control is commonly utilized in many organizations because of its ability to achieve relatively immediate results. Its negative effects can be reduced by incorporating several **hot stove principles,** including

- *Providing ample and clear warning.* Many organizations have clearly defined disciplinary steps. For example, the first offense might elicit an oral warning; the second offense a written warning; the third offense, a disciplinary layoff; the fourth offense, discharge.

- *Administering the discipline as quickly as possible.* If a long time elapses between the ineffective behavior and the discipline, the employee may not know what the discipline is for. | Positive strategies can get more predictable results than negative strategies.

- *Administering the same discipline for the same behavior for everyone, every time.* Discipline has to be administered fairly and consistently.

- *Administering the discipline impersonally.* Discipline should be based on a specific behavior, a specific person.

Because it is the immediate supervisor or manager who plays the integral role in administering discipline, to increase its effectiveness the organization should

- Allow managers and supervisors to help select their own employees
- Educate managers and supervisors about the organization's disciplinary policies and train them to administer the policies

▪ Set up standards that are equitable to employees and that can easily and consistently be implemented by managers and supervisors[11]

Preventive Strategies

The following strategies are useful for many of the undesired behaviors; however, some work better for some behaviors than for others. Thus, the strategies-behaviors discussed represent the most frequently found and most effective combinations. Although these strategies are used here as a means of preventing undesirable behavior they can also be used to help control and reduce existing undesirable behavior.

Positive Group and Individual Incentives. The quotation about the General Motors absenteeism problem sets up this discussion of using group incentives and peer pressure to prevent/reduce absenteeism:

> Peer pressure is an effective means for making the behavior of individuals conform to the collective will of the group. The education of employees concerning the costs of absenteeism coupled with a mechanism for distributing the savings realized from reduced absences are necessary steps toward focusing group pressure upon the chronic absentee to develop better work habits. Employees, cognizant of the monetary rewards stemming from reduced absenteeism, have an incentive to "persuade" problem workers to adjust their behavior to conform to the wishes of the group.
>
> The profit sharing provisions of the new General Motors/United Automobile Workers contract provide an excellent opportunity for implementing collective incentives to reduce absenteeism. Employees with good attendance records could be issued General Motors stock in an amount equal to 35 percent of the cost savings resulting from reduced worker absences. This percentage represents the proportion of total production costs due to worker compensation and is generally accepted as an equitable method for distributing productivity gains. Assuming that peer pressure leads to a reduction in the absenteeism rate from 5 percent to 4 percent (as discussed earlier), the work force would be entitled to 35 percent of the resulting savings of $834 million—or $292 million in General Motors stock. Given a labor force of 479,000 employees, each worker would receive $610 in General Motors stock.[12]

In addition to these positive group incentives to reduce absenteeism, organizations can also use positive individual incentives. One general positive individual incentive program is to attach rewards or at least the potential for rewards, such as money or prizes, for perfect attendance. A specific program of this nature is similar to a poker game. Each day a worker comes to work on time she or he receives a playing card. At the end of the week, the worker with the best hand wins. If a worker misses a day, she or he is ineligible to play. Although this program can succeed in reducing absenteeism if the prizes are big enough, it may fail where the employees are opposed to gambling (for example, for religious reasons). Do you see any other potential disadvantages to it?[13]

Eliminate Rewards for Undesirable Behavior. Often absenteeism goes unattended. It seems always easier to ignore it, at least until it becomes extremely disruptive. This is the case even where there are contractually specified disciplinary procedures and penalties. Not only is failure to discipline those who are absent unfair to the rest, but it rewards those who are absent. Those absent enjoy the benefits of being off work without any punishments for missing work. True, they may not be paid for the day absent, but even this can be avoided by calling in sick.[14]

Generally, however, when workers are absent they do not get paid. But they do continue to receive indirect, fringe benefits. For example, the employer is still paying health and medical insurance benefits for the worker who is not working. In essence then the worker is partially being paid for missing work. One suggested way to deal with this situation is to tie indirect benefits to only the hours worked. Since the employer has already paid for the benefits for the worker, when she or he is absent, the cost of the indirect benefits can be a payroll deduction.

Participation.   Bottom-up management, employee participation in decisions, and consensus development are all ways used by management to bond workers to their organizations in more meaningful ways. The effects of this stronger bond are more loyalty and less absenteeism and turnover. As discussed in Chapter 16, participatory management styles and strategies can also result in enhanced performance and reduction of marginal performance.

Job Rotation.   Another way organizations have tried to increase the bond between worker and organization is by job rotation. It also increases the level of understanding workers have for each other. In turn, empathy replaces friction and close working relationships facilitate communication.

Firing.   Often the final step in a progressive disciplinary program (see Chapter 8, p. 252) is dismissal or just plain firing or displacing an employee. But firing can be exceedingly painful, even though it is well organized and planned. And many individuals are capable of effective performance but only in certain types of situations. Thus some organizations reassign employees to different parts of the organization and trade top-level managers to other organizations. These alternatives may not be available, however, particularly if the organization needs to reduce its labor force by layoffs or if it believes that certain employees would be ineffective any place. Consequently increasing numbers of organizations have adopted career counseling and outplacement services for employees being terminated for whatever reason.[15]

Employee Assistance Programs (EAPs).   EAPs are programs designed specifically to assist employees with chronic personal problems that hinder their job performance, attendance, corporate citizenship and even off-the-job behaviors. They are often used with employees who are alcoholics or who have severe marital problems. Since these problems may in part be caused by the job, some employers are taking the lead in establishing EAPs to assist these individuals in their problems.[16]

A company that establishes an EAP generally thinks that it has a responsibility to the employee and that the employee should be given a chance to correct any undesirable job behavior. Nevertheless, it is the employee who must help himself or herself. If she or he fails to participate in an EAP or recover through other means, the employer may have no other choice but to terminate the employee. The philosophy of most EAPs is to help individuals help themselves within a context of fairness yet firmness.[17]

Employees should be treated with fairness and firmness.

EVALUATING STRATEGIES TO MOTIVATE EMPLOYEES

Evaluating strategies or programs such as the ones described above to motivate employees is essential. The measures against which to evaluate the success of our programs include:

- Number of marginal performers
- Rate of absenteeism
- Rate of turnover
- Incidence and severity of avoidance behaviors

In turn, the significance of these four can be shown in terms of dollars and cents. Thus what is necessary for the personnel manager is to

1. Gather data on each of these four measures for all parts of the organization;
2. Establish and implement programs designed for the undesirable behaviors that company wants to eliminate;
3. Gather data again on the measures that are relevant to the program implemented;
4. Compare the data gathered before the program was implemented and after it was implemented; and
5. Translate these differences into the actual dollars. For example, if turnover was reduced, the dollar value of this reduction should be determined. Also the cost of the program should be stated in dollars. The differences between the dollars expended and saved thus represent the value of the program.

Although these are critical steps, they are not always easy to do, especially costing out the effects of the program. To illustrate the complexity yet feasibility of costing out just one of the measures, see Appendix E.

FACING THE CRITICAL ISSUES IN MOTIVATING EMPLOYEES

Now it is appropriate to address the Critical Issues presented at the start of this chapter. Remember, only highlights of the Critical Issues are presented. You should, however, be more thorough in developing your responses to the four issues.

Issue: *How can managers motivate their people? It seems as if people aren't motivated any more or the way they used to be.*

Many managers, both personnel and line managers, ask this question all the time. It seems as if people aren't motivated. However, as we know, everyone is motivated. It is just a question of motivated to do what and with how much intensity.

Personnel managers can aid line managers in motivating their employees to engage in desired behaviors by presenting the factors that help determine motivation: (1) consequences; (2) feedback; (3) task interference; and (4) goal setting. Then the personnel manager must make sure the line manager identifies the desired behaviors and communicates them to the employees. When the employee engages in behaviors, the manager then must be ready to provide rewards and punishments as appropriate. If the employee does not have the ability, the manager must spot this and have the personnel department suggest training programs.

Issue: *Can organizations reduce our absenteeism and turnover? How?*

Of course! A key to reducing either of these undesirable behaviors is to identify the causes. Using the framework discussed in the first response, the consequences of turnover and absenteeism for the employees should be identified. Many employees are absent because the consequences for doing so are greater than those for not doing so. Generally, the punishments for being absent are not too severe.

To reduce absenteeism it may be necessary to make absenteeism more costly. Progressive discipline may be needed. (See Chapter 8). Absenteeism may also be reduced by providing more rewards for attendance.

To reduce turnover the entire organization needs to be examined. This is assuming that the good people are leaving in higher than reasonable numbers. What needs to be done is to get them more involved and committed to the organization. Perhaps jobs can be enriched and employees can be given a greater voice in decision making. Inequities need to be removed and consistency needs to be practiced.

Issue: *Organizations are having trouble with the growing number of employees with drinking and other drug problems. How can these be solved?*

With understanding, fairness, and firmness. In some cases, the organizations recognize their contribution to employee alcoholism. Especially when this is true, organizations have been inclined to establish EAPs. EAPs are established to aid employees with chronic, undesirable behaviors. The treatment of the behaviors, however, is done with *fairness* to the other employees. It is also done with *firmness* such that employees are dismissed if they fail to improve. Clearly not all cases can be solved. There are times when the employee's alcoholism is due solely to nonjob factors.

Issue: *It's getting harder and harder to get employees to do even the smallest things. Employers are supposed to be lucky if the employee just comes to work! What happened to the good employees?*

This is also a common thought of managers. Fortunately surveys reveal that folks such as you still value doing a good job. In fact, the importance of work to young people is on the upswing. This suggests that there are good employees. It is just up to organizations to identify them.

Perhaps what is more critical, however, is for organizations to provide an environment that allows employees to care to do a job. This requires looking at the organizational structure, the nature of jobs, and the practices of supervisors. In addition, organizations must be ready to change these.

Remember, there are many large organizations in the United States, such as Delta Airlines, Xerox, IBM, and Proctor and Gamble, that appear to have few people problems. A close look reveals that what these organizations do for their employees is often not done elsewhere. Fortunately, their practices can often be done elsewhere. Yes, there is hope.

SUMMARY

Motivating employees to engage in desirable behaviors is important for organizations. The costs of undesirable behaviors are enormous. Effectively managing human resources is based in large part upon motivating employees to engage in above average performance, minimal absenteeism, and turnover good corporate citizenship. Since these are critical criteria for total personnel effectiveness the personnel manager must be intimately involved in motivating employees.

Fortunately, it is quite feasible, though not necessarily easy, to motivate employees. What the personnel manager should do first is to become aware of what motivates people. With this understanding, it is easier to develop strategies to more effectively motivate employees to engage in desired behaviors. Critical to getting these behaviors, however, is a diagnosis of what is causing the current undesired behaviors. With this knowledge, the appropriate strategies can be developed and implemented. Once they are implemented the personnel manager should carefully monitor and evaluate their effectiveness. Changes should be made as deemed necessary.

Successfully motivating employees often rests upon the proper use of positive consequences. Although these need not be financial, often they are. Since using financial consequences can be costly to the organization, it must be done with care. And since it is complex, it must be done with an understanding of the total compensation system of the organization. Thus total compensation is discussed in the next three chapters.

KEY CONCEPTS

outplacement	behavior-outcome expectancy
positive discipline	outcome attractiveness
preventive discipline	effort-behavior expectancy
high performance	extrinsic outcomes
marginal performance	intrinsic outcomes
scheduled absenteeism	equity
unscheduled absenteeism	task conflict
rate of absenteeism	task uncertainty
turnover	positive behavioral control strategy
rate of turnover	negative behavioral control strategy
corporate citizenship	earned time
avoidance behavior	hot stove principles
expectancy model of motivation	employee assistance programs

DISCUSSION QUESTIONS

1. What is the key to getting employees to exhibit desired behaviors, and what are these behaviors?

2. What is the purpose of motivating employees, and why is it so important?

3. Explain the expectancy model of motivation.

4. What is the concept of equity, and how does it apply to worker motivation in the expectancy model? Give an example.

5. Identify and describe the determinants of employee behavior.

6. What are the critical aspects of well-established rules and policies governing employee behavior?

7. Describe the positive behavioral control strategy.

8. When should the negative behavioral control strategy be used? What is its primary weakness?

9. What is meant by outplacement, and who is it designed for?

10. Do workers really need to be motivated?

CASE

Whether to Kick or to Pat

"Ladies and gentlemen, as I promised, this meeting will be as short in time as the agenda is short in content. Our charter is a simple one: Employee absenteeism is getting out of hand and I want it stopped," said plant manager William Fine in a manner that left the nature of his disposition on this particular subject quite clear. "Very frankly, I'm not all that concerned about the manner you choose to reduce the incidence of employee absenteeism. But, I say again, I want it stopped. May I have your recommendations?"

"Yes, Bill, if I may. I've given this matter some thought," answered the first shift supervisor, Tom May. "I'm thinking about an incentive program designed to reward those employees who maintain regular attendance. Maybe we could give out a single playing card per day. At the end of the week, the best poker hand would win $50 or something like that. The point is that you can't win without five cards: If you are absent during the week, you can't win."

"You have to be kidding," retorted Jane West, second shift supervisor. "For instance, does the city reward you if you *don't* get a parking ticket over some period of time? Does the IRS reward you if you *don't* cheat on your taxes for some number of years? Certainly not! Those are expected behaviors. I don't know that I can agree with rewarding people for engaging in responsible behavior. I think that regular attendance is part and parcel of the employment contract. We agree to pay some amount of money and benefits in return for a modicum of reasonable behavior at work; one of those behaviors is reasonable attendance.

"I am, therefore, in favor of a strict new policy for absenteeism with progressive discipline, which in extreme cases will lead to termination," Ms. West concluded sharply.

Case Questions

1. What do you think of the position of Tom May, first shift supervisor?

2. What do you think of the position of Jane West, second shift supervisor?

3. In your opinion which of the programs is more likely to reduce absenteeism?

4. Which recommendation would you choose if you were in Bill Fine's position?

FOR YOUR CAREER

▪ How an organization treats employees who *don't* behave appropriately is as important as how it treats employees who *do* behave appropriately.

▪ Remember one day you may not perform as well as you might like. Working for an organization that is concerned is then especially critical.

▪ Any good manager should have a basic understanding of what motivates employees.

▪ You probably work hardest when you know that you'll be rewarded and are relatively certain you can do it.

▪ Rewards that you can give yourself can be more satisfying than those given to you by others.

▪ Perhaps being treated fairly is one of the most important feelings that an individual in an organization can have.

ENDNOTES

1. Frank E. Kuzmits, "How Much Is Absenteeism Costing Your Organization," *Personnel Administrator,* June 1979, pp. 29–32.

Frank E. Kuzmits, "The Impact of a Legalistic Control Policy upon Selected Measures of Absenteeism Behavior." Paper presented at the Academy of Management Meeting, Eastern Division, May 1981.

Job Absence and Turnover, Bureau of National Affairs Quarterly Report, 2nd Quarter 1981, copyright 1981, Washington, D.C.

2. *Job Absence and Turnover.*

3. D. R. Dalton, "Absenteeism and Turnover: Measures of Personnel Effectiveness," in R. S. Schuler, J. M. McFillen, and D. R. Dalton, eds., *Applied Readings in Personnel and Human Resources Management* (St. Paul: West Publishing, 1981), pp. 20–38.

L. W. Porter and R. M. Steers, "Organizational, Work and Personal Factors in Employee Turnover and Absenteeism," *Psychological Bulletin* 80 (1973):151–176.

R. M. Steers and S. R. Rhodes, "Major Influences on Employee Attendance: A Process Model," *Journal of Applied Psychology* 63 (1975):391–407.

4. Clarence R. Deitsch and David A. Dilts, "Getting Absent Workers Back on the Job: The Case of General Motors," *Business Horizons,* Fall 1981, pp. 52–58.

5. Owens/Corning Fiberglass, Inc. *The Employee Assistance Program* (Toledo: Owens/Corning Fiberglass, Inc., 1978).

6. This section is adapted from Edward E. Lawler, III, *Pay and Organization Development* (Addison-Wesley Publishing Co.: Reading, Mass.) pp. 20–22.

7. R. F. Mager and P. Pipe, *Analyzing Performance Problem or 'You Really Oughta Wanna'* (Belmont, Calif.: Fearon Pitman Publishers, Inc., 1970).

8. "Actions and Reactions in the Field of Fair Employment," *FEP Guidelines,* September 14, 1981, pp. 1–8.

9. *Bulletin to Management,* September 10, 1981, p. 3. Reprinted by permission from *Bulletin to Management,* copyright 1981 by the Bureau of National Affairs, Inc., Washington, D.C.

10. *FEP Guidelines,* September 14, 1981.

11. James E. Belohlav and Paul O. Papp, "Making Employee Discipline Work," *Personnel Administrator,* March 1978, pp. 22–24.

12. Deitsch and Dilts, pp. 57–58.

13. Hilde Behrend, "Absence Problems—Are Attendance Bonus Schemes the Answer?" *Management Decisions* 18, no. 4 (1979):212–216.

Frank E. Kuzmits, "No Fault: A New Strategy for Absenteeism Control," *Personnel Journal,* May 1981, pp. 387–390.

J. Michael McDonal, "What Is Your Absenteeism I.Q.?" *Personnel,* May–June 1980, pp. 33–37.

Clarence R. Deitsch and David A. Dilts, "To Cut Casual Absenteeism: Tie Benefits to Hours Worked," *Compensation Review,* 1st Quarter, 1981, pp. 41–46.

Thomas E. Hall, "How to Estimate Employee Turnover Costs," *Personnel,* July–August 1981, pp. 43–52.

Richard E. Kopelman, George O. Schneller IV, and John J. Silver, Jr., "Parkinson's Law and Absenteeism: A Program to Rein in Sick Leave Costs," *Personnel Administrator,* May 1981, pp. 57–64.

Martin Lasder, "Cut Turnover With a Japanese Pattern," *Computer Decisions,* September 1981, pp. 135–140, 144–148.

John S. Piamonte, "An Employee Motivational System That Leads to Excellent Performance," *Personnel,* September–October 1980, pp. 55–66.

14. Haluk Bekiroglu and Turan Gonen, "Labor Turnover: Root, Costs and Some Potential Solutions," *Personnel Administrator,* July 1981, pp. 67–72.

Gary P. Latham, Larry L. Cummings and Terence R. Mitchell, "Behavioral Strategies to Improve Productivity," *Organizational Dynamics,* Winter 1981, pp. 5–23.

Fred Luthans and Mark Martinko, "An Organizational Behavior Modification Analysis of Absenteeism" *Human Resource Management,* Fall 1976, pp. 11–18.

Mary Coeli Meyer, "Demotivation—Its Cause and Cure," *Personnel Journal,* May 1978, pp. 260–266.

Miriam Rothman, "Can Alternatives to Sick Pay Plans Reduce Absenteeism?" *Personnel Journal,* October 1981, pp. 788–790.

15. Ronald A. Brooks, "Don't Fire Your Executives—Trade Them," *Personnel Journal,* May 1979, pp. 308–310.

16. D. J. Kravetz, "Counseling Strategies for Involuntary Terminations," *Personnel Administrator,* October 1978, p. 24.

17. Edwin J. Busch, Jr., "Developing an Employee Assistance Program," *Personnel Journal,* September 1981, pp. 708–711.

Merrill Douglass and Donna Douglass, "Time Theft," *Personnel Administrator,* September 1981, pp. 13.

H. Joe Featherston and Robert J. Bednarek, "A Positive Demonstration of Concern for Employees," *Personnel Administrator,* September 1981, pp. 43–47.

Christine A. Filipowicz, "The Troubled Employee: Whose Responsibility?" *Personnel Administrator,* June 1979, pp. 17–22, 33.

Robert C. Ford and Frank S. McLaughlin, "Employee Assistance Programs: A Descriptive Survey of ASPA Members," *Personnel Administrator,* September 1981, pp. 29–35.

Richard T. Hellan and William J. Campbell, "Contracting for AEP Services," *Personnel Administrator,* September 1981, pp. 49–51.

Robert W. Hollman, "Beyond Contemporary Employee Assistance Programs," *Personnel Administrator,* September 1981, pp. 37–41.

Frank E. Kuzmits and Henry E. Hammons II, "Rehabilitating the Troubled Employee," *Personnel Journal,* April 1979, pp. 238–242, 250.

Hermine Zagat Levine, "Consensus," *Personnel,* March–April 1981, pp. 4–10.

Thomas N. McGaffey, "New Horizons in Organizational Stress Prevention Approaches," *Personnel Administrator,* November 1978, pp. 26–32.

Roger Ricklefs, "Firms Offer Employees A New Benefit: Help In Personal Problems," *Wall Street Journal,* August 13, 1979, pp. 1, 21.

Leon B. Sager, "The Corporation and the Alcoholic," *Across the Board,* June 1979, pp. 79–82.

Phillipp A. Stroberl and Marc J. Schniederjans, "The Ineffective Subordinate: A Management Survey," *Personnel Administrator,* February 1981, pp. 72–76.

Compensating Employee Behavior

Chapter 11
Total Compensation

Chapter 12
Performance-Based Pay

Chapter 13
Indirect Compensation

Chapter Outline

Critical Issues in Total Compensation

Total Compensation
Purposes and Importance of Total Compensation
Total Compensation Relationships with Other Personnel Activities

Environmental Impact on Compensation
Federal and State Laws
Unions
The Market

The Basic Pay Structure
Job Evaluation
Determining Job Classes
Wage and Salary Surveys
Individual Wage Determination

CHAPTER 11

Total Compensation

Issues in Wage and Salary Determination
Participation Policies
Pay Secrecy
Satisfaction with Pay
All-Salaried Work Force

Evaluating Total Compensation

Facing the Critical Issues in Total Compensation

Summary

Key Concepts

Discussion Questions

Case

For Your Career

Endnotes

Personnel in the News

A $12.50 Minimum Wage?

Assuming the best, there are a number of trends which, at least in part, indicate the types of issues and changes in the foreseeable future. Certainly, one is that people will earn more. They will earn substantially more. By the year 2006, 25 years from now, the minimum hourly wage will exceed $12.50. Secretaries will be making $60,000 per year or more. MBAs with little or no experience will start at more than $120,000 per year. MBAs coming straight out of school will start at the 50 percent tax bracket— assuming, of course, that the maximum tax on earned income is not increased. Of course, by then it will cost more than $6 to ride the subway in New York City, and a local telephone call will be $1.50. But the very fact that people are earning more and paying higher taxes is part of the future of the compensation manager. (From Robert E. Gibson, Compensation, rev. ed. [New York: AMACOM, 1981], pp. 4–5.)

The U.S. Wage Woes

Increases in hourly wage rates among manufacturing workers in industrialized countries outpaced rises in the cost of living during the 1970's, according to a recent Citibank analysis of gross pay rates and employer contributions to Social Security and other employee benefit programs. Since tax and benefit systems vary so widely from country to country, estimates of take-home pay were not attempted.

In terms of local currencies, gains ranged from just 11 percent in the United States, where lagging output per man-hour put a lid on inflation-adjusted wage gains, to 73 percent in Belgium.... They rose by 63 percent in West Germany, 57 percent in the Netherlands, 56 percent in France, 54 percent in Japan and 53 percent in Sweden. Productivity in the United States rose 29 percent during the 1970–1979 period, according to the Bureau of Labor Statistics, while at the other end of the scale Japanese and Belgian workers recorded increases of 90 and 84 percent, respectively.

*In dollar terms, there was more bad news. American workers began the decade as the world's most highly paid, taking in $4.89 an hour, more than four times the average rate in Japan, and $1.18 an hour higher than the country with the next highest rate of compensation, Canada. But they ended up in seventh place, at $10.14 an hour. Workers in Belgium were earning $13.08 an hour in 1979, in Denmark $10.92, in West Germany $11.39, in the Netherlands $13.30, in Sweden $13.06 and in Switzerland $11.33. However, the dollar's weak performance against those local currencies influenced the comparison. (*The New York Times, *March 8, 1981, p. 18-F. © 1981 by the New York Times Company, reprinted by permission.)*

The Dawning of "Comparable Worth"

While admitting that great strides in equal employment opportunity concerning the compensation issue have been made by EPA and interpretations of the other anti-discrimination laws, there are those who say that the facts and figures still show women and minorities are not reaping a fair share of rewards for their labor. Statistics indicate that in female or minority dominated occupations, wages are consistently lower than in occupations dominated by white males. And in fields with the highest rewards—male occupations—regardless of age, education, or occupational status,

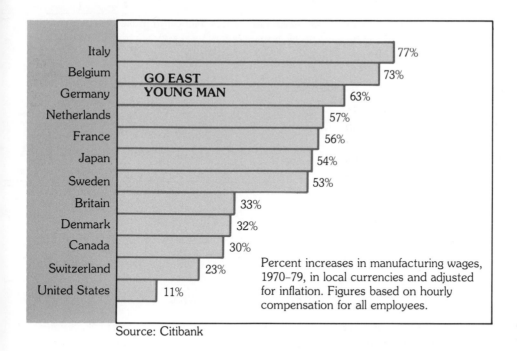

Italy		77%
Belgium	**GO EAST**	73%
Germany	**YOUNG MAN**	63%
Netherlands		57%
France		56%
Japan		54%
Sweden		53%
Britain		33%
Denmark		32%
Canada		30%
Switzerland		23%
United States		11%

Percent increases in manufacturing wages, 1970–79, in local currencies and adjusted for inflation. Figures based on hourly compensation for all employees.

Source: Citibank

women and minorities who manage to break into these fields are still earning less on the average than men.

That is why the "comparable worth" issue has been raised. Should male and female employees be paid the same for jobs that might not be "substantially equal" but are worth the same to an employer? Should a municipal employer, for instance, have to pay hospital nurses as much as trash collectors? Should librarians employed by a county be paid only $14,000 when county liquor store clerks get $21,000? In private employment, should secretaries be paid as much as warehousemen, or female assemblers as much as forklift operators? Essentially this issue boils down to an attack on the persistent wage gap between "men's work" and "women's work."

The Supreme Court has touched on this issue in its much publicized Gunther v. County of Washington *decision. In that case the Court said female prison guards could sue for sex discrimination in compensation under Title VII even though they had no Equal Pay Act claim because their jobs were not "substantially equal" to those of the higher paid male guards. Although the Court did not specifically endorse comparable worth, it did open the door to a potential flood of cases which will test the limits of Title VII on this issue from every conceivable angle over the next few years. (From FEP Guidelines 195 [10], p. 3.)*

Together these quotes illustrate several significant points about compensating employees in organizations. One is that compensation is a very dynamic activity. The level of compensation is a very dynamic activity. The level of compensation can change quickly, especially during periods of inflation. Closely related to the first point is the growing awareness of U.S. compensation levels (pay per dollars an hour) in relation to the rest of the world. This awareness has already become critical to the automobile industry, where the wage rates of U.S. auto workers are comparatively higher than those of the Japanese. This awareness will continue to grow in importance as the world becomes the marketplace and production site for most goods produced in the United States and consumed by the United States. Although these first two points are significant, the one that appears to be having the most significant impact now is the notion of comparable worth. This is the one that you are likely to hear about frequently for the next decade.

Other points in compensation that are and have been important are (1) How are wages really determined? (2) How do we know when people are paid fairly; and (3) How do we decide the wage rate for a given individual? Since all of these points are important in compensating employees, they are addressed in this chapter after the Critical Issues are identified.

CRITICAL ISSUES IN TOTAL COMPENSATION

Here are the four Critical Issues identified by our group of personnel managers:

1. *What is the notion of comparable worth? What is the potential impact of comparable worth on organizations?*
2. *Can market surveys still be used to help determine what a job will be paid?*
3. *What is the best way to determine the "true worth" of a job?*
4. *Should employees set their own wages? Can they be responsible?*

What, specifically, is total compensation? **Total compensation** is the activity by which organizations evaluate the contributions of employees in order to distribute fairly direct and indirect monetary and nonmonetary rewards within the organization's ability to pay and legal regulations.

TOTAL COMPENSATION

Total compensation for employees includes monetary and nonmonetary rewards and direct and indirect rewards. As Exhibit 11.1 indicates, there are two categories of **direct compensation**—the basic wage and performance based pay—and three categories of **indirect compensation**—protection programs, pay for time not worked, and employee services and perquisites. The basic wage category of direct compensation is discussed in this chapter, performance-based pay in Chapter 12, and indirect compensation in Chapter 13.

Purposes and Importance of Total Compensation

Compensation is important because of four major purposes:

- To attract potential job applicants
- To motivate employees
- To retain good employees
- To administer pay within legal constraints

Exhibit 11.1

Components of Compensation (Adapted from J. F. Sullivan, "Indirect Compensation: The Years Ahead," © 1972 by the Regents of the University of California. From *California Management Review* vol. XV, no. 2, p. 65, table 1 by permission of the Regents.)

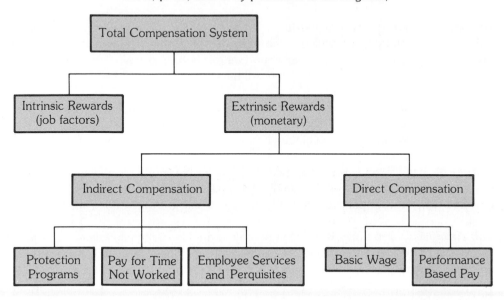

The importance of compensation to the organization is highlighted by the fact that approximately 50 percent of an organization's costs are those of compensation. Furthermore, an ever-growing percentage of these compensation costs is going to indirect rather than direct compensation.

The importance that money has to an individual is related to the needs it serves. Money is able to satisfy almost all employee needs, including so-called higher-level needs. Because money has the potential to serve several needs and because individuals differ in the importance of their needs, money can take on varying degrees of importance.

Although money means different things to different people, it's almost always important.

However, employees are often willing to join an organization and to perform in it for more than just the money.[1] They are often willing to perform for nonmonetary rewards an organization may offer. Some of the nonmonetary rewards an organization can provide are job status and prestige, job security, safety, job responsibility, and variety.[2] Although these rewards can be critical, the next three chapters on compensation primarily discuss monetary rewards, which are usually regarded as the major part of compensation in most organizations. But keep in mind the value of nonmonetary rewards, especially when the limits of monetary rewards become apparent.[3]

Total Compensation's Relationships with Other Personnel Activities

Compensation is one of the most important personnel activities in organizations. This is because money is so important to people and because compensation is so extensively related to other personnel activities.

Recruitment and Selection. Employees differ in the value they put on pay. If personnel departments can determine how important pay is to individuals, they can recruit people to fill specific jobs with specific pay policy options. Some jobs could be very interesting but pay little, whereas other jobs could be very dull but pay well. Individuals could be recruited and selected on the basis of their job and pay values.

Union-Management Relationships. Wage levels and individual wage determinations can be influenced greatly by the existence of a union or association in the organization. A union can also play an important role in the job evaluation process and may determine whether an organization will have a merit or incentive pay plan.

Personnel Planning. Compensation also plays an important part in personnel planning. If the planning activity identifies shortages of personnel, or at least potential shortages, the compensation level may have to be raised to attract more individuals.

Career Management. From the individual's point of view, a compensation policy clearly identifying the levels of pay and pay ranges for jobs can be a valuable aid in deciding which career path to take and whether to stay with the organization.

Job Analysis. Job analysis and compensation are also integrally related. The job evaluation process that determines the relative worth of jobs is based in large measure on how the job is described in the formal job description and specification.

Performance Appraisal. Perhaps the most important relationship for individuals in the organization is that between compensation and performance appraisal. Especially where merit pay exists, the results of the performance evaluation are significant. Where promotions are available, the performance evaluation system can have added significance to the extent that promotion is a reward for performance.

A summary of these relationships, along with a list of administrative issues discussed in Chapters 12 and 13, is shown in Exhibit 11.2.

ENVIRONMENTAL IMPACT ON COMPENSATION

Three major aspects of the environment influencing compensation are federal and state laws, unions, and the market.

Federal and State Laws

The federal government has imposed several laws influencing the level of wages that employers may pay, pay structures, and individual wage determinations.

Davis-Bacon and Walsh-Healy. The first federal law to protect the amount of pay employees received for their work was the Davis-Bacon Act of 1931, which requires that organizations holding construction contracts with federal agencies pay laborers and mechanics the prevailing wages of the locality in which the work is performed. The Walsh-Healey Public Contracts Act of 1936 extended the Davis-Bacon Act to include all federal contracts exceeding $10,000 and specified that pay levels conform

Exhibit 11.2

The Aspects and Processes of Compensating Employees

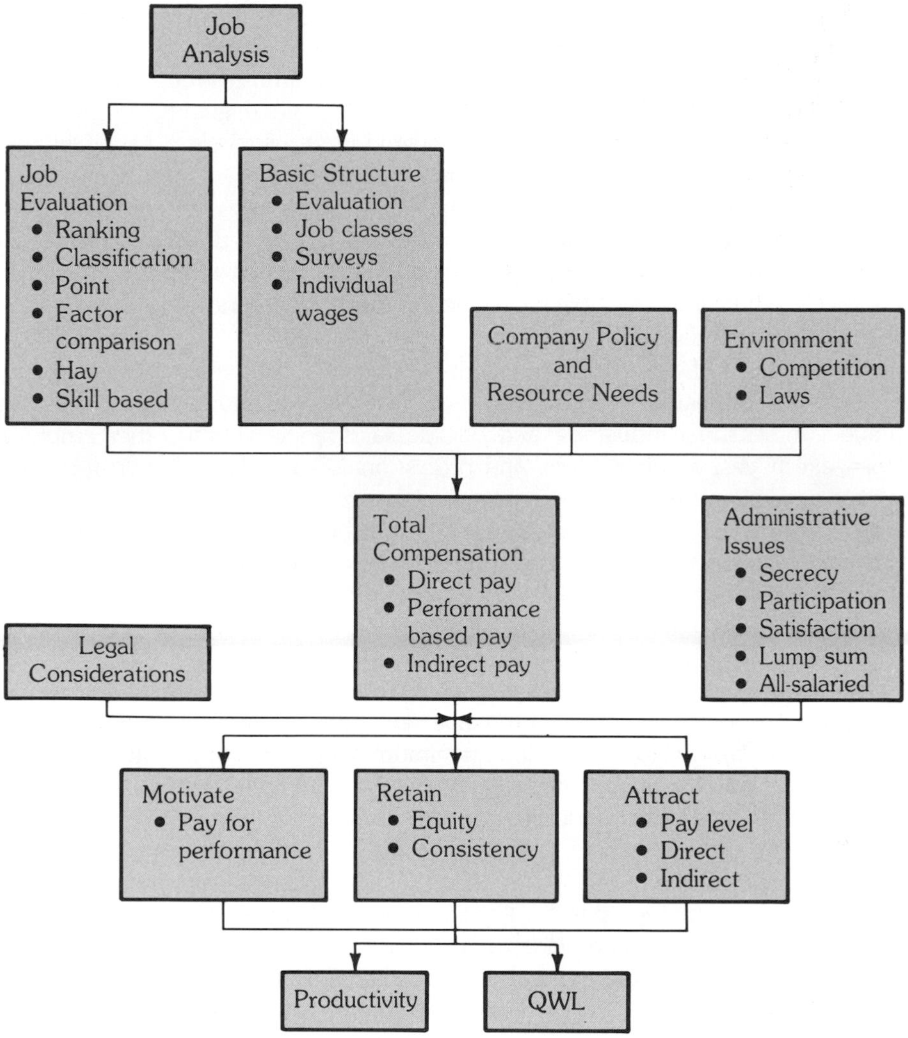

to the industry minimum rather than the area minimum, as specified in Davis-Bacon. The Walsh-Healey Act also established overtime pay at one and one-half times the hourly rate. The wage provisions do not include administrative, professional, office, custodial, and maintenance employees or beginners and handicapped persons.

Fair Labor Standards Act. Partially because Davis-Bacon and Walsh-Healey were limited in their coverage of employees, the Fair Labor Standards Act of 1938 (FLSA, the wage and hour law) was enacted. The FLSA set minimum wages, maximum hours, child labor standards, and overtime pay provisions for all workers except domestics and government employees. A 1974 amendment extended FLSA coverage to domestic and government employees. In 1976, however, the Supreme Court ruled that state and local government employees are covered only by state minimum wage laws. The 1974 amendment also revised the minimum wage, which was 25 cents per hour in 1938, to $3.35 in 1981. As suggested in the quotation at the start of this chapter, the minimum wage in 2006 will probably exceed $12.50 per hour. Small businesses whose sales do not exceed $362,500 are exempt from all FLSA requirements. They are now covered, however, under the *Minimum Wage Law of 1977*.

The overtime pay provisions of the FLSA established who is to be paid overtime for work and who is not. Most employees covered by the FLSA must be paid time-and-a-half for all work exceeding forty hours per week. There are special regulations for employees in such organizations as hospitals, nursing homes, and bowling alleys. In hospitals, for example, the computation for overtime is based not on a forty-hour work week but on an average of forty hours per week over two consecutive weeks. These special regulations have been designed to recognize the needs of the organization as well as the individual.

Several groups of individuals are exempt from both overtime and minimum-wage provisions. These include employees of firms not involved in interstate commerce, employees in seasonal industries, and outside salespeople. Three other employee groups—executives, administrators, and professionals—are also exempt from over-time pay and minimum-wage laws in most organizations. In fact, they are called **exempt employees,** meaning that they may not be paid overtime for work after forty hours per week. All employees subject to being paid for overtime work are called **nonexempt employees.** Although nonexempt employees are usually paid less than exempt employees, practices and policies regarding their treatment are much more clearly defined than they are for exempt employees.[4]

Several state laws also influence wages paid to employees and the hours they can work. Thirty-nine states have minimum-wage laws covering intrastate employees and other employees not covered by federal minimum-wage laws. Although many states at one time had laws limiting the number of hours women could work, the number of states with these laws has now declined to about ten.

Wage Deduction Laws. Three other federal laws influence how much employers may deduct from employee paychecks. The *Copeland Act of 1934* authorized the Secretary of Labor to regulate wage deductions for contractors and subcontractors doing work financed in whole or part by a federal contract. Essentially, the Copeland Act was aimed at illegal deductions. Protection against a more severe threat from an employer with federal contracts was provided in the *Anti-Kickback Law of 1948*. The Federal Wage Garnishment Law of 1970 also protects employees against deductions to pay for indebtedness. It provides that only 25 percent of one's disposable weekly earnings or thirty times the minimum wage, whichever is less, can be deducted for repayment of indebtedness.

Antidiscrimination Laws. Several federal antidiscrimination laws passed since 1960 also influence individual wage determination. They are the Equal Pay Act of 1963, the Civil Rights Act of 1964, and the Age Discrimination Act of 1967. All are meant to ensure that employees with similar seniority, performance, and background doing the same work are paid the same, regardless of sex, age, race, national origin, or religion. Although the laws are on the books, the practice in organizations suggests that employees are still being paid differentially because of sex and race. There are several reasons used to explain this differential. Outright discrimination where women on the same job are paid less than men is also a reason. Another reason is that women work in jobs that are valued less than those jobs in which men work. This notion has given rise to the issues of **comparable worth,** and the demand for equal pay for jobs of comparable value. Note that the Equal Pay Act provides legal coverage for only equal pay for equal work, that is, when men and women are performing the same job they are entitled to identical pay, unless there are differences in performance, seniority, or factors other than sex.

Comparable Worth Issue. Since the comparable worth issue is so critical and is likely to be the most significant compensation issue in the 1980s, it is important to discuss it separately. As suggested in the opening quotation, the heart of the comparable worth theory is the contention that men's jobs are paid more than they are worth and women's jobs are paid less. Resulting differences in pay that are disproportionate to the differences in the "true worth" of jobs, therefore, amount to wage discrimination. Consequently, legal protection should be provided according to the comparable worth advocates.[5]

Although the courts have not yet said jobs of comparable worth must pay the same, the Supreme Court has ruled that Title VII of the Civil Rights Act can cover workers who are working on similar though not equal jobs (*Gunther* v. *County of Washington,* 1981). The Supreme Court's disinclination to rule specifically on the comparable worth issue is in part related to the notion of determining **true worth** (the real value of jobs) and the cost of realizing equal pay for jobs of comparable worth.

Currently organizations determine the worth of jobs through job evaluation (discussed shortly). Although this is a subjective process, it appears as if the alternatives are limited, largely because the notion of true worth is more hypothetical than real. Whether it can be determined is anyone's guess at this point. Even if true worth could be determined, the cost of settlement, according to some observers, "would create an economic and social upheaval of the most radical proportions."[6]

Unions

Unions and associations have had a major impact on wage structures, wage levels, and individual wage determinations regardless of whether specific organizations organized or not.[7] This impact is present from the early stages of job analysis and job evaluation to the final determination of specific wage rates and the selection of the criteria used to set those roles. Although unions generally do not conduct job evaluation programs, in many instances they do help design, negotiate, or modify company programs. Even if union interests are not completely served in the job evaluation process, they can be served at the bargaining table. In fact, serving the interests of members at the bargaining table puts job evaluation into perspective for the union as well as the management.

Final wage levels are reached on the relative power of the union and management. It is important to note that individual wage determinations are generally not of concern to the union. It is the union philosophy that all employees on the same job are doing essentially the same work and, therefore, should be paid the same. That philosophy and collective bargaining appear to have paid off, however, for individual members. Their wages have generally been higher than without collective bargaining, especially where the unions are strong.[8]

Since 1978, however, the trend toward higher pay and benefit demands by

Unions play a critical role in an organization's compensation plan even if the organization is not unionized.

To save some companies and industries, wages may have to be decreased rather than increased.

unions has slowed dramatically. This in large part has been due to the serious financial difficulties of organizations and the need to survive. In fact, conditions have become so severe in several industries that workers have actually voted to take *pay cuts* as a consequence of *take-back negotiations* between the union and management.

The Market

Although both union and management base the final wage rates and levels on far more than the results of job evaluation and *wage surveys*, both often use wage surveys.[9] The surveys are used to determine wage rates for comparable work in other sections of the industry and wages paid in the locality. Other criteria for wage determinations are labor market conditions (the number of people out of work and looking for work), traditions and past history of the organization's wage structure, fringe benefits, indexes of productivity, company profit figures or turnover data, and the Consumer Price Index and the Urban Workers' Family Budget figures, both of which help determine cost-of-living increases.

Although many organizations do use and have used wage survey results to help set pay levels for jobs, the courts say this, "Paying what the market will bear, paying women and minorities less because they are willing to accept less just to land a job, is no excuse for wage discrimination." This is nicely illustrated in the *Personnel in Action* entitled "Economics 101."

THE BASIC PAY STRUCTURE

Among basic wage issues are three that represent most activities in many compensation departments: (1) determination of the pay structures in the organization; (2) setting of pay levels; and (3) individual wage determinations.

Pay structures are important when organizations are concerned about establishing internal equity among the different jobs in the organization. The amount paid for a job could be decided on the basis of a manager's impression of what the job should pay or is worth, but to help ensure internal equity, more formal methods are often used. After jobs are formally evaluated, they are grouped into classes, families, or grades. Within each class, jobs are then arranged in order of importance, and ranges of pay are established with the aid of wage surveys.

Job Evaluation

Job evaluation is the basis for determining the worth of jobs.

Organizations offer rewards to individuals on the basis of their job performance and personal contributions. "Organizations implicitly recognize job-related contributions by assigning pay in accordance with the difficulty and importance of jobs."[10] Most organizations also use some type of formal job evaluation or informal comparisons of job content for determining the relative worth of job-related contributions. It is usually only in the formal job evaluation process, however, that job-related contributions are explicitly specified. **Job evaluation** is the comparison of jobs by the use of formal and systematic procedures to determine their relative worth within the organization.[11]

There are *four essential steps in job evaluation*. The *first step* is a thorough job analysis (see Chapter 3). This step provides information about the job duties and

PERSONNEL IN ACTION
Economics 101

If an employer is charged with wage discrimination in violation of the Equal Pay Act, it can beat the charges by showing jobs held by the higher paid sex involve more skill, effort, or responsibility. But even if the jobs are basically the same on that score, an employer can still defend differentials if it can prove that they are based on a seniority system, a merit system, a system which measures earnings by quantity or quality of work, or any other factor besides sex. A university relied on two of these defenses when it was sued by female professors who charged that they were invariably paid less than their male colleagues, regardless of status, experience, or credentials.

But Women Accept Lower Pay

The university said it could explain the wage discrepancies. It was a simple matter of market economics—supply and demand—which was a "factor other than sex." Since there was a greater supply of prospective female teachers and a willingness on the part of females to accept lower beginning salaries, naturally the university paid them less. The university was not responsible for the realities of an open labor market. And since women started at lower salaries, they remained behind their male colleagues because raises were figured as a percentage of annual salary. The university insisted it had done nothing wrong.

But a federal district court in Georgia shot down this argument. Market forces do not fall under the "factor other than sex" exception to the Equal Pay Act, ruled the court. Even if they did, said the court, to be a credible defense the university would have had to inform itself of the going rates for professors, which it had not done, and the hiring process would have had to include the kind of bargaining over beginning salaries that would normally be expected in the context of a competitive marketplace. But the university didn't bargain over salaries.

Wages Based on Merit?

Nevertheless, said the university, if its female faculty members earned less it was really because they deserved less. Pay at the school was based on merit, the university claimed, and surely that was a legitimate defense against Equal Pay Act charges.

Yes, the court agreed, but a merit system means duties and qualifications for each job must be determined and documented, and every job must be officially assigned a beginning salary grade with increases to be awarded as a result of time in grade, superior performance, or increased qualifications (such as advanced degrees). Had the university established a system like that?

Well, the university replied, not quite like that.

In fact the court found the university's merit system was not at all acceptable. It operated in an informal and unsystematic manner with evaluations carried out on an *ad hoc* and subjective basis by the dean and division heads (all men). No teachers were even aware that any system existed. Worse still, salary decisions were based on personal, and in many cases, ill-informed judgments of an individual teacher's expertise. This was no merit system that would justify pay differentials under the Equal Pay Act, the court said firmly.

Price Tag

The court proceeded to teach the university a basic lesson in economics. Because the school had violated the law, it would have to raise the wages of female professors to bring them into line with those of male faculty and pay back wages to all the female teachers who had been discriminated against. In addition, the court extended the usual two-year period for which back wages must be paid to three years, because the university was well aware of the requirements of the Equal Pay Act. (It had been investigated several years before, concerning the wage differentials between male and female custodians.) Although the court did not determine the exact amount of this employer's back-pay liability, you can get a pretty good idea of what it might be by multiplying the number of women on the faculty who would be in line for back wages (at least half a dozen) by about $4,000 (the average difference in annual pay between male and female teachers) and then multiplying that total by three years. Add to that attorneys' fees and court costs, and the final price tage climbs well into six figures.

(*Marshall* v. *Georgia Southwestern College,* 489 FSupp 1322), *FEP Guidelines* 195 [10, pp. 7–8, 1981)].

responsibilities and about employee requirements for successful performance of the job.

The *second step* in job evaluation is deciding what the organization is paying for—that is, determining which factors will be used to evaluate jobs (although not all methods of job evaluation explicitly use factors). The factors are like yardsticks used to measure the relative importance of jobs. Since these factors help determine what jobs are paid, they are called **compensable factors.** The factors used by organizations vary widely, but they all presumably reflect job-related contributions. Such factors might include accountability, know-how, problem-solving ability, and physical demands. After the determination of compensable factors, their relative importance must be decided.

The *third step* is to choose and adapt a system for evaluating jobs in the organization according to the compensable factors chosen in the second step. There are many basic methods of job evaluation that organizations can adapt to their own needs.

Since the *fourth step* in the process of job evaluation is to decide who will do the job evaluation and then actually use the evaluation methods, it is important to examine the operation of job evaluation methods in detail. There are two common non-quantitative methods of job evaluation—*ranking and job classification*. The *point rating method, Hay plan,* and *factor-comparison method* are more quantifiable.

You should note that job evaluation is the crux of many of the discussions of equal pay and job comparability. As you read the discussion on job evaluation, be thinking about the issue of "true worth" and how slippery this concept really is.

Steps in Job Evaluation:

- Job analysis
- Pick factors
- Choose system
- Use system

Compensable Factors:

- Must exist in all jobs evaluated
- Should not overlap in meaning
- Should be important to the jobs
- Should be identified by several groups

Job Evaluation Methods:

- Ranking
- Job classification
- Point (factor) rating
- Hay plan
- Factor comparison
- Skill based

Ranking Method.   Job analysis information can be used to construct a hierarchy or ladder of jobs that reflects their relative difficulty or value to the organization. This is the core of the **ranking method.** Although any number of compensable factors could be used to evaluate jobs, the job analyst often considers the whole job on the basis of just one factor, such as difficulty or value.

This method is convenient when there are only a few jobs to evaluate and when one person is familiar with them all. As the number of jobs increases and the likelihood of one individual knowing all jobs declines, job analysis information becomes more important and ranking is often done by committee. Especially with a large number of jobs to be ranked, key or benchmark jobs are used for comparison.

One of the difficulties in the ranking method is that jobs are forced to be different from others. Often it is difficult to make fine distinctions between similar jobs, and thus disagreements arise. One way of avoiding this difficulty is to place jobs into classes or grades.

Job Classification Method.   The **job classification method** is similar to the ranking method, except that classes or grades are established, and then the jobs are placed into the classes. Jobs are usually evaluated on the basis of the whole job, often using one factor such as difficulty or an intuitive summary of factors. Again, job analysis information is useful in the classification, and benchmark jobs are frequently established for each class. Within each class or grade, there is no further ranking of the jobs.

Although many organizations use job classification, the largest is the U.S. government, which has eighteen distinct classifications from GS 1 to GS 18 (*GS* stands for "general schedule") with the top three referred to as supergrades. GS 11 and above usually denote general management and highly specizlized jobs; while GS 5 to GS 10 are assigned to management trainee and lower-level management positions; GS 1 to GS 4 are for clerical and nonsupervisory personnel.

A particular advantage of this method is that it can be applied to a large number and wide variety of jobs. As the number and variety of jobs in an organization increase, however, the classification of jobs tends to become more subjective. This is particularly true when an organization has a large number of plant or office locations, and thus jobs with the same title may differ in content. Because it is difficult to evaluate each job separately in such cases, the job title becomes a more important guide to job classification than job content is.

A major disadvantage of the job classification method is the basis of job evaluations. Evaluations either use one factor or an intuitive summary of many factors. The problem with using one factor, such as difficulty (skill), is that it may not be important on all jobs. Some jobs may require a great deal of skill, but others may require a great deal of responsibility. Does this mean that jobs requiring much responsibility should be placed in a lower classification than jobs requiring much skill? Not necessarily. Perhaps both factors could be considered together. Thus each factor becomes a compensable factor, valued by the organization. Jobs would be evaluated and classified on the basis of both factors. However, "this balancing of the compensable factors to determine the relative equality of jobs often causes misunderstandings with the employee and the labor leaders."[12] To deal with this disadvantage, many organizations use more-quantifiable methods of evaluation.

Point Rating Method. The most widely used method of job evaluation is the **point rating** or **point factor method**, which consists of assigning point values for previously determined compensable factors and adding them to arrive at a total. The advantages of the point rating method are several:

1. *The point rating plan is widely used throughout industry, permitting comparisons on a similar basis with other firms.*

2. *The point rating plan is relatively simple to understand. It is the simplest of quantitative methods of job evaluation.*

3. *The point values for each job are easily converted to job and wage classes with a minimum of confusion and distortion.*

4. *A well-conceived point rating plan has considerable stability—it is applicable to a wide range of jobs over an extended period of time. The greatest assets here are consistency and uniformity and its widespread use throughout industry.*

5. *The point rating method is an objective, definitive approach requiring several separate and distinct judgement decisions. Thus errors tend to* cancel *one another.*[13]

The limitations of the point rating method are few, but an especially critical one is the assumption that all jobs can be described with the same factors. Many organizations avoid this limitation by developing separate point rating methods for different groups of employees. In Exhibit 11.3 there are eleven compensable factors used by one organization to evaluate the jobs in supervisory, nonsupervisory, and clerical categories. Exhibit 11.3 also shows a description of what's associated with one of the factors (complexity and judgment) and sets forth the specifications for the degrees or levels within that factor. Some factors are more important than others, as shown by the different point values. For example, the second degree of practical experience is worth four times as much as the second degree of job conditions. In essence, each job is evaluated on its compensable factors. The personnel department determines which

The appropriateness of the compensable factors depends upon the type of jobs being evaluated.

Exhibit 11.3
Sample of Point Rating Method

Compensable Factor	1st Degree	2nd Degree	3rd Degree	4th Degree	5th Degree
Basic knowledge	15	30	45	60	—
Practical experience	20	40	60	80	—
Complexity and judgment*	15	30	45	60	—
Initiative	5	10	20	40	—
Probable errors	5	10	20	40	—
Contacts with others	5	10	20	40	—
Confidential data	5	10	15	20	25
Attention to functional detail	5	10	15	20	—
Job conditions	5	10	15	—	—
For Supervisory Positions Only					
Character of supervision	5	10	20	—	—
Scope of supervision	5	10	20	—	—

COMPLEXITY AND JUDGMENT

This factor appraises the scope and complexity of the job in terms of the consistent variety of functions, their intricacy and general level of importance. It appraises also the amount of discretion and judgment involved, as measured by the importance of recommendation preliminary to or tantamount to decisions. It is frequently referred to as the "headwork" factor.

1st Degree—15 Rating Points
Simple repetitive duties involving little or no choice as to course of action and requiring only common sense judgment in carrying out detailed instructions.

2nd Degree—30 Rating Points
Routine duties which generally follow a prescribed course of action or involve the application of readily understood rules and procedures. Standard practices restrict independent action and judgment to a limited number of procedural decisions.

3rd Degree—45 Rating Points
Semi-diversified work involving a thorough practical knowledge of a restricted field of activity, and which involves decisions based on a wide range of procedures and the analysis of facts in situations to determine what action should be taken, within the limits of standard practice.

4th Degree—60 Rating Points
Work is diversified and involved. Duties require independent thought and action in working toward general objectives which, in turn, may necessitate devising new methods or in modifying or adapting standard principles and practices to new or changed conditions common to administrative, executive, professional or sales function. Requirement for discretion and judgment in making decisions which in general are based upon precedent or standard operating policies and procedures.

degree of a factor is appropriate for the job, and then the points assigned to each degree of each factor are totaled. Levels of compensation are determined on the basis of the point totals. The description provided on complexity and judgment is similar to that written on all of the compensable factors.

The point factor method, as with other job evaluation plans, incorporates the potential subjectivity of the job analyst. As such it has the potential for wage discrimination. *Bias or subjectivity* can enter (1) in the selection of the compensable factors;

Exhibit 11.4
Hay Plan Compensable Factors

Mental Activity (Problem Solving)	Know-How	Accountability
The amount of original, self-starting thought required by the job for analysis, evaluation, creation, reasoning, and arriving at conclusions.	The sum total of all knowledge and skills, however acquired, needed for satisfactory job performance (evaluates the job, not the person)	The measured effect of the job on company goals
Mental Activity has two dimensions:	Know-How has three dimensions:	Accountability has three dimensions:
▪ The degree of freedom with which the thinking process is used to achieve job objectives without the guidance of standards, precedents, or direction from others	▪ The amount of practical, specialized, or technical knowledge required	▪ Freedom to act, or relative presence of personal or procedural control and guidance; determined by answering the question, "How much freedom has the job holder to act independently?"; for example, a plant manager has more freedom than a supervisor under his or her control
▪ The type of mental activity involved; the complexity, abstractness, or originality of thought required	▪ Breadth of management, or the ability to make many activities and functions work well together; the job of company president, for example, has greater breadth than that of a department supervisor	▪ Dollar magnitude, a measure of the sales, budget, dollar value of purchases, value added, or any other significant annual dollar figure related to the job
Mental Activity is expressed as a percentage of Know-How for the obvious reason that people think with what they know. The percentage judged to be correct for a job is applied to the Know-How point value; the result is the point value given to Mental Activity.	▪ Requirement for skill in motivating people	▪ Impact of the job on dollar magnitude, a determination of whether the job has a primary effect on end results or has instead a sharing, contributory, or remote effect
	Using a chart, a number can be assigned to the level of Know-How needed in a job. This number—or point value—indicates the relative importance of Know-How in the job being evaluated.	Accountability is given a point value independent of the other two factors.

The total evaluation of any job is arrived at by adding the points for Know-How, Mental Activity, and Accountability. Points are not shown here.

(2) in the relative weights (degrees) assigned to factors; and (3) in the assignment of degrees to the jobs being evaluated. What's at stake here are equal pay and job comparability. Consequently the organization should make sure its point factor evaluation system is free from potential bias and is implemented as objectively as possible.

Hay Plan.   A method with only three factors is shown in Exhibit 11.4. This method, generally known as the **Hay plan,** is a widely used method for evaluating managerial and executive positions. The three factors—know-how, problem solving, and accountability—are used because they are assumed to be the most important aspects of managerial and executive positions. Although the Hay plan appears to use only three factors, there are for all practical purposes eight: three subfactors in know-how, two in problem solving, and three in accountability. In deriving the final point profile for any job, however, only the three major factors are assigned point values. The Hay Plan was used in the San Jose job comparability case described earlier.

Factor-Comparison Method.   The point rating method, regardless of the number of factors and degrees of each factor, derives a point total for each job. Several very different types of jobs can have the same total points. After the total points are determined, jobs are priced—often according to groups or classes, similar to the job classification method. The **factor-comparison method** avoids this step between point totaling and pricing by assigning dollar values to factors and comparing the amounts directly to the pay for **benchmark jobs.**

Benchmark jobs are those jobs selected by the organization from which to determine the value of other jobs. Once benchmark jobs are selected, the amount or degree of each compensable factor in each of the benchmark jobs is determined. Since dollar values have already been assigned to each factor, the dollar value of each compensable factor on each benchmark job can be determined. Once this is done, other jobs can be compared (in terms of degrees) relative to the benchmark jobs. Since the dollar values for the factors are known, the wage rates for the non-benchmark jobs are now readily determined.

In short, factor-comparison is similar to point rating in that both use compensable factors. But the point method uses degrees and points for each factor to measure jobs, whereas factor-comparison uses benchmark jobs and dollar values on factors.

The **prices** or **wage rates** for the benchmark jobs are determined by the market. Although this is a quick method by which to set wage rates, it has the potential to perpetuate the traditional pay differentials between jobs. As such it has come under attack from the job comparability advocates. What do you think those advocates would say about the market method of pricing jobs?

Use of benchmark jobs can further perpetuate traditional pay differentials since it is against these jobs that the wage rates for other jobs are determined. Since this process of determining the rates of other jobs is really in the hands of the wage and salary analyst, it can be subjective, furthering the potential for wage discrimination.[14]

Skill based evaluation is useful where employees rotate from job to job.

Skill Based Evaluation.   Whereas the first five job evaluation plans "pay for the job," **skill based evaluation** is based on the idea of "paying for the person." As such, this type of evaluation is concerned with the skills of the employees and in developing training programs to facilitate skill acquisition by employees.[15]

The idea of paying for the person, or at least the person-job combination rather than for just the job, is not new. Many professional organizations have been doing this for a long time, for example, universities, law offices, and research and development labs. What is new, however, is paying for the person in blue-collar jobs. One of the more visible examples of skill based evaluation for blue-collar jobs is the Topeka, Kansas, dog food plant of General Foods (described further in Chapter 16). Their plan is based on a starting rate given to all new employees. After coming on board, employees are advanced one pay grade for each job they learn. Jobs can be trained in any order and at any price. Members of each employee's team, however, ensure that the jobs are learned correctly. They decide when the employee has mastered a job. Employees reach the top pay grade in the plant after learning all jobs.

Determining Job Classes

Determining **job classes** or **job families** means grouping together all jobs of nearly the same difficulty, for example, grouping all clerical type jobs together or grouping all managerial jobs together. The jobs within the same class may be quite different, but they must be about equal or comparable in value to the organization. All jobs in each class are assigned one salary or range of salaries.

Why group jobs into classes? For efficiency of salary administration, for one thing. Also, it is hard to justify the small differences in pay that would exist without classes of jobs, and small errors that occur in evaluating the jobs can be eliminated in the classification process. Of course, employees can also find fault with the classification if their jobs are grouped with what they feel are less important jobs. Sometimes the jobs that are grouped together are too dissimilar. This may occur because there are too few classes of jobs. Few classes are appropriate, however, if many of the jobs in the organization are of similar value. It is when there is a wide range of job difficulty that too few job classes may lead to employee complaints of inequity. It is also under this same condition that validation of a selection procedure or a performance appraisal technique would be suspect. The Uniform Guidelines (described in Chapter 4) make it clear that, when validation procedures are done for job families or classes, the families or classes must contain jobs that are substantially equivalent so that a selection procedure is likely to be valid for all jobs in a class.

Determining job classes is more an art than a science.

Although job classes are determined for the purpose of establishing wage rates, job classes are often based on wage rates that have already been established. This practice may seem somewhat bizarre, but it is typical in most organizations. Most organizations are already paying their employees and thus need to determine job classes only when many new jobs are introduced or if it has never really had a sound job analysis program. In addition, if the organization has grown and incorporated many more jobs, it may need to group them into classes for purposes of salary administration. On the other hand, an organization that is just being established is most likely small, and the price of its jobs would be determined by surveys of what other organizations are paying.

Wage and Salary Surveys

In order to attract and retain adequate employees, the salary structure must not only be internally equitable but also externally equitable. Wage surveys of other organizations in the same labor market provide the information for establishing external equity.

Wage surveys can be used to develop compensation levels, wage structures, and even payment plans (the amount and kind of direct and indirect compensation). Survey results can also be used to indicate compensation philosophies of competing organizations. For example, a large electronics company may have a policy of paying 15 percent above the market rate (the average of all rates for essentially the same job in an area); a large service organization may choose to pay the market rate; a large bank may decide to pay 5 percent less than the market rate.

Most organizations use wage surveys extensively. Separate surveys are published for different occupational groupings; thus many larger organizations subscribe to several surveys. For example, there are surveys for clerical workers, professional workers, managers, and executives. Separate surveys are conducted not only because there are such wide differences in skill levels but also because labor markets are so different. An organization surveying clerical workers may need only to survey companies within a 10-mile radius, whereas a survey of managerial salaries may cover the entire country.

Individual Wage Determination

Pay differentials are based on performance and personal contributions.

Once the job analysis and job evaluation have been completed, the job classes have been established, and the wage structure has been determined through wage surveys, the question is how much do we pay Anne and John, both of whom work on the same job? If the rate range were $1,500 to $2,000 per month, Anne might be paid $2,000 and John $1,750. What difference might account for the pay differential? Although the performance contribution seems like the best criterion, seniority, sex, age, size of family, experience, and appearance (personal contributions) have also been found to influence individual wages. Age and seniority, in fact, are frequently perceived to be rather important factors.[16]

In actuality, the individual wage determinations combine both personal contributions and performance. Thus age and seniority as well as their performance may influence Anne's and John's pay. However, many managers would argue that pay differences based on performance are more equitable than those based on such personal contributions as seniority. On what criteria do you think the salaries of the baseball players in the *Personnel in Action* insert, "A Look at the Free-Agent Class of 1980," are determined?

The market can help determine what performance and personal contributions are worth.

But if performance is the criterion, is it past, current, or future performance? Many employees are given raises on the basis of their performance potential although athletes are usually paid on the basis of the last year's performance (this is not true for certain sports, such as race-car driving, tennis, and horse racing). There are several difficulties in giving merit raises based on past performance, however. One of those difficulties is employees' perceptions of their performance. Anne and John, like many people, are apt to rate themselves in at least the top 50 percent in terms of performance. Thus both may perceive that they performed well. Using performance as the sole criterion may, therefore, upset John—unless he has a significantly lower level of performance, knows it, and accepts it. More issues related to paying for performance are discussed in the next chapter.

The answers to the question of how much to pay Anne and John can be as varied as the number of people answering the question. Compensation managers should also ask questions like "What does the rest of my compensation program look like?" "What was the initial understanding or contract with Anne and John?" and "Can I defend my decision?" *Defensibility* and *consistency* are perhaps the two most important aspects of compensation management. Regardless of the method used or the decision reached, there will always be criticism from others. But being able to defend the decision and show that it is consistent with others goes a long way in reducing criticism. What arguments would you use to defend pay differentials in the salaries of Rusty Staub and Dave Winfield versus the $102,307 salary of Lane Kirkland, president of the AFL-CIO or the $100,000 salary of Edward T. Hanley, president of the Hotel, Restaurant Employees Union?[17]

ISSUES IN WAGE AND SALARY ADMINISTRATION

There are several contemporary issues in wage and salary administration, but three have particular importance: To what extent should employees be able to set their own wages? What are the advantages and disadvantages of pay secrecy? What is needed for employees to be satisfied with their pay? And should all employees be salaried? More administration issues are addressed in the next two chapters.

PERSONNEL IN ACTION

A Look at the Free-Agent Class of 1980

Despite the owners' insistence every year that they won't give free agents the lucrative contracts free agents have received in the past, they do. Here are details of the contracts worth $1 million or more given to last year's free agents (where there are two sets of figures, the first is the money that is guaranteed, the second—in parentheses—the total including non-guaranteed salaries):

Rusty Staub
Mets (.317,5hr,21rbi)

Three years, $1,070,000: $150,000 signing bonus; $250,000 salary each year, $100,000 deferred with interest, $10,000 relocation expenses. Bonuses each year of $25,000 for 1.5 million attendance and $50,000 for two million attendance and $50,000 for general performance at general manager's discretion.

Dave Winfield
Yankees (.294,13,68)

Ten years, minimum of $15 million, maximum of $22,473,763: $1 million signing bonus, first-year salary of $1.4 million with maximum cost-of-living increase of 10 per cent per year applied every other year. Yankees can buy out last two years at 50 per cent of salary. Bonuses each year of $25,000 for 130 games, $25,000 for Gold Glove, $50,000 for mvp.

Ron LeFlore
Chicago White Sox (.246,0,24)

Three years, $2,425,000 (4 years, $3,235,000): $520,000 signing bonus, salaries of $535,000; $635,000; $735,000; $810,000 not guaranteed for fourth year. Moving expenses Detroit to Chicago. Bonuses each year of $10,000 for All-Star team, $15,000 for post-season all-star team selection, $25,000 for mvp.

Tug McGraw
Philadelphia (2won–4lost,2.66ERA)

Three years, $1.35 million (4 years, $1.65 million): $250,000 signing bonus, salaries of $350,000 first three years and $350,000 not guaranteed for the fourth year; $50,000 if released before the fourth year.

Jim Essian
Chicago White Sox (.308,0,5)

Four years, $1.1 million: $250,000 signing bonus, salaries of $175,000; $200,000; $225,000; $250,000. Bonus; salaries of $250,000 the first three years, $300,000 the fourth, $300,000 not guaranteed for the fifth. Bonus each year of $25,000 for 200 innings pitched or 40 games and $25,000 for 240 innings or 50 games.

Darrell Porter
St. Louis (.224,6,31)

Five years, $3.5 million: $200,000 signing bonus, salaries of $500,000 the first year and $700,000 in each of the next four.

Geoff Zahn
California (10–11,4.42)

Three years, $1,173,000: $166,000 signing bonus deferred; salaries of $225,000 the first year, $391,000 each of the next two with $166,000 deferred in second and third years.

Dave Roberts
Houston (.241,1,5)

Five years, $1.1 million: $100,000 signing bonus; salaries of $150,000; $175,000; $200,000; $225,000; $250,000. Bonuses each year of $15,000 for 100 games or 250 plate appearances, $15,000 for 125 games or 375 plate appearances, $20,000 for 145 games or 435 plate appearances, $25,000 for All-Star game, $25,000 for post-season all-star team, $100,000 for mvp for total possible bonuses of $200,000 a year.

(From *The New York Times*, November 8, 1981, S7, © 1981 by the New York Times Company. Reprinted by permission.)

Participation Policies

For many employees, total compenstion generally represents a mixture of direct salary and indirect benefits. These indirect benefits may represent as much as 45 percent of total compensation, but employees generally have no choice as to what indirect benefits they receive. Management defends this policy on the grounds that it ensures that employees have the proper benefits and there is a cost advantage in buying the same benefits for all employees.[18] Yet the proliferation of indirect pay arrangements has created a kind of smoked-glass effect through which the attitudes and desires of the recipient can be seen only darkly, if at all. Employees often receive costly benefits they neither want nor need and, in many cases, do not even know about. And even in cases where employees know they are receiving particular forms of compensation, they tend to undervalue the benefits.[19]

What are the alternatives? The popular form of participation for executive-level employees is the **cafeteria approach,** in which individuals select from a variety of compensation "entrees" those items they want. Another form incorporates employee-management negotiations on compensation levels and forms.

The cafeteria approach tends to be favored by a majority of executives, even if the administrative costs are deducted from their annual pay.[20] If given the choice, executives would also select heavier doses of supplemental (indirect) compensation than they are now receiving.

Because the cafeteria approach allows individuals to make some pay decisions, they are more likely to be satisfied with their compensation package. Allowing employees to participate in the compensation package also helps increase their understanding of what they are actually receiving from the organization.

Although the cafeteria approach appears to have several positive benefits, it has generally been limited to executives and has also generally restricted participation to initial decisions on the proportion and type of direct and indirect benefits.

A newer method of employee participation is allowing employees to set their own wage rates. One way of doing this is by letting the employees decide who should get a raise by voting on the matter. At Romac, a pipe fitting plant in Seattle, Washington, an employee requests a pay raise by completing a form that includes information about his or her current pay level, previous raise, the raise requested, and reasons why she or he thinks a raise is deserved. The employee then "goes on the board." His or her name, hourly wage, and photograph are posted for six consecutive working days. Then the employees vote. Majority rules. Although top-level managers can't vote, they can veto a raise. This, however, hasn't happened yet since management has learned that employees can responsibly set their own wages given that they trust management and have a sufficient understanding of the "cost of doing business."[21]

Employees can set their own wages responsibly.

Pay Secrecy

Ask anyone who works for a living how much money he or she makes, and you are likely to encounter a range of responses from evasion to outright hostility. Such responses, however, should not be surprising. According to organizational etiquette, it is generally considered gauche to ask others their salaries. In a recent study of E. I. du Pont de Nemours, all employees were asked if the company should disclose more payroll information so that everyone would know everyone else's pay. Only 18 percent voted for an open pay system.

Nevertheless some companies practice open salary administration because they feel it is the right thing to do.[22] For example, the Polaroid Corporation has established a pay-level structure for its exempt salaried employees and, in keeping with its policy of openness, involves those employees in making salary decisions. Employees are also involved in the job evaluation process to get a broad understanding of the process by which job value is established.[23]

Satisfaction with Pay

If organizations want to minimize absenteeism and turnover, they must make sure that employees are satisfied with their pay. And since satisfaction with pay and motivation to perform are not necessarily highly related, it is necessary to know the determinants of pay satisfaction. With this knowledge, organizations can develop pay practices more likely to result in satisfaction with pay. Perhaps the three major determinants of satisfaction with pay are pay equity, pay level, and pay administration practices.

Pay Equity. **Pay equity** refers to the relationship between what people feel they should be receiving and what they feel they are receiving. If they regard this comparison as fair or equitable, they will be satisfied.

Pay Level. **Pay level** is an important determinant of the perceived amount of pay, which is compared to what should be received. The result of the comparison is satisfaction with pay if the "should" level of pay equals the action level of pay. Pay dissatisfaction results only if the actual level is less than the "should."

Pay Administration Practices. What does this suggest for pay administration practices? First, if the employer is to attract new employees and keep them satisfied with their pay, the wages and salaries offered should approximate the wages and salaries paid to other employees in comparable organizations.[24]

Second, the pricing of jobs can enhance pay satisfaction when it is perceived as embodying a philosophy of equal work or equal pay for jobs of comparable worth. The determination of equal pay for equal work can be aided by sound job evaluations. But the worth of jobs must be evaluated according to the factors considered most important by the employees and the organization.

Third, pay-for-performance systems must be accompanied by a method for accurately measuring the performance of employees and must be open enough so employees can clearly see the performance-pay relationship.[25]

A final pay administration practice is trust and consistency. Employees must perceive that the organization is looking out for their interests as well as its own. Without trust and consistency, pay satisfaction is not only low, but pay also becomes a target for complaints regardless of the real issues.[26]

All-Salaried Work Force

How people were paid often indicated whether they were management or workers. Today this isn't always the case.

Although there is some evidence that all employees prefer to "be on salary" than to be paid on an hourly basis, most organizations distinguish between their employees by method of pay. That is, salary status is usually reserved (along with a parking space) for management, and the nonmanagement (except clerical workers) employees are paid on an hourly basis.

Some organizations, nevertheless, have put all their employees on salary. IBM has had an all-salary work force since the 1930s. Eaton Corporation, Cleveland, Ohio, is using the all-salary concept in its newer plants along with throwing out the time clocks. Of course some employees abuse being on salary (for example, they can come in late or miss a day and still be paid), but overall the all-salary concept awards employees more mature treatment and a sense of trust by management.

Though there is little hard evidence to support the effectiveness of the all-salaried concept, it appears to be a practical way to increase productivity and QWL.

EVALUATING TOTAL COMPENSATION

In evaluating how effectively an organization administers its compensation program, remember the four major purposes of total compensation:

- To attract potentially qualified employees
- To motivate employees
- To retain qualified employees
- To administer pay within legal constraints

In order to attain these purposes employees generally need to be satisfied with their pay. This means that the organization's pay levels should be competitive, that employees should perceive pay equity, and that the compensation program should be properly administered. It also means that the compensation must adhere to the various state and federal wage and hour laws. It also strongly suggests that the notion of comparable worth be strongly considered in pay administration practices.

Thus there are many bases on which to evaluate the effectiveness of an organization's compensation program. The size and quality of the applicant pool can easily be measured and compared over time, and its turnover rate among qualified employees can be determined. Of course, serious problems may exist if there is a high turnover rate amongst the most qualified employees yet a very low rate amongst the least qualified employees. Furthermore, an organization can track the number of legal violations and employee charges of pay discrimination. All of these methods can also prove quite useful in helping to determine the relative effectiveness of a new pay program over a previous one.[27]

FACING THE CRITICAL ISSUES IN TOTAL COMPENSATION

Based upon our discussion of compensating employees, it is appropriate to address the Critical Issues presented at the start of this chapter. Only the highlights of responses to the Critical Issues are presented here. You, however, should be more thorough in developing responses to the four Issues.

Issue: *What is the notion of comparable worth? What is the potential impact of comparable worth on organizations?*

The notion of comparable worth is that the true value of jobs should be used in determining compensation rates. What exists now, say the proponents of comparable worth, is that the compensation rates of jobs really reflect the fact that men occupy certain jobs and women occupy others.

If the notion of comparable worth were to be realized it would (will) have far-reaching effects on compensation rates and costs. It would raise them significantly, but probably remove previous wage discrimination. It would also involve some changes in the job evaluation procedures of many organizations.

Issue: *Can market surveys still be used to help me determine what a job will be paid?*

Yes, but primarily for those jobs that have identical or nearly identical counterparts in the marketplace. Doing market surveys to price jobs that are not found in other organizations should be avoided. It involves too much subjectivity; therefore, it is more open to potential wage discrimination charges. Remember, however, to be careful in using market rates to perpetuate wage differentials that are obviously discriminatory. Fair evaluations should be conducted to help reduce that likelihood.

Issue: *What is the best way to determine the true worth of jobs?*

Although it is unlikely that the true worth of jobs can be determined, using sound job evaluation procedures can certainly enable an organization to move in that direction. Sound procedures, for example, using a point factor system would involve (1) Using a single set of factors (that is, just one evaluation system or plan) rather than one for the clerical staff, one for the blue-collar workers and yet another for the supervisory group; (2) selecting factors that reflect the working environment and the organization's objectives; (3) developing factors and relative weights free of bias; (4) eliminating as much as possible the subjective measurement error in evaluating positions; (5) eliminating bias in the evaluation committee that reviews job evaluation results on jobs; and (6) sustaining an updated system to ensure that factors or evaluations do not become outdated.

Issue: *Should employees set their own wages? Can they be responsible?*

Nowhere is it set in stone that managers make better decisions than nonmanagers, nor that managers are more responsible than nonmanagers. In fact, in the few companies that have tried it, employees have set their own wages without management having to alter the procedures or change decisions. Where the method is most successful, however, is where employees trust management and vice versa and employees are provided with information to help them understand the financial status of the company.

SUMMARY

We have now taken a look at many of the important aspects of one of the most significant personnel activities in an organization. Perhaps no single issue evokes as much emotion as learning that one's level of pay is less than another's or finding out that another person got a bigger raise even though he did less.

With the importance and purposes of compensating employees in mind, you should begin to gain an appreciation for the notion of comparable worth. For although not yet a legal issue, it appears to be only a matter of time before it may be one. But even if it doesn't become one, the basic underlying issues of job evaluation are important for any good personnel practitioner to know. We considered many of those issues, directly and indirectly, in this chapter.

We also examined several critical issues related to the administration of compensation programs. There are many still to be discussed, such as how to deal with merit raises in times of rapid inflation and big demands for huge cost-of-living increases. To this issue and many others we turn in the next two chapters.

KEY CONCEPTS

compensable factor	job classification method
total compensation	job evaluation
exempt employee	nonexempt employee
direct compensation	pay equity
indirect compensation	pay secrecy
comparable worth	pay level
true worth	point rating method
factor-comparison method	ranking method
Hay plan	price or wage rates

benchmark jobs   job classes

skill-based evaluation   cafeteria approach

job families

DISCUSSION QUESTIONS

1. What are the four major purposes of total compensation in effective personnel management?
2. What other area of personnel management is most directly relevant to compensation activities? Why is this area so salient?
3. What is meant by the concept of comparable worth?
4. What types of categories and rewards comprise total compensation?
5. What are some examples of wage deduction laws and what is their intended purpose?
6. What roles do unions play in compensating employees?
7. What other criteria besides market surveys are used for wage determinations?
8. What are the four essential steps in job evaluations?
9. How is skill-based evaluation different from other evaluation methods? Give examples of skill-based evaluation.
10. What measures can be used for evaluating compensation policies and practices?

CASE

What Motivates Employees?

For each of the individual cases discussed here, select from the following list, *in order of importance,* the three rewards or inducements that you think a personnel manager could use to effectively motivate each of the four individuals. Justify your selection.

1. job security
2. a raise in salary
3. more life insurance
4. less supervision
5. more recognition for achievement
6. more status—for example, title, own office
7. a group profit-sharing plan
8. an individual incentive plan
9. more participation in managerial decisions

10. job enlargement—for example, opportunity for creativity, a wider range of activities
11. eye care/dental care
12. day care facilities
13. more time off

Case A

Bob Baker is office manager for a medium-sized firm. He is forty-one, unmarried and lives in an uptown apartment in New York City. He has been office manager for three years and earns $38,200 per year. He started in the mailroom and has been with the company for nearly 20 years.

Case B

Frank Folley is an insurance investigator for a company whose main line is automobile insurance. He is fifty-eight years old, widowed, and has three married children. His annual salary is about $40,000. He has been with this company for eleven years. Previously, he worked for two other insurance companies, as an investigator in one and as an agent in the other.

Case C

Sue Stoner is purchasing agent for a small machine tool company. She is twenty-seven. She started with the company four years ago as a shipping clerk. After one year, she became a material requisition clerk; last year, she assumed her present position under Tom Garvey, the purchasing agent, who is forty-two years old. Sue is now earning $17,200 per year. She is getting married next month.

Case D

Eugene Trail is a successful hair dresser in a small salon in a small town near Washington, D.C. He is single and enjoys traveling. Due to the nature of the business he is required to work late Fridays and all day Saturday. He has a good relationship with the owner and customers and enjoys his work a great deal.

FOR YOUR CAREER

- Pay is one topic with which almost everyone in an organization is concerned. Pay not only determines how well you *live* but also how well you *feel*.
- The area of compensation is a critical personnel activity and one that carries a great deal of weight in many organizations.

- The compensation controversy that may affect you most in the 1980s is the issue of comparable worth. You should be familiar with this issue.

- Pressure from international competition is forcing companies and unions to examine the current level of wages. The result may be wage reductions in the years ahead. You may actually make less than your parents in the years ahead.

- Although job evaluation may be used to determine the value/worth of the job you get, the market may determine how much you'll get paid.

- The job/compensation analyst is an important person. She or he helps determine the worth of jobs and what the job incumbent may eventually be paid.

ENDNOTES

1. A. Gouldner, *Patterns of Industrial Bureaucracy*, (New York: Free Press, 1954).

2. D. W. Belcher, *Compensation Administration* (Englewood Cliffs, N.J.: Prentice-Hall, 1974), p. 383.

   R. E. Gibson, *Compensation*, rev. ed. (New York: AMACOM, 1981).

3. E. E. Lawler III, *Pay and Organizational Effectiveness: A Psychological View* (New York: McGraw-Hill, 1971), p. 35.

4. W. G. Hoke, "Equity and Exempt Personnel," *Personnel Administrator*, July 1976, pp. 41–46.

5. James T. Brinks, "The Comparable Worth Issue: A Salary Administration Bombshell," *Personnel Administrator*, November 1981, pp. 37–40.

   Michael F. Carter, "Comparable Worth: An Idea Whose Time Has Come," *Personnel Journal*, October 1981, pp. 792–794.

   Michelle Celarier, "The Paycheck Challenge of the Eighties—Comparing Job Worth," *Ms.*, March 1981, pp. 38–44.

   Julius N. Drazin, "Labor Relations," *Personnel Journal*, September 1981, p. 684.

   Laura N. Gaseway, "Comparable Worth: A Post-Gunther Overview," *Georgetown Law Journal* 69 (1981):1123–1169.

   Bruce A. Nelson, Edward M. Opton, Jr., and Thomas E. Wilson, "Wage Discrimination and Title VII in the 1980's: The Case Against 'Comparable Worth,'" *Employee Relations Law Journal* 6, No. 3:380–405.

   David Thomsen, "Compensation and Benefits," *Personnel Journal*, April 1981, pp. 258–260.

   "Bias Against Jobs Dominated by Women Found by Federal Study on Pay Inequities," *Wall Street Journal*, September 2, 1981, p. 8.

   See also the entire April 1982 issue of the *Personnel Administrator*.

6. Nelson, Opton, and Wilson, p. 381.

7. H. D. James, "Union Views on Job Evaluation: 1971 vs. 1978," *Personnel Journal*, February 1979, pp. 80–85.

8. "Fewer Firms Grant Whitecollar COLA's," *Industry Week*, August 21, 1978, p. 18.

9. *New York Times*, Sunday, January 25, 1981.

B. Shiskin, "Job Evaluation: What It Means to Unionists," *Personnel,* August 1947, pp. 20–22.

Shiskin, "Job Evaluation: What Unions Should Do About It," *Personnel,* September 1947, pp. 22–23.

10. Belcher, p. 175.

11. David J. Thomsen, "Compensation and Benefits," *Personnel Journal,* May 1981, pp. 348–354.

12. J. D. Dunn and F. M. Rachel, *Wage and Salary Administration: Total Compensation Systems,* p. 175, copyright © 1971 by McGraw-Hill Book Company.

13. Dunn and Rachel, pp. 177.

14. Thomsen, May 1981, p. 348–354.

15. E. E. Lawler, *Pay and Organizational Development* (Reading, Mass.: Addison-Wesley, 1981).

16. Robert J. Greene, "Which Pay Delivery System Is Best for Your Organization?" *Personnel,* May–June 1981, pp. 51–58.

17. "For Union Executives, A Lag in Take-Home Pay," *Business Week,* May 11, 1981, pp. 114–116.

18. E. E. Lawler III, "Workers Can Set Their Own Wages-Responsibly," *Psychology Today,* February 1977, pp. 109–112.

19. W. G. Lewellen and H. P. Lanser, "Executive Pay Preferences," *Harvard Business Review,* September–October 1973, p. 115–123.

20. Lawler, 1977, p. 110.

21. Mary Zippo, "Roundup," *Personnel,* September–October 1980, pp. 43–45.

22. E. E. Lawler III, "Managers' Perceptions of Their Subordinates' Pay and Their Supervisors' Pay," *Personnel Psychology,* no. 18 (1965), pp. 413–422.

23. Zippo, "Roundup," *Personnel,* May–June 1981, pp. 43–50.

24. L. Dyer, D. P. Schwab, and J. A. Fossum, "Impacts of Pay on Employee Behaviors and Attitudes: An Update," p. 56. Reprinted with permission from the January 1978 issue of the *Personnel Administrator,* copyright 1978, The American Society for Personnel Administration, 30 Park Drive, Berea, OH., 44017.

25. Dyer, Schwab, and Fossum, p. 56.

26. W. F. Whyte, ed., *Money and Motivation: An Analysis of Incentives in Industry* (New York: Harper & Row, 1955).

27. Marvin G. Dertien, "The Accuracy of Job Evaluation Plans," *Personnel Journal,* July 1981, pp. 566–570.

Stanley B. Henrici, "A Tool for Salary Administrators: Standard Salary Accounting," *Personnel,* September–October 1980, pp. 14–23.

Chapter Outline

Critical Issues in Performance-Based Pay

Performance-Based Pay Systems
Conditions When Performance-Based Pay Plans Work Best
Importance of Performance-Based Pay
Prevalence of Performance-Based Pay Plans

Merit Pay Plans
Merit versus Cost-of-Living Increases

Types of Incentive Plans
Individual-Level Incentive Plans
Group-Level Incentive Plans
Organization-Level Incentive Plans

CHAPTER 12

Performance-Based Pay

Administrative Issues in Performance-Based Pay
Lump Sum Salary Increases
Participation in Performance-Based Pay Plans

Evaluating Performance-Based Pay Systems

Facing the Critical Issues in Performance-Based Pay

Summary

Key Concepts

Discussion Questions

Case

For Your Career

Endnotes

Personnel in the News

Up-Front Bonuses

The relatively new development of granting CEOs [Chief Executive Officers] spectacular bonuses for signing new-job contracts has added to the furor over executive compensation. One such upfront payment which raised eyebrows was the $1.5 million that International Harvester Co. gave Archie R. McCardell, its chairman and CEO, in 1978. But another CEO contends: "If he makes the turnaround he's expected to, it will be the biggest bargain the shareholders ever had."

Turnaround is, likewise, the key word for Chrysler Corp.'s Lee A. Iacocca, who was awarded a $1.5 million bonus for signing on with the struggling automaker. He collected $1 million of the bonus as part of his $1,266,000 compensation in 1979. But his remuneration took a nosedive last year when the Chrysler CEO voluntarily agreed to work for a salary of $1. Under a proviso, he will recoup the foregone amount of his salary if the company's stock price rebounds to $8.50 a share by Aug. 31 of this year. However, the prospects of that happening now seem slim; last month Chrysler stock was selling at below $4.

U.S. Steel's Mr. Johnston draws a comparison to the world of sports and entertainment. "A CEO surely is worth to his shareholders, for one year, as much as the entertainment world pays its top performers for only a week in Las Vegas," he says. And he wonders if outfielder Dave Winfield, who signed a contract with the New York Yankees worth $20 million, is really more valuable than a man like Harry Gray, (chairman and CEO of United Technologies Corp). "Winfield makes far more: but the point is that no one has to buy a ticket to Yankee Stadium—and Boeing doesn't have to buy a Pratt & Whitney engine [from United Technologies]."

"People who question the motivational value of money," says TPF/C's Mr. Crystal, "tend to be mostly in academia or the news media. They have a much lower greed content than executives in industry and are motivated by other things. And that's good, because if they measured their success by the money they make, they'd probably kill themselves." (Industry Week, May 4, 1981, pp. 66, 74. Copyright 1981, Penton IPC, Inc. Reprinted by permission of Industry Week.)

Employee Profit-Sharing in Japan

Twice each year, in midsummer and at year-end, employees throughout Japan become even more acutely aware than usual of the relationship between productivity, profitability and personal gain. It is the time of the semiannual bonus negotiation, a distinguishing feature of the Japanese compensation system.

In addition to a base salary, workers in Japan receive a supplementary wage allowance, popularly known as the semiannual bonus. The precise amount awarded is determined through company-union negotiation, and reflects both the national economy and that of the individual enterprise. Generally, the amount is the equivalent of five to six months salary.

The tendency on the part of American managers is to shudder at the thought of such a system, though most likely it is the aspect of the compulsory negotiation that causes such an adverse reaction. In actuality, however, the plan is a means of relating employee compensation to company profits.

Once or Twice a Year?

Though a typical American annual profit-sharing is a reflection of a year's overall success (or lack of), such an end-of-the-year approach suffers from the one-shot syndrome. Once a year, employees know that they will be awarded a certain amount of money, determined according to the success of the company over the past year. Depending upon the amount awarded, there may be feelings of satisfaction or discontent, though ambivalence is more likely.

Maybe the frequency of bonus negotiations in Japan is a good idea. Perhaps it doesn't hurt to give employees, on an ongoing basis, tangible reinforcement of the advantages of working harder to increase profits. A more frequent focus on profit sharing, tied in with quarterly or semiannual results, would serve to paint a more realistic picture of the business ups and downs, and would more effectively drive home the cause and effect relationship of productivity and profitability. (Mary S. O'Connor, Personnel Journal, *August 1981, p. 614. Reprinted with the permission of* Personnel Journal, *Costa Mesa, Calif.; all rights reserved.)*

Together these two quotations illustrate how money is used and can be used in organizations. "Up-Front Bonuses" also illustrates how large sums of money to single individuals can be justified. You might use this to help you defend the salaries of Rusty Staub and Dave Winfield versus Lane Kirkland and Edward Hanley presented in Chapter 11. "Employee Profit-Sharing in Japan" shows that the effects of money are found worldwide and often used to the competitive disadvantage of the United States. The quotation also shows how the United States might benefit from studying personnel practices in other countries. In the meantime let's see what more we can learn about the personnel practices in the United States.

In Chapter 11, the first of three chapters on employee compensation, aspects of total compensation related most closely with attracting and retaining employees within legal guidelines are discussed. Those aspects include the environment of compensation, job evaluation, selected administration issues, and determination of the basic pay structure.

Now in this chapter, the primary aspect of total compensation related most closely with motivating employees for desired behaviors is discussed. This aspect is referred to as performance based pay. The two components of performance based pay to be examined are merit pay systems and incentive systems. Note that while in Chapter 10 we examined several behaviors desired by organizations of their employees, performance is the behavior of primary focus in this chapter. Remember, however, that pay is also critical in motivating the employees for the other behaviors discussed in Chapter 10, especially attendance and membership (which help attain the purpose of retaining employees).

CRITICAL ISSUES IN PERFORMANCE-BASED PAY

While performance-based pay can be quite effective in motivating, its use does raise a number of critical issues for personnel managers. Four Critical Issues include

1. *Although it's nice to give merit raises to good performers, a salary budget during rapid inflation is eaten up by cost-of-living adjustments. What can be done under these conditions?*

2. *How can a company really reward people for good performance? Can companies afford to do it?*

3. *What are the limits on a company's decision to use performance-based pay system? Which system is best?*

4. *Should employees help set up and administer the performance-based pay system if a company decides to use one?*

In order to respond to these issues, both merit pay systems and incentive pay systems have to be discussed in detail.

Pay systems that relate pay to performance are called **performance-based pay systems.** The extent of the relationship and the measure of performance used differentiate the two major types of performance-based pay systems or plans:

- Incentive Pay Plans
- Merit Pay Plans

PERFORMANCE-BASED PAY SYSTEMS

Incentive pay plans generally have more incentive value than merit pay plans.

Although there are many types of incentive pay plans, they all link rewards with performance. Performance is often, but not always, measured by standards of productivity and direct indexes of individuals, groups, or organizations. By contrast, merit pay plans generally use less direct measures of performance, such as rankings or ratings made by supervisors. Another aspect of many incentive pay plans is that the major portion of an individual's compensation, such as that of a salesperson on commission, is from incentive pay. Since the level of compensation varies with performance, the level of an individual's compensation can vary greatly. Merit pay plans, on the other hand, affect a relatively small percentage of an individual's total salary, because merit pay is generally used only to move an individual's compensation within a rate range (and this adjustment is made only once a year). Traditionally, incentive pay plans have used only money as a reward. More recently, such nonmonetary rewards as praise, participation, and feedback are also being tied to performance.

Thus **merit pay plans** are methods of monetary compensation, generally related to subjectively evaluated performance, that represent only a small percentage increment in an employee's direct compensation. **Incentive pay plans** are methods of monetary and nonmonetary compensation related to direct indexes of performance for the individual, group, or organization and generally represent a substantial proportion of an individual's direct compensation.

Keep in mind that, although many people are rewarded under one of these two performance-based pay plans, the majority of people are rewarded under merit pay plans. Consequently much of the total compensation people receive is not related to performance but rather related to the results of the job evaluation and steps in rate ranges discussed in Chapter 11. Nevertheless, when the conditions are right, performance-based pay plans, especially incentive plans, can really get workers to perform at high levels.

Conditions When Performance-Based Pay Plans Work Best

If pay is going to influence employee performance, employees must perceive a close relationship between performance and pay.[1] Pay, of course, must also be important to employees, and they must be able to perform. Being able to perform means they must have the ability, know what's expected, and perceive minimal conflicts in performing the rewarded behaviors.

Other conditions are also needed for performance-based pay to motivate performance. These conditions include

- The amount of money offered must be sufficiently large to make the extra effort worthwhile; this often is between 3 percent and 10 percent more money;
- The employee must not be placed in jeopardy or conflict by working for the extra pay. For example, she or he must not fear physical injuries, rate cutting, job insecurity, or ridicule from coworkers;
- Performance must be measurable and fair;
- There must be a high level of trust between the organization and the employees;
- The employee must know and understand how the pay program works; and
- The employee must be able to control the performance on which the performance-based pay is based.

Importance of Performance-Based Pay

When all of these conditions (and others to be discussed later) exist, which isn't often, money can be an extremely powerful motivator of performance. Studies of performance-based pay systems (especially incentive systems) have shown that individual incentive plans can improve performance on an average of almost 30 percent over nonperformance based pay plans. Group incentive plans can increase performance 15 percent to 20 percent.[2] These figures are really impressive. These are even more impressive given that other personnel programs such as goal setting, participation plans, and job enrichment have less of an impact on productivity. Thus, the personnel manager must, not only keep these figures in mind when selecting compensation systems, but must also keep them in mind when thinking about ways to improve the organization's productivity and QWL.

By the way, not all performance-based plans produce the same results. (An evaluation of these plans is presented in Exhibit 12.3.) Some are much better than others under certain conditions. Thus knowing the conditions and the plans to choose from is critical in successfully using performance-based pay plans. A list of plans to choose from is shown in Exhibit 12.1. We examine the qualities of each and the conditions that make each of them effective in the rest of this chapter.

Performance-based pay plans cannot only get people to perform at high levels but also get high performing people to join the organization.

Exhibit 12.1
Performance-Based Pay Plans by Level

Individual		*Group*	*Organization*
▪ Merit pay	▪ Piecework plan	▪ Production incentive	▪ Profit-sharing
	▪ Standard hour plan	▪ Department head	▪ Scanlon
	▪ Measured day work	▪ Staff/professional	
	▪ Sales incentive plan	▪ Senior officer	
	▪ Managerial incentive plans		
	▪ Suggestion systems		

Prevalence of Performance-Based Pay Plans

Since rewarding performance can be an effective way to get increased performance (see Chapter 10), one would expect organizations to do so by having performance-based pay plans. This is the case.

Merit Pay Plans.   According to the most recent survey on merit pay plans conducted by the Conference Board, merit pay plans are widely used. Of the companies surveyed, merit pay is granted to 96 percent of their nonexempt salaried employees, 99 percent of exempt, and 98 percent of top management. In contrast, only 7 percent of the unionized hourly employees receive merit pay hikes, which usually are awarded in combination with a general increase. Nonunion hourly workers are granted merit hikes by 39 percent of the companies, with 45 percent of the merit-paying firms also granting a general increase. Nonexempt salaried employees earned a median merit increase of 8 percent in 1977 and 1978—a figure that declined to 7.7 percent in 1979. Exempt salaried employees receive median merit increases of 8 percent in each of the surveyed years, while the median merit hikes for top management were 8.1 percent in 1977, 8.2 percent in 1978, and 8 percent in 1979.

Incentive Pay Plans.   In the United States, most incentive plans are either piecework or standard hour plans, although small-group plans and plantwide incentives are increasingly being used.[3] Yet fewer than 15 percent of the work force is paid under an incentive plan. A survey by the U.S. Bureau of Labor Statistics showed that only about 20 percent of plant employees in manufacturing worked under incentive plans.[4] In most other industries, the percentage is smaller; it is almost zero for office employees. There is a great deal of variation in these percentages, however, by type of industry and area of the country. For example, over 60 percent of the employees in the textile, clothing, cigar, and steel industries are covered by incentive plans, but fewer than 10 percent are covered in the aircraft, bakery, beverage, chemical, and lumber industries. In addition, almost no public employees are paid under an incentive plan. "In some cities in the Northeast and North Central areas, from 35 to 40 percent of plant employees work under incentive plans; in the South some cities range from 20 to 25 percent; and on the West Coast the percentage is less than ten."[5] In general, it is more likely that incentive plans will be used if labor costs are large, the market is cost-competitive, technology is not advanced, and an employee's output is relatively independent of another employee's.[6]

MERIT PAY PLANS

Because most large private organizations have some type of merit plan, it may be useful to look at a specific example of such a plan.[7] This merit plan tends to be rather typical. As shown in Exhibit 12.2, the pay increments depend not only on employee performance but also on employee position in the salary range. Position is determined by expressing the employee's current salary as a percentage of the salary that is the midpoint of the range of salaries for that job. The lower the position in the range (the first quartile is the lowest), the larger the percentage of the merit raise.

Merit based plans are based on performance appraisal and evaluation.

    An important component of compensation administration is monitoring the number of people in each quartile. Although the percentage of merit increases is greater in the lower quartiles, the absolute size of increases is often larger in the higher quartiles. The more people in the higher quartiles, the larger the budget necessary for merit increases. Therefore, the compensation manager must monitor the line managers, who attempt to get their employees pushed to the top of the ranges in each job as a way to offer more rewards to their employees. The compensation manager ends up playing the role of police officer, especially in a highly centralized operation. Unpleasant as it may be, this role is necessary for budget purposes and to assure equity for all employees in the organization. Employees who perform equally well should not be paid different salaries and given different merit increases.

Exhibit 12.2
Sample Merit Pay Plan

Performance Rating	Current Position in Salary Range			
	First Quartile	Second Quartile	Third Quartile	Fourth Quartile
Truly outstanding	13–14% increase	11–12% increase	9–10% increase	6–8% increase
Above average	11–12% increase	9–10% increase	7–8% increase	6% increase or less
Good	9–10% increase	7–8% increase	6% increase or less	delay increase
Satisfactory	6–8% increase	6% increase or less	delay increase	no increase
Unsatisfactory	no increase	no increase	no increase	no increase

    Although under merit pay plans, money is the reward for performance, it may not always be. At Allied Bancshares, employees receive stock shares for performing well as described in the *Personnel in Action* insert on Allied Bancshares.

PERSONNEL IN ACTION

Noble Goal at Allied Bancshares: Make More Employes Millionaires

Allied Bancshares Inc. thinks it has found a sure-fire way to hang onto employes: Make them rich.

"We have a number of Allied millionaires now, and our goal is to have a larger number of staff members with significant net worths than any other institution," says Gerald H. Smith, the bank's president and chief executive officer.

The bank pays salaries in line with other banks. But it rewards performance with shares of Allied stock. At many banks, that would be no reward at all. But Allied is in Texas, where banks are booming like everything else, and its stock has been rising steadily.

In 1975, a share of Allied common sold for $9. The price now is $45 a share. Of Allied's 2,000 employes, 86% own stock. At the end of 1980, 31 workers had Allied stock valued at more than $500,000 each, says D. Kent Anderson, an executive vice president who owns 16,506 shares. And, he says, "The price has gone up since then."

Joan Schaumburger, an Allied teller for eight years, says she is "thrilled to death" with the stock program. "I've talked to a broker who I ride the bus with, and he tells me to keep buying the stock," she says. "He says it will make me totally independent one day." Mrs. Schaumburger has accumulated 330 shares.

The stock is distributed through a savings plan in which the worker earmarks 3% of his or her salary for stock. The bank contributes an equivalent amount, and stock is purchased with the total. Workers can take their stock and sell it anytime, but most choose to keep it in the plan, letting dividends and new purchases swell their total holdings.

Allied also has a profit-sharing plan—paid, of course, in stock. The staff voted last year to dissolve the previous plan in favor of a stock-based plan.

Mr. Smith, the president, says, "Our goal is to have our staff benefit or perish on their stock." Since its creation in 1972, Houston-based Allied has had 22.3% annual compound growth in earnings per share, and has increased its assets to $2.85 billion from $250 million.

But the bank's incentive plan hasn't satisfied everyone. Recently one of Allied's senior vice presidents was accused of embezzling $17 million over a period of nearly 10 years.

Merit versus Cost-of-Living Increases

It's hard to give large merit increases if COLAs are large due to high inflation.

Many large organizations grant **cost-of-living adjustments (COLAs)** to their employees, especially firms in which unions have written COLAs into their contracts. Although this type of salary increase is not based on performance, yet it can take the lion's share of money available for compensation increases. And where unionized workers have COLA guarantees, the pressures are great to provide the same benefits to nonunion, often white-collar, employees. But many firms are trying to elminate their COLAs in favor of merit pay plans,[8] primarily because they aren't "getting any bang for their buck." In addition to not getting performance from pay, COLAs often take some salary control out of the hands of the organization and the compensation manager. Since most COLAs are tied to the Consumer Price Index (CPI), all the organization can do is watch salaries increase as the CPI does. The more the CPI increases, the more the organization must pay. The more the COLA budget, the smaller the pot for merit increases. And as some argue, for merit increases to really work, they must be pretty big.[9] Thus the issue is really whether the salary budget should be used for COLAs or merit increases. This issue, however, is less important in times of low inflation rates.

TYPES OF INCENTIVE PLANS

There are numerous types of incentive plans. The easiest way to discuss them is by the level at which they are applied—individual, group, or organization. Each type of plan is generally unique to a specific level. Regardless of the level at which a plan is implemented, the intended beneficiaries are always the organization and the individuals covered by the plan.

Individual-Level Incentive Plans

There are several types of individual-level incentive plans. They differ basically on how closely additional pay is related to each additional piece of output.

The Piecework Plan.   Piecework is the most common type of incentive pay plan. Under this plan, employees are guaranteed a standard pay rate for each unit of output. The pay rate per unit is frequently determined by the time-and-motion studies and the current base pay of the job. For example, if the base pay of a job is $20 per day and the employee can produce at a normal rate twenty units a day, the piece rate may be established at $1 per unit. Thus the incentive pay rate is based on the standard output and the base wage rate. The "normal" rate obviously is more than what the time-and-motion studies indicate. However, it is supposed to represent 100-percent efficiency. The final rate also reflects the bargaining power of the employees, economic conditions of the organization and community, and what the competition is paying.

The Standard Hour Plan.   This plan is the second most-used incentive plan. It is essentially a piecework plan, except that standards are denominated in time per unit of output rather than money per unit of output. Tasks are broken down by the amount of time it takes to complete them. This can be determined by historical records, time-and-motion studies, or a combination of both. The time to perform each task then becomes a "standard time."

Measured Day Work.   An individual-level incentive plan that removes some of the relationship between rates and standards is **measured day work.** Again, formal production standards are established, and employee performance is judged against these standards. But with measured day work, the typical standards are less precise. For example, standards may be determined by the results of a rating or ranking procedure rather than by an objective index such as units produced.[10] Consequently, one employee may be paid more than another because he or she received an "outstanding" performance rating while the other received only an "average" performance rating.

Sales Incentive Plans.   All the incentive plans discussed thus far share an important characteristic: they are usually applied to blue-collar employees and in some cases office employees. This is not to say that other employees do not participate in incentive programs with similar characteristics or incentive values. To the contrary, there are many managerial employees and salespeople who participate in incentive plans that have rather large incentive values. Incentive plans for salespeople are referred to as **commissions.**

About two-thirds of all salespeople are paid a salary plus commission.[11] In real estate sales, however, almost 75 percent of the people are paid straight commissions; straight commissions are paid to only 22 percent of all salespeople. As with the individual incentive plans for blue-collar and office employees, very few salespeople (11 percent) work without some guaranteed minimum pay.[12]

Managerial Incentive Plans. Incentive plans for managers generally take the form of cash bonuses for good performance of the department, division, or organization as a whole.[13] The magnitude of these cash bonuses is illustrated in the opening quotations of this chapter.

Other forms of compensation that can be used as managerial incentives are stock options and performance shares. A **stock option** is an opportunity for a manager to buy stocks of the organization at a later date but at a price established when the option is granted. The idea is that managers will work harder to increase their performance and the profitability of the company (thus increasing the price of the company's stock) if they can share in the profits over the long run. If the market price of the stock increases over time, managers can use their options to buy the stock at a lower price and to realize financial gain.

Managers often have their pay linked to the goals they have attained.

Performance shares provide a very close connection between individual performance (as reflected in company profitability) and rewards. This is because the manager or executive is rewarded only if established goals are met. The goals are usually stated in earnings per share (EPS). Furthermore, if the EPS goal is met, the manager receives shares of stock directly. Usually the manager receives cash (called **bonus units**) as well as stock in order to pay taxes on the equity (stock) reward. Receipt of just the shares, however, can result in a substantial reward.[14]

Although suggestion systems are made fun of, under the right conditions they can be quite beneficial for everybody.

Suggestion Systems. This form of incentive compensation, which rewards employees for money-saving or money-producing suggestions, is important because it is used so extensively. The 1,000 members of the National Association of Suggestion Systems (NASS) realized aggregate savings of $470 million from useful suggestions in 1975 alone.[15] The organizations belonging to NASS represent only a fraction of the organizations using suggestion systems. The average award per suggestion in 1973 was $78.65 and, for every dollar spent to run these systems, companies saved approximately $5.70.[16]

Nonetheless, it is not always easy to have an effective suggestion system. The characteristics of successful systems are shown in Chapter 7.

Group-Level Incentive Plans

Although individual-level incentive plans can be very effective, not all organizations can use them. One of the major reasons for this is that jobs are too interdependent.

As organizations become more complex, a growing number of jobs become interdependent with other jobs in either of two senses. Some jobs are part of a sequence of operations so that performance on jobs that precede them and follow them affect their performance; other jobs require joint efforts to achieve results.[17]

In either case, measurement of individual performance is difficult at best and often impossible. Individual-level incentives are not appropriate under these conditions because they fail to reward cooperation. Group-level incentives can do this. Thus individual-level incentive plans may become less common if changing technologies make jobs even more interdependent and individual performance more difficult to measure. However, most group-level incentive plans are adaptations of individual incentive plans. The standard hour and sharing plans are frequently used, but in group applications base rates are paid for a group standard output, and group performance above this standard determines the premium for the individuals in the group.

For group-level incentive systems to effectively motivate performance, they should have an objective measure of performance for the group. The individuals in the group must believe that they can affect the measure by their performance. Also, the system must be perceived as rewarding cooperation as well as group performance.

The Nucor Corporation Example.   Thus incentive plans can be effective in motivating employees to perform. However, each incentive plan does have its drawbacks that can limit its effectiveness. Consequently, to minimize the limitations and maximize the benefits of incentive plans, organizations use several incentive plans at one time. An example is the Nucor Corporation of Nebraska.

> In 1971 Nucor Corporation had sales of $64.8 million dollars and profits of $2.7 million dollars. In 1980 Nucor Corporation had sales of $482.4 million dollars and profits of $45.1 million dollars. This growth of more than 60 percent in sales and 1,500 percent in profits was entirely internally generated and due to a number of factors such as modern technology, aggressive management style and, most importantly, substantial improvements in productivity.[18]

Nucor is an excellent example of how useful incentive plans can be.

And the substantial improvement in productivity has been due in large part to the various group incentive plans. Since these plans can be adopted by other organizations, it is appropriate and useful to use Nucor as the basis for discussing group incentive plans.

Nucor has four group incentive compensation plans. The plans are for production employees, department heads, secretaries, accounting clerks, accountants, engineers and senior officers. The four plans (bonus groups) are

1. *Production Incentive Program.* About 2,500 employees within Nucor work under this program. Employee incentive groups, however, are no larger than 25 or 30 people. Consequently there are many bonus groups. For each of the steel mills there are nine bonus groups: three in melting and casting, where the bonus is based on good billet tons per hour for the week; three in rolling, where the bonus is based on good shear tons produced; and three in straightening, where the bonus is based on good straightened tons produced. The bonuses are paid together with employees' regular pay the next week. To help ensure that these bonus plans work well, Nucor makes sure that the operation and output of each group are definable and measurable.

Nucor uses several different types of incentive plans.

2. *Department Head Incentive Program.* At the department head level the company has an incentive compensation program based on the *division* contribution of the particular division in which the *department* manager works or the profits of the division relative to the expenses it directly controls.

3. *Staff/Professional Incentive Program*. This third program covers those neither in production nor at the departmental manager level. Thus included in this program may be groups composed of an accountant, an engineer, a secretary and an accounting clerk. The bonus incentive for these groups is based on either the division return on assets or the company's return on assets.

4. *Senior Officer Incentive Program*. The senior officers at Nucor receive no profit sharing, no pension plans, nor many other executive "perks." Pay for these executives are at 70 percent of the salary executives at similar levels in other companies receive. All other compensation is in the form of a bonus, half of which is paid in cash and half is deferred. The bonus derives from 10 percent of pretax earnings set aside for the senior officers according to their salary.

Organization-Level Incentive Plans

Many organizations need high levels of cooperation among their employees and so provide some form of incentive on an organizationwide basis. Approximately 7 percent of the firms in the United States have either plantwide bonus plans or profit-sharing arrangements.[19] The **bonus** is typically a percentage of the base wage rate of the employee if the organization reaches some goal. Employees receiving the same base wage or salary rate therefore receive the same incentive. Profit-sharing plans are often not considered a form of incentive compensation because individual employees have only partial and indirect control over organizational profits. However, since the extent of employee control over performance in a profit-sharing plan is a matter of degree rather than kind, profit-sharing plans are included here as an organization-level incentive.

Profit Sharing Plans. All profit-sharing plans must be approved by the Internal Revenue Service to comply with current tax laws. There are two major types of profit-sharing plans that organizations can use. **Cash plans** provide for payment of profit shares at regular intervals, typically ranging from monthly to yearly. The percentage of profits distributed ranges from 8 to 75 percent.[20] If profits are not realized by the company, no cash payments are made to employees. **Wage-dividend plans** (a special type of cash plan) set the percentage of profits paid to employees according to the amount of dividends paid to stockholders. These plans are assumed to increase understanding between employees and stockholders and are often perceived as more fair to employees than regular cash plans.

The Scanlon Plan. The Scanlon plan represents as much a philosophy of management-employee relations as it does a companywide incentive system. It emphasizes employer-employee participation and sharing in the operations and profitability of the company. As such, Scanlon plans are adaptable to different companies and changing needs.[21] The plan is used in union as well as nonunion plants.

The **Scanlon plan** reflects the fact that efficiency of operations depends on companywide cooperation and that bonus incentives encourage cooperation. The bonus is determined on the basis of savings in labor costs, which are measured by comparing the payroll to the sales value of production on a monthly or bimonthly basis. Previous months' ratios of payroll to sales value of production help establish expected labor costs. Savings in labor costs are then shared by employees (75 percent) and the employer (25 percent). Because all employees share in the savings, one group does not gain at the expense of another. Each employee's bonus is determined by converting the bonus fund to a percentage of the total payroll and applying this percentage to the employee's pay for the month. Although Scanlon plans can be successful, their real incentive value can be short lived. This can occur if the employees feel they can no longer work smarter or harder and, therefore, feel they cannot improve upon previous months' payroll to sales value of production ratios. At this point, employee performance levels off, and the Scanlon plan loses its incentive value. This effect is greatly minimized where work methods and products are always changing. Under these conditions employees are more likely to feel they can always find better ways to work.

ADMINISTRATIVE ISSUES IN PERFORMANCE-BASED PAY

In addition to paying attention to the conditions listed above, which can increase the effectiveness of performance based pay, there are several broader administrative issues that the personnel manager needs to consider.

Lump Sum Salary Increases

Although merit increases are generally given at the end of a six-month or a one-year interval, the additional pay is given out in only small weekly or monthly portions.[22] Let's take an example of an individual with a $50,000 yearly salary who has just received a 10 percent merit increase, which means a $5,000 bonus. Assume the individual is paid every two weeks. Approximately how much more does the individual get in his or her check? Since this individual is in the 50 percent tax bracket (federal, state, and local taxes combined), she or he takes home approximately $100 more in every check. In times of rapid inflation the real value of what the individual gets in every check is less than $100.00!

> Would you rather have one check for $10,000 or 10 checks for $1,000 spread over 12 months?

Recognizing that this method may reduce the motivational impact of the salary increase, companies such as B. F. Goodrich, Timex, and Westinghouse have started lump sum programs. Specifically, they give the employee the choice of receiving salary increases in the traditional way (divided up into parts for each check) or as a lump sum. Although this is a relatively new idea, it appears that a majority of the employees choose the lump sum payment unless the payment is treated as a loan for one year and interest is charged. When interest is charged, the attractiveness and motivational value of the lump sum declines substantially.

Participation in Performance-Based Pay Plans

Employee participation can take place at two critical points in performance-based pay plans: (1) in the design stage and (2) in the administration stage.

Design Stage Participation.   Many pay plans are designed by top management and installed in a fairly authoritative fashion. It appears, however, that employees cannot only do the same things, but do them more effectively. That is, employees can

Employees often act responsibly when given responsibility.

be responsible in designing the pay plan. Furthermore, they understand and accept the plan more readily because of this involvement. Participation in plan design also helps to reduce the potential resistance to change that accompanies almost any change in an organization. As a consequence of all of these factors, employees are more motivated to increase performance.

Despite these potential advantages of employee participation in pay plan design, they don't always occur. They fail to occur when management is not truly participative but rather tries to manipulate the employees with the participation. And they fail to occur when the employees prefer not to participate. These reasons for failure also apply to employee participation in the administration of the pay plan.

Administration Participation. As indicated in Chapter 11, employees can responsibly determine when and if other workers should receive pay increases. Another twist to this issue is individuals determining their *own* pay increases. At the Friedman-Jacobs Company, a small appliance firm in Oakland, California,

> Friedman decided to allow his employees to set their own wages based on their perception of their performance. This radical approach apparently has worked well. Instead of an all-out raid on the company coffers, the employees displayed responsible behavior. They set their wages slightly higher than the scale of the union to which they belonged and apparently find their pay quite satisfactory. When one appliance serviceman who was receiving considerably less than his co-workers was asked why he did not insist on equal pay, he replied, "I don't want to work that hard."[23]

EVALUATING PERFORMANCE-BASED PAY

Regardless of organizational conditions and constraints, performance-based plans can be measured by how well they relate motivation to performance.[24] The three criteria for judging incentive plans are (1) the relationship between performance and pay—that is, the time between performance and the administration of the pay (actual and as perceived by employees); (2) how well the plan minimizes the perceived negative consequences of good performance, such as social ostracism; and (3) whether it contributes to the perception that rewards other than pay (such as cooperation and recognition) stem from good performance, the more it minimzes the perceived negative consequences, and the more it contributes to the perception that other good rewards are also tied to performance. Exhibit 12.3 presents an evaluation of individual, group, and organizational plans based on these three criteria.

Four objective measures used to determine the level of performance to be rewarded are sales, units made, cost effectiveness, and savings below budget; subjective measures include things like traditional supervisor ratings. The more objective measures generally have higher credibility, are more valid, and are more visible and verifiable than the subjective measures. As shown in Exhibit 12.3, the objective measures (productivity and cost effectiveness) are more likely to link pay to performance than they are to minimize negative side effects. This evaluation is based on the notion that people do what's rewarded. More objective measures tend to make it very clear what's rewarded and what's not. This may produce more keen competition with other workers, result in more social ostracism, and lead workers to perceive that good performance may reduce the work available to them.[25]

Exhibit 12.3

Effectiveness of Performance-Based Pay Plans* (From E. E. Lawler
III, *Pay and Organizational Effectiveness*, p. 165. Copyright © 1971 by
McGraw-Hill Book Company. Reprinted with permission.)

	Type of Plan	Performance Measure	Tie Pay to Perfor- mance	Minimize Negative Side Effects	Tie Other Rewards to Perfor- mance
SALARY REWARD	Individual plan	Productivity	+2	0	0
		Cost effectiveness	+1	0	0
		Superiors' rating	+1	0	+1
	Group	Productivity	+1	0	+1
		Cost effectiveness	+1	0	+1
		Superiors' rating	+1	0	+1
	Organizationwide	Productivity	+1	0	+1
		Cost effectiveness	+1	0	+1
		Profit	0	0	+1
BONUS	Individual plan	Productivity	+3	−2	0
		Cost effectiveness	+2	−1	0
		Superiors' rating	+2	−1	+1
	Group	Productivity	+2	0	+1
		Cost effectiveness	+2	0	+1
		Superiors' rating	+2	0	+1
	Organizationwide	Productivity	+2	0	+1
		Cost effectiveness	+2	0	+1
		Profit	+1	0	+1

*A higher positive score indicates greater effectiveness and a lower negative score indicates less effectiveness.
Salary reward is essentially merit pay and bonus is incentive pay.

The overall evaluation of plans suggests that group and organizationwide incentive plans, although not high in relating individual performance with pay, result in no negative side effects (the exception is with intergroup competition with good performance besides pay, such as esteem, respect, and social acceptance from other employees.

Among the three levels of performance based pay plans there are no clear winners by all criteria. Incentive plans, however, have more incentive value than stock-option plans, seniority increases, across-the-board raises, and even merit pay plans. Thus the situation for motivating performance with pay is not hopeless. In fact, in a recent study of fifty-four companies with incentive programs, average increase in productivity over their previous nonincentive programs was 22.8 percent. Furthermore, it appears that even larger gains are possible and are more certain to be maintained when these conditions exist:

More
conditions to
increase the
effectiveness of
performance
based pay
plans.

- The plan is clearly communicated.

- The plan is understood, and bonuses are easily calculated.

- The employees have a hand in establishing and administering the plan.

- The employees feel they are being treated fairly.

- The employees have an avenue of appeal if they feel they are being treated unfairly.
- The employees feel they trust the company; therefore, that they have job security.
- The bonuses are awarded as soon as possible after the desired performance.

FACING THE CRITICAL ISSUES IN PERFORMANCE-BASED PAY

Now that we have considered performance-based pay systems, it is appropriate to return to the Critical Issues presented at the beginning of this chapter. Remember, only brief responses are presented here. You, however, should be able to expand on each of the four responses.

Issue: *Although it's nice to give merit raises to good performers, a salary budget during rapid inflation is eaten up by cost-of-living adjustments. What can be done under these conditions?*

This is a question that many personnel managers and compensation managers have been asking during the past several years of rapid, often double-digit inflation. What these managers face is the question of how to divide up the new pool of money that is added to the budget for salaries. Note that this is a situation where some attempt is being made to use the merit plan to pay for performance. But as with merit pay plans, raises are generally less than 15 percent of an individual's salary. The average merit increase is generally 8 or 9 percent.

During times when inflation is quite low, the personnel manager doesn't have a problem. The problem only comes during rapid inflation. The reason for this is the concern of many organizations to keep people from falling behind. During inflation, an employee's actual (real) income declines. A raise may only keep the person from falling behind under inflationary times. But the essence of merit pay is to reward employees and make them better off than they were before performing well. But to do this, organizations have to grant raises that exceed the rate of inflation. The crunch, however, comes now. Generally organizations had allocated 8 to 9 percent additional to salary budgets to support merit pay. That's when inflation averaged 2 or 3 percent. With inflation around 9 or 10 percent, to maintain the same real impact, the salary budget would need to be increased 15 to 16 percent. The organization simply can't afford that. Where does the money come from? Should they not prevent people from falling behind?

Issue: *How can a company really reward people for good performance? Can companies afford to do it?*

Can you afford not to do it? If you can really measure performance and everyone thinks the system is fair and tied to the objectives of the organization, paying for performance increases performance that should increase profitability. This increased profitability should more than enable you to pay for the cost of performance-based pay plan.

What plan you go with must be determined by several factors, such as the level at which performance can be accurately measured (individual, group, or organization) for given individuals, the extent of cooperation needed between groups and level of trust between management and nonmanagement. Remember that several plans can be used together to reward different groups of employees for good performance.

Issue: *What are the limits on a company's decision to use performance-based pay systems? Which system is best?*

Limits on a company's decision should include management's desire to have performance-based pay; management's commitment to take the time to design and implement one or several systems; the extent to which employees really influence the output; the extent to which there is a good performance appraisal system; the existence of a union; and the degree of trust in the organization. Note that whether the organization is public or private influences the decision too. Generally, only private organizations utilize incentive systems. Both types, however, can and do use merit pay systems.

Which pay system is best depends upon many factors. One is that the level of performance can be measured. Another is the control a person has over the level of performance, and another is the extent of cooperation needed between individuals and groups. Another consideration is the degree of negative consequences produced by a system. A final major consideration is the extent to which the employees will understand and accept the plan.

Issue: *Should employees help set up and administer the performance-based pay system if a company decides to use one?*

Yes, if the employees are used to and desire participation and the management generally runs the company in an open, participative way. The experience from other companies indicates that employees can responsibly set their own wages as well as design the system to be used. It really helps, however, if the employees have some economic information and understanding of the cost structure of the organization.

As a consequence of employee participation, it appears as if they are more committed to the organization and are absent less. In broad terms, participation in system design and/or administration appears positively related to productivity and QWL.

SUMMARY

Although performance based pay plans (except merit pay) are used in relatively few organizations, they continue to attract the attention of many personnel managers, and line managers continue to ask whether pay can be used as a motivator with their employees. Yet their experiences with merit pay convince them that pay cannot motivate. The success of many incentive plans indicates, however, that pay can motivate performance, although there can of course be many problems.

Implementation of incentive pay plans requires an effective performance appraisal program. The more objective the measures of performance, the more value incentive plans have. But many organizations do not have effective appraisal programs. As a result, pay is not based on performance (even though some people may actually be doing more work than others) but rather on nonperformance factors, such as the cost of living or seniority. To retain some appearance of rewarding performance, some organizations may use merit pay plans. Consequently, most organizations do not or are not able to provide the full incentive value of pay. Nevertheless, a few organizations are attempting to change the incentive plans, generally organizationwide plans that allow a great deal of employee participation in implementation and administration. The future for this type of plan looks much more promising than for any other type of incentive plan because of its wider applicability.

Even when organizations adopt some type of incentive plan, they still need to provide employees with indirect compensation, such as pension and retirement benefits, holidays, and other benefits related only to organization membership.

KEY CONCEPTS

performance-based pay systems	managerial incentive plans
merit pay plans	stock options
incentive pay plans	performance shares
cost-of-living adjustments (COLAs)	suggestion systems
piecework plan	bonus
standard hour plan	cash plans
measured day work	wage dividend plans
sales incentive plans	Scanlon plan
commissions	bonus units

DISCUSSION QUESTIONS

1. What is performance-based pay?
2. Compare and contrast incentive pay plans with merit pay plans.
3. What are the conditions under which performance-based pay systems are most effective?
4. Why don't suggestion systems generally have a favorable reputation?
5. What is necessary for group-level incentive systems to effectively motivate employees?
6. What lessons can be learned from the group-level incentive program developed by the plant?
7. What is the philosophy behind the Scanlon plan and to what level does it apply as a performance-based pay plan?
8. List some of the potential beneficial results of the Scanlon plan.
9. What is the rationale underlying improved motivation and increased performance by employee participation in developing performance-based pay plans?
10. What factors are considered to be important in designing performance-based pay plans?

CASE

The Merit Award: A Pat on the Back or a Push Out the Door?

GeoChemCo is a firm engaged in the manufacture and distribution of chemicals. Since much of the manufacturing, storage, and distribution processes of GeoChemCo are monitored and controlled by computer technology, the firm's computer operations expenditures are substantial. Fred Jenkins, the director of the firm's computer operations division, estimated that the projected annual budget for his division would amount to approximately $25,000,000. The comptroller of GeoChemCo felt that this amount was excessive and directed Jenkins to reduce costs wherever possible. To accomplish this objective, Jenkins assigned a number of systems analysts to review the current level and type of computer services provided to the organization. These analysts were instructed to streamline operations and eliminate unnecessary or infrequently used management reports and computer equipment.

Jack Rollins was one of the best and brightest system analysts who worked for Jenkins. After weeks of intensive investigation, Rollins submitted a proposal which permitted a $450,000 reduction in the computer operations budget. These budgetary reductions were accomplished by (1) consolidating the existing elements of the management/production control monitoring system; (2) elimination of redundant reporting and data collection procedures; (3) the utilization of less expensive "batch" computer processing where feasible; (4) the elimination of unnecessary or infrequently used computer equipment; and (5) better utilization and coordination among existing computer resources. Thus, Rollins was able to reduce operational costs while not reducing the level or quality of services provided to management.

Jenkins was greatly impressed by Rollins's activities and felt that he deserved some special form of recognition. Therefore, he informed Rollins that he was recommending him for a cash bonus/merit award. These awards, which were administered by the comptroller's office, constituted an important part of the firm's motivational program. Under this program, the employee's supervisor would make a recommendation as to the amount of the cash award to be received by the employee. In general, the dollar value of the reward was expressed as a percentage of the amount of cost savings the employee was responsible for. Jenkins recommended that Rollins receive a monetary bonus equivalent to 3 percent of the cost savings he generated (that is, $13,500).

Two months after Jenkins recommended Rollins for the cash bonus/merit award, Jenkins received a letter from the comptroller indicating that Rollins did not qualify for an award. The comptroller justified this decision by stating that the development of plans to reduce computer operational costs was an integral part of Rollins's job and, therefore, did not merit additional compensation. Jenkins felt that this decision was both unjustified and characteristic of an "accounting mentality." For the next several months, both of these individuals exchanged letters and telephone calls arguing for their respective viewpoints. When Rollins inquired as to the status of his award, Jenkins was forced to tell him of the long-running dispute between himself and the comptroller. However, Jenkins assured Rollins that the cash bonus would be awarded even if the firm's president had to be brought in to settle the dispute.

Approximately sixteen months after Jenkins submitted the original award recommendation, a compromise agreement was worked out with the comptroller. According to this agreement, Rollins was to receive a $250 cash award and a printed certificate of achievement. At the awards ceremony, Rollins accepted the monetary award and certificate from the comptroller. The following day, Rollins informed Jenkins that he was submitting his resignation in order to accept a job offered to him by another firm.

Case Questions

1. Are cash bonus/merit award systems desirable for enhancing employee motivation?

2. What are the advantages/disadvantages of the cash bonus/merit award program used by GeoChemCo?

3. What factors might have influenced Rollins in his decision to leave GeoChemCo?

4. What changes would you recommend in GeoChemCo's cash bonus/merit award program?

FOR YOUR CAREER

- It is likely you will work in an organization that has a merit based pay plan. If you strongly prefer to be paid for every piece of work you do, selling may be an area worth considering for your career.

- If you could choose, how much of your total pay would you like to be related directly to how much you produced?

- Organizations find it really difficult to reward outstanding performers during times of rapid inflation when the salary budget is eaten up by COLAs.

- There are significant differences among organizations. Some emphasize COLAs more than merit pay increases while others do the reverse. It may pay you to find out when looking for a job.

- If you work under a merit pay plan, knowing what performance is expected of you and knowing how your performance will be evaluated are critical. Find this out early.

- Working in a company like Nucor can be exciting as well as profitable.

ENDNOTES

1. Douglas L. Fleuter, "A Different Approach to Merit Increases," *Personnel Journal*, April 1979, pp. 225–226, 262.

   James G. Goodale and Michael M. Mouser, "Developing and Auditing a Merit Pay System," *Personnel Journal*, May 1981, pp. 391–397.

2. Keith W. Bennett, "Employee Incentives Plus New Technology Equals Productivity," *Iron Age,* February 2, 1981, pp. 43–45.

"Roundup," *Personnel,* November–December 1979, pp. 57–59.

Edward E. Lawler III, *Pay and Organization Development* (Reading, Mass.: Addison-Wesley Publishing Company, 1980).

3. R. B. McKersie, C. F. Miller, Jr., and W. E. Quarterman, "Some Indicators on Incentive Plan Prevalence," *Monthly Labor Review,* March 1964, pp. 271–276.

4. D. W. Belcher, *Compensation Administration* (Englewood Cliffs, N.J.: Prentice Hall, 1974), p. 401.

5. S. H. Slichter, J. J. Healy, and E. R. Livernash, *The Impact of Collective Bargaining on Management* (Washington, D.C.: The Brookings Institution, 1960), p. 301.

6. Lawler, p. 92.

7. Lawler.

David J. Thomsen, "Salary Increases vs. Incentives," *Personnel Journal,* December 1980, p. 974.

8. B. L. Metzger, *Profit Sharing in Perspective,* 2nd ed. (Evanston, Ill.: Profit Sharing Research Foundation, 1966), p. 45.

Howard Risher, "Inflation and Salary Administration," *Personnel Administrator,* May 1981, pp. 33–38, 68.

David J. Thomsen, "Compensation Trends in 1981," *Personnel Journal,* January 1981, p. 22.

Charles A. Peck, *Compensating Salaried Employees During Inflation: General vs. Merit Increases.* (New York: The Conference Board, 1981).

9. S. Barkin, "Labor's Attitude Toward Wage Incentive Plans," *Industrial and Labor Relations Review,* July 1948, pp. 553–572.

10. J. D. Dunn and F. M. Rachel, *Wage and Salary Administration: Total Compensation Systems* (New York: McGraw-Hill, 1971), p. 236.

11. *Incentive Plans for Salesmen,* Studies in Personnel Policy 217 (New York: National Industrial Conference Board, 1970).

12. *Compensating Field Representatives,* Studies in Personnel Policy 202 (New York: National Industrial Conference Board, 1966).

13. "Pay at the Top Mirrors Inflation," *Business Week,* May 11, 1981, pp. 58–59.

"Surge in Executive Job Contracts," *Dunn's Business Month,* October 1981, pp. 86–88.

Kenneth E. Foster, "Does Executive Pay Make Sense," *Business Horizons,* September–October 1981, pp. 47–58.

Donald B. Thompson, "Are CEOs Worth What They're Paid?" *Industry Week,* May 4, 1981, pp. 65–74.

14. Richard J. Bronstein, "The Equity Component of the Executive Compensation Package," *California Management Review,* Fall 1980, pp. 64–70.

"After the Qualified Stock Option," *Business Week,* May 25, 1981, pp. 100–102.

15. M. A. Tather, "Turning Ideas Into Gold," *Management Review,* March 1975, pp. 4–10.

16. V. G. Reuter, "A New Look At Suggestion Systems," *Journal of Systems Management,* January 1976, pp. 6–15.

17. Belcher, pp. 323–324.

18. John Savage, "Incentive Programs at Nucor Corporation Boost Productivity," *Personnel Administrator,* August 1981, pp. 33–36, 49.

19. J. Corina, *Forms of Wage and Salary Payment for High Productivity* (Paris: Organization for Economic Cooperation and Development, 1970).

20. Metzger, p. 45.

21. R. W. Davenport, "Enterprise for Everyman," *Fortune*, January 1950, pp. 55–59, 152, 157–159.

22. Lawler.

23. Lawler, p. 110.

24. E. E. Lawler III, *Pay and Organizational Effectiveness: A Psychological View* (New York: McGraw-Hill, 1971) pp. 157–177.

25. Samuel R. Collins, "Incentive Programs: Pros and Cons," *Personnel Journal*, July 1981, pp. 571–575.

   Ronald B. Goettinger, "Compensation and Benefits," *Personnel Journal*, November 1981, pp. 840–842.

Chapter Outline

The Critical Issues in Indirect Compensation

Indirect Compensation
The Purposes and Importance of Indirect Compensation

Legal and Environmental Impact on Indirect Compensation
Environmental Conditions
Legal Conditions

Protection Programs
Public Protection Programs
Private Protection Programs

Pay For Time Not Worked
Off the Job
On the Job

Employees Services and Perquisites

CHAPTER 13

Indirect Compensation

Administrative Issues in Indirect Compensation
Determining the Benefits Package
Providing Benefit Flexibility
Communicating the Benefits Package

Evaluating the Benefits of Indirect Compensation

Facing the Critical Issues in Indirect Compensation

Summary

Key Concepts

Discussion Questions

Case

For Your Career

Endnotes

Personnel in the News

Why Benefits Don't Benefit

Underlying our entire approach to benefits—with management and union in complete agreement, for once—is the asinine notion that the workforce is homogeneous in its needs and wants. As a result, we spend fabulous amounts of money on benefits which have little meaning for large groups of employees and leave unsatisfied the genuine needs of other, equally substantial groups. This is a major reason why our benefit plans have produced so little employee satisfaction and psychological security. (Reprinted by permission of the Harvard Business Review. *Excerpt from "What Can We Learn from Japanese Management?" by Peter Drucker [March–April 1981, p. 110]. Copyright © 1981 by the President and Fellows of Harvard College; all rights reserved.*)

Equal Pay Act Interpreted

EEOC's interpretation of the U.S. Supreme Court's 1978 ruling on fringe benefits in Los Angeles Department of Water v. Manhart *(421:618) is that an employer is required to provide equal benefits to employees under both Title VII and the Equal Pay Act. Before Manhart, the Labor Department permitted either equal contributions or equal benefits under the EPA. EEOC's newly proposed interpretation states that it would be unlawful for an employer to discriminate between men and women with regard to fringe benefits and that "it shall not be a defense under the Act to a charge of sex discrimination that the cost of such benefits is greater with respect to one sex than the other." Included in the definition of fringe benefits are "medical, hospital, accident, life insurance and retirement benefits; profit-sharing and bonus plans; leave; and other terms, conditions, and privileges of employment." The interpretations also address for the first time the relationship between EEOC's jurisdiction over the Equal Pay Act and Title VII. The proposals note that where the jurisdictional prerequisites of both Acts are satisfied, "any violation of the Equal Pay Act is also a violation of Title VII." However, stressing Title VII's broader scope in the area of wage discrimination, EEOC says that a policy or practice that does not violate the EPA nevertheless may be prohibited by Title VII.* (From Fair Employment Practices 429, September 10, 1981, pp. 1–2. Reprinted by permission from Fair Employment Practice Service, copyright 1981 by The Bureau of National Affairs, Inc., Washington, D.C.)

The Changing Role of Employee Support Programs

Past assumptions about the needs, values and expectations of the American worker are no longer necessarily valid. Technology has advanced so rapidly that machines have become the cheap resource and people the expensive one. Sophisticated technology requires sophisticated technologists. The pool of appropriately trained and qualified employees diminishes with each technological advance. Further employees with high-demand skills are in the enviable position of being able to highly influence the terms and conditions of their employment.

Workers of the '80s will come to the workplace with the clear expectation of finding a network of support programs to satisfy their needs and help them cope with the rigors of a constantly changing world. Employees expect their companies to provide suitable programs to insure their good health, to guarantee adequate leisure, and to contribute to their psychological and emotional well-being. What began as an incentive has become an obligation. (Gerries Mallof, Director of Personnel, Software Products Group, Informatics Inc., Canoga Park, California, Personnel Journal *November 1981, p. 844. Reprinted with the permission of* Personnel Journal, *Costa Mesa, Calif.; all rights reserved.)*

Together these quotations highlight several important aspects of indirect ("fringe") benefits. One is that many U.S. companies have failed to benefit from their benefit programs because employees often aren't pleased with the benefits. This, as Drucker points out, has been the result of companies' assuming and treating all employees alike, when in fact they are not.

A second aspect is the continued legal presence in personnel activities. Thus far, almost every personnel activity discussed is influenced by federal and state laws or court decisions. The indirect benefits area continues in that tradition. In addition to the Equal Pay Act (EPA) application to benefits, there are several other important laws or acts influencing benefits, such as the *Multiemployer Pension Plan Amendment Act of 1980* and the *Economic Tax Act of 1981.*

The third aspect based on these quotations is the changing role of benefits and the desire for new types of benefits such as support benefits. Since this aspect has many more facets, it is discussed much more extensively under Administrative Issues later in this chapter.

As with direct compensation, many employees are vitally concerned with indirect compensation. After all, this is a form of compensation—in addition to being very valuable—on which they do not have to pay income taxes. But as the cost of indirect benefits in proportion to the total payroll cost grows, organizations are becoming more concerned about how they benefit or can benefit and what they must do to really satisfy employees. Consequently, their critical concerns are many as reflected in the following Critical Issues.

CRITICAL ISSUES IN INDIRECT COMPENSATION

The four Critical Issues identified by our personnel managers include ones that you can help answer right now. For example:

1. *What types of benefits do people really want?*
2. *How can an organization get anything in return for the tremendous benefits it gives its employees?*
3. *How many more benefits will people want? What does the future hold for benefits?*
4. *Should employees be allowed to select their own benefits? Can companies afford to do that?*

Almost all organizations offer some form of indirect compensation—also known as fringe benefits or supplemental compensation. For some of these organizations, indirect compensation may make up as much as 50 percent of the cost of total compensation. Furthermore, the percentage of total compensation devoted to indirect compensation is expected to increase. Since the cost of indirect compensation is becoming so significant, it is important to ask whether organizations are getting their money's worth. The answer depends on the purposes or objectives of indirect compensation and its definition.

INDIRECT COMPENSATION

Indirect compensation is defined as those rewards provided by the organization to employees for their membership or participation (attendance) in the organization. Indirect compensation is divided into three categories:

Protection Programs
- Public
- Private

Pay for Time Not Worked
- On the job
- Off the job

Employee Services and Perquisites
- General
- Limited[1]

Although several of these rewards are mandated by federal and state governments and must, therefore, be administered within the boundaries of laws and regulations, many others are provided voluntarily by organizations. Indirect rewards are much more diverse than direct compensation and as a result are not always valued or seen as a reward by all employees. It is only when indirect compensation is seen as a reward, however, that many of the purposes of indirect compensation can be attained.

The Purposes and Importance of Indirect Compensation

The most recent survey on indirect benefits indicates that their value/cost as a percentage of direct compensation is growing and is substantial. As shown in Exhibit 13.1, the percentage increase from 1979 to 1980 averaged about 2 percent for employers in each of the three types of industries and in each of the salary groups. Note also that the percentage of indirect benefits is greatest at the lowest salary levels. Regardless of salary level, however, the cost of benefits to organizations is enormous.

In return for these benefits, organizations would like to attain several purposes, including

- Attracting good employees
- Increasing employee morale
- Reducing turnover

Exhibit 13.1
Noncash Benefit Values as Percentage of Salary (From
Compensation Review, First Quarter, 1981, p. 6.)

Employer Group	Annual Salary	Noncash as a Percentage of Cash	
		1979	1980
Industrial	$100,000	29.4%	31.0%
	70,000	30.6	32.4
	50,000	32.0	34.2
	30,000	35.0	37.7
	20,000	38.0	41.0
Financial	$100,000	31.6%	33.3%
	70,000	32.9	34.6
	50,000	34.2	36.2
	30,000	37.0	39.3
	20,000	39.5	42.0
Service	$100,000	29.5%	30.3%
	70,000	30.9	31.9
	50,000	32.4	33.8
	30,000	35.7	37.3
	20,000	38.5	40.5

- Increasing job satisfaction
- Motivating employees
- Enhancing the organization's image among employees
- Making better use of compensation dollars
- Keeping the union out[2]

Only rarely, however, are all these purposes attained.[3]

Benefits may not be successful in attaining these purposes because many employees do not think they are as important as rewards such as opportunity for advancement, salary, geographic location, and even prestige of the job and company.[4] By communicating the *real value* of indirect benefits, however, organizations may reverse this relatively low level of importance of benefits.

LEGAL AND ENVIRONMENTAL IMPACT ON INDIRECT COMPENSATION

Although many employees may not place much importance on benefits, there has been and is substantial legal and environmental impact on them. This is because benefits, such as social security, are really important to employees.

Environmental Conditions

Generally
employee
benefits are a
recent
phenomenon.

The Depression of the 1930s gave the necessary impetus for the beginning of extensive indirect benefits. The *Social Security Act,* passed in 1935, provided old age, disability, survivor, and health benefits and the basis for federal and state unemployment programs. The unions have also had a significant impact on indirect benefits, and their growth was enhanced by the *National Labor Relations Act (NLRA) of 1935.* There were indirect benefits before 1930, but the rapid growth of federally mandated benefits began then, also sparking the growth of voluntary benefits. In fact, in 1929 indirect benefits were less than 5 percent of the cost of total compensation. By 1949 this cost rose to 16 percent.

Legal Conditions

Before World War II, the significant legal conditions affecting benefits were the Social Security Act and the NLRA. Both of these acts continue to play a significant role in the administration of benefits, especially with the impact of the Age Discrimination in Employment Act on mandatory retirement.

After the war, two court cases helped to expand benefit coverage by declaring that pension and insurance provisions were bargainable issues in union and management relations. The right to bargain over pensions was decided in *Inland Steel* v. *National Labor Relations Board* (1948), and the right to bargain over insurance was decided in *W. W. Cross* v. *National Labor Relations Board* (1949).

Age Discrimination in Employment Act of 1967. Although the Social Security Act allows women to retire earlier than men (at age sixty-two as opposed to age sixty-five), the U.S. Supreme Court, by refusing to hear a lower-court ruling, affirmed that it is illegal to require women to retire earlier than men. On the issue of mandatory retirement, neither men nor women can now be forced to retire before the age of seventy if they are working for a private business with at least twenty persons on the payroll. Exceptions to this are top-level executives, who can be retired at age sixty-five. These provisions, which are contained in a 1978 amendment to the 1967 *Age Discrimination in Employment Act,* took effect on January 1, 1979. Employees, however, may still choose to retire at sixty-five and receive full benefits. But because social security is almost broke, there is the desire on the part of some congressmen to increase the age at which full social security benefits can start to sixty-eight.

ERISA of 1974 and Private Employees' Pensions. ERISA (Employees' Retirement Income Security Act) was enacted to protect employees covered by private pension programs. Before ERISA, employees in such plans often found themselves without any real benefits by the time they reached retirement. Sometimes employees who left an organization after working there many years would receive no retirement benefits or only a small proportion of the benefits due to them because they had no **vested rights.** The term *vested rights* refers to the legal right of an employee to be part of an organization's pension program. If vested employees quit, they still receive a pension when they reach retirement age; without vesting, employees who quit must remove their pension contribution and may not receive the employer's contribution. Sometimes the pension programs were not adequately funded or were mismanaged.

ERISA specified numerous minimum requirements for private employee pension programs if organizations chose to have them at all. Organizations with existing programs can either comply with these requirements or drop their programs, which many have done. Between the enactment of ERISA and 1977, about 18,000 private pension programs were terminated by organizations.[5] Critics of ERISA say this is primarily due to the requirements of ERISA; its supporters claim that this many would have been dropped with or without ERISA.

Multiemployer Pension Plan Amendments Act (MEPPAA) of 1980.   Because ERISA did not address problems unique to multiemployer plans, Congress felt it necessary to amend provisions of ERISA.[6] It did so with the **MEPPAA.** This act is really important for personnel departments because it, for the first time, forces them to get involved in the fixing of multiemployer plan benefit levels and the payment of those benefits. Whereas ERISA covers only single pension plans funded and administered by one company, MEPPAA covers those plans that cover employees in many different companies. Because multiemployer plans are generally collectively bargained they are considered "union" plans.

Pregnancy Discrimination Act of 1978.   There was a trend in recent years to treat pregnancy as a disability. Opponents of this trend argued that pregnancy is a voluntary condition, not an involuntary sickness and, therefore, should not be covered by disability benefits. The *Pregnancy Discrimination Act of 1978*, however, states that pregnancy is a disability and, furthermore, must receive the same benefits as any other disability. In the same year the U.S. Supreme Court added that all indirect benefits must be administered without respect to sex under the *Equal Pay Act of 1963 (Los Angeles Department of Water v. Manhart).*

Economic Recovery Tax Act of 1981.   Under this act, which became effective January 1, 1981, employees may make tax-deductible contributions to Individual Retirement Accounts (IRAs) or their employers' pension, profit-sharing, or savings plan (all retirement type programs) of up to $2,000.

PROTECTION PROGRAMS

Of the three groups of indirect compensation protection programs, pay for time not worked, for employee services, and perquisites, protection programs are generally the most significant to employee as well as to employer. **Protection programs** of indirect compensation are designed to protect the employee and family if and when the employee's income (direct compensation) is terminated and to protect the employee and family against the burden of health care expenses. Protection programs required by federal and state governments are referred to as public programs, and those voluntarily offered by organizations are called private programs. An outline of typical private and public protection programs appears in Exhibit 13.2.

Protection Programs:
- Public
- Private

Public Protection Programs

Many public protection programs are for the most part direct products of the Social Security Act of 1935. The protection programs of social security were initially funded

Public
Protection
Programs:

- Pension
benefits
- Unemploy-
ment
compensa-
tion
- Disability and
worker
compensa-
tion
- Medical and
hospital

by old age, survivor's, and disability insurance. The act initially set up systems for retirement benefits, disability, and unemployment insurance. Health insurance, particularly Medicare, was added in 1966 to provide hospital insurance to almost everyone sixty-five and older.

The Social Security System. Funding of the social security system is provided by equal contributions from employee and employer. Employees' contributions are deducted from paychecks under the terms of **FICA** (Federal Insurance Contribution Act). Initially, employee and employer each paid 1 percent of the employee's income up to $3,000. Currently the employee and employer each pay social security tax on the first $29,700 of the employee's income at a rate of 6.65 percent ($1,975 from each). The rate is scheduled to go to 7.15 percent by 1987 on a base income up to $42,500. This amounts to employee and employer contributions of $3,045 each per year.

Exhibit 13.2
Protection Programs (Adapted from J. S. Sullivan, Indirect Compensation: The Decade Ahead, *California Management Review*, Winter 1972, Vol XV, no. 2, p. 65.)

Hazard	Private Plans	Public Plans
Old age	■ Pensions ■ Deferred profit sharing ■ "Thrift" plans	■ Social Security old age benefits
Death	■ Group term life insurance (including accidental death and travel insurance) ■ Payouts from profit-sharing, pension, and/or thrift plans ■ Dependent survivors' benefits	■ Social Security survivors' benefits ■ Worker's compensation
Disability	■ Short-term accident and sickness insurance, sick leave ■ Long-term disability insurance	■ Worker's compensation ■ Social Security disability benefits ■ State disability benefits
Unemployment	■ Supplemental unemployment benefits and/or severance pay	■ Unemployment benefits
Medical/dental expenses	■ Hospital/surgical insurance ■ Other medical insurance ■ Dental insurance	■ Worker's compensation ■ Medicare

Social Security
benefits were
never intended
to be the sole
means of
support for
retired
individuals.

Presently, the social security system is facing a potential financial crisis. Although there have been numerous proposals to avert the crisis, none as yet has been adopted. It is unlikely, however, that the system will be allowed to fail.[7]

Social Security Pension Benefits. The average pension check from social security is now about $275 per month. In 1972 Congress passed a law providing that increases in pension benefits be determined by an inflation escalator clause. As a result, recipients receive increases in benefits greater than the inflation rate of the preceding year. Consequently, the maximum benefits from social security are $653.80 per month plus 50 percent for an aged dependent spouse. In addition, individuals receiving pension benefits can now earn up to $6,000. Presently federal employees are not eligible for social security coverage, but other employees, including self-employed individuals, are eligible.

Unemployment Compensation Benefits.   In order to control the pension provisions of social security, the unemployment provisions dictate that benefits from unemployment compensation be determined jointly through federal and state cooperation. As a result, employer costs and employee benefits can vary from state to state. The unemployment compensation fund is supported solely by employers, except in Alabama, Alaska, and New Jersey, where employees also contribute. The base rate for employer contributions varies depending on the number of unemployed people an organization has drawing from the state's unemployment fund. Thus it pays for an organization to maintain relatively stable employment and to avoid layoffs.

The current rate an employer has to pay into the unemployment fund is 3.4 percent of each employee's salary, up to $6,000 per year. The employer, however, can obtain a credit of 2.7 percent, thus paying only 0.7 percent. The credit can be obtained by making payments to the state unemployment fund through the company's experience rating (the more people on layoff, the higher the rating). Thus a company with a good rating may pay only 1 percent of employee's salaries to the state fund and 0.7 percent to the federal fund. The remaining 2.7 percent is not paid, because it is a bonus for having a good rating. The exact percentages assigned for good experience ratings varies from state to state, but the potential savings for stable employment and good human resource planning are significant.

The purpose of unemployment compensation is to provide income to an individual who is employed but not currently working (indefinite layoff) or who is seeking a job. To be eligible for benefits, an employee must first have worked a minimum number of weeks (exact number set by the state), currently be without a job, and be willing to accept an appropriate job offered through the State Unemployment Compensation Commission. It was recently declared in New York that even individuals on strike may collect unemployment benefits. Although the typical period of time a person may receive unemployment benefits is twenty-six weeks, the period has often been extended. Extended benefit periods and the rising number of people collecting unemployment compensation has put many state unemployment funds in severe financial condition.

FOR YOUR CAREER

Pension programs are funded in two major ways. One way is totally by contributions from the employer for the employee. This type of program is called **noncontributory.** The second way is by contributions by both the employer and the employee. This is called a **contributory** program. Generally private pension programs are noncontributory and public pension programs are contributory. Social security is a contributory program.

Disability and Worker's Compensation Benefits. These benefits are provided in public programs by the social security system and by state systems. At both the state and federal level, compensation benefits are administered to assist workers who are ill or injured and cannot work due to work or occupational injury or ailment. Totally disabled employees can receive payments from social security until retirement. Usually these payments are minimal (less than $100), but state compensation benefits can add substantially to that amount. State compensation benefits are usually paid for permanent partial, temporary total, partial, or permanent total disability.[8]

Medical and Hospital Benefits. The major public program providing medical and hospital benefits is Medicare which is funded by social security.

Medicare applies only to people over sixty-five, but the Health Maintenance Organization Act of 1973 is an attempt to provide medical and hospital benefits for younger people as well. The act established and regulates health maintenance organizations (**HMOs**), which incorporate the services of hospitals, clinics, doctors, nurses, and technicians at a single monthly rate.[9] The act also requires employers of at least twenty-five persons to offer an HMO plan option if they offer traditional health benefits. If HMOs organized for both group and individual practice operate in an employer's area, the employer is required to offer enrollment in both types.[10]

Private Protection Programs

Private Programs:

- Retirement
- Insurance
- Supplemental

Private protection programs are those offered by organizations (private and public) that are not required by law, although their administration may be regulated by law. The programs provide benefits for health care, income after retirement, and insurance against loss of life and limb. Almost all employers provide them for their employees. In contrast, only about 2 million employees, or about 2 percent of the work force, are covered by programs providing income before retirement in the form of supplemental unemployment benefits and guaranteed pay and work programs.

Retirement Benefits. About 78 percent of all plant workers and 85 percent of all office workers are covered by private pension programs, none of which is required by law. Although these percentages may appear to be rather high, only about one-third of the entire U.S. work force is covered.[11]

Because the benefits from social security are generally not sufficient—nor were they intended to be—to provide a comfortable retirement private pension benefits are critical to the survival of many people.[12] However, many people work many years only to find out they are not eligible for a company's pension benefits. There are many reasons for ineligibility so it is important to find out early in your career with an organization answers to questions such as "when will I become vested?"[13]

Insurance Benefits. There are three major types of insurance programs: *life*, *health*, and *disability*. These insurance programs are provided by most organizations at a cost far below what would be charged to employees buying their own insurance. They are essential benefits, although employees do not always recognize them as being very important. Nevertheless, these programs have grown substantially, both in the dollar amount of benefits and the percentage of employees covered.

Life insurance programs cover almost all employees. The benefits are equal to about two years' income, but this tends to be true more for managerial employees than for nonmanagerial employees.[14] Nonmanagerial, clerical, and blue-collar employees are generally covered for an amount less than one year's income. After retirement the benefits continue for most employees, but they may be reduced by as much as two-thirds.[15]

A similar philosophy dictates the offering of *health insurance programs.* The extent of health coverage has increased greatly over the past few years. Some organizations now offer, in addition to the typical hospital (Blue Cross), surgical (Blue Shield), and major medical coverage, insurance for eyeglasses, dental care, prescription drugs, and hearing aids. As with life insurance programs, almost all employees are provided with the typical health insurance package (hospital, surgical, and major medical), although managerial employees have slightly more extensive coverage.[16] Often health programs for managerial employees also have a deductible feature, which obligates employees to pay the first $50 to $100 of their health expenses for each sickness or accident before receiving the benefits of the insurance coverage. Nonmanagerial employees, especially those who are unionized, generally do not pay any part of their health expenses.

Whereas health insurance programs offered by the employer generally cover *short-term disability insurance,* longer-term absences due to sickness or disability are covered by *long-term sickness and disability insurance.* Note that this insurance is also referred to as **worker compensation insurance.** Both types of disability insurance generally supplement state and federal disability programs. However, short-term disability protection is generally offered by more organizations than is long-term disability protection. About 70 percent of all organizations provide short-term sickness and accident protection, but only 60 percent provide long-term coverage.[17]

Although broadening the coverage of benefits is helpful to individuals, it, along with rising medical costs, more frequent litigation, and legislative mandates, has threatened the viability of worker compensation programs.[18] This is illustrated in the *Personnel in Action* insert on "On-the-Job Injuries."

Insurance benefits are critical for most employees.

PERSONNEL IN ACTION
On-the-Job Injuries: Now, Suits Against the Boss

William Bell, a route salesman for Industrial Vangas Inc., was delivering gas to a customer of the Fresno (Calif.) supplier when a fire broke out as he was transferring propane from his truck to small tanks, badly burning him. In California, Bell's apparent sole remedy was workers' compensation—an insurance system that pays an employee a flat amount (in Bell's case, $30,000) for on-the-job injuries, whether or not anyone is at fault. The 1911 Workers' Compensation Act specifically prohibits employees from suing em-

ployers, as do comparable laws in virtually all states.

But Bell sued anyway, seeking several million dollars for his injuries and charging that since Industrial Vangas had assembled the propane truck it should be liable—not as the employer but as a maufacturer. Late last year the California Supreme Court agreed. The court ruled that an employer's shield against being sued can be stripped away when it acts in a "dual capacity." The decision threatens to upset the very foundation of workers' compensation—the delicate balance between swift compensation payments for injured employees and immunity from legal liability for the employer—and could cost California companies millions of dollars. It could "virtually double insurance costs" for all employers, concludes Vangas Senior Vice-President Paul H. Jones.

'Coincidental' Employment

The Bell case is not the only challenge to the longtime compensation system, but it is the most far-reaching. It follows the California high court's 1980 decision against Johns-Manville Products Corp. that an employee who contracted asbestosis on the job could sue the asbestos manufacturer for fraudulently concealing the origins of the disease. And the current ruling will be closely watched in a recent decision against International Paper Co., now on appeal, that held that an injured employee was entitled to $825,000 in damages (reduced by about $120,000 received in workers' compensation benefits) because the company is self-insured. Under the dual-capacity doctrine, International Paper is liable for the worker's injuries as a "third-party insurer," not as the employer, said a state superior court. If this decision is not reversed on appeal, says Michael G. Lowe, a San Francisco attorney specializing in employer-liability defense work, "it will virtually end self-insurance in the state of California."

In a strongly worded dissent in the Bell case, Justice Frank K. Richardson branded the majority's conclusion "absurd" and pointed out that under the dual-capacity logic, a company could be held liable for injuries attributable to its status as "landowner, motor vehicle operator, or cafeteria proprietor." Plaintiffs' lawyers have already gotten the point. Lowe notes that injured workers going to court are calling the fact of their employment "coincidental."

As a result, corporate officials have begun to worry about a broader impact of the dual-capacity rulings. Fixed compensation schedules for employee injuries provide a high degree of certainty in figuring insurance costs and, in turn, product prices. "If there is unlimited liability, companies don't know how to estimate their costs or how to price their product," says Lowe. Moreover, most general liability policies exclude injuries arising out of the course of employment, while workers' compensation insurance covers only work-related injuries. According to Alan Tebb, general manager at the California Workers' Compensation Institute, the courts "may have created an uninsured and uninsurable hazard."

The cumulative effect of the erosion of legal immunity in these cases has led some companies to reevaluate doing business in California. Bethlehem Steel, Uniroyal, and Ford Motor, among others, have named California's workers' compensation system as part of the reason that they recently have closed down certain operations in the state or expanded elsewhere. Although few observers expect any mass corporate exodus, the cost of doing business in California, and in many of the states such as Ohio, Illinois, and New Jersey that follow its lead in the workers' compensation area, is likely to climb considerably.

Already workers' compensation insurance costs are more than half again as high for California employers as for the average U.S. employer ($3.04 per $100 payroll in California compared with less than $2 nationwide, according to the Workers' Compensation Institute). Premiums for insured employers in California have jumped from $774 million in 1972 to more than $3 billion today. Although California ranks fourth in the nation in terms of compensation costs to employers, it is only 39th in terms of benefits to injured parties, in part because a relatively high proportion of such cases go to court, consuming $300 million annually in litigation costs and in part because of overcompensating some workers who have no long-term handicaps. With benefits to injured workers lagging behind most other states, plaintiffs see lawsuits as a way around inadequate coverage.

Benefits Trade-Off

The California legislature is under pressure to defuse the recent court decisions. One pending measure would end the erosion of legal immunity in return for perhaps $445 million in additional benefits for workers. Although California industry is unlikely to support such a high-priced trade-off now, changes may be better for a $100 million package later this year.

Without some restriction, the exposure of companies to such suits could become huge. "The Bell decision is only an indication of future legal liability," observes Paul P. Gladfelty, director of workers' compensation for the California Manufacturers Assn. "But it's like a cavity; it's better to get it when it's small."

Supplemental Unemployment Benefits.　　A small number of organizations offer employees protection against loss of income and loss of work before retirement. **Supplemental unemployment benefits (SUB)** are for people laid off from work. When SUB benefits are combined with unemployment compensation benefits, laid-off employees can receive as much as 95 percent of their average income. The size of these benefits makes it easier for employees with more years of service to accept layoffs, thus allowing employees with less service, often younger, to continue working. SUB programs exist in a limited number of industries, and all are the product of labor-management contracts. The industries in which they are found include the automotive, steel, rubber, glass, ceramic, and ladies' garment industries.

PAY FOR TIME NOT WORKED

The second most significant group of indirect compensation for the employer and employees is **pay for time not worked.** This benefit is not so complex to administer as benefits from protection programs, but it is almost as costly to the organization. Pay for time not worked continues to grow, in amount as well as in kind.[19] For example, in 1955 the average number of paid holidays per year was approximately six; in 1978 it was ten. During the same period, the average number of weeks of paid vacation went from three to four.[20]

　　There are two major categories of pay for time not worked. Holidays and vacations belong to the *off-the-job category;* the other category is *on the job.*

Off the Job

Payments for time not worked, especially those referred to primarily as off-the-job benefits, constitute a major portion of the total cost of indirect compensation. Almost 16 percent of indirect compensation is pay for time not worked of which 11 percent is for off-the-job payments. The most common paid off-the-job components are vacations, sick leave, holidays, and personal days. It is common for organizations to pay for ten holidays per year, with many giving employees their birthday off.

Increasing costs are forcing companies to reduce the number of holidays given employees.

On the Job

Paid benefits for time not worked on the job include rest periods, lunch periods, wash-up time, and clothes-change and get-ready times. Together these benefits are the fifth most expensive indirect compensation benefit. One benefit growing in popularity is time for and facilities for physical fitness.

Physical Fitness Benefits.　　With increased awareness of the relationship between job stress and coronary heart disease and other physical and mental disabilities, organizations have become more concerned with finding ways to alleviate stress whenever possible. People who are in good physical condition can often deal with stress better and suffer fewer negative symptoms than people in poor physical condition. In addition, physical exercise is a good way to cope with stress and reduce its effects. Consequently, organizations are encouraging their employees to be physically fit and to engage in exercise by providing athletic facilities on company premises. These facilities are essentially a service to employees.

EMPLOYEE SERVICES AND PERQUISITES

The third and final component of indirect compensation is **employee services and perquisites,** which may consist of

- Food service costs or losses
- Employee discounts
- Day care centers
- Employer-sponsored scholarships (or tuition assistance) for employees and their dependents
- Employee counseling and advisory services (legal, tax, and personal problems)
- Low-cost loans
- Company-leased or -owned vehicles for business and personal use
- Service/suggestion awards

Primarily for top executives are such perquisites as

- Annual company-paid physical examinations
- Company-paid memberships in country, athletic, and social clubs
- Use of company expense accounts to cover personal travel, meals, and entertainment
- Business and personal use of corporate aircraft
- Relocation costs[21]

Blue-collar workers generally have fewer perquisites than white-collar workers.

Although this component represents the smallest percentage of indirect compensation, services and perquisites are rewarding as well as necessary for many employees. To some, they represent an important element in the status system of the organization; to others, they represent a means by which working is made possible. For example, day-care centers make it more practicable for some individuals to start working and make it more feasible for them to continue working and with less absenteeism.[22] To others, services and perquisites, since they are generally not taxed are seen as desirable as shown in the *Personnel in Action* insert.[23]

ADMINISTRATIVE ISSUES IN INDIRECT COMPENSATION

Although indirect compensation is often used and seen as a reward, it is not used or seen as a reward by everyone.[24] Because organizations prefer to get at least something for something, they become concerned with their package of indirect compensation benefits and how they are administered.

Determining the Benefits Package

The benefits package should be selected on the basis of what's good for the employee as well as the employer. Often knowing employee preferences can help determine what benefits package the employer should offer.

PERSONNEL IN ACTION

Unions Eye the Three-Martini Lunch

Item: The Painters & Allied Trades Union in northern California has a contract that makes every other Friday a no-pay holiday. Instead of earning regular income, many members want a steady opportunity to moonlight for cash. Since a painter's weekly take-home pay averages $460, taxes make the difference between a four-day and five-day week only $50. "On that fifth day, a guy doesn't like working for so little," says union spokesman Don Heino.

Item: Flight attendants, who earn as much as $32,000 a year, have negotiated meal allowances as well as pay increases. "You are looking at $200 to $300 of tax-free expense money a month," says Linda Puchala, president of the Association of Flight Attendants. "We keep saying it's not salary. But if the expenses are not incurred, it's the same thing."

Item: General Motors has set up a stock ownership plan for hourly employees, under which the firm credits stock to assembly-line workers with two or more years of service. Workers pay no taxes on stock in the plan, which becomes deferred income. There is a sweetener for management: The corporation can claim a tax credit for its contribution.

Right now, tax-free perks like these aren't the main concern of unions. Those at the top of the pay scale—auto workers, coal miners, steelworkers and building tradesmen—are worried about rising unemployment. But as recovery comes and their yearly paychecks hit $25,000 and more, such perks are certain to become a key part of bargaining strategy. Union leaders see these benefits as one important way to blunt the impact of falling real wages and higher marginal tax rates. In 1981, for example, first-year wage increases in major union contracts are expected to average 10%, but inflation may well average 12%. "Workers are finally realizing that real wages have been falling

for ten years," says Audrey Freedman, chief labor economist for the Conference Board.

Like their counterparts in the executive suite, rank-and-file workers are victims of tax-bracket creep. Fat increases have pushed hard hats into top-tier marginal tax brackets. Skilled auto workers will be up to $30,000 annually in a few years, and that worker with a wife and two children, for example, loses almost one-third of a 10% raise to taxes. If his wife works and they earn $40,000 a year, nearly 40% drops out of their paychecks up front. Beyond this, the Social Security cutoff has risen to $29,700, making the total income of millions of union members subject to withholding.

The result is that many workers are beginning to think like executives when it comes to dealing with the taxman. Historically, unions won what amounts to tax-free income mainly through medical insurance plans. While these have been expanding—to include dental care, for example—they can go only so far. Notes the Conference Board's Freedman, "It's like adding a fourth martini to a three-martini lunch—more benefits don't really improve things."

Union leaders are more blunt. "The guys have had it," says Reese Hammond, director of education for the International Union of Operating Engineers in Washington, D.C. "I never used to believe it when they said, 'Don't give me a raise. I can't afford it.' But I do now."

Hammond predicts that all forms of sheltered income are going to become popular. In his own union, where master mechanics command $25,000 to $30,000 a year and more, some of the locals have expanded traditional insurance benefits to include dental care and eye care, and may soon negotiate free legal services as well. "The master mechanic is probably quite a bit like the lawyer that lives next door" when it comes to concern over taxes, Hammond says.

Congress made the negotiating for such fringes easier in 1978, when it barred the Internal Revenue Service from issuing rules that set limits on tax-free benefits. As a result, unions pressing for more perks haven't had to worry about the taxman. Though that congressional prohibition expires in June, it is likely to be extended.

Two other factors, however, may ease the trend, at least for a bit. A substantial reduction in federal taxes, as Ronald Reagan has promised, will make the pressure for off-paycheck earnings less intense. "The tax cuts," says economist Freedman, "will make everybody feel better." Also, normally aggressive unions

like the United Auto Workers and the United Steelworkers now confront employers in depressed industries—so most of the new inventive benefit packages are being implemented by less militant bargainers.

Still, there are already straws in the wind. "Our employers have almost everything they want in traditional benefits," says Victor Zink, director of employee benefits for GM's 460,000 hourly wage earners. "Now, they are talking about peripherals like legal aid, group auto insurance and child care." When business improves, such talk is likely to be heard loud and clear at the bargaining table.

Carol E. Curtis, *Forbes*, March 2, 1981, page 41. Reprinted by permission. Copyright 1981, Forbes Inc.

Employee Preferences. Indirect compensation programs and benefits are often provided without any specific knowledge of what employees really want or prefer. Employees, however, have indicated strong preferences for certain benefits over others, regardless of cost considerations. Employees in one company indicated a strong preference for dental insurance over life insurance, even though dental insurance was only one-fourth the cost of life insurance to the company.[25] The most desired benefit appears to be time off from work in large chunks.[26] There are, of course, differences in employee preferences. As workers get older, there is a consistent increase in the desire for increased pension benefits. This is also the case for employees with rising incomes. Employees with children prefer increased hospitalization benefits compared to those without children.[27]

With new lifestyles becoming common, companies should start providing more varied benefits.

Providing Benefit Flexibility

Since employees have many preferences, it pays to offer benefit flexibility.

Flexible benefit plans are called cafeteria compensation.

When employees can design their own benefits package, both they and the company benefit. At least that's the experience at companies such as American Can Company, TRW, and the Educational Testing Service (ETS). At ETS, the company provides a core package of benefits that covers such basic needs as personal medical care, dental care, disability, vacation and retirement to all employees. Then each individual can choose, just like food in a cafeteria, from optional benefits and/or increase the benefits in the core package. Employees are allowed to change their packages once a year. The cost? At ETS the entire benefit package represents 37.8% of total payroll costs and 49% of this is the cost due to providing the flexibility. The benefits to individuals and companies offering benefit flexibility are highlighted in the *Personnel in Action* insert.[28]

Communicating the Benefits Package

Providing benefit flexibility is good not only because it gives employees what they are more likely to want but also because it makes employees aware of what benefits they are gaining.[29]

PERSONNEL IN ACTION

More Workers Are Getting a Chance To Choose Benefits Cafeteria-Style

James Bechtel, a 34-year-old senior associate at Morgan Stanley & Co., figures his wife's employer is covering the family's doctor bills so he skips extra medical coverage and loads up on life insurance.

Jean Choffe, an American Can Co. marketing manager, skimps on medical and life insurance to increase company contributions to a capital accumulation plan for employes. Last month, by borrowing against the fund, she was able to buy a house in Fairfield County, Conn.

Both employes are taking advantage of a trend toward dishing out fringe benefits cafeteria-style. Workers are given a package of benefits that includes "basic" and "optional" items. Basics might include modest medical coverage, life insurance equal to a year's salary, vacation time based on length of service and some retirement pay. But then employes can use credits to choose among such additional benefits as full medical coverage, dental and eye care, more vacation time, additional disability income and higher company payments to the retirement fund.

Among the first to offer its employes flexible benefits was Educational Testing Service, Princeton, N.J., in 1974. TRW Inc., American Can and the city of Batavia, N.Y., followed. Within the past year, PepsiCo Inc., Northern States Power Co., Morgan Stanley and the Kingsport Press division of Arcata Corp. have started similar programs.

And "that's just the tip of the iceberg," says Thomas Paine, a senior partner at Hewitt Associates, a Lincolnshire, Ill., benefits consulting company. He believes many more will start the programs in the next three years. Sixty to 70 large companies are considering a switch, he says, including Girard Co., a Philadelphia bank-holding company, and Loews Corp., which makes cigarets and watches, owns theaters and operates hotels.

There are problems, though.

Under most of the plans, employes can readjust their benefit packages once a year, which requires a lot of extra bookkeeping. In addition, to create a pool of flexible benefits without increasing costs, employers have to scale back existing benefit programs, which may alienate employes.

Unions say they are studying the plans. So far, according to John Zalusky, an AFL-CIO economist, most of the people receiving flexible benefits are non-unionized, salaried people, not hourly wage workers. If an employer offered flexible benefits at the bargaining table, the union would insist on finding out the value of the package. "We are going to be looking far more closely at the employers' cost than ever before," Mr. Zalusky says. "Under the NLRB guidelines, we would want to know what each and every benefit costs."

Employers say the plans have a lot of bonuses for them. Educational Testing Service says its employe turnover has been "minimal" since the plan went into effect. Mary Jane Klansky, director of employe benefits, says flexible benefits are also "a great recruitment tool." And she says the plan makes employes more aware of their total benefit package.

Changes in the tax laws have made the plans even more attractive. A 1974 law required taxation of all benefits chosen by employes. Its effect was to freeze "the growth of the plan, because employers want to offer benefits that will be attractive to their employes," says Theresa Thompson, a principal of Towers, Perrin, Forster & Crosby, benefit consultants. Since the revisions, she says, "companies think it's clear to go ahead with the plans."

The plans also have the advantage of allowing companies to give the illusion of providing employes with more benefits without increasing costs. "When companies can't afford to keep pace with inflation, offering raises, they can give other forms of compensation" through the plans, says Ronald C. Palinzo, president of the American Society of Personnel Administrators.

Some insurers worry that employes will load up on medical options they can make claims against, running up costs for the carrier. "You lose the notion of sharing costs among a lot of people" in cafeteria plans, says David Klein, senior vice president, marketing, for Blue Cross Association.

But Prudential Life Insurance Co. isn't worried. Late last year it formed a flexible compensation services unit to design and consult on the plans. "It's a natural extension for us. We've got the experience of administering insurance systems," says David Balak, vice president of the unit.

As part of its marketing campaign, the unit holds seminars on the plans for businessmen. A recent session in Philadelphia attracted 60 people. Mr. Balak showed charts of suggested plans and gave advice. He urged companies to start the plans gradually, with a few options, and add more when possible. "You need to learn about the concept," he said, "and get the word out to employes."

Many employees are not only unaware of the costs of the benefits they are receiving but also unaware of which benefits they are receiving.[30] If employees have no knowledge of their benefits, then there is little reason to believe that the organization's benefit program objectives will be attained. Many organizations indicate that they assign a high priority to telling employees about their benefits, although a majority spend only $10 per employee per year doing this.[31] Recall that the average benefits package costs over $5,000 per employee.

Often employees don't seek out benefits information; they must be told about them.

Considering that most benefits program objectives are not currently attained, it is likely that assessment of communication effectiveness would produce unfavorable results.[32] This may in part be due to the communication techniques used. Almost all organizations use impersonal, passive booklets and brochures to convey benefits information; only a few use more personal, active media, such as slide presentations and regular employee meetings. A technique that is especially good at communicating the benefits package is one that communicates the *total compensation every day!* This can be done through giving employees calendars. Each month of the calendar shows a company employee receiving a compensation benefit. For example, one month may feature a photo of an employee building a new home made by through the company's incentive program and savings plan. Another month may feature the usefulness of the company's medical plan.

EVALUATING THE BENEFITS OF INDIRECT COMPENSATION

Listed at the beginning of this chapter are several purposes of indirect compensation. The impact of the indirect benefits on these purposes is one-half of the way to measure the effectiveness of the benefits package. The other half is by determining the costs. Another way is to determine the effectiveness of the indirect benefit program and then compare the costs and benefits.

An organization can determine the costs of indirect compensation in four ways:

- Total cost of benefits annually for all employees
- Cost per employee per year divided by the number of hours worked
- Percentage of payroll divided by annual payroll
- Cost per employee per hour divided by employee hours worked.[33]

These costs can then be compared with the benefits such as reduced turnover, absenteeism, or an enhanced company image among employees.

After the company determines these cost/benefit ratios, it can further evaluate the benefits of its indirect compensation by

- Examining the internal cost to the company of all benefits and services, by payroll classification, by profit center, and for each benefit.

- Comparing the company's costs for benefits to external norms. For example, compare its costs to average costs, averages by industry, and so on, as reported in surveys such as those conducted by the Chamber of Commerce, for the package as a whole and for each benefit. The April 28, 1980, issue of *Business Week* had an excellent supplement explaining how companies can determine the usefulness/competitiveness of their indirect compensation program.[34]

- Preparing a report for the decision maker contrasting the above two items and highlighting major variances.

- Analyzing the costs of the program to employees. Determine what each employee is paying for benefits, totally and by benefit.

- Comparing the data in the above step with external data such as Chamber of Commerce data.

- Analyzing how satisfied the employees are with the organization's current program—and as compared to competitors' programs.[35]

These steps highlight the cost and benefit consideration of indirect compensation to an organization as well as the strategic choices for remaining competitive with other organizations.[36]

FACING THE CRITICAL ISSUES IN INDIRECT COMPENSATION

Now that we have covered many important topics associated with providing indirect compensation to employees, it is appropriate once again to respond to the Critical Issues presented at the start of this chapter. Because the responses offered here are only partial ones, you should be able to add a great deal more information to each one.

Issue: *What type of benefits do people really want?*

It appears that, in general, different people want different benefits. For example, younger employees may have a stronger preference for insurance benefits, time off, and educational benefits while older employees may have a greater interest in retirement benefits, and preretirement counseling opportunities. To the extent, however, that it is possible to speak of the preferences of people in general, Exhibit 13.3 illustrates what they want.

Issue: *How can an organization get anything in return for the tremendous benefits it gives its employees?*

By first making sure that the employees know they are receiving tremendous benefits and what they are. COMMUNICATE YOUR BENEFITS! To the extent possible, allow the employees a choice in the benefits they get. It is also important for your benefits

Exhibit 13.3

Perceived Importance of Indirect Benefits (Adapted from R. P. Quinn and G. L. Staines, *The 1977 Quality of Employment Survey* [Ann Arbor, Mich.: Survey Research Center, University of Michigan], p. 60.)

"Which of the fringe benefits you get are most important to you?"

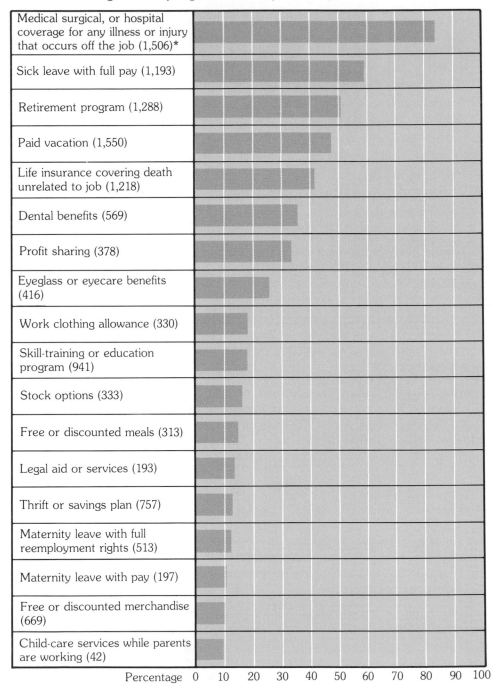

	Percentage
Medical surgical, or hospital coverage for any illness or injury that occurs off the job (1,506)*	
Sick leave with full pay (1,193)	
Retirement program (1,288)	
Paid vacation (1,550)	
Life insurance covering death unrelated to job (1,218)	
Dental benefits (569)	
Profit sharing (378)	
Eyeglass or eyecare benefits (416)	
Work clothing allowance (330)	
Skill-training or education program (941)	
Stock options (333)	
Free or discounted meals (313)	
Legal aid or services (193)	
Thrift or savings plan (757)	
Maternity leave with full reemployment rights (513)	
Maternity leave with pay (197)	
Free or discounted merchandise (669)	
Child-care services while parents are working (42)	

Percentage 0   10   20   30   40   50   60   70   80   90   100

*The numbers in parentheses indicate how many employees in the sample receive this benefit.

package to be competitive with what other organizations provide. Again, where possible, tie some of the benefits to performance, hours worked, or attendance. In return for doing these things you increase the chances of obtaining good employees, retaining them, and instilling a sense of loyalty.

Issue: *How many more benefits will people want? What does the future hold for benefits?*

It appears that, as with direct compensation, employees will continue to want more benefits in terms of the ones they now have and in terms of ones they presently do not have. For example, employees want greater private retirement benefits, health and insurance coverage, and more time off. Demands for dental coverage, eye care, and legal services will probably increase. Greater educational and career development opportunities are also likely to be demanded by employees.

Although the trend in many benefits is for more, one benefit that may stand out as being the most important of all is job security. As the economy continues to shift and dislocate employees and as international competition increases, job security will continue to take on even greater importance.

Issue: *Should employees be allowed to select their own benefits? Can companies afford to do that?*

This issue is similar to the ones raised in the other two chapters on compensation on whether individuals can responsibly determine their own wage levels or wage increases. The response here is also similar to the responses of those issues. Specifically, it is probably useful to let employees select their own benefits. It is a way to get more "bang for the buck" (of indirect benefits). If employees get to choose their benefits, it is likely the benefits will mean more to them. This will in turn make the organization more attractive to them, especially if other organizations do not offer a choice. Consequently employees may be more loyal to the organization, and it may be easier for the organization to attract new qualified job applicants.

With these advantages from offering employees a choice in benefits, it appears that an organization cannot afford to *not offer* employees a choice. Companies that have done so, report that employees can select their own benefits without much trouble if sufficient information is available to them. Companies also report that it is economically feasible to offer this choice. This, of course, is within some constraints. Generally, all employees have to take some benefits (to make offering these cost effective, such as insurance coverage) and then have a choice among another set of benefits.

SUMMARY

Chapters 11, 12, and 13 address what are often the most frequently asked questions in organization orientation programs: "How much do I get paid?" and "How much and when is my vacation?" Although most organizations have been responding to both questions with "More than ever before," the growth in indirect compensation has been double that of direct compensation. This doubling has occurred despite the lack of evidence that indirect compensation is really helping to attain the purposes of total compensation. Money, job challenge, and opportunities for advancement appear to serve the purposes of compensation as much as, if not more than, pension benefits, disability provisions, and services, especially for employees aspiring to managerial careers.

This is not to say, however, that employees do not desire indirect benefits. It is in part because employees desire them that organizations are offering them at such a rapid rate. The specific indirect benefits offered by an organization are, however, not always valued by all employees, nor do all employees know what benefits are offered. As a result, some organizations solicit employee opinions about their preferences for compensation programs. Organizations are also becoming more concerned with the communication of their benefits programs, partly because of the requirements of ERISA. The current evidence suggests that employees' lack of awareness of benefit programs and their value may partially explain why they are not perceived as valuable. Increased communication and more employee participation in the benefits packages may, therefore, increase the likelihood that organizations will receive some benefit from providing benefits.

KEY CONCEPTS

indirect compensation	worker compensation insurance
ERISA	wage loss
MEPPAA	employee services and perquisites
FICA	pay for time not worked
HMOs	protection programs
contributory program	supplemental unemployment
noncontributory program	benefit (SUB)
vested rights	

DISCUSSION QUESTIONS

1. What are the purposes of indirect compensation? How can these purposes be attained?

2. What are some of the historical/legislative events that shaped the growth of indirect compensation?

3. What is the benefit to the organization of providing time off with pay for physical fitness programs?

4. What are the protection programs, and who are they designed for? Give some examples.

5. List three reasons why the viability of worker compensation is threatened.

6. List and discuss two ways employees can reduce the costs of worker compensation, thus making it a more effective cost-benefit form of indirect compensation.

7. Discuss the two categories of pay for time not worked. Contrast these forms with benefits from other protection programs.

8. Compare and contrast different types of employee services and perquisites for different types of employees.

9. What facts must organizations take into consideration if they are to develop and maintain indirect compensation benefits that are in line with changing employee preferences?

10. What is the major reason for the failure of indirect compensation packages? In other words, why are they ineffective?

CASE

Flowers: Fiasco or Fringes?

Although secretaries, like any group of good employees, should be complimented and recognized for good work throughout the year, many organizations save their plaudits for secretaries' week. Generally secretaries' week occurs in the spring, just the time the doldrums of winter are leaving and the fragrances of the new season most inviting. Thus, the secretaries of the University were especially delighted to be given a day off during secretaries' week last year. Like the students and faculty, they were able to enjoy a beautiful, sunny spring day. Though this fringe benefit of a day off was not planned nor formally agreed to, the secretaries were looking forward to the same thing this year. This was especially true because the winter was a severe one and many of the secretaries had put in extra hours without pay during the year.

Consequently the secretaries were extremely displeased, some even angry, when, on the first day of secretaries' week, the dean of the school sent them flowers. Since last year they had received no flowers but a day off, they assumed that if they received flowers this year, they would not get a day off. They were right! Feeling offended as well as angered, they "forgot" to send the dean a note thanking him for the flowers. Several weeks passed and the dean realized he had not been thanked by the secretaries. Interpreting this as a sign of ingratitude, the dean told what had happened to Professor Freedman, a human relations specialist on the faculty. Professor Freedman, being sensitive to the needs of both the dean and the secretaries, later that day, asked the head secretary to tell him about secretaries' week. After learning the secretaries' interpretation of what had happened during secretaries' week, Professor Freedman, several days later, shared with the dean how the secretaries had perceived the flowers. After the professor left, the dean muttered to himself "It doesn't pay to try to be nice to people nowadays."

Case Questions

1. Do you agree with the dean's final statement?

2. Where did the dean go wrong?

3. Do you think the secretaries should have been happy with the flowers? Were they ungrateful?

4. What should the dean do next year? Is there anything he should do now?

FOR YOUR CAREER

- It pays for you to inquire about the benefits an organization provides. After all, if you had to buy these benefits yourself they would be quite expensive. Furthermore, benefits are tax free.

- If you had your choice of benefits, which ones would you select? What percentage of your total compensation would you want to be indirect?

- Although public protection programs help, you'll need also the protection from private programs that most organizations provide.

- Disability from stress is increasingly being covered by worker compensation benefits. This may be important to you, especially if you get a job in a stress-prone job situation.

- Although benefits have increased dramatically, it is likely this trend will stop. It may even reverse itself.

- In your job interviews find out about all the benefits the company provides. In the process you can learn how much the interviewer knows.

ENDNOTES

1. John F. Sullivan, "Indirect Compensation: The Years Ahead," *California Management Review*, Winter 1972, pp. 65–76.

2. R. C. Huseman, J. D. Hatfield, and R. W. Driver, "Getting Your Benefit Programs Understood and Appreciated," *Personnel Journal*, October 1978, p. 562.

3. D. W. Belcher, *Compensation Administration*, (Englewood Cliffs, N.J.: Prentice-Hall, 1974).

4. Allen Flamion, "The Dollars and Sense of Motivation," *Personnel Journal*, January 1980, pp. 51–52, 61.

   William L. White and James W. Becker, "Increasing the Motivational Impact of Employee Benefits," *Personnel*, January–February 1980, pp. 32–37.

5. P. S. Greenlaw and W. D. Biggs, *Modern Personnel Management* (Philadelphia: Saunders, 1979), p. 513.

6. Joseph A. LoCicero, "How to Cope With the Multiemployer Pension Plan Amendments Act of 1980," *Personnel Administrator*, May 1981, pp. 51–54, 68.

   Joseph A. LoCicero, "Multiemployer Pension Plans: A Time Bomb for Employers?" *Personnel Journal*, November 1980, pp. 922–924, 932.

   Paul T. Shultz and Howard J. Golden, "Current Developments in Employee Benefits," *Employee Relations Law Journal* 6, No. 3:494–497.

7. Vicky Cahan and Stephen H. Willstrom, "Can Reagan Revolutionize Social Security?" *Business Week*, May 25, 1981, p. 42.

   "The Battle Over Repairing Social Security," *Business Week*, September 28, 1981, pp. 116–120.

Richard Schulz, Peter J. Ferrera, and Richard C. Keating, "Social Security: Three Points of View," *Personnel Administrator,* May 1981, pp. 45–49.

8. R. M. McCaffery, *Managing the Employee Benefits Program* (New York: American Management Associations, 1972).

9. R. I. Henderson, *Compensation Management: Rewarding Performance in the Modern Organization* (Reston, Va.,: Reston Publishing Company, 1976).

10. *Congressional Quarterly Almanac* 29 (Washington, D.C.: Congressional Quarterly Service, 1973), p. 507.

11. D. R. Bell, "Prevalence of Private Retirement Plans," *Monthly Labor Review* 98 (1975):17–20.

12. "Inflation Is Wrecking The Private Pension System," *Business Week,* May 12, 1980, pp. 92–99.

"Pension Liabilities: Improvement is Illusory," *Business Week,* September 14, 1981, pp. 114–118.

Mary Zippo, "Roundup," *Personnel,* pp. 43–45.

Insurance Decisions, Insurance Company of North America, 1981.

13. Carol Krucoff, "Money: The Pension Crisis," *Washington Post,* September 11, 1980, Section D, p. 5.

14. M. Meyer and H. Fox, *Profile of Employee Benefits* (New York: Conference Board, 1974), p. 8.

15. *Employee Health and Welfare Benefits,* Personnel Policies Forum Survey 122 (Washington, D.C.: Bureau of National Affairs, 1978), p. 7.

16. Meyer and Fox, pp. 11–15.

Employee Health and Welfare Benefits, pp. 15–23.

17. *Employee Health and Welfare Benefits,* p. 10.

"Insurance Survey," *Personnel Journal,* July 1981, p. 525.

18. Martin W. Elson and John E. Burton, Jr., "Worker's Compensation Insurance: Recent Trends in Employer Costs, *Monthly Labor Review,* March 1981, pp. 45–50.

Insurance Decisions, Insurance Company of America, 1981.

K. Per Larson, "Taking Action to Contain Health Care Costs, Part II," *Personnel Journal,* September 1980, pp. 735–739.

Larson, "Taking Action to Contain Health Care Costs, Part I," *Personnel Journal,* August 1980, pp. 640–644, 675.

Larson, "How Companies Rein in Their Health Care Costs," *Personnel Administrator,* November 1979, pp. 29–33.

19. *Employee Benefits,* 1975, p. 28.

Hermine Zagat Levine, "Consensus," *Personnel,* September–October 1981, pp. 4–12.

20. Adapted from *Basic Patterns in Union Contracts,* 9th ed. (Washington, D.C.: Bureau of National Affairs, 1979).

21. David Gibson, "Why Lunch Is Free at Texasgulf," *New York Times,* September 20, 1981, Sec. F, p. 9.

22. G. Milkovich and L. Gomez, "Day Care and Selected Employee Work Behaviors," *Academy of Management Journal,* March 1976, pp. 111–115.

23. Arthur Young and Co., "Compensating Executives: Meeting the Needs of Management Today," *Financial Executive,* July 1974, pp. 46–47.

Bruce R. Ellig, "Perquisites: The Intrinsic Form of Pay," *Personnel*, January–February 1981, pp. 23–31.

24. "Employees Shun Free Education," *Small Business Report*, September 1979, p. 17.

25. S. Nealy, "Pay and Benefit Preferences," *Industrial Relations*, October 1963, pp. 17–28.

26. A. N. Nash and S. J. Carroll, Jr., *The Management of Compensation* (Monterey, Calif.: Brooks/Cole, 1975), p. 241.

27. "New Benefits for New Lifestyles," *Business Week*, February 11, 1980, pp. 111–112.

28. J. H. Foeger, "Compensation and Benefits," *Personnel Journal*, July 1981, p. 530.

    George W. Hettenhouse, "Compensation Cafeteria For Top Executives," *Harvard Business Review*, September–October 1971, pp. 113–119.

    James H. Shea, "Cautions About Cafeteria-Style Benefit Plans," *Personnel Journal*, January 1981, pp. 36–38, 58.

    "Flexible Benefits," *Personnel Journal*, August 1981, p. 602.

    Judith Willis, "Benefits Buffet," *Minneapolis Star,* June 1, 1981, Sec. D, pp. 1, 12.

29. Ray Foltz, "Communique," *Personnel Administrator*, May 1981, p. 8.

    Huseman, Hatfield, and Driver, pp. 560–566, 578.

    "How Do You Tell Employees About Benefits?" *Personnel Journal*, October 1980, p. 798.

    Robert M. McCaffery, "Employee Benefits: Beyond the Fringe?" *Personnel Administrator*, May 1981, pp. 26–30, 66.

30. J. A. Gilden, "What's Happening in Employee Benefit Communications?" *Pension and Welfare News*, March 1972, pp. 31–38.

    W. H. Holley, Jr., and E. Ingram III, "Communicating Fringe Benefits," *Personnel Administrator*, March–April 1973, pp. 21–22.

31. Huseman, Hatfield, and Driver, p. 563.

32. Ibid., p. 578.

33. B. Ellig, "Determining the Competitiveness of Employee Benefits Systems," *Compensation Review*, 1st quarter, 1974 (New York: AMACOM, a division of American Management Associations, 1974), p. 9.

34. "Fringe Benefits and Inflation," *Business Week*, April 28, 1980, pp. 130–138.

35. Ellig, pp. 8–34.

36. Ibid. See also R. B. Dunham and R. A. Formisano, "Designing and Evaluating Employee Benefit Systems," *Personnel Administrator*, April 1982, pp. 29–36 for an excellent model to determine the worth of alternative benefit plans.

SECTION SEVEN

Training and Career Development

Chapter 14
Training and Developing Employees

Chapter 15
Career Planning and Development

Chapter Outline

Critical Issues in Training and Development

Training and Development
The Importance and Purposes of Training and Development
Training and Development Relationships with Other Personnel Activities
Legal Considerations in Training and Development

Determining Training and Development Needs and Targets

Implementing Training and Development Programs
Training and Development Considerations
Training and Development Programs
Selecting a Program

CHAPTER 14

Training and Developing Employees

Evaluating Training and Development Programs
Evaluation Designs

Facing the Critical Issues in Training and Development

Summary

Key Concepts

Discussion Questions

Case

For Your Career

Endnotes

Personnel in the News

The Basic Skills, Company Style

Banks, financial houses, insurance companies and a variety of industries throughout the nation are becoming increasingly involved in basic-skills training. Their new interest in the business of education is in response to some of the complaints heard in its upper echelons: Secretaries cannot proofread letters, machinists cannot read equipment manuals, engineers cannot spell, and vice presidents cannot write a literate memorandum.

So, they have taken education matters into their own hands. A study four years ago by the Conference Board Inc., an independent, nonprofit business research organization in New York, estimated that 35 percent of the companies in the nation provided remedial education for employees.

At Continental Bank, the nation's seventh largest, for example, there is a 20-week course in spelling, punctuation and grammar. At the home office of the Metropolitan Life Insurance Company in New York City, 800 employees brush up on basic skills each year. At the American Telephone and Telegraph Company, 14,000 employees attend classes on basic writing and basic arithmetic during office hours, at a yearly cost of $6 million, according to W. Frank Blount, assistant vice president for training and development. The Polaroid Corporation, which, like Xerox and the Connecticut General Life Insurance Company, has had a remedial program for more than a decade, has 15 part-time teachers for nearly a thousand employees yearly in its "Fundamental Skills Program."

Other banks, including First Federal Savings and Loan in Chicago, the State Street Bank and Trust Company in Boston and Chase Manhattan in New York, have extended remedial-education courses such as "English Fundamentals" and "Writing Fundamentals" for their employees.

At Metropolitan Life, 40 percent of the training and development programs are on English usage and arithmetic, according to Lott Moroney, manager for employee education and training.

Who takes these courses? The students are primarily recent high school graduates who, with training, can fill immediate needs, and employees who want to improve their skills because of supervisor pressure or a desire for promotion. Company personnel usually prepare the instructional material and teach the courses.

The catalogue listings look like those for any university computer science department: Introduction to Computer Architecture; Data Logic and Set Theory; Man and Machine. Each course is listed with its prerequisites, meeting times, instructor and textbooks. But the Systems Research Institute is not an academic place. "It's all business," said its associate director, Joseph E. Flanagan.

The institute is a school in New York City run by the International Business Machines Corporation for its employees, and offers courses geared to I.B.M. Although restricted to one company, Systems Research has a faculty, a student body and a budget that would be the envy of many university departments of computer science.

Systems Research is just one aspect of corporate education at I.B.M., a company that has a reputation for stressing employee education. I.B.M. will not say how much it *spends on education for its 340,000 employees, but Robert Craig, vice president of the American Society for Training & Development, said it is not unusual for a company like I.B.M. to spend between $1,000 and $2,000 per employee.*

Merrill Lynch, Pierce, Fenner & Smith Inc. has opened its own college for brokers—the Donald T. Regan School of Advanced Financial Management, apparently thinking it could match the business schools at teaching financial management. But Merrill Lynch is not a breed apart in this. McDonald's Hamburger University in Elk Grove, Ill., is not just flipping burgers; it teaches management, personnel, finance, taxation—just like any other business school. (Henry M. Brickell and Carol B. Aslanjan, p. 37.) (From "Survey of Continuing Education," New York Times, August 30, 1981. © 1981 by The New York Times Company. Reprinted by permission.)

Targeting Future Training Topics

U.S. businesses spend approximately $30 billion a year—or about one half of the total cost of higher education in America—on employee training and development, asserts Carnie Lincoln, president of the American Society for Training and Development. Testifying at Senate hearings on the future of the nation's employment and training policies, Lincoln stresses that employers are increasing their "investments in human capital for pragmatic purposes—to improve job performance and job satisfaction." (From Bulletin on Training, *July 1981 issue. Reproduced with permission BNA Communications, Inc., Rockville, Md., 20850.)*

In addition, several major organizations testified as to need for joint-training efforts with the federal government or the granting of tax incentives by the government so that private employers would have greater incentive to train. Of the many organizations to testify, here is what three said:

- U.S. Chamber of Commerce—*By 1990, the Chamber warns, the nation will face a shortage of skilled workers, including a shortfall of 210,000 machinists and 196,000 machine operators. The Chamber notes that it is studying a "voucher" plan that would utilize available training capabilities in vocational institutions and proprietary schools in order to better match instructional programs with available jobs.*
- Business Roundtable—*Providing greater incentives for companies to invest in employee training and development programs "offers a major new route to national productivity growth—particularly in the existing era of limited capital," the Roundtable maintains.*
- Associated General Contractors—*Industry-operated training systems generally are preferable to government-operated ones, AGC maintains, except for vocational education programs that could be set up in partnership with industry.* (Bulletin on Training, *July 1981, BNA Communications Inc., 9417 Decoverly Hall Road, Rockville, Maryland.)*

Together these quotations provide us with a great deal of information about employee training and development. One significant piece of information is that many organizations spend a great deal of time and money in training and developing their employees. Another is that no level or group of employees is excluded or exempt from training and development. Rank-and-file employees all the way through to top management are provided with the opportunity to learn everything from basic job skills to upper-level management skills such as strategic and operational planning. A final piece of information from these quotations is that government can play a role in providing training, especially to the unskilled workers, through offering tax incentives to companies.

Because training and development is so important and costly, organizations want to do it right. This desire to do it right, however, raises a number of critical issues that our group of personnel managers identified and think necessary to address if they and their companies are to do an effective job of training and developing their employees.

CRITICAL ISSUES IN TRAINING AND DEVELOPMENT

Of the many issues identified by the personnel managers, the four which emerged as most critical are:

1. *What is the best way to train employees? Should companies even have training and development programs?*
2. *Training never seems to work. After a training program, people just go about doing what they did before. How can training be made to work?*
3. *Who should be trained? How can companies really determine what type of training and development is needed?*
4. *How can companies evaluate the effectiveness of their programs to show management they are really worthwhile?*

With these issues in mind, let us examine training and development in detail.

Employee training and development is any attempt to improve current or future employee performance by increasing an employee's ability to perform through learning, usually by changing the employee's attitudes or increasing his or her skills and knowledge.[1] The need for training and development is determined by the employee's performance deficiency, computed as

> Standard or desired performance (present or future)
> − Actual (present or potential) performance
> = Training and development need[2]

TRAINING AND DEVELOPMENT

Although this is a rather simple formula, it is often rather difficult for an organization to determine exactly what performance is really desired, especially in the future, and what level of performance employees are currently exhibiting or are likely to exhibit in the future. Nevertheless, organizations engage in training and development because they have a pretty good idea as to what is needed. Though this may not be true for all organizations, it is certainly true for those named in the opening quotations.

The Importance and Purposes of Training and Development

The main goal of training and development programs is to remove performance deficiencies, whether current or anticipated, that are the result of the employee's inability to perform at the desired level. And as the pace of technological innovation increases, the potential for employee inability will increase. Consequently this main goal of training will grow in importance in the years ahead. Indeed, it is already important to many companies. The *Personnel in Action* insert shows how important training is to Control Data Corporation. It is important because it can make organizations and employees much more productive.[3] Training and development is also important because it is increasingly recognized that society can benefit by enabling individuals to be productive and contributing members of organizations.[4]

Training is becoming more critical as the pace of technological innovation accelerates.

Training and Development Relationships with Other Personnel Activities

As shown in Exhibit 14.1, training and development really consist of a large number of procedures and processes that are extensively related to many of the personnel activities we have discussed so far.

Planning.   The determination of the organization's training and development needs depends initially on its personnel planning requirements. These requirements are derived from the organization's overall plans and objectives, its projected human resource needs (by skill, type, and number), and the anticipated supply of human resources to fill these needs. As implied in the beginning quotations, organizations are finding it increasingly difficult to fill some of their human resource needs with already-trained employees. As a result, they find it necessary to do more of their own training.

If you can't get the people with the skills you need, you train them yourself.

Performance Appraisal and Job Analysis.   Training and development needs are also determined by comparing the current performance of employees with the desired levels of performance. Job analysis helps establish the desired performance and skill levels for a job. This analysis helps to determine what training is needed by new employees. Performance appraisal describes the current performance of employees. It is important in the appraisal of an employee's performance to ascertain whether there is a training problem or a motivational or organizational problem. (Refer to Chapter 10 to review the determinants of performance.)

Recruitment.   Although an organization may determine that it has need for training and development, it may still choose to recruit trained individuals rather than train its

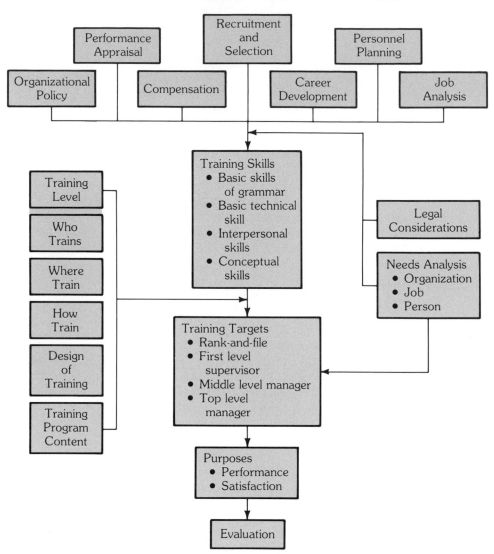

Exhibit 14.1
Training and Development Processes and Procedures

current employees. By "going outside," an organization may get somebody who is already trained, but it does so at the expense of reducing the promotional rewards that could be used as incentives for its current employees. The many organizations that do promote from within have training and development programs both for employees needing abilities for future jobs and for those needing abilities for current jobs. But occasionally these organizations need a uniquely skilled individual and therefore go outside to recruit.

Compensation. It is important for rewards to be attached to any training and development activity, because an employee may not be interested in performing

PERSONNEL IN ACTION

Norbert R. Berg
Deputy Chairman of the Board
Control Data Corporation
Minneapolis, MN

Control Data Corporation in Minneapolis recently announced it was "gearing up on an unprecedented scale" to train its employees. We asked Norbert R. Berg, deputy chairman of the board, about the reasons for this commitment, and what types of training it includes.

BERG: The long-term success of any corporation depends a great deal on its human resources. At Control Data, we've made a commitment to enhance ours by taking a holistic approach to employee training. Not only are we providing more opportunities for our employees to learn skills they can use in their jobs, we also are giving them opportunities to plan and develop new careers within the company by offering appropriate training to reach their individual career goals. In addition, we are increasing the number of education courses that can help employees become more effective individuals, not only on the job, but in all aspects of their lives.

TRAINING: Your company has about 47,000 employees across the United States. How can you implement such a broad training program?

BERG: Obviously such a task would not be possible or affordable if we used only traditional methods of training. We are in the process of replacing those older methods with PLATO, our computer-based education system.

We have more than 100 Learning Centers in the United States, each equipped with PLATO terminals. If an employee in Houston needs to take a specific course, for example, that employee simply calls our Learning Center there and schedules a time to use a PLATO terminal. Without this expanding network, we'd have no economical way of reaching all employees with the same consistency. In fact, it would be virtually impossible. The system is convenient for employees and cost-effective for the company. We don't have the expense of transportation, instructors or classrooms.

TRAINING: How much employee training does Control Data deliver now and what portion of that is computer-based?

BERG: Last year our employees received approximately one million hours of formal training. About one-third of that was computer-based. We're in the process of developing a tremendous array of computer-based education courses to add to the significant number already available to employees.

TRAINING: How will you determine if all that training is relevant to your employees?

BERG: We feel that all employees deserve a thorough orientation to the company, to the unit in which they work and to their jobs. In addition, they deserve specific skills training that can be applied to their jobs, adequate counseling in planning their careers and the training necessary for that career development.

With those training objectives in mind, we've taken a coordinated corporate approach to the question of relevancy. You have to understand that curriculum planning and course design for computer-based education both require longer lead times than for traditional training methods. So we have to consider our long-range business strategy, what technology changes are down the pike and even trends in education.

We also are using some of our programs to determine the relevance of our training. One of them, Comprehensive Job Analysis, identifies various functional groups within the company and the tasks those groups are asked to perform. Another, our Performance Appraisal System, helps us determine what skills our employees possess.

In addition to the front-end work of needs identification, we evaluate our courses as carefully as possible. That involves more than getting a user's reaction to a course. We are trying to pinpoint barriers in the work place that prevent newly acquired skills or knowledge from being fully utilized. In the years ahead, we'll be working with managers to increase their ability to help employees transfer training to their jobs.

TRAINING: Will that be part of a training curriculum for management?

BERG: Yes. Management training already has undergone some changes. Every newly appointed manager is required to complete 50 hours of training—all computer-based—within 90 days. In addition, we now require managers to complete 40 hours of relevant training a year. Last year, more than 5,000 Control Data managers in the United States averaged nearly 46 hours of formal training each.

TRAINING: How have your employees reacted to the increased emphasis on training?

BERG: The results of our employee attitude survey this year showed that 86% of our employees think Control Data is a good company to work for. I think that reflects a positive attitude about our commitment to provide opportunities for employees to grow. In the same survey, 62% reported they were satisfied with the opportunities for training and development at Control Data, compared with 59% last year. We're convinced that percentage will climb even higher as we meet our commitment to provide every employee, regardless of job level, with opportunities for training.

(Reprinted with permission from page 42 of the October 1981 issue of *Training, The Magazine of Human Resources Development.* Copyright 1981, Lakewood Publications, Minneapolis, MN (612) 333-0471. All rights reserved.)

---

better if there are no monetary or promotional rewards for doing so. For instance, to encourage managers to train their employees, organizations often evaluate managers on how well they perform this function. The use of incentives is important not only for getting employees into training and development programs but also for maintaining the effects of these programs. Employees will revert to the old performance if that is the one that is rewarded (again, refer to Chapter 10 to review the role of consequences on employee behavior).

Organizational Policy and Support. In order for any training and development program to be successful it must have the support and commitment from top management. Often support and commitment are initially provided by an organization's policy regarding the treatment of human resources. An example of such a policy is shown in the *Personnel in Action* insert about General Electric.

PERSONNEL IN ACTION

Principles of Sound Management Development at General Electric

Described by Carrol D. Houser of GE's Executive
Manpower Staff

Acknowledging that every company has to tailor executive manpower plans to its own needs, Houser recommended GE's generally applicable principles:

—*Top-level commitment.* GE's chief executive of-

ficer expresses a deep commitment to management development through policies and speeches, but most important, through actions. He plans regularly for top management succession, reviews plans and progress, rewards results, and rejects business plans that show inadequate manpower planning.

—*Long-term viewpoint.* GE recognizes that management development does not get quick, miraculous results.

—*Responsibility of all executives.* The CEO's involvement is an example to all managers. They know they are accountable for developing subordinates and are the principal implementers of the system. They meet their obligations to delegate, coach, encourage, and help subordinates to get promoted, and they remove employees who do not perform.

—*Recognition that work develops people.* Work assignments are planned and used for development, on the premise that development occurs mainly through getting good results on a tough job. Formal educational and training sessions are also used.

—*Performance/achievement orientation.* GE's system is designed to reward excellent performance and accomplishment and successful risk taking. Longevity and loyalty carry little weight in reward, recognition,

and progress. A strong effort is made to eliminate nepotism, favoritism, or other kinds of bias.

—*Chance for growth to the top.* According to Houser, GE employees can realistically aspire to positions at all levels—even the very top. No classes or layers of positions are reserved for a special elite or external group of candidates.

—*Recognition of unique staff role.* Although line managers make the GE management development system work, a corporate staff reports directly to the chairman and serves the CEO and other senior executives. In addition, a network of manpower planners is assigned to general managers at each of the top five planning and operating levels, serving as communications links among various GE Businesses on manpower matters.

(From *Behavioral Sciences Newsletter* "Special Report on Managing Human Resources for Increased Productivity," pp. 1–4, Behavioral Sciences Newsletter, Whitney Road, Mahwah, N.J. 07430.)

Legal Considerations in Training and Development

Discrimination in training is banned by all three major employment discrimination laws—Title VII, Equal Pay Act (EPA), and Age Discrimination in Employment Act (ADEA)—as well as many state and local laws. Bans on discrimination extend to on-the-job training and one-day introductions to new jobs or equipment, as well as to affirmative action and other more formal apprenticeship/training programs. You can limit formal training programs to those under a certain age, but you lose that exception with women and minorities if they've previously been denied training opportunities.[5]

The Big Question. How do employers detect discriminatory training practices before they go to court? To begin with, they find the answers to the following questions:

- Are minorities and/or women given the same training opportunities as white males? Be careful! Advertising and recruiting practices come into play here.
- Are requirements for entry into a training program (i.e., tests, education, experience, etc.) job related, or are they arbitrary?
- Are nearly all machine functions or other specialized duties that require training performed by white or male workers?
- Does one class of trainees tend to get more challenging assignments or other special training opportunities?
- Do supervisors know what constitutes training? It could be almost any learning experience from how to fit a drill bit to a two-week seminar on complex sales procedures.
- Who evaluates the results of instruction or training—only white males?

- Are all trainees given equal facilities for instruction? Are they segregated in any way?
- Do a disproportionate number of females and/or minorities fail to pass training courses? If so, find out if it is because they are more often unqualified or because they receive inferior instruction. Adverse impact here is treated the same as it is in selection.

Write About It. If employers land in court on a charge of discrimination in training practices, they will be required to provide evidence that their program was conceived and administered without bias. This will be exceedingly difficult to produce unless companies have had the foresight to document their training practices. Thus they should follow these guidelines:

- Register affirmative action training and apprenticeship programs with the Department of Labor (DOL). Include the goals, timetables, and criteria for selection and evaluation of trainees. Such a record will help prove job relatedness and/or that there was no intent to discriminate. It can also be valuable in proving that an organization's program was not used as a pretext to discriminate. This is consistent with the *Weber* decision described in detail in Chapter 4.
- Keep a record of all employees who wish to enroll in your training program. Detail how each trainee was selected. Keep application forms, tests, questionnaires, records of preliminary interviews, and anything else that bears on an employee's selection or rejection for at least two years or as long as training continues.
- Document all management decisions and actions that relate to the administration of training policies.
- Monitor each trainee's progress. Provide progress evaluations and make sure counseling is available. Continue to evaluate the results even after completion of training.

DETERMINING TRAINING AND DEVELOPMENT NEEDS AND TARGETS

The three levels of needs analysis are

- Organizational
- Job
- Individual

The successful implementation and maintenance of training and development programs depend on establishing a sound record-keeping system and an effective set of relationships with many of the other personnel activities. Success, however, begins with the proper assessment of training and development needs and identification of training targets. Since assessment and identification are important in successful training, both are discussed here in detail.

This section focuses on the *assessment phase*, which consists of the analysis of:

- Organizational needs
- Job needs
- Person needs[6]

Organizational Needs Analysis

Organizational needs analysis begins with an examination of the short-term and long-term objectives of the organization and the trends that are likely to affect these objectives.[7] According to one expert "organizational objectives should be the ultimate concern of any training and development effort."[8] In addition to examining the organization's objectives, the organizational needs analysis also consists of human resource analysis, analysis of efficiency indexes, and analysis of the organizational climate.[9] Although analysis of the organizational climate helps to locate training needs, it is primarily useful in the evaluation of training and development programs.

Human resource analysis consists of the activities of translating the organization's objectives into the demand for human resources, skills required, and programs for supplying the needed skills and human resources. Training and development programs play a vital role in matching the supply of human resources and skills with the demands of the organization.

The analysis of the *organizational climate*—a summary term used to describe the quality of the organization, how the employees feel about it, and how effective they are—is the final aspect of the organizational needs analysis. Like the analysis of efficiency indexes, it can help identify where training and development programs may be needed and provide criteria against which to evaluate the effectiveness of the programs that are implemented. Measures of the quality of the organizational climate include absenteeism, turnover, grievances, productivity, suggestions, attitude surveys, and accidents.[10]

Job Needs Analysis

Just as important as analyzing the organization's needs, and perhaps just as frequently overlooked, is the second phase of any needs analysis. The organizational needs analysis is too broad to spot training and development needs for specific jobs, so it is necessary to conduct a **job needs analysis.**[11] Essentially, this analysis provides information on the tasks to be performed on each job (the basic information contained in job descriptions), the skills necessary to perform those tasks (from the job specifications or qualifications), and the minimum acceptable standards (information that is often not a part of the traditional job analysis). These three pieces of information are gathered independently from current employees or job applicants.

The skills necessary to perform a task are next ranked by one or more people in order of their importance to the task. Only when all the people rating the task agree that the skills are related to an independent measure of performance is the job needs analysis validated.

After the information about the necessary skills and their importance and the minimal acceptable standards of proficiency has been collected, only the person needs analysis remains to be done before the potential training and development needs can be determined.

Person Needs Analysis

The **person needs analysis** can be accomplished in two different ways. Employee performance discrepancies may be identified either by comparing actual performance with the minimal acceptable standards of performance or by comparing an evaluation of employee proficiency on each required skill dimension with the proficiency level required for each skill. Notice that the first method is based on the actual, current job performance of an employee; therefore, it determines training and development needs for the current job. The second method, on the other hand, really identifies training and development needs for future jobs.

A relevant training question for the first method is can the employee do his or her current job? For the second method, the relevant question is can this employee or new job applicant do some job he or she has yet to do? Both these questions have important implications for equal employment opportunity and affirmative action. To ensure equal opportunity and affirmative action, the basis for the above answers must be a validated set of measures that will enable the organization to determine current performance or future performance potential.

Type of Training Needs Identified

After completing the organizational, job, and person needs analyses, the appropriate level or type of training is determined. Although there are many types of training, for ease of discussion, we group them into four categories as shown in Exhibit 14.1. These categories correspond to the skills and abilities that are being increased by the training. These are:

Four Skill
Categories:

▪ BSG
▪ BST
▪ IPS
▪ CIS

▪ *Basic skills* (**BSG**) *of grammar, math, safety, reading, listening and writing.* As shown in the opening quotations, these skills are often missing in new employees. They are, however, also missing in many executives who have been around a long time. For example,

> Ask most business executives how they would like to improve their reading on the job, and they will probably answer, "I would like to read faster. I can't keep up with all the reading material that comes across my desk."
> Employees have begun to recognize their reading limitations and are now requesting reading improvement courses. Many corporations, such as Scott Paper Company, Provident National Bank, Western Electric Company, and Getty Oil have appreciated this need and have implemented programs for their employees. The response of industry in general indicates a belief on its part that efficient reading by employees should be a major goal for business.[12]

▪ *Basic skills* (**BST**) *of a technical nature to do the specific job.* These skills might include how to type, file, or how to weld a pipe or fix a car. Budgeting and scheduling skills are included here. Other basic skills can be more specific to a particular company. For example at McDonald's

> Management skills, such as handling "bin supply," are most important. "We learn how to handle situations such as when you're taking it easy at around 3 P.M., and a big bus pulls into the parking lot," said Gary Rose, a franchiser from Sudbury, Ont. "You've got to know when to join in and start cooking along with the crew, and when you're more efficient doing something else."[13]

▪ *Interpersonal skills* (**IPS**) *including communications, human relations, leadership, and labor relations.* Also included here are skills related to legal considerations, and even skills in how to be better organized and use time more effectively. Perhaps nowhere is the demand and need for IPS greater than at the level of the first line supervisor or what used to be called the "foreman."

▪ *Broader-based conceptual, integrative skills* (**CIS**), *such as strategic and operational planning and organizational design and policy skills.* Also included here are decision-making skills and skills in adapting to complex and changing environments.

Targeting the Types of Training

Now that the types of need have been identified, they need to be matched with those employees who are most appropriately in need of them as determined by the needs assessment.[14] As shown in Exhibit 14.1, there are four major groups of employees:

▪ Rank and file
▪ First level supervisors
▪ Middle level managers
▪ Top level managers

You should regard these groupings are being pretty general. Many organizations break training target groups down even farther. For example, Chase Manhattan Bank identifies three distinct segments of management. These are, according to Alan Lafley, Executive Vice President of Human Resources at Chase Manhattan:

> (1) The highest potential individuals most capable of development and growth to fill senior executive and business manager positions; (2) individuals identified as having the highest potential for filling senior functional or more individually focused positions (these are jobs calling for strong functional, professional, or specialized experience and capability); and (3) talented and experienced individuals who, though consistently identified as high performers, have little or no potential or interest in higher positions with increased responsibility (this segment includes both managers and nonmanagers whom the organization critically needs to retain and to utilize (effectively.)[15]

Large retail stores, such as Hecht's in Washington, D.C., may break out target groups by function as well as level in the function. For example, Hecht's has training programs for assistant buyers and for buyers and for group managers (sellers) and department managers.

Regardless of how a specific organization breaks out its target groups, it usually tailors specific programs for those groups only. Each program is unique to the extent it emphasizes different skills and different proportions of those skills. In general, training programs for the rank-and-file employees have more BSG and BST than the programs for supervisors. In turn, programs for supervisors generally have more IPS and less CIS than those programs for managers. A summary of these training skills-training target relationships are shown in Exhibit 14.2.

No doubt for training programs to be effective they must be targeted.

IMPLEMENTING TRAINING AND DEVELOPMENT PROGRAMS

There are several considerations associated with implementing training and development programs. Each of these must be appropriately addressed in order to increase the chances of the program being effective.[16] These considerations are

Exhibit 14.2

Relative Amounts of Training Received by the Four Different Groups of Employees

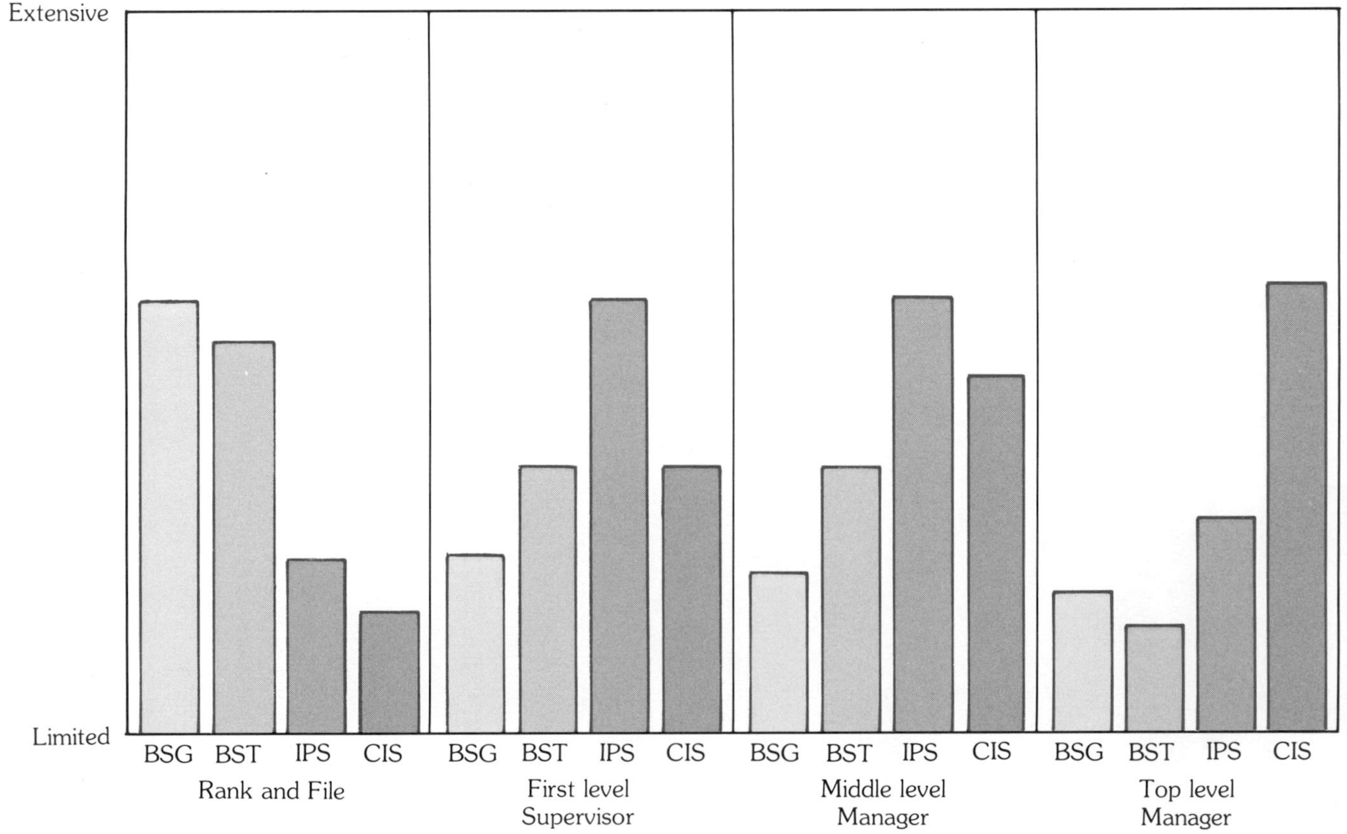

- Who participates in the program?
- Who teaches the program?
- What media are used to teach?
- What's to be the level of learning?
- What design principles are needed?
- Where is the program conducted?

For a training program to be successful, many things have to be considered.

With these considerations in mind, the personnel manager selects a training and development program from among the many that are available. Effective selection depends upon a knowledge of the programs that are available and the types of skills and level at which the program is best directed.[17]

Training and Development Considerations

Who Participates?   Generally, training and development programs are designed specifically to teach particular skills. This is because in most programs only one target audience is in attendance. There, however, are times when having two or more target audiences together may be helpful. For example, rank-and-file employees and their supervisors may more effectively learn about a new work process or machine together so they have a common understanding about the new process and their respective roles.

Who Teaches the Program?   Training and development programs may be taught by one of several people including

- Immediate supervisors
- Coworkers, as in buddy systems
- Members of the personnel staff
- Specialists in other parts of the company
- Outside consultants
- Industrial associations
- Faculty members at universities

Which of these sources is selected to teach often depends on where the program is held and the skill that is being taught. For example, programs teaching the basic skills are usually done by members of the personnel staff or specialists in other parts of the company.

What Media Are Used to Teach the Program?   There are several ways to learn. In many colleges and universities, the basic ways used are the lectures, lecture-discussion combinations, and some self-programmed instructions.[18] These are also the ways used in many training and development programs. Some additional training media or techniques are

Training programs are more effective when they use several teaching media.

- Role playing
- Behavior modification
- Group participation exercise

- One-on-one counseling
- Demonstrations
- Videotape recording and playback
- Modeling

Often combinations of these techniques are used. For example, some retail stores are training their department managers by a videotape-modeling combination. Managers in training view a videotape of a manager (really an actor) behaving in an ideal way. Then the managers watching are given a chance to "model" the ideal behavior themselves. Perhaps a more novel way to learn is through wilderness adventures as described in the Personnel in Action insert.

What's to Be the Level of Learning? As discussed earlier, there are four major *categories* of skills that can be taught:

- Basic skills
- Basic job skills
- Interpersonal skills
- Broader-based conceptual skills

In addition to these categories of skills are the *levels* at which these skills can be learned.

PERSONNEL IN ACTION

For Some Managers, Training Program Is Real Obstacle Course

HURRICANE ISLAND, Maine—Last month, 10 executives from Dayton Power & Light Co. met for a week-long management-training course on this windblown, granite island. The most luxurious accommodations are a scattering of tents and cabins.

The island is 12 miles off the Maine Coast, at the mouth of Penobscot Bay. And if the site seems unlikely for management training, consider some of the executives' activities during the week: jogging for three miles over treacherous boulders; diving into the 48-degree ocean water for a quick dip; and rappelling

down a 70-foot cliff before clambering right back up to the top.

"The things I am doing here will help me back in Dayton," Peter H. Forster, the utility's 39-year-old executive vice president, said at the time. And that, of course, was the point of the training, which was conducted by Outward Bound, the wilderness-adventure school.

(David E. Sanger, *Wall Street Journal*, July 27, 1981, p. 1. Reprinted by permission of *The Wall Street Journal*, © Dow Jones and Company, Inc., 1981. All rights reserved.)

There are three levels of skill learning: (1) **fundamental knowledge,** such as what you are doing reading this text; (2) **skill development,** where you learn how to do some of the things being discussed; and (3) **operational efficiency,** where you are actually using and benefiting from what you learn. Note that all of the four skill categories can be learned at any one or all of these three levels of skill learning.

Training Design Principles.   Training and development programs are much more likely to be effective when they incorporate several critical learning principles. They include

- Employee motivation
- Recognition of individual differences
- Practice opportunities
- Reinforcement
- Knowledge of results (Feedback)
- Goals
- Follow-up

Having employees motivated to change and acquire different behavior certainly makes training easier and more likely to be successful.[18]

Remember our equation in Chapter 10 where:

$$\text{Performance} = \text{Employee Motivation} \times \text{Ability}$$

Well, this also applies to training. That is:

$$\text{Training Effectiveness} = \text{Employee Motivation} \times \text{Ability}$$

This equation is important because it alerts us to the role of individual ability. Since ability is a crucial component in determining training effectiveness, the ability level of each individual must be considered. Other individual differences must also be considered. Some individuals learn more rapidly than others, some have had more experience than others, and some may be more physically able to exhibit the behaviors resulting from the training.

People learn better under some conditions than under other conditions.

Regardless of individual differences, whether a trainee is learning a new skill or acquiring knowledge of a given topic, the person should be given the opportunity to practice what is being taught. Practice is also essential even after the individual has been successfully trained. It is hard to find a professional tennis player who doesn't play several hours daily as a rule. But you say "why practice?" Perhaps because the results from practicing are very reinforcing.

According to the principles of **reinforcement,** people will do what's rewarded and avoid doing what is not rewarded or what is punished.[19] And although learning can be rewarding for its own sake, it is generally regarded as a difficult and distasteful process which must be rewarded extrinsically to ensure its effectiveness. This fact may be useful for training and development programs, because extrinsic rewards are often at the disposal of the organization and the trainer. For example, managers may praise their employees for learning a new skill, and the organization may provide promotional opportunities for those who successfully complete a training and development program. These extrinsic rewards are said to reinforce an individual's behavior (for example, learning a new skill) because they are given on the basis of that behavior. Another term used to describe these extrinsic rewards is **contingent rewards.** Because the principles of reinforcement are so important in learning, the implementation and maintenance of effective training depend in part on the effective management of contingent rewards.[20]

Although the evidence indicates that contingent rewards and punishments are effective if they are administered properly, managers occasionally claim that there are few rewards to give. Yet they often fail to provide what is probably the single most important reinforcement and incentive: **knowledge of results.**[21] In learning a new behavior, people sometimes cannot judge whether they are behaving correctly. Managers can play an important role at this point simply by telling employees how well they are doing. Adding rewards for properly performed behaviors and imposing punishments for improper behaviors accelerates learning considerably.

Note that the characteristics that help learning are the same ones discussed in Chapter 10 to help explain any employee behavior.

Goal setting can also accelerate learning, particularly when it is accompanied by knowledge of results.[22] Individuals generally perform better and learn more quickly when they have goals, particularly if the goals are specific and reasonably difficult. Goals that are too easy or too difficult have little motivational value. It is only when people have some chance of reaching the goal that they can really become motivated.[23] The motivational value of goals setting may also increase when employees participate in the goal-setting process.[24] When the manager or trainer and the employee work together to set goals, the employee's unique strengths and weaknesses can be identified. Then aspects of the training and development program can be tailored to specific employees, which may increase the effectiveness of the training program.

A final design principle to remember is **follow-up.**[25] Once a participant leaves the training program, the personnel manager should provide a means of follow-up to help ensure that she or he will actually do what was taught. All too often, participants who do want to change their current behavior, get back to work and slip into the old patterns. This in turn results in a significant loss of effectiveness of the training program. One approach to help prevent this from happening is the **contract plan.** Its simplicity is a key factor in its success. Basically it is an informal agreement written by each participant near the end of a training program stating which aspects of the program she or he feels will have the most beneficial effect back on the job and then agreeing to apply those aspects. Each participant is also asked to pick another participant from the program to whom a copy of the contract is given and who agrees to "check up on" the participant's progress every few weeks. Sound good? Try it with a friend. If you want to break a habit, tell your buddy and have your buddy ask you occasionally how you're doing.

Training can be most effective when employees enter into a contract plan.

Where the Program Is Conducted. A final consideration is where the training and development program is to be conducted. Actually the decision is from among three choices:

- *At the job* itself
- *On site* but not on the job—for example, in a training room in the company

■ *Off the site,* such as in a university or college classroom, a hotel room, or the wilderness, such as with the Outward Bound program described in the *Personnel in Action* insert earlier.

Typically the basic job skills are taught at the job and the basic grammar skills are taught on site. Much of the IPS and CIS training is done off the site. For purposes of the following discussion and to be consistent with how training is often discussed in organizations, the term *on the job* encompasses both at the job and on site, and *off the job* refers to off the site.

Training and Development Programs

Organizations can pick from a large variety of training and development programs. These programs take into account, though somewhat differently, many of the above characteristics.

Exhibit 14.3
Major Training and Development Program Availability

OJT: On-the-Job Training and Development
   Job Instruction Training (JIT)
   Apprentice Training*
   Internship* and Assistantships
   Job Rotation
   Multiple Management (Junior Board)
   Supervisory Assistance—coaching; feedback; performance appraisal
OFFJT: Off-the-Job Training and Development
   Formal courses—self (PI); other (lecture/reading/correspondence course)
   Simulation—vestibule, management games, assessment centers
   Human relations, role playing
   Human relations, sensitivity training
   Case Discussion (conference)
   Wilderness training

*These programs are actually composed of off-the-job as well as on-the-job components.

On-the-Job Programs. As shown in Exhibit 14.3 several programs can be conducted on the job. These programs are often formally developed and implemented by the organization, but some training and development is informal. One such informal method is supervisory assistance, which can be provided for both nonmanagerial and managerial employees.

Generally, on-the-job training programs are used by organizations because they provide "hands-on" learning experience that facilitates learning transfer and because they can fit into the organizations' flow of activities. Separate areas for training and development are thus unnecessary, and employees can begin to make a contribution to the organization while still in training.[26] On-the-job training programs, however, are not without their disadvantages. For example, have you ever been waited on by a trainee in a restaurant? Or have you ever had to wait in line a particularly long time because the bank was breaking in two teller trainees? On-the-job programs may result not only in customer dissatisfaction but also in damage to equipment, costly errors, and frustration for both the trainer (most likely a coworker or supervisor) and the trainee.

The disadvantages of on-the-job training can be minimized by making the training program as systematic and complete as possible. **Job instruction training (JIT)** represents such a systematic technique. JIT was developed "to provide a guide for giving on-the-job skill training to white- and blue-collar employees as well as technicians."[27] Since JIT is a technique rather than a program, it can be adapted to training efforts for all employees in off-the-job as well as on-the-job programs.

JIT consists of four steps: (1) careful selection and preparation of the trainer and the trainee for the learning experience to follow; (2) a full explanation and demonstration by the trainer of the job to be done by the trainee; (3) a trial on-the-job performance by the trainee; and (4) a thorough feedback session between the trainer and trainee to discuss the trainee's performance and the job requirements.[28]

Another method for minimizing the disadvantages of on-the-job training is combining it with off-the-job training. Apprenticeship training, internships, and assistantships are programs based on this combination. **Apprenticeship training** is mandatory for admission into many of the skilled trades, such as plumbing, electronics, and carpentry. These programs are formally defined by the U.S. Department of Labor's Bureau of Apprenticeship and Training and involve a written agreement "providing for not less than 4,000 hours of reasonably continuous employment . . . and supplemented by a recommended minimum of 144 hours per year of related classroom instruction."[29] To be really effective, the on- and off-the-job components of the apprenticeship program must be well integrated and appropriately planned, recognize individual differences in learning rates and abilities, and be flexible enough to meet the changing demands and technology of the trades.[30]

Somewhat less formalized and extensive than apprenticeship training are the internship and assistantship programs. **Internships** are often part of an agreement between schools and colleges and local organizations.[31] As with apprenticeship training, individuals in these programs earn while they learn but at a rate that is less than that paid to full-time employees or master craftworkers. The internships, however, function not only as a source of training but also as a source of exposure to job and organizational conditions. Students on internship programs are often able to see the application of ideas taught in the classroom more readily than students without any work experience. **Assistantships** involve full-time employment and expose an individual to a wide range of jobs. However, since the individual only assists other workers, the learning experience is often vicarious. This disadvantage is eliminated by programs of job or position rotation and multiple management.

Both job rotation and multiple-management programs are used to train and expose employees to a variety of jobs and decision-making situations. Although **job rotation** does provide employee exposure, the extent of training and long-run benefit it provides may be overstated. This is because the employees are not in a single job for a long enough period to learn very much and are not motivated to dig in because they know that they will move on in the near future. As a personal career strategy, you may want to avoid job rotation and opt instead for job assignments that are more fixed but that provide a greater challenge. This choice is discussed more fully in Chapter 15 which deals with career management.

In **multiple-management programs,** lower- and middle-level managers participate formally with top management in the planning and administration of corporate affairs.[32] In essence, the top level of management makes decisions with the advice of the middle and lower levels. Using multiple managers provides an opportunity for top management to identify and select top-management candidates. In a sense, it becomes an on-the-job assessment process. Being part of a multiple-management program can be an important step in an individual's career. Because of a relatively limited number of positions in the multiple-management program, competition for them can be great, but the potential rewards are even greater. If such an opportunity is provided, you may not wish to pass it up.

If possible, get into a multiple management training program.

The final and most informal program of training and development is **supervisory assistance**.[33] This method of training is a regular part of the supervisor's job. It includes day-to-day coaching and counseling of workers on how to do the job and how to get along in the organization. The effectiveness of coaching and counseling as a technique for training and development depends in part on whether the supervisor creates feelings of mutual confidence, provides opportunities for growth to employees, and effectively delegates tasks.[34]

Off-the-Job Programs.   Exhibit 14.3 lists six categories of off-the-job training and development programs. The first two—formal courses and simulation—are applicable to both nonmanagerial and managerial employees; the last four are primarily for managerial employees.[35]

The **formal course method** of training and development can be accomplished either by self-training, which is facilitated by programmed instruction, computer-assisted instruction, and reading and correspondence courses, or by others-training, as in formal classrooms and lectures. Although many training programs use the lecture method, because it efficiently conveys large amounts of information to large groups of people at the same time, it does have several drawbacks:

■ It perpetuates the authority structure of traditional organizations and hinders performance because the learning process is not self-controlled.

■ Except in the area of cognitive knowledge and conceptual principles, there is probably limited transfer from the lecture to the actual skills and abilities required to do the job.

■ The high verbal and symbolic requirements of the lecture method may be threatening to people with low verbal or symbolic experience or aptitude.

■ The lecture method does not permit individualized training based on individual differences in ability, interests, and personality.[36]

Because of these drawbacks, the lecture method is often complemented by self-training methods based on auto-instructional technologies.

The two predominant auto-instructional methods are the linear programing method and the branch programing method, both of which are types of **programed instruction** (**PI**). In each, the learning material is broken down into "frames." Each frame represents a small component of the entire subject to be learned, and each frame must be learned successfully before going on to the next. To facilitate the learning process, feedback about the correctness of the response to a frame is provided immediately.

The successful use of PI requires that the skills and tasks to be learned be broken down into appropriate frames. Once this is done, the probability of an individual learning by PI is high, because PI allows individuals to determine their own learning pace and to get immediate and impersonal feedback. Nevertheless, there are many skills and tasks that are impossible to break down into appropriate frames. Thus other methods, such as simulation, are used for off-the-job training and development.

Simulation, a training and development technique that presents participants with situations that are similar to actual job conditions, is used for both managers and nonmanagers. A common technique for nonmanagers is the *vestibule method*, which simulates the environment of the individual's actual job. Since the environment is not real, it is generally less hectic and safer than the actual environment; as a consequence, there is the potential for adjustment difficulties in going from the simulated training environment to the actual environment. Because of this, some organizations prefer to do the training in the actual job environment. But the arguments for using the simulated environment are compelling: It reduces the possibility of customer dissatisfaction that can result from on-the-job training; it can reduce the frustration of the trainee; and it may save the organization a great deal of money, because fewer training accidents occur. Even though these arguments may seem compelling, however, not all organizations, even in the same industry, see the situation the same way. Some banks, for example, train their tellers on the job, whereas others train them in a simulated bank environment.

An increasingly popular simulation technique for managers is the **assessment center method.**[37] The assessment center is discussed in Chapters 4 and 6 as a device for selecting managers. The center can also be used to spot training needs. However, certain aspects of the assessment center, such as the management games and in-basket exercises, are excellent for training and do not have to be confined to assessment center programs.

Another method of training that is a part of many managerial training programs is the **case discussion,** or conference. This method emphasizes individual or group analysis of a case that describes an organization and its sometimes not-so-apparent problems. Based on the information in the case, the individual trainee or group of trainees presents a solution to the problems faced by the organization.

Whereas the simulation exercises and case discussions may be useful for developing conceptual and problem-solving skills, there are two types of *human relations* or process-oriented training that are used by organizations to develop in its managers "interpersonal insights—awareness of self and of others—for changing attitudes and for practice in human relations skills, such as leadership or the interview."[38] These two types are role playing and sensitivity training.

Role playing, in comparison with the simulation and case discussion methods, generally focuses on emotional (that is, human relations) issues rather than on factual ones. The essence of role playing is to create a realistic situation, as in the case discussion method, and then have the trainees assume the parts of specific personalities in the situation. The usefulness of role playing depends heavily on the extent to which the trainees really get into the parts they are playing. If you have done any role playing, however, you know how difficult this can be and how much easier it is to do what amounts to just reading the part. But when the trainee does get into the role, the result is a greater sensitivity on the part of the trainee to the feelings and insights that are presented by the role.

A method of training and development that has been quite popular is **sensitivity training,** or laboratory training. Individuals in an unstructured group exchange thoughts and feelings on the "here-and-now" rather than the "there-and-then."

Although the experience of being in a sensitivity group often gives individuals insight into how and why they and others feel and act the way they do, critics claim that these results may not be beneficial.[39] The **wilderness training** program introduced earlier is used by some organizations for executive (top- and middle-management) development:

> The theory underlying Outward Bound's executive course is that people learn their own capabilities and limitations far better when they are faced with immediate, physical tasks that require cooperative decision-making. Roy H. Yamahiro, manager of training, education and employee development for Martin Marietta, the Maryland-based aerospace and construction-materials manufacturer, says the participants in the Outward Bound executive program "should come away with the thought that if they put their minds to a task there is virtually nothing they can't do."
>
> Martin Marietta runs a program with the Colorado Outward Bound school that this year will involve more than 200 employes. The four-and-a-half-day program now is in its third year, and Mr. Yamahiro is pleased with the results. "When they come back to the office," he says of the participants, "people who didn't believe they could be creative start acting creatively." Mr. Yamahiro also says that preliminary surveys indicate that 25% to 30% of the program's graduates "make significant changes in their life."
>
> But the program also has detractors. W. R. Worman, vice president of operations for Kaiser Steel Corp.'s steel-mills group, says his company isn't likely to repeat an Outward Bound raft trip taken two years ago by 13 department heads in the Fontana, California plant. The trip down the Rio Grande River "had beautiful scenery," he says, "but I don't think it had any carryover whatsoever when we got back to the job."[40]

A summary of the advantages and disadvantages of all these programs is shown in Exhibit 14.4.

Special Programs for Women?   During the 1970s many training programs for women sprang up but largely as a reaction to the equal opportunity pressures. The results of those reactive programs were not always very favorable. The decade of the 1980s, however, can be different. With two-thirds of the next twenty-five million new workers entering the labor force being women, organizations will want to be ready to take advantage of this relatively untapped source for future management talent. Organizations can seize this opportunity by developing proactive training.[41]

Proactive training occurs *prior* to the need for making training a response to a negative situation. Proactive training appears to be particularly suitable for women, especially those having a low level of self-esteem and confidence in their ability to be good managers and operate effectively in an organization. Actually any of the training programs for managers discussed above can be used to increase women's self-esteem and confidence and additionally their proficiency, productivity, and promotability. All that is really necessary is that they be used before they are moved into positions requiring needed skills, not after.

Special training programs may be necessary to reach agreed-to goals and timetables in AAPs. Special programs should also be developed for any group needing them.

Selecting a Program

A knowledge of the principles of learning, the four categories of skills needed by individuals in organizations, and the methods of training and development available

Exhibit 14.4

A Summary of the Advantages and Disadvantages of the On-the-Job and Off-the-Job Training Programs

	Advantages	Disadvantages
JIT	Facilitates transfers of learning No need of separate facilities	Interferes with performance Damages equipment
Apprenticeship	Does not interfere with real job performance Provides extensive training	Takes a long time Expensive May not be related to job
Internships Assistantships	Facilitates transfer of learning Gives exposure to real job	Not really a full job Learning is vicarious
Rotation	Exposure to many jobs Real learning	No sense of full responsibility Too short a stay in a job
Multiple management	Involves high-level responsibility Good experience	Not many positions available May be costly
Supervisory assistance	Informal, integrated into job Inexpensive	Effectiveness rests with supervisor Not all supervisors may do it
Formal courses	Inexpensive for many Does not interfere with job	Requires verbal skills Inhibits transfer of learning
Simulation	Helps transfer Creates lifelike situations	Can't always duplicate real situations exactly
Role playing	Good for interpersonal skills Gain insights into others	Can't create real situations exactly— still role playing
Sensitivity	Good for self-insight More aware of others	May not transfer to job May not relate to job
Case	Good for problem-solving skills Inexpensive	Not useful for interpersonal skill learning
Wilderness training	People learn limits and capabilities	Costly May not transfer

and their advantages and disadvantages provide the information necessary to select the training and development programs that are most appropriate for a specific organization. Program selection is based on the answers to three questions:

- What skills do the employees need to learn?
- At what level do these skills need to be learned?
- What training and development programs are most appropriate for the required skills and level?

Skills Needed.   The answers to the first two questions are determined by the results of the needs analyses. Referring back to Exhibit 14.2, you can see that the question of what skills employees need to learn can be answered in part by knowing what types of employees need the training. For example, if there are performance deficiencies among the supervisory and rank-and-file employees, most of the training should be aimed at increasing technical skills; on the other hand, interpersonal skills would be the primary need of middle-management employees, and top-level managers would most be in need of conceptual or managerial and administrative skills.[42] These matches between type of employee and the predominant type of skill training needed are useful guides to training employees for their current jobs and for future jobs they might assume. Thus knowledge of these matches can be used to facilitate employee career development and the organization's planning of what training and development programs it will need to offer.

Level Needed.   But to use these matches for the benefit of the individual and the organization, it is still necessary to know the appropriate level of skill training: increased operational proficiency, skill development, or fundamental knowledge. The results of the job and person needs analyses determine the necessary level, particularly for current job training. The levels required for future job training depend on the organizational needs analysis as well as on the job and person needs analyses.

Program Needed.   The final step is to determine which programs are most appropriate for the skill and level of training needed. A guide for this determination is shown in Exhibit 14.5.[43] For example, apprenticeship training is appropriate for those who need to increase their operational proficiency in basic technical skills, whereas the case discussion method is appropriate for conceptual or managerial and administrative skill training at all three levels.

Unfortunately, selection of the appropriate program does not ensure the success of a training and development effort. Success also depends on effective use of the principles of learning (such as reinforcement and feedback), provisions for learning transfer, well-trained trainers, and systematic and supportive organizational policies for the training and development of employees.[44]

EVALUATING TRAINING AND DEVELOPMENT PROGRAMS

> If we cannot judge whether an action has led forward or backward, if we have no criteria for evaluating the relation between effort and achievement, there is nothing to prevent us from making wrong work habits. Realistic fact-finding and evaluation is a prerequisite for any learning.[45]

And yet,

> historically very little evaluation of employee training has been carried out in industry, business or government. Managers, needless to say, expect their manufacturing and sales departments to yield a good return and will go to great lengths to find out if they have done so. When it comes to training, however, they may expect the return but rarely do they make a like effort to measure the actual results.[46]

Exhibit 14.5

Selecting a Training and Development Program (Adapted from T. J. Von der Embse, "Choosing a Management Development Program: A Decision Model," *Personnel Journal,* October 1973, p. 911. Reprinted with the permission of *Personnel Journal,* Costa Mesa, Calif.; all rights reserved.)

		Skills Required		
		BSG/BST	IPS	CIS
Level of Skill Required	Fundamental Knowledge	job rotation multiple management apprenticeship training job instruction training	role playing sensitivity training formal courses	job rotation multiple management simulation case discussion
	Skill Development	job rotation multiple management simulation supervisory assistance	role playing sensitivity training job rotation multiple management simulation	job rotation multiple management simulation case discussion
	Operational Efficiency	job rotation multiple management apprenticeship training job instruction training simulation internship and assistantship supervisory assistance	role playing job rotation multiple management apprenticeship training job instruction training simulation	job rotation multiple management simulation case discussion

Evaluation of employee training and development programs may be lacking for several reasons. The organization may be willing to accept the programs at face value, or it may be unaware of the importance and value of evaluation. Managers may be fearful of finding out that the programs really are not working. There may be a lack of understanding of the methods of evaluation and a lack of agreement on the bases or criteria of evaluation. The people in the organization may not be totally committed to the support of any training or change. Finally, a general design or framework for planning the evaluation of training and development programs and organizational change programs may be lacking.[47]

Nevertheless, the importance and necessity for evaluating the impact of any program remains. Evaluation is necessary to determine how well a program achieves its goals, the efficiency with which the goals were attained by the program, and the extent to which the changes that occurred were due to the program. Evaluation should therefore be regarded as a necessary aspect of any employee training and development program. Criteria against which the effectiveness of a training program can be evaluated include productivity, attitude surveys, and accidents (all aspects or organizational climate). The criteria selected to evaluate the training program should depend upon what the program is aimed to improve. If it is aimed to increase employee job skills, then productivity may be the most appropriate criterion. If it is aimed to make employees more aware of safety procedures, then accidents may be the most appropriate criterion.

Regardless of the criteria selected to evaluate the program, the personnel manager must select an *evaluation design*. Evaluation designs are important because they help the personnel manager determine if improvements have been made and if the training program caused the improvements. In addition to aiding in the evaluation of training programs, evaluation designs can (1) aid in evaluating any personnel program to improve productivity and the quality of work life; and (2) aid in evaluating the effectiveness of any personnel activity. Combining the data collection tools discussed in Chapter 7 with knowledge of evaluation designs can prove essential for personnel in demonstrating its effectiveness, and the effectiveness of any of its programs and activities, to the rest of the organization. Because the combination of data collection and evaluation design is vital for personnel, evaluation design is discussed in more detail here. Review chapter 7 and the evaluation sections of all the other chapters to see how these evaluation designs can be used with data collection techniques to help measure personnel effectiveness.

Evaluation Designs

There are three major classes of **evaluation designs:** *pre-experimental, quasi-experimental,* and *experimental.*[48] Although each can be used to evaluate the effectiveness of a program or personnel activity, it is preferable to use the experimental design. Evaluation using the experimental design allows the personnel manager to be more confident that

1. A change has taken place, for example, that employee productivity has actually increased;
2. The change is caused by the program or personnel activity; and
3. A similar change could be expected if the program were done again with other employees.

Due to many organizational constraints, however, the personnel manager is generally only able to use the quasi-experimental design. But in reality, the personnel manager frequently uses the pre-experimental design. This design is used because it is easier and quicker. To convey how much easier and quicker the pre-experimental design is, an illustration of all three designs is shown in Exhibit 14.6. This exhibit is also used to convey how, using these designs, programs can be evaluated and what is required determined.

Although it is desirable to use the experimental design, many organizations find it difficult to assign employees randomly to training programs. Organizations generally want all employees in a section trained, not just a few who are randomly selected. Consequently, more typical of the type evaluations organizations use is the preexperi-

Exhibit 14.6
The Three Major Classes of Evaluation Designs to Help
Determine Program Effectiveness (Source: Adapted from I. L.
Goldstein, *Training: Program Development and Evaluation* (Monterey,
Calif.: Brooks/Cole, 1974), pp. 49–88.)

Pre-Experimental	Quasi-Experimental	Experimental
1. One-shot case study design $\quad$ X $\qquad$ T_2	1. Time-Series Design $\quad$ $T_1 T_2 T_3$ X $T_4 T_5 T_6$	1. Pretest/Posttest Control Group Design $\quad$ T_1 $\quad$ X $\quad$ T_2 $\quad$ T_1 $\qquad$ T_2
2. One-Group Pretest-Posttest design $\quad$ T_1 $\quad$ X $\quad$ T_2	2. Non-equivalent Control Groups $\quad$ T_1 $\quad$ X $\quad$ T_2 $\quad$ T_1 $\qquad$ T_2	2. Solomon Four-Group Design $\quad$ T_1 $\quad$ X $\quad$ T_2 $\quad$ T_1 $\qquad$ T_2 $\qquad$ X $\quad$ T_2 $\qquad$ T_2

Note: X indicates that the program was administered. T_1 indicates that a measure of the variable against which the program is to be evaluated is taken, for example, productivity or the level of accidents.

T_2 indicates that a second measure is taken on the same variable. Then the results of T_1 and T_2 are compared.

Note: the two designs in the experimental class are different from the other two classes of designs because all of the individuals used in the evaluation are randomly assigned. Thus if there are differences between T_1 and T_2 the personnel manager can be more confident that the changes were due to the program (X) and that the results can be repeated in future programs.

mental design. An example of how one large retailer evaluates one of its training and development programs is shown in the *Personnel in Action* insert.

PERSONNEL IN ACTION

HECHT's

F Street at Seventh, N.W.
Washington, D.C. 20004

To: Tom Tortoriello

From: Gary Turner

Date: May 15, 1980

Subject: Results of Merchandise Math II Training

Copy: D. Giles, D. Smith, H. Lehrer, M. Buzan

A training effectiveness evaluation was made for the Merchandise Math II class conducted by Mike Buzan for the Assistant Buyer Training Program.

Before Mr. Buzan's classes began on April 29 and May 1 the attached Pre-Test was given the participants in order to test seven concepts. The 54 participants were asked to complete the seven questions and when they completed them we gathered the test before the session began. The average score at that time was 33.4%.

Before the May 14 class on Inventory Reconciliation began, I handed out the same test as a Post-Test. The Post-Test was completely unannounced and surprised many class participants. There were 25 participants who had gone through The Merchandise Math II class. The average score at that time was 78.3%.

I personally feel that the 45% increase is indicative of the efforts that went into the program and the good

results will be reflected on the job. I had one Assistant Buyer tell me this morning that after the session she was of great help to her Buyer in calculating out average stocks and turnover for projections in their Six-Month Plans.

Reprinted by permission of Thomas R. Tortoriello, Director, Executive Training and Development, Hecht's, Washington, D.C.

FACING THE CRITICAL ISSUES IN TRAINING AND DEVELOPMENT

Now that you have a better understanding of employee training and development, it is much easier to face the Critical Issues raised at the start of this chapter. Because only partial responses to the Critical Issues are presented here, you should expand the responses with more detailed information.

Issue: *What is the best way to train employees? Should companies even have training and development programs?*

There is no one best program to use to train employees since program effectiveness depends in part on the skills to be learned and the level at which they need to be learned. There are, however, several program design qualities that help make any program much better. Those qualities include providing feedback, reinforcement, follow-up, practice, goals, sufficient employee motivation, and consideration for individual differences.

Making sure that these are a part of the program can help ensure that actual changes in employee behavior will occur. As the emphasis on productivity increases, organizations will become more concerned about having behavior changed to improve productivity. Although programs that increase an employee's awareness or understanding are useful and will continue, behavioral and performance changes will also be expected.[49]

Remember, however, you don't need training and development programs if you don't have any current performance discrepancies nor expect to have any. But if you do, it makes good sense (cents) to have these programs (assuming they are effective). Whether they are run by the company or provided by someone else depends on the costs, skills to be learned, and availability of programs.

Issue: *Training never seems to work. After a training program, people just go about doing what they did before. How can training be made to work?*

You're right. People generally don't change unless they desire to change. Without sufficient employee motivation, training will not work. Thus, get your employees motivated to learn and change. Make them dissatisfied with their current level of performance or make it rewarding for them to exhibit a new or different behavior. (Remember our discussion of how to correct employee behavior in Chapter 10?) Then you need to make sure that the program offers sufficient time for practice of the new skills. Goals should also be established. They help direct and motivate employees to change.

Three other critical qualities needed to make programs work include reinforcement, feedback, and then follow-up. These help ensure that the program will have an immediate benefit and a long-term benefit, regardless of what type of program it is.

Issue: Who should be trained? How can companies determine what type of training and development is really needed?

Anyone with an important performance discrepancy should be trained. The type of training needed can be determined by a more general, intuitive method. That is, programs to be offered are usually determined by who will attend, or vice versa. If it is decided who should attend, then the type of program is determined. This determination can be made along the lines of the match between type of skills needed and type of employee described in this chapter.

Issue: How can companies evaluate the effectiveness of their programs to show management that they are really worthwhile?

Although it is *technically* very complex to really show that a training program has been solely responsible for producing a change, many organizations use a *practical* method to demonstrate a change due to training.

The practical method is to take a baseline measure of what the training program should change, for example, competency in math or job performance. Then the program is conducted. After the program, another measure is taken. The results of this measure are then compared with the results of the first measure.

Most personnel managers claim success of a training program if the difference between the first and second measures is reasonably large and in the right direction. Most personnel managers, however, still do not use this method to determine if their programs are worthwhile. Often they just measure how the participants (the employees) felt about the program, whether they thought it was well done or worthwhile, and whether or not they would send someone else. These are all based on measures taken only after the program is conducted.

Another more technically sound approach to use is in addition to the practical method. That is, take before and after measures on the group being trained and do the same for another similar group not being trained. This latter group is called the "control" group, and the former group is called "experimental."

SUMMARY

The training and development of employees is becoming an increasingly important and necessary activity of personnel and human resource management. Rapidly changing technologies increase the potential obsolescence of employees more quickly today than ever before. And as reflected in the initial scenario of this chapter, some skills are just dying off, so that in some areas of the nation, local, state, and federal governments are entering into training and development.

As employee training and development become more important, it also becomes more necessary that the training and development be done effectively. This requires careful attention to the three phases of training and development: assessment or needs analysis, program development and implementation, and evaluation. The three types of needs analysis discussed in this chapter are a careful and systematic diagnosis of the short- and long-range human resource needs of the organization; a determination of the skills and abilities necessary for specific jobs in the organization; and an analysis of the current and expected performance levels of employees in the organization compared with the performance levels desired of them. It is really this difference between actual and desired employee performance (either present or expected) that defines a training and development need. This performance deficiency, however, only becomes a training and development need when it is the result of employee ability.

Although removing performance deficiencies is vital to the organization, training and development must consider the needs of the employees. Recognition of this fact helps make employee training and development a mutual process between the organization and the individual.

KEY CONCEPTS

training and development
BSG
BST
IPS
CIS
organizational needs analysis
job needs analysis
person needs analysis
fundamental knowledge
skill development
operational efficiency
reinforcement
contingent rewards
knowledge of results
goal setting
follow-up
contract plan
on-the-job programs (OJT)

job instruction training (JIT)
job rotation
apprenticeship training
role playing
internships
assistantships
multiple management programs
supervisory assistance
off-the-job programs (OFFJT)
evaluation designs
formal course method
programed instruction (PI)
simulation
case discussion
wilderness training
sensitivity training
proactive training

DISCUSSION QUESTIONS

1. Why should an organization be concerned with training and development of its employees when employees can learn by experience on the job?
2. What relationships do training and development have with other functions of personnel management?
3. What is important for organizations to have if and when they are required to substantiate training and development efforts that are nondiscriminatory?

4. What are the four categories of skills in training, and what types of employees are generally the targets for these skills?

5. What considerations are essential during the implementation stage of training and development programs?

6. What is a contract plan, and when is it used?

7. List some of the disadvantages of using on-the-job training programs, and discuss how they might be minimized using a job instruction training (JIT) strategy.

8. What is the theory behind wilderness training programs that make them viable learning experiences for executive employees? Do they work?

9. What three aspects are important in selecting a training and development program?

10. What reasons are there for the scarcity of evaluations of training and development programs?

CASE

A Training Misdiagnosis or Mistake?

Sue Campbell, the Training Representative for the regional office of a large service organization, had been very excited about the new training program. The Personnel Department at the headquarters office had informed her six months ago that it had purchased a speed-reading training program from a reputable firm, and statistics showed that the program had indeed proven to be very effective in other companies.

Sue knew that most individuals in the regional office were faced, on a daily basis, with a sizable amount of incoming correspondence, including internal memoranda, announcements of new and revised policies and procedures, reports of federal legislation, and letters from customers. So, a course in speed reading should certainly have helped most employees.

The headquarters office had flown regional Training Representatives in for a special session on how to conduct the speed-reading program. Sue had, therefore, begun the program in her regional office with great confidence. She led five groups (30 employees each) through the program, which consisted of nine two-hour sessions. Sessions were conducted in the on-site training facilities. Altogether, 1,200 employees in the organization participated in the training, at an approximate cost to the company of $110 per participant (including training materials and time away from work). The program was very well received by the participants, and speed tests administered before and after training showed that, on average, reading speed increased 250 percent with no loss in comprehension.

A couple of months after the last session, Sue informally asked a couple of employees who had gone through the training if they were applying the speed-reading principles in their work and maintaining their reading speed. They said they were not using it at work but did practice their new skills with their off-the-job reading. Sue checked with several other participants and heard the same story. Although they were applying what they had learned in their personal reading and for school courses, they were not using it on the job. When Sue asked them about all of the reading material which crossed their desks daily, the typical response was, "I never read those memos and policy announcements anyway!" Sue was concerned about this information but didn't know what to do with it.

Case Questions

1. Did Sue really waste valuable training funds?
2. Should Sue now start a program to get the employees to read the memos and policy announcements?
3. How could Sue have avoided the situation she now faces?
4. Should organizations provide training programs to help improve employee skills to be used off the job?

FOR YOUR CAREER

- Stay away from companies that do not provide training and development programs. Someday you may need retraining or want some management training.
- If the top management of the organization is not committed to training and development, it is likely that the company's effort in this activity will not be very effective.
- As the pace of technological change accelerates, you and organizations will find it increasingly necessary to have training programs.
- Many of our behaviors we have learned by modeling others. Lower-level managers often benefit by modeling the behavior of middle-level managers.
- If you are considering taking a training program, wait until you are really motivated to learn the subject matter.
- If possible, get into a multiple-management training program. Internships are valuable preemployment training opportunities.

ENDNOTES

1. Irwin L. Goldstein, "Training in Work Organizations," *Annual Review in Psychology* 31 (1980):229–272.

    R. J. House, *Management Development: Design Evaluation and Implementation* (Ann Arbor, Mich.: Bureau of Industrial Relations, Graduate School of Business, The University of Michigan, 1967).

    Thomasine Rendero, "Roundup," *Personnel,* July–August 1981, pp. 53–58.

    K. N. Wexley and G. P. Latham, *Developing and Training Human Resources in Organizations* (Glenview, Ill.: Scott, Foresman and Company, 1981).

2. T. F. Gilbert, "Proxeconomy: A Systematic Approach to Identifying Training Needs," *Management of Personnel Quarterly,* Fall 1967, pp. 20–33.

3. E. Mandt, "Managing the Knowledge Worker of the Future," *Personnel Journal,* March 1978, p. 139.

Wexley and Latham.

4. Hermine Zagat Levine, "Consensus," *Personnel,* July–August 1981, pp. 4–11.

Francis X. Mahoney, "Targets, Time, and Transfer: Keys to Management Training Impact," *Personnel,* November–December 1980, pp. 25–34.

Arthur E. Wallach, "System Changes Begin in the Training Department," *Personnel Journal,* December 1979, pp. 846–848, 872.

5. C. J. Bartlett, "Equal Opportunity Issues in Training," *Public Personnel Management,* November–December, 1979, pp. 398–405.

6. Robert E. Boynton, "Executive Development Programs: What Should They Teach?" *Personnel,* March–April 1981, pp. 60–70.

I. L. Goldstein, *Training: Program Development and Evaluation* (Monterey, Calif.: Brooks/Cole, 1974).

W. McGehee and P. W. Thayer, *Training in Business and Industry,* (New York: Wiley, 1961).

M. L. Moore and P. Dutton, "Training Needs Analysis: Review and Critique," *The Academy of Management Review,* July 1978, pp. 532–545.

7. Goldstein, 1974.

8. T. J. Vonder Embse, "Choosing a Management Development Program: A Decision Model," *Personnel Journal,* October 1973, p. 908.

9. McGehee and Thayer.

10. Moore and Dutton.

11. McGehee and Thayer.

Goldstein, 1974.

12. Timothy Hornberger and Roy Trueblood, "Misused and Underrated: Reading and Listening Skills," *Personnel Journal,* October 1980, p. 808. Reprinted with the permission of *Personnel Journal,* Costa Mesa, California; all rights reserved.

13. "Survey of Continuing Education," *New York Times,* Section 12, August 30, 1981, p. 27. Reprinted by permission of *The New York Times,* © 1981 by Dow Jones and Company. All rights reserved.

14. Lester A. Digman, "Management Development: Needs and Practices," *Personnel,* July–August 1980, pp. 45–57.

Marilyn Hachey, "A Checklist for In-House Secretarial Training," *Personnel Journal,* January 1980, pp. 59–60.

Stanley D. Truskie, "Guidelines for Conducting In House Management Development," *Personnel Administrator,* July 1981, pp. 25–32.

15. Rendero, "Roundup," *Personnel,* July–August 1981, p. 54.

16. Robert F. Reilly, "Corporate Assistance in Professional Development," *Personnel Journal,* February 1981, p. 124.

17. Goldstein, 1980.

Wexley and Latham.

18. James E. Holbrook, "Here's How to Sell Your Ideas for Audio-Visual Training Programs to Top Management," *Personnel Administrator,* July 1981, pp. 34–39.

Wexley and Latham.

19. B. M. Bass and J. A. Vaughan, *Training in Industry: The Management of Learning* (Belmont, Calif.: Wadsworth, 1966), p. 62.

Fred Luthans and Tim R. V. Davis, "Beyond Modeling: Managing Social Learning Processes in Human Resource Training and Development," *Human Resource Management,* Summer 1981, pp. 19–27.

Bernard L. Rosenbaum, "A New Approach to Changing Supervisory Behavior," *Personnel,* March–April 1978, pp. 37–44.

Donald D. White and Bill Davis, "Behavioral Contingency Management: A Bottom-Line Alternative for Management Development," *Personnel Administrator,* April 1980, pp. 67–75.

20. C. W. Hamner, "Worker Motivation Programs: Importance of Climate, Structure, and Performance Consequences," in W. C. Hamner and F. L. Schmidt, eds., *Contemporary Problems in Personnel,* (Chicago: St. Clair Press, 1977).

21. Bass and Vaughan, p. 66.

22. Rebecca Thacker Baysinger and Richard W. Woodman, "The Use of Management by Objectives in Management Training Programs," *Personnel Administrator,* February 1981, pp. 83–89.

D. R. Ilegan, C. D. Fisher, and M. S. Taylor, "Consequences of Individual Feedback on Behavior in Organizations," *Journal of Applied Psychology* 64 (1979):349–371.

E. A. Locke, "Effects of Knowledge of Results, Feedback in Relations to Standards, and Goals on Reaction-Time Performance," *American Journal of Psychology* 81 (1968): 566–575.

23. Bass and Vaughan.

Locke.

24. R. Likert, "Motivational Approach to Management Development," *Harvard Business Review,* 37 (1959), pp. 75–82.

25. S. R. Siegel, "Improving the Effectiveness of Management Development Programs," *Personnel Journal,* October 1981, pp. 770–773.

26. Goldstein, 1974.

27. Bass and Vaughan, pp. 88.

28. John E. Dittrich, James R. Lang, and Sam E. White, "Nurse Management Problems and Their Training Implications," *Personnel Journal,* May 1979, pp. 314–317.

P. S. Greenlaw and W. D. Biggs, *Modern Personnel Management,* Philadelphia: Saunders, 1979), pp. 270–272.

Goldstein, 1974.

29. Bureau of National Affairs, "Planning the Training Program," *Personnel Management: BNA Policy and Practice Series,* No. 41 (Washington, D.C.: The Bureau of National Affairs, 1975), p. 205. See also, Bass and Vaughan, pp. 89–90.

30. Bass and Vaughan.

Goldstein, 1974.

31. D. T. Hall, *Careers in Organizations* (Santa Monica, Calif.: Goodyear, 1976).

32. K. B. Watson, "The Maturing of Multiple Management," *Management Review* 63 (1974):5.

33. Thomas DeLone, "What Do Middle Managers Really Want From First-Line Supervisors," *Supervisory Management,* September 1977, pp. 8–12.

W. Earl Sasser, Jr., and Frank S. Leonard, "Let First Level Supervisors Do Their Job," *Harvard Business Review,* March–April 1980, pp. 113–121.

The Woodlands Group, "Management Development Roles: Coach, Sponsor, and Mentor," *Personnel Journal,* November 1980, pp. 918–921.

34. M. Mace, "The Supervisor's Responsibility Toward His Subordinates," *Developing Executive Skills* (New York: American Management Association, 1958), pp. 89–135.

35. For further discussion of these programs, see W. F. Glueck, *Personnel: A Diagnostic Approach,* rev. ed. (Dallas, Texas: Business Publications, Inc., 1978).

Greenlaw and Biggs.

36. J. R. Hinrichs, "Personnel Training in M. D. Dunnette, ed., *Handbook of Industrial and Organizational Psychology,* (Chicago: Rand McNally, 1976), pp. 829–860.

37. Louis Olivas, "Using Assessment Centers for Individual and Organizational Development," *Personnel,* May–June 1980, pp. 63–76.

38. Hinrichs, p. 855.

39. Bob Mezoff, "Human Relations Training: The Tailored Approach," *Personnel,* March–April 1981, pp. 21–27.

J. P. Campbell, M. D. Dunnette, E. E. Lawler III, and K. E. Weick, Jr., *Managerial Behavior, Performance and Effectiveness,* (New York: McGraw-Hill, 1970).

40. "For Some Managers Training Program Is Real Obstacle Course," *Wall Street Journal,* July 27, 1981, p. 1.

41. Ellyn Mirides and Andre Cote, "Women in Management: Strategies for Removing All Barriers," *Personnel Administrator,* April 1980, pp. 25–28, 48.

Joan Harley and Lois Ann Koff, "Prepare Women Now for Tomorrow's Managerial Challenges," *Personnel Administrator,* April 1980, pp. 41–42.

Christine D. Hay, "Women in Management: The Obstacles and Opportunities They Face," *Personnel Administrator,* April 1980, pp. 31–39.

42. Mandt.

43. Note that Von Der Embse suggested a table for the selection of training programs for managerial employees only. I revised the table, adding more training programs and adapting it to cover nonmanagerial as well as managerial employees.

44. "Ten Serious Mistakes in Management Training Development," by J. W. Taylor, *Personnel Journal,* May 1974, pp. 357–362.

House.

45. K. Lewin, "Feedback Problems in Social Diagnosis and Action," in W. Buckley, ed., *Modern Systems Research for the Behavioral Scientist* (Chicago: Aldine, 1968), p. 442.

46. "An Organized Evaluation of Management Training," by M. H. Steel, p. 724, Reprinted with permission *Personnel Journal,* Costa Mesa, Calif., Copyright October 1972.

47. Ira G. Asherman and Sandra Lee Vance, "Documentation: A Tool for Effective Management," *Personnel Journal,* August 1981, pp. 641–643.

P. Horst, J. N. Nay, J. W. Scanlon, and J. S. Wholey, "Program Management and the Public Evaluator," *Public Administration Review* 34 (July–August 1974), pp. 300–308.

Laird W. Mealiea and John F. Duffy, "Nine Pitfalls for the Training and Development Specialist," *Personnel Journal,* November 1980, pp. 929–931.

Jonathan S. Monat, "A Perspective on the Evaluation of Training and Development Programs," *Personnel Administrator,* July 1981, pp. 47–52.

John W. Newstrom, "Evaluating the Effectiveness of Training Methods," *Personnel Administrator,* January 1980, pp. 55–60.

48. See Goldstein, pp. 49–88 for an excellent discussion of these designs.

49. George S. Odiorne, "Ten Technologies of Training," *Training and Development Journal,* October 1975, pp. 61–65.

Frank Hoy, W. W. Buchanan, and B. Vaught, "Are Your Management Development Programs Working?" *Personnel Journal,* December 1981, pp. 953–957.

Stanley D. Truskie, "Getting the Most from Management Development Programs," *Personnel Journal,* January 1982, pp. 66–68.

Rich Treadgold, "At Last, a Training Program that Works," *Personnel Journal,* February 1982, pp. 110–112.

Chapter Outline

Critical Issues in Career Planning and Development

Career Planning and Development
The Purposes and Importance of Career Planning and Development
Relationships of Career Planning and Development

Organizational Career Development Programs
Career Pathing
Success without Promotion
Career Stress Management

Your Career Planning Activities
Personal Appraisal and Career Thinking—Step 1
Identify Types of Jobs, Organizations and Industries—Step 2
Prepare for Organizational Life—Step 3
Getting Job Offers—Step 4
Choosing an Offer—Step 5
Doing Well—Step 6

CHAPTER **15**

Career Planning and
Development

Evaluating Career Planning and Management Activities
The Individual Perspective
The Organizational Perspective

Facing the Critical Issues in Career Planning and Development

Summary

Key Concepts

Discussion Questions

Case

For Your Career

Endnotes

Personnel in the News

Career Growth versus Upward Mobility

If business is to meet the challenges of the 1980s, it will surely need to release new reserves of employee energy and talent. Faced with slower growth and no longer able to offer unlimited advancement in return for performance, companies must continue to find opportunities to help employees enlarge their skill base and put these skills to work. Employees can thus maintain, and even increase, the contributions they make to their organizations and can continue to earn substantial rewards, without benefit of a promotion.

In a slow growth economy, the promotion process will be more deliberate, more closely tied to management objectives and based on the organization's timetable. But a promotion need not be the only way positions can be filled or people get new jobs within organizations. More than ever, both individual career and organizational needs should or will be met through lateral transfers, i.e., moves from one job to another within the organization, at the same hierarchical level. (From William T. McCaffrey, reprinted with permission from the May 1981 issue of Personnel Administrator, *p. 81. Copyright by the American Society for Personnel Administration, 30 Park Drive Berea, Ohio 44017).*

The Personal and Business Costs of "Job Burnout"

Jack T. works long hours, but his department's productivity is low. Everybody else, he says, is to blame. For comfort and escape, he occasionally sneaks an extra lunchtime hour to tryst with a divorced woman, a trainee in the department. Jack is a victim of "job burnout," a newly recognized syndrome that's thought to be costing employers a large if unmeasured amount of time, effort and thus productivity.

Sufferers generally show symptoms of "chronic fatigue, low energy, irritability and a negative attitude toward themselves and their jobs," Diane Ryerson and Nancy Marks say in a recent paper presented to the American Psychological Association, the professional group. The two women are psychological consultants in Teaneck, N.J., who specialize in burnout. They and other specialists are being retained by employers to deal with burnout that seems near epidemic in some occupations.

Psychologists say job burnout differs from mid-life crises that affect many people. Burnout is a specific set of symptoms brought on by severe or chronic stress directly related to the job rather than to personal difficulties, such as divorce, death of a spouse, money problems or aging. Burnout more often affects employees who deal extensively with other people on the job.

Service Professionals Suffer

For that reason, it has become notable in healing and service professions such as medicine, social service and the law. Among the people who seem especially vulnerable to burnout are nurses, and some specialists think it accounts for the shortage of nurses. Other vulnerable people are divorce and criminal lawyers, policemen, teachers, and business people. (Jerry E. Bishop, Wall Street Journal, *November 11, 1980, page 33. Reprinted by permission of* The Wall Street Journal. *Copyright 1980 by Dow Jones and Company. All rights reserved.)*

452

Together these quotations highlight several significant aspects associated with the careers of individuals in organizations. One is that organizations must be involved in the management of employees' careers in organizations because the costs of not doing so are potentially too great. In addition to cost, organizations should also be concerned because they often are the source of many employee career problems such as burnout. But employers cannot be expected to be completely responsible for their employees' problems. The employee must also assume a significant share of that responsibility. Indeed, this approach to sharing the responsibility is probably most effective because it is more likely to produce the needed commitment and motivation by both employer and employee to make career development efforts work.

Because these aspects of career management and development are important, much of this chapter provides information related to them. Consequently by the end of this chapter you should be capable of preventing unfavorable or unfortunate events from happening to you. By the end of this chapter you should be able to help our personnel managers address their Critical Issues so that they can provide better career management activities for their organizations.

CRITICAL ISSUES IN CAREER PLANNING AND DEVELOPMENT

Although our group of personnel managers identified many critical issues, the four that stand out are

1. *What can organizations do to help their employees in their career planning and development efforts?*

2. *Why should companies even offer career development programs? After going through training and development programs, the best people may jump to competitors.*

3. *What can we do to help employees manage stress, to reduce or prevent their people from being burned out? Indeed, should they do anything since only a few people actually burn out?*

4. *What can/should people do themselves to plan and develop their own careers?*

Having these two components planning and development underlines the need and importance for the individual (you) as well as the organization to be involved in career management. You should therefore, be aware what organizations can do for your career and what you can do for your career. The two components are:

- **Development programs** that an organization can provide its employees in order to help match employees' needs, goals, and abilities with organizational job demands and rewards.
- **Planning activities** that you, as an individual apart from the organization, should do to help ensure your own career success, job security, self-esteem, growth, and comfort.

CAREER PLANNING AND DEVELOPMENT

Until recently, an individual's career was decided by the organization. If the organization needed someone in another location, someone was transferred. The success of one's career was often indicated by the number of moves that were made, since these moves were generally rewarded by promotions to more important and better-paying jobs. The organization was rarely concerned with whether the new job was really what the individual wanted, and the individual had very limited control over his or her career.

Now, organizations are becoming concerned about whether an individual's abilities and needs are really matched to the job. For example, organizations are beginning to accept the fact that not all people want to be promoted. As a result, it has become more legitimate to have a successful career without climbing to the top of the organization. Organizations are also responding by offering stress management programs and programs for women in management.

Most career development programs offered by organizations are based on the premise that both the employee and the organization must be responsible for career planning and development. Nevertheless, you the individual must evaluate your personal strengths and weaknesses, needs, values, interests, and motivations and be responsible for seeking out and taking advantage of opportunities afforded by an organization's career development programs. Thus you must be ready and able to engage in career planning activities.

Career development programs make an organization more attractive.

The Purposes and Importance of Career Planning and Management

It is both costly and time consuming for organizations to offer career development programs and for individuals to plan their careers. The investments of money and time, however, are worthwhile. Career planning and management fulfill many important purposes.

Career Development Programs. The general purpose of career development programs is to match an employee's needs, abilities, and goals with current or future opportunities and challenges within the organization. In other words, the purpose of career development programs is to increase the employee's likelihood of achieving personal fulfillment and to ensure that the organization places the right people in the right place at the right time. Career development programs are, therefore, aimed at satisfying the two matches that were discussed in the recruitment and selection chapters: the match between individual ability and job demands and the match between individual needs and job rewards.

Career programs help an organization obtain and retain the right people.

There are also several specific purposes for conducting career management programs. "For the organization, career programs serve to assure maximum contributions from individual employees, as well as reduce underemployment."[1] In addition, these programs enable organizations to identify pools of talent and to practice a policy of promotion from within. They enable organizations to fulfill equal employment obligations by developing female and minority employees. They also help reduce absenteeism and turnover to the extent that they are successful in meeting the individual need-job reward match. "Overall, organizations encourage these career programs, hoping to improve performance and profitability."[2]

Career Planning Activities. Although organizations may offer career planning activities, you can engage in them yourself. When you do, the purposes of career planning activities are to help *you* attain for yourself:

- Job security
- Career success
- High self-esteem
- Growth
- Comfort and peace

These purposes are behind what makes career planning activities so important both for you as well as for organizations offering career planning activities. Also making career planning activities important is the fact that, without conscious planning, you are less likely to attain those career purposes.[3]

Relationships of Career Planning and Development

Career development programs and career planning activities have important relationships with several other personnel and human resource activities, as shown in Exhibit 15.1. Among the most important are relationships with personnel planning, training and development, job analysis, staffing activities, performance appraisal, and personal appraisal.[4]

Exhibit 15.1
Career Planning and Development Processes and Procedures

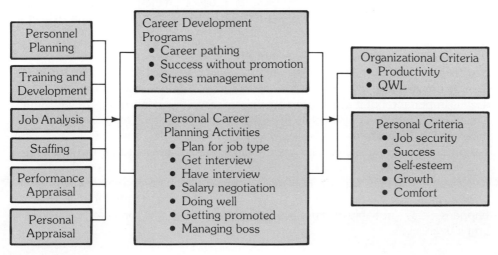

Personnel Planning.   Until recently, the personnel planning activity was the traditional way an organization dealt with career management. That is, potential job demands are forecast, and then supplies of employees were forecast to fill those needs. The primary concern was making sure that the job demands were filled, and thus the one match—between individual ability and job demands—received much attention. Now, however, with the increased necessity of accommodating employees, personnel planning must also consider the individual needs-job rewards match. Since a critical part of career management is the identification of and accommodation to individual needs and values, it is an activity that complements planning. Organizations such as Nationwide Insurance Company, XEROX Corporation, and IBM have recognized this relationship by adding personal data, such as employee preferences regarding promotion and transfer, to their employment records of employees. These data, in turn, are used in constructing employee replacement charts (see Chapter 2).

Training and Development.   Training and development programs are quite complementary to career planning and management. Often training programs are a part of a set of career management programs an organization may offer its employees. You may be thinking that it's really hard to tell the difference between training and development programs and career development programs. For some organizations there may be little difference, but in others the differences most likely lie in the focus and degree of specificity. Where training programs are more likely to focus on a specific skill to be taught in order to improve an employee's performance in the short term, career development programs are more likely to focus broadly on creating skills that will serve an employee in many situations often for the longer-run benefit of both the individual and the organization.

Job Analysis.   Sears, Roebuck and Company has an extensive job-based career development program that depends heavily on its job analysis. As Chapter 3 explains, job analysis identifies the critical job duties and necessary employee qualifications. At Sears this information is used to develop career paths or routes of job progression. Career paths are constructed to provide employees with an increase in at least one skill area on each new assignment, an increase of at least 10 percent in total points (based on the Hay job evaluation plan) on each new assignment, and assignments in several different functional areas.[5] The Sears program is based on the Hay plan, but that plan could be supplemented by an analysis of what new skills employees can expect to acquire.

Staffing Activities.   An organization is more likely to be attractive to and successful in recruiting qualified job applicants if it has a career development system. The system itself is important, but it also represents the organization's concern for the individual. An effective system suggests that the organization regards its relationship with the individual as mutually beneficial.

In spite of these benefits, however, organizations are reluctant to have career development systems for fear they will actually lose rather than gain employees as a result of the employees finding out that they really belong in some other line of work. Organizations like the Ameritrust of Cleveland, however, have found that, even if this happens, it is probably in the best interests of both the organization and the employee.[6]

Performance Appraisal.   Many organizations use performance appraisals to find out employees' career aspirations and to provide an outside assessment of employees' abilities. Performance appraisal is also an important part of a career development system, since it identifies how well and, with the job analysis, under what conditions an employee performs. This information can then be used to map that employee's career path.

Personal Appraisal.   Although this is not a common personnel activity, it's hard to run effective career management programs without knowing what employees want. They, however, most likely don't know what they want unless they do a personal appraisal. So the personnel manager should encourage employees to do it. It is also something you should do. **Personal appraisal** is really the basis of your career planning activities. It consists of your identifying abilities, values, and goals that are important to you. It also consists of your identifying the strengths and weaknesses you possess. Before you finish this chapter, please take some time to list your important

- Abilities
- Values
- Goals

Identify goals for several areas of your life including work, family, physical fitness, community involvement, friends, education, and travel. Then list your five major strengths (things about you that are just great) and your five major weaknesses (things about you that you would like to have better or at least different).

FOR YOUR CAREER

What Do You Want from Your Career?

Rank order what you most want from your career.

What You Can Get	Rank Order*
Intellectual challenge	_____
Money	_____
Independence	_____
Security	_____
Prestige	_____
Opportunity to contribute to society	_____
Power	_____

*Rank these from 1 to 7. Use each number only once. For example, if prestige is most important, rank it 1; and if security is least important, rank it 7.

ORGANIZATIONAL CAREER DEVELOPMENT PROGRAMS

Career development programs are offered by organizations to assist employees in career planning and development. Of the many career development programs, only a few can be examined here.[7] These few, however, illustrate the diversity of needs that are filled by the programs and the wide range of concerns that are considered by organizations to be important in career management.[8]

Career Pathing

Three key programs are

- Career pathing
- Success without promotion
- Stress management

Career pathing programs consist of two major activities. One helps an employee identify his or her abilities, values and goals, and strengths and weaknesses.[9] The other provides a set of job experiences that helps an employee (1) satisfy some of those values, goals; (2) utilize some of those strengths and abilities; and (3) improve upon some of those weaknesses identified in the career planning activity. Let us examine both of these activities.

Career Planning. The career planning activity is very similar to your personal appraisal activity. The major difference is that the career planning activity is offered by the organization and directly related to it and its specific jobs, and your personal appraisal (done here at least) is unrelated to a specific organization and done at your initiative. Other than that, they are pretty similar.

Organizations should:

- Aid individual career planning
- Conduct employee assessment
- Develop career paths
- Counsel and coach employees

Job Progression. The **job progression program** at Sears mentioned earlier was developed to enhance the relationship between career planning and development and to serve the practical needs of the employees and the organization. To do this, Sears focuses on the job as the vehicle for career development. There are four principles on which Sears bases its approach:

- The most important influences on career development occur on the job.
- Different jobs demand the development of different skills.
- Development can occur only when a person has not yet developed the skills demanded by a particular job.
- By identifying a rational sequence of job assignments for a person, the time required to develop the necessary skills for a chosen target can be reduced.[10]

The essence of the Sears job progression program is the identification of job demands or dimensions. Sears uses the Hay plan to analyze their job on three basic dimensions: *know-how, problem solving,* and *accountability.* Since these dimensions require different employee skills, a rational sequence of job assignments for an employee's career development would consist of jobs with different dimensions. As a consequence, Sears can use its program to identify rational paths to target jobs (those that represent the end of employees' path); to classify paths according to speed and level of development obtained; to justify and identify lateral moves and even downward moves; and to assess training needs and provide input into a human resource planning program.

Used appropriately, such a job progression program can be very helpful in aiding an organization's equal employment efforts and in opening up career opportunities. "This kind of system can lift career planning out of the informal corporate 'old boy' network and reduce the employee's dependence upon a well-informed boss."[11]

Success Without Promotion

As indicated in the first quotation at the start of this chapter, many organizations are experiencing and will continue to experience slower growth and less ability to offer unlimited advancement in return for performance. This, combined with the bulge of the twenty-four to fifty-four age group in the 1980s and 1990s as discussed in Chapter 2, will really limit, for many employees, the traditional route to "success"—the promotion.

You may need to redefine your measure of success in an organization.

Organizations are responding to this potential crisis by redefining the essence of success, that is, by reducing the level of importance of promotion in the definition of success. One way they are doing this is through cross-functional lateral transfers. Where once employees shunned lateral transfers, they are beginning to value them. The benefits go to both the organization and the individual. Here's how this happens.

Cross-functional or **cross-departmental transfer** means moving an employee from one type of job activity to another; both, however, are comparably evaluated. When offered early in an employee's career this type of lateral transfer every nine to twelve months can prepare the employee for second-level management (a promotion) within a few years and as his or her career progresses, a greater degree of flexibility in moving from job to job. This job rotation program opens up promotion opportunities that were previously blocked to a person because she or he lacked the necessary experience. Thus, though promotion time may be slowed down with lateral transfer programs, they help ensure an employee that there will be promotion opportunities down the road.

Career Stress Management

Jack T. in the quotation at the start of this chapter is a real person. He is regional sales manager for a large manufacturer.

> Jack dropped out of college at the age of 20 because of financial problems. When he first started work as a salesman, he worked harder to get ahead than his college-educated peers. He was spotted as bright and aggressive. He kept getting promotions until he became a regional sales manager. He earns a salary that permits him to pay for a suburban home, membership in a country club that his wife uses for tennis and bridge, and college for his two children.

Hitting Dead End

> But he's blocked in his job, and he knows it. The national sales manager, whom Jack once stood a chance of succeeding, won't retire. So far as he's concerned, Jack's peers, the other regional sales managers, some of them younger and more aggressive, are getting the pick of new salesmen hired by the company. Jack looks upon his own staff as the culls. He knows that it's only a matter of time before the "baby boom brighties" in his company are going to force him out. He has high blood pressure. His sex life, at home at least, has deteriorated.[12]

Not everyone
suffers from
stress, even
under the
same
conditions.

Fortunately, not all employees experience **job burnout** (career stress) as has Jack T., but even if they did, they would not all react as he did. Nevertheless, many employees experience other stress symptoms at work that are just as damaging to an individual's career as it is to the organization.[13] Such symptoms include apathy, withdrawal, dissatisfaction, irritability, absenteeism, ulcers, hypertension, increased likelihood of coronary heart disease and accident proneness.

It is important to note that this discussion of stress is limited to ideas most relevant and useful for an individual's career. Other stress ideas more relevant and useful for the total organization are discussed in Chapter 17.

Two key
sources of
stress are

• Uncertainty
• Lack of
   control

Reasons for Career Stress. In order to help alleviate or reduce the occurrence of these stress symptoms, it is important to know two of the major reasons individuals experience career stress in organizations: **uncertainty** and the **lack of control.** For example, Jack T. is suffering from burnout because he feels out of control of his fate. In addition he knows he's on his way out, but he's not sure exactly when. Using these two reasons we can explain why many aspects of organizations are sources of stress.

Managing Career Stress. As a consequence of these two reasons for stress, organizations can offer career stress management programs to help individuals get back in control (for example, by implementing a program to increase the level of employee participation in decisions that most closely affect how and when one does a job) and to clarify uncertainties. One way of clarifying uncertainties is by effective performance planning programs.[14] (Other ways are examined in Chapter 17 on health and safety). By clarifying uncertainties, effective performance planning can reduce the stress associated with job responsibilities.[15]

One company implemented effective performance planning by training its managers in management by objectives. One of the managers' objectives was to help their employees identify, clarify, and become committed to work goals.[16] Before the managers received their training, however, the employees were surveyed on six goal-oriented dimensions:

■ Difficulty of work goals
■ Clarity of work goals
■ Quality of performance feedback from the supervisor
■ Amount of performance feedback from the supervisor
■ Employee participation in setting work goals
■ Peer competition for goal accomplishment

Five months after the program began, the employees were resurveyed on the same six dimensions. Comparison of the two surveys indicated considerable improvement. And as a result, uncertainty declined, and absenteeism within the organization declined.

The results of this strategy illustrate that a change in just one personnel activity—in this case, performance appraisal—can be useful in managing career stress. The results also indicate that organizations should pay particular attention to their performance appraisal systems, especially to the phenomenon of the "vanishing performance appraisal"—the performance appraisal that never takes place—because of the adverse effects they can have on employees' stress levels.

What someone like Jack T. can do to manage career stress is to get back in control of his life as described in the *Personnel in Action* insert, "Getting Back in Control." Notice that the insert discusses getting back in control for those individuals most out of control: those out of a job. Although you (and Jack T.) may never be out of control that much, many of the seven points may still be quite useful for your own career. In addition to managing your career stress, there are several other career planning activities that you may find useful for a successful career.

PERSONNEL IN ACTION

Getting Back In Control

Some advice, gleaned from the formerly unemployed:

1. *Structure your time stringently at first.* You can ease up later on, but it's best to gradually move into a less structured time frame. Make lists of activities every day and force yourself to do them. Read Alan Lakein's "How to Get Control of Your Time and Your Life."

2. *Marshal your social support system.* Use every friend and family member that you can count on to give you a boost when your spirits are sagging. Experts agree that the strength of this system is the crucial factor in how well you cope with unemployment. In addition to moral support, these people should be tapped as information resources. Have they been through a similar experience and what did they learn that can help you?

3. *Find your most effective and constructive escape routes.* Use them when necessary or when tempted to use a negative escape, e.g., TV, overeating, drinking. Get more than your regular amount of exercise. If reading is an effective relaxation for you, decide what kind of books are most likely to lift your spirits, make you feel positive about yourself, and motivate you to act. Self-improvement books, while often positive, may encourage you to continue passive behavior.

4. *Balance work and leisure.* Restrict your work activities to a certain area of your home and a certain part of your day. Do the same with leisure. Make sure you schedule some of both.

5. *Reward yourself.* When you finish a task, call up an understanding friend and brag.

6. *Do something for someone else.* A tried-and-true cure for the blues that still works.

7. *Recognize that ultimately no one cares quite so much about your happiness or your life as you do.* Do everything you can to activate your own motivation, even though it may be dormant from years of inactivity in an organization.

For friends and family of the unemployed, Tom Jackson and Davidyne Mayleas, authors of "The Hidden Job Market," suggest that you:

- Look on this time as an opportunity rather than a time of depression.

- Take a practical interest in the person's job-finding and reward successes, no matter how small.

- Try to interest the person in other activities besides job-hunting.

(*Washington Post*, January 26, 1981, p. C5. Used by permission.)

YOUR CAREER PLANNING ACTIVITIES

The basic idea of this section is: By actively managing your career, you'll do better than by not managing it. "Better" is measured by any standard you choose—personal fulfillment, climbing to the top of the organization, happiness, salary level. By planning and managing, you'll increase your chances of getting whatever you realistically identify as most important.

Exhibit 15.2 outlines one strategy for getting into the right company. To obtain the most from this model, you should carefully review and do each step.[17]

Exhibit 15.2
Personal Career Planning Activities

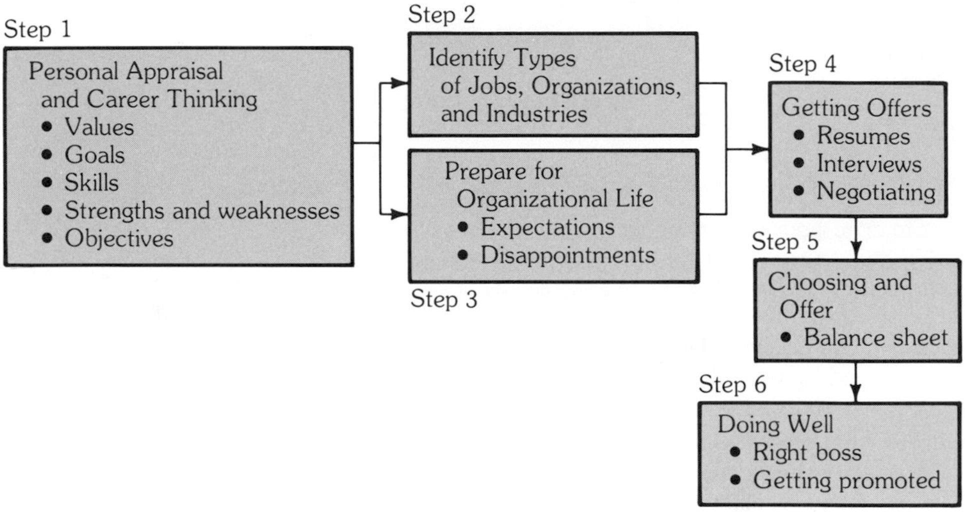

Step 1

Personal Appraisal
and Career Thinking
- Values
- Goals
- Skills
- Strengths and weaknesses
- Objectives

Step 2

Identify Types
of Jobs, Organizations,
and Industries

Step 3

Prepare for
Organizational Life
- Expectations
- Disappointments

Step 4

Getting Offers
- Resumes
- Interviews
- Negotiating

Step 5

Choosing and
Offer
- Balance sheet

Step 6

Doing Well
- Right boss
- Getting promoted

Personal Appraisal and Career Thinking—Step 1

You have done a large portion of this step already if you have identified your

Personal
appraisal is
critical for your
personal
success.

- Values
- Goals
- Skills
- Strengths and weaknesses
- Objectives

The remaining part of your personal appraisal here is to start identifying your career objectives. Do this on only a broad level, but try to relate career objectives with your values, goals, skills, strengths, and weaknesses. For example, if you really value interacting with other people and have a great deal of singing talent, perhaps it is reasonable to aim for an entertainment career.

FOR YOUR CAREER

Are You Lucky?

Although career planning certainly helps people get what they want, some people get what they want without career planning, or so it seems, because they're lucky. But you can be lucky too. Luck is really not something you're born with but something that you have because of what you do (such as career planning!). Here are ten characteristics of lucky people:

1. Lucky people are extroverted.
2. Lucky people have magnetic personalities.
3. Lucky people are in touch with their feelings.
4. Lucky people know the difference between a hunch and a hope.
5. Lucky people do their homework.
6. Lucky people recognize opportunities.
7. Lucky people take risks.
8. Lucky people are skeptics.
9. Lucky people quit while ahead.
10. Lucky people admit their mistakes.[18]

Identify Types of Jobs, Organizations, and Industries— Step 2

Because the job or jobs you choose can have such an impact on your life, it is important to analyze carefully what you want for your first job and your first company. You may want to start by first identifying industries in which you may want to work.[19] For example, you may want to choose to work in an industry with great growth potential such as

- Banking
- Insurance
- Medical care
- Computer science, data processing
- Communications

Then within these industries, or any others, you next want to gather information on a particular company. Summer work experience, internships, and part-time work are valuable ways to gain exposure to new companies. Although some work experience may be boring to you, it sometimes helps if you consider them as learning experiences, ways of getting to know yourself better. Other sources of information are newspapers and professional magazines, school placement offices, libraries, direct mail, job-search firms, friends, and family.

Don't Exclude Nontraditional Jobs. In thinking about the types of job, organizations, and industries in which you would like to work, think creativity. Consider jobs, organizations and industries that you would label as nontraditional.

Many people hate their jobs because they dislike being closely supervised or confined to the same work area every day. Or they may feel they never have the satisfaction of seeing a finished product of their labor. Yet they see no escape.

There are actually numerous high-paying jobs (often $10 an hour and up) which permit great freedom of movement, require little supervision and offer lots of personal satisfaction. If you are skilled with your hands and you enjoy working with things, consider becoming any of the following: air-conditioning, refrigeration and heating mechanic; appliance serviceperson; television and radio service technician; business machine, computer or industrial machinery serviceperson; truck or bus mechanic; vending machine mechanic.

Though most of these jobs are commonly thought of as men's work, the U.S. Department of Labor points out that they are equally suited to women. The Labor Department bases its opinion on the fact that the majority of repair occupations require relatively little physical strength and are performed indoors in warm surroundings. Most important, career-aptitude research indicates that the same high finger dexterity which allows women to excel at typing and factory assembly jobs also enables them to do very well at these highpay repair occupations.

Other research by the Department of Labor indicates that if you do learn one of these skills, you'll have plenty of job opportunities through the 1980's.[20]

> *Seek out as much job information as possible. Never leave a stone unturned.*

There are, of course, many other types of jobs including self-employment and the more traditional entry-level jobs in larger organizations that are the first step in a series through promotions to senior management positions. Within larger organizations these traditional paths are available in many functional areas such as personnel and across functional areas as described in the first part of this chapter. There are also a few job opportunities in the relatively new field of internal corporate consulting.

Management consulting has long been a springboard to lofty corporate positions for men, and as far back as the late 1960's a handful of women also used it to move up in corporations. For instance, Mary C. Falvey, 40, who currently earns a salary estimated at well above $100,000 as vice-president of finance at Shaklee Corp. in San Francisco, joined the management consulting firm of McKinsey & Co. back in 1967. But only in the past four or five years have substantial numbers of women discovered consulting as a shortcut to corporate achievement, a demanding—but rewarding—way of bypassing lower managerial jobs.[21]

Prepare for Organizational Life—Step 3

It is one thing to know the type of jobs you might want and the type of industry or organization in which you want to work, but it's an entirely different thing to know the realities of living and working in an organization. Two qualities of organizational life, in almost any organization, that you should be aware of are (1) organizational expectations, and (2) organizational disappointments.

Organizational Expectations. One thing you should realize is that most organizations expect new employees to have certain characteristics:

- Competence to get a job done
- Ability to accept organizational realities
- Ability to generate and sell ideas
- Loyalty and commitment

- High personal integrity and strength
- Capacity to grow[22]

Organizational Disappointments.   Although organizations have high expectations of you, they may not always live up to their end of the bargain. What they do or
don't do may bring you disappointments (**reality shock**). Here are several likely
reasons why:

- *Low initial job challenge:* Although some findings have indicated the usefulness of
  giving new recruits a challenging initial job, many organizations continue to ease the
  new recruit into the organization. This, of course, is consistent with the organization's perception of the new recruit as a novice.

- *Low self-actualization and need satisfaction:* The new recruit may fail to experience   These points
  the autonomy and challenge necessary to grow and to develop self-esteem and   describe
  competency. Some researchers have suggested that an individual may actually lose   "Reality
  competency of the job if not given the opportunity to advance in the direction of the   Shock."
  growth and independence characteristic of mature adults.

- *The vanishing performance appraisal, or inability to determine what the real criteria
  are:* New recruits come on board with the expectation of receiving clear and unambiguous evaluations of their performance. In reality, new recruits report having little
  feedback on their performance, although their supervisors may claim the opposite.

- *Unrealistically high aspirations:* As it turns out, most recruits have higher expectations of being able to use their skills and abilities than actually occur. The gap
  between an individual's skills and the skills actually used on the job is probably
  increased because of the manager's belief that the new recruit really is not capable
  of assuming responsibility.

- *Inability to create challenge:* Although new recruits may not be given challenging
  assignments, they are also often incapable of creating their own challenge. They
  have been conditioned to receive well-defined projects from others. As a result, they
  find it more difficult to create challenge from an ill-defined or unstructured situation.

- *Source of threat to the boss:* A new recruit's first boss plays a critical role for the
  recruit's future in the organization. This role tends to be negative, especially if the
  boss feels threatened. The threat may occur to the supervisor who is in a terminal
  position and can't go any further in the organization. The new recruit may be seen
  as a "comer" with a great deal more potential than the boss. In addition, the new
  recruit is probably younger and has different values and styles. As a result, the
  supervisor may not be very supportive of the new employee and may not provide
  many positive experiences.

- *Amount of conflict and uncertainty in the organization:* New recruits think that rules
  and procedures, directions, and communications will be clear, crisp, and without
  conflict. The reality in many situations is just the opposite.[23]

Getting Job Offers—Step 4

Now that you've narrowed down (but not too much) the types of jobs, organizations,
and industries you want and are prepared for organizational life, the next thing to do is
get some job offers. Three aspects of getting job offers are

- Resume Writing
- Interviewing
- Negotiating

Resume Writing.   The **standard resume** lists work experience from your current job or student status to those two years you spent delivering the daily paper (to show youthful vitality, industry, and responsibility for customers and money). Often it's a chronology of dates, titles, and responsibilities (whether they are previous jobs or positions held in school organizations). An example of a standard resume is Appendix D.

PERSONNEL IN ACTION

Reference Letters Lose their Appeal as an Employment Screening Tool

Increasingly, bosses are skittish about giving candid, written references for fear ex-employees may sue. This hurts letters' value and prompts many employers to stop requiring them. Letters "aren't as reliable as they used to be," says Northrop Corp. Or the notes just contain employment dates and a salary scale says Allied Corp. One New York recruiter has found a few financial executives fake reference letters.

Some concerns just ask for references' names. Southern California Edison Co. doesn't check those out unless "we feel there's a reason to." GAF Corp. and others phone applicants' prior bosses. Even this method creates problems. The information you get may be "very subjective," notes a Grumman Corp. personnel official.

But Security Pacific Bank puts more emphasis on lists and letters of reference, because other firms "are becoming more lax."

*   *   *

(*Wall Street Journal*, November 3, 1981, page 1. Reprinted by permission of *The Wall Street Journal.* Copyright 1981 by Dow Jones and Company. All rights reserved.)

Job Interviewing.   Step 1 has great value as preparation for job interviews. If you know yourself inside and out, you will find it easier to "sell" yourself to potential employers. Here are six suggestions for participating in job interviews:

Job interviews are critical. Prepare carefully for them.

- "Sell" yourself to the recruiter with the same determination you would use in selling a product or service to a customer. Remember that the interview period is brief. Yet a favorable impression of your appearance, sense of purpose, and clarity of self-expression will probably weigh more heavily with the recruiter than your transcript, your resume, or your references.
- Familiarize yourself ahead of time with the employer to be interviewed—know what the company does and what products or services it offers. Ask only pertinent questions during the interview, and suggest how your skills and abilities may benefit the organization.

- Develop your ability to communicate, but do not come on too strong or be overly confident.

- Cite academic achievements, especially if they appear to relate to the job area you are interested in. Remember that recruiting companies often view your college work as a preparatory period. Hence, cite your academic efforts as evidence that you can attain long-range goals and objectives.

- Mention extracurricular activities that demonstrate your leadership or initiative.

- Learn the art of interviewing by accepting as many interview opportunities as you can, even with organizations you think you may not prefer. Enroll in psychology and management courses where interviews are practiced by role playing.[24]

Remember, you only get one chance to make a good first impression.

Negotiating. An important topic that will surely arise in your interviewing is salary. How you handle this topic could make a substantial difference in how much you get paid. Here are a few tips on how to handle this aspect in your job search.

> It's "dumb" for a job candidate to raise the question of salary early in the hiring process, says Pfizer divisional vice-president Max Hughes. And it is. Until the employer has had time to make up his or her mind to hire you, you aren't worth anything to the employer. To negotiate the highest possible salary, listen and ask questions so that you can identify the other person's needs and communicate how you can help meet them. It's best to delay the subject of salary until later in the interview. Loaded with information about your strengths, the employer should see you as a more valuable asset than when you began to talk. . . .
>
> Inevitably, the employer who wants you on his or her team will ask, "What are your salary requirements?" Unlike some career consultants who encourage you to get the employer to name the first figure, executive recruiter Richard Irish, career consultant John Crystal, job-market analyst Richard Lathrop, and others say (and I agree) that you should name the first figure and make it high.[25]

Choosing An Offer—Step 5

Now that you have all the skills necessary to get several offers, it's equally necessary to have the skills to choose one from among several offers. Although choosing the best offer may be more an art than a science to be taught and learned, one method that may help is the **career balance sheet.** On this you enter positive and negative aspects of given job offer. Enter aspects of each job offer with consideration for how they affect you personally and how they affect others, for example, your spouse, friends, or family. While a job offer may have many positive aspects for you, it may have several negative aspects for others. You have as many sheets as you do job offers. Balance sheets help you make your job choice because it requires you to organize and lay out job information in a systematic way.[26]

Doing Well—Step 6

Doing well involves getting what you want from the organization in which you are working. It means having things go your way. It may mean getting promoted, and it certainly means staying valuable and useful to the organization. As such it requires that you know about

■ Dealing with your boss

■ Getting promoted

It pays to work for a good boss. A bad boss is as bad as a bad job.

The Right Boss. People are more likely to develop strong leadership qualities if they work for a boss who has something to teach, who is on the move, and who is capable of taking others along. The preference for being on a winning team is a survival mechanism. And people are less dependent and uncertain if they're allied with bosses who are strong leaders. Consequently it pays you to try to be in a position to select your boss. This is especially true for your first boss. You can enhance your chances of working for the boss of your choice by being an outstanding performer and by becoming a critical subordinate for your boss but one who doesn't threaten the boss.[27]

Getting Promoted. Getting promoted is much easier when you

■ Have credibility with senior managers

Managers with credibility can take greater risks and make more mistakes because they have the known ability to produce results. It's necessary to have credibility with superiors before developing it with subordinates. For example, a manager was brought in from the outside to run a division that designs aerospace equipment. He could barely get information he needed from headquarters—he had few connections and no clout. And when senior managers wanted answers, they went straight to his subordinates because the senior managers believed the subordinates had a better idea of what was going on. Without the support of top management, his subordinates thought little of him.[28]

■ Have a reputation as being an expert

When a manager has the reputation of being an expert, others tend to defer to that manager on issues involving his or her expertise. This is important in large organizations where many people have only second-hand knowledge about one's professional competence.[29]

■ Are the first in the position

A manager who is the first in a new position, takes risks, and succeeds is more likely to be rewarded than a manager who does something second. While excellent performance on routine tasks is usually valued, being innovative is a big plus.[30]

■ Know and use networks

Grow and prune your career networks.

Knowing about and using networks can be critical to your job success. Essentially a **network** is a collection of friends and acquaintances, both inside and outside one's workplace, that can be counted on for some kind of help. Networks can provide many kinds of help including information, services, support and access.

■ Know how to unstop a career bottleneck[31]

To avoid getting stuck in a job or a company that no longer provides growth or promotional opportunities, investigate the possibility of a lateral move. If that doesn't work, figure out ways to increase job responsibilities and, if that fails to work, consider changing companies or changing career fields altogether.[32]

EVALUATING CAREER PLANNING AND MANAGEMENT ACTIVITIES

Evaluating the effectiveness of career planning and development must be done from the individual and the organizational perspectives. Although the overall purpose of career management is to match individual ability to job demands and individual needs to job rewards, there are several specific purposes that relate primarily to the individual or the organization.

The Individual Perspective

From the individual's perspective, effective career planning should result in several beneficial outcomes:

- A more realistic awareness of one's skills, abilities, and weaknesses
- An awareness of one's needs, values, and goals
- An awareness of realistic job and career opportunities that match one's abilities and needs
- A greater sense of self-worth and self-esteem from doing what one is able to do and wants to do
- A more satisfied and productive individual

There is, however, little evidence to indicate how well career planning activities actually help to attain these outcomes. The evidence that does exist suggests that employees are more satisfied as a result of job placement activities that match them on needs as well as abilities (see Chapter 5). More informal evidence indicates, however, that the initial stages of gaining self-awareness and career awareness are often difficult and even frustrating if appropriate opportunities are not available. People who gain greater self-awareness may even leave an organization in search of better matches. How do organizations respond to this? If they offer career programs for their benefit as well as for that of the individual, organizations often wish the individual well.

The Organizational Perspective

From the organization's perspective, effective career development programs should also result in several beneficial outcomes, including

- More effective use of its current work force
- Reduced absenteeism, since employees are better fitted to their job situation
- Reduced turnover after employees go through career planning and find an appropriate job in the current organization
- Improved morale among employees who decide to remain

- A work force with lower potential for obsolescence and a higher level of flexibility and adaptability to changing circumstances
- More employees suitable for potential promotion
- A better image as an organization to work for and, as a result, a larger pool of job applicants to select from
- A greater likelihood of fulfilling equal and employment obligations and using the skills of all employees
- And, last but not least, improved performance

Again the evidence on how well career management programs provide these outcomes is limited. However, those organizations that have them—for instance, Sears, Roebuck and Company, IBM, Ameritrust, Standard Oil (Ohio), J. C. Penney Company, and Procter & Gamble—indicate that they are able to identify more potentially promotable employees and have an easier time attracting qualified candidates because of being known for offering career development opportunities. Career development is becoming more and more necessary in order for companies to remain effective.

FACING THE CRITICAL ISSUES IN CAREER PLANNING AND DEVELOPMENT

Now that we have discussed many important aspects of career planning and development, it is appropriate to return to the Critical Issues presented at the start of this chapter. Because you now are able to add a lot of information on each Critical Issue yourself, only a brief response to each is presented here.

Issue: *What can organizations do to help their employees in their career planning and development efforts?*

There's really a lot you can do. You can perhaps be most effective in helping employees by offering career development programs and encouraging them to do their own career planning. Some programs you might offer, such as career pathing and job progression, can fit quite nicely into your employees' own career planning efforts. Other programs include preretirement counseling, stress and time management, employee assistance, and extensive training and development programs.

Issue: *Why should companies even offer career development programs? After going through training and development programs, the best people jump to competitors.*

That's a good point. What you have to ask yourself then is why are the best people leaving? Just like any other personnel activity, career development programs must be coordinated with the other personnel activities. In fact, your example is a nice one, illustrating the waste that occurs when personnel activities are not coordinated.

If the career development programs are properly coordinated, the best employees are less likely to leave (some will always leave); they are likely to be more satisfied with the organization, and the organization will get a reputation as a good place to work. Thus recruiting good people will be easier.

Should you offer career programs? Only if you're ready to coordinate them with other personnel activities and want the many desirable results from having them.

Issue: *What can companies do to help employees manage stress and to reduce or prevent their people from being burned out? Indeed, should they do anything since only a few people actually burn out?*

People do indeed respond differently to the same situations. One person's poison is another's meat, as the saying goes. This is certainly true with stress and burnout. But it's also true with accidents. Do you avoid efforts to reduce accidents because only a few employees have them? Just as you are legally responsible for accidents, increasingly you may also be responsible for stress symptoms. There are several cases in courts now addressing this issue.

But even if you are not legally responsible, the costs of running programs to help employees manage or reduce stress could be much less than the benefits. Programs that you might run include time management, exercise routines, and almost anything that helps reduce uncertainty. This may even involve changing parts of the organization or aspects of other personnel activities such as performance appraisal and compensation.

Issue: *What can/should people do themselves to plan and develop their own careers?*

People should definitely assume some responsibility for their own careers. As such they should identify their own goals, values, strengths, and weaknesses. They should also prepare for the realities of organizational life.

Everyone should also be responsible for knowing how to write resumes and for doing effective interviews. People should also know the ropes of surviving and doing well in organizations.

SUMMARY

Career management is an important activity that provides benefits to both organizations and individuals. The benefits include better use of human resources, more satisfied and productive employees, and more personally fulfilling careers.

Organizations have only recently become involved in career management activities. Previously, organizations were concerned only with matching an employee's abilities to the demands of the job. Now they are also concerned with matching an employee's needs to the rewards of the job. The result of this dual concern in recruitment and selection is reduced absenteeism and turnover and increased performance. In addition, when organizations are concerned with employee needs, it becomes easier for them to attract new employees.

It is important for any prospective employee to become attractive to organizations. This involves several steps that must be followed in order to manage one's career effectively. Once hired by the company, the individual must then know how to remain attractive. One aspect of this task is always knowing what your goals and needs are. What are yours now?

KEY CONCEPTS

career balance sheet

reality shock

career development programs

career pathing

career planning

uncertainty

lack of control

job progression program

cross-functional or cross-departmental transfer

network

standard resume

job burnout

personal appraisal

DISCUSSION QUESTIONS

1. What is the dual match in career planning and development?

2. In what ways can the organization benefit from offering career development programs to its employees?

3. Who is responsible for career development—the organization or the individual?

4. What is the difference between training and development programs as they are related to career planning?

5. What is a personal appraisal, and how is it related to career management?

6. What are the causes of career stress? How can they best be dealt with?

7. List the six steps in planning your career.

8. What are some critical points to keep in mind about job interviewing?

CASE

Retired on the Job: Career Burnout or the Nonmotivated Employee?

George Benson, the newly appointed manager of Pentarecon Corporation's Production Control and Methods Improvement Division, faced a rather perplexing personnel problem. One of the long-time employees of his division, Harry Norton, wasn't performing his job properly. In questioning subordinates, Benson learned that Norton had not performed any real or substantive work for years. Furthermore, his current job actions were a source of embarrassment to the entire division. "Hangover Harry" Norton was observed to arrive at work approximately 45 minutes late each morning and proceeded to begin the work day by attempting to recover from the previous evening's outing with his "Scotch friends." Norton's method of recovery appeared to involve (1) reading the paper for about an hour while smoking and drinking coffee; (2) "office hopping" with his coffee cup in order to visit, talk, and interact with his many friends who were employed within the division; (3) a two-hour, three-martini lunch break; and (4) an afternoon nap while secluded back in his office. Benson had expected the employees of his division to resent Norton's behavior and obvious poor or nonperformance. Thus, he was quite surprised when he learned that Norton was almost universally liked and considered somewhat of a folk hero among nonsupervisory employees. Therefore, Benson decided to thoroughly investigate Norton's case before taking any type of personnel action.

From company records, Benson learned that Norton had been employed by Pentarecon Corporation for twelve years. He began his employment with the firm as an internal management specialist. The duties of this position involved the development of methods improvements to facilitate both management and manufacturing operations. Initially, Norton was quite successful in this position. His performance appraisals routinely cited him for both his ingenuity and complete understanding of the complex production control systems used by the firm. Norton was credited with the introduction of new work procedures that lessened both worker fatigue and industrial accidents. Additionally, several of his suggestions resulted in substantial improvements in product quality within the manufacturing department. Recognizing this performance excellence, the firm promoted Norton once and issued to him several cash bonuses during his first five years of employment.

During his seventh year of employment, Norton was being considered for a supervisory position within the division. Everyone was surprised when Pentarecon's top management finally decided to fill this supervisory vacancy with another employee from the Research and Development Group. Norton appeared to accept this career setback with some degree of indifference. He still seemed to exhibit his friendly and engaging interpersonal style that had won him many friends within the division. Yet six months later, a project he was assigned to direct seemed to "never get off the ground" because of his failure to exhibit proper levels of leadership and enthusiasm when dealing with other project analysts. Subsequent job assignments also revealed a substantial deterioration in performance. Norton's failure to consider a variety of relevant variables in his work assignments resulted in the development of nonusable work methods and production control techniques. Norton's supervisor noted that Harry appeared to be drinking heavily during this period of time and was said to be experiencing marital difficulties. This pattern of poor performance, tardiness, and alcohol abuse continued to the point where Norton's supervisor was afraid to assign him projects of any real significance. Therefore, Harry was either given small, noncritical work assignments or no work at all.

Case Questions

1. What are the underlying causes of Norton's performance?
2. Who's responsible for the current state of Norton's performance?
3. Should Benson have taken action much earlier?
4. What should Benson do now? Should Benson fire Norton?

FOR YOUR CAREER

- ▪ Organizations may be reluctant to provide career development opportunities for fear employees will leave after taking advantage of the opportunity.
- ▪ If possible, go to work for an organization with a reputation for really good development opportunities, such as Procter and Gamble or General Electric.
- ▪ You must take responsibility for your own career. If the organization treats you poorly, realize you need to change the relationship or leave. Changing an organization, however, is hard.
- ▪ It pays to maintain contacts with friends in other organizations. Develop networks and work with them.
- ▪ You should engage in personal appraisal and evaluation continuously. We change just as our environment does.
- ▪ It pays to monitor your stress levels. Develop social support groups and engage in time management activities in order to better handle your stress.

ENDNOTES

1. D. A. Morgan, D. T. Hall, and A. Martier, "Career Development Strategies in Industry: Where Are We and Where Should We Be?" *Personnel,* March–April 1979, p. 14.

2. Ibid.

3. J. Rago, "Career Management and Obsolescence" (Cleveland State University, 1979).

4. John J. Leach, "The Career Planning Process," *Personnel Journal,* April 1981, pp. 283–286.

   Nan Strauss and Anthony Castino, "Human Resource Development: Promise or Platitude?" *Personnel Administrator,* November 1981, pp. 25–27.

   Richard M. Vosburgh, "The Annual Human Resource Review (A Career Planning System)," *Personnel Journal,* October 1980, pp. 830–837.

5. M. Jelinek, *Career Management for the Individual and the Organization* (Chicago: St. Clair Press, 1979).

   J. W. Walter, "Let's Get Realistic About Career Paths," *Human Resource Management,* Fall 1976, pp. 2–7.

   H. L. Wellbank, D. T. Hall, M. A. Morgan and W. C. Hamner, "Planning Job Progression for Effective Career Development and Human Resources Management," *Personnel,* March–April 1978, pp. 54–64.

6. R. E. Hastings, "Career Development: Maximizing Options," *Personnel Administrator,* May 1978, pp. 58–61.

7. For an extensive discussion of CDPs and career issues related to males and females in organizations, see R. S. Schuler, "Male and Female Routes to Managerial Success," *Personnel Administrator,* February 1979, pp. 35–38.

8. Albert R. Griffith, "Career Development: What Organizations Are Doing About It," *Personnel,* March–April 1980, pp. 63–69.

J. Van Mannen and E. Schein, "Career Developments," in J. R. Hackman and J. L. Sattle, eds. *Improving Life at Work* (Santa Monica, Calif.: Goodyear, 1977).

James F. Wolf and Robert N. Bacher, "Career Negotiation: Trading Off Employee and Organizational Needs," *Personnel,* March–April 1981, pp. 53–59.

9. Donald Grass, "A Guide to R & D Career Pathing," *Personnel Journal,* April 1979, pp. 227–231.

Eugene E. Jennings, "How to Develop Your Management Talent Internally," *Personnel Administrator,* July 1981, pp. 20–23.

Carol Krueoff, "Careers: When Less Is More," *Washington Post,* July 21, 1981, sec. B, p. 5.

William T. McCaffrey, "Career Versus Upward Mobility," *Personnel Administrator,* May 1981, pp. 81–87.

10. Wellbank et al., p. 55.

11. Ibid.

12. Jerry E. Bishop, "The Personal and Business Costs of 'Job Burnout,'" *Wall Street Journal,* December 1980, pp. 33, 37.

Robert S. Greenberger, "How 'Burnout' Affects Corporate Managers and Their Performance," *Wall Street Journal,* April 23, 1981, p. 1.

13. Sandy Graham, "Macbeth Lands Top Scotland Job; Wife Viewed as Motivating Force," *Wall Street Journal,* March 26, 1981, p. 29.

Susan Harrigan, "For Managers, Stress May Be An Addiction," *Wall Street Journal,* March 26, 1981, p. 29.

Bruce Horovitz, "Suicide: An Executive Suite Hazard?" *Industry Week,* March 9, 1981, pp. 40–44.

Robert Kreitner, Steven D. Wood, and Glenn M. Friedman, "Warning: Your Job May Be Killing You," *Business,* January–February 1981, pp. 2–6.

Berkeley Rice, "Can Companies Kill?" *Psychology Today,* June 1981, pp. 78–85.

14. Arthur P. Brief, "How to Manage Mangerial Stress," *Personnel,* September–October 1980, pp. 25–30.

15. W. C. Duemer, N. F. Walker, and J. C. Quick, "Improving Work Life Through Effective Performance Planning," *Personnel Administrator,* July 1978, pp. 23–26.

16. F. H. Cassell, "The Increasing Complexity of Retirement Decisions," *MSU Business Topics,* Winter 1978, pp. 15–24.

Phil Farish, "Pair Potpourri," *Personnel Administrator,* December 1980, pp. 18–20.

Paul F. Hagstrom, "The Older Worker: A Travelers Insurance Companies' Case Study," *Personnel Administrator,* October 1981, pp. 41–44.

Morgan Lyons, "The Older Employee as a Resource Issue for Personnel," *Personnel Journal,* March 1981, pp. 178–186.

Thomas McCarroll, "Rehiring Retirees," *New York Times,* November 22, 1981, sec. F, p. 8.

Mary Zippo, "Roundup," *Personnel,* January–February 1980, pp. 65–70.

17. S. A. Culbert, *The Organization Trap and How to Get Out of It* (New York: Basic Books, 1974).

18. "The Luck Factor at Work," *Working Woman,* October 1981, pp. 75–78.

19. Shirley Sloan Faber, *Family Weekly,* January 18, 1981, p. 11.

20. Ibid.

21. "The Consulting Springboard," *Business Week,* August 17, 1981, pp. 101–104.

22. E. H. Schein, "How to Break in the College Graduate," *Harvard Business Review* 42 (1964):70.

23. D. E. Berlew and D. T. Hall, "Some Determinants of Early Managerial Success," Working Paper #81–64 (Cambridge, Mass.: Sloan School of Management, MIT, 1964).

R. A. Webber, "Career Problems of Young Managers," *California Management Review* 4 (1976):19–33.

24. J. H. Conley, J. M. Hueghi, and R. L. Minter, *Perspectives on Administrative Communication* (Dubuque, Iowa: Kendall/Hunt, 1976), p. 172.

William J. Morin, "The 4 Interviewer Breeds: How to Tame Them," *The New York Times Recruitment Survey,* October 11, 1981, pp. 59, 62.

James T. Yenckel, "Careers: Facing the Interview," *Washington Post,* October 20, 1981, Sec. D, p. 5.

25. Sherry Chastain, "On the Job: The Winning Interview," *Winning the Salary Game: Salary Negotiations for Women,* eds., Diane Littman, Connie Siegel (New York: Wiley, 1980).

26. Irving Janis and Dan Wheeler, "Thinking Clearly About Career Choices," *Psychology Today,* May 1978, pp. 67–76, 121–122.

27. "Managers Who Are No Longer Entrepreneurs," *Business Week,* June 20, 1980, pp. 74–82.

John J. Gabarro and John P. Kotter, "Managing Your Boss," *Harvard Business Review,* January–February 1980, pp. 92–100.

Betty Lehan Harragan, "Outwitting the Impossible Boss," *Savvy,* December 1980, p. 22.

Michael Korda, "The Woman Who Wants to Succeed Ought to Appear to Be in Charge," *New York Times,* September 4, 1977, pp. 1, 10.

James T. Yenckel, "Careers: Tell It to the Boss," *Washington Post,* May 5, 1981, sec. B, p. 5.

28. "Living With the New Guidelines on Sexual Harassment," *People and Business,* July 1981, p. 3.

29. Ibid.

30. Ibid.

31. Christopher Wellisz, "Darker Days for College Grads," *The New York Times National Recruitment Survey,* October 11, 1981, pp. 44, 50. Copyright 1981 by The New York Times Company. Reprinted by permission.

32. Ibid.

Improving the Work Environment

Chapter 16
Improving Productivity and
Quality of Work Life

Chapter 17
Improving Safety and Health

Chapter Outline

Critical Issues in Improving Productivity and QWL

Productivity and Quality of Work Life
The Importance and Purposes of QWL and Productivity
Relationships of QWL and Productivity

Programs for QWL Improvement
Quality Circles
Semiautonomous Work Groups
Organization Restyling
The Tarrytown Project—A Case Example in QWL Improvement

Programs for Productivity Improvements
Task Changes
Automation
Office Design
Delta: The World's Most Profitable Airline—A Case Example in Productivity
Improvement

CHAPTER 16

Improving Productivity and Quality of Work Life

Evaluating QWL and Productivity Programs
QWL Programs
Productivity Programs

Facing the Critical Issues in Improving QWL and Productivity

Summary

Key Concepts

Discussion Questions

Case

For Your Career

Endnotes

Personnel in the News

Managers Invite Workers to Help Them Call The Plays

BALTIMORE—To a small but rapt audience, Pete Freeman was describing the way Sperry Univac got workers and supervisors at its St. Paul defense systems plant to sit down together and solve problems mutually.

"It's a very, very difficult process, said Freeman, director of organization effectiveness. "Because as supervisors become leaders of action teams, they have to give up being autocrats. Employees, for their part, have to speak up. But it works. For the first time, we had computer programmers and users of programs thinking together—and for the first time, programmers saw what their programs were being used for."

It was just the sort of practical example that the personnel managers, labor leaders, and consultants had come to hear: an encounter with that notorious beast known as the quality circle. (Dave Hage, Minneapolis Star, November 19, 1981, page 1-C.)

Better Output

You can obtain productivity increases while making organizations into better places for people to work, according to TRW's Paul Hubert. He told the American Management Association's annual Human Resource Conference some people believe that one is achieved at the expense of the other, but this has not been the case at his company and cited cases to back his point. The key is to do things which will achieve both, he said. Many ideas and programs are useful: gains-sharing plans, improved systems and procedures, automated work teams and the like. The important point, Hubert said, is to keep expected results in mind. TRW experiences which he cited:

- *A long-established nonunion plant with 100 employees was changed in 1973 to put all employees on a salaried basis. Time clocks were discarded. Job classifications were reduced from 42 to five. A team-performance gains-sharing plan was established. The plant consistently has improved its output by five percent a year. Sales have increased by 13 percent a year and absenteeism went down by a third and has stayed at that level.*

- *A new plant was set up in 1975 to make blades and vanes for jet engines. The 160 employees were set up in work teams. They do their own production planning and cost control work. Employees are paid on the basis of the number of skills they have and the degree of proficiency they demonstrate rather than on the particular job they do. In mid 1977 the operation was redesigned and expanded to double production and performance levels were brought up to the former level in three months. (Phil Farish, reprinted with permission from the June 1980 issue of Personnel Administrator, page 19. Copyright 1980 by The American Society for Personnel Administration, 30 Park Drive, Berea, Ohio 44017.)*

Productivity: The Search for the Old Magic

When complex ideas make that big leap from the textbook to the political theater, something is often lost in the translation. So it seems to be with the lagging growth in American productivity, a problem that in some circles has become a symbol of the decline of all our basic virtues.

Shrouded in the politics is a real problem, experts say, that will continue to have a profound effect on the job market for the rest of the century. While much of the discussion about improving productivity has issues such as tax incentives and de-regulation, about which there are great disputes, there is general agreement that much of the answer to productivity problems can be found at the level of the individual company. "I believe that we top managers bear the major responsibility for poor productivity," said John F. Donnelly, chairman of Donnelly Mirrors Inc., a manufacturer of automotive-glass equipment.

American workers continue to be among the most productive in the world, but improvement lags. Productivity, literally a measure of output per hour, improved 14.2 percent in the private-business sector during the 1970's, less than half the increase of 33.2 percent in the 1960's or 37.1 percent for the 1950's, said Samuel M. Ehrenhalt, regional commissioner of the Bureau of Labor Statistics. In the 1940's the increase was 29.9 percent and in the depression-era 1930's, 16 percent.

Regardless of who is responsible for the lag in productivity, business managers are looking for new ways to do things, and the job seeker who can help—either by finding those new ways, by being able to adjust to them or by helping others to do so—will be at a distinct advantage.

While much of this effort is still in the early stages, and Howard Risher, a vice president of William M. Mercer Inc., a management-consultant concern, companies are starting to look for managers who can blend technical skill with an understanding of how to get people to work better. "The productivity-improvement guy is going to be one who has jumped around," Mr. Risher added, "who has spent some time in engineering and in the production process and also has a basic knowledge of the people implications of what's going on out there."

At the heart of this is the seemingly simple idea that you can get more out of workers by paying more attention to them and making them more a part of the process. "The workers in both the private and public sectors are a virtually untapped natural resource of ingenuity and enthusiasm," said Thomas R. Donahue, secretary-treasurer of the A.F.L.-C.I.O. (Michael Oreskes, The New York Times National Recruitment Survey, October 11, 1981, p. 6. © 1981 by the New York Times Company. Reprinted by permission.)

The Times Call for Revised Game Plan

BALTIMORE—There was a time in U.S. industrial circles when managers had three ways to motivate workers: fear, company loyalty and the old-fashioned work ethic.

But time and change have conspired to force a new era of labor relations on U.S. industry, and people on both sides find that the shifting ground leaves them unsure of where they stand.

Referring to a variety of participatory management programs, one leading thinker in the field noted: "You're not talking about some new technology here. You're talking about changes in institutions and the way human beings get along."

Droping productivity and foreign competition have pressed the giants of U.S. industry—auto and steel producers in particular—to get more out of their workers. Revolutions in technology are forcing similar changes on high-tech companies such as Honeywell and Martin Marietta Aerospace.

At a recent national conference here to discuss work life conditions, representatives of no less a corporation than General Motors and no less a union than the United Steelworkers of America told 450 labor-relations professionals that a new era of work place collaboration—"quality of work life"—is upon us. (Dave Hage, Minneapolis Star, November 19, 1981, p. 1-C.)

It's getting easier and easier to obtain quotes about productivity and the quality of work life (QWL). That's because one (productivity) is seen as a real problem facing American industry and the other (QWL) is seen as a major solution to the problem.

Together the quotations support this problem-solution relationship between productivity and QWL. They also indicate that effective management of human resources is the essence of QWL. Yet QWL is not the only way to effectively manage human resources and increase productivity as the final quotation describes. Nevertheless, QWL through its basic philosophy of labor-management participation and involvement is receiving the bulk of attention today. Consequently this is the time for the personnel manager to be at the forefront of productivity improvement. It's also the time for you to plan your career so you can focus on techniques to improve the quality of an organization's work life and its productivity. By the end of this chapter, you should have several techniques you can recommend to an organization. In addition you should be able to effectively address the Critical Issues facing personnel managers.

CRITICAL ISSUES IN IMPROVING PRODUCTIVITY AND QWL

The four major Critical Issues identified by our personnel managers are:

1. *What can be done to increase productivity? Can companies really depend on their people to change and help out?*
2. *Is the issue of quality of work life really fundamental to understanding why the United States is facing a productivity crisis?*
3. *Can companies in the United States really learn from the Japanese? Is the quality circle concept one companies should adopt? Can companies use Theory Z Management?*
4. *What other ways can companies improve productivity without increasing employee participation as in QWL programs?*

Declining U.S. productivity is a dilemma increasingly discussed in executive suites and by almost all personnel managers. Reversing the decline and improving productivity is thus a major goal for many organizations and their personnel managers. Yet one of the most perplexing aspects of improving productivity is defining and measuring it. While almost no one challenges productivity's most basic, traditional *definition—output divided by input—*the debate enters in deciding what *is* output and what *is* input. At first glance, however, it appears impossible to *measure* the output or input of a nursing home, a bank, a big city orchestra, or any of the thousands of service and professional organizations. It appears equally impossible to measure the work that individual employees do in these types of organizations. At second glance, organizations are discovering that the task is not impossible just difficult. Furthermore, they are discovering that measures of productivity have to be tailored to each organization. Thus while we leave it to each organization to measure its productivity, **productivity** is defined here as the output of an individual, group, or organization divided by the input needed by the individual, group, or organization for the creation of the outputs.

PRODUCTIVITY AND QUALITY OF WORK LIFE

Quality of work life, while quite different from the notion of productivity, shares a similar degree of elusiveness in definition and measurement. Nevertheless, **QWL** is defined here as a situation in which all members of the organization, through appropriate channels of communication set up for this purpose, have some say about the design of their jobs in particular and the work environment in general. In this kind of participative and responsive organizational climate, suggestions, questions, and criticism that might lead to improvement of any kind are encouraged and welcomed. In such a setting, creative discontent is viewed as a manifestation of constructive caring about the organization rather than destructive griping. Management encouragement of such feelings of involvement often leads to ideas and actions for upgrading of operational effectiveness and efficiency as well as environmental enhancement. Increased productivity thus is likely to result as a natural byproduct.[1]

QWL is also improved when employee rights are respected.

The Importance and Purposes of QWL and Productivity

Just as QWL and productivity are separate concerns for EPM, each serves separate purposes and has its own importance for organizations.

QWL. The attention now being paid to the quality of work life reflects the growing importance being attached to it. It is clear that a substantial number of workers are unhappy with their jobs and are demanding more meaningful work. Workers are beginning to demand improvements in both economic and noneconomic outcomes from their jobs. The importance of noneconomic rewards is increasing relative to the importance of economic ones, especially among white-collar and highly educated

It is important to remember that all workers are not unhappy.

workers. Thus, there is a need for improvement, and considerable room for improvement, in the quality of work life of many contemporary American workers.[2]

The importance of QWL is reflected in the effects of its absence.[3] Some people attribute part of the present productivity slowdown in the United States to deficiencies in the quality of work life and to changes in the needs and values that employees consider important. People are demanding greater control and involvement in the jobs. They don't want to be treated as a cog in a machine. When they aren't treated as a cog, but rather with respect, by being given a chance to voice their opinions and by being given more self-control, employees respond favorably:

> "[General Motor's quality of work life] program was initially explained to us that it would make a worker feel as important when he walked through the door of a plant as he felt before he walked in there. It dignified him. It made him feel important where he's working as well as in his community. Why should walking through the door of a factory—or whatever—change you suddenly into a nothing, when you're someone?"[4]

But not all QWL projects are meant exclusively to improve conditions for the employee:

> The "blue collar blues" may promote the adoption and diffusion of innovative work designs in a wide range of industries, from blue collar manufacturing work to white collar and service work and in both the private and the public sectors, but a major reason companies are trying work improvement projects is competition. Another is the changing expectations of workers, whose consciousness of quality of work life issues continues to rise. Another is the implicit threat of legislation that might require workers to participate in the governance of private industry.[5]

Productivity. An equal if not greater level of attention is being paid to productivity since companies and managers are evaluated by the level of profitability of the company. Since the level of productivity is generally a major factor in determining profitability, ways to improve productivity are always of interest to companies. This is especially true now, however, as the rate of productivity growth in the United States is declining while at the same time it is rising in other countries. Thus if the United States increases its productivity, it should become more competitive in the international as well as national markets.[6]

Increasing productivity is also seen as important because more Americans are realizing that their standard of living is actually declining. Furthermore, if the current trend continues, you and your children will live less well than your parents, the first time this would have ever happened in America.

In summary, interest in the quality of work life and productivity usually focuses on techniques for changing the organization in order to improve employee satisfaction and productivity and to reduce turnover and absenteeism. Since all of these are beneficial, it would be good if they can be attained together. It appears as if this is possible. In the words of Gundy Gundvaldson, the late president of the northwest region of the International Woodworkers of America:

> The workers see many ways of improving the quality of a product and improving productivity at the same time. If a management climate can be developed in which workers are encouraged and rewarded for taking an interest in worksite improvement; if communication structures are set up to invite meaningful participation in arriving at work-related decisions; if it stimulates a reduction in absenteeism; if the

Exhibit 16.1
Programs for Productivity and Quality of Work
Life Improvements

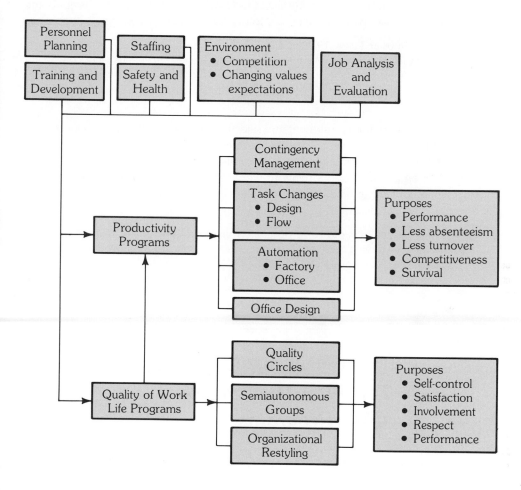

quality of the product improves; if the safety record improves; if the worksite becomes more pleasant; if the workers begin to feel a sense of ownership, then a quality of work life project is a success.[7]

Even though productivity and QWL improvements can be achieved together, they can be achieved independently.[8] How they are treated in this chapter is illustrated in Exhibit 16.1. Note that although QWL can influence productivity, many other programs can also. Consequently, those programs are discussed in the section on productivity improvement. QWL programs designed to improve QWL are discussed in a separate section of QWL improvement. However, both sets of programs are critical for effective personnel management.

Relationships of QWL and Productivity

QWL and productivity have a significant influence on several personnel activities. The consequences of a low QWL are aptly illustrated by the following quotations about the Tarrytown, New York, plant of General Motors before its QWL program began:

> In the late 1960s and early 1970s, the Tarrytown plant suffered from much absenteeism and labor turnover. Warnings, disciplinary layoffs and firings were commonplace. At certain times, as many as 2,000 labor grievances were on the docket.[9]

Staffing.   Naturally, the recruitment and selection activities of the plant were directly affected by these occurrences. "Because of the high labor turnover, the plant was hiring a large number of young people" who were not so conscientious about their work as older employees. Labor relations were difficult at best in this environment of mistrust. Union officers and committee members battled constantly with management. As one union officer describes it,

> "we were always trying to solve yesterday's problems. There was no trust and everybody was putting out fires. The company's attitude was to employ a stupid robot with hands and no face."[10]

PERSONNEL IN ACTION

CEOs Tell Why They Support QWL Programs

There is universal agreement that participation cannot be created through top-down imposition or executive fiat. But, as William Ouchi, author of *Theory Z*, writes: "Ultimately, the process of organizational change cannot succeed without the direct and personal support of the top person in the hierarchy." The degree of involvement depends on management style: while some CEO's have chosen to give the go-ahead and demonstrate a willingness to "let it happen," others lead the way.

AT&T's Chairman Charles L. Brown sent a memo last year to presidents of all Bell System operating companies announcing a long-term commitment to QWL: "We are dealing with nothing less than management style here . . . I am speaking of an insistence on your part that the principles involved be tried out— and 'tolerated' where they cause waves—with the end objective of a gradual spread to the whole organization."

Xerox's President David T. Kerns is circulating an in-house videotape in which he candidly lays out the company's strategies, capital investment plans and competitive threats. He states: "I pledge to you that management of this company at all levels will listen to you and put your ideas to work."

Congressional Representative Stanley Lundine, former mayor of Jamestown, NY, initiated cooperative efforts there: "As the Mayor of Jamestown, I was actively involved in the creation and development of . . . a community-wide labor/management committee . . . By making work in the manufacturing sector more efficient and rewarding . . . the people of Jamestown were able to make the most of their human resources and turn their economy around."

Sidney Harman, Chairman of Harman International Industries Inc., facilitated ground-breaking programs: "We cannot hope to see [QWL programs] truly develop if we begin only at the blue-collar level.

This material must work at the level of middle management, must work at the level of top management, and it is my personal experience, and it is my conviction . . . that, in the end, the principal beneficiary of such programs as this is, in fact, the person at the top . . . he discovers . . . you don't have to be right all the time . . ."

CEO of Ford Motor Company, Canada, Roy F. Bennett says: "Employee involvement is not a substitute for good management or labor practices . . . It is a program that requires a tremendous amount of thought, ground-laying processes and time . . . the greatest likelihood of mistakes being made is in people charging into it too quickly and expecting immediate returns . . . The '60s were probably the MBO decade. The '80s are likely to be the decade of employee involvement in QWL . . . It's a natural evolution from MBO to involving everyone in reaching those objectives."

Lincoln National Life Insurance Company's CEO Ian M. Rolland describes his continuing belief in QWL: "[We] introduced a new style of management we call Quality Commitment . . . in 1978 . . . I felt at that time that it would be our most important management effort for the next five years. Now, as we consider our experience to date, I am even more convinced of its importance. We have placed in motion a process based on the belief that all work can be done better by the continuous application of creative thinking, problem solving and energetic job performance. That is what we believe 'productivity' really means."

(Reprinted from the October 1981 issue of *Training, The Magazine of Human Resources Development,* p. 57. Copyright 1981, Lakewood Publications, Minneapolis, MN [612] 333–0471. All rights reserved.)

Job Analysis and Job Evaluation.　All of these consequences eventually prompted the company to engage in management and organizational development. This resulted in many jobs being enriched. To the extent that job enrichment techniques are used to improve QWL, job analysis and job evaluation are affected. After working in a job enrichment program, one employee commented,

> I like branch coding but because you get such a variety of work, it is hard to make your efficiency. I think the [basic job classification] should be raised.[11]

Personnel Planning.　QWL projects also influence personnel planning. Since turnover and absenteeism may be reduced by these projects, human resource needs may also be reduced. Training needs may increase, however, at least initially. This is especially so for supervisors who are having to adjust to the new role of the supervisor as a consequence of QWL programs. A nice illustration of these implications is shown in the *Personnel in Action* insert, "A View from the Union Hall."

Training and Development.　It is often the first-level supervisor whose cooperation is most needed to ensure the success of QWL programs and whose role is often most changed by them:

> Suddenly we asked foremen to develop a rather different set of skills. We wanted them to be "good managers of people." Instead of people receiving discipline from the supervisor, the new climate emphasized self-discipline. We redefined the foreman's role rapidly, and this created problems during the change. The problems were exacerbated by the fact that formal training for foremen was traditionally less important than on-the-job training, so they tended to be reluctant to take courses at first.
>
> Yet in the new circumstances foremen needed considerable training to regard themselves as information-gatherers, as aides to the employees, as teachers and

consultants, rather than as bosses. And in many cases the attitude change was only partial, stimulated and, at the same time, hampered because it was forced by pressure from employees and management, rather than from the foremen's own convictions.[12]

Safety and Health.   As discussed in more detail in Chapter 17 on "Improving Safety and Health," many programs to improve QWL are also capable of improving occupational safety and health. In large part this results from workers, as a consequence of QWL programs such as job redesign, being more involved and motivated. Often workers have accidents due to the boredom experienced on the job. QWL programs can reduce this boredom and, therefore, reduce those accidents.

PERSONNEL IN ACTION

A View from the Union Hall

"There are still some supervisors from the old school who like to hold a club, but we are past the halfway mark toward the new lifestyle."

That is the assessment of the new foreman through the eyes of a union man, Raymond Calore, president of United Automobile Workers Local 664 at the General Motors assembly plant in Tarrytown, N.Y.

"A supervisor is now a supervisor; he is not a boss," he said, a change Mr. Calore feels represents a major overhaul at G.M. in its view of how to increase productivity and improve quality at the plant.

"It used to be that the foreman would say, 'This is the job and here's how you do it, or out the door you go,'" Mr. Calore said. "Today, the good ones come in and say, 'This is the job we have to do, here's how the guys in engineering have planned for us to do it, let's start out this way, and you let me know if you have any problems or suggestions on how to improve it.'"

As Mr. Calore sees it, the new approach is the only one that makes sense at a plant where more than 75 percent of the 1,200 most recently hired employees have at least two years of college background. "We have some very talented people on the line now be-

cause they can earn better money than at jobs like teaching," he said.

The search for a more cooperative formula for turning out cars with a minimum of defects and delays has been accompanied by a new attitude toward discipline. An employee who years ago would have been summarily sent home for arriving late is now likely to be put to work and later taken aside and asked for an explanation. If there is a personal problem, such as a sick child, the supervisor may well adjust the employee's hours until the illness is past.

"They recognize that workers today may have other priorities, such as family," Mr. Calore said. "We no longer try to determine who is right or wrong. We try to find the problem."

What about the old-fashioned supervisors who still prefer giving orders to cooperative efforts? Eventually, Mr. Calore said, the higher absenteeism and poorer quality work in their departments focuses negative attention on them. "Things are changing slowly," he said.

(From *The New York Times*, May 17, 1981, p. 4-F. © 1981 by The New York Times Company. Reprinted by permission.)

Union-Management Relations.   Unions also have an important responsibility in QWL projects:

> We as a union knew that our primary job was to protect the worker and improve his economic life. But times had changed and we began to realize we had a broader

obligation, which was to help the workers become more involved in decisions affecting their own jobs, to get their ideas, and to help them to improve the whole quality of life at work beyond the paycheck.[13]

Not all unions, however, embrace the notion that workers are concerned with QWL issues or that unions should be a party to QWL projects with management. As Thomas Donahue, executive assistant to the late AFL-CIO president George Meany, said:

> We do not seek to be a partner in management, to be, most likely, the junior partner in success and the senior partner in failure. We do not want to blur in any way the distinction between the respective roles of management and labor in the plant.[14]

You may be concluding from these statements that there is no uniform union position or that not all unions represent the best interests of the workers. This may be true, but you should remember that many job enrichment projects have been less than successful, although some for reasons unrelated to worker acceptance of QWL principles and ideals.[15] Also consider that of the more than 5 million organizations in the United States, there have been only about 500 QWL projects.[16] Thus it becomes apparent that there is no uniform management position on QWL programs either. Moreover, since unions represent only about 25 percent of all employees, the responsibility for initiating and implementing QWL projects rests more directly on management. QWL projects may require not just that these personnel activities be changed or modified to fit the situation but also that they be shared with line managers, supervisors, employees, and employee representatives. For example, work groups may begin to make some recruitment, selection, and compensation decisions. The personnel manager must be there to assist the work groups with these decisions, even though the work group may initially seem to be reducing the power and responsibility of that manager.[17]

PROGRAMS FOR QWL IMPROVEMENT

Programs for QWL improvements range from those limited to only certain parts of an organization to the entire organization. What they all have in common is some element of increased participation by workers in decisions that were previously considered "management decisions." What typically vary in QWL programs are the *scope* of decisions in which workers are allowed to participate and the *extent* to which they actually make the decisions.[18] Workers may only provide input (limited final decision influence) to a manager who makes the final decision, or workers may be allowed to make the final decision (extensive final decision influence).

In general, the more varied and vast the scope of issues in which workers participate and the more decision-making power they have, the greater is the impact on the entire organization, the more the organization is characterized by a nontraditional, decentralized structure (style). (Refer to Chapter 2). If the organization is characterized by a traditional centralized structure (style), the change to the nontraditional structure requires a tremendous change in style of management (from point B to point A shown on Exhibit 16.2). Nonetheless, movement along the line from B to A is what usually occurs as organizations become more deeply committed to QWL. Representative of varying levels of commitment are three groups of QWL programs or activities shown in Exhibit 16.2:

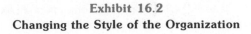

Exhibit 16.2
Changing the Style of the Organization

- ▪ Quality Circles
- ▪ Semiautonomous Groups
- ▪ Organizational Restyling

Remember that all employees do not prefer to participate in decision making.

Since each is important, all three are discussed in detail. Before discussing these, however, it is important to point out that there are limits on the extent to which participation in organizations can be increased. Indeed, there are limits on its effectiveness in organizations. The effectiveness of participation in decision making (such as found in quality circle programs) depends upon several factors: (1) the need of the employees for participation in decision making; (2) The type and extent of decisions in which employees participate—that is, do employees decide only issues related to their jobs or to the total organization? (3) The amount of information the organization is willing to share with employees; (4) The willingness of supervisors and managers to allow their employees to participate; and (5) The availability of problems and situations for which decisions are necessary. Other potential factors influencing the appropriateness of participation and the topics in which employees may participate are shown in Exhibit 16.3.

Quality Circles

QCs allow employees to identify and solve productivity problems.

Quality Circles (QCs) are an innovative management concept that helped contribute to Japan's dynamic industrial growth. The concept amounts to a targeted philosophy that taps a company's own work force as its most valuable resource because it is often the most qualified to identify and solve work-related problems.

Since Honeywell and Lockheed first introduced the circles in America, more and more corporations have developed similar programs. Among the more than 500 companies using QCs are Bethlehem Steel, Westinghouse, Ford, Solar Turbine, Hughes Aircraft, General Electric, Boeing, Martin Marietta, RCA, Control Data, and

Exhibit 16.3
Topics Appropriate for Participation and Potential Constraints
on Their Use

Topics
  Performance appraisal
  Compensation
  Job assignment/job design
  Safety
  Employment decisions (hiring, firing)
  Work schedules
  Stress management strategies
  Change

Potential Constraints
  Limited change frequency
  Extensive rules and procedures
  Current leadership styles and beliefs
  Top management preferences
  Willingness to change—management and employees
  Personnel department climate and leadership
  Information access and availability

General Motors. A great many more are seriously considering installing programs as a means of obtaining greater productivity, quality, and morale.[19]

QC Teams. A **quality circle** consists of seven to ten people from the same work area who meet regularly to define, analyze, and solve quality and related problems in their area. Membership is strictly voluntary, and meetings are usually held once a week for an hour. During the group's initial meetings, members are trained in problem-solving techniques borrowed from group dynamics, industrial engineering, and quality control. These techniques include brainstorming, pareto analysis, cause-and-effect analysis, histograms, control charts, stratification, and scatter diagrams.[20]

QCs and Unions. According to Dan Dewar, past president of the International Association of Quality Circles in Midwest City, Oklahoma, unions have not opposed the introduction of quality circles and he sees no reason why they should in the future. The fact that participation is voluntary forestalls possible union objections. If participation were mandatory, the union might decide to make the circles a bargaining issue, reasoning that workers were being ordered to do something that was leading to greater profits for the company. "One way the company can get into the union's good graces is to explain the circles to the union before they are actually implemented, and invite it to send a representative to a meeting of the steering committee," Dewar suggests.[21]

Supervisor as Team Leader. In many instances, the first-line supervisor runs the team meeting. In essence she or he acts as the facilitator. This is important in terms of the existing organizational authority pattern as well as creating better communications

Good communication skills are critical for supervisors in QCs.

between the supervisor and employees. The team leader undergoes a basic training course (often given by personnel) in group dynamics, problem solving and other techniques, while members often receive preliminary training on establishing priorities and brainstorming.[22]

Results of QCs. Do workers really have the expertise to improve production and work life?

There are a few spectacular examples where knowledge of day-to-day production intricacies benefited companies enormously. At the General Motors Packard Electric plant in Warren, Ohio, creation of worker-management teams to advise on construction of four factories resulted in a $13.5 million cost reduction and a $4.5 million reduction in inventory of supplies; it also achieved the lowest injury, grievance, and absenteeism rates in the division.

In just one example from the steel industry, Bethlehem Steel's Los Angeles works reduced operating costs by $225,000 over two months after worker-management teams identified ways to exploit mill downtime for production. At the Westinghouse Electronic Corporation Defense and Electronic Systems Center near Baltimore, a purchasing department quality circle noticed waste in the way vendors were sending supplies and saved the plant $636,000.[23]

Essentials for QCs. There are several characteristics essential for quality circles. For example,

Personnel helps ensure these essentials for QCs are provided.

- The role of the facilitator is the most important aspect of a QC program. Whoever fills the function must be able to work with people at all levels of the organization, be creative and flexible, and be aware of the political atmosphere of the organization.

- Management must support the quality circle program. If a union is involved, it also should support the program, and its support and views should be solicited.

- The program is voluntary for employees, but management should encourage the establishment of circles.

- Within established limits, circle members must feel free to work on problems of their choosing.

- Facilitators must keep management informed of what the circles are working on and on their progress.

- Quality, not quantity, should be the first consideration. The program will expand as word-of-mouth spreads success stories.

- A successful program must adhere to the concept and principles of the program. One of the facilitator's most crucial tasks is to see that circles follow correct procedures. Once the circles forego using the procedures, they become non-productive and eventually dissolve.[24]

Semiautonomous Work Groups

Although quality circles bring individuals together, it is for a relatively short period of time and for the sole purpose of generating and evaluating ideas. Individuals can also be brought together and used for longer periods of time and for many purposes. This is the essence of semiautonomous work groups.

> A human group is a collection of individuals (1) who have significantly interdependent relations with each other, (2) who perceive themselves as a group by reliably distinguishing members from nonmembers, (3) whose group identity is recognized by nonmembers, (4) who have differentiated roles in the group as function of expectations from themselves, other group members, and nongroup members, and (5) who, as group members acting alone or in concert, have significantly interdependent relations with other groups.[25]

This definition of a human group describes what generally happens in effective semiautonomous work groups. This is because individuals in these work groups work together to produce final products or major segments of final products. In addition to making a product, they make a number of employment decisions partially independent of the personnel department (hence the name **semiautonomous work groups**). For example, they make decisions on how to discipline their colleagues, what salary increases members should receive, and even who should be hired and who should be terminated. The General Foods' dog food plant is an example of where this has been done.

The General Foods Dog Food Plant.   Despite several turbulent years in adjusting to the semiautonomous work group concept (especially by the supervisors), the General Foods dog food plant in Topeka, Kansas, has been an apparent success.[26] Overhead costs are low and productivity and satisfaction are high. There is only one level of direct supervision in this plant with 250 employees. Work groups (teams) exist both in the office and the factory. Teams perform their own maintenance, quality control, warehousing, and hiring of replacements. The personnel manager helps with skills training, problem solving, and corporate-level coordination. Discipline is handled by peer pressure.

Efforts and results similar to those at the dog food plant have been reported at a General Motors battery plant in Georgia, at the Manufacturer's Life Insurance Company in Toronto, and at the famous Volvo Kalmar plant in Sweden. Although all of these examples are small plants (less than 1,000 employees) and nonunion, there are a growing number of larger unionized plants using the semiautonomous work group design. These plants, such as at Buick and Oldsmobile, are discussed in the labor-management chapters (18 and 19).

At Ford Quality is Job 1.

Organizational Restyling

Beyond improving QWL through individual and group based changes is a change in the total organization. Such an all-encompassing change can restyle the organization.

Honeywell's Corporate Restyling.   While quality circles and semiautonomous work groups go a long way in improving QWL, they represent limited changes to the organization itself. Far more extensive and dramatic are QWL efforts that combine several programs and that have a major impact on the way an organization treats its people and regards its people.[27] QWL efforts that have this type of impact do what amounts to a restyling of the corporation. An excellent example of a restyling effort is the one at Honeywell emphasizing quality circles. In addition to the use of quality circles, Honeywell is adopting many organizational concepts described by "Theory Z" management.[28]

Theory Z Management.   Since Theory Z management is currently an approach to QWL being used in many corporations such as Honeywell and Westinghouse, it is useful to describe its characteristics.[29] Theory Z essentially represents a modification of more traditional American management (**Theory A**) using some of the ideas from traditional Japanese management (**Theory J**). The characteristics of these two are illustrated in Exhibit 16.4. Theory Z essentially falls in the middle of Theory J and Theory A. The result is

- Employment of a longer-term nature, informally stated
- A relatively slow promotion and evaluation period
- Some "wandering around" of career paths through different functions in the organization
- Extensive planning data and accounting data but used for purposes of information and collective decision making rather than for control
- Decisions made on the basis of sound data and on whether they "fit" the entire organization rather than just one subpart
- Sharing of responsibility for making and implementing decisions although often guided by one individual

As do the Japanese, we can benefit by learning from others.

As with Theory J and Theory A, in practice Theory Z takes many forms. It is adapted not only to the American culture but also to the unique styles and needs of each management and corporation. This modification of Theory J recognizes the fact that the cultures of the United States and Japan are quite different. Thus it is really impossible to do here exactly what is done in Japan. The advice from Richard Pascale reinforces the importance of this point and cautions U.S. firms against wholesale adoption of Japanese practices. His advice is presented in the *Personnel in Action* insert.

Exhibit 16.4
The Contrast Between Theory J and Theory A Management. Based on W. Ouchi, *Theory Z: How American Business Can Meet the Japanese Challenge* (Reading, Mass.: Addison-Wesley Publishing Company, 1981).

Theory J	Theory A
Lifetime employment	Short-term employment
Slow evaluations and promotions	Rapid evaluations and promotions
Nonspecialized career paths	Specialized career paths
Implicit control mechanisms	Explicit control mechanisms
Collective responsibility	Individual decision making
Holistic concern	Individual responsibility
	Segmented concern

Although an insufficient number of companies have adopted Theory Z to really measure its effectiveness, it appears to be an important and significant alternative to managing human resources with which personnel and line managers must be famliar as they consider approaches to improving productivity as well as QWL.

quality of work life

PERSONNEL IN ACTION

Firms Advised To Do More Than Just Plug In Japan Style

Richard Tanner Pascale is a student and admirer of the Japanese style of management. He believes that the Japanese have much to teach American executives about using ambiguity instead of shoot-from-the-hip candor, emphasizing cooperation and interdependence rather than competition and individualism.

In the last few years many American executives have come to share Pascale's fascination with the Japanese. But the writer, lecturer and consultant is concerned that their interest is too narrow, limited just to the Japanese phenomenon of quality circles.

Quality circles are small groups of workers who informally share ideas on improving production and quality with their bosses. For many American firms, quality circles will be just another management fad, Pascale predicts, because they will start them and change nothing else.

"These things are quick fixes," he said. "A lot of managers see them like electric appliances: They plug them in and they work.

"If you have a desire to change quality by putting in quality circles, but all the systems remain cost-oriented and top management is not participative, you're just going to confuse people . . . You may make matters worse by making people cynical."

For this reason Pascale is skeptical about the chances for success of more than 400 quality circles at Honeywell Inc. James Renier, president of the Honeywell control systems, is a strong advocate of quality circles and a variety of other techniques to change the corporation's management to a more participative style. But Renier's personal management style is characterized as autocratic, Pascale noted.

"Renier's role model to his people is a very powerful signal about the real nature of things in that corporation," Pascale said. "If they see him as a hipshooter, not a good listener, that's a complete countersignal to what they're trying to pull off (with quality circles).

"American managers often try to fix things as though the problem were someone other than themselves."

(Renier, who has never met Pascale, characterized himself as aggressive rather than autocratic.)

An outside consultant's recent report showed that the conclusion shared by Renier's subordinates in some recent interviews was that he's tough, comes on hard at times but that he's generally an evenhanded, people-oriented manager, Renier said.

("While we're learning these techniques (the Japanese style), some of us may lapse into the old methods. I see no benefit on the part of theoreticians criticizing people who are trying to put this into practice.")

In choosing top managers, Pascale complained, American firms put too much emphasis on toughness, attractiveness, charisma and facility with financial data. "In the process," he said, "we pass up a lot of people who are more humble, better listeners, extraordinarily good at getting things done in the trenches . . . They are more Walter Matthaus than Rock Hudsons."

They often are more effective managers, he said, adding: "Our culture blinds us. It makes us believe that a business leader must be decisive or lose face. . . . But in Japan it's considered tacky for a senior manager to stand out."

(Renier said he believes that the quality-circles approach will only work 80 to 90 percent of the time. There are times of crisis, he said, when a manager must make quick, tough decisions.)

Pascale, a lecturer at the Stanford graduate school of business, was in the Twin Cities last week to promote "The Art of Japanese Management," the book he wrote with Anthony Athos.

He observed that Americans often regard management style as an extension of personality, which is not easy to change. Instead, he argued, management style is the way a manager chooses to use his or her time and attention—primarily via the inbasket, telephone and calendar.

If the manager's appointments and calls emphasize year-end profit goals and an old-boy network for hiring, subordinates will get one message. If the manager stresses customer service and a thoughtful, thorough means of hiring and pomoting people, subordinates will get another message.

Pascale's book notes that many of the most successful American corporations—companies like IBM, ITT and Boeing—are led by managers who are more

Japanese than American in their style: low-key, emphasizing participation, human relations and loyalty to company goals.

Americans traditionally have prized individuality, Pascale said, and journalists and professors still behave as though it is the average American's most prized value. "We have this great distrust of our employers intruding or having a hold on us greater than the labor we're exchanging," he said.

He believes that most Americans have a different value system: "Most Americans are rather rootless and rather lonely and rather in search for meaning in their lives. In fact, people create meaning in their work even when their employers don't.

"When a company taps into that with a central value like IBM's 'We stand for service,' when people believe that, it creates a tremendous force for trust and commitment" between workers and their employer.

(Lynda McDonnell, *Minneapolis Tribune*, September 8, 1981, p. 17-A. Reprinted with permission from *The Minneapolis Tribune*.)

The Tarrytown Project—A Case Example in QWL Improvement

The Tarrytown project is QWL program at a General Motors car assembly plant in Tarrytown, New York, that employs more than 3,800 employees.[30] This cooperative project between the union and management began in 1970, when the plant had one of the poorest labor and production records at GM. The project was initiated by the plant manager because it was necessary to make substantial changes in the operations of the plant. The plant workers were asked to participate in making the necessary changes. Although top management was behind the project, many supervisors doubted that the workers could produce useful ideas. Yet according to those supervisors, "We found they did know a lot about their own operations. They made hundreds of suggestions and we adopted many of them."[31]

Management, the union, and the workers continued to cooperate. In 1973, the United Auto Workers and GM explicitly addressed QWL in their contract agreement. This reflected a new atmosphere of trust between the union and the plant management. In 1974 a professional consultant was brought in to conduct joint training programs in problem solving for supervisors and workers, because the project was expanding. Although participation in the project was voluntary, out of 600 workers in two volunteering sections, 95 percent said they wanted to be involved in the project. In 1977 the participation and problem-solving training sessions were launched plantwide. "Each week, 25 different workers reported to the training rooms on Tuesdays, Wednesdays and Thursdays, for nine hours a day."[32] Included in these sessions were discussions of the QWL concept, plant operations, and problem-solving skills. While the employees were in training, the company continued to pay their regular hourly rate of about $7.

Although the Tarrytown project cost approximately $1.6 million, the quality of performance improved substantially, and absenteeism fell from $7\frac{1}{4}$ percent to between 2 and 3 percent. In December 1978 there were 32 grievances on the docket, in contrast to 2,000 in 1971.[33]

Managers can benefit greatly by listening and acting on the ideas of their employees.

It is clear from this project that workers do not desire to take over the management of the operations but that they do want to become involved in pragmatic, immediate, and localized problems and issues. The principles learned from the Tarrytown project and many others conducted in the private and public organizations are numerous.

- Management must be wholly competent in running the company.
- The union must be strong and must be trusted by the members.
- Management, in most instances, has to be the first party to suggest the program.
- QWL should never be used to circumvent the labor-management agreement.
- Top management and union officials should be strongly committed to QWL.
- Middle management and first-line supervisors must be involved, trained, and behind the QWL programs.
- QWL can't be used by management primarily as a way to speed up the workers' pace. Better quality, lower absenteeism and turnover, and better production methods, however, may result from QWL.
- QWL programs should have voluntary participation.
- QWL programs should be started on a limited scale and with flexibility to adapt and change.
- Workers must be trained in group process methods, problem solving, decision making, interpersonal relationships and communication skills.
- QWL programs should not be seen as injections but rather a continuous way of doing things, a new philosophy of labor-management relationships, and a renewed commitment to mutual respect.[34]

PROGRAMS FOR PRODUCTIVITY IMPROVEMENTS

As with QWL, improvements for productivity can represent the results of a wide range of programs as well as untraditional philosophies of how to do things and deal with people in organizations. Here's an example of one such untraditional philosophy:

> "You can't simply sell a program like this, because what you're trying to do is win hearts and minds. You're attempting to change basic assumptions about the way people have traditionally done their jobs. That's not an easy thing to do. It casts individuals in unconventional situations, which makes many people acutely uncomfortable."
>
> Thomas Graham, president and chief executive officer of Jones & Laughlin Steel Corp. (J&L), was speaking from his spacious, well-appointed office in Pittsburgh's Gateway Center. But as his comments suggest, his mind was focused on the company's searing furnaces and incessant production lines.
>
> Specifically, he was discussing J&L's facility at Louisville, Ohio. There, management and labor alike have been struggling with a small portion of a pressing problem for corporate America: withering productivity growth.
>
> Clearly, the dilemma is immense. Its solution involves nothing less than revitalizing that growth—and American industry.
>
> It also transcends getting people to simply "work harder," reminds another Pittsburgh-based executive, Edward A. Loeser, vice president of operations at Rockwell International Corp. Most of the nation's bluecollar and whitecollar workers do work hard, he and others would submit. Productivity's solution, then, lies in harmonizing a company's efforts in as efficient a manner as possible. That is a management task.
>
> There is no one answer to organizing in a way that will improve productivity. Some companies may need to overhaul their entire organization to purge ineffi-

ciencies. Others may need only a strong dose of common sense, a reexamination of selected operations, or a modest fine tuning in order to run with a leaner mix of people, resources, and money.[35]

There are many ways to improve productivity.

Keeping in mind that programs to improve productivity do not have to rest on untraditional philosophies, let us examine what techniques or programs are being implemented to get something useful for less. Note that only a few, select programs or techniques are examined here. There are, however, many ways that organizations can improve productivity including doing all of the personnel activities more effectively. For example, Citizens & Southern National Bank in Georgia completely turned around its operations with a new top management that emphasized a hard-nosed management-by-objectives program.[36] Now "all bank officers participate in setting their own goals—and are held accountable for them." Programs clarifying performance expectations, job descriptions and job duties not only reduce stress as discussed in Chapter 15 but also go a long way toward improving productivity.

A less frequently used approach to improving productivity was Intel's "work more hours" solution. Intel Corporation, based in Santa Clara, California, asked its 5,100 professional managers to work 50 hours a week instead of 40, for the same pay. Intel's purpose in using this solution was to increase the pace at which new money-making products are produced.[37]

Task Changes

What people do at work has two significant effects on productivity. One impact is a result of how the worker reacts to the job or task itself and the other impact is the arrangement of the separate tasks distributed among the employees and departments in the organization in order to produce the final product. Whereas the first effect is through task design, the second is through the work flow.

Redesign tasks for the individual or for the group.

Task Redesign. In Chapter 3, various approaches to task redesign are discussed. Although all of these can be used, job enrichment and sociotechnical designs are more likely to improve QWL and productivity.

The first job redesign approach that can be used to improve productivity is the individual contemporary form called job enrichment. Jobs can be enriched by altering the levels of five core job duties described in Chapter 3. These duties are (1) skill variety, (2) task identity, (3) task significance, (4) task autonomy, and (5) task feedback.

The potential effectiveness that job enrichment programs can have on productivity and bottom-line dollar savings is shown in Exhibit 16.5. Nevertheless, the relationships among the five core job dimensions and the outcomes and the potential effectiveness may not apply equally to everyone. Not all employees value satisfying the psychological needs. And even for those who do value these needs there are limits to the impact of job enrichment on employees. In fact, there are limits to the extent that jobs can be enriched. These limitations result from the fact that the job is really embedded in a social and technological network in the organization. This network acts as a constraint on redesigning individual jobs. In addition, job enrichment is limited in its impact on employees because it can only serve some of the employees' psychological needs. The sociotechnical approach to job design overcomes some of these limitations.

Exhibit 16.5
Job Enrichment at AT & T (Reprinted by permission of the publisher, from Robert N. Ford, *Motivation Through the Work Itself*, p. 44. Copyright © 1969 by American Management Association. All rights reserved.)

Projected Savings, First 18-Month Period, After a Shareholder Correspondent Job Was Enriched in the AT & T Treasury Department

1. 27 percent drop in turnover: nonsupervisory specialists	$245,000
2. Investigation and file clerks: annual salaries (force reduced from 46 to 24 clerks, three management jobs eliminated)	135,000
3. Correspondents' group: salaries (five management, four verifier jobs eliminated)	76,000
4. Stock transfer group: salaries eliminated	40,000
5. Merger of employee stock-pension unit and dividend reconciliation unit: salaries eliminated	100,000
6. Improved productivity (not priced)	?
7. Improved service indexes (not priced)	?
8. Improved tone of exit interviews (not priced)	?
9. Personnel section: job rearrangements (not priced)	?
10. Must offset half the salary of the six employees working on job-enrichment program part-time	(38,000)
	$558,000

The second major job redesign strategy uses the team contemporary, **sociotechnical approach**. This approach to job design arose in response to the views that: (1) Jobs, as organizational units, are not conceptually appropriate bases for the analysis and design of work systems and (2) Jobs are not a practically appropriate unit for making changes in organizations to improve the quality work life. The sociotechnical approach rests on the notions that jobs are man-made inventions designed to suit a number of technical and social systems needs and are constantly changing. The objective of the sociotechnical design such as the famous one at Volvo, is to bridge the two worlds (the technical and social) so that the resources of the two are optimally used to coproduce an outcome that is desired by the employees of the organization. More often than not, it is the sociotechnical approach that is an important part of semiautonomous work groups discussed earlier. Nevertheless, the decision as to which job redesign to implement is a complex one. The number of steps and what should be done in each of those steps includes

Step 1 ■ Recognizing a need for a change; gathering data for evaluation (Step 7)
Step 2 ■ Determining task redesign is the appropriate change
Step 3 ■ Diagnosing the organization, work flow, group processes, and individual needs
Step 4 ■ Determining how, when, and where to change jobs
Step 5 ■ Providing for training and support if necessary
Step 6 ■ Making the job changes
Step 7 ■ Evaluating the change; comparing with Step 1[38]

Work Flow. Work flow changes result in improved productivity based largely on the principles of industrial engineering and organization design.[41] These principles include

- Breaking operations (tasks) into discrete, small duties (elements)
- Measuring how long the duties take
- Setting standards of performance on the duties
- Devising methods of meeting the standards and performing the duties
- Measuring how well the duties are performed and the standards are attained
- Feeding back the results to the employees and organization
- Monitoring the task flow
- Correcting the task flow as needed[39]

These principles, as those of job enrichment, can be applied in the office as well as in the factory and to white-collar service work as well as blue-collar manufacturing work. An excellent example of how it is applied to white-collar service work in an office is provided by the *Personnel in Action* insert, "Boosting Productivity at American Express."

PERSONNEL IN ACTION

Boosting Productivity at American Express

Until recently anyone who reported the loss of an American Express card had to wait two or more weeks to get a replacement. AmEx clerks would note the rough details down on a telephone sheet, copy them onto a 3x5 card, and then ship the cards out for another group to process. Half the time the cards were buried under later requests. Now the recopying step has been eliminated, and the phone clerks track the replacement requests. Result: Cards are being replaced in as little as two days.

Things are moving faster in the traveler's check operation, too. It once took 12 days for American Express Co. to rule on a merchant's request to reconsider a check that it had refused to honor—one that had been reported lost, for instance. The division has streamlined the flow of such requests from the mail room through the word processing unit. Result: While the time frame for processing appeals was targeted at six days, they are now processed in five.

When AmEx merges its credit card and traveler's check operations into a new Consumer Financial Services Div. on Oct. 1, it will find that the similarities in

the two groups' customer service departments already outweigh the differences. Both have gone through the type of productivity improvement program that is becoming commonplace in the manufacturing sector but is rare in the service sector. "Economists always have found measuring input and output on an assembly line easier than measuring the productivity of service businesses, where 'the product' is often the customer's intangible experience," explains Ruth C. Finley, regional vice-president for commercial sales. Finley, formerly the card division's vice-president for customer service, spearheaded the productivity program three years ago.

Heavy Competition

The timing was not coincidental. Over the last few years, AmEx has run into heavy competition from bank cards such as MasterCard and Visa. The bank cards are less expensive for both cardholders and merchants to use. And merchants can get same-day reimbursement from the banks, a service AmEx has never offered. Diners' Club International and Carte Blanche, now owned by Citibank, are also coming back as competitors to AmEx.

Thus, slow customer service—particularly in replacing lost cards or issuing new ones—hits AmEx with double barrels. The company loses about $2.70 in charge volume for every day that a user is without a card. And the charge customer winds up using—and possibly learning to prefer—the competitive cards.

Finley's program to speed up and improve service had all the earmarks of a classic industrial engineering study. It broke operations into discrete elements, measured how long each one took, set performance standards, and devised methods of meeting them. It was predicated on looking at the end products of customer service as though they were as tangible as a new car. Customers, she notes, are interested in the ultimate timeliness, accuracy, and responsiveness of the company, and the original pilot program, which took place at AmEx's Phoenix card center, concentrated on breaking down all service operations into the elements that feed into those three factors. Task forces, which included both headquarters people and local managers, first identified and measured the elements, then devised ways to improve them.

Forcing Down Walls

For example, one task force discovered that it was taking an average of 35 days to process applications for personal charge cards. It checked patterns of customer inquiries and found that applicants got impatient before three weeks went by. Thus, it set a standard of two weeks to issue cards. Only then did it study the flow of applications from the mail room to the card-issuing staff to see how the standard could be met. Because the task forces included local managers from several different departments, they were able to coordinate specific process improvements. "The system forces the walls between departments to come down," notes Randy Williams, regional director for customer service in Phoenix. Finley adds a more subtle, but equally important, reason for including local management from the beginning. "We had to make sure that no one thought the project was a headquarters-directed witch-hunt," she says.

The original Phoenix program turned up 180 different criteria—from simple courtesy to complex financial approvals—by which customer service could be measured. Most have since been applied at AmEx's card centers in Fort Lauderdale, Fla., and New York, and Finley cites some dramatic nationwide productivity improvements. Response to cardholder inquiries

has been reduced to 10 days from a prior 16 days, and response to financial inquiries from merchants is down to 4 days from a high of 14. While Finley insists that increased customer satisfaction is the most important by-product, there have been tangible bottom-line effects as well. Speeding up the replacement of lost cards and the issuance of new ones has resulted in $2.4 million in added revenue and $1.4 million in added profit, she says.

Defining 50 Services

Taking the program nationwide yielded unexpected synergies. Regional card centers are sharing productivity improvement suggestions for the first time. For example, Williams recalls that her staff in Phoenix set up a specially trained unit to handle incoming calls that required more research than most. The other operators could then expedite routine calls quickly. In all, "we reduced by 23% the average time for phone calls, and we shared that information with the other two centers," she notes. In the past, she says, the procedure would have remained Phoenix's secret.

At the traveler's check operation, where a similar program has been in force for 18 months, the quality control staff had to define and improve service to four different customer categories: check purchasers, check sellers (usually banks), merchants who accept checks, and refund agents who reimburse the merchants. According to Corinne S. Licata, director of quality engineering, some 100 managers joined with her quality staffers to define 50 separate services provided to these customers and devised methods to improve them. For example, to speed up response time to written inquiries, Licata's group designed 13 new form letters and batched similar correspondence to help the word processing center better organize its workload.

The productivity improvement program is by no means completed for either the credit card or traveler's check operations. In both groups, quality assurance staffers take daily samples of work and measure each manager's performance against standards. For instance, a "statistically valid" sample of telephone calls on lost checks is recorded each day. The 54 telephone representatives in the traveler's check group meet regularly to review the recordings and to discuss ways to improve the handling of calls. Licata says the percentage of calls that did not meet the criteria for responsiveness is down from 16% in January, 1980 to 7.5% in August, 1981. "We're still looking to meet a standard of 2%," she says.

Resistance

While the quality assurance people insist that the daily monitoring is meant purely to help supervisors quickly spot potential backlogs or trouble areas, both Finley and Licata acknowledge that some managers still view it as a "Big Brother" approach. "We continue to have a level of resistance and defensiveness," Licata admits.

Both executives are counting on a continued emphasis on training and education to attain total acceptance of the programs. In Phoenix, for example, new employees at all levels are routinely indoctrinated into the workings of each department so that each under-stands the impact of his or her function on the customer's perception of service. "Managers are starting to manage by priorities of results, not by blind adherence to operational procedures," Finley says. And Licata notes that the main change has been one of attitude. "Jim Robinson [AmEx's chairman] told us we have a charter to deliver optimum service from the customer's viewpoint," she sums up. "And we really are becoming a customer-driven service organization."

(Reprinted from the October 5, 1981, issue of *Business Week*, pp. 62–66, by special permission, © 1981 by McGraw-Hill, Inc., New York, NY 10020. All rights reserved.)

Automation

After a decade of decline in the face of low-cost, high-quality imports, U.S. industry is beginning to automate at a pace that will soon change the face of American factories and offices. Within reach are computer-controlled systems of robots that will replace and are replacing most humans on plant floors and will produce and are producing unprecedented gains in productivity. Automated equipment is also moving into offices. Altogether these changes will affect more than forty-five million U.S. jobs, many during the next twenty years.[40]

Since automation is so significant and likely to be a major contributor to improving productivity, it is critical for personnel to understand it and utilize it to improve productivity and the QWL. Automation is especially critical to personnel since it has the potential of changing the nature of so many jobs and in creating many new jobs. These changes in turn will impact employee recruitment and selection, performance appraisal, and training.

Factory Automation. U.S. manufacturing companies are finally leaping into total automation. Although the United States is behind Japan and Germany now in automation use, many executives predict this will change by 1990.[41] "We are gathering momentum in the U.S. today, and as the momentum builds we are going to make quantum leaps in factory automation," according to Joseph Tulkoff, director of manufacturing technology for Lockheed-Georgia Company.[42]

Evidence to support these forecasts comes from these examples of increased capital spending:

Factories will never be the same.

- U.S. industry will triple its automation spending to $5 billion by the mid-1980's
- Sales of robots in the U.S. will go from 2,000 in 1981 to over 5,000 in 1985
- U.S. corporations will spend $2.3 billion in 1985 on minicomputers, numerical controls, and programmable controls as compared to only $510 million in 1980
- Spending on computer-aided design (CAD) systems, to aid the building of the total CAD-computer–aided manufacturing (CAM) system, will reach $2.5 billion in 1985, up from $610 million in 1979.[43]

Office Automation. What's happening to the factory is also happening to the office. Eventually almost 80 percent of the white-collar jobs in the United States will be automated; this includes managers and professionals as well as the clerical staff. In fact, the really big gains in office productivity are predicted to come from automating the jobs of the professionals and managers.[44]

The consulting firm of Booz-Allen & Hamilton in Washington, D.C., reported that less than half of the $50 billion spent by U.S. business each year for office automation goes for equipment for managers and professionals. Yet the yearly compensation for these two groups is nearly double ($500 billion) that of the clerical group. Consequently, with more office automation for managers and professionals, Booz-Allen predicts that by 1985 U.S. companies could increase their productivity by 15 percent and save up to $125 billion annually. They can do this

Offices will never be the same again.

■ By using automated calendars, tickler files, and other forms of equipment that replace the hand-written lists made by businesspeople to keep track of their time and others.

■ By using word and image processors that allow managers and professionals to better review and edit their work. Personal computers could reduce the time these individuals spend in making decisions and analyzing data, and audio-visual conferences could replace the face-to-face meeting—and eliminate the accompanying travel time.

■ By installing retrieval-of-information services and electronic mail (the latter a broad term encompassing facsimile, keyboard, and speech or voice-activated mail) that could increase productivity and also help connect other types of automated tools with each other.[45]

Office Design

Corning Glass Works, a recognized leader in using behavioral science principles on the job, redesigned its division of engineering by consolidating four physically separate departments into one well-designed building. It is estimated that productivity might increase by as much as 15 percent since the new design allows for close, personal interaction and engineers get more than 80 percent of their ideas through face-to-face contact with colleagues.

The physical environment influences employee performance and QWL.

The major design aspects of the building include

—The building centers on a glassed atrium that includes a cafeteria through which most employees enter from the parking area. Thus many employees start their day meeting casually with colleagues over coffee.

—A variety of stairways, escalators, ramps and elevators encourage easy circulation from floor to floor.

—Twelve more coffee lounges are scattered throughout the building. They are equipped with beverage machines, high stools, and wall-size washable writing boards. The aim is to encourage informal gatherings and casual brainstorming.

—Except for lab areas, all offices are enclosed only by 62-inch high partitions or floor-to-ceiling glass screens. Everyone has access to daylight and a view. Most labs have a view to the outside, and executive offices overlook the atrium.

—Ample strategic use of mirrored glass on balcony areas lets engineers glimpse activities on other floors and in other areas.[46]

While the Corning engineers find easy access and interaction vital to productivity, many people who work in offices experience too much interaction which proves to be more hindrance than help. Consequently, office design should allow employees to have some privacy, some time to work uninterrupted and to have quiet.[47] Individuals can, and do, implement quiet time on their own, but the greatest benefits occur when groups do it together. An entire office, department, division, or company can help make all employees successful when they observe quiet time as a unit. Everyone should be included. When all employees in the office are making a special effort to do their work quietly and not bother their coworkers, the level of internal office interruptions is greatly reduced. External interruptions are minimized where possible. The greater the number of interruptions that are eliminated during this quiet period, the more work will be successfully accomplished.[48]

Delta: The World's Most Profitable Airline—A Case Example in Productivity Improvement

While it is important to be acquainted with the individual techniques or programs to improve productivity, it is necessary to realize that programs for productivity improvement rarely work well in isolation. They work best under conditions where

- Top management visibly supports the programs
- There is a philosophy of productivity improvement
- Employees are adequately trained
- Employees are fairly rewarded
- Employees are involved and receive feedback and
- Appraisal systems are seen as fair and used in compensation decisions

In other words, productivity programs work best only when part of a total management approach to productivity. An example of such an approach is Delta Airlines.

Delta Is Ready—Are You? During the past ten years Delta has amassed almost $1 billion in earnings. The next most profitable airline during that period was Northwest Airlines, Inc. Its accumulated earnings for that same period have been about half Delta's total. How does Delta do it? It combines good planning—fifteen years ahead for flight equipment and facilities—with a massive effort to motivate employees, aspects of which are similar to some in Theory Z. Those aspects include

Many personnel activities must be tied together to really achieve high productivity.

- Management by teamwork and consensus.
- Employees are treated like members of a family. Delta didn't lay off a worker for economic reasons all the time between 1955 and 1980.
- The employees' benefit plan is one of the most generous in the airline industry.
- Unusually outstanding behavior by employees leads to recognition and praise by management.
- A willingness on the part of supervisors to listen to employees and make suggested changes if appropriate.
- A promotion from within system. All Delta employees start at the entry level.
- An open-door, open-communications policy that is practiced; and

■ A consistent application of fair and human resource-oriented personnel policies.[49]

Although Delta is very successful with these management qualities (most of which are personnel practices), not all organizations would be. As with job redesign efforts, a thorough diagnosis of many aspects of the company must first be done to see what management style and personnel practices are appropriate. That is the first step for any improvement in QWL or productivity. Since the essence of diagnosis is the organizational survey, refer back to Chapter 7.

EVALUATING QWL AND PRODUCTIVITY PROGRAMS

As shown in Exhibit 16.1, the programs aimed at improving QWL and productivity have several intended purposes. Although the two sets of programs have different intended purposes, QWL programs can also result in the intended purposes of the productivity programs. Consequently QWL programs can be evaluated by how well they attain all of the outcomes or purposes in Exhibit 16.1.

QWL Programs

In contrast to many of the other personnel activities discussed, evaluating the benefits of QWL programs solely on the basis of dollars and cents is almost impossible. Consider for a moment how you would evaluate in dollars the benefits of raising the level of employee self-control or satisfaction by 10 percent. How much would you pay for 10 percent more satisfaction or self-control? It's really hard to say. But more importantly, should it have to be said at all? Do you think QWL programs have to be justified on the basis of dollars and cents? Or do you think they can be justified solely on the basis of increasing self-control, satisfaction, involvement, and self-respect (essentially all employee benefits)?

Although corporations certainly think benefits to the individual are important, many QWL programs are supported by corporations and employees because they also reap benefits to the organization, that is, individual performance and productivity gains. Thus the difficulty of evaluating QWL in dollars and cents is diminished. Some difficulty remains, however, because the productivity gains (which, of course, can be evaluated in dollars and cents) resulting from QWL programs may not occur for several years after the QWL program, as described in the Tarrytown case.

But even if the individual benefits from QWL programs cannot easily be evaluated in dollars and cents, they can still be evaluated by the level to which the individual benefits increase in relationship to the type and cost of the QWL program. If individual satisfaction is valued in itself, increasing it at a lower cost (in dollars and cents) rather than a higher cost is beneficial for all. Measuring the changes in the level of employee benefits can be done by the organizational survey methods discussed in Chapter 7.

Productivity Programs

The process of evaluating productivity programs is made less complex than that for QWL programs because individual outcomes are much more measurable. For example, productivity programs are most likely to be evaluated in individual performance, absenteeism, and turnover. Productivity programs at the organizational level can be evaluated in terms of profitability, competitiveness, and survival measures.[50]

FACING THE CRITICAL ISSUES IN IMPROVING QWL AND PRODUCTIVITY

Now that we have covered many aspects involved in improving productivity and QWL, it is appropriate to respond to the Critical Issues raised by our personnel managers and listed at the start of this chapter. Although only brief responses are provided here, you should be able to generate an outline of a much more extensive response.

Issue: *What can be done to increase productivity? Can companies really depend on their people to change and help out?*

Many things can be done to increase productivity. However some of these may not work as well as others in your organization. It is really important to do a diagnosis of your place and see which is more likely to be needed and thus have a bigger impact. Once this is done, you may be able to choose from among several programs, many directly related to your personnel activities. For example, the total compensation system could be changed to being more performance based.[51]

Yes, you really can count on your employees helping out if you are ready to communicate openly with them. They need to have the same information you are working with. If they do and if they trust you, they will not only help out but have many good suggestions. (Refer back to Chapter 7 for the skills involved in communicating effectively with employees).

Issue: *Is the issue of quality of work life really fundamental to understanding why the United States is facing a productivity crisis?*

It is to some extent. Really there are many reasons for the current productivity crisis, such as the way managers are rewarded and promoted, the decline in research and development, and the much larger segment of the U.S. economy that is not producing goods and services. The increasing age of the capital equipment in the United States and increased international competition certainly are important also in understanding our current productivity crisis.

Since the volume of goods and services is the basis for productivity measurement, the fewer people we have producing them the harder it becomes to increase the average output of goods and services for each person employed. You see, many people are employed who do not contribute to the actual production of goods and services, but who are counted when figuring the level of productivity.

Issue: *Can companies in the United States really learn from the Japanese? Is the quality circle concept one companies should adopt? Can companies use Theory Z management?*

We can probably learn from everyone. Certainly we took many QWL ideas from the European countries such as Germany and Sweden.

But just as with those countries, when we look at Japanese techniques like quality circles, we must consider the cultural differences. Wholesale adoption of the techniques of others is rarely likely to be successful.

Theory Z management essentially is a modification of Japanese techniques for the U.S. environment. It represents perhaps a midpoint between traditional Japanese management and traditional American management. While some large companies here are shifting to Theory Z, it is too early to tell if it will be successful. Perhaps something else, not even labeled yet, might be more appropriate for your company.

Issue: *What other ways can companies improve productivity without increasing employee participation as in QWL programs?*

Really, many productivity programs require minimal, if any, employee participation. Task redesign, office redesign, and automation programs may not require employee participation, but some participation may prove to be quite useful. It can provide many good ideas in the design stage and can reduce potential resistance to change at the implementation stage. Sometimes, of course, participation may be necessary—if there is a union contract involved, and major work place changes are to occur.

SUMMARY

Faced with increasing international competition, U.S. companies are confronted with a productivity crisis of major proportions. Faced with changing social values and individual values, U.S. companies are confronted with a quality of work-life crisis of similar proportions.

Faced with these two crises, some U.S. companies are responding by implementing programs for productivity and QWL improvements. It should be noted that some U.S. companies are not responding this way. Some are not facing a crisis because they have had productivity and QWL programs for many years. Those faced with these crises, however, are now doing what others have done. In some cases, crises or not, many organizations are engaged in new productivity and QWL programs as they are developed.

In this chapter, we examined only a few of many programs (some newer than others) that are being used by U.S. companies to improve their productivity and QWL. Many of these programs appear to be having some success. In some cases success is better than in others due to many situational differences. This suggests that a careful diagnosis of the organization is needed as a critical first step in helping to ensure the success of any effort to improve productivity or QWL. Wholesale adoption of programs because they are popular or "everyone else is doing them" is not likely to result in success.

KEY CONCEPTS

Semiautonomous work groups   Quality of work life

Theory Z management   Productivity

Theory J   Quality circle

Theory A   Sociotechnical approach

DISCUSSION QUESTIONS

1. What is the problem-solution relationship between QWL and productivity?
2. What other personnel activities are affected by QWL and productivity programs, and in what ways are these programs related?
3. What are the three groups of QWL activities? Discuss some pertinent topics for these QWL activities, and identify some potential constraints.
4. Discuss the essentials of any effective quality circle program.
5. Compare and contrast Theory A with Theory Z management.
6. Identify three productivity programs by classification and their appropriate techniques.
7. What are the conditions under which productivity programs work best?
8. Why is Delta Airlines' approach to increasing productivity and QWL successful?
9. What evaluation strategy can be used to document success or failure in QWL activities?
10. What evaluation strategy can be used to document success or failure in productivity programs?

CASE

The 25% Solution: A Case In Organization Productivity

Imagine that you have just accepted a position with a well-known management consulting firm that specializes in quality of work life and productivity improvement projects. Your firm has been called by the vice president for operations of a major national insurance company, who feels that there are some significant productivity and morale problems in the company's large eastern claims processing division. In your initial conversation with him, you learn that the division's primary task is to process the paper work resulting from financial claims made by the company's clients. The VP's concern stems from the fact that the average time a case is processed has increased from 1-½ hours to 2 hours over the last year, a 25% decline in productivity. This has resulted in a substantial backlog of pending cases and thus decreased the company's responsiveness to its clients when they make claims. The vice president is very concerned about finding the causes of the problem and fixing it as soon as possible. To that end, he contracts with your firm to identify the causes of the problem.

You decide to proceed by interviewing the different levels of management in the division, and your first step is to arrange a meeting with the manager. Speaking to her on the phone to set a date, you find her cordial enough but note that she sounds somewhat ambivalent about having you, an outsider, ask questions about her division. During the interview you find out that she has been with the company only five years and has successfully held a series of progressively senior supervisory positions leading up to her current job, which she has held for only nine months. You also learn that she is very task oriented and is very committed to improving the operations of the division. She feels that the increase in claims processing time results from employees simply not feeling they have to do the work as fast as they used to. In fact, she has already developed a plan to improve their work unit and the amount of time they have to meet the objective. She tells you that, if the plan is successful, average processing time per case should begin to show significant improvement. She is also frank in telling you that she is quite annoyed that the vice president has hired "hot shot" consultants before she has had a chance to try her plan. She complains to you that if the VP in this company would stop breathing down her neck, everyone would be better off.

Your next step is to arrange a group interview with the three branch supervisors who report to the manager of the claims division. You start the meeting by explaining why you are there and ask if there are any questions. They don't have any, and you proceed to ask them if they are aware of the recent decline in average processing time. Two of the three remain silent, but the third quickly states that of course they are aware, aren't they reminded about the problem every other day. You then ask them what they believe are the reasons for these problems, and the same person once again exclaims, "what difference does it make? The boss has already developed a plan that will give each of us monthly objectives to meet." In the discussion that ensues you determine that they feel the new plan simply takes the problem off their boss's shoulders and places it squarely on theirs. After all, they are the ones that will be held accountable for meeting each month's performance objectives. Probing further, you learn that they believe her objectives to be based on arbitrary numbers and totally unobtainable. You also learn that the company's headquarters modified the case processing procedure about a year and a half ago, adding about fifteen minutes of processing time to each case. The supervisors conclude that it should have been expected that processing time would increase, especially since they were not given any additional personnel to compensate for the additional time taken by the new procedure. Besides, they continue, they have never been told the reason for the change and see it as an unnecessary administrative procedure.

Next you arrange a number of group interviews with a representative sample of the employees. You find the employees quite vocal in their views of why productivity has declined. First of all they feel that no one really cares about them at all. In fact, if any one would ask them, she or he would learn that one of their biggest problems is that the continually increasing volume of incoming claims has simply overloaded the capacity of the computer. Frequently they are denied rapid access to necessary information because the computer is down, making it necessary for the employees to come back or look the information up manually. Also you find out that few of the employees have a thorough understanding of the whole claims processing procedure. Each only performs a minor function on each case and then passes it on to the next person. Your most notable reaction resulting from the employee interviews is that they have many things to say about how their jobs are performed and have many interesting reasons for why there has been an increase in claim processing time.

Now that the data collection phase is complete, you should write a short report for the vice president explaining what you found out and what you recommend.

Case Questions

1. Is the company a Type Z or Type A organization?

2. Why did you take the time to interview personnel at each level of the organization?

3. Is quality of work life an important issue for this organization to address?

4. How might quality circles work in this organization?

5. What are your recommendations to the management of this company?

FOR YOUR CAREER

▪ You'll be a valued employee if you can develop strategies to improve an organization's productivity and QWL.

▪ You should be very familiar with quality circles. You may ask to volunteer for one someday.

▪ It's important to learn to work well in groups, even with people you may not like personally.

▪ Being a "productivity specialist" could be a very rewarding career.

▪ Your career well be significantly influenced by office and factory automation. You need to be prepared for automation.

▪ When looking for a job, be on the lookout for companies that have active programs in productivity and QWL improvements. Those companies are likely to do well in the long run and so will you if you're with them.

ENDNOTES

1. E. W. Glaser, "Productivity Gains Through Worklife Improvements" *Personnel*, January–February 1980, p. 72.

2. J. R. Hackman and J. L. Suttle, *Improving Life at Work*, p. 8. Copyright © 1977 Goodyear Publishing Company, Inc.

3. F. Herzberg, "The Human Need for Work," *Industry Week*, July 24, 1978, pp. 49–52.

  D. C. McClelland, "N Achievement and Entrepreneurship: A Longitudinal Study," *Journal of Personality and Social Psychology*, no. 1, (1965), pp. 389–392.

4. Reprinted by permission of the *Harvard Business Review*, Excerpt from "Europe's Industrial Democracy: An American Response" by T. Mills (November–December 1978), p. 151. Copyright © 1978 by the President and Fellows of Harvard College; all rights reserved.

5. Reprinted by permission of the *Harvard Business Review*. Excerpt from "Work Innovations in the United States" by R. E. Walton (July–August 1979), p. 93. Copyright © 1979 by the President and Fellows of Harvard College; all rights reserved.

6. "Organizing for Productivity: Part II" *Industry Week*, February 9, 1981, pp. 55–60.

7. Mills, p. 151.

8. R. R. Blake and J. S. Mouton, "Increasing Productivity Through Behavioral Science," *Personnel,* May–June, 1981, pp. 59–67.

D. S. Cohen, "Why Quality of Work Life doesn't always mean quality," *Training/HRD,* October, 1981, pp. 54–60.

9. Reprinted by permission of the *Harvard Business Review.* Excerpt from "Quality of Work Life: Learning from Tarrytown" by R. H. Guest (July–August 1979), p. 77. Copyright © 1979, by the President and Fellows of Harvard College; all rights reserved.

10. Ibid.

11. P. J. Champagne and C. Tausky, "When Job Enrichment Doesn't Pay," *Personnel,* January–February 1978, pp. 30–40.

12. Reprinted by permission of the *Harvard Business Review.* Excerpt from "How Volvo Adapts Work to People" by P. G. Gyllenhammar (July–August 1977), p. 112. Copyright © 1977 by the President and Fellows of Harvard College; all rights reserved.

13. Guest, p. 79. See also, M. Beer, and J. W. Driscoll, "Strategies for Change," in J. R. Hackman and J. L. Suttle, eds., *Improving Life at Work* (Santa Monica, Calif.: Goodyear, 1977), pp. 364–447.

14. Mills, p. 148.

15. Champagne and Tausky, p. 35.

16. Walton, p. 94.

17. "Stonewalling Plant Democracy" *Business Week,* March 28, 1977, pp. 78, 81–82.

18. J. F. Donnelly, "Participative Management at Work" *Harvard Business Review,* January–February 1977, pp. 117–127.

19. "Quality circle boom part of growing American trend, *Supervision,* September 1981, pp. 8–11.

20. T. Rendero, "Productivity and Morale Sagging? Try the Quality Circle Approach," *Personnel,* May–June 1980, pp. 43–45.

21. Ibid.

22. "Quality circle boom part of growing American trend."

23. D. Hage, "Goal is improving work place," *Minneapolis Star,* November 19, 1981, p. 1-C.

24. "Quality Circles on the Rise," *Performance,* United States Office of Personnel Management, May 1981, p. 2.

25. Hackman and Suttle, p. 230.

26. "Stonewalling Plant Democracy,"

27. L. McDonnell, "Honeywell ponders altering corporate style," *Minneapolis Tribune,* July 26, 1981, p. 1-D.

28. J. Main, "Westinghouse's Cultural Revolution," *Fortune,* June 15, 1981, pp. 74, 76, 80, 84, 88, 93.

W. Ouchi, "Going from A to Z: Thirteen Steps to a Theory Z Organization," *Management Review,* May 1981, pp. 9–16.

29. W. Ouchi, *Theory Z: How American Business Can Meet the Japanese Challenge* (Reading, Mass.: Addison-Wesley Publishing Company, 1981).

30. Guest, p. 76.

31. Ibid., p. 78.

32. Ibid., p. 83.

33. Ibid., p. 85.

34. B. A. Macy, "A Public Sector Experiment to Improve Organizational Effectiveness and Employees' Quality of Work Life: The TVA Case," Paper presented at the Forty-first Annual Meeting of the Academy of Management, August 2–5, 1981, San Diego, Calif.

35. "Organizing for Productivity: Part II," p. 58.

36. "How one troubled bank turned itself around," *Business Week,* August 24, 1981, pp. 117, 122.

37. "Intel's 125% solution," *Business Week,* November 9, 1981, p. 50.

38. Adapted from Ricky Griffin, *Task Design—An Integrative Approach* (Glenview, Ill.: Scott, Foresman and Company, 1982), p. 205.

39. "Boosting productivity at American Express," *Business Week,* October 5, 1981, pp. 62, 66.

40. "The Speedup in Automation," *Business Week,* August 3, 1981, pp. 58–67.

41. M. Kanabayashi, "A March of the Robots, Japan's Machines Race Ahead of America's," *Wall Street Journal,* November 24, 1981, p. 1.

42. "The Speedup in Automation," *Business Week,* August 3, 1981, p. 59.

43. Ibid., p. 58.

44. "Office Automation, Personnel and the New Technology," *Personnel Journal,* October 1980, pp. 815–820.

45. T. Rendero, "Want to Boost Managerial Productivity and Cut Costs? Try Automation," *Personnel,* March–April 1981, pp. 39–40.

46. "Corning Builds for Productivity," Behavioral Sciences Newsletter, October 12, 1981, p. 2.

47. "Work Environment: Its Design and Implications," *Personnel Journal,* January 1981, pp. 27–31.

48. M. E. Douglass and D. N. Douglass, "Quiet Time Increases Productivity," *Personnel Administrator,* September 1980, p. 22.

49. "Delta: The World's Most Profitable Airline," *Business Week,* August 31, 1981, pp. 68–72.

50. C. R. Day, Jr., "Solving the Mystery of Productivity Measurement," *Industry Week,* January 26, 1981, pp. 61–66.

51. J. W. Forrester, "More Productivity Will Not Solve Our Problems," *Business and Society Review,* Spring 1981, pp. 10–19.

B. Jonsson, "We have to be willing to let others in the organization take some risks," *Personnel Journal,* August 1980, pp. 633–636.

Chapter Outline

Critical Issues in Improving Safety and Health

Occupational Safety and Health in Organizations
What Is Occupational Safety and Health?
Importance and Benefits of Improving Safety and Health
Model of Occupational Safety and Health
Safety and Health's Relationships with Other Personnel Activities

Legal Environment of Safety and Health
Occupational Safety and Health Act of 1970
Legal Responsibility for Safety and Health: Who Has It?

Sources of Safety and Health
Factors Affecting Occupational Accidents
Factors Affecting Occupational Diseases
Factors Causing a Low Quality of Work Life
Sources of Organizational Stress

CHAPTER 17

Improving Safety
and Health

Safety and Health Strategies for Improvement
Safety and Health Rates
Strategies for Improving Occupational Safety and Health in the Physical Work Environment

Evaluating Safety and Health Activities
Evaluating the Occupational Safety and Health Administration
Evaluating Organizational Safety and Health Activities

Facing the Critical Issues in Improving Safety and Health

Summary

Key Concepts

Discussion Questions

Case

For Your Career

Endnotes

Personnel in the News

OSHA Is Now Trying To Help You

Revenge was not the reason Thorne G. Auchter wanted to head the Occupational Safety and Health Administration. His family-owned construction company in Jacksonville, Fla., had been cited by OSHA for a couple of dozen minor violations and fined $1,400 over the past 10 years, but Auchter had another motive. "President Reagan asked me, 'Can that agency work?' I said yes. I've always believed its mission was to protect the worker, not penalize the employer. We're going to accomplish that mission."

But how? In building its reputation as the agency you love to hate, OSHA started off on the wrong foot and has been out of step with some portion of its constituency ever since. Its health and safety standards have been attacked as either too lax to do any good or too rigid to be economically possible. Its rule-making and standard-setting processes have been described as biased by both sides, and as cumbersome, complex and ill-conceived. Its inspectors have been accused of acting like the Mod Squad and its administrators characterized as inaccessible functionaries, publicity pursuers or political payoffs. OSHA in a short decade has produced enough regulatory horror stories to ensure itself a spot in the Bureaucratic Hall of Infamy.

Undismayed, Auchter talks calmly about what he calls the agency's "two-stage development." In the first half of OSHA's existence, he says, "it tried to enforce thousands of standards written by various industrial trade groups as voluntary guidelines. That produced great confusion. In the past four or five years OSHA has concentrated on promulgating health standards. That has been equally difficult."

Now, Auchter says, the 2,800-staff agency is in Stage Three, in which he believes he can make OSHA a catalyst that will change the present adversary relationship between employers and employees into a partnership to achieve a "safe and healthful workplace." (Phil Farish, reprinted by permission from Nation's Business, *August 1981, p. 20. Copyright 1981 by* Nation's Business, *Chamber of Commerce of the United States.)*

The Employer's Responsibility

OSHA's poor performance gives credence to the theory that voluntary safety and health preservation programs by employers are the only viable solution to protecting workers. Without the arbitrary and bureaucratic barriers presented by OSHA, with its often inflexible and nit-picking regulation and the exorbitant paper work and administrative burdens it places on businesses, industry may be able to effect greater protection of its own workers through its own efforts. Although industry can be aided by governmental encouragement, incentive, and consultation, the ultimate source of protection of worker safety and health must be the employers themselves.

A compelling reason why employers voluntarily assume safety responsibilities themselves is the prohibitive cost of workmen's compensation. Mary Jane Bolle, a Library of Congress analyst, stated in a 1977 cost/benefit study that company expen-

ditures for insurance and workmen's compensation claims have run nearly five times as high as safety expenditures.

Finally, the lack of OSHA impact also supports the theory that most workplace injuries are the result of pure accidents. For instance, slips and falls are not the type of accidents which even daily visits by compliance officers could prevent. Similarly, as Safety Sciences' Kelly King points out, "you can't enforce skill. For example, felling a tree takes a certain amount of skill. An inspector could stand there all day and not be able to tell if it was done in a safe way."

Estimates vary as to what percentage of injuries are even potentially preventable, regardless of how much OSHA effort is expended. An OSHA-funded State of Wisconsin study attributed 75 percent of all accidents to "behavioral problems or momentary (nonpersistent) hazardous condition." A California Department of Industrial Relations' study concluded that 82 percent of occupational accidents were of the genre which a governmental inspection system could not possibly affect. Finally, Business Week has reported that the prevailing view among safety experts is that 85 percent of all accidents are caused by worker unsafe acts and only 15 percent by unsafe conditions which the employer can control. Regardless of the exact percentages, it is clear that OSHA, even if optimally administered (which it surely is not), could not rectify the majority of workplace safety and health problems. (M. A. DeBernado, "A Summation of OSHA's Gaucheries," Business and Society Review, Spring 1980, p. 46.)

A Religion of Safety

DuPont's effective safety program works because it is part of the company philosophy and various kinds of communication are used to make it accepted and understood, according to David Willette. He told the National Safety Congress that everyone—wage earners, managers, even the chairman—is held responsible for safety. It amounts to a religion, in fact. "This is not a simple system of paternalism, however, because every employee is responsible for his safety and the safety of the employees he or she works with. If we cannot convince an employee to accept this responsibility, then we admit our failure and dismiss the employee. Safety is, in summary, a condition of employment at DuPont."

The rigor with which safe working practices are pursued is such that, according to National Safety Council figures, DuPont is 28 times safer than the chemical industry—and 64 times safer than industry as a whole. The off-the-job safety record of DuPont employees, as with industry at large, is not as good as the record at work, but even so, the rate for DuPont employees is better than average, Willette noted.

"Our basic policy—and this is written down and every departmental vice president knows it by heart—is that employees must be kept informed of any potential hazard which might affect them. We cannot and would not say to an employee, 'You are responsible for safe practices,' and then deprive that employee of vital information, whether that information concerns a carcinogen the employee works with or an electrical hazard, or a mechanical hazard," he stated.

Safety communication goes through line management. Information alone, warnings, for example, are only passive communication, Willette noted. Active involvement in safety meetings and training sessions is standard practice. One way is through employee-conducted safety meetings. Employees are required to attend these sessions, held on company time, and they are expected to participate. And, from time to *time employees lead the sessions. Safety guidelines are continually reworked and revised to incorporate employee suggestions. Willette said, "We also use incentive programs to keep people thinking about safety and to keep a continuing internal communication—including peer pressure—among employees at a particular site." (Phil Farish, reprinted with permission from the February 1981 issue of* Personnel Administrator, *p. 23. Copyright 1981 by The American Society for Personnel Administration, 30 Park Drive, Berea, Ohio 44017.)*

Together these three quotations illustrate many interesting, if not controversial, aspects of safety and health in organizations. Perhaps the most controversial is the role of the federal government in safety and health. Currently this role is played by the **Occupational Safety and Health Administration** (**OSHA**). OSHA's role is to promulgate and enforce safety and health standards. As shown in the first two quotations, however, there is not complete agreement that OSHA is doing this effectively nor that it even should or need to be doing this.

These quotations suggest that safety and health in organizations can best be handled by management and its employees (or with the union). In line with this, in 1982, Thorne Auchter, head of OSHA, began shifting the position of OSHA vis-à-vis public and private organizations from one of distrust and conflict to one of trust and cooperation. The potential effectiveness of this strategy rests upon the same premises as much of the QWL movement: a spirit of cooperation ("We're all in it together") yields better results at the work place than a spirit of conflict and confrontation ("You do it your way, and I'll challenge it and do it my way"). At this point, what's your opinion? Which spirit do you think works better? It's a question raised by many of our personnel managers in our survey for the Critical Issues in safety and health.

CRITICAL ISSUES IN IMPROVING SAFETY AND HEALTH

Interestingly enough, many of our personnel managers, being from nonmanufacturing service companies, had less identification with this personnel activity than with any other. They, however, did raise a few issues increasingly being asked in office settings (questions 1 and 2), and the personnel managers representing manufacturing firms raised two more traditional safety and health issues (questions 3 and 4):

1. *What are the effects of office automation on employees?*
2. *What can companies do to reduce the incidences of stress-related accidents and deaths?*
3. *What can companies do to make the work environments better? Can companies get their employees involved in their efforts?*
4. *Why doesn't OSHA put some of the responsibility for health and safety on the employee?*

W ith a mandate to be more cost-effective and to play a more significant role in the management of human resources, the personnel manager can benefit greatly by being concerned with occupational health in organizations. Indeed, many personnel functions and activities are related to occupational health, and a neglect of occupational health can result in substantial costs for the organization. By ignoring occupational health, the personnel manager may be passing up a great chance to demonstrate another area where personnel can show its effectiveness. Thus the personnel manager may want to develop an awareness of occupational health in his or her organization and develop strategies for improving occupational health in the organization. [1]

Improving health and safety is a great way to increase personnel effectiveness.

OCCUPATIONAL SAFETY AND HEALTH IN ORGANIZATIONS

What is Occupational Safety and Health?

Occupational safety and health refers to the physiological/physical and psychological conditions of an organization's work force. If an organization is more effective from the occupational safety and health perspective, fewer of its employees are suffering from harmful physiological/physical or psychological conditions than in an organization that is less effective. What are these harmful conditions?

Physiological/Physical Conditions. These conditions include actual loss of life or limb, cardiovascular diseases, death, various forms of cancer (such as of the lungs), emphysema, and arthritis. This set of conditions also includes leukemia, white-lung disease, brown-lung disease, black-lung disease, sterility, central nervous system damage, and chronic bronchitis.

Psychological Conditions. Common harmful psychological conditions include dissatisfaction, apathy, withdrawal, projection, tunnel vision, forgetfulness, inner confusion about roles or duties, mistrust of others, vacillation in decision making, inattentiveness, irritability, procrastination, and a tendency to become distraught with trifles.

Importance and Benefits of Improving Safety and Health

In order to help develop strategies to improve conditions, it is necessary to know what it is that is to be improved.

Costs. On an average yearly basis in theUnited States there are over 10,000 deaths and 6 million lesser injuries from **occupational accidents.** On the same basis, there are approximately 400,000 new incidences of **occupational disease** and as many as 100,000 workers who die as a result of occupational diseases.

Although determining the exact cost of occupational accidents and diseases is difficult, these estimates should be regarded as conservative. In addition, there are enormous costs associated with **organizational stress** and a **low quality of work life.** For example, alcoholism, often used as a way to cope with the stress of the job and a low quality of work life, costs organizations and society over $43 billion annually. Of this, $20 billion are attributed to lost productivity and the remainder to the direct costs of insurance, hospitalization, and other medical costs.[2] Perhaps more difficult to quantify, but just as symptomatic of stress and a low quality of work life, is the worker's lack of psychological meaningfulness and involvement in his or her work and the loss in feeling of importance as an individual.

Workers protect themselves by psychologically withdrawing from the job.

Benefits. If organizations can reduce their rates and severity of occupational accidents, diseases, and stress and improve the quality of work life for their employees, they will be more effective. Fewer incidences of accidents and diseases, a reduced level of occupational stress, and the presence of QWL result in (1) more productivity due to fewer work days lost because of absenteeism; (2) more efficiency from workers who are more involved with their jobs; (3) reduced medical and insurance costs; (4) lower worker compensation rates and direct payments because of far fewer claims being filed; (5) greater flexibility and adaptability in the work force as a result of increased participation and feeling of ownership in changes from QWL projects; and (6) better selection ratios because of the increased attractiveness of the organization as a place to work.

A safe place is a good place to work.

Preventable. An important aspect of the concern for occupational safety and health is the fact that the costs associated with occupational accidents, diseases, and stress and lack of quality of work life can be reduced. For example, until 1973 Massachusetts had a forty-year average of five workers killed digging ditches (trenches) each year. After modifying the construction sites around trenches according to standards set by the Occupational Safety and Health Administration, there were only two fatalities in the trenches in more than a thirty-month period.[3]

Model of Occupational Safety and Health

A good work environment is safe and sane.

When treating harmful conditions (indicators of ill health) in the organization, it is useful to attack their sources. The two general sources are the **physical work environment** and the **sociopsychological work environment.** The consequences of these sources and harmful conditions are the *outcomes* associated with a lack of organizational effectiveness, such as loss of productivity, absenteeism, turnover, worker compensation claims, and medical costs. A model of these conditions, sources, and outcomes is illustrated in Exhibit 17.1.

Safety and Health's Relationships with Other Personnel Activities

Safety and health activities have extensive relationships with other personnel activities. A summary of the many relationships is shown in Exhibit 17.2.

Exhibit 17.1
Model of Occupational Ill Health in Organizations

SOURCES	CONDITIONS	OUTCOMES
Physical work environment 　Occupational accidents 　Occupational diseases	Physical/physiological 　■ Loss of limb 　■ Cancer 　■ Leukemia	High turnover/absenteeism Dissatisfaction Medical claims Low productivity Low efficiency
Sociopsychological work *　environment* 　Low quality of work life 　Organizational stress	Psychological 　■ Dissatisfaction 　■ Apathy 　■ Confusion	High worker compensation 　costs Low job involvement

Staffing.　To the extent that an organization can provide a safe, healthy, and comfortable work environment, it may increase its success in staffing and maintaining the human resource needs of the organization. Obviously, when organizations have high rates of accidents, particularly fatal ones, they need to recruit more employees. And if organizations develop reputations for being unsafe places to work, they will find it extremely difficult to recruit and select qualified employees.

Indirect Compensation.　The administration of indirect compensation is also affected by characteristics of the work environment. Worker's compensation benefits

Exhibit 17.2
Aspects of Safety and Health in Organizations

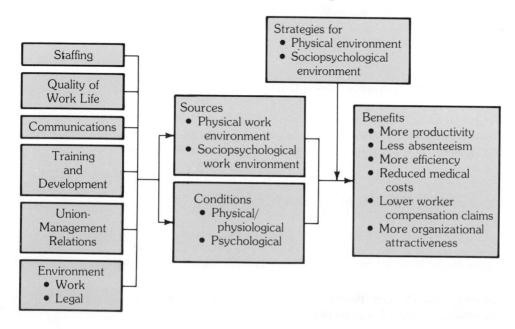

The more money spent on indirect compensation, the less left for direct compensation.

increased from $2.6 billion in 1969 to $8.5 billion in 1977.[4] As the costs for indirect compensation rise, so do the costs of the total compensation package. This in turn may make it necessary for the organization to hold down the rate of increase in direct compensation, and organizations that cannot offer good salaries will not be able to attract and retain able employees or to motivate the work force.

Quality of Work Life. QWL is directly associated with safety and health since a low QWL can result in poor safety and health as shown in Exhibit 17.1. Improving the QWL by engaging in many of the QWL programs discussed in Chapter 16 may thus alleviate many undesirable conditions, resulting in a better and more productive work environment.

Training and Development. Strategies to improve health and safety often involve an education process. Sometimes knowledge and awareness of safety and health in organizations are sufficient to help improve them. Thus the personnel manager can play a significant role in improving safety and health through training and development programs.

Safety committees work well at companies such as DuPont.

Communications. Two-way communications (discussed in Chapter 7), especially through methods like a safety committee, do much to create a concern for improving safety and health and to develop strategies to improve the work environment.[5] The effectiveness of communications for improving the work environment is nicely illustrated in the third opening quotation (about DuPont).[6] Here again the personnel manager can play a critical role by developing techniques to facilitate open communications.

Union-Management Relations. Occupational safety and health is one of the major concerns of unions. Many union contracts have some type of safety provision ranging from the right to refuse unsafe work to a union-employer pledge of cooperation in the development and operation of safety and health programs. The sanctity of the union contract regarding safety has been upheld by the courts (*Irvin H. Whitehouse & Sons Co.* v. *NLRB*, 1981).

LEGAL ENVIRONMENT OF SAFETY AND HEALTH

Because the consequences of not having a safe and healthy work environment are so severe, federal and state governments have passed laws and the courts have made several decisions to help make the work place safer and healthier.

Occupational Safety and Health Act of 1970

Ignoring health and safety can result in substantial fines.

The federal government's main response to the issue of safety and health in the work place has been the *Occupational Safety and Health Act of 1970,* which prescribed inspections of organizations for safety and health hazards; reporting by employers; and investigations of accidents and allegations of hazards.[7] Although this act was well-intentioned, it soon was perceived as emphasizing minor safety matters while overlooking major ones and, even more vital, of failing to focus attention on health standards.[8] Actually, this perception developed around one of the three organizations established by the act, the Occupational Safety and Health Administration. The other two organizations are the **National Institute for Occupational Safety and Health (NIOSH)** and the Occupational Safety and Health Review Commission (OSHRC).

Inspection. OSHA was given responsibility for establishing and enforcing occupational safety and health standards and for inspecting and issuing citations to organizations that violate these standards. The fact of the matter is, however, that there are over 5 million organizations and a very limited number of OSHA inspectors. Thus there is general agreement that the 65,000 inspections that OSHA makes annually, affecting less than 2 percent of the 5 million work places, must be aimed more specifically at frequent and flagrant violations of OSHA rules. In response, OSHA is moving toward a new policy on inspections to include

- A new targeting system so that companies with injury rate at a certain low level, e.g., 6 lost work-day cases per 100 workers would be exempt from inspection.
- Fewer immediate inspections in response to worker complaints unless OSHA perceives an imminent danger and then only if the problem weren't corrected after written OSHA notification to the company.
- Exemption from inspections for companies with in-plant labor-management commitees that would respond to worker complaints, conduct monthly inspections and ensure hazards were eliminated.[9]

Note that these changes significantly alter the previous legal privilege of OSHA to conduct inspections. Previously, OSHA inspectors were given the right to enter at reasonable times any factory, plant, establishment, construction site, or other area, work place, or environment where work is performed.[10] However, this inspection mandate was changed by the Supreme Court's decision in **Marshall** v. **Barlow's, Inc.** handed down in May 1979. According to this decision, employers are not required to let OSHA inspectors enter their premises unless the inspectors have search warrants.[11]

Another court decision also influenced OSHA inspections. In *Chamber of Commerce* v. *OSHA* the U.S. Court of Appeals for the District of Columbia Circuit struck down the *walk-around pay requirement.* The requirement had made it mandatory for companies to pay the wages of employees during the time they spent accompanying an OSHA inspector on the tour of the work site.

But, regardless of whether organizations are inspected, they are required to keep safety and health records so that OSHA can compile accurate statistics on all disabling, serious, or significant work injuries and illnesses—*whether or not* involving loss of time from work—other than minor injuries requiring only first-aid treatment and not involving medical treatment, loss of consciousness, restriction of work or motion, or transfer to another job.[12]

The records must contain information on the accidents and illnesses occurring in the organization. (See Exhibit 17.5 for an illustration of what OSHA considers a recordable accident or illness.) Falsification of records results in a fine of up to $10,000, imprisonment for up to six months, or both.

Establishing Standards. As with inspections, the way OSHA establishes standards has been changing. It has also been affected by several Supreme Court deci-

There is a critical difference between "no-risks" and "significant risks."

sions. Previously OSHA could set **no-risk standards.** That is, OSHA could tell companies that they had to make a work environment absolutely free of *any* risk from employee exposure. Now, however, OSHA has the burden of making an assessment that an existing exposure level poses **significant risks** to employee health before OSHA can force companies to adhere to the more stringent *no-risk* standard (*Industrial Union Department, AFL-CIO* v. *American Petroleum Institute*, 1980). However, if "significant risks" from exposure are shown to exist, OSHA can demand compliance regardless of the costs (*United Steelworkers of America, AFL-CIO* v. *Marshall*, 1981).[13]

Legal Responsibility for Safety and Health: Who Has It?

Who's Responsible?

- Employees
- Personnel manager
- Line manager
- Supervisor
- Safety director

Although the new policies regarding inspections being set by OSHA are geared towards making OSHA more effective, they also help spread the apparent responsibility for safety and health in organizations from top management through line and personnel managers all the way to the rank-and-file workers. After all, safety and health should be the concern of everyone in the organization. In a formal sense, however, the top management of the organization often has the responsibility for ensuring that employees are aware of health and safety and that the organization meets federal and state health and safety requirements. This is especially true in smaller organizations. In organizations with over 2,000 employees, the responsibility shifts to the personnel department or line managers.[14] There may even be a safety director or even an industrial engineer directly responsible for safety and health who reports to the personnel manager or the plant or office manager. In most organizations, however, the day-to-day enforcement of safety rules falls into the hands of the supervisor. The personnel manager or safety director then plays the role of assisting that supervisor, often by providing administrative research and advice. The personnel department often relies on experts in safety and health. To provide this expertise and to establish standards regarding health and safety at the federal level, the Occupational Safety and Health Act established the National Institute for Occupational Safety and Health (NIOSH). Nonetheless, the issue of who's responsible is far from resolved.[15]

SOURCES OF SAFETY AND HEALTH

Four sources of health and safety:

- Diseases
- Accidents
- QWL
- Stress

As shown in Exhibit 17.1 there are two major aspects of the work environment that influence occupational safety and health—the physical and the sociopsychological. Within each of these two aspects are two more sources of health and safety. For the physical, it is diseases and accidents and for the sociopsychological it is QWL and stress. Though it is these *two* major aspects of the work environment that influence the indicators of poor health and safety, traditionally only the physical environment has received the attention of most companies and OSHA. Increasingly, however, both OSHA (especially through the efforts of NIOSH) and companies are admitting to the impact of the sociopsychological environment on indicators of poor health and safety.

Consequently efforts to improve occupational safety and health must include strategies for both aspects of the work environment. Developing effective strategies depends upon knowing about each of the four sources of safety and health in organizations.

Factors Affecting Occupational Accidents

Certain organizations, and even certain departments within the same organization, have higher accident rates than others. There are several factors that explain this difference.

Organizational Qualities.   Accident rates vary substantially by industry. For example, firms in the construction and manufacturing industries have higher incidence rates than firms in services, finance, insurance, and real estate.

Small and large organizations (those with fewer than 100 employees and more than 1,000) have lower incidence rates than medium-size organizations. This may be because supervisors in small organizations are better able to detect safety hazards and prevent accidents than those in medium-size organizations. And larger organizations have more resources than medium-size organizations to hire staff specialists who can devote all their efforts to safety and accidents.[16]

Although data on incidence, severity, and frequency rates by type of industry and size of organization are important, these rates often veil differences between same-size organizations in the same industry. For example, DuPont's accident rate is twenty-eight times safer than the chemical industry and sixty-four times safer than industry as a whole. These differences can in part be attributed to the effectiveness of DuPont's safety programs.

Safety Programs.   Organizations differ in the extent to which they develop techniques, programs, and activities to promote safety and prevent accidents. The effectiveness of these techniques and programs varies by the type of industry and size of organization. For example, in large chemical firms, greater expenditures for off-the-job safety, medical facilities and staff, safety training, and additional supervision are associated with decreased work-injury costs.[17] On the other hand, work-injury costs have actually increased with additional expenditures for correction of unsafe physical conditions, for safety staff, for employee orientation, and for safety records if these expenditures are applied ineffectively. As a result, some organizations in the same industry may have higher injury costs per employee than others. This is very clearly illustrated by the DuPont statistics cited in one of the opening quotations. And of course, those organizations that have no safety programs generally have higher injury costs than similar companies that have implemented such programs.

The Unsafe Employee?   Although organizational factors play an important role in occupational safety, many experts point to the employee as the cause of accidents. Accidents depend on the behavior of the person, the degree of hazard in the work environment, and pure chance.

The degree to which the person contributes to the accident is often regarded as an indicator of proneness to accidents. There are certain psychological and physical characteristics that make some people more susceptible to accidents. For example, employees who are emotionally "low" have more accidents than those who are emotionally "high," and employees who have had fewer accidents have been found to be more optimistic, trusting, and concerned for others than those who have had more accidents.[18] Employees under greater stress are likely to have more accidents than those under less stress, and those with better vision have fewer accidents than those with poorer vision. Older workers are likely to be hurt less than younger workers.[19] People who are quicker in recognizing differences in visual patterns than in making muscular manipulations are less likely to have accidents than those who are faster in muscular manipulation than in recognition of visual patterns. Many psychological conditions that may be related to accident proneness—for instance, hostility and emotional immaturity—may be temporary states. Thus they are difficult to detect until after at least one accident.

Since none of these characteristics are related to accidents in all work environments, and since none is ever-present in employees, selecting and screening job applicants on the basis of accident proneness is difficult. But even if it were possible, aspects of the organization—such as its size, technology, management attitudes, safety programs, and quality of supervision—would still be important sources of accidents for those job applicants who are actually hired.

Factors Affecting Occupational Diseases

The potential sources of work-related diseases are distressingly varied:

> Typical health hazards include toxic and carcinogenic chemicals and dust, often in combination with noise, heat and other forms of stress. Other health hazards include physical and biological agents. The interaction of health hazards and the human organism can occur either through the senses, by absorption through the skin, by intake into the digestive tract via the mouth or by inhalation into the lungs.[20]

Ten major health hazards contributing to worker diseases are described in Exhibit 17.3.

Categories of Occupational Diseases. The fastest-growing category of occupational disease includes illnesses of the respiratory system. "Chronic bronchitis and emphysema are the fastest growing diseases in the country, doubling every five years since World War II, and [they] account for the second highest number of disabilities, under Social Security."[21] Cancer, however, tends to receive the most attention, since it is a leading cause of death in the United States (second after heart disease). Many of the known causes of cancer are physical and chemical agents in the environment. And because physical and chemical agents are theoretically more controllable than human behavior, OSHA is placing increasing emphasis on eliminating them from the work place.[22]

OSHA's emphasis on health, however, is not aimed solely at eliminating cancer and respiratory diseases. OSHA is concerned with all seven categories of occupational diseases and illnesses on which employers are required to keep records:

- Occupational skin diseases and disorders
- Dust diseases of the lungs
- Respiratory conditions due to toxic agents
- Poisoning (systemic effects of toxic materials)
- Disorders due to physical agents
- Disorders associated with repeated trauma
- All other occupational illnesses[23]

Exhibit 17.3

Ten Suspected Hazards in the Work Place (Reprinted from *U.S. News & World Report*, February 5, 1979, p. 42. Copyright 1979 U.S. News & World Report, Inc.)

As cited by federal agencies, here are some of the major agents linked to on-the-job diseases—

Potential Dangers	Diseases That May Result	Workers Exposed
Arsenic	Lung cancer; lymphoma	Smelter, chemical, oil refinery workers; insecticide makers and sprayers—estimated 660,000 exposed
Asbestos	White-lung disease (asbestosis); cancer of lungs and lining of lungs; cancer of other organs	Miners; millers; textile, insulation, and shipyard workers—estimated 1.6 million exposed
Benzene	Leukemia; aplastic anemia	Petrochemical and oil refinery workers; dye users; distillers; painters; shoemakers—estimated 600,000 exposed
Bischloromethylether (BCME)	Lung cancer	Industrial chemical workers
Coal dust	Black-lung disease	Coal miners—estimated 208,000 exposed
Coke-oven emissions	Cancer of lungs, kidneys	Coke-oven workers—estimated 30,000 exposed
Cotton dust	Brown-lung disease (byssinosis); chronic bronchitis; emphysema	Textile workers—estimated 600,000 exposed
Lead	Kidney disease; anemia; central-nervous-system damage; sterility, birth defects	Metal grinders; lead-smelter workers; lead storage-battery workers—estimated 835,000 exposed
Radiation	Cancer of thyroid, lungs, and bone; leukemia; reproductive effects (spontaneous abortion, genetic damage)	Medical technicians; uranium miners; nuclear-power and atomic workers
Vinyl chloride	Cancer of liver, brain	Plastic-industry workers—estimated 10,000 directly exposed

Certain occupations are definitely less safe and healthy than others.

Occupational Groups at Risk. "Miners, construction and transportation workers and blue-collar and lower-level supervisory personnel in manufacturing industries experience the bulk of both occupational disease and injury."[24] In addition, large numbers of petrochemical and oil refinery workers, dye users, textile workers, plastic-industry workers, and industrial chemical workers are also particularly susceptible to some of the most dangerous health hazards (See Exhibit 17.3.). Interestingly enough, skin diseases are the most common of all reported occupational diseases, with the group most affected being leather workers.[25]

PERSONNEL IN ACTION

Toxic Paint Chemicals Raise Alarm as Threat To Health of Workers

WASHINGTON, April 11—Three years ago, in response to an increasing number of its members who were reporting strange and debilitating illnesses, the International Brotherhood of Painters and Allied Trades started running an "Ask the Doctor" column in its journal. The letters poured in.

"I told the foreman I was getting numb around the mouth and in my hands," one painter wrote. "A stationary object would move as I walked toward it," wrote another. And according to another, "When we came in to work each day we had to haul dead rats out of the rooms we had painted the night before."

There are about 400,000 painters, paint makers, sign painters, silk screen printers and tile and carpet layers in the United States who work with coatings or adhesives made with aromatic hydrocarbons and other solvents, often in places without enough ventilation. Many of them have complained for years of dizzyness or intoxication while on the job.

But recently, as paint manufacturers have incorporated new chemicals in their products and as the toxicity of some, such as toluene and benzene, have become more widely known, many industry, Govern-ment and union officials have come to share the conclusion of Frank Raftery, the painters' union president, who said:

"Toxic chemicals are a major threat to painters that rivals or exceeds the better-known health threats to asbestos workers and even to coal miners."

Dr. John Froinds, a Government toxicologist who is acting director of the National Institute for Occupational Safety and Health, agreed that the chemical compounds in paint presented "new and serious problems."

"We are concerned about the hazards of painting to such an extent," he said, "that we are conducting extensive research into the carcinogenic and neurotoxic effects in the workplace. Obviously, further research is needed to evaluate these problems."

Neurotoxins are poisons that destroy nerves or nervous tissue, resulting in neuropathy, or a dysfunction of the way the nervous system usually works.

(Ben A. Franklin, *New York Times*, April 12, 1981, p. 34. © 1981 by The New York Times Company. Reprinted by permission.)

Of course occupational diseases are not the exclusive privilege of employees in manufacturing industries. The "cushy office job" has evolved into a veritable nightmare of physical and psychological ills. Among them are varicose veins, bad backs, deteriorating eyesight, migraine headaches, hypertension, coronary heart disorders, respiratory problems, and digestive problems. The causes of these in an office?

- Too much noise
- Interior air pollutants such as cigarette smoke and chemical fumes, for example, from the copy machine
- Uncomfortable chairs[26]
- Poor office design (see Chapter 16)
- Chemically treated paper
- New office technology such as video display terminals (VDTs) from office automation.[27]

Hazards of the office are numerous.

In addition, dentists are routinely exposed to radiation, mercury, and anesthetics, and cosmetologists suffer from high rates of cancer and respiratory and cardiac diseases connected with their frequent use of chemicals.

PERSONNEL IN ACTION

Computer Controls In Other Countries

"The problems associated with video display terminals are being studied at an increasingly frantic pace by government agencies, unions and universities around the world," writes Joel Makower in *Office Hazards: How Your Job Can Make You Sick.*

"Most of the earliest [studies] were done outside the United States, primarily in European countries like Sweden, Austria and West Germany, which have aggressive government-sponsored programs examining a wide range of occupational health and safety issues."

In Scandinavian countries, this research has resulted in regulations to protect workers, says Swedish engineering psychologist Olov Ostberg, a pioneer in the still-emerging field of "technology health science."

"Sweden is the most computerized country in the world," notes Ostberg, who says 10 percent of Swedish workers now use VDTs extensively and 45 percent rely on VDTs occasionally. "These numbers are, of course, growing."

Unions are largely responsible for prompting regulations concerning worker safety. "But you have to understand," says Ostberg, "that our unions are very different from those in America. Eighty-five percent of eligible workers belong to the Central Organization of Salaried Employees of Sweden.

"In Sweden, work must be organized in such a way that the [VDT operator] can intermittently be given periods of rest or work involving more conventional visual requirements. Employers must provide eye exams for employees who start using VDTs. They must provide eyeglasses, if required."

Norway has gone "even further," says Ostberg. "They now have recommended a regulation that no one must work more than 50 percent of their time in front of a VDT."

(Reprinted from The *Washington Post*, August 26, 1981, p. B-5.)

Factors Causing a Low Quality of Work Life

For many workers a low quality of work life is associated with many conditions in the organization. Although these conditions are different, what they do have in common is that they fail to satisfy many important needs and values of workers, such as a feeling or sense of responsibility, challenge, meaningfulness, self-control, recognition, achievement, fairness or justice, security, and certainty.

Here are the things that make for a low QWL.

Some of the conditions that exist in organizations resulting in these needs and values not being satisfied include: (1) jobs with low significance, variety, identity, autonomy, feedback, and qualitative underload (see Chapters 3 and 16 for discussion of these); (2) minimal involvement of employees in decision making and a great deal of one-way communicating with employees; (3) pay systems not based on performance, or based on performance that is not objectively measured or under the control of the employee; (4) supervisors, job descriptions, and organizational policies that fail to convey to the employee what's expected and what's rewarded; (5) personnel policies and practices that are discriminatory and with low validity; and (6) employment conditions that may only be temporary and/or where employees are dismissed at will (employee rights don't exist).

One person's meat may be another person's poison.

Please note that there are many conditions in organizations that are associated with a low quality of work life just as there are with organizational stress. Remember, however, that a condition of stress or low QWL for one individual may not be for another (largely because of differing needs and values). Thus it is always important to survey employees, as discussed in Chapter 7.

Sources of Organizational Stress

There are many sources of stress in organizations (that is, there are many organizational stressors).[28] Only the more prevalent ones are described here. These extend our discussion of career management stress in Chapter 15, where causes of career stress are presented.

The Four S's.   The four S's, which are sources of stress for many employees are

- Supervisor
- Salary
- Security
- Safety[29]

Uncertainty is a major component of stress.

The two major stressors that employees associate with the supervisor are petty work rules and relentless pressure for more production. Both deny workers fulfillment of the need to control the work situation and of the need to be recognized and accepted.

Salary is a stressor when it is perceived as being given unfairly. Many blue-collar workers feel that they are underpaid relative to their white-collar counterparts in the office. Teachers think they are underpaid relative to people with similar education who work in private industry.[30]

Employees experience stress when they are unsure whether they will have their jobs next week, next month, or even the next day. For many employees, lack of job security is even more stressful than jobs that are really unsafe. At least the employees know the jobs are unsafe, whereas with a lack of job security, the employees are always in a state of uncertainty.

Organizational Change.   Changes made by organizations are often stressful, because usually they involve something important and are accompanied by uncertainty.

Many changes are made without advance warning. Although rumors often circulate that a change is coming, the exact nature of the change is left to speculation. People become concerned about whether the change will affect them, perhaps by displacing them or by causing them to be transferred. The result is that the uncertainty surrounding a change yet to come causes many employees to suffer stress symptoms.

Work Pace.   Work pacing, particularly who or what controls the pace of the work, is an important potential stressor in organizations. **Machine pacing** gives control over the speed of the operation and the work output to something other than the individual. **Employee pacing** gives the individual control of the operations. The effects of machine pacing are severe, since the individual is unable to satisfy a crucial need for control of the situation. It has been reported that workers on machine-paced jobs feel exhausted at the end of the shift and are unable to relax soon after work because of increased adrenaline secretion on the job. In a study of twenty-three white- and blue-collar occupations, assembly workers reported the highest level of severe stress symptoms.

Work Overload.   While some employees complain about not having enough to do, others have far too much. In fact, some have so much to do that it exceeds their abilities and capacities. The result of this situation can be fatal, as described in the *Personnel in Action* insert, "Can Companies Kill?"

PERSONNEL IN ACTION

Can Companies Kill?

On the morning of January 31, 1979, Roger Berman left for work early, as usual, and drove into the city to his office at the corporate headquarters of a large international conglomerate. Instead of putting in his customary long day, however, he left the office abruptly during the morning. He may have driven around for some time, but eventually he went home and pulled into his garage. With the motor still running, he got out of the car, closed the garage door, and apparently sat down to wait. His body was found there later, slumped on the floor. The autopsy report listed carbon monoxide as the cause of death, but in this case "cause" is a matter of some dispute.

Though tragic, suicides are not uncommon. Berman's is, because his widow is suing his former employer for $6 million, claiming it caused her husband's death by failing to respond to his repeated complaints of overwork and by displaying a "callous and conscious disregard" for his mental health.

Berman joined the company as a management trainee soon after he graduated from high school. A

hard worker, he put himself through college at night while rising steadily through the ranks of the giant corporation. Eventually he became manager of a large department, with a salary of about $50,000, plus substantial fringe benefits. In time, however, the job became increasingly difficult for him, demanding more and more of his evening and weekend hours. The pressure became so great that he asked several times to have his work load lightened. According to the legal complaint, his superiors promised to ease up on him, but nothing changed.

Approaching 50, and with 30 years of service to the company, Berman decided in 1978 to take early retirement, largely to escape from the strain of his job. According to the suit, his superiors talked him into staying on, promising to ease his work load. Relying on those promises, he agreed, but again, the complaint charges, no relief came. Some time after that, Berman discovered that he would not become eligible again for early retirement and pension for another five years.

With escape by retirement thus effectively blocked, Berman became increasingly anxious about his ability to accomplish his work. His company doctor referred him to an outside psychiatrist. According to the suit, the psychiatrist reported back to the company, warning that Berman's mental health was "precarious" and would be "further impaired" without some relief in the conditions of his work. Still, apparently, nothing changed.

On January 10, 1979, Berman's colleagues found him sitting at his desk in a dazed stupor. They could not snap him out of it, nor could the company doctor. During this "catatonic" episode, according to the complaint, he was not sent to a hospital; he was not sent home; no one called his wife. After a few hours, he came out of it on his own. He stayed in the office for the rest of that day, and left for home, alone. Three weeks later he committed suicide.

(Berkeley Rice, reprinted from *Psychology Today Magazine*, June 1981, p. 78. Copyright © 1981 Ziff-Davis Company.)

Physical Environment.   Although office automation, discussed in Chapter 16, is a way to improve productivity, it does have its stress-related drawbacks. One aspect of office automation with a specific stress-related drawback is the VDT. Currently the findings aren't complete on just how serious an effect VDT screens have on workers. As discussed earlier in this chapter, other countries have taken more steps to deal with VDTs than has the United States. Nevertheless, NIOSH is gathering data on VDTs.

SAFETY AND HEALTH STRATEGIES FOR IMPROVEMENT

To improve the occupational health of an organization's work force, the sources of the harmful conditions must be identified. Then, based on the sources, strategies for improving the organization's occupational safety and health ratings can be developed. Then to determine the success of the strategies, the occupational safety and health ratings before a strategy was implemented must be compared to the ratings after they have been in effect. Only by doing this can organizations determine if what they're doing is really effective. Thus since occupational safety and health ratings are so critical and because they are required by OSHA, you should know how to compute them as well as the possible strategies to use.

A summary of these strategies to be discussed is shown in Exhibit 17.4.

Safety and Health Rates

Rates of
- incidence
- frequency
- severity

Safety and health rates are described in terms of their frequency, severity, and occurrence. Although organizations are required by OSHA to maintain records only of the incidence of accidents and disease (illness) for comparison purposes, many organizations also maintain frequency and severity records of accidents and illnesses. Exhibit 17.5 is an OSHA guide to determining what constitutes an accident or illness that must be recorded. Note that these procedures are only designed to measure poor health and safety from the physical environment. They can also be adapted to be used for the psychological environment.

Exhibit 17.4
Summary of Sources and Strategies for Occupational Health

SOURCES	STRATEGIES
Physical Work Environment	
Occupational Accidents	Redesigning the work environment
	Setting goals and objectives
	Establishing safety committees
Occupational Diseases	Measuring the work environment
	Setting goals and objectives
Sociopsychological Work Environment	
Quality of Work Life	Redesigning jobs
	Increasing participation in decision making
Organizational Stress	Establishing organizational stress programs
	Establishing individual stress strategies

Exhibit 17.5
OSHA Guide to Recording Cases

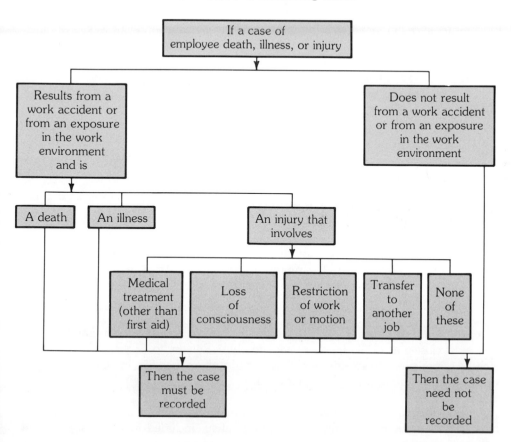

The **incidence rate** is most explicit in combining both illnesses and injuries, as shown by this formula:

$$\text{Incidence rate} = \frac{\text{Number of recordable injuries and illnesses} \times 1 \text{ million}}{\text{Number of employee exposure hours}}$$

Suppose an organization had 10 recorded injuries and illnesses and 500 employees. To get the number of exposure hours, it would multiply the number of employees by forty hours and by fifty work weeks—$500 \times 40 \times 50 = 1$ million. In this case, the incidence rate would be 10. In 1977, the average incidence rate for all private organizations was 9.3. That is, there were 9.3 recorded injuries and illnesses for each 100 employees.

The **severity rate** reflects the hours actually lost due to injury or illness. It recognizes that not all injuries and illnesses are equal. Four categories of injuries and illnesses have been established: deaths, permanent total disabilities, permanent partial disabilities, and temporary total disabilities. OSHA assigned each category a specific number of hours to be charged against an organization. The severity rate is calculated by this formula:

$$\text{Severity rate} = \frac{\text{Total hours charged} \times 1 \text{ million}}{\text{Number of employee hours worked}}$$

Obviously, an organization with the same number of injuries and illnesses as another but with more deaths would have a higher severity rate. However, because OSHA decided the assignment of hours charged for each type of accident and illness was arbitrary, it dropped the idea of using a severity rate.

The **frequency rate** is similar to the incidence rate except that it reflects the number of injuries and illnesses per million hours worked rather than per year:

$$\text{Frequency rate} = \frac{\text{Number of disabling injuries} \times 1 \text{ million}}{\text{Number of employee hours worked}}$$

Strategies for Improving Occupational Safety and Health in the Physical Work Environment

There are two major categories of strategies to improve safety and health in the physical work environment. One represents strategies to reduce the likelihood of occupation accidents. The other represents strategies to reduce the incidence of occupational disease.

Occupational Accidents. This aspect of the physical work environment describes that most closely associated with immediate physical injury to workers. Such injuries include minor cuts and sprains as well as loss of limb or even life. In developing ways to deal with accident rates and improve safety, organizations can use several alternative responses.[31]

First, designing the work environment to make accidents difficult is perhaps the best way to prevent accidents and increase safety. Included in the design of the physical environment are guards on machines, hand rails in stairways, safety goggles and helmets, warning lights, and self-correcting mechanisms and automatic shutoffs. Even though all of these physical environment responses are designed to help reduce accidents, the extent to which they actually do depends upon employee acceptance and utilization. For example, whether there are fewer eye injuries because of the availability of safety goggles depends on whether or not the employee wears them correctly. Whether or not the employee wears them correctly often depends on the process used in implementing the use of goggles and whether there is a conflict in complying with the goggles. If the employee has been a part of the decision to wear goggles (or any other physical change) she or he is more likely to accept the decision than if she or he was not part of the decision-making process.

There are many alternative ways to reduce or prevent accidents.

    Second, implementing programs and maintaining records of accidents can also increase safety. Many organizations have set up management by objectives programs to deal with occupational health. The four basic steps of these programs are

1. Awareness and recognition of the hazards of existing harmful conditions. This awareness and recognition can be obtained from the personnel records.

2. On the basis of personnel records, an evaluation of the severity and risk of these hazards can be made.

3. Formulation and implementation of appropriate programs to control, prevent, or reduce the possibilities of accidents and the setting of objectives regarding reduction of accidents.

4. After hazardous situations are identified, a system of objectively assessing improvements and giving positive feedback for correct safety procedures needs to be established; and

5. Monitoring and evaluating the progress of programs against stated goals and objectives, and making revisions in the program as needed.[32]

    Third, another strategy that incorporates the group in accident prevention is the use of the safety commitee and two-way talk. The personnel department can serve as the coordinator of a safety team or committee composed of several representatives of the employees. Where unions exist, the committees reflect union representation as well. Often organizations have several safety committees. Several may exist at the department level for implementation and administration purposes with one larger committee at the organizational level for the purpose of policy formulation. For these safety committees to work, however, there must be two-way talk or communication. Without it, the committee idea is likely to fail. To further spur the effectiveness of these committees, several of them can be established and compete against each other for the best safety record. Sound unlikely? Read a true story (in the *Personnel in Action* insert) of what happened at a bakery shop operating in a grocery store chain where the use of a safety committee was not working because the talk was all one way.

Two-way communication comes to the rescue.

    Another way of altering the work environment to improve safety is to alter the nature of the task, make the job itself more comfortable and less fatiguing.[33] This approach is generally referred to as ergonomics. Ergonomics considers changes in the job environment in conjunction with the physical and physiological capabilities and limitations of the employees (see Chapter 3). As a result, employees are less likely to make mistakes due to fatigue and tiredness.

    A final strategy for increasing safety is by just making the employees more aware of safety. For example, many companies put up Safety First posters or post the number of days without an accident. The National Safety Council in Chicago is a good source of posters, statistics, and even safety movies.

PERSONNEL IN ACTION
Safety Idea Rises in Bakery

The accident rate in the bakery had been increasing for several years at an intolerably high rate of 30 percent. Appearance before the committee by an employee who had sustained an injury was an uncomfortable experience. When the plant manager put accident reduction at the top spot on his agenda, he first set up teams among the employees headed by captains who were chosen for leadership qualities. These team captains became the working body on the safety committee and the supervisors who had run the committee before were recast as consultants. The committee became a vehicle for correcting conditions which had contributed to accidents. As employees realized that the upward communication through the body was paying off for them in improved working conditions, the flow of ideas increased and matters which had a bearing on morale became part of the committee's agenda. The result was not only an improvement in the safety record but also in reduction of turnover and better attendance at work.

Part of the good result came through setting up a competition among the teams. Points were won for accident-free periods and lost when mishaps occurred. Similarly for promptness and attendance, a consistent record of arriving on time won points which could be reduced or cancelled by team members being late. In the early stages, all the teams turned in negative scores, but these gradually improved. Prizes and publicity give an additional spur to keeping a good record.

(Reprinted with permission from the June 1981 issue of *Personnel Administrator,* p. 12, copyright 1981 by The American Society for Personnel Administration, 30 Park Drive, Berea, Ohio 44017.)

Occupational Diseases. More harmful and costly to organizations and employees than occupational accidents are occupational diseases. Furthermore, the impact of the physical environment on occupational diseases is often far more subtle than on occupational accidents.[34] Thus it is generally more difficult to develop strategies to reduce the incidence of occupational diseases. Nevertheless, three strategies can be suggested.

The first organizational approach to reducing the incidence of occupational diseases is measurement of the chemicals and other hazards in the work environment. What organizations measure is often determined by OSHA standards and requirements, unless, of course, an organization chooses to ignore them. One OSHA requirement is that organizations measure the chemicals in the work environment and keep records on these measurements. The records must include the date, number of samples taken, length of period over which the sampling was done, procedure used, analytical method, the employees' names, social security numbers, and job classifications, where the employees work in the organization, and the protective equipment used. Often a physician is involved in the process of gathering this information, but the responsibility for having the information lies with the organization.

The organization is required to keep this information "for as long a period as is associated with the incubation period of the specific disease—it could be 40 years of medical surveillance of the environment."[35] If the organization is sold, the new owner must assume responsibility for storing the old records and continuing to gather the required data. If the organization goes out of business, the administrative director of OSHA must be informed of the whereabouts of the firm's records.

Compliance with OSHA standards and requirements is not the only approach organizations can take to occupational health hazards. They can also become more active in the process by which OSHA establishes those standards. OSHA must publish its intent to review or establish standards, and it must hold a hearing. At this hearing, organizations can contribute information regarding what they believe the standard should be. A past administrator of OSHA, Morton Corn, advised organizations that

Organizations should take the initiative in making work places safe and healthy.

> When the government promulgates some regulations then it is too late—you are coming from behind. Use your facts to maneuver what the government is doing so that good standards result, otherwise your evidence will not be accepted to put down a standard. They can't regulate every industry because they don't know every industry. You know the industry.[36]

The second strategy is setting objectives, implementing programs, and maintaining records of diseases. This strategy uses the information collected in the first occupational disease strategy and follows the same steps as those management by objective-type programs in reducing occupational accidents.

A third strategy is for organizations to recognize the importance of previously neglected ailments and make a committed effort to help workers with those ailments. For example, Burlington Industries has jointly undertaken with the Arthritis Foundation and the University of North Carolina School of Medicine to assist employees with arthritis. Although arthritis is usually not part of dinner conversation, it is a serious ailment. Last year alone arthritis sufferers lost 27 million working days and over $1 billion in disability payments (about 15 percent of all social security disability payments) were made to U.S. workers.

A final strategy is utilizing worker educational programs and awareness.[37] Educational programs on arthritis are now being conducted at General Motors, Johns-Manville Corporation, Western Electric, Sentry Insurance, and Samsonite Company. A part of worker awareness is informing them of clinics across the nation to which workers can go if they suspect they are ill due to work-place exposures.

Strategies for Improving Occupational Safety and Health in the Sociopsychological Work Environment

There are many techniques that can be used to improve the sociopsychological work environment. Techniques to improve the QWL include job redesign, quality circles, organizational restyling, and even training programs to change supervisory communication styles.[38] Since these are described in Chapter 16 (see Exhibit 16.2), emphasis here is given to techniques to manage organizational stress.

Organizational Stress. Organizational stress can come from a large number of conditions. Consequently several strategies can be used to help alleviate organizational stress. First, one of several organizational stress management programs can be used. Specific programs that may be implemented on the basis of the information gathered are in large part related to the organization's stressors. Thus, specific programs can be designed to improve aspects of the organization such as the supervisor, work overload, the physical environment, the salary structure, job security, and career development opportunities for the employees.[39] And while it is unlikely that one organization would use all of these programs, many are using at least a few of them.

At TRW (due in part to employee demand, general dissatisfaction, and new policies and procedures to conform to federal and state legislation), several steps to reduce stress are being implemented: (1) Crisis-counseling training sessions with the industrial relations staff; (2) increasing the employees' general awareness of stress and what they can do about it; (3) adding stress discussions to the supervisory training program; (4) adding a module on stress to middle management programs and; (5) offering after-hours programs such as workshops in the use of biofeedback, meditation exercises, and other relaxation techniques. Pennsylvania Bell has adopted special seminars where executives can discuss their personal and job changes, identify their own strengths and weaknesses in adapting to the changes, and then develop methods to adapt.

We sometimes deceive ourselves by thinking we are in good health.

Second, one of several individual stress management programs can be used. Time management is an effective individual strategy to deal with organizational stress. Other individual strategies that should be included in individual stress management programs are those that recommend: (1) good diets; (2) regular exercise; (3) monitoring of physical health; and (4) the building of good social support groups. Many large organizations, such as Xerox, encourage employees to enroll in programs of regular exercise and careful monitoring of their physical health. It appears, however, that enrollment in these programs has to be strongly encouraged because many employees have highly favorable perceptions of their fitness and health. These perceptions are generally more favorable than what the results of "**wellness tests**" indicate. "Wellness tests" include measures of blood pressure, blood cholesterol, high-density cholesterol, skin-fold evaluation of diet, life-change events, smoking, drinking, and family history of coronary heart disease.[40]

EVALUATING SAFETY AND HEALTH ACTIVITIES

The evaluation of safety and health activities can be divided into two specific categories: those associated with OSHA and those associated with the health and safety programs undertaken by organizations.

Evaluating the Occupational Safety and Health Administration

How effective has OSHA been? According to one General Motors spokesperson, GM "had a good safety program going long before anybody ever heard of OSHA, and we haven't seen any effect from all the money ($79 million in 1974 alone) that's been spent, so far as any reduction in our accident rate is concerned."

Judging from this statement, it would appear that OSHA is not effective. But consider the result of OSHA's requirement that trenches in construction projects be shored adequately, as stated at the start of this chapter.

Unfortunately, such successes occur only in selected organizations. Meanwhile, in 1980 alone, the estimated cost to organizations of implementing OSHA requirements was approximately $4 billion. In fact, it is often more cost-effective for an organization to comply with OSHA regulations only when forced to by an OSHA inspector, since there is such a slight chance that an inspection will ever occur. This, however, appears to be changing along with the entire thrust of OSHA and its relationship with employees under the present administration of OSHA. Yet what are the alternatives to OSHA? Many would argue that employees should assume more of the responsibility for their own health and safety. This may be possible to the extent that employees contribute to their own accidents, but "how can employees be responsible for diseases such as lung cancer, cancer of liver and brain and kidney disease from exposure to arsenic, radiation and asbestos, vinyl chloride and lead?"[42] Others would argue that employers should assume more responsibility, especially when it comes to stress in organizations and the quality of work life.

Evaluating Organizational Safety and Health Activities

The effectiveness of safety and health activities run by organizations can be evaluated against the outcomes associated with safety and health or the reasons for wanting to reduce poor safety and health shown in Exhibit 17.1. However, evaluating strategies or activities for improving safety and health targeted at the physical work environment differs from the evaluation of the strategies targeted at the sociopsychological work environment.

Physical Work Environment Strategies.   The effectiveness of these strategies is often measured by the effects of a specific strategy on employee absenteeism and turnover, medical claims and worker compensation rates and costs, productivity and efficiency. The effects of these strategies can also be seen in the rates of accidents or the incidences of specific diseases, that is, the physical/physiological indicators of safety and health levels in an organization.

Sociopsychological Work Environment Strategies.   In contrast to the physical work environment strategies, the effectiveness of this class of strategies is measured against the psychological indicators of safety and health levels and employee dissatisfaction and job involvement. Their effectiveness can, however, also be measured against the same factors as are the physical work environment strategies. Indeed, it is very appropriate to measure the effectiveness of stress management strategies against the physical/physiological indicators. Since evaluating the effectiveness of safety and health strategies against the psychological indicators and dissatisfaction and job involvement raised questions similar to those raised when evaluating QWL programs, refer back to Chapter 16 for the discussion in the evaluation section.

FACING THE CRITICAL ISSUES IN IMPROVING SAFETY AND HEALTH

Now that we have examined several aspects associated with improving safety and health in organizations, it is appropriate to respond to the Critical Issues listed at the start of this chapter. Remember that the responses here are just meant to get you started. You should be able to develop a much longer response.

Issue: *What are the effects of office automation on employees?*

It appears that there are many stress-type symptoms associated with office automation. This, however, is only true for some aspects of office automation, those involving video display terminals (VDTs). Many of the other office automation tools are too new to be or just haven't been researched. VDTs, of course, are widespread now. The effects on those who use VDTs range from back pains and headaches to eye strain. The severity of these symptoms and whether or not they really result from VDTs, however, is disputed, at least in the United States. Concern and action regarding VDT use is much greater in Europe at this time.

Issue: *What can companies do to reduce the incidences of stress-related accidents and deaths?*

There are currently many organizational and individual stress management strategies. You can set up programs such as time management or physical exercise so employees essentially help themselves cope, or you can alter conditions in the organizations associated with the stress. To do the latter, however, requires a diagnosis of the organization to see what is happening, where, and to whom before really deciding how best to proceed. Since there are so many possible sources of stress and because not all people react the same way to them, it may be more efficient to implement individual stress management strategies. This would not be the case, however, if many people were suffering very similar stress symptoms in a specific part of the organization. Given this, an organizational strategy may be more appropriate.

Issue: *What can companies do to make the work environments better? Can companies get their employees involved in their efforts?*

As with many quality of work life programs being implemented in organizations, employee involvement in improving safety and health is not only a good idea but one likely to be desired by the employees.

Many things can be done to make work environments better. But it is important to distinguish two types of environment. One is the physical and the other is the sociopsychological. Each is quite different and has its own unique subparts. While some improvement strategies may work well for one part of the work environment, they will not work in other parts. Thus, again, a careful diagnosis is recommended before anything else.

Issue: *Why doesn't OSHA put some of the responsibility for health and safety on the employee?*

The Occupational Safety and Health Act of 1970 places the burden of safety and health on the employer. At the time the act was being formulated Congress must have thought that poor safety and health were largely the result of the work environment rather than individual workers. Even if they thought individuals did contribute to poor safety and health, Congress probably thought organizations could do more to help than could the employees.

SUMMARY

The health of employees in organizations will become increasingly important in the years ahead. Employers are becoming more aware of the cost of ill health and the benefits of having a healthy work force. The federal government through OSHA is also making it more necessary for employers to be concerned with employee health. The government's concern, however, is primarily with employee health as related to occupational accidents and diseases, both aspects of the physical environment. Now organizations can choose to become involved in programs dealing with employee health and the workers' sociopsychological environment. However, if the choice is not to, the government *may* in the near future prescribe regulations for them to do so. Thus it pays organizations to be concerned with both aspects of the work environment now. Effective programs for both environments can significantly improve employee health and the effectiveness of the organization.

Because employee health is so important and the benefits so significant, the personnel manager should be at the forefront in the organization's concern for employee health. Involvement in employee health will be entirely consistent with the new measurement imperative facing personnel and human resource management and the increasing role being played by personnel in organizations in the effective management of human resources.

KEY CONCEPTS

occupational safety and health

Occupational Safety and Health Administration (OSHA)

Marshall v. *Barlow's, Inc.*

no-risk standard

National Institute of Occupational Safety and Health (NIOSH)

significant risk

physical work environment

sociopsychological work environment

occupational disease

occupational accidents

organizational stress

low quality of work life

machine pacing

employee pacing

frequency rate

severity rate

wellness tests

DISCUSSION QUESTIONS

1. Who is responsible for health and safety in organizations? Who should be responsible?

2. What are some of the reasons that an organization such as DuPont has been able to deal effectively with occupational health and safety problems?

3. What are the two major types of conditions that define and contribute to an organization's health and safety in the working environment? How are they different? What are their effects?

4. What relationships do occupational safety and health have with other personnel activities?

5. What is the difference between the "no-risk" standard and the "significant risk" standard? How are these related to the evolution of OSHA?

6. What are three sources of occupational accidents? Give examples of each.

7. While certain occupational groups may be more at risk for occupational disease—for example, miners and construction workers—what physical and psychological ills, if any, are associated with white-collar office jobs, and why?

8. What is NIOSH, and what is its role in occupational health and safety?

9. What strategies are available for organizations wishing to reduce and control occupational accidents, occupational diseases, quality of work life, and organizational stress?

CASE

The Reluctant Employee

Sharon Hawkins is plant manager of Dalton Manufacturing's eastern facility. Just after noon she was approached by a production supervisor who told her of a problem he had encountered earlier in the day. One of the production employees had refused to do an assigned job that he had never done before. The employee argued that the job was unsafe and that he was therefore not obligated to perform it.

The production supervisor told Ms. Hawkins that he called the employee aside and explained that other employees routinely performed the job without complaining about safety. As he told Ms. Hawkins, this refusal seemed a clear case of insubordination, and since it had taken place in front of several other employees, he was concerned that it had eroded his authority.

The job in question, like many in an automated plant, does have an element of risk to it; however, every reasonable safety precaution is regularly followed by employees. Moreover, the equipment is periodically inspected for both operation and the integrity of its many safety features.

Ms. Hawkins has several concerns: First, if the employee performs the job and is injured, there is an issue of who's to blame. Second, given that the job is reasonably safe and that precautions are taken, there is an issue of insubordination. Third, who should judge the safety of this or any operation? Should this decision be made by management or by individual employees? Most jobs in manufacturing plants carry an element of risk. Therefore, any employee could refuse to work most jobs if the only criterion for refusal were the existence of some risk.

Case Questions

1. What would you advise Ms. Hawkins to tell the supervisor about the reluctant employee?

2. Can the employee refuse to do this assignment? Is this insubordination?

3. Who should judge the safety of a job?

4. Suppose that the employee agrees to work the job and is injured. Could the company argue the employee is to blame to relieve its liability?

FOR YOUR CAREER

- Although stress is not always harmful, you should be aware of how much stress you are under and how well you deal with it.
- Organizations are recognizing the importance of having a healthy work force. In your job interviews, check to see how important it is to the companies you are interviewing.
- The costs of accidents and diseases for many organizations are rather large. Knowing how to reduce these costs can make you a valuable employee.
- Safety and health are just as important whether you work in a factory or in an office. You should be aware of the unique hazards of each.
- It's really in your best interest to act safely regardless of whose fault an accident may be.
- You have the right to refuse unsafe work assignments.

ENDNOTES

1. This discussion is based in part on an article that appears in R. S. Schuler, J. McFillen, and D. Dalton, *Applied Readings in Personnel and Human Resources Management* (St. Paul: West Publishing, 1981).

2. J. G. Nelson, "Health: A New Personnel Imperative," *Personnel Administrator*, February 1980, pp. 69–71.

3. "Why Nobody Wants to Listen to OSHA," *Business Week*, June 14, 1976, p. 64.

4. P. S. Greenlaw and W. D. Biggs, *Modern Personnel Management*, (Philadelphia: Saunders, 1979), p. 588.

5. "New OSHA Tack," *Personnel Administrator*, June 1981, p. 12.

6. Phil Farish, "PAIR Potpourri," *Personnel Administrator*, February 1981, pp. 23–26.

7. American Federation of Labor and Congress of Industrial Organizations, *The Occupational Safety and Health Act*, Publication No. 149 (Washington, D.C.: American Federation of Labor and Congress of Industrial Organizations, September 1971).

8. "Why Nobody Wants to listen to OSHA," p. 64.

9. Vicky Cahan, "The Overhaul that Could Give OSHA Lite Under Reagan," *Business Week,* January 19, 1981, pp. 88–89.

"OSHA Is Now Trying to Help You." *Nation's Business,* August 1981, pp. 20–26.

"A Lighter Schedule of OSHA Inspections," *Business Week,* September 14, 1981, p. 38.

10. *The Occupational Safety and Health Act,* Public Law 91–596, December 29, 1970, Sec. 2, p. 1.

11. "Now OSHA Must Justify Its Inspection Targets," *Business Week,* April 9, 1979, p. 64.

12. *The Occupational Safety and Health Act,* Public Law 91–596, December 29, 1970, Sec. 12, p. 6.

13. Neil J. Sullivan, "The Benzene Decision: A Contribution to Regulatory Confusion," *Administrative Law Review,* 1981, pp. 351–365.

"From the Editor," *Employee Relations Law Journal* 6, No. 3 (1981):361–363.

Robert H. Sand, "Current Developments in OSHA, "*Employee Relations Law Journal* 6, No. 3 (1981):484–493.

14. J. Gardner, "Employee Safety," in J. Famularo, ed., *Handbook of Modern Personnel* (New York: McGraw-Hill, 1972).

15. "Suits That Are Searing Asbestos," *Business Week,* April 13, 1981, pp. 166–169.

16. J. V. Frimaldi and R. H. Simonds, *Safety Management,* (Homewood, Ill.: Irwin, 1975).

17. F. C. Rineford, "A New Look at Occupational Safety," *Personnel Administrator,* November 1977, pp. 29–36.

18. R. B. Hersey, "Rates of Production and Emotional State," *Personnel Journal,* April 1982, pp. 355–364.

19. Norman Root, "Injuries at Work Are Fewer Among Older Employees," *Monthly Labor Review,* March 1981, pp. 30–34.

20. N. A. Ashford, "The Nature and Dimension of Occupational Health and Safety Problems," p. 45. Reprinted with permission from the August 1977 issue of the *Personnel Administrator,* copyright 1977, The American Society for Personnel Administration, 30 Park Drive, Berea, Ohio 44017.

21. Ibid., p. 48.

22. M. Corn, "An Inside View of OSHA Compliance," *Personnel Administrator,* November 1979, pp. 39–42, 44.

23. C. L. Wang, "Occupational Skin Disease Continues to Plague Industry," *Monthly Labor Review,* February 1979, pp. 17–22.

24. Ashford, p. 48.

25. Wang, p. 17.

26. James T. Yenckel, "Careers: So You Think Your Job Is Cushy?" *Washington Post,* September 23, 1981, Sec. B, p. 5.

27. Eliot Marshal, "FDA Sees No Radiation Risk in VDT Screens," *Science,* June 5, 1981, pp. 1120–1121.

28. Berkeley Rice, "Can Companies Kill?", *Psychology Today,* June 1981, pp. 78–85.

29. A. B. Shostak, *Blue Collar Stress* (Reading, Mass.: Addison-Wesley, 1980), p. 28.

30. Ibid., p. 37.

31. "Editor to Reader," *Personnel Journal,* April 1981, pp. 242–246.

32. H. M. Taylor, "Occupational Health Management-by-Objectives," *Personnel,* January–February 1980, pp. 58–64.

33. V. Reinhart, "Ergonomic Studies Improving Life on the Job," *Job Safety and Health,* December 1975, pp. 16–21.

34. "Dubious Tactics in the War on Cancer," *Business Week,* June 14, 1976, p. 76, copyright 1976, McGraw-Hill. Reprinted with permission.

35. Corn, p. 42.

36. Ibid.

37. "Editor to Reader," *Personnel Journal,* July 1981, pp. 514–520.

38. R. E. Walton, "Work Innovations in the United States," *Harvard Business Review,* July–August 1979, p. 90.

39. A. P. Brief, R. S. Schuler, and M. Van Sell, *Managing Job Stress,* (Boston: Little, Brown and Company, 1981).

L. J. Warshaw, *Stress Management,* (Reading, Mass.: Addison-Wesley Publishing Company, 1980).

40. R. Kreitner, S. D. Wood, and G. M. Friedman, "Just How Fit Are Your Employees?" *Business Horizons,* August, 1979, pp. 39–45.

Union—Management Relations

Chapter 18
Unionization of Employees

Chapter 19
Collective Bargaining, Negotiating,
Conflict Resolution, and Contract
Administration

Chapter Outline

Critical Issues Facing the Unionization of Employees

Unionization of Employees
Importance and Purposes of Unionization
Relationships of Unionization with Other Personnel Activities

The Legal Framework for Unionization and Collective Bargaining
Railway Labor Act
National Labor Relations Act
Labor-Management Relations Act
Labor-Management Reporting and Disclosure Act
Federal Employee Regulations
State and Local Employee Regulations
Court Decisions

The Attraction of Unionization
The Decision to Join a Union
The Decision Not to Join a Union

The Development and State of Unionization
The Early Days: Tough Times
The Recent Days
Structure of Unionization in America
Operations of Unions

CHAPTER **18**

Unionization of Employees

The Organizing Campaign
The Campaign to Solicit Employee Support
Determination of the Bargaining Unit
The Preelection Campaign
Election, Certification and Decertification

Evaluating the Unionization of Employees

Facing the Critical Issues in the Unionization of Employees

Summary

Key Concepts

Discussion Questions

Case

For Your Career

Endnotes

551

Personnel in the News

Do We Still Need Labor Unions?

It is common knowledge today that organized labor is losing strength in both numerical and political terms, as well as in the influence it exerts over the rest of the labor force. Numerically, labor unions have gone from 42% of the labor force in the 1950s to less than 20% today, with every indication that this downward trend will continue. Were it not for the large number of newly organized public employees, the outlook would be even more ominous for labor unions. And many labor students contend that because of the restrictions on unions in the public sector (many cannot discuss wages and are prohibited from striking), the value to labor as a whole of a certain number of public employees organizing is not nearly as great as a like number of privately employed workers' organizing. Thus, even the decreasing numbers may not tell the whole story of labor's deteriorating position.

While organized labor has long been considered the trend setter for wages and terms of employment, even here we are witnessing the declining strength of unions. Except in a few big industries (steel, auto, etc.) where unions enjoy a virtual monopoly, the increasing number of nonunionized firms have reintroduced the cost of labor as a competitive factor in market strategies. More and more frequently, unions have had to consider the impact of their economic demands on the employers' ability to attract enough business to maintain employment levels. The construction industry is the most dramatic and widely known example of this phenomenon, but it is happening in an increasing number of less publicized instances. The "Southern strategy" of the auto employers, the move to the South of the big steel companies, and the inability of the mining unions to organize new mines are all indicators that even in industries long considered union strongholds, this factor will become increasingly important in the future. (Kenneth A. Kovach, Personnel Journal, *December 1979, p. 849. Reprinted with the permission of* Personnel Journal, *Costa Mesa, California; all rights reserved.*)

Hospital Labor Relations

Employee unrest, especially among women, and stepped-up union organizing activity will characterize labor relations in the health-care industry during the 1980s.

Today's hospital workforce, stresses Anthony F. McKeown, a Bannockburn, Ill., consultant, is the best educated, the most highly motivated, and the most aggressive of modern times. They are no longer quiescent and obedient in times of economic stress and high unemployment, he continues, adding that unions are making inroads in the traditionally unorganized health-care field.

Noting that the vast majority of nurses and service and maintenance workers are female while most doctors and administrators are male, McKeown says that the situation is "ripe for confrontation." The women's movement, he predicts, will be the single most important factor governing health-care employee relations in the next decade. Unions already have come "light years in realizing how the women's movement can benefit them," McKeown notes. In union representation elections over the

552

past two years, he points out, unions have been successful in 59 percent of the elections where women's rights were an issue, compared with less than 50 percent of elections overall. (Bulletin to Management, April, 1981, p. 7. Reprinted by permission from Bulletin to Management, Copyright 1981 by The Bureau of National Affairs, Inc., Washington, D.C.)

Divorce Union Style

If "unionism" is a dirty word to some corporations, "decertification" has an even more vile meaning to those in the labor movement. To be unceremoniously drummed out of a plant where a union already has a foothold constitutes the ultimate disgrace within organized labor.

"Decertification is a real stigma for the local union guy," says an official with the International Assn. of Machinists (IAM). "He's usually held responsible for it by the international." Thus, decertification is rarely accepted gracefully by unions.

It's not always an unexpected trauma. Sometimes the union senses a growing alienation from its membership, and simply fades away rather than fight a losing battle for worker loyalty. All that remains is for the employees to stamp out the last vestiges of the union through an unchallenged and perfunctory decertification vote.

But more often than not, particularly when large units or workplaces with established unions are involved, a decertification attempt can leave scars that go far beyond election day—and the plant gate as well.

Hence, few in either management or labor who've been through decertification like to talk about it. "It's kind of like divorce," says the IAM official. "You can get somebody to talk about it until you ask about theirs." The divorce analogy is an apt one, too: a relationship effected by law is legally voided, accompanied by the emotional strain of the breaking up of two parties who once thought they were meant for each other. When survivors do discuss a decertification, it's generally with bitterness and regret. (Daniel D. Cook, Industry Week, June 25, 1979, p. 37. Reprinted by permission of Industry Week. Copyright 1979, Penton/IPC, Inc.)

Together these quotations point to many important aspects of the unionization of employees. One is the rapid decline of the percentage of the work force that is unionized just in the last thirty years. Concurrent with this percentage decline in unionization has been the decline in union economic and political power. Unions, as well as managements, are having to fight for survival of the very industries they organized many years ago. And now instead of getting wage gains in those industries, they are having to take wage cuts.

All is not unfavorable for unionization, however. There are still industries that appear ripe for unionization. One is the health care industry. And as union campaigns in the health care industry continue to succeed, unionization can continue to survive and perhaps even grow. One mild trend, however, that threatens to put a damper on these hopes is decertification. Management, noting this trend, is increasing its efforts to make unionization a less attractive alternative to their employees—either ones currently unionized or still unorganized. In some cases they are succeeding. Among other things, management's desire to make unions less attractive is recognition that unions are still a force to be dealt with. Consequently, the topic of unionization raised a number of critical issues from our group of personnel managers.

CRITICAL ISSUES IN THE UNIONIZATION OF EMPLOYEES

The four most critical issues came equally from our group of personnel managers from unionized companies and from nonunionized companies. The issues are:

1. *Why would employees be most likely to start a unionization drive? Can employers legally stop them from starting one?*
2. *What can a company do to help prevent its employees from organizing?*
3. *If a company already has a union, how can it get rid of it? Is it really in a company's best interest not to have a union?*
4. *Since a union may be suspicious of a company's motives in establishing quality circles, how can a company convince them otherwise?*

Employees sometimes think that they are at a disadvantage in dealing with their employers. Organizations are certainly larger and more powerful than any single employee. The organization appears to the employee to practically "call all the shots." In an effort to redress this imbalance, employees unionize.

UNIONIZATION OF EMPLOYEES

Unionizing or **organizing** is the effort by employees and outside agencies (unions or associations) to band together and act as a single unit when dealing with management over issues related to their work. The most common form for organizing employees is the **union,** an organization with the legal authority to negotiate with the employer on behalf of the employees—over wages, hours, and other conditions of employment—and to administrate the ensuing agreement. In the public sector, employees are sometimes represented by employee associations like the National Education Association. Although **employee associations** may not be involved in as many functions as a union (they may not bargain with the employer, for example), most of the large associations do engage in the same activities and have become very similar to private-sector unions.

Importance and Purposes of Unionization

Unionization is often as important to employers as it is to employees, although for different reasons.

To Employers.   Understanding the organizing process, its causes, and its consequences is an important part of personnel and human resource management. The personnel department can play a key role in designing the organization and management structure to prevent unionization of employees. If unionization occurs, personnel managers will probably be given the task of dealing with the organizing effort: presenting management's view to the employees; responding to statements or behaviors of the unions, such as boycotts or picketing; and representing management at the certification proceedings. The personnel department may even need to create a labor relations department to deal with the union.

Unionization is important to organizations because it often results in management having less flexibility in hiring, job assignments, and the introduction of new work methods such as automation, a loss of control, inefficient work practices, and inflexible job structures. And as indicated in Chapter 8, unions get for their members rights that employees without unions do not legally have. This, of course, makes the management with unions consider their employees' reactions to many more decisions than management without unions.[1] This, however, is not always true. Employers who are nonunion and who want to remain that way often give more consideration and benefits to their employees. Consequently, the claim that it is more expensive for a company to operate with unionized employees than with nonunionized employees is not always the case.

Some employers claim that unions handcuff their ability to manage the work force.

To Employees.   Although it has been suggested that unions are attractive because they directly satisfy people's social or growth needs, this function does not appear to be so important as the union's influence in changing the work setting. A national survey of workers by the University of Michigan Survey Research Center indicates that workers perceive the union's goals to be related primarily to job context factors. Of all the goals listed, 80.5 percent were related to wages, benefits, working conditions, or job security; 1.3 percent were concerned with job content; 6.5 percent had to do with union power, such as dominating business or obtaining political power; and 11.7 percent had negative associations, such as hurting employees, business, or the country. The same survey showed that 89 percent of the workers felt unions have power to improve wages and working conditions, 87 percent felt they had power to improve job security, and 80 percent felt they could protect workers.[2]

Employees perceive many benefits from unions.

These perceptions and goals that workers have of unions help indicate the importance and purpose of unions to employees. This is because surveys continue to show the four most common and important goals of employees to be:

- Earning a living wage
- Working in a safe environment
- Having decent hours of work
- Having comfortable physical surroundings[3]

These goals are particularly interesting in light of the recent emphasis on other issues often associated with the quality of work life, issues such as employee participation, quality circles, and job enrichment. Though not diminishing the importance of participation and job enrichment, this does suggest that, for many workers, having a quality of work life means first having decent income and working conditions.

Exhibit 18.1
Relationships and Aspects of the Unionization of Employees, the
Union-Management Relationship

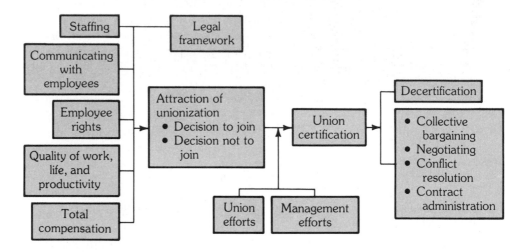

Relationships of Unionization with Other Personnel Activities

As shown in Exhibit 18.1 the unionization of employees is related to many other personnel functions and has an extensive set of legal relationships. Because these legal relationships influence organizing as well as other collective bargaining activities, an entire section is devoted to the discussion of the legal framework for unionization and collective bargaining.

Staffing.   Unionization has a direct impact on who is hired and the conditions under which applicants are hired. In the construction industry, union hiring halls are generally the source of employees for any employer hiring construction workers who are union members. In states with **union shop** provisions (approximately three-fifths of the states), employees must join the union (if the company has one for the particular group of employees) after a set number of days, often sixty or ninety days. In the remaining states where **right-to-work** laws exist (mainly in the sunbelt states), employees do not have to join a union even if one exists.

Communicating with Employees.   A common source of employees' desire for unionization is the way that supervisors communicate with them. As discussed in Chapter 7, supervisory communication behaviors and style can be associated with very productive and satisfied employees or very unproductive and dissatisfied employees. The quality of communications from top management is also critical in how employees feel about unionization. If a feeling of one big happy family can be communicated by top management, employees are more likely to be loyal to the company and less likely to be attracted to unionization.

Employee Rights.   When employers treat individuals with fairness and respect, employees are also more likely to feel loyal towards their employers. Since treating employees fairly and with respect results from recognizing and observing employee rights, the more rights that employers recognize and observe, the better employees feel. Consequently it really pays an organization, if it wants to remain union-free, to observe all the legal rights of employees and to recognize and observe many of the "humane" rights of employees described in Chapter 8. If employers fail to do this, employees are more likely to unionize. Once unionized, the union will help ensure that many employee rights (legal and humane) are recognized and observed.

It pays to respect the rights of employees.

Quality of Work Life and Productivity. As described in Chapter 16, many programs for QWL and productivity improvement are undertaken jointly by union and management. Although not all unions support these programs, thinking that management uses them to help weaken the union, many unions do offer active support and the involvement (generally voluntary) of their members. In addition to union impetus for QWL and productivity programs, employers often initiate these programs to ward off the threat of unionization. Thus in either case, unionization can be a potent force behind these programs.

Unions and the threat of unions can be very helpful for employees.

Compensation. Since one of the most important goals of employees is a decent wage and adequate indirect benefits and since unions are perceived as causing employers to provide them, if employers are not providing them, employees are likely to turn to unionization. The threat of possible unionization is often enough to cause employers to provide even more than decent wages and benefits.

THE LEGAL FRAMEWORK FOR UNIONIZATION AND COLLECTIVE BARGAINING

The federal government entered the labor scene in an attempt to stabilize the rather violent and disruptive labor situation in the 1920s and 1930s.[4] Court actions and efforts by employers at the time appeared to be suppressing the rights of workers to act collectively to protect their interests.

Federal legislation specifically addressing labor relations dates back to 1926, when the Railway Labor Act was passed. Since then, several statutory labor laws (listed in Appendix A) have become the basis for today's labor relations.

Railway Labor Act

The **Railway Labor Act** (**RLA**) was passed by Congress in 1926 to prevent the serious economic consequences of labor unrest in the railway industry. It has since been expanded to include air carrier employees as well.

The RLA was the first act to protect "the fundamental right of workers to engage in labor organizing actively without fear of employer retaliation and discrimination."[5] Other objectives of the act were to avoid service interruption, to eliminate any restrictions on joining a union, and to provide for prompt settlement of disputes and grievances.[6]

The act specified that employers and employees would maintain an agreement over pay, rules, working conditions, dispute settlement, representation, and grievance settlement. A Board of Mediation (later to be called the National Mediation Board) was created to aid in the settlement of disputes through encouragement of, first, negotiation, then arbitration, and finally the President's emergency intervention. A second Board—the National Railway Adjustment Board—was created in 1934 to deal with grievances. This board has exclusive jurisdiction over questions relating to grievances or the interpretation of agreement concerning pay, rules, or working conditions; it makes decisions and awards that are binding on both parties.

National Labor Relations Act

The success of the Railway Labor Act led Congress to enact a comprehensive labor code in 1935. The purpose of the National Labor Relations Act (NLRA), also known as the **Wagner Act,** was to "restore the equality of bargaining power arising out of employers' general denial to labor of the right to bargain collectively with them."[7] Such employer refusal resulted in poor working conditions, depression of wages, and a general depression of business.

The NLRA affirmed employees' rights to form, join, or assist labor organizations, to bargain collectively, and to choose their own bargaining representative through majority rule. The second significant portion of the act identified five unfair labor practices on the part of employers:

- Interference with the efforts of employees to organize
- Domination of the labor organization by the employer
- Discrimination in the hiring or tenure of employees to discourage union affiliation
- Discrimination for filing charges or giving testimony under the act
- Refusal to bargain collectively with a representative of the employees

Court interpretation of these unfair labor practices has made it clear that bribing, spying, blacklisting union sympathizers, moving a business to avoid union activities, and other such employer actions are illegal.[8]

The **National Labor Relations Board** (**NLRB**) was established to administer this act. Its major function is to decide all unfair labor practice suits. It also has authority over the election of bargaining representatives.[9]

Labor-Management Relations Act

Employer groups criticized the Wagner Act on several grounds. They argued that the act, in addition to being biased toward unions, limited the constitutional right of free speech of employers, did not consider unfair labor practices on the part of unions, and caused employers serious damage when there were jurisdictional disputes.

Congress responded to these criticisms in 1947 by enacting the Labor-Management Relations Act, often called the **Taft-Hartley Act.** This act revised and expanded the Wagner Act in order to establish a balance between union and management power and to protect the public interest. Among the changes it introduced:

- Employees were allowed to refrain from union activity as well as to engage in it.
- The closed shop was outlawed, and written agreement from employees was required for deducting union dues from workers' paychecks.
- Unions composed of supervisors did not need to be recognized.

- Employers were ensured of their right to free speech, and they were given the right to file charges against unfair labor practices. The unfair practices that were identified were coercing workers to join the unions, causing employers to discriminate against those who do not join, refusing to bargain in good faith, requiring excessive or discriminatory fees, and engaging in featherbedding activities.

- Certification elections (voting for union representation) could not be held more frequently than once a year.

- Employees were given the right to initiate decertification elections.[10]

These provisions indicated the philosophy behind the act—as Senator Taft put it, "simply to reduce the special privileges granted labor leaders."

From time to time amendments are added to the Taft-Hartley Act. For example, the 1980 amendments to the act provided for an identical accommodation for employees with religious objections to union membership or support. Thus employers and unions must accommodate (within reason) the religious beliefs of employees as protected by Title VII. For example, an employee may, on religious grounds, contribute to a charity in lieu of paying union dues (*Tooley* v. *Martin-Marietta Corp.* [1981]).

Labor-Management Reporting and Disclosure Act

Although the Taft-Hartley Act included some regulation of internal union activities, abuse of power and the corruption of some union officials led to the passage of a "bill of rights" for union members in 1959. The Labor-Management Reporting and Disclosure Act, or the **Landrum-Griffin Act,** provided a detailed regulation of internal union affairs. Some of the provisions include

- Equality of rights for union members in nominating and voting in elections
- Controls on increases in dues
- Control of suspension and firing of union members
- Elections every three years for local offices and every five for national or international offices
- Restriction of the use of trusteeship to take control of a member group's autonomy for political reasons
- Definition of the type of person who can hold union office
- Filing of yearly reports with the secretary of labor

The intention of this act was to protect employees from corrupt or discriminatory labor unions. By providing detailed provisions for union conduct, much of the flagrant abuse of power was eliminated, and the democratic rights of employees were protected to some degree. The United Mine Workers, for example, held their first election of international officers in 1969. This event may not have been likely to occur even then without the provisions of the Landrum-Griffin Act.

Federal Employee Regulations

These labor laws were enacted to govern labor relations in the private sector. In fact, the Wagner Act specifically excludes the U.S. government, government corporations, states, and municipal corporations in its definition of employer. Therefore, for a long time government employees lacked the legislative protection afforded private-sector workers. Until recently, federal employee labor relations were controlled by executive orders issued by the president.

The government's view of its employees differs from its view of private-sector employees. Several of the rights of unions in the private sector are not included in public-sector regulations, although the content of these regulations often is lifted from private-sector acts.

There are several significant differences between labor relations in the private sector and those in the public sector.

Executive Orders. The first set of regulations for federal employee labor relations was Executive Order 10988, introduced by President John Kennedy in 1962. This order forbade federal agencies from interfering with employee organizing or unlawful union activity and provided for recognition of employee organizations. Employee organizations were denied the right to strike, however, and economic issues were not part of the bargaining process, since these are fixed by the Civil Service classification system. Agency heads were made the ultimate authority on grievances, and managers were excluded from the bargaining units.

Executive Order 11491, issued in 1969 and amended in 1971 (EO 11616) and 1975 (EO 11838), addressed some of the difficulties presented by the first executive order. It created a Labor Relations Council to hear appeals from the decisions of agency heads, prescribed regulations and policies, and created a Federal Services Impasses Panel to act on negotiation impasses. The council and the employee representatives could meet and discuss personnel practices and working conditions, but all agreements had to be approved by the council head. Unfair labor practices by both agency management and labor organizations were delineated. The council was restricted from interference, discrimination, sponsorship of union discipline against an employee for filing a complaint, and was required to recognize or deal with a qualified union. Labor organizations also were restrained from interfering, coercing management or employees, discriminating against employees, calling for or engaging in a strike, or denying membership to an employee.

These controls on employers and labor organizations are similar to those found in private-sector legislation. Yet federal employees do not have the same bargaining rights. They lack rights in four areas:

- No provision is made for bargaining on economic issues.
- Although the parties can meet and confer, there is no obligation to do so.
- The ultimate authority is the agency head rather than a neutral party.
- There is no provision for union security through the agency shop, which requires all employees to pay dues but not to join the union.

Civil Service Reform Act. In 1978 the Federal Service Labor-Management Relations Statute was passed as **Title VII of the Civil Service Reform Act,** which has been referred to as "the most significant change in federal personnel administration since the passage of the Civil Service Act in 1883."[11] Several significant changes were made by the statute, prime among them the following:

- Passage of the statute removed the president's ability to change the act through executive order and in general made it more difficult to change the legislation.

- It established the **Federal Labor Relations Authority (FLRA)**, modeled after the NLRB, as an "independent, neutral, full-time, bipartisan agency"[12] created, as President Jimmy Carter said, "to remedy unfair labor practices within the Government." Interpretation of the act is the province of the FLRA and the courts. Agency heads, including the president, cannot define the meaning of the act.

- An aggrieved person may now seek judicial review of a final order of the FLRA. The FLRA may also seek judicial enforcement of its order.

- Negotiated grievance procedures, which must be included in all agreements, must provide for arbitration as the final step.

State and Local Employee Regulations

Employee relations regulations at the state and local level are varied. Not all states have legislation governing their employees, but some states have legislation covering municipal employees as well. One widespread regulation can be noted. **Collective bargaining** is permitted in most states, and it covers wages, hours, and other terms and conditions of employment. The other terms and conditions have caused the most difficulty in interpretation. Managerial prerogatives are usually quite strong, especially for firefighters, police, and teachers. The requirement to bargain over certain issues in the private sector is not so stringent at the state or local level. In addition, some twenty states have passed "**right-to-work**" laws, which prohibit union membership as a condition of employment.

Although the rights and privileges of public-sector labor organizations are not so extensive as those in the private sector, the greatest growth in unionization in recent years has come in the public sector. This will become an increasingly important area of labor relations in the 1980s.

Court Decisions

One of the most significant court decisions of the 1980s is *First National Maintenance Corp.* v. *NLRB.*[13] In this case the Supreme Court held that an employer is not obligated to bargain with the union about a decision to close a portion of its business. As discussed in Chapter 8, however, many employers are discussing plant closings and relocation plans with employees and unions. Not only does this imply a recognition of the employee's right to know, but it also bodes well for future relationships between the employees and management and for the ease of the facility being closed.[14]

Management can still decide when and where it wants to run its business.

The cornerstone of labor relations, the grievance-arbitration process, was established in *Textile Workers Union* v. *Lincoln Mills* (1957). In that case decided by the Supreme Court, it was held that the agreement to arbitrate grievances is the quid pro quo for an agreement not to strike through the years. This agreement, however, has been afflicted with the problem of **unfair representation** by the union of its members.[15] Over the past ten years, cases filed by employees with the NLRB against their unions for unfair representation (breach of duty) have more than tripled to several thousand annually. Although the union's obligation of fair representation is clear, the parameters of the specific duties of this obligation have been left unclear by numerous court decisions, including *Ford Motor Co. v. Huffman* (1953); *Hines v. Anchor Motor Freight Co.* (1976); *Milstead v. Teamsters, Local 957* (1979) and the NLRB ruling in *Miranda Fuel Co.* (1962). (See also Chapter 19, p. 612).

Finally, in the area of seniority systems the Supreme Court has ruled that "bona fide" seniority systems are protected under section 703(h) of Title VII of the 1964 Civil Rights Act. Thus equal employment considerations in general do not replace seniority systems in employment decisions where a seniority system has been in existence for some time or where its intention is not discriminatory (*California Brewers Association v. Bryant* (1980) and *International Brotherhood of Teamsters v. United States* (1977) and *American Tobacco v. Patterson* (1982) as discussed in Chapter 5. Recall from Chapter 4, however, that the Court in the *Weber* case held that employers and unions may establish formal, voluntary affirmative action plans. At this time, however, the Civil Rights Division in the Justice Department is attempting to get the Supreme Court to reverse its ruling in *Weber*.[16] Thus the legal framework surrounding unionization is extensive. This framework, however, does not ensure union membership. Union must *attract* members.

THE ATTRACTION OF UNIONIZATION

Unions were originally formed as a response to management's exploitation and abuse of employees. To understand the union movement today, however, it is necessary to consider the reasons employees decide to join unions and the reasons they decide not to.

The Decision to Join a Union

Unions are attractive due to employee:
- dissatisfaction
- lack of power

There are two major conditions that prompt an individual to decide to join a union or at least give serious consideration to joining a union. They are dissatisfaction and the lack of power.

Dissatisfaction. When an individual takes a job, certain conditions of employment (wages, hours, type of work) are specified in the **employment contract.** There is also a **psychological contract** between employer and employee, which consists of the unspecified expectations of the employee—expectations about reasonable working conditions, requirements of the work itself, the level of effort that should be expended on the job, and the amount and nature of the authority the employer has in directing the employee's work.[17] These expectations are related to the employee's desire to satisfy certain personal needs in the work place. The degree to which the organization fulfills these needs determines the employee's level of satisfaction.[18]

Dissatisfaction with either the employment or the psychological contract will lead employees to attempt to improve the work situation, often through unionization. A major study has found a very strong relationship between level of satisfaction and the proportion of workers voting for a union.[19] Almost all workers who were highly dissatisfied voted for a union, but almost all workers who were satisfied voted against the union (see Exhibit 18.2).

Thus if management wants to make unionization less attractive to employees, it

Exhibit 18.2
**Relationship between Employee Satisfaction and Voting for
Unionization** (From *Union Representation Elections: Law and Reality,* by
Getman *et al.,* copyright © 1976 by Russell Sage Foundation. Reprinted
by permission of the publisher.)

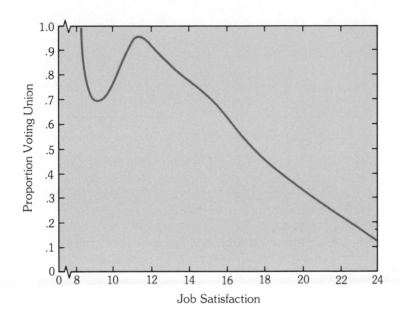

should make more satisfying work conditions. Yet management and the personnel
department often contribute to the level of work dissatisfaction by

- Giving unrealistic job previews creating expectations that can't be fulfilled
- Designing jobs that fail to use the skills and abilities of employees and fail to satisfy
  their needs and values
- Practicing day-to-day management and supervisory behaviors, such as poor supervisory practices, unfair treatment, and lack of upward communication
- Failing to tell employees that management would prefer to operate without unions
  and that they are commited to treating employees with respect. A recommended
  way employers can communicate this preference and commitment is through a
  policy statement similar to this example:

> Our success as a company is founded on the skill and efforts of our employees.
> Our policy is to deal with employees as effectively as possible, respecting and
> recognizing each of them as individuals.
> In our opinion, unionization would interfere with the individual treatment, re-
> spect and recognition the company offers.
> Consequently, we believe a union-free environment is in the employee's best
> interest, the company's best interest and the interest of the people served by the
> corporation.[20]

Power is enhanced by essentiality and exclusivity.

Lack of Power. Unionization, however, is seldom the first recourse of employees who are dissatisfied with some aspect of their job. The first attempt to improve the work situation is usually made by an individual acting alone. Someone who has enough power or influence can affect the necessary changes without collaborating with others. The features of a job that determine the amount of power the job holder has in the organization are **essentiality,** or how important or critical the job is to the overall success of the organization, and **exclusivity,** or how difficult it is to replace the person.[21] An employee with an essential task who is difficult to replace will be able to force the employer to make changes. If, however, the individual task is not critical and the employee can easily be replaced, employees are likely to consider other means, including collective action, to increase their power to influence the organization.

To summarize, there are *two factors* on which the decision or motivation to unionize is based: dissatisfaction with the employer's fulfillment of the written or psychological contract, which impairs satisfaction of needs, and the individual's lack of ability of power to change the situation or to influence the employer to change the situation.[22]

The *processes* involved in the decision to unionize are summarized in Exhibit 18.3. The expectation that work will satisfy personal needs may induce satisfaction or dissatisfaction with work. As the level of dissatisfaction increases, individual workers seek to change their work situation. If they fail, and if the positive consequences of unionization seem to outweigh the negative consequences, individuals will be inclined to join the union. This, however, will not always be the case. Employees may choose not to join a union.

The Decision Not to Join a Union

The question of whether to join a union involves an assessment of the negative consequences of unionization. Employees may have misgivings about how effectively a union can improve unsatisfactory work conditions. Collective bargaining is not always successful; if the union is not strong, it will be unable to make an employer meet its demands. Even if an employer does respond to union demands, the workers may be affected adversely. The employer may not be able to survive when the demands of the union are met, and thus the company may close down, costing employees their jobs. The organization may force the union to strike, inflicting economic hardship on employees who may not be able to afford being out of work, or it may in some cases attempt reprisals against pro-union employees, although this is illegal.[23]

Exhibit 18.3
Processes in the Decision to Organize (Source: William D. Todor).

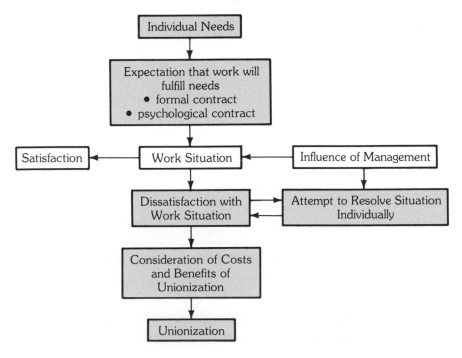

Beyond perceptions of unions as ineffective in the pursuit of personal goals, employees may also resist unionization because of general attitudes toward unions. Employees may identify strongly with the company and have a high level of commitment to it. They would, therefore, tend to view the union as an adversary and would be receptive to company arguments against unions. Employees may also perceive the goals of the union to be objectionable, intending to harm the company and the free enterprise system in general. They may object to the concept of seniority or even to the political activities of the unions. Moreover, certain employees—for example, engineers or college professors—view themselves as professionals and find collective action to be contrary to such professional ideals as independence and self-control.[24]

Good management involves care and consideration of employees.

The decision not to unionize can be influenced by management as well. Many companies successfully avoid unionization through good management practices: fostering, opening channels of communication, setting up processes for handling employee problems and grievances, developing employee trust, and offering competitive wages[25]—all characteristics of effective personnel management discussed throughout this book. It should be noted that, along with the many benefits employees may receive from joining a union, employers may also benefit from their employees unionizing. This is especially so when the union brings some certainty and discipline to the work force. In essence, a union can help management manage the work force.

THE DEVELOPMENT AND STATE OF UNIONIZATION

The study of labor unions is enhanced a great deal by an appreciation of their historical context.[26] You may also better understand some of the attitudes and behaviors of both unions and management through a knowledge of past labor-management relations.

The Early Days: Tough Times

Labor unions in the United States can be traced back to the successful attempt of journeymen printers to win a wage increase in 1778.[27] By the 1790s, unions of shoemakers, carpenters, and printers had appeared in Boston, Baltimore, New York, and other cities. The Federal Society of Journeymen Cordwainers, for example, was organized in Philadelphia in 1794, primarily to resist employers' attempts to reduce wages. Other issues of concern to these early unions were union shops and regulation of apprenticeship to prevent the replacement of journeymen employees.

The early unions had methods and objectives that are still in evidence today. Although there was no collective bargaining, the unions did establish a price below which members would not work. Strikes were used to enforce this rate. These strikes were relatively peaceful and for the most part successful.

One negative characteristic of early unions was their susceptibility to depressions. Until the late 1800s, most unions thrived in times of prosperity but died off during depressions. Part of this problem may have been related to the insularity of the unions. Aside from sharing information on strikebreakers or scabs, the unions operated independently.

The work situation at the end of the nineteenth century evidenced several important changes. Transportation systems (canals and turnpikes) expanded the markets for products and increased worker mobility. Increases in capital costs prevented journey-men from reaching the status of master craftworker (that is, from setting up their own businesses), thereby creating a class of skilled workers. Unionism found its start in these skilled occupations, largely because "the skilled worker . . . had mastered his craft and was no longer occupationally mobile" and the alternatives were "to pas-sively accept wage cuts, the competition of nonapprentice labor and the harsh working conditions, or to join in collective action against such employer innovations."[28]

Employers reacted to the unions by forming employers' associations and taking court action. The major legal tool was the conspiracy law, which was used to prosecute workers' organizations as illegal conspiracies in restraint of trade. The Cordwainers of Philadelphia were found guilty of such a conspiracy in 1806, and the courts estab-lished a "conspiracy doctrine" that was used against unions in the ensuing decades. This doctrine, along with a depression in 1819, successfully repressed the union movement.

The unions continued to experience highs and lows that were largely tied to economic conditions. Employers took advantage of the depression to combat unions: In "an all out frontal attack . . . they engaged in frequent lockouts, hired spies . . . summarily discharged labor 'agitators,' and [engaged] the services of strike breakers on a widespread scale."[29] These actions, and the retaliations of unions, established a tenor of violence and lent a strong adversarial nature to labor-management relations, the residual of which is in evidence today.

The history of union-management relations is filled with turmoil and bloodshed.

The Recent Days

The union movement has had its highs and lows. Recently it has been in one of its lows.

The Decline in Membership.   In 1980 the number of employees belonging to unions or employee associations was about 24 million. The distribution of these members among unions and employee associations is shown in Exhibit 18.4. Mem-bership grew to a peak of 23.4 million in 1974 and then leveled off.

The proportion of the labor force represented by unions has been declining steadily since the mid-1960s. In 1980, only 20.8 percent of nonagricultural workers were represented by unions, the lowest proportion since the mid-1930s and down from 22.3 percent in 1978. Factors that contribute to this decline include the increase in public sector employment and white-collar jobs, both of which have historically had a low proportion of union members, and the decline in employment in industries that are highly unionized. In the future, however, economic conditions and legislation may make unionization more feasible in white-collar and public sector jobs. Indeed, most organizing activities today are focused on the public sector services and health care as described in the quotation at the beginning of this chapter.[30]

In addition to this focus on particular industries for expansion of membership, unions are targeting areas of the country, particularly the sunbelt. For example, the AFL-CIO is embarking on a costly multiyear campaign to organize workers in all industries in the Houston area. Practically all industries in this area are tempting organizing targets. In Houston between 1970 and 1977 employment increased 90 percent in services, 60 percent in financial institutions, 54 percent in retail trade, 49 percent in construction and 32 percent in manufacturing. In other words, only 15 percent of Houston's work force are union members.[31]

Some parts of the country are key unionization targets.

Exhibit 18.4
Union and Association Membership in the United States, 1980
(in thousands) (Adapted from Eugene Becker, Bureau of Labor
Statistics, U.S. Department of Labor, Washington, D.C., May 1982,
personal communication.)

National unions affiliated with AFL-CIO	13,940	
Unaffiliated unions	7,113	
Total union membership		21,053
Professional and state employee associations	2,623	
Municipal employee associations	235	
Total employee association membership		2,858
Total union and association membership		23,911

The Distribution of Membership. Historically, membership has been concentrated in a small number of large unions.[32] In 1976, sixteen unions represented 60 percent of union membership, and eighty-five unions represented just 2.4 percent. Similarly, the National Education Association accounted for 62 percent of all association members. Many employee associations are small because they are state organizations; their membership potential, therefore, is limited. Moreover, unions have been acquiring members at the expense of some associations.[33] Exhibit 18.5 lists the ten largest unions and six largest employee associations and their membership as of 1981.

It is interesting to examine the distribution of union membership by industry. Manufacturing accounted for 33.4 percent of union and association membership in 1978, nonmanufacturing for 41.8 percent, and government for 34.8 percent. There has been a steady drop in the proportion of union membership in manufacturing—

Exhibit 18.5
Union and Employee Association Membership, 1981 (Adapted
from Eugene Becker, U.S. Department of Labor, Bureau of Labor
Statistics, personal communication, May, 1982.)

Union	Membership (in thousands)	Employee Association	Membership (in thousands)
Teamsters	1,891	Teachers (National	1,684
Automobile workers	1,357	Education Association)	
Steelworkers	1,238	Civil service	255
Electrical workers	1,041	employees	
(International Brotherhood		Nurses	180
of Electrical Workers)		Police	150
Machinists	754	California	105
Carpenters	784	employees	
State, county and	1,098		
municipal employees			
Laborers	608		
Service employees	650		

Exhibit 18.6
Proportion of Employees Unionized, by Industry (Adapted from
U.S. Department of Labor, Bureau of Labor Statistics, *Directory of
National Unions and Employee Associations, 1977,* Bulletin No. 2044
[Washington, D.C.: Government Printing Office, 1979], p. 70.)

75 percent and over	50 percent to 75 percent
Transportation	Telephone and telegraph
Contract construction	Transportation equipment
	Primary metals
	Petroleum
	Food and kindred products
	Apparel
	Tobacco manufactures
	Stone, clay, and glass products
	Mining
	Fabricated metals
	Electrical machinery
	Federal government
	Paper
	Manufacturing

25 percent to 50 percent	Less than 25 percent
Rubber	Chemicals
Machinery	Nonmanufacturing
Lumber	Textile mill products
Leather	Instruments
Electric and gas utilities	Service
Furniture	Finance
Federal government	Agriculture and fishing
Local government	Trade
Printing and publishing	
State government	

from 48.2 percent in 1958 to 33.4 percent in 1978—and a steady increase in government—from 5 percent in 1958 to 34.8 percent in 1978.

The proportion of employees in different industries is presented in Exhibit 18.6. Many of the major industries—transportation, construction, mining, telephone and telegraph—have over half their employees unionized, whereas service, finance, agriculture and fishing, and trade are the least represented. Since the effectiveness of unions depends on their ability to increase membership, unions in industries that are highly unionized have begun to look to these less-organized industries for members.

Unions today are exhibiting a substantial and increasing amount of diversification of membership. For example, in 1958, 73 percent of the unions had at least four-fifths of their members in a single industry; this had dropped to 55 percent in 1976. The most pronounced diversification has occurred in manufacturing. For example, of the twenty-nine unions that represent workers in chemicals and allied products, twenty-six presently have less than 20 percent of their membership in a single industry.[34]

Structure of Unionization in America

The basic unit of labor unions in the United States is the **national union** (or international union), a body that organizes, charters, and controls member **union locals.** The national union develops general policies and procedures by which locals operate and provides assistance to them in such areas as collective bargaining. National unions provide clout for the locals because they control a large number of employees and can influence large organizations through national strikes or slowdown activities.

The major umbrella organization for national unions is the **AFL-CIO**—the American Federation of Labor and Congress of Industrial Organizations. It represents about 77 percent of the total union membership and contains 106 national unions. Although several major unions are not members, including the two biggest (the Teamsters and United Auto Workers), the AFL-CIO is an important and powerful body.

Every two years the AFL-CIO holds a convention to develop policy and amend its constitution. Each national union is represented in proportion to its membership. Between conventions, an executive council (the governing body) and a general board direct the organization's affairs; a president is in charge of day-to-day operations. The executive council's activities include evaluating legislation that affects labor and watching for corruption within the AFL-CIO. Standing committees are appointed to deal with executive, legislative, political, educational, organizing, and other activities.

FOR YOUR CAREER

The American Federation of Labor began in 1886 and quickly assumed a leading role in the union movement. Much of its early success can be traced to the pragmatic approach of its president, Samuel Gompers, and to the principles he adopted:

- The national unions were to be autonomous within the AFL.
- Only one national union would be accepted for each trade or craft.
- The AFL would focus on the issues of wages, hours, and working conditions and avoid reformist goals.
- The AFL would avoid permanent political alliances.
- The strike would become a key weapon for achieving union objectives.

The AFL also accepted and endorsed the free enterprise system, choosing to operate within it rather than to change the whole system. The policy of giving national craft unions substantial control over their own affairs successfully attracted these unions and allowed the AFL to grow substantially despite employer campaigns to inhibit growth. Legislation passed in the 1930s made the legal climate more conducive to union growth.

The Congress of Industrial Organizations (CIO) was formed in 1935 as a rival union organization that focused on industrywide unions rather than craft unions. The competition between the AFL and the CIO intensified unionizing efforts, and by 1941, 10.2 million workers were union members. The labor movement had become representative of the full spectrum of American workers.

Eventually the CIO and the AFL, realizing that their competition was not in the best interests of labor, merged into the AFL-CIO. The merger of these organizations eliminated jurisdictional squabbles and gave union leaders a stronger voice. The new organization had great expectations for a significant growth in membership.

In spite of these expectations, the AFL-CIO lost membership over the next two decades. Several factors accounted for this decline: The Teamsters and the United Auto Workers left the organization, corruption among unions tarnished their image, and increasingly high wage demands resulted in a lack of public confidence. Changing attitudes among employees and the public also reduced the appeal of labor unions. Membership today continues to grow at a slow pace, and hopes for large-scale unionization seem to be fading. The United Auto Workers, however, have come back into the fold, and the concern for job security and wages is more important than ever.

The Department of Organization and Field Services, for instance, focuses its attention on organizing activities. Outside of headquarters, three structures exist to organize the local unions. Many of the craft unions are organized into the Trade Department and the Industrial Department, which represent them to the national union. The remaining locals are organized directly into national unions, which are affiliated with headquarters but retain their independence in dealing with their own union matters.

Sixty-three national unions, representing 4.5 million workers, operate independently of the AFL-CIO. This separation is not considered desirable by the AFL-CIO, and at its 1980 convention Lane Kirkland, the AFL-CIO president, indicated that affiliation talks were underway with the Teamsters, the largest independent union.

At the heart of the labor movement are the 70,000 or so local unions, varying in size up to 40,000 members. The locals represent the workers at the work place, where much of the day-to-day contact with management and the personnel department takes place. Most locals elect a president, a secretary-treasurer, and perhaps one or two other officers from the membership. In the larger locals, a business representative is hired as a full-time employee to handle grievances and contract negotiations. The other important member of the union local is the **steward,** an employee elected by his or her work unit to act as the union representative on the work site and to respond to company actions against employees that may violate the labor agreement. The steward protects the rights of the worker by filing grievances where the employer has acted improperly.

Women in Unions. The 6.6 million women who belong to unions and employee associations comprise 22 percent of union membership and 59 percent of association membership. In spite of this, representation of women in union governing bodies has been extremely low.[35] In 1976 only 8 percent of union board members were women. The membership of the International Ladies Garment Workers, for example, is 80 percent female, but only one woman sits on that union's board of directors. This, however, is very similar to the conditions in Japan. Only one of the 16 top executives in the Japanese Federation of Electrical Machine Workers Union is a woman even though nearly one-fifth of its 530,000 members are female.[36]

In America, as in Japan, women are getting increasing attention from labor leaders. This is for two major reasons: (1) As women become increasingly better educated and move into top-management positions, unions will be forced to deal with them; and (2) women are in the industries, such as health care, that are a major territory and hope for union membership expansion. So in addition to labor's concern for social equality and fair treatment, unions must more completely integrate women and minorities for union survival and growth.

Women in the work force represent a large group of potential union members.

Operations of Unions

Activities of union locals revolve around collective bargaining and handling griev-ances. In addition, locals hold general meetings, publish newsletters, and otherwise keep their members informed. Typically, however, the membership is apathetic about union involvement. Unless a serious problem exists, attendance at meetings is usually very low, and often even elections of officers draw votes from less than one-fourth of the membership.

At headquarters, the AFL-CIO is involved in a variety of activities. Staff and committees work on a wide range of issues, including civil rights, community service, economic policy, education, ethical practices, housing, international affairs, legislation, public relations, research, safety, social security, and veterans' affairs. There is also a publication department, which produces a variety of literature for the membership and outsiders.

National union headquarters also provide a variety of specialized services to regional and local bodies. Specialists in organizing, strikes, legal matters, public rela-tions, and negotiations are available to individual unions.

Unions must fight to survive and grow.
Another important role for national unions and the AFL-CIO is in the political arena. Labor maintains a strong lobbying force in Washington, D.C., and is also involved at the state and local level. A recent development is the international political activities of some of the large national unions. The United Auto Workers have held discussions with Japanese car manufacturers concerning the level of imports into the United States and the construction of assembly plants here. They have threatened to lobby in Washington to restrict imports of cars in an attempt to bolster U.S. auto makers and to increase jobs. Thus, in an attempt to help their membership, unions are expanding their activities on all levels, and in some cases they work with organizations to attain mutual goals.

Without doubt, times are tough for unions. Recent indications are that the lobby-ing clout of unions in Washington has diminished substantially when compared to that of business. Most large unions have always had political action committees in Wash-ington, but the number of business committees has increased tenfold from 1974 to 1981. This increase in activity and a concern for the abuse of influence by big business has encouraged labor, consumer, and public-interest groups to unite to curb the power of business.[37] This adversity, however, is forcing the union movement also to get tough. It's also causing factions of the union movement to band together for political and economic reasons.

THE ORGANIZING CAMPAIGN

Now that there is a well-established legal environment for the unionization of em-ployees, it is much easier for employees to organize. This, combined with employee dissatisfaction and lack of power, helps start the organizing campaign.

> The process by which a single union is selected to represent all employees in a particular unit is crucial to the American system of collective bargaining. If a major-ity vote for union representation, all employees are bound by that choice and the employer is obligated to recognize and bargain with the chosen union.[38]

One of the major functions of the National Labor Relations Board is to conduct the selection of unions to represent nongovernment employees. This is accomplished

Exhibit 18.7
Certification Process (Source: William D. Todor).

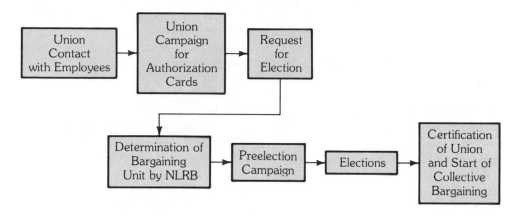

through a **certification election** to determine if the majority of employees want the union. Under American labor law, the union that is certified to represent a group of employees has sole and exclusive right to bargain for that group. Because unions thereby acquire significant power, employers are anxious to keep them out. To add to this potentially turbulent situation, there may be more than one union attempting to win certification as representative of a group of employees, creating competition between unions.

Several stages in the certification process can be identified: (1) a campaign to solicit employee support for union representation; (2) the determination of the appropriate group the union will represent; (3) the preelection campaign by unions and employers; (4) the election itself; and (5) the certification of a union. These steps are outlined in Exhibit 18.7. The next stage of the organizing process—negotiation of a collective bargaining agreement—is discussed in Chapter 19.

Here are several stages in the certification process.

The Campaign to Solicit Employee Support

The campaign usually begins with the initial contact between the union(s) and the employees. From this point on, the certification process is generally a very active one.

Establishing Contact between the Union and Employees.   Contact between the union and employees can be initiated by either party. National unions usually initiate contact with employees in industries or occupations that they have an interest in or are traditionally involved in. The United Auto Workers, for example, would be likely to contact nonunion employees in automobile plants and have done so for the new plants that have been built in the South. Another prominent example of union initiative was the attempt by two competing unions—the United Farm Workers and the Teamsters—to organize the agricultural workers in California. Often these unions were aggressive, even violent, during their campaigns for worker support. One consequence of their precertification activities, which included national boycotts of grapes and lettuce, was the California Agricultural Relations Act, passed in 1975. The purpose of this act is to regulate union-management relations in the agriculture industry.

In many cases the union is approached by employees interested in union representation, and the union is usually happy to oblige. Employees may have strong reasons for desiring union representation—low pay, poor working conditions, and other factors relating to dissatisfaction.[39] Since workers tend to be apathetic toward unions, their concern generally becomes quite serious before they will take any action.[40]

Authorization Cards and the Request for Elections. Once contact has been made, the union begins the campaign to get sufficient **authorization cards,** or signatures of employees interested in having union representation. This campaign must be carried out within the constraints set by law. If the union collects cards from 30 percent of an organization's employees, it can petition the National Labor Relations Board for an election. (Procedures in the public sector are similar.) If the NLRB determines that there is indeed sufficient interest, it will schedule an election. If the union gets more than 50 percent of the employees to sign authorization cards, it may petition the employer as the bargaining representative. Usually employers refuse, whereupon the union petitions the NLRB for an election.

The employer usually resists the union's card-signing campaign. For instance, companies usually prohibit solicitation on the premises. However, employers are legally constrained from interfering with an employee's freedom of choice. Union representatives have argued that employers ignore this law because the consequences for doing so are minimal—and they can effectively discourage unionism. One employer who has been very aggressive in resisting unionization is the J. P. Stevens Company, a large textile manufacturer. The Amalgamated Clothing and Textile Workers Union has been trying since 1963 to organize the Stevens employees. As of early 1980, only eleven of eighty-four J. P. Stevens plants had been organized. Much of this lack of success is attributed to unfair labor practices by J. P. Stevens and "wholesale violations of the rights of workers to join a union."[41] The company has been found guilty of many violations over the years and has been accused of being the "most flagrant labor law violator in this country."[42] Presently, however, it appears as if some harmony between labor and management has been established. But this may reflect a preoccupation with profits more than a change in philosophy about unions:

> On Oct. 19, 1980, J. P. Stevens signed an agreement with the Amalgamated Clothing and Textile Workers Union approving the first collective bargaining contracts in the company's history. The agreement marked the end of one of the ugliest episodes in recent labor history; a 17 year war during which Stevens repeatedly harassed or fired union activists, and the union countered with a boycott of Stevens products and a campaign to isolate the company by pressuring companies that dealt with Stevens or had Stevens officers on their boards.
>
> At the time, the agreement was hailed as an historic breakthrough by labor leaders. They hoped that the surrender by Stevens—the second-largest textile manufacturer in the nation after Burlington Industries, and long a symbol of resistance to unions—might be the first of a series of capitulations by recalcitrant Southern companies. Stevens, for its part, said that the agreement was "clearly in the company's best interest," reaffirmed its opposition to unions and hoped that "the controversy which has surrounded Stevens" would abate.
>
> One year later, Stevens seems closer than the union to fulfilling its hopes. The company continues to battle the union's organizing efforts at its other nonunionized

Southern mills and to fight its way through a snarl of legal cases, the legacy of its years of unrelenting opposition to Amalgamated.

But in the past year, it has become evident that Amalgamated won only a battle and not the war. Organizers have turned their attention to other companies, and Stevens, now belatedly trying to improve its flagging sales and profits, is no longer preoccupied with its union quarrel. "We've got plenty of problems, and that isn't one of our top priorities," Whitney Stevens, the company's 54-year-old chairman and chief executive officer, said in a recent interview.[43]

During the union campaign and election process, it is important that the personnel manager caution the company against engaging in unfair labor practices. Unfair labor practices, when identified, generally cause the election to be set aside. Severe violations by the employer can result in certification of the union as the bargaining representative, even if it has lost the election.

Determination of the Bargaining Unit

When the union has gathered sufficient signatures to petition for an election, the NLRB will make a determination of the **bargaining unit,** the group of employees that will be represented by the union. This is a crucial process, for it can determine the quality of labor-management relations in the future:

> At the heart of labor-management relations is the bargaining unit. It is all important that the bargaining unit be truly appropriate and not contain a mix of antagonistic interests or submerge the legitimate interests of a small group of employees in the interest of a larger group.[44]

In order to assure "the fullest freedom of collective bargaining,"[45] there are legal constraints and guidelines for the unit. Professional and nonprofessional groups cannot be included in the same unit, and a craft unit cannot be placed in a larger unit unless both groups agree to it. Physical location, skill levels, degree of ownership, collective bargaining history, and extent of organization of employees are also guidelines that are considered. Some of these considerations are reflected in the *Personnel In Action* insert, "Court Widens Office Worker Union Rights."

From the union's perspective, the most desirable bargaining unit is one whose members are prounion, so that they can win certification. The unit must also have sufficient influence over the operations of the employer to give the union some power once it wins representation. Employers generally want a bargaining unit that is least beneficial to the union; this will help to maximize the likelihood of failure in the election and to minimize the power of the unit.[46]

The Preelection Campaign

After the bargaining unit has been determined, both union and employer embark on a **preelection campaign.** Unions claim to provide a strong voice for employees, emphasizing improvement in wages and working conditions and the establishment of a grievance process to ensure fairness. Employers emphasize the costs of unionization—union dues, strikes, and loss of jobs.

The impact of preelection campaigns is not clear. A study of thirty-one elections

PERSONNEL IN ACTION

Court Widens Office Worker Union Rights

The Supreme Court, in a major decision for organized labor, ruled yesterday that office workers with access to their employers' confidential information can join labor unions.

The decision, written by Justice William J. Brennan Jr., said that only those employees who deal directly with labor-management issues can be excluded from protection under the nation's labor laws.

This "labor-nexus" test has been the policy of the National Labor Relations Board, but it was contested by two employers who said workers with access to confidential business information were excluded from protection under the National Labor Relations Act.

Justices Byron R. White, Thurgood Marshall, Harry A. Blackmun and John Paul Stevens joined in the decision. Chief Justice Warren E. Burger and justices Lewis F. Powell, William H. Rehnquist and Sandra D. O'Connor concurred in part and dissented in part.

The decision, which resolves a 40-year-old labor-management dispute, "is pretty important because if the Labor Board lost it, a lot of white collar employees and possibly some blue collar employees who had access to some confidential information might have lost protection under the [National Labor Relations] Act," an NLRB official said. At least "several hundreds of thousands of employees" are affected by the ruling, the official said.

Powell said in his separate opinion that he agreed with the majority that persons privy to confidential business information are not excluded from protection by labor laws merely because they have that access.

But he said, "By its rigid insistence on the labor nexus in the case of confidential secretaries, the [National Labor Relations] Board and now this court have lost sight of the basic purpose of the labor nexus test itself and of the fundamental theory of our labor laws.

"Thus, it makes little sense to exclude 'expediters,' 'assistant buyers' and 'employment interviewers' as managerial but include within the rank and file confidential secretaries who are privy to the most sensitive details of management decision-making, who work closely with managers on a personal and daily basis and who occupy a position of trust incompatible with labor-management strife," Powell said. "To include employees so clearly allied to management within the ranks of labor does a disservice to management and labor alike."

The high court's decision reversed an appeals court ruling in the case of Mary Weatherman, a nine-year employee of a rural electric membership cooperative who was fired after signing a petition to reinstate a close friend who had lost his arm while employed with the cooperative.

Weatherman filed an unfair labor practice charge with the NLRB, but her former employer claimed she was not protected by the National Labor Relations Act because she was a confidential secretary. The cooperative didn't dispute that Weatherman's duties were unrelated to labor policies.

However, the court added in a footnote, "We do not suggest that personal secretaries to the chief executive officers of corporations will ordinarily not constitute confidential employees." Weatherman was specifically restricted from handling labor decisions and "it is unlikely that Weatherman's position mirrored that of executive secretaries in general," the court said.

(Jane Seaberry, *Washington Post*, December 3, 1981, p. C-13. Reprinted by permission.)

showed very little change in attitude and voting propensity after the campaign.[47] People who will vote for or against a union before the election campaign generally vote the same way after. Severe violations of the legal constraints on behavior, such as using threats or coercion, could be effective, but the NLRB watches the preelection activity carefully to prevent such behavior.

Election, Certification, and Decertification

Generally, elections are associated with the process of determining if the union will win the right to *begin* representing the employees. Elections can, however, be associated with the process of determining if the union will *continue* to have the right to represent the employees.

Election and Certification. The NLRB conducts the election and certifies the results. If a majority vote for union representation, the union will be certified. If the union does not get a majority, another election will not be held for at least a year. The NLRB holds about 9,000 elections a year involving about 500,000 employees. Generally about a third to a half of the elections certify a union, with less union success in larger organizations. Once a union has been certified, the employer is required to bargain with that union.

The success rate of union campaigns and the number of elections held is critical to the survival and growth of the union movement. Thus in Houston the AFL-CIO faces a real tough battle since the number of elections has declined dramatically. Between 1977 and 1980, the number of elections went from 301 to 201. On a national scale, union success in elections has also declined dramatically. In 1969 it was 55 percent, and in 1979 it was 45 percent. Of the many reasons for this decline, one in particular is management's use of consultants to keep unions out.[48]

Decertification Elections. The NLRB also conducts **decertification elections,** which remove a union from representation. If 30 percent or more of the employees request such an election, it will be held. These decertification elections most frequently occur in the first year of a union's representation, when the union is negotiating its first contract. Union strength has not yet been established, and employees are readily discouraged about union behavior. Recently there has been a substantial increase in decertification elections and actual decertification (849 elections were held in 1977, five times the number in 1955). However, the impact on the union movement is small, with less than 1 percent of union members being affected.[49] But while decertification may not be a direct threat to the union movement as a whole, it is having a particularly severe effect in the service industry. There were only six cases for decertification filed in 1954 compared with 296 in 1978.

Here and in other industries, consultants aid management in decertification efforts just as they do in preventing unionization in the first place.[50] Nevertheless, employer-initiated decertification elections haven't increased as much as those initiated by employees. This fact alone provides labor with reason for optimism, since most employee-initiated votes for decertification are antiunion rather than procompany. Thus the union can turn around this trend toward decertification by convincing the employees that unionization is in their interests. In other words, the ball is in the union's court, and what can be done is shown in the Personnel in Action.

PERSONNEL IN ACTION

Labor Strikes Back at Consultants That Help Firms Keep Unions Out

WASHINGTON—A sticker on a file cabinet in the AFL-CIO's organizing department here reads: "Bust the Union Busters!"

Organized labor is rallying behind that slogan in a fight against the growing number of consultants and law firms that help employers avoid or end unionization. The fight is often bitter and shrill, punctuated by pickets, protests and smears.

"It seems in every campaign, we're running into a hired union buster or the personnel people have attended a union-busting school," says Charles Bradford, organizing director for the Machinists' union. He says his union's counteroffensive, which is typical, consists of "compiling the tactics used against us" and "having our people infiltrate management training sessions."

Unions Lose Ground

Keeping unions out has become a big business. A House labor subcommittee reported last month that outside labor-relations advisers gross more than $500 million a year. Meanwhile, labor's success in representation elections has dropped significantly—to 45% in 1979 from 54.6% in 1969. Workers also have been rejecting unions in an increasing proportion of decertification elections.

Union organizers charge that many of their defeats were caused by unethical or illegal techniques used by many of the estimated 1,000 "union busters." They—and Democrats on the House subcommittee—contend that the advisers prevent workers from exercising free choice by teaching managers to harass, intimidate and threaten their subordinates.

Such conduct "is so un-American that you can't let this kind of thing go on behind closed doors," says Robert Muehlenkamp, executive vice president of the National Union of Hospital and Health Care Employees. Citing the consultant's methods, the union was able to get support from community groups and persuade five hospitals to fire the consulting firms.

Nevertheless, a leading consultant scoffs at the critics' allegations. "We don't use illegal tactics," says

Herbert Melnick, chairman of Modern Management Inc., Bannockburn, Ill. His firm, also known as 2M, charges more than $700 a day (plus expenses) for each consultant and boasts a 93% success rate. But Mr. Melnick insists that "we aren't an anti-union company." He says "our purpose in every campaign is to give employes the right to make an informed choice" and to improve communications.

The unions' counterassault against 2M and other consulting firms includes such tactics as:

- Publishing a monthly Report on Union Rosters, also called the RUB Sheet. The AFL-CIO newsletter profiles law firms and consultants, and it lists managers who attend seminars on how to avoid unions or get rid of them. About 7,500 union officials subscribe to the RUB Sheet, up from 500 when it started in 1979.

- Picketing and attempting to interfere with management seminars. In the past two years, demonstrations by hundreds of unionists have occurred in more than a half-dozen cities, including Los Angeles, Miami, Fla., Washington, and Albuquerque.

- Pressing for a federal crackdown on consultants. In response to union pressures, the National Labor Relations Board has brought unfair labor-practice complaints against 2M and West Coast Industrial Relations Association Inc., Santa Clara, Calif.

Meanwhile, the Labor Department is stepping up enforcement of a law requiring financial reports by consultants and by employers that use consultants. The department recently sued a Pittsburgh hospital for refusing to provide the reports. Earlier this year, the Health and Human Services Department rejected hospital-industry efforts to weaken its ban on federal reimbursement for anti-unionization efforts.

- Advanced training for union organizers. In an AFL-CIO course, organizers pretend they're management consultants for a half-day. The federation also is forming teams of knowledgeable organizers to help individual unions.

Raising a fuss about the consultants sometimes pays off. By a 13-vote margin, nearly 200 Pittsburgh Press advertising employees agreed to join the International Typographical Union in August 1979. The union had publicized the newspaper's costly use of Thomas Geist, executive vice president of West Coast Industrial. Quoting Labor Department records, a flier noted that his firm had billed 30 employers $153,000 to help fight unionization the previous year.

The literature "had a great effect on the vote. When people found out how much he was making, it really helped the cause," recalls Elaine Cirocco, a classified advertising saleswoman. Mr. Geist also "lost a lot of credibility," she says, when workers learned of his firm's "union-busting" reputation. "All along, he had said he was there for employee relations," and he wouldn't identify his company.

Geist's Version

Mr. Geist disagrees. Workers "don't really care about the use of consultants," he says. He maintains the ITU won because management failed to recognize "problems in day-to-day employee relations."

But because Mr. Geist became an issue, says Dean Stuart, the newspaper's personnel manager, "we wouldn't use him again. Nor would we use a consultant from the outside" in future unionizing drives. (Mr. Stuart emphasizes that his views aren't necessarily those of top management of E. W. Scripps Co., owner of the newspaper.)

In an organizing campaign last fall, a hospital workers' union was less successful confronting Modern Management. The Hospital of St. Raphael, New Haven, Conn., learned the union had solicited a letter from local political figures. In it, the politicians objected strongly to 2M's alleged use of intimidation during a bid to organize service employees, and they suggested that the firm be fired. But before the union could release the letter, the hospital refuted the charges in large advertisements in two local newspapers, and the union lost the vote.

Protests about consultants' seminars also have produced mixed results. The programs typically run for a day or two and cost up to $550 a person. Unionists claim their publicity, pickets and subsequent needling of corporate participants have hurt attendance and have forced the cancellation of some sessions.

Locking Up Listeners

At a seminar in Chicago in January, Executive Enterprises Inc. locked up participants and brought in their meals after union leaders stole registration lists, according to Harry Kurshenbaum, the business manager for a Service Employees International Union local.

But Lewis Abrams, president of the New York consulting firm, denies the story. "I think they're blowing their own horns," he says. Unions' picketing, which has occurred at most of Executive Enterprises' programs for the last year or so, hasn't "hurt at all," he says, and the sessions' annual attendance of 2,500 to 3,000 individuals "has stayed fairly stable through the years."

Some union officials advocate tougher measures to combat "union busters." At SEIU's urging, Chicago-area unions may soon urge supporters to halt contributions to social agencies that hire the advisers. And another union's top organizer predicts "more confrontations in the street against these consultants. I'm talking about strikes to the bitter end. Either we go down or the employers go under."

(Joann S. Lublin, *Wall Street Journal,* April 2, 1981, p. 28. Reprinted by permission of *The Wall Street Journal,* © Dow Jones and Company 1981. All Rights Reserved.)

FOR YOUR CAREER

Union locals are more likely to be decertified when there is

- Lack of local leadership
- Little support of the local union by the international
- Low union member involvement in union activities
- Changing nature of the work force

EVALUATING THE UNIONIZATION OF EMPLOYEES

Although there may be occasions when management desires to have its employees unionized, its general preference is for its employees to be nonunionized. Consequently, the pressure is on the personnel manager to prevent the employees from becoming dissatisfied and joining a union. In other words, the effectiveness of the personnel manager can be determined by how satisfied and involved the employees are with the company.

Since union-management activities are encased in a network of laws, another element of effectiveness is how well the personnel manager avoids violating any of these laws in maintaining a nonunionized work force. This element also applies to how effectively the personnel manager negotiates and administers contracts if the employees are unionized.

FACING THE CRITICAL ISSUES IN THE UNIONIZATION OF EMPLOYEES

Now that many aspects involved in the unionization of employees have been briefly examined, it is appropriate to respond to the Critical Issues presented at the start of this chapter. In addition to expanding on the responses provided here, you may wish to provide rebuttals to these responses. It's really important to be familiar with all the sides of an issue, however critical.

Issue: *Why would employees be most likely to start a unionization drive? Can employers legally stop them from starting one?*

Employees are generally attracted to unionization because they are dissatisfied with work conditions and they feel powerless to change those conditions. Some major sources of dissatisfaction are inequity in pay administration, poor communications, and poor supervisory practices. By correcting these, or not allowing them to occur in the first place, organizations can help prevent unions from being attractive. However, once a union-organizing campaign begins, a company can't legally stop it unless an unfair labor practice is committed. At this point it is best to hire a labor attorney familiar with the NLRB and labor law to monitor the practices of the union. But even if a charge is filed with NLRB, it takes a long time for the charge to be heard. There are, nonetheless, other ways to delay the organizing campaign, such as challenging the bargaining unit, challenging the election procedures, and even conducting a campaign telling of the benefits provided by the company.

Issue: *What can a company do to help prevent its employees from organizing?*

Assuming you want to do this peacefully and legally, you can establish a number of good personnel practices. You should make sure your compensation package is in good order. Pay should be competitive, and the principles of equal pay for equal worth and equal pay for comparable worth should be observed. Supervisors should be trained in effective communication styles and methods. Employee rights must be recognized and observed, both the legally protected rights and the so-called humane rights. QWL programs and safety programs are also worth considering. If you do all of these, as some companies do, you should be able to attain your objective.

Issue: *If a company already has a union, how can it get rid of it? Is it really in a company's best interest not to have a union?*

The second question should be answered first. You may decide a union is in your best interest, in which case you will not want to get rid of it. Unions can bring an element of peace and stability among the workers and actually help you manage. At the same time, unions may cause too much inflexibility and block attempts to make improvements where you want to, for example, in QWL or productivity. If this weighing of the costs and benefits of having a union results in the decision to attempt to get rid of it, you may want to contact a consultant who specializes in this area. These people can help ensure that you don't violate any labor-management laws and that your chances for success are reasonably high. A failure at this effort on your part could be costly. You may just hope that your employees initiate a decertification election.

Issue: *Since a union may be suspicious of a company's motives in establishing quality circles, how can a company convince them otherwise?*

This is a frequent question faced by managers. Since your union doesn't trust you, the best you can do is make sure that participation in the quality circle is voluntary and that it can be stopped by the union at any time. In this way you have little to lose. If the quality circle program is not going well, stopping the program is appropriate. If the program is going really well, union efforts to stop it may be to its peril.

SUMMARY

A labor union is attractive to employees when the union is perceived as being able to reduce dissatisfaction at work by providing for their needs. The attractiveness of unions is, therefore, related to management's behavior. If the company is able to deal successfully with employee dissatisfaction, employees will be less likely to unionize.

Unions represent about a fifth of the work force. They have obtained a good deal of power through organizing important industries. Currently the greatest opportunity for union growth is in the public sector. The labor union structure includes union locals, which deal with the work organization on a daily basis; national unions, which are the source of power in the union movement; and the AFL-CIO, an association of most of the national unions.

Union-management relations are regulated by a series of labor laws governing the interactions between unions, management, and employees in both the public and private sectors. These laws attempt to maintain stable relations by facilitating collective bargaining and the settlement of disputes.

Historically, labor and management have operated as adversaries, because many of their goals are in conflict. But since conflict is detrimental to both management and labor, effective labor relations have been established to reduce this conflict. For instance, unions and management have begun to cooperate to achieve mutual goals. Although cooperation is not widespread, it may be the style of union-management relations in the future. Its effects are particularly apparent in collective bargaining, contract negotiation, and grievance processing, all topics discussed in the next chapter.

KEY CONCEPTS

AFL-CIO

authorization card

bargaining unit

certification election

collective bargaining

decertification election

employee association

Federal Labor Relations Authority (FLRA)

employment contract

Landrum-Griffin Act

National Labor Relations Board (NLRB)

national union

preelection campaign

psychological contract

Railway Labor Act (RLA)

steward

Taft-Hartley Act

Title VII of the Civil Service Reform Act

unionizing

union locals

Wagner Act

union

right-to-work law

union shop

unfair representation

essentiality

exclusivity

conspiracy doctrine

DISCUSSION QUESTIONS

1. Discuss the pros and cons of unionization of employees during the current time and in the future.
2. Why is unionization important for organizations?
3. What is the importance of the Taft-Hartley Act? Has it affected unionization of employees?
4. Identify and discuss the factors that make unionization attractive to employees.
5. Describe the history of unionization by providing a brief yet cogent historical sketch.
6. For what reasons will women's involvement in unions continue to increase?
7. Outline the process by which a union can become certified in an organization.
8. What is a "bargaining unit," and why is its formation important?
9. What are decertification elections, and why do they occur?
10. On what basis can unionization be evaluated?

CASE

A Bad Place to Work

Brenda C. is a nursing aide at a nursing home. She has been a diligent employee there for two-and-one-half years and enjoys her work. She has been considered a good worker by her supervisor. Recently she has become increasingly concerned with the pay and the working conditions at the home.

Although the nursing aides often work extra to help a patient and as a group are dedicated to their work, the pay scale is significantly below that of other homes in the area. In addition, the nursing aides and other hospital staff have no area where they can get away from the patients for a break; in fact, the nursing home does not provide for a coffee break at all. The nursing staff do, however, take informal breaks whenever they can get a few minutes, and Brenda has found that these help her function better in the sometimes hectic work situation. Since the staff are not allowed to eat in the cafeteria, they must provide for their lunch by eating out or bringing a bag lunch. This has also caused problems, because sometimes the staff are delayed at the restaurant when they go out for lunch.

It seems to Brenda that providing a lounge area for coffee and lunch breaks would make the job much easier for the staff and would result in better care for the patients. She approached her supervisor about the matter, but he was not receptive and suggested that she concentrate on her job. Brenda persisted and was told that the budget is too tight and space is too limited.

Brenda knows that her nursing aide friends in other homes have such facilities, and she is fairly certain that those homes are no better off financially than hers. She feels she can get no further on her own, so she contacts the union that represents nursing aides in some of the other homes and arranges for a meeting after work on Friday, expecting a good turnout. She discusses the situation with her coworkers and many of them are very interested.

On Friday afternoon the manager of the nursing home calls her into his office and tells her that her performance has recently been inadequate (although her last review was good), that her attitude toward the patients has changed, and that he is terminating her employment as of that day. Brenda is shocked. She tells her coworkers what has happened, and they are also very surprised. Four people attend the union meeting that night. They soon leave expressing fear for their jobs.

Case Questions

1. Why is Brenda interested in getting a union involved in her situation?
2. What are the major aspects of the nursing home that you find objectionable and would prefer not to have?
3. Can unionization help Brenda and her coworkers? How?
4. What can the nursing home do to change Brenda's mind?

FOR YOUR CAREER

■ You may one day be a member of a union or association. On the other hand, you may be negotiating for a company with a union.

■ Unionization efforts often develop because of poor personnel practices rather than because of good union practices.

■ As a supervisor, you will be greatly influenced by whether or not your employees are unionized.

■ One of the most explosive topics you can discuss with others is the value and function of unions in America.

■ Unions are organizations too and must comply with all the relevant equal opportunity legislation.

■ Women will play an increasingly greater role in the union movement in the 1980s.

ENDNOTES

1. Steven Briggs, "The Grievance Procedure and Organizational Health," *Personnel Journal,* June 1981, pp. 471–474.

   "A Creaky System of Collective Bargaining," *Business Week,* June 30, 1980, pp. 82–83.

   James F. Rand, "Preventive Maintenance Techniques for Staying Union Free," *Personnel Journal,* June 1980, pp. 497–499.

2. R. P. Quinn and G. C. Staines, the 1977 Quality of Employment Survey (Ann Arbor, Mich.: Institute for Social Research, Survey Research Center, University of Michigan, 1979).

3. Phil Farish, "PAIR Potpourri," *Personnel Administrator,* September 1981, pp. 23–24.

4. A good discussion of earlier contributions to Labor Law can be found in D. P. Twomey, *Labor Law and Legislation,* 6th ed. (Cincinnati, Ohio: Southwestern, 1980).

5. H. B. Frazier II, "Labor Management Relations in the Federal Government," *Labor Law Journal,* March 1979, p. 131.

6. Twomey, p. 75.

7. Twomey, p. 77.

8. A. Sloan and F. Whitney, *Labor Relations,* 3rd ed. (Englewood Cliffs, N.J.: Prentice Hall, 1977), p. 35.

9. Ibid.

10. J. A. Fossum, *Labor Relations: Development, Structure, Process* (Dallas, Texas: Business Publications, Inc., 1979), pp. 395–396.

11. Frazier, p. 133.

12. Ibid.

13. Julius N. Draznin, "Labor Relations," *Personnel Journal,* October 1981, pp. 764–766.

14. Herbert Hammerman and Marvin Rogoff, "Communications," *Monthly Labor Review,* April 1976, pp. 34–37.

15. George W. Bohlander, "Fair Representation: Not Just A Union Problem," *Personnel Administrator,* March 1980, pp. 36–40, 82.

James P. Swann, Jr., "Misrepresentation in Labor Union Elections," *Personnel Journal,* November 1980, pp. 925–926.

16. Paul I. Weiner, "Seniority Systems Under Teamsters and Bryant," *Employee Relations Law Journal* 6, No. 3:437–457.

17. E. H. Schein, *Organizational Psychology* (Englewood Cliffs, N.J.: Prentice Hall, 1965), p. 17.

18. For a discussion of the concept of met expectations and satisfaction, see

A. C. Kalleberg, "Work Values and Job Rewards: A Theory of Job Satisfaction," *American Sociological Review* 42 (1977):124–143.

E. A. Locke, "What Is Job Satisfaction?" *Organizational Behavior and Human Performance* 4 (1969):309–335.

19. J. G. Getman, S. B. Goldberg, and J. B. Herman, *Union Representation Elections: Law and Reality* (New York: Russell Sage Foundation, 1976), 46–55.

20. Rand, p. 498.

21. R. Dubin, *The World of Work* (Englewood Cliffs, N.J.: Prentice Hall, 1958), p. 237.

22. J. M. Brett, "Behavioral Research on Unions," in B. M. Staw and L. L. Cummings, eds., *Research in Organizational Behavior,* Vol. 2 (Greenwich, Conn.: JAI Press, 1980), pp. 177–213.

Jeanne M. Brett, "Why Employees Want Unions," *Organizational Dynamics,* Spring 1980, 47–59.

W. Clay Hamner and Frank J. Smith, "Work Attitudes as Predictors of Unionization Activity," *Journal of Applied Psychology,* August 1978, pp. 415–421.

23. Getman, Goldberg, and Herman, p. 12.

24. F. Bairstow, "Professionalism and Unionism: Are They Compatible," *Industrial Engineering,* April 1974, pp. 40–42.

P. Felville and J. Blandin, Faculty Job Satisfaction and Bargaining Sentiments," *Academy of Management Journal,* December 1974, pp. 678–692.

B. Husaini and J. Geschwender, "Some Correlates of Attitudes Toward and Membership in White Collar Unions," *Southwestern Social Science Quarterly,* March 1967, pp. 595–601.

L. Imundo, "Attitudes of Non-Union White Collar Federal Government Employees toward Unions," *Public Personnel Management,* January–February 1974, pp. 87–92.

A. Kleingartner, "Professionalism and Engineering Unionism," *Industrial Relations,* May 1969, pp. 224–235.

A. Vogel, "Your Clerical Workers are Ripe for Unionism," *Harvard Business Review,* March–April 1971, pp. 48–54.

25. J. H. Hopkins and R. D. Binderup, "Employee Relations and Union Organizing Campaigns," *Personnel Administrator,* March 1980, pp. 57–61.

26. Interesting discussions of early American labor history can be found in R. B. Morris, "A Bicentennial Look at the Early Days of American Labor," *American Monthly Labor Review,* May 1976, pp. 21–26.

27. Fossum, p. 10.

28. Sloan and Whitney, p. 59.

29. Ibid., p. 64.

30. Julius N. Draznin, "Labor Relations," *Personnel Journal,* November 1981, p. 836.

31. "The Navy's Truce with Its Shipbuilders," *Business Week,* October 19, 1981, p. 43.

32. U.S. Department of Labor, Bureau of Labor Statistics, *Directory of National Unions and Employee Associations,* Bulletin No. 2044 (Washington, D.C.: Government Printing Office, 1979), p. 60.

33. Data supplied to the author by the offices of The Bureau of Labor Statistics, Washington, D.C., May 1982.

34. Charles J. Janus, "Union Mergers In the 1970's: A Look at the Reasons and Results," *Monthly Labor Review,* October 1978, pp. 13–23.

"Building Trades Lose Ground," *Business Week,* November 9, 1981, p. 103–104.

"A Union Fight That May Explode," *Business Week,* March 16, 1981, pp. 102–104.

35. U.S. Department of Labor, Bureau of Labor Statistics, *Directory of National Unions and Employee Associations, 1975,* Bulletin No. 1937 (Washington, D.C.: Government Printing Office, 1977).

36. "A Changing Work Force Poses Challenges," *Business Week,* December 14, 1981, pp. 116–120.

37. "Reagan Is Arousing AFL-CIO Activism," *Business Week,* October 5, 1981, p. 35.

"Labor Moves in on the Democrats," *Business Week,* October 5, 1981, p. 143.

"A Hard Line on Soviet Trade," *Business Week,* June 22, 1981, p. 143.

38. Getman, Goldberg, and Herman, p. 1.

39. Ibid., p. 10.

Hopkins and Binderup.

40. William E. Fulmer, "Step by Step Through a Union Campaign," *Harvard Business Review,* July–August 1981, pp. 94–102.

Edward L. Harrison, Douglas Johnson, and Frank M. Rachel, "The Role of the Supervisor in Representation Elections," *Personnel Administrator,* September 1981, pp. 67–72, 82.

41. K. A. Kovach, "J. P. Stevens and the Struggle for Union Organization," *Labor Law Journal,* May 1978, p. 307.

42. Twomey, p. 137.

43. Sandra Salmans, "J. P. Stevens: One," *New York Times,* October 18, 1981, Sec. F, p. 8. Copyright 1981 by The New York Times Company. Reprinted by permission.

44. Twomey, p. 134.

45. Getman, Goldberg, and Herman, p. 72.

46. William Bitler, Jr., "Unionization of Security Guards: A Unique Problem," *Personnel Administrator,* June 1981, pp. 79–83.

"An Acid Test at DuPont," *Business Week,* December 14, 1981, pp. 123–127.

47. W. Imberman, "How Expensive is an NLRB Election?," *MSU Business Topics,* Summer 1975, pp. 13–18.

48. J. Krislov, "Decertification Elections Increase but Remain No Major Burden to Unions," *Monthly Labor Review,* November 1979, p. 31.

49. Ibid.

50. Daniel D. Cook, "Divorce Union Style," *Industry Week,* June 25, 1979, p. 37–42.

William E. Fulmer and Tamara A. Gilman, "Why Do Workers Vote for Union Decertification," *Personnel,* March–April 1981, pp. 28–35.

Chapter Outline

Critical Issues in Collective Bargaining, Negotiating, Conflict Resolution, and Contract Administration

The Collective Bargaining Process
Union-Management Relationships
A Model of the Collective Bargaining Process
Management Strategies
Union Strategies
Joint Union-Management Strategies

Negotiating the Agreement
Negotiating Committees
The Negotiating Structure
Issues for Negotiation

Conflict Resolution
Strikes and Lockouts
Mediation
Arbitration

CHAPTER 19

Collective Bargaining, Negotiating, Conflict Resolution, and Contract Administration

Contract Administration
Grievance Procedures
Grievance Issues
Management Procedures
Union Procedures

Public Sector Collective Bargaining

Evaluating the Effectiveness of the Entire Union-Management Relationship
Effectiveness of Negotiations
Effectiveness of The Grievance Procedure

Facing the Critical Issues in Collective Bargaining, Negotiating, Conflict Resolution and Contract Administration

Summary

Key Concepts

Discussion Questions

Case

For Your Career

Endnotes

Personnel in the News

The Labor Management Cooperation Act

With the passage of the Labor Management Cooperation Act, the 95th U.S. Congress established a national policy which may change the direction of American labor-management relations. Those of you who are professionally engaged in industrial relations and human resources development may very well be key people in any constructive efforts to place this policy into practice.

The new law encourages joint labor and management efforts to promote innovation, cooperation and communications supplemental to the traditional adversarial relationship. A statement of purpose taken directly from the Labor Management Cooperation Act may help you to understand its intent:

1) To improve communication between representatives of labor and management

2) To provide workers and employers with opportunities to explore innovative joint approaches to achieving organizational effectiveness

3) To assist workers and employers in solving problems of mutual concern not susceptible to resolution within the collective bargaining process

4) To study and explore ways of eliminating potential problems that could inhibit the economic development of the plant, area or industry

5) To enhance the involvement of workers in making decisions that affect their working lives

6) To expand and improve working relationships between workers and managers

7) To encourage free collective bargaining by establishing communication links between employers and their employees. (Robert E. Steiner, Personnel Journal, May 1981, p. 344. Reprinted with the permission of Personnel Journal, Costa Mesa, California; all rights reserved.)

At G.M.'s Buick Unit

A year ago, Eddo Brantley's biggest responsibility was blowing dust off equipment with an air hose. Now, she can shut down one of the principal production lines of an automobile factory whenever she wants.

And she does. On a recent day, the slender, 49-year-old laborer strode assertively to a control panel and pushed a fat maroon button. A rolling line of metallic saucers, destined for a spot in every new front-wheel-drive car produced by the General Motors Corporation, jerked to a halt.

"I could never do this before," said Mrs. Brantley, one of 2,500 Buick workers who has been trained in what are termed "Quality of Work Life" principles. "Now, I stop the line whenever there is a problem."

She and hundreds of other production line workers at Buick's huge assembly plant here make decisions on adjusting machine settings, rejecting faulty raw materials and moving machinery into step-saving positions overlooked by engineers. In return for taking on this added responsibility, they no longer have to answer to foremen, punch timeclocks or work continually at the same monotonous job. And they can get more money.

"I think I've found myself a home," said Fred Bailey, 41, a welder and another work team member. "People get along better here and they let you put out a better product."

The Buick operation represents one of the more clearcut examples of a growing trend in industrial relations: enhancing quality and productivity through delegating more responsibility to frontline laborers. For more than three decades, management theorists have argued that employees are more productive when given wide latitude in performing tasks. The late Douglas R. McGregor, in "The Human Side of Enterprise," wrote in 1960 that most workers identify with a job and contribute to their company's success if managers permit them to find fulfillment in it. (Thomas C. Hayes, New York Times, July 5, 1981, p. 7 © 1981 by The New York Times Company. Reprinted by permission.)

More Support for Arbitration

Arbitration as a means of resolving a dispute that would otherwise wind up in litigation got a boost from the U.S. Court of Appeals for the Fourth Circuit when the court halted a pending state lawsuit in favor of a contractual commitment to arbitrate. A contractor and a hospital had agreed that any disputes that might arise out of a construction contract must first be submitted to the architect, then to arbitration. The contractor demanded more money; discussions with the architect lasted for months. One day before the contractor finally asked formally for an arbitrator to decide his claim, the hospital filed suit, calling on the state court to rule that the contractor had waited too long and had consequently lost the right to press for arbitration. The contractor then filed suit in federal court under the federal Arbitration Act, which applies to all written arbitration provisions in contracts dealing with interstate commerce. The federal trial court stayed the contractor's suit, holding that the state court was competent to decide whether arbitration was warranted. The Court of Appeals, however, reversed that ruling and ordered the state suit stayed pending the arbitration. The Arbitration Act, the appeals court ruled, plainly calls for a stay of all litigation that would obstruct the speedy arbitration of the dispute. In re Mercury Construction Corp., U.S. Ct. App., Richmond, Va. (Reprinted from p. 132 of the October 5, 1981, issue of Business Week, by special permission, © 1982 by McGraw-Hill, Inc., New York, N.Y. 10020. All rights reserved.)

Together these quotations highlight several important aspects of the union-management relationship. One of the most recent and important developments is the trend toward increased union-management cooperation. This represents a shift away from the more traditional adversarial relationship between labor and management. Although the trend toward cooperation has been spurred by the **Labor Management Cooperation Act,** it has also been encouraged by the declining productivity in the United States and the growing international competition.

The results of labor-management cooperation are reflected in the establishment of productivity and QWL programs such as those at Buick in Flint, Michigan. It appears thus far that when labor and management cooperate both can benefit, rather than one winning and the other losing.

But cooperation cannot cover all aspects of the labor-management relationship. Labor and management have many different goals. Consequently there is bound to be conflict between them. When this conflict occurs over a provision in the labor-management contract, arbitration is often used as the final point for resolving the conflict. When arbitration fails, a strike is likely to occur.

At this time the quality of the relationship between labor and management has never been more important. This is reflected by the amount of attention given this topic in daily newspapers and magazines and by the comments made by our personnel managers.

CRITICAL ISSUES IN COLLECTIVE BARGAINING, NEGOTIATING, CONFLICT RESOLUTION, AND CONTRACT ADMINISTRATION

For this chapter, only the personnel managers who deal with unionized employees raised critical issues. Here are the four they regarded as most critical:

1. *Since productivity is so critical, companies want to do everything possible to increase it. Can they get the unions to help? How?*
2. *Why don't unions cooperate with companies more? Why do they always take an adversarial position?*
3. *Should public employees have the right to strike?*
4. *Is it likely to expect unions to settle for wage increases that are less than the cost-of-living increases and just equal to productivity increases?*

The core of union-management relations is collective bargaining. It may include two types of interaction. The first is the negotiation of work conditions that, when written up as the collective agreement, become the basis for employee-employer relationships on the job. The second is the activity related to interpreting and enforcing the collective agreement and the resolution of any conflicts arising out of it. This is often referred to as the **administration of the collective agreement.**

This chapter discusses both of these interactions. First, however, the quality of the labor-management relationship is discussed since it has such a powerful influence on the negotiating process, the settlement of grievances, and the rest of the collective bargaining process.

THE COLLECTIVE BARGAINING PROCESS

Collective bargaining is a complex process in which union and management negotiators maneuver to win the most advantageous contract. As in any complex process, a variety of issues come into play. How these issues are dealt with and resolved depends upon

- The quality of the labor-management relationship;
- The type of bargaining used by labor and management;
- Management's strategies in the collective bargaining process; and
- Labor's strategies in the collective bargaining process.

Union-Management Relationships

An understanding of union-management relationships is facilitated by seeing them set in a **labor relations system.** The labor relations system is composed of three subunits—employees, management, and the union—with the government influencing the interaction among the three. Employees may be managers or union members, and some of the union members are part of the union management system (local union leaders). Each of the three interrelationships in the model is addressed by specific government regulations: union and management by the *National Labor Relations Act;* management and employees by the *National Labor Relations Act,* and *Title VII of the Civil Rights Act,* and union and employees by the *Labor-Management Reporting and Disclosure Act* and *Title VII of the Civil Rights Act.*

Labor relations systems have:

- Employees
- Management
- Union

Each of the groups identified in the labor relations model has different goals, as shown in Exhibit 19.1. Workers are interested in improved working conditions, wages, and opportunities; unions are interested in their own survival, growth, and acquisition of power, which depend on their ability to maintain the support of the employees by providing for their needs. Management has overall organizational goals (profit, market share, growth, and others), and it also seeks to preserve managerial prerogatives to direct the work force and to attain the personal goals of the managers (promotion, achievement). Government is interested in a stable and healthy economy, protection of individual rights, and safety and fairness in the work place.

It's a challenge to serve all of these goals.

An Adversarial Relationship. These goals are not compatible in most cases. Conflict arises when two groups, typically union and management, attempt to achieve incompatible goals simultaneously. Thus an **adversarial system** has emerged, with labor and management attempting to get a bigger cut of the pie while government looks on to protect its interests.

> In an adversarial system of union-management relations, the union's role is to gain concessions from management during collective bargaining and to preserve those concessions through the grievance procedure. The union is an outsider and critic.[1]

Exhibit 19.1

Traditional Goals of Parties to the Labor Relations System (From
J. Brett, "Behavioral Research on Unions and Union Management
Systems," In *Research in Organizational Behavior*, vol. 2, eds. B. M.
Staw and L. L. Cummings. Copyright 1980. JAI Press Inc. Reprinted
with permission.)

Workers
Good extrinsic working conditions—wages, benefits, fair supervisor, safe and pleasant
   working conditions, job security
Good intrinsic working conditions—interesting work that provides a sense of accomplishment
Participation in decisions which affect work and working conditions
System for redressing grievances

Unions
Achievement of members' goals for working conditions
Survival and growth
Political security for union leaders

Management
Profitability
Preservation of management's prerogative to direct the work force
Job security/advancement

Government
Democratic unionism
Healthy economy
Safe working conditions
Profitable firms
Fair wages
Fair and nondiscriminatory employment
Noninflationary wage agreements and pricing policies

Historically, unions have adopted an adversarial role in their interactions with management. Their focus has been on wages and working conditions as they have attempted
to get "more and better" from management. This approach works well in economic
boom times but becomes difficult when the economy is not healthy. High unemployment and the threat of continued job losses have recently induced unions to expand
their role, especially since many of their traditional goals—better pay and working
conditions—have been achieved. Many unions have begun to enter into new, collab-
orative efforts with employers. Some of the reasons for this are described in the *For
Your Career* "Taking Combat Out of Labor Relations."

A Cooperative Relationship

> In a cooperative system, the union's role is that of a partner, not a critic, and the
> union becomes jointly responsible with management for reaching a cooperative
> solution. Thus, a cooperative system requires that union and management engage
> in problem solving, information sharing, and integration of outcomes.[2]

Cooperative systems have not been a major component of labor relations in
the United States. Other countries—Sweden, Yugoslavia, and West Germany, for
example—have built a cooperative mechanism (codetermination is discussed in

Chapter 20) into the labor system. There have been occasions, however, when American management and labor have worked together to solve a problem. Most changes and job redesign projects undertaken by management need the acceptance of the union to be successful. Active involvement of the union is one of the best ways to gain this acceptance.[3]

Successful projects like the Tarrytown, New York, plant of General Motors and the Buick plant in Michigan (briefly introduced in the opening quotations) involve the union in a cooperative effort to solve problems of concern to both parties.[4] Another example of a cooperative approach is the use of an in-house fact-finder appointed by mutual agreement of management and union to develop and suggest alternative solutions to problems associated with labor relations. The fact-finder is a neutral party who has the trust and confidence of both labor and management and whose primary concern is employee participation in decision making. The fact-finder is often able to alter an adversarial relationship between union and management.

Union-management cooperation is increasing in the United States.

A Model of the Bargaining Process

The most widely used model of the bargaining process incorporates four types of bargaining in contract negotiations: distributive bargaining, integrative bargaining, attitudinal structuring, and intraorganizational bargaining.[5]

Distributive Bargaining.   This type of bargaining takes place when the parties are in conflict over an issue and the outcome represents a gain for one party and a loss for the other. Each party tries to negotiate for the best possible outcome. The process is outlined in Exhibit 19.2.

Exhibit 19.2
Distributive Bargaining Process (From U.S. Department of Labor, Bureau of Labor Statistics, *Occupational Safety and Health Statistics: Concepts and Methods*. BLS report 438 [Washington D.C. Bureau of Labor Statistics, 1975], p. 2).

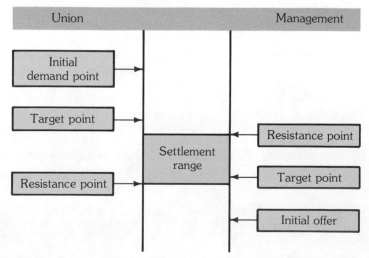

Distributive bargaining is very common—for unions, management, and even individuals.

On any particular issue, union and management negotiators each have three identifiable positions. The union has an **initial demand point,** which is generally more than it expects to get; a **target point,** which is its realistic assessment of what they may be able to get; and a **resistance point,** which is the lowest acceptable level for that issue. Management has three similar points: an **initial offer,** which is usually lower than the expected settlement; a target point, which is the point it would like to reach agreement at; and a resistance point, which is its upper acceptable limit. If, as shown in Exhibit 19.2, management's resistance point is greater than the union's resistance point, there is a **positive settlement range** where negotiation can take place. The exact agreement within this range depends on the bargaining behavior of the negotiators. If however, management's resistance point is below the union's, there is no common ground for negotiation. In such a situation, there is a **negative settlement range,** and a bargaining impasse exists.[6]

FOR YOUR CAREER

Taking Combat Out of Labor Relations

Collective bargaining in the '80s must evolve from a form of warfare into the means for governing the workplace with respect to wage matters, working conditions, and those items that relate to the work force. We have an opportunity to institutionalize a form of private government, uniquely American and free of Government domination.

The labor-management relationship has been moving toward a structure that legislates (the formation of the contract terms), administers (day-to-day implementation of its terms), and adjudicates (through the grievance procedure). In fact, the final step in resolving complaints of violation of the contract is being placed in the hands of privately selected and privately paid judges. The labor relations judicial process is called arbitration.

The development is a logical and essential response to our society's economic needs. The warfare and hostility that have typified most of the nation's bargaining history are luxuries our society can no longer afford. What we need are strong unions, self-assured, secure and capable of serving as cooperative partners in the labor-management relationship. What we need is management genuinely willing to accept unions and their role as full partners in the labor-management relationship.

This seems to be the gradual development of our own history and experience. It has become urgent, however, because of external problems such as foreign penetration of our markets, intensified domestic competition, inadequate capital investment, and the scourge of inflation.

A supportive environment. The dramatic response has been a series of programs for cooperation to improve productivity, to improve the quality of work life and to resist foreign competition. If these programs are to be effective over a period of time, they must take place in a collective bargaining environment that is supportive. Workers are unlikely to have high morale and constructive interests in improved performance while they are engaged in periodic or incessant combat.

The key to the '80s may well be more attention to how bargaining is carried on. If warfare is not the name of the game, then the institutions of combat should be displaced by new ways more conducive to effectuate cooperative rule making, administration, and arbitration.

What might these new ways be? All we can do is indicate some general considerations because collective bargaining must vary widely in response to the infinite combinations of circumstances that exist throughout our economy.

The notion of a union making demands and a company making offers is counterproductive. It persists because of inertia. Some of the most successful relationships have long since abandoned this route.

Instead, parties should bring their problems and needs to each other. The bargaining table should be the place for thorough exploration of the matters brought there. In fact, such exploration should take place long before a contract expires so that facts and opinions can be gathered in a responsible and, if possible, a joint manner.

The object is not to win but to reach agreements that best serve the needs of the enterprise and the workers. The wide variety of issues that now occupy the attention of bargainers makes agreement difficult to achieve, but the demand-offer route increases the difficulty, complicates the process of balancing the issues, and, too often, leaves unsettled or badly settled issues that have substantial impact on all concerned.

What workers want. The process whereby representatives meet and exchange proposals and finally come up with agreement often ignores the opinions and knowledge of the constituents. This is especially true on the union side.

The issues that concern workers are no longer the simple matter of how much. As workers increase their income, they can afford to become concerned about other matters, including quality of life at the workplace. These workers do not react to a settlement only in terms of how much but express great concern over a wide array of other issues.

The bargainers on both sides have to appreciate that the worker of the '80s is not like his predecessor. Therefore, the representatives must know what goes on and must develop channels of ongoing consultation, not only to keep people informed but also to test out various proposals. By the time agreement is reached, a substantial consensus should already be assured. Springing an agreement on the members to see if it meets their approval confuses and defeats the objective of achieving a fair and useful settlement.

And, finally, collective bargaining does not stop with the signing of an agreement. The parties have the job of assuring the proper implementation of its terms and an efficient, fair means of handling grievances.

Grievances do not do harm. Failure to address them is the culprit. If the parties approach settlement without hostility, most grievances will be resolved fairly and promptly. Those that go to arbitration will be handled not as lawsuits but as matters that both parties want settled fairly.

In this kind of atmosphere, the labor-management community can address the many problems that plague companies and unions. High morale is essential to high levels of performance. An ongoing cooperative atmosphere can unleash the ideas and energies of workers and provide our economy with needed productivity boosts.

Warfare was yesterday's agenda. Aggressive achievement of effective performance and satisfied workers is the need for the '80s.

(Ben Fischer, reprinted from the September 21, 1981, issue of *Business Week* by special permission, © 1981 by McGraw-Hill, Inc., New York, N.Y. 10020. All rights reserved.)

Using wages as an example, the union may have a resistance point of $5.40 per hour, a target of $5.60, and an initial demand of $5.75. Management may offer $5.20 but have a target of $5.45 and a resistance point of $5.55. The positive settlement range is between $5.40 and $5.55, and it is very likely that this is where the settlement will be. Note, however, that only the initial wage demand and offer are actually made public at the beginning of negotiations.

Since many issues are involved in a bargaining session, the process becomes much more complicated. Although each issue may be described by the above model, in actual negotiations there is an interaction among issues. Union concessions on one issue may be traded for management concessions on another. Thus the total process is dynamic.

The ritual of the distributive bargaining process is well established, and deviations are often met with suspicion. The following story illustrates this point:

A labor lawyer tells the story of a young executive who had just taken over the helm of a company. Imbued with idealism, he wanted to end the bickering he had seen take place during past negotiations with labor. To do this, he was ready to give the workers as much as his company could afford. Consequently he asked some members of his staff to study his firm's own wage structure and decide how it compared with other companies, as well as a host of other related matters. He approached the collective bargaining table with a halo of goodness surrounding him. Asking for the floor, he proceeded to describe what he had done and with a big smile on his face made the offer.

Throughout his entire presentation, the union officials stared at him in amazement. He had offered more than they had expected to secure. But no matter, as soon as he finished, they proceeded to lambaste him, denouncing him for trying to destroy collective bargaining and for attempting to buy off labor. They announced that they would not stand for any such unethical maneuvering, and immediately asked for 5 cents more than the idealistic executive had offered.[7]

Integrative Bargaining. **Integrative bargaining** is the situation in which management and the union work to solve a problem to the benefit of both. For instance, issues of work crew size may be addressed or union concerns for job security. Most quality-of-work life changes involve integrative bargaining. The new work setting will benefit employees as well as the employer. Given the adversarial nature of labor-management relations, integrative bargaining is not common, although the recent interest in cooperative relations may change that.

Attitudinal Structuring. The relationship between labor and management results in **attitudinal structuring,** or the shaping of attitudes toward one another. Four dimensions of this relationship have been identified: motivational orientation, or tendencies that indicate whether the interaction will be competitive and adversarial or cooperative; beliefs about the legitimacy of the other, or how much a party believes the other has a right to be bargaining; level of trust in conducting affairs, or belief in the integrity and honesty of the other party; and degree of friendliness, or whether the interactions are friendly or hostile. As the bargaining process proceeds, these attitudes may be altered. The attitudes emerging from the negotiations will have a serious impact on the administration of the contract and on future negotiations.

Intraorganizational Bargaining. During negotiations, the bargaining teams from both sides may have to engage in **intraorganizational bargaining,** or conferring with their constituents over changes in bargaining positions. Management negotiators may have to convince management to change its position on an issue—for instance, to agree to a higher wage settlement. Union negotiators must eventually convince their members to accept the negotiated contract, so they must be sensitive to the demands of the membership but be realistic as well. When the membership votes on the proposed package, it will be strongly influenced by the opinions of the union negotiators.

Management Strategies

Prior to the bargaining session, management negotiators prepare by developing the strategies and proposals they will use. Four major areas of preparation have been identified:

▪ Preparation of specific proposals for changes in contract language

- Determination of the general size of the economic package that the company anticipates offering during the negotiations
- Preparation of statistical displays and supportive data that the company will use during negotiations
- Preparation of a bargaining book for the use of company negotiators, a compilation of information on issues that will be discussed, giving an analysis of the effect of each clause, its use in other companies, and other facts[8]

An important part of this preparation is calculation of the cost of various bargaining issues or demands. The relative cost of pension contributions, pay increases, health benefits, and other provisions should be determined prior to negotiations. Other costs should also be considered. For instance, what is the cost to management, in terms of its ability to do its job, of union demands for changes in grievance and discipline procedures or transfer and promotion provisions? The goal is to be as well prepared as possible by considering the implications and ramifications of the issues that will be discussed and by being able to present a strong argument for the position management takes.

An example of preparation to the extreme is the bargaining practice called **Boulwarism,** in which management presents the union with an offer early in the negotiations and holds firm to that offer. This practice, used successfully by General Electric in the 1960s and early 1970s, involves preparing for negotiations by effecting what company representatives describe as "the steady accumulation of all facts available on matters likely to be discussed." This information will be modified only on the basis of "any additional or different facts" the company is made aware of, either by its unions or from other sources, before or during the negotiations. The company offers at an "appropriate" but invariably very early point during the bargaining "what the facts from all sources seem to indicate that we should," and it changes this offer only if confronted with "new facts."[9]

Along with these bargaining strategies, GE engaged in a massive communication program aimed at convincing workers that GE was looking out for their interests. During the 1960 negotiations and subsequent strike, GE sent out 246 written communications to its employees.[10] Using these tactics, GE was able to have its proposal accepted by the International Brotherhood of Electrical Workers. Union leaders protested that these tactics constituted an unfair labor practice because the company refused to bargain.[11] To be sure, this bargaining approach made the union look bad and further weakened its position with union members. (The union had already been relatively weak due to internal problems and conflicts with other unions.)

GE is having less success in getting its offers accepted in recent negotiations, because the union has since become stronger and better prepared. Other companies have not adopted GE's strategy because the NLRB declared Boulwarism illegal because it represented a lack of good faith, and partly because they do not want to give up potential gains at the bargaining table or risk higher costs when a strong union responds to this strategy. Since the court upheld the NLRB ruling, GE has also dropped this strategy.

Union Strategies

Like management, unions need to prepare for negotiations by collecting information. More and better information gives the union the ability to be more convincing in negotiations. Since collective bargaining is the major means by which a union can convince its members that it is effective and valuable, this is a critical activity.

Unions should collect information in at least three areas:

Unions are beginning to get more financial information from management as management seeks more concessions from unions.

- The financial situation of the company and its ability to pay
- The attitude of management toward various issues, as reflected in past negotiations or inferred from negotiations in similar companies
- The attitudes and desires of the employees

The first two areas give the union an idea of what demands management is likely to accept. The third area is important but is sometimes overlooked. The union should be aware of the preferences of the membership. For instance, is a pension increase preferred over increased vacation or holiday benefits? The preferences will vary with the characteristics of the workers. Younger workers are more likely to prefer more holidays, shorter work weeks, and limited overtime, whereas older workers are more interested in pension plans, benefits, and overtime. The union can determine these preferences by using a questionnaire to survey its members, as discussed in Chapter 7.

Joint Union-Management Strategies

There are two important types of bargaining that represent the joint efforts of union and management—productivity and continuous bargaining.

Productivity Bargaining. A relatively recent procedure in negotiations is **productivity bargaining.** This is a special form of integrative bargaining. Labor agrees to scrap old work habits for new and more effective ones desired by management, and in exchange management returns some of the gains of modernization and increased efficiency to labor in the form of new and better work incentives.[12]

Some unions have been hesitant to agree to this approach, because they fear that their members will lose jobs, that the company will require excessive work, or that technological change will eventually eliminate more jobs. Despite this hesitancy, productivity bargaining has been used successfully. One of the notable changes is that the bargaining process changes from distributive to integrative. "Labor and management work together, not only to create the agreement itself, but to create an atmosphere of ongoing cooperation."[13]

Continuous Bargaining. As affirmative action, safety and health, and other government regulations continue to complicate the situation for both unions and employers, and as the rate of change in the environment continues to increase, some labor and management negotiators are turning to **continuous bargaining.** A joint committee meets on a regular basis to explore issues of common interest. These committees have appeared in retail food, over-the-road trucking, nuclear power, and men's garment industries.[14]

Several characteristics of continuous bargaining have been identified:

- Frequent meetings during the life of the contract
- Focus on external events and problem areas rather than internal problems
- Use of outside experts in decision making
- Use of a problem-solving (integrative) approach[15]

The intention is to develop a union-management structure that is capable of adapting to sudden changes in the environment in a positive and productive manner. This continuous bargaining approach is different from, but an extension of, the emergency negotiations that unions have insisted on when inflation or other factors have substantially changed the acceptability of the existing agreement. Continuous bargaining is a permanent arrangement intended to help avoid the crises that often occur under traditional collective bargaining systems. Although not a formal adoption of continuous bargaining, the renegotiation of contract terms between the United Auto Workers and Ford, Chrysler, and GM before contract expiration was done and is being done to help avert a crisis in the U.S. automobile industry.

NEGOTIATING THE AGREEMENT

Once a union is certified as the representative of a work unit or bargaining unit, it becomes the only party that can negotiate an agreement with the employer for all members of that work unit, whether or not they are union members. This is, therefore, an important and potent position. The union is responsible to its members to negotiate for what they want, and it has the "duty to represent all employees fairly."[16] The union is a critical link between employees and employer. The quality of its bargaining is an important measure of union effectiveness.

Negotiating Committees

The employer and the union select their own representatives for the **negotiating committee.** Neither party is required to consider the wishes of the other. Management negotiators, for example, cannot refuse to bargain with representatives of the union because they dislike them or do not think they are appropriate.

Negotiation involves:

- Committees
- Structure
- Issues

Union negotiating teams typically include representatives of the union local, often the president and other executive staff members. In addition, the national union may send a negotiating specialist, who is likely to be a labor lawyer, to work with the team. The negotiators selected by the union do not have to be members of the union or employees of the company. The general goal is to balance bargaining skill and experience with knowledge and information about the specific situation.

At the local level, when a single bargaining unit is negotiating a contract, the company is usually represented by the manager and members of the labor relations or personnel staff. Finance and production managers may also be involved. When the negotiations are critical, either because the size of the bargaining unit is large or because the effect on the company is great, such specialists as labor lawyers may be included on the team.

In national negotiations, top industrial relations or personnel executives frequently head a team made up of specialists from corporate headquarters and perhaps managers from critical divisions or plants within the company. Again, the goal is to have expertise along with specific knowledge about critical situations.

The Negotiating Structure

Most contracts are negotiated by a single union and a single employer. In some situations, however, different arrangements can be agreed on. When a single union negotiates with several similar companies—for instance, the construction industry or supermarkets—the employers may bargain as a group with the union. At the local level this is called **multiemployer bargaining,** but at the national level it is referred to as **industrywide bargaining.** Industrywide bargaining occurs in the railroad, coal, wallpaper, and men's suits industries.[17] National negotiations result in contracts that settle major issues, such as compensation, whereas issues relating to working conditions are settled locally. This split bargaining style is common in Great Britain and has been used in the auto industry in the United States. When several unions bargain jointly with a single employer, they engage in **coordinated bargaining.** Although not so common as the others, coordinated bargaining appears to be increasing, especially in public-sector bargaining.[18]

The incentive to use these bargaining structures usually is related to efficiency and the relative strength of union and management. In multiemployer bargaining, the companies negotiate very similar contracts to eliminate the time and cost of individual negotiations. Since it too will save time and money, the union may be willing to accept this type of bargaining if its own bargaining position is not weakened. Where local conditions vary substantially, there may be a need for splitting the bargaining between the national and local levels—settling the major issues at the national level and leaving specific issues for the local level, where they can be adjusted to meet local needs.

Issues for Negotiation

The issues that can be discussed in collective bargaining sessions are specified by the Labor-Management Relations Act of 1947 (which is discussed in Chapter 18). The act differentiates among three categories: mandatory issues, permissive issues, and prohibited issues.[19]

Issues for negotiation include:

- Wages
- Economic supplements
- Institutional issues
- Administrative issues

Employers and employee representatives (unions) are obligated to meet and discuss "wages, hours, and other terms and conditions of employment." These are the **mandatory issues.** Historically there has been a debate over what specific topics fall into this category. The Supreme Court's decision in the Borg Warner case (1958) suggests that the distinction between mandatory and permissive bargaining issues is based on whether the topic regulates the relations between the employer and its employees.[20] Any issue that changes the nature of the job itself or compensation for work must be discussed in collective bargaining. Mandatory issues therefore include subcontracting work, plant closings, changes of operations, and other actions management might take that will have an impact on employees' jobs.

Permissive issues are those that are not mandatory but are not specifically illegal. They are issues not specifically related to the nature of the job but still of concern to both parties. For example, issues of price, product design, and decisions about new jobs may be subject to bargaining if the parties agree to it. Permissive issues usually develop when both parties see that mutual discussion and agreement will be beneficial. Management and union negotiators cannot refuse to agree on a contract if they fail to settle a permissive issue.[21]

Prohibited issues are those concerning illegal or outlawed activities, such as the demand that an employer use only union-produced goods or, where it is illegal, that it employ only union members. Such issues may not be discussed in collective bargaining sessions.

Mandatory bargaining issues, therefore, are the critical factors in the bargaining process. They are the issues that may affect management's ability to run the company efficiently or clash with the union's desire to protect jobs and workers' standing in their jobs.[22]

Wages. Probably no issues under collective bargaining continue to give rise to more difficult problems than do wage and wage-related subjects. Wage conflicts are the leading cause of strikes. Difficulties here are understandable: A wage increase is a direct cost to the employer.

The wages that an employee is paid are primarily determined by the basic pay rate for a certain job. Then this pay may be increased by several other factors. All of these payments are subject to collective bargaining. Although management would prefer that basic pay be related only to productivity, this is seldom the case. Three additional standards are frequently used: comparative norms, where rate of pay is influenced by the rates provided for similar jobs in other companies within an industry or even by comparative rates between industries; ability to pay, where the pay rate is influenced by the financial capability of the company and especially the amount of its profit; and standard of living, where changes in the cost of living influence the rate of pay.[23]

Recently, due to the productivity crisis and increased international competition, firms are having profitability problems. In turn they are asking unions to hold the line on wage increases and in some cases to take a wage reduction.[24] As described in the *Personnel in Action* insert, taking wage reductions is an anathema to organized labor, but sometimes there's little choice.

> Some firms are asking employees to take wage cuts or lose their jobs.

PERSONNEL IN ACTION

Saving Jobs by Cutting Wages

Chrysler's production workers, now in the process of voting on a package of $622 million in pay cuts, face an excruciating decision in determining whether to "give back" wages and benefits negotiated in previous contracts. But they need not feel alone in their agony.

In the last year sluggish demand in the economy along with persistent inflation and vanishing profits have led several beleaguered companies in declining industries to demand cost savings concessions from their employees.

In recent months, such companies as Armour, Conrail and Firestone, in addition to Chrysler and Uniroyal have won substantive changes in previously negotiated wages or work rules. International Harvester took a bitter and costly six-month strike last year to change its work rules and reduce its labor costs.

Some economists see these developments as one of the more encouraging trends in the fight against inflation. One school of economic thought has long held that steadily increasing wages are a major cause of inflation, especially when accompanied by expansive monetary policy. These analysts believe that the "give-backs" can play a role in slowing price increases and reversing the decline in productivity.

"The Chrysler agreement may be the big breakthrough of the 1980's" says Melvin W. Reder, professor of urban and labor economics at the University of Chicago Graduate School of Business. "We'll have a good deal of conflict in the next few years but wage adjustments are coming."

Many free-market theorists have long been troubled by what they call "the stickiness" of wages during an economic downturn. That is, wages have not fallen, mainly because of union contracts, during times of rising unemployment. Consequently, they say, prices have not softened as much in recent recessions as they did in the days of less effective unionization.

Union leaders, on the other hand, say that the real problems of the industries currently in distress are high energy prices and the competition from imports rather than high labor costs.

"The cost of labor isn't the villain of this inflation," says Saul Miller, director of information for the American Federation of Labor and Congress of Industrial Organizations. "Oil, interest rates and food are the causes. You aren't going to change that by cutting anyone's wages." In troubled industries, the labor leaders say, jobs can be saved by legislation to curb imports and by bailouts similar to those for Chrysler and Lockheed.

But Professor Reder disagrees. "When unions insist on keeping money wages equal with the rate of inflation," he says, "they're actually redistributing income to union members from others." He says that pensioners, stockholders and nonunion members suffer from that kind of redistribution.

Whatever the case, as more industries face up to the challenges of low-priced imported products and lower wage rates in other countries, individual companies are trying to bring down their own costs in order to survive.

For example, Uniroyal demanded and got last summer a 13 percent reduction in wages and benefits, including a 58-cent reduction in hourly wage rates and suspension and deferral of cost-of-living increases.

Other companies are eagerly watching the progress of companies fighting for concessions. The Ford Motor Company has indicated that it may seek concessions from the United Automobile Workers to maintain its labor cost parity with Chrysler. And the A.F.L.-C.I.O. is worried that the electronics and textile companies shortly will be demanding "give-backs" similar to those agreed upon at Chrysler.

"It's not just Chrysler. It's spreading and becoming an increasingly difficult problem," says Mr. Miller. "The employers feel that this is the time to move in on the union."

It is a page torn from the negotiating books of state and local governments. A few years ago public employees began to feel the sting of budget deficits and the fallout from California's Proposition 13, as local governments got tough with their unions. But the government employees seldom yielded anything except a few fringe benefits—a holiday here, a coffee break there.

Nonunion employees have been affected also. International Harvester recently froze the wages of its nonunion workers and Chrysler is demanding wage and benefit concessions of $161 million from its white-collar force.

Despite their objections to giving up previously won wages, union leaders are sanguine about the prospect. Douglas Fraser, president of the United Automobile Workers, put it bluntly after the outlines of the U.A.W. agreement with Chrysler were made public: "This is the worst economic settlement we've ever made," Mr. Fraser said. "The only thing worse is the alternative—which is no jobs."

At the same time, Mr. Fraser said he may have trouble selling the agreement to the union ranks. Predictably the provisions for wage reductions have been the most troublesome.

"I won't vote for it," said an irritated William Jones, as he reported to work following a shutdown of a month and a half at Chrysler's Belvidere, Ill., plant, where the company assembles its Omni and Horizon models. "They say this is supposed to guarantee our jobs but that's what they said the last time."

This is the third time that Chrysler workers have had to reopen their contract, which was negotiated last year. All the concessions should save the company more than $1 billion by the time the contract expires in 1982. U.A.W. members this time are being asked to forgo two 3 percent increases and to forfeit cost-of-living increases, in effect freezing average wages at $10.22 an hour for assemblers, compared to $10.55 an hour at General Motors and Ford. There are more concessions on personal holidays and pension increases.

Hostility to outright wage cuts is typified by the feelings of workers at Firestone's industrial products plants in Noblesville, Ind. Firestone announced in late October that it would close the rambling old multistory shop in six months if sufficient cost-saving measures could not be carried out. Its first proposal, that workers take pay and benefit cuts amounting to $1.60 an hour, was rejected by a margin of 567 to 67.

"I've worked here for 30 years and they want me to give up what we've won in the last 20," said Lucille Hurst, shivering in a light snow as she waited for a ride home after the first shift. She said she would rather retire and collect a pension than accept the company's request. Some workers at the Noblesville plant said they had heard rumors that Firestone's proposals would actually amount to a 40 percent cut.

Her co-worker, Harold Gibson, chimed in, "Let them freeze the COLA [cost-of-living allowance] for a while," he said. "But don't take anything off the card. Leave the card alone."

Because cutting wages is such an emotional issue, most of the troubled companies have focused on adjustments to their cost-of-living clauses. In fact, labor specialists at many companies, including prosperous ones, say that the cost-of-living adjustments are a main cause of inflation when the Consumer Price Index is rising rapidly. The more liberal agreements generally grant a wage increase of 0.75 percent wage for each percentage rise in the index.

But that change in emphasis has hardly softened employee resistance. Last year American Telephone and Telegraph during its contract negotiation with the Communications Workers of America tried with only limited success to put a cap on its cost-of-living clauses, arguing that the C.P.I. had overstated the actual rate of inflation.

The A.F.L.-C.I.O. backed off an attempt to put a cap on the cost-of-living clause of its staff. And the bankrupt Delaware & Hudson Railroad said a few weeks ago that it would request a six-month deferral of such increases, but the railroad changed its mind when it despaired of getting the agreement of all the unions involved.

The workers' resistance is fueled by a belief that many of the troubled companies will fail or merge eventually anyway and that their sacrifices would either be in vain or downright stupid.

The companies have had far more success with nonwage concessions, such as changing work rules. American industry, hit since 1978 by a 1.2 percent annual decline in the rate of output per hour, has been hard-pressed to find ways to increase productivity.

"In times of adversity everybody gets on the same side," says Steve Clem, research director of the United Rubber Workers. "We certainly don't want to push anybody over the brink."

After the workers at the Firestone Noblesville plant rejected the wage cut, union members and plant managers formed a committee to focus on measures to improve productivity and reduce unit labor costs. Earlier this month, Firestone workers approved a contract change for workers at its Memphis plant.

The changes allow Firestone's management to schedule regular Saturday and Sunday shifts with no premium pay. In addition, all job classifications will be reviewed and the strict work rules that prevent craftsmen from crossing jurisdictional lines will be eased. Firestone estimates that the changes will increase productivity of the plant by 30 or 40 percent. International Harvester won similar concessions after its long strike.

The Delaware & Hudson Railway is seeking to reduce its train crew sizes and to win special work rules for new services that would attract new business. The United Transportation Union says it has granted such concessions already to Conrail, the bankrupt Milwaukee Road, and the Boston & Maine, also bankrupt. It says it expects such applications from other railroads to accelerate this year.

Several labor experts say that non-wage provisions of the Chrysler agreement bear watching, specifically a contingency profit-sharing plan. The details of the plan must still be worked out but in its rough form it provides that Chrysler workers will get a share of corporate earnings when they exceed 10 percent of stockholders' equity.

"Unions will have to face up to the fact that if they want high average pay, they'll have to take below average pay when things are bad," says Professor Reder, the labor economist. "Under this agreement the workers share the risk. They become stockholders."

Of course, the workers are less certain. "We aren't responsible for the mess they're in," said a worker at the Belvidere plant. "We didn't decide which models to push or what size they should be. Why should we pay for their mistakes?"

But another, Orville Wilson, was more amenable. "I don't like it very much, but you can't live in the street," he said.

(Winston Williams, *New York Times*, January 25, 1981, p. 3 © 1981 by The New York Times Company. Reprinted by permission.)

Economic Supplements. An increasingly important part of the pay package is the section covering **economic supplements,** fringe benefits such as vacations, holidays, pensions, and insurance. These benefits run as high as 45 percent of the cost of wages and are now a major factor in collective bargaining.

It is important to realize that provisions written into the bargaining agreement are very difficult to remove. If the union wins a new medical plan, for example, management will not be able to negotiate for its removal at the next bargaining session. Since management has less control over fringe benefits than over wages, it tends to be cautious about agreeing to costly benefits.

Occasionally, economic circumstances are so extreme that the union will agree to reductions in fringe benefits. The response of the United Auto Workers to the financially troubled Chrysler Corporation is a case in point. The union agreed to a reduction in paid personal holidays, a modification of the sick-pay provisions, and smaller increases in pension benefits to help the ailing company survive.[25] The general rule, however, is that once something becomes part of the agreement, it is difficult to eliminate.

Some of the more common economic supplements:

▪ *Pensions:* Once management has decided to provide a pension plan, the conditions of the plan must be determined (when the benefits will be available, how much will be paid, and whether they become available according to age or years of service). Finally, the organization must decide how long employees must work for the company in order to receive minimum benefits (vesting) and whether the organization will pay the whole cost or whether employees or the union will be asked to help.

▪ *Paid vacations:* Most agreements provide for paid vacations. The length of vacation is usually determined by length of service, up to some maximum. The conditions that qualify an individual for a vacation in a given year are also specified. Agreements occasionally specify how the timing of vacations will be determined. For example, employees may be given their choice of vacation time according to seniority.

▪ *Paid holidays:* Most agreements provide time off with pay on Independence Day, Labor Day, Thanksgiving, Christmas, New Year's Day, and Memorial Day. Several others may also be included.

▪ *Sick leave:* Unpaid sick leave allows the employee to take time off for sickness without compensation. Paid sick leave is usually accumulated while working. Typically one-half to one-and-one-half days of paid sick leave are credited for each month of work.

▪ *Health and life insurance:* The employer may be required to pay some or all of the costs of health and life insurance plans.

▪ *Dismissal or severance pay:* Occasionally employers agree to pay any employee who is dismissed or laid off due to technological changes or business difficulties.

▪ *Supplemental unemployment benefits:* In the mid-1950s, the United Auto Workers negotiated a plan to supplement state unemployment benefits and to make up the difference when these state benefits expired. Most contracts with this provision are found in the auto and steel industries, where layoffs are common, but workers in other industries are beginning to negotiate them as well.

Institutional Issues.   Some issues are not directly related to jobs but are nevertheless important to both employees and management. Institutional issues are those that affect the security and success of both parties.

▪ *Union security:* About 63 percent of the major labor contracts stipulate that employees must join the union after being hired into its bargaining unit. However, twenty states that traditionally have had low levels of unionization have passed "right-to-work" laws outlawing union membership as a condition of employment.

- *Checkoff:* Unions have attempted to arrange for payment of dues through deduction from employees' paychecks. By law, employees must agree to this in writing, but about 86 percent of union contracts contain this provision anyway.

- *Strikes:* The employer may insist that the union agree not to strike during the life of the agreement, typically when a cost-of-living clause has been included. The agreement may be unconditional, allowing no strikes at all, or it may limit strikes to specific circumstances.

- *Managerial prerogatives:* Over half the agreements today stipulate that certain activities are the right of management. In addition, management in most companies argues that it has "residual rights"—that all rights not specifically limited by the agreement belong to management.

Administrative Issues.   The last category of issues is concerned with the treatment of employees at work.

- *Breaks and cleanup time:* Some contracts specify the time and length of coffee breaks and meal breaks for employees. Also, jobs requiring cleanup may have a portion of the work period set aside for this procedure.

- *Job security:* This is perhaps the issue of most concern to employees and unions. Employers are concerned with restriction of their ability to lay off employees. Changes in technology or attempts to subcontract work are issues that impinge on job security. A typical union response to technological change was the reaction of the International Longshoremen's Association in the late 1960s to the introduction of containerized shipping: The union operated exclusive hiring halls, developed complex work rules, and negotiated a guaranteed annual income for its members. Job security continues to be a primary issue for longshoremen, telephone workers, and most other blue-collar occupations.

  > Job security is a very critical issue today.

- *Seniority:* Length of service is used as a criterion for many personnel decisions in most collective agreements. Layoffs are usually determined by seniority. "Last hired, first fired" is a common situation. Seniority is also important in transfer and promotion decisions. The method of calculating seniority is usually specified to clarify the relative seniority of employees.

- *Discharge and discipline:* This is a touchy issue, and even when an agreement addresses these problems, many grievances are filed concerning the way employees are disciplined or discharged.

- *Safety and health:* Although the Occupational Safety and Health Act specifically deals with worker safety and health, some contracts have provisions specifying that the company will provide safety equipment, first aid, physical examinations, accident investigations, and safety committees. Hazardous work may be covered by special provisions and pay rates. Often the agreement will contain a general statement that the employer is responsible for the safety of the workers so the union can use the grievance process when any safety issues arise.[26]

- *Production standards:* The level of productivity or performance of employees is a concern of both management and the union. Management is concerned with efficiency, but the union is concerned with the fairness and reasonableness of management's demands. This was a key issue in the New York City transit negotiations.

- *Grievance procedures:* This is a significant part of collective bargaining, and is discussed in more detail later in this chapter.
- *Training:* The design and administration of training and development programs, and the procedure for selecting employees for training may also be bargaining issues.
- *Duration of the agreement:* Agreements can last for one year or longer, with the most common period being three years.

CONFLICT RESOLUTION

Although the desired outcome of collective bargaining is agreement on the conditions of employment, there are many occasions when negotiators are unable to reach such an agreement at the bargaining table. In these situations several alternatives are used to resolve the impasse. The most visible response is the strike or lockout, but third-party interventions such as mediation and arbitration are also used.

Strikes and Lockouts

Three modes of conflict resolution:

- Strikes
- Mediation
- Arbitration

When the union is unable to get management to agree to a demand it feels is critical, it may resort to a strike. A **strike** may be defined as the refusal by employees to work at the company. Management may refuse to allow employees to work, which is called a **lockout,** but this is not a frequent occurrence.[27] In 1979 there were 4,788 strikes involving 1,735,000 workers.[28] This was lower than the rate for previous years, which had peaked at 6,074 strikes in 1974. The frequency of strikes is affected by a variety of circumstances, including the general health of the economy, union-management relations, and internal union affairs.[29]

In order to strike, the union usually holds a strike vote to get its members' approval for a strike if the negotiations are not successful. Strong membership support for a strike strengthens the union negotiators' position. If the strike takes place, union members picket the employer, informing the public about the existence of a labor dispute and preferably, from the union's point of view, convincing them to avoid this company during the strike. A common practice is the refusal of union members to cross the picket line of another striking union. This gives added support to the striking union.

Employers usually attempt to continue operations while the strike is in effect. They either run the company with supervisory personnel and people not in the bargaining unit or hire replacements for the employees. Although the company can legally hire these replacements, the union reacts strongly to the use of "scabs," and they may be a cause of increasingly belligerent labor relations. The success of a strike depends on its ability to cause economic hardship to the employer. Severe hardship usually causes the employer to concede to the union's demands. Thus it is paramount, from the union's point of view, that the company not be able to operate successfully during the strike and that the cost of this lack of production be high. The union is, therefore, very active in trying to prevent replacement employees from working. In addition, the timing of the strike is often critical. The union attempts to hold negotiations just prior to the period when the employer has a peak demand for its product or services, when a strike will have maximum economic impact.

Although strikes are common, they are costly to both the employer, who loses revenue, and employees, who face loss of income. If the strike is prolonged, it is likely that the cost to employees will never fully be recovered by the benefits gained. In part because of this, employers are seeking more no-strike guarantees from labor. Because times are tough for labor, especially in manufacturing, labor is increasingly agreeing to this guarantee as a concession for job security.

Moreover, public interest is generally not served by strikes. They are often an inconvenience to the public and can have serious consequences to the economy as a whole. Conflict resolution that avoids work stoppage, which may occur regardless of whether or not no-strike clauses exist, by interventions like mediation and arbitration, is, therefore, desirable from several perspectives.

Mediation

Mediation is a procedure in which "a neutral third party assists the union and management negotiators in reaching voluntary agreement."[30] Having no power to impose a solution, the mediator attempts to facilitate the negotiations between union and management. The mediator may make suggestions and recommendations and perhaps add objectivity to the often emotional negotiations. To have any success at all, the mediator must have the trust and respect of both parties and have sufficient expertise and neutrality to convince the union and employer that he or she will be fair and equitable. The U.S. government operates the Federal Mediation and Conciliation Service to make experienced mediators available to unions and companies.

Arbitration

Arbitration is a procedure in which a neutral third party studies the bargaining situation, listening to both parties and gathering information, and then makes recommendations that are binding on the parties. The arbitrator, in effect, determines the conditions of the agreement.[31]

Two types of arbitration have developed.[32] The first is an **extension of bargaining;** the arbitrator attempts to reach a rational and equitable decision acceptable to both parties. The second type is called **final-offer arbitration.** It involves the arbitrator choosing between the final offer of the union and the final offer of the employer. The arbitrator cannot alter these offers but must choose one as it stands. Since the arbitrator chooses the offer that appears most fair, and since losing the arbitration decision means settling for the other's offer, there is pressure to make as good an offer as possible. The intention of final-offer arbitration is to encourage the parties to make their best offer and to reach an agreement before arbitration becomes necessary.

CONTRACT ADMINISTRATION

The collective agreement, once signed, becomes "the basic legislation governing the lines of the workers."[33] That is, the daily operation and activities in the organization are subject to the conditions of the agreement. Since it is impossible to write an unambiguous agreement that will anticipate all the situations occurring over its life, there will inevitably be disputes over interpretation and application of the agreement. The most common method of resolving these disputes is a **grievance procedure.** Virtually all agreements negotiated today provide for a grievance process to handle employee complaints.

Grievance Procedures

Basically a grievance is a "charge that the union-management contract has been violated."[34] A grievance may be filed by the union for employees or by employers, although management rarely does so. The grievance process is designed to investigate the charges and to resolve the problem.

Five sources of grievances have been identified:

■ Outright violation of the agreement

■ Disagreement over facts

■ Dispute over the meaning of the agreement

■ Dispute over the method of applying the agreement

■ Argument over the fairness or reasonableness of actions[35]

In resolving these sources of conflict, the grievance procedure should serve three separate groups: the employers and unions, by interpreting and adjusting the agreement as conditions require: the employees, by protecting their contractual rights and providing a channel of appeal; and society at large, by keeping industrial peace and reducing the number of industrial disputes in the courts.[36]

Grievance procedures typically involve several stages. The collective bargaining agreement specifies the maximum length of time that each step may take. For example, it may require the grievance to be filed within five days of the incident that is the subject of dispute. The most common grievance procedure, shown in Exhibit 19.3, involves four steps, with the final step being arbitration.

Step 1. An employee who feels that the labor contract has been violated usually contacts the union steward, and together they discuss the problem with the supervisor involved. If the problem is simple and straightforward, it is often resolved at this level. Many contracts require the grievance to be in written form at this first stage. However, there may be cases that are resolved by informal discussion between the supervisor and the employee and, therefore, do not officially enter the grievance process.

Step 2. If agreement cannot be reached at the supervisor level, or if the employee is not satisfied, the complaint can enter the second step of the grievance procedure. Typically, an industrial-relations representative of the company now seeks to resolve the grievance.

Step 3. If the grievance is sufficiently important or difficult to resolve, it may be taken to the third step. Although contracts vary, top-level management and union executives are usually involved at this step. These people have the authority to make the major decisions that may be required to resolve the grievance.

Step 4. If a grievance cannot be resolved at the third step, most agreements require the use of an arbitrator to consider the case and reach a decision. The arbitrator is a

Exhibit 19.3
Typical Grievance Procedure (Source: William D. Todor)

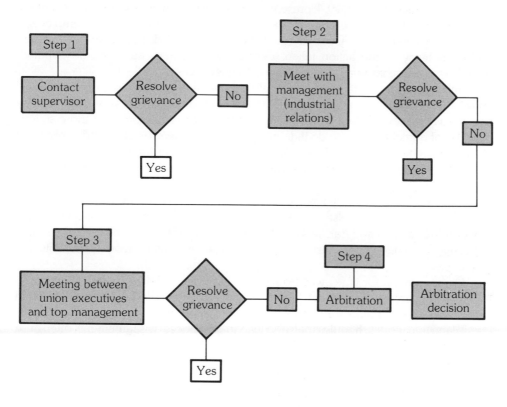

neutral, mutually acceptable individual who may be provided by the Federal Mediation and Conciliation Service or some private agency. The arbitrator holds a hearing, reviews the evidence, then rules on the grievance. The decision of the arbitrator is usually binding.

Since the cost of arbitration is shared by the union and employer, there is some incentive to settle the grievance before it goes to arbitration. The average fee for each arbitration case is $1,434, and there are other expenses involved. An added incentive in some cases is the requirement that the loser pay for the arbitration.[37] The expectation is that the parties will screen or evaluate grievances more carefully, because pursuing a weak grievance to arbitration will result in a loss and the costs of arbitration.

Occasionally the union will call a strike over a grievance in order to resolve it. This may happen when the issue at hand is so important that the union feels it cannot wait for the slower arbitration process, which takes an average of 223 days.[38] This "employee rights" strike may be legal, but if the contract specifically forbids strikes during the tenure of the agreement, it is not legal and is called a **wildcat strike.** Wildcat strikes are not common, however, since most grievances are settled through arbitration.

Grievance Issues

Grievances can be filed over any issue relating to the work place that is subject to the collective agreement, or they can be filed over interpretation and implementation of the agreement itself. The most common type of grievance reaching the arbitration stage is concerned with discipline and discharge, although many grievances are filed over other issues. Exhibit 19.4 presents a list of common categories of grievances.

It is generally conceded that management has the right to discipline employees. The grievance issue usually relates to "just cause" for the discipline and the fairness and consistency of the action taken. Because what is just cause can be disputed, discipline and discharge actions are prone to grievances.

There are many grievance issues that help protect the employee.

Although it is accepted that absenteeism can be grounds for discharge, the critical issue is the determination that the absenteeism in question is excessive. Insubordination usually is either failure to do what the supervisor requests or the more serious problem of outright refusal to do it. If the supervisor's orders are clear and explicit and if the employee is warned of the consequences, discipline for refusal to respond is usually acceptable. The exception is when the employee feels that the work endangers health.

Since seniority is usually used to determine who is laid off, bumped from a job to make way for someone else, or rehired, its calculation is of great concern to employees. Promotions and transfers also use seniority as one of the criteria to determine eligibility, so management must be careful in this area so as to avoid complaints and grievances.

Compensation for time away from work, vacations, holidays, or sick leave is also a common source of grievances. Holidays cause problems because there are often special pay arrangements for people working on those days.

Wage and work schedules may also lead to grievances. Disagreements often arise

Exhibit 19.4
Types of Grievances (Adapted from Bureau of National Affairs,
Grievance Guide, 4th ed. [Washington, D.C.: Bureau of National Affairs,
1972].)

Discipline and discharge	**Vacation**
Absenteeism	Eligibility
Insubordination	Scheduling
Misconduct	Pay
Poor Work	**Holidays**
Seniority	Eligibility for pay
Calculating seniority	Pay for holiday work
Layoffs	**Wages and hours**
Bumping	Incentive pay plans
Worksharing	Job evaluation
Rehiring	Overtime
Leave of absence	Premium pay
Paid sick leave	Pay for reporting
Personal leave	Scheduling
Union business	Wage guarantee and SUB plans
Promotion	**Management rights**
Posting and bidding	**Union rights**
Basis for promotion	**Administration of benefits**
Measurement of ability	**Union security**
Transfer	

over interpretation or application of the agreement relating to such issues as overtime pay, pay for reporting, and scheduling.

Grievances have been filed over the exercise of management rights—that is, its right to introduce technological changes, use subcontractors, or change jobs in other ways. This type of behavior may also be the source of charges of unfair labor practices, since these activities may require collective bargaining.

The Taft-Hartley Act gives unions the right to file grievances on their own behalf if they feel their rights have been violated. This act also gives unions access to information necessary to process the grievance or to make sure the agreement is not being violated. In addition, unions may file grievances for violations of union shop or check-off provisions.

Occasionally other activities prompt grievances. Wildcat strikes or behavior that is considered to be a strike (mass absences from work, for example) may result in a management grievance. The major focus of grievances, however, is in the administration of the conditions of the agreement.

Management Procedures

Management can significantly affect the grievance rate by adopting proper procedures when taking action against an employee. One of the most important areas for such procedures is discipline and discharge. Since the issue of just cause and fairness is central to most discipline grievances, employers must ensure that the employee is adequately warned of the consequences, that the rule involved is related to operation of the company, that a thorough investigation is undertaken, and that the penalty is reasonable. The following activities have been identified as being useful in meeting these conditions:

- Explanation of rules to employees
- Consideration of the accusations and facts
- Regular warning procedures, including written records
- Involvement of the union in the case
- Examination of the employee's motives and reasons
- Consideration of the employee's past record
- Familiarization of all management personnel, especially supervisors, with disciplinary procedure and company rules[39]

In areas outside of discipline and discharge, management can avoid some grievance problems by educating supervisors and managers about labor relations and about the conditions of the collective agreement. It has been found that supervisors with labor knowledge are an important factor in the reduction of grievances.

Union Procedures

The union has an obligation to its members to represent them fairly in the grievance process. Thus it should have a grievance-handling procedure that will aid in effectively processing grievances.

Unions may have an additional interest in grievances as a tool in collective negotiation. They may attempt to increase grievance rates to influence management as collective bargaining approaches. Grievances may also be a way to introduce or show concern for an issue in negotiations. In some cases, grievances may be withdrawn by unions in exchange for some management concessions, although this may be dangerous, since it may be an unfair representation of the employee.

Unfair representation, according to the National Labor Relations Board, is usually related to one of four types of union behavior:

▪ *Improper motives of fraud:* The union cannot refuse to process a grievance because of the employee's race or sex or because of the employee's attitude toward the union.

▪ *Arbitrary conduct:* The union must investigate the merits of the grievance. Unions cannot dismiss a grievance without investigating it.

▪ *Gross negligence:* The union cannot display a reckless disregard of the employee's interests.

▪ *Union conduct after filing the grievance:* The union must process the grievance to a reasonable conclusion.[40]

Because the employer can also be cited for unfair representation, management should attempt to maintain a fair grievance process. Company labor-relations managers should avoid taking advantage of union errors in handling grievances lest this action affect fair representation.

Another important influence on the grievance process is the union steward. Since the union steward is generally the first person to hear about an employee's grievance, the steward has substantial influence on the grievance process. A steward can encourage an employee to file a grievance, can suggest that the problem is really not a grievance, or can informally resolve the problem outside the grievance procedure. The steward, being in such a key position, can have a profound effect on the situation. Personality characteristics of stewards may, in fact, influence the number of grievances filed.[41] Since stewards are selected from the ranks of employees and may have little knowledge of labor relations, the union should provide training to improve their effectiveness. The company, since it may also be liable in a fair-representation suit, should support such training.

PUBLIC-SECTOR COLLECTIVE BARGAINING

Collective bargaining in the public sector differs somewhat from that in the private sector. Federal employees do not have the right to strike. The Civil Service Reform Act, however, changed the situation by creating an independent agency to remedy unfair labor practices. Yet federal employees still do not have the same collective bargaining rights as private workers. In the federal sector, management must bargain over a limited number of issues.

Arrangement for collective bargaining at the state and local level vary considerably. All but fourteen of the states have collective bargaining provisions. There is a wide range of coverage among the states: some include municipal employees, some include state employees, and some include both. Special legislation for police officers, firefighters, and teachers are also often found.

One distinctive characteristic of public-sector collective bargaining is the tendency to have multilateral bargaining. **Multilateral bargaining** occurs when more than two parties are involved in the negotiation and there is no clear union-management dichotomy. Governments tend to have so many levels of authority that unions can sometimes go outside the government negotiating team to higher authorities to seek a settlement. However, such actions tend to disrupt the bargaining process and can lead to distrust and difficulties in future negotiations. Until recently the penalty for striking in the public sector has rarely been enforced.[42] The firing of the air traffic controllers, who as members of PATCO went on strike against the United States government, however, suggests that penalties may begin to be enforced. The enforcement of penalties appears to be one way to reduce the incidence of strikes in the public sector. Other methods can accomplish the same result.

Arbitration procedures for bargaining impasses have been effective in reducing the incidence of strikes in police and firefighter negotiations.[43] Mediation and arbitration are becoming common methods for resolving difficulties in the public sector as a whole. These issues are illustrated in the Personnel in Action.

PERSONNEL IN ACTION

Municipal Officials Getting Tougher In Bargaining With Public Workers

From the Cambria County courthouse in western Pennsylvania to city hall in Dallas, government is taking a tough stance toward public workers.

Even before President Reagan's confrontation with striking air traffic controllers, public officials across the country had started to approach bargaining with a "take-it-or-leave-it" attitude.

This strategy marks a reversal from the past, when government negotiators acquired a reputation for acquiescing to union demands on everything from higher wages to lucrative pension plans.

"There are more strikes being lost by unions, and government is becoming more rigid and unwilling to simply go to the bargaining table and listen to the demands of unions," says Ralph Vatalaro, executive director of the New York Public Employment Relations Board, which mediates labor disputes. "It's becoming more and more prevalent."

Inspirational Effect

And, if President Reagan prevails in his firing of the air traffic controllers, it's likely to inspire more politicians to take on unions at contract time.

"Reagan's popularity has put him in the position of being a role leader. What he does others will imitate, especially if it works," argues Mario Bognano, an industrial relations professor at the University of Minnesota. "If management wins, then other unions that negotiate contracts will have to ask themselves, 'Gee, should we run the cost (of a strike)?' " President Reagan's firing of the air-traffic controllers, for instance, could discourage a strike by postal workers, who haven't yet accepted a new contract.

Labor experts cite several reasons for government's new approach to bargaining. Inexperienced government negotiators who were out-bargained by seasoned union negotiators in the late 1960s and early 1970s have finally learned the ins and outs of collective bargaining. As strikes have become common, politicians and citizens alike have found that many walk-outs will cause only minor inconveniences and that they needn't be feared.

What's more, "unlike manufacturing concerns, when (public) employes go on strike, we make money. Taxes keep coming in and users' charges keep coming in," notes Kermit Francis, employe relations director in Pasadena, Calif., and president of the National Public Employer Labor Relations Association.

Politically Popular

Above all, the taxpayer revolt of recent years has made it financially necessary—and politically popular—to confront public workers unions. "Public employes aren't held in high regard by the public these days, and there is more of a willingness to take a strike because of this," concedes Marcia Caprio, director of economic affairs for the American Federation of State, County and Municipal Employees.

The city of Dallas fired 478 transit workers last October after they conducted an illegal walkout demanding a 13% pay raise instead of the 7% raise the city was giving all its employees.

"The city was in the process of raising real estate taxes and was having a real problem with taxpayers," notes Robert N. Taylor, personnel director for the transit system. "The strike disrupted transportation considerably for some time, but it was better to do that. Otherwise, you would have somebody else going out on strike if we gave in."

After 54 days, the strike ended. Transit workers didn't get any additional pay increase—only an agreement that the city would rehire the fired workers as job openings occurred.

A showdown between city hall and city workers in Providence, R.I., this summer also ended with firings. About 50 garbage collectors who staged an illegal two-day walkout in July were dismissed and then rehired a couple of days later. But they were put on a 90-day probationary status.

Two weeks later, Providence sanitation workers went on strike after the city eliminated overtime hours, and some 1,500 city workers—including the garbage collectors—struck to support them. Mayor Vincent S. Cianci Jr. promptly fired the garbage collectors for violating the probationary status, and the city signed a five-year contract for private garbage collection. Threatened with violence, the mayor refused to budge; instead he stationed a police guard outside his home.

"There has never been as tough a stance here as this one, and I think people were more than pleased," says an aide to Mr. Cianci. "We were amazed at the reaction, and obviously delighted." The city did negotiate a compromise with the sanitation workers, and the strike ended after a couple of weeks.

More often, government negotiators try to outlast illegal strikers instead of firing them. Cambria County, Pa., had two strikes last year—a four-week walkout by nursing home workers and a 22-week strike by county office workers—that ended in settlements only marginally better than the county offered before the strike.

Supervisors cleaned floors and cooked meals at the nursing home and opened mail and filed papers at the county offices during the strike. "Certain things were neglected that had to be picked up afterwards, but it was no crisis," says Andrew J. Gleason, an attorney who acted as the county's negotiator.

Whittling Away Gains

Government also is showing more determination to curtail costly contract provisions won by unions in the past. Throughout the 1970s, the Chicago Transit Authority entered each round of contract talks intent on whittling away at a cost-of-living clause that increased wages in lock-step with inflation on top of general pay increases that were negotiated.

But, threatened with a strike, the transit authority caved in every time—until December 1979. The workers struck and the authority won a court injunction ordering them back to work. The issue went to arbitration, as required by the contract, and as a result cost-of-living increases are limited to about 60% of the inflation rate.

Many strikes, of course, still end in compromises, with neither side scoring a clear victory. Both union and government bargainers are claiming success in a new tentative contract ending a 22-day strike by Minnesota state employes that was legal under state law. In effect, the state paid for a slightly higher settlement with money it saved by not paying wages during the strike.

But, perhaps sensing the penny-pinching mood of taxpayers, Democrats largely refrained from criticizing Republican Gov. Albert Quie for accepting the strike. The governor's aides say his stance may have helped his image, which has been harmed by the state's financial difficulties. "He demonstrated he has the resolve to take a strike for three weeks without caving in. I don't think it can hurt him," says an official.

(Lawrence Ingrassia, *Wall Street Journal*, sec. 2, p. 35. Reprinted by permission of *The Wall Street Journal*, © Dow Jones & Company, Inc. 1981. All rights reserved.)

The new Civil Service Reform Act requires a grievance procedure with arbitration to be included as the last step in all agreements. Thus the mechanism for grievance settlement is similar to that in the private sector. However, unlike the private sector, personnel practices in the public sector tend to be more formalized, and the discretion of management in discipline, promotion, transfers, and work assignments is reduced.[44]

EVALUATING THE EFFECTIVENESS OF THE ENTIRE UNION-MANAGEMENT RELATIONSHIP

The effectiveness of the entire union-management relationship can be measured by the extent to which each party attains its goals, but there are difficulties associated with this approach. Because goals are incompatible in many cases and can, therefore, lead to conflicting estimates of effectiveness, more useful measures of effectiveness may be found in two major components of the union-management relationship: negotiations and grievances.[45]

Effectiveness of Negotiations

Since the purpose of negotiations is to achieve an agreement, agreement becomes an overall measure of bargaining effectiveness. A healthy and effective bargaining process encourages the discussion of issues and problems and their subsequent resolution at the bargaining table. In addition, the effort required to reach agreement is a measure of how well the process is working. Some indications of this effort are the duration of negotiations, the outcome of member ratification votes, the frequency and duration of strikes, the use of mediation and arbitration, the need for government intervention, and the resulting quality of union-management relations (whether conflict or cooperation exists). Certainly joint programs for productivity and QWL improvements could be regarded as successes resulting from the quality union-management relations.

Effectiveness of the Grievance Procedure

How successful a grievance procedure is may be assessed from different perspectives. Management may view the number of grievances filed and the number settled in management's favor as measures of effectiveness. Unions may also consider the number of grievances, but from their point of view, a larger number, rather than a smaller number, may be considered more successful.

Although the views of management and the union may differ, an overall set of measures to gauge grievance procedure effectiveness may be related to the disagreements between managers and employees. Some of the measures that might be included are frequency of grievances; the level in the grievance procedure at which grievances are usually settled; the frequency of strikes or slowdowns during the term of the labor agreements; the rates of absenteeism, turnover, and sabotage; and the necessity for government intervention.

The success of arbitration is often judged by the acceptability of the decisions, the satisfaction of the parties, innovation, and the absence of biases in either direction.

The effectiveness of any third-party intervention rests in part on its ability to reduce or avoid strikes, since the motivation for third-party intervention is the realization that strikes are not a desirable form of conflict resolution.

FACING THE CRITICAL ISSUES IN COLLECTIVE BARGAINING, NEGOTIATION, CONFLICT RESOLUTION AND CONTRACT ADMINISTRATION

Now that we have examined many aspects of collective bargaining, negotiating, conflict resolution and grievance procedures, it is useful to respond to the Critical Issues presented at the start of this chapter. As in the last chapter, in addition to expanding upon the brief responses provided here you may want to prepare rebuttals to each of the four responses.

Issue: *Since productivity is so critical, companies want to do everything possible to increase it. Can they get the unions to help? How?*

Productivity is important to unions also, especially when it results in the survival of the company and jobs. When jobs are lost through the introduction of ways to improve productivity, then unions rightly are concerned (See Chapters 2 and 16 for examples of these ideas).[46]

Thus getting the union to cooperate means thinking through your willingness to address the job security issue. Let's assume that over the long run new workers will not be hired and the present work force is to have job security. Productivity increases in the short run then come from better methods of production.

Workers often have many good ideas to improve the productivity of a work group or the entire organization. This is what Buick and the UAW are betting on. This is what the U.S. steel industry and the United Steel workers are betting on. The Japanese have been collecting on this bet for many years. The cornerstone of most of the union-management efforts to improve productivity is worker participation, getting the ideas from those who know the job best. This participation can be conducted in quality circles, semiautonomous work groups, or other types of team arrangements such as in the Scanlon plan.

Issue: *Why don't unions cooperate with companies more? Why do they always take an adversarial position?*

Of course management is the reason for the existence of unions. If management had looked out for the interests of the worker, unions may not have arisen. Unions remain attractive because management still fails to look after the interests of the worker.

Unions have, then, grown up representing the interests of workers, which evidently were not the interests of management. In essence, the union-management relationship developed on the basis of two different sets of interests. An adversarial relationship was thus natural. Now, however, union and management do not always feel that each represents a separate set of interests. On some issues, for example, company survival, both share an interest. When issues of common and similar interests are found union-management relationships can be cooperative.

Unions, however, have been tricked before by management. Who's to say that some companies won't use the current situation and the QWL movement to *their* advantage rather than the *mutual* advantage of labor and management. Cooperation without trust is difficult. Even if trust exists, however, there will always be a place for adversarial relationships because workers and management do have different interests.

Issue: *Should public employees have the right to strike?*

As you know, public employees strike all the time. Many of these strikes are by teachers, local sanitation workers, police, and firefighters. These are public servants who have agreed to work for a local or state government or a board of education with the understanding that strikes are illegal. The air traffic controllers made the same agreement with the federal government. Most people getting married make a similar binding agreement—not to get divorced.

As with marriage, it takes two—labor and management—to make the relationship work. Would you argue that someone *has to* stay married to someone who becomes a drunk, runs around, and abuses the rest of the family? Would you argue that someone *should* stay married to that someone? So would you argue that public employees *have to* keep working even if their employers fail to provide pay increases to merely keep up with the cost of living increases? Did the public employees agree to continue working under even the most adverse conditions, that is, where management disregards the rights and welfare of the employees?

Historically the threat of a strike is necessary to bring concessions by management. Without the threat, these concessions become less likely, though some managements may grant them even without the threat. The strike threat is an integral part of union-management relations in the private sector. Is the public sector really different from the private sector? Arguments go both ways, of course. It's hard to tell the difference, however, between an irresponsible management in the private sector from one in the public sector regardless of how essential the services are to the community.

Unless public managers are required to take vows of responsibility (and those in the private sector not), public employees deserve to have the same rights and obligations as private employees. What do you think?

You should note that some observers argue that giving public unions the right to strike as a part of their right to bargain gives them the right to supersede the electorate in setting public policy. Thus if public unions are given the *right* to strike, the concept of government *sovereignty* (the power of government to rule) is compromised. However, without this right, the numerous strikes by public unions in the 1970s resulted in significant political power. This is because violations against "no strike" provisions by public unions were essentially ignored. President Reagan's handling of the air traffic controllers and the decertification of the controllers' union (PATCO), however, have appeared to reverse this policy of "looking the other way." These two events have also significantly influenced the "political strength" of public unions.

Issue: *Is it likely to expect unions to settle for wage increases that are less than the cost-of-living increase and just equal to productivity increases?*

Would you be willing to work year after year and only receive wage increases based on the level of your productivity over which you have only a little control when inflation is 15 percent?

Though you may have answered no to this question, some workers are saying yes. The five white-collar unions representing the workers at the Tennessee Valley

Authority essentially agreed to do this. Three locals of the United Steelworkers at Timken in Canton, Ohio, did this.[48] The UAW at the U.S. auto companies are doing this. But in these cases it's a matter of survival. Where it is not, it may not only be unlikely that unions will settle for increases less than the cost-of-living increases, but it may be irresponsible management behavior to expect unions to settle *unless* you and all of management are also willing to do the same.

SUMMARY

Both management and the union should be well prepared for bargaining negotiations by collecting information and evaluating possible solutions. A management strategy that has been used is Boulwarism, where management makes an offer and then refuses to budge from this position. Productivity bargaining is an attempt to encourage increased effectiveness in the work place by passing some of the economic savings of modernization or increased efficiency on to the employees. A recent innovation is continuous bargaining, where a joint union-management committee meets on a regular basis to deal with problems. Influencing this trend toward greater productivity and continuous bargaining is the shift from the traditional adversarial relationship between union and management toward cooperation.

Although there are obstacles to union-management cooperation—a history of adversarial relations, hesitancy on the part of the union to give up the traditional roles of labor, and both parties' fear of losing power—present economic conditions and the threat of an influx of foreign products are prompting many organizations to act for their mutual benefit. In one notable example, the president of the United Auto Workers lobbied in both Washington and Japan to reduce imports, which would aid the auto companies by lessening competition and the union by preserving jobs. The success of such cooperative activities can be measured first by the attainment of specific goals and second by the effect they have on labor-management relations in general. The need for cooperation has been recognized by some union leaders who recommend more decision-making participation with management. It appears that cooperation may become more common in the future as unions reexamine their role.

The quality of the union-management relationship can be extremely important. It can have a strong influence on contract negotiations. In negotiations labor and management each select a bargaining committee to negotiate the new agreement. The negotiations may be between a single union and a single company or multiple companies or between multiple unions and a single company.

Bargaining issues are either mandatory, permissive, or prohibited. Mandatory issues must be discussed, permissive issues can be discussed if both parties agree, and prohibited issues cannot be discussed. The issues can be grouped into wage issues, economic supplements issues, institutional issues, and administrative issues.

Almost all labor contracts outline grievance procedures for handling employee complaints. The most common grievance is related to discipline and discharge, although wages, promotions, seniority, vacations, holidays, and management and union rights are also sources of complaints.

Management can influence the results of grievances by developing a procedure that ensures their actions are for just cause and are fair. Written records of actions taken are useful for potential arbitration. Unions have a legal responsibility to represent the employee fairly in grievances; therefore, they also need a grievance-handling procedure.

The effectiveness of collective bargaining and contract administration is usually assessed by measures of how well the process is working. Bargaining can be evaluated using such measures as the duration of negotiations, the frequency of strikes, use of third-party intervention, and the need for government intervention. The effectiveness of the grievance process can be assessed by number of grievances, level in the grievance process that settlement occurs, frequency of strikes or slowdowns, rate of absenteeism, turnover, and sabotage, and need for government intervention.

KEY CONCEPTS

arbitration

attitudinal structuring

Boulwarism

continuous bargaining

coordinated bargaining

distributive bargaining

economic supplement

grievance procedure

industrywide bargaining

integrative bargaining

intraorganizational bargaining

lockout

mandatory issue

mediation

multiemployer bargaining

multilateral bargaining

permissive issue

productivity bargaining

prohibited issue

strike

wildcat strike

Labor Management Cooperation
  Act

collective bargaining

Adversarial system

initial demand point

final offer arbitration

resistance point

target point

initial offer

cooperative system

positive settlement range

negative settlement range

extension of bargaining

unfair representation

DISCUSSION QUESTIONS

1. Why has there been a recent trend toward cooperation between unions and management?
2. What is collective bargaining, and what two types of interaction does it include?
3. Identify and discuss the important issues in the collective bargaining process.
4. Outline and explain the distributive bargaining process.

5. Define productivity bargaining, and explain why it may be an effective bargaining strategy in the future.

6. Why are some union employees willing to take pay cuts even in the face of high inflation and increased costs of living?

7. Discuss three methods that are available to unions and management when they cannot reach agreement at the bargaining table.

8. Outline and discuss a typical grievance procedure.

9. Compare and contrast public versus private sector unions.

10. What indications or measures can be used to effectively evaluate the union-management relationship?

CASE

Quality Circles or Quality Problems

The Place

A large plant of a heavily unionized, medium-sized consumer products manufacturer. The company has been in business for many years, and while traditionally financially successful, has never had a reputation as a progressive work place.

Main Characters

Harvey Lee. Mr. Lee has spent all of his career with the company working his way up from a line worker to general manager of this facility. He will retire in two years and would like these final years to go as smoothly as possible; but recently it seems that troubles loom large on the horizon. Profits have dropped considerably. While a major portion of this decline is attributable to a national economic downturn, he feels that another problem is that the company's products have lost their competitive edge because of quality control problems. His personal opinion for this loss is that workers no longer care anymore about their work. He wonders how to rekindle the work ethic employees used to have.

James Duncan. Mr. Duncan is the president of the local union, a position he has held for about ten years. When he was first elected to this position, working conditions in the plant were, in his opinion, abysmal. Furthermore, he believed workers had little power to change prevailing conditions. During his second year in office, contract negotiations had completely bogged down and in response he arranged a strike. The strike lasted only a few days, but quite effectively laid the groundwork for achieving some employee rights then and in subsequent years. However, from then on, union and management relations have been characterized by suspicion and mistrust. Currently his major concern regards possible layoffs resulting from the company's financial troubles.

Thomas Stein. Mr. Stein is the labor relations manager at the plant, a position he has occupied for some years. In fact, he was appointed to the position shortly before the strike several years ago. While he knows the technical aspects of his job very well, he no longer is hopeful about improving the state of his relationship with the union.

The Employees. These are the employees covered by the bargaining agreement in the manufacturing area. They are of all ages and persuasion but, by and large, feel alienated from the company. Their attitudes could be characterized by the following statements: "Why should we have any commitment to the company; obviously the company doesn't give a damn about us. Profits have dropped only slightly in the last year, and already there is talk of laying people off. Besides what's the incentive to do a good job? We feel we could offer the company more than physical labor, but no one in management would ever listen."

Ruth Henderson. Ms. Henderson joined the company three years ago after graduating from college with a B.A. in business administration. She spent her first two years at the company's Chicago headquarters rotating through a variety of assignments including personnel, marketing, production planning, and so on. This program was to prepare her for the initial supervisory position that she now holds. However, as the supervisor for the past eight months of two foremen and thirty employees, she sometimes wonders if the training program was useful at all. Certainly, the heavy dose of reality she is now experiencing is much different from anything she learned in the program or in school. It seems to her that the employees don't have any respect for their work and are simply not motivated. Nevertheless, she is bright, eager to be successful, and has much to contribute.

The Situation

One of Ms. Henderson's ideas involved the concept known as quality circles, where employees from a work unit volunteer to identify, analyze, and solve work-related problems. She knew that the concept had been widely used in this country and there were many reports of successful applications in popular business publications. As far as she was concerned, it was exactly what was needed to get employees interested and motivated once again. In addition, the reports often indicated that the circles' suggestions often saved the company money and improved the quality of the product.

After receiving permission from the general manager, Ms. Henderson implemented a quality circle in one of the two units she directly supervised. In the beginning, the employees were skeptical, but a few volunteered for the necessary training. To everyone's amazement, the circle members produced some useful suggestions. In fact, one of their suggestions resulted in a substantial improvement in the reject rate of one of the company's "problem" products. Even more surprisingly, some circle members seemed to be more committed to the company and more satisfied with their work. Absenteeism among circle members dropped about 25 percent.

Given the initial success of the project, Ms. Henderson sought to publicize the case throughout the company. Some enlightened managers showed interest in the concept. Before long the "secret" was out, and even Mr. Lee asked Ms. Henderson for a report. After reading the report and doing some follow-up research, he decided that quality circles might hold a fair amount of potential for the plant and initiated a plan to try ten circles in different parts of the organization. At this point he held a meeting with a number of his managers to discuss implementation of the program.

With all the attention given quality circles, it was natural that word about the program would spread throughout the plant. Upon learning about quality circles through the grapevine, Mr. Duncan's reaction was, "What the hell is management up to this time?" By the next morning, all union members were told that quality circles were just one more attempt by managers to exact more work from them with no additional compensation. To support this he produced articles that harped on circles as a productivity improvement technique. The effect of this, of course, was that employees were unwilling to participate in circles and they had cause to feel even more alienated from the company. In fact, even the one circle that had been operating effectively was forced by peer pressure from other union members to shut down.

Case Questions

1. Characterize your perceptions of union-management relations in this company.
2. What type of bargaining likely takes place in this company during union-management negotiations?
3. Was it legitimate for the union president to react the way he did when he learned about quality circles?
4. Which management official was not included during the implementation of quality circles?
5. Should the company try to implement quality circles again?

FOR YOUR CAREER

- It is important for you to know and appreciate the views of organized labor as well as management.
- More than ever, innovative ways are needed for labor and management to work together to improve QWL and productivity. If you can provide these ways, you'll be a valuable employee.
- What's your style of interacting with others? Do you tend to compete with them, problem-solve, compromise, accommodate, or avoid them?
- You may want to consider working for a union. Such a job could have considerable influence and impact on the lives of many people.
- Being an effective collective bargainer (whether for union or management) takes real skill. Jobs are always available for individuals who can bargain well.
- Would you agree to a wage reduction of 20 percent in order to help save the jobs of other workers, even though your job was very secure?

ENDNOTES

1. J. M. Brett, "Behavioral Research on Unions," In B. M. Staw and L. L. Cummings, eds, *Research in Organizational* Behavior, Vol. 2 Greenwich, Conn.; (JAI Press, Inc., 1980), p. 200.

2. Ibid.

3. "The New Industrial Relations," *Business Week,* May 11, 1981, pp. 85–98.

   "A Partnership to Build the New Workplace," *Business Week,* June 30, 1980, pp. 96–101.

   "Hot UAW Issue: Quality of Work Life," *Business Week,* September 17, 1979, pp, 120–122.

   "A Try at Steel-Mill Harmony," *Business Week,* June 29, 1981, pp. 132–136.

   "Quality of Work Life; Catching on," *Business Week,* September 21, 1981, pp. 72–80.

   Julius N. Draznin, "Labor Relations," *Personnel Journal,* October 1980, pp. 805.

   Robert E. Steiner, "Labor Relations," *Personnel Journal,* May 1981, pp. 344–346.

4. Thomas C. Hayes, "At G.M.'s Buick Unit, Workers and Bosses Get Ahead by Getting Along," *New York Times,* July 5, 1981, Sec. F, pp. 4–5.

5. Interesting discussions of early American labor history can be found in R. B. Morris, "A Bicentennial Look at the Early Days of American Labor," *American Monthly Labor Review,* May 1976, pp. 21–26.

6. J. A. Fossum, *Labor Relations: Development Structure, Process* (Dallas, Texas: Business Publications, Inc., 1982), p. 10.

7. Reprinted by permission of the *Harvard Business Review.* Excerpt from "Collective Bargaining: Ritual or Reality?" by A. A. Blum (November/December 1961). Copyright © 1961 by the President and Fellows of Harvard College; all rights reserved.

8. A. Sloan and F. Whitney, *Labor Relations,* 3rd ed. (Englewood Cliffs, N.J.: Prentice Hall, 1977), p. 59.

9. Sloan and Whitney, p. 64. Boulwarism was so named after the vice president of General Electric, Lemuel Boulware, who initiated this management bargaining practice.

10. Ibid., pp. 83–84.

11. A good discussion of earlier contributions to labor law can be found in D. P. Twomey, *Labor Law and Legislation,* 6th ed. (Cincinnati, Ohio: Southwestern, 1980).

12. H. B. Frazier II, "Labor Management Relations in the Federal Government," *Labor Law Journal,* March 1979, p. 131.

13. Daniel D. Cook, "Labor Faces the Productivity Challenge," *Industry Week,* March 9, 1981, pp. 61–65.

   Twomey, p. 77.

14. Sloan and Whitney, p. 95.

15. Fossum, pp. 395–396.

16. *1979 Guidebook to Labor Relations,* 18th ed. (Chicago: Commerce Clearing House, 1978), p. 282.

17. D. Greenberg, "The Structure of Collective Bargaining and Some of Its Determinants," *Proceedings,* Industrial Relations Research Association, Albany, N.Y., December 1966.

18. A. Leonard, "Collective Bargaining with Multinational Firms by American Labor Unions," *Labor Law Journal,* December 1974, pp. 746–759.

   R. Mansfield, "The Advent of Public Sector Multi-Employer Bargaining," *Personnel Journal,* May 1975, pp. 290–294.

19. Fossum, p. 171.

20. E. Platt, "The Duty to Bargain As Applied to Management Decisions," *Labor Law Journal,* March 1968, p. 145.

21. Fossum, p. 173.

22. Platt, p. 144.

23. Examples of these are discussed in *Business Week,* "The Oil Workers Vow to Catch Up on Wages," December 31, 1979, p. 34, and *Business Week,* "Taking Aim at Union Busters," November 26, 1979, pp. 67–72.

24. "Why the URW Will Be More of a Team Player," *Business Week,* September 28, 1981, pp. 97–99.

"The Demands Airlines are Pressing on Labor," *Business Week,* December 7, 1981, p. 37.

"Tough Choices for the UAW," *Business Week,* December 7, 1981, p. 105.

"Detroit Gets a Break from UAW," *Business Week,* November 30, 1981.

"A New Moderation in Rail Talks," *Business Week,* August 31, 1981, p. 50.

"The IBT Pact Could be a Model of Moderation," *Business Week,* September 28, 1981, p. 38.

Mark N. Dodosh, "Companies Increasingly Ask Labor to Give Back Past Contract Gains," *Wall Street Journal,* November 27, 1981, p. 21.

25. "The Price of Peace at Chrysler," *Business Week,* November 12, 1979, pp. 93–96.

26. T. A. Kochan, *Collective Bargaining and Industrial Relations* (Homewood, Ill.,: Irwin, 1980).

27. William E. Lissy, "Use of Temporary Replacements During a Lockout," pp. 18–21.

28. Stephen J. Cabot and Jerald R. Cureton, "Labor Disputes and Strikes: Be Prepared," *Personnel Journal,* February 1981, pp. 121–123, 136.

"Current Labor Statistics," *Monthly Labor Review,* March 1980, p. 103.

29. "Why Labor Militancy Has Abated," *Business Week,* January 19, 1981, pp. 22–23.

30. T. A. Kochan, "Collective Bargaining in Organizational Research," in B. M. Staw and L. L. Cummings, eds., *Research in Organizational Behavior,* Vol. 2 (Greenwich, Conn.: JAI Press, Inc. 1980).

31. "More Support for Arbitration," *Business Week,* October 5, 1981, p. 132.

Julius N. Draznin, "Labor Relations," *Personnel Journal,* April 1981, p. 256.

Dennis King, "Three Cheers for Conflict!," *Personnel,* January–February 1981, pp. 13–22.

James F. Rand, "Creative Problem-Solving Applied to Grievance Arbitration Procedures," *Personnel Administrator,* March 1980, pp. 50–52.

Derek Sheane, "When and How to Intervene in Conflict," *Personnel Journal,* June 1980, pp. 515–518.

"Arbitration Cases Increase," *Personnel Journal,* November 1981, p. 832.

Samuel C. Walker, "The Dynamics of Clear Contract Language," *Personnel Journal,* January 1981, pp. 39–41.

32. Kochan, 1980, p. 151.

33. A. Cox, "Rights Under A Labor Agreement," *Harvard Law Review* 69 (February 1956): 601–657.

34. S. H. Slichter, J. J. Healy, and E. R. Livernash, *The Impact of Collective Bargaining on Management* (Washington, D.C.: The Brookings Institution, 1960), p. 694.

35. Slichter, Healy, and Livernash, pp. 694–696.

36. Julius N. Draznin, "Labor Relations," *Personnel Journal,* July 1981, p. 528.

Ibid., August 1980, p. 625.

Bruce A. Jacobs, "Don't Take 'No' for an Answer," *Industry Week,* January 26, 1981, pp. 38–43.

Kochan, 1980, pp. 385–386.

Irving Paster, "Collective Bargaining: Warnings for the Novice Negotiator," *Personnel Journal,* March 1981, pp. 203–206.

37. B. R. Skeleton and P. C. Marett, "Loser Pays Arbitration," *Labor Law Journal,* May 1979, pp. 302–309.

38. G. W. Bolander, "Fair Representation: Not Just A Union Problem," *Personnel Administrator,* March 1980, p. 39.

39. Bureau of National Affairs, *Grievance Guide,* 4th ed. (Washington D.C.: Bureau of National Affairs, 1972), pp. 8–9.

40. Memorandum 79–55, National Labor Relations Board, July 7, 1979.

41. D. R. Dalton and W. D. Todor, "Manifest Needs of Stewards: Propensity to File a Grievance," *Journal of Applied Psychology,* December 1979, pp. 654–659.

42. "Talking Tough to Public Workers," *Business Week,* April 27, 1981, pp. 114–116.

43. Kochan, 1980, p. 471.

44. Kochan, 1980, p. 472.

45. Brett, 1980, p. 210.

Kochan, 1980, p. 452

46. Joann S. Lublin, "As Robot Age Arrives, Labor Seeks Protection Against Loss of Work," *Wall Street Journal,* October 26, 1981, pp. 1, 21.

47. Gerald I. Susman, *A Guide to Labor Management Committees in State and Local Government* (U.S. Department of Housing and Urban Development and U.S. Office of Personnel Management, Washington, D.C., Spring 1980).

Susan G. Clark, *Executive Report on a Guide to Labor Management Committees,* (U.S. Department of Housing and Urban Development and U.S. Office of Personnel Management, Washington, D.C., Spring 1980).

48. "Timken Talks Tough to Win Concessions," *Business Week,* November 9, 1981, pp. 43–44.

"TVA's Hard Line Ends Years of Labor Peace," *Business Week,* September 21, 1981, pp. 31–32.

Trends and Comparisons

Chapter 20
Effective Personnel Management
in the 1980s

Chapter Outline

Critical Issues for Personnel Management in the 1980s

Trends in Personnel Management
Planning for Personnel Management
Staffing
Establishing Relationships with Employees
Appraising and Motivating Employee Behavior
Compensating Employee Behavior
Training and Career Development
Improving the Work Environment
Union-Management Relations

Personnel Practices in Other Countries
Japan

Effective
Personnel Management
in the 1980s

Evaluating Personnel Management in the 1980s

Facing the Critical Issues of Personnel Management in the 1980s

Summary

Key Concepts

Discussion Questions

For Your Career

Endnotes

Personnel in the News

The Highly Motivated Work Force

Some of us laugh at the Japanese when we read that a shift going on the job in Japan applauds the shift leaving the job. But when you examine it, the practice is not really something to laugh about. The Japanese are highly motivated—their increase in productivity clearly demonstrates that. And the Japanese appreciate and understand the dignity of work. The shift leaving the plant, having done its job well and having produced a high-quality product, is deserving of applause. (From B. S. Murphy, "The Past is Prologue: Building Better Industrial Relations in the 1980s," Personnel Journal, *January 1980, p. 24. Reprinted with the permission of* Personnel Journal, Costa Mesa, Calif.; *all rights reserved.)*

Managing the Impending Promotion Squeeze

A highway traffic controller would never expect a rush hour flow of ten cars abreast to safely squeeze into only two lanes—unless he created a system of lights and signs to regulate that flow. Similarly, without a well-conceived management plan, top executives can't expect to properly control the flow—more accurately the flood—of the postwar "baby boom" generation into management positions. The time for making such plans is now; the baby boom traffic jam is upon us.

In the next ten years, though the total labor force will shrink, the number of workers in the 25–44 age group—the baby boom generation—will increase by one-third. With large percentages of women in this age bracket choosing to enter or reenter the job market—an unprecedented 69% of all women born in the later '50s are now working—this 25–44 year-old group will grow to more than 53% of the workforce by 1990.

Many of the potential problems that this baby boom bulge will create, as greater numbers of younger workers try to begin and then enhance their careers in management-level positions, have become familiar to us through journalistic accounts and government reports. More elusive, however are the solutions to these problems. (Kenneth P. Shapiro, Personnel Journal, *October 1981, p. 800. Reprinted with the permission of* Personnel Journal, Costa Mesa, Calif., *all rights reserved.)*

Together these two quotations indicate why personnel management will continue to become even more important to organizations. On the one hand, it will become even more important because there are so many changes occurring in the work force. Not only are their demographics changing, but so are their needs, values, and what it will take to motivate them—you and me. These changes in turn are imposing many changes upon the personnel activities. And on the other hand, it will become more important because international competition will continue to make productivity and quality of work life central concerns for the United States. Since the impact of the demographic changes and the international competition are right up the alley of personnel management, its role in the 1980s may be far-reaching. Most personnel managers are well aware of this and see this as an opportunity to improve their credibility with the organization. Consequently, they want to be prepared for the 1980s. This desire is reflected in the final set of Critical Issues raised by our group of personnel managers.

CRITICAL ISSUES FOR PERSONNEL MANAGEMENT IN THE 1980s

1. *How can personnel manage the impending promotion squeeze? What will it take to satisfy employees?*
2. *What will be the likely events happening in each of the personnel management activities?*
3. *How can personnel show it is worth its salt and doing worthwhile things for the organization?*
4. *Do the Japanese really work harder? Are they really better workers?*

Personnel executives of the 1980s, facing increased responsibilities and new challenges, will be viewed as key decision makers. They will have to meet not only organizational goals but also individual and social goals. Moreover, all personnel activities will continue to grow in importance as discussed in Chapter 1.

The first part of this chapter discusses the significant trends in personnel management in the 1980s. Then some aspects of personnel management in Japan are examined.

The same factors that are making personnel management more important are also creating new trends in this field. Although we could speculate about many of these trends, we will analyze here only those that are most significant and that have the greatest likelihood of occurring. These trends are analyzed for each personnel function presented in the preceding chapters.

TRENDS IN PERSONNEL MANAGEMENT

Planning for Personnel Management

Two major categories of personnel planning influence the organization. One category helps the organization decide upon and fulfill its strategic plans, and the other helps the organization do these as effectively and legally as possible.

Personnel Planning. Many organizations have long engaged in various forms of planning. In most, however, personnel plans were built around decisions that had already been made.[1] This was possible when human resources were abundant and organizations had a great degree of freedom to hire and fire, but it is no longer possible. Organizations must now integrate personnel plans with the strategic plans of the total organization. This involves forecasting the human resources needed to carry out the organization's plans—for instance, for expansion or even for retrenchment or reduction in operations involving plant closing or relocation.

Personnel policies will be linked more with corporate policies.

This corporate-level integration of personnel planning offers top management the opportunity to generate more understanding of and support for the organization's personnel objectives. Corporate-level integration is also a necessity if the personnel planning is to be effective:

> When human resources issues are not included in the formal planning process, directives from top management about employee relations policy often are met by lower managers with indifference or in some instances, outright hostility.[2]

Employees will help redesign their own jobs.

Job Design and Analysis. As organizations attempt to meet equal employment and affirmative action requirements, there is an increased need to justify staffing procedures and performance appraisal results. A critical basis for this justification is the job analysis, which provides adequate details of both the duties that a job entails and the skills needed to perform those duties. Thus organizations without a formal job analysis program will be likely to institute one, and those that already have such a program will review their job analyses to ensure that they are current and that the skills listed are really necessary.

In addition to having the conventional descriptions of job duties and employee skill qualifications, more job analyses will include a description of the results expected and even the rewards that are part of the job. Such a description might also include design characteristics and context of the job.

As it becomes more difficult to promote employees, job redesign will become an alternative way to keep the employees motivated. Job redesign will continue to be used as a critical feature of many QWL programs.

Staffing

Obtaining a pool of qualified or potentially qualified job applicants will continue to be an important activity for most personnel departments. Skilled labor shortages, managerial surpluses, and declining economic growth will make effective staffing a real challenge.

Recruitment. Because fewer younger individuals will be entering the labor force in the 1980s than previously, entry positions may remain open even though there is a surplus of middle and senior managers. Consequently, recruiting efforts will have to be increased for entry-level positions and reduced at higher levels.

In addition, fewer managers will be hired from other organizations. The rare middle- and upper-level management positions that open up will be reserved for people who are already part of the organization. Because there will be fewer opportunities for upward movement, promotion will also come to include lateral movements.

Rapid technological changes and the growing potential for employee obsolescence may make demotions more necessary. The impact of obsolescence and demotion will be eased by renaming it a **downward transfer.**

Selection. Because of the trends in recruiting, there will be a need to select more entry-level employees. And although it would appear that selection for higher-level positions will become easier because fewer positions will be available, the opposite will actually be the case. The better an organization's affirmative action program, the more employees there will be going after these scarce positions.

But an organization must still be careful to fill vacancies with qualified employees. The burden will be on the organization to defend its selection procedures, so it will have to spend more time making each selection decision. It will also need to defend and explain its decisions to those who are passed over, particularly if they are passed over because the organization is complying with a consent decree or an affirmative action program.

Selection decisions will also become more important because of the declining percentage of employees who can be promoted. Although the organization will get a more favorable selection ratio, fewer people will be selected. That means more people wanting to know why they are not selected. Not only will this *desire* on the part of employees to know why they were not selected increase in the 1980s, but also their feeling that they have a *right* to know. In other words, employees will demand the organization communicate with them and recognize many more rights.[3]

> Personnel decisions must be valid.

Establishing Relationships with Employees

Once spending the time, money, and effort to recruit and select the right employees, organizations will increasingly want to hold onto them. Effectively communicating with them and respecting their rights are certainly integral in retaining the right employees.

Communicating with Employees. As the work force becomes more diverse in values and preferences, organizations will find it more necessary to accommodate to the needs of their employees than ever before. In order to do this, organizations will need to communicate effectively with employees. This means they will have to engage in two-way communication. Quality circles will be one key way organizations will facilitate this type of communication.

> More than ever, personnel will have to find out what the "troops are thinking."

Personnel will also engage in more survey work to find out how the employees are doing and what they are thinking. Data collection will grow in importance as personnel seeks to show the effectiveness of what it does.

Employee Rights. Increasingly employees are demanding more rights, for example, the right to a job and the right to participate in making decisions that affect them. While some of these desired rights are legally protected, others are not. In the 1980s organizations will face a growing number of desired rights not legally protected. Organizations will have to decide whether they want to recognize and provide these desired rights or ignore them. By ignoring them organizations may run the risk of the desired

> Organizations should anticipate and accommodate employee rights.

rights becoming legally protected. The personnel manager can be very influential in deciding on the course of action the organization should take. She or he can also decide on how best to appraise and motivate the work force.

Appraising and Motivating Employee Behavior

As organizations become more concerned with productivity, they become more concerned with employee performance. Organizations become concerned with determining who are the best performers and how the others can be motivated to improve.

Appraising and Evaluating Employees. With the increased emphasis on fair employment practices, greater care will be taken in appraising employee performance. This care will manifest itself in the use of more objective measures of performance and a decline in the use of more subjective, less performance-related measures. In addition, the system in which an employee's performance is embedded will increasingly be taken into account.

Managing ineffective performance will become even more important in the years ahead. Thus organizations will become more concerned about feeding back the results of performance appraisals to employees as frequently as possible. However, the idea of mandatory retirement will become less popular, so it will no longer be so easy to wait for poor performers to retire. As a means of correcting poor performance, **performance contracts** will be brought into use. Employees agree to achieve clearly specified objectives within a given time period, and failure to do so results in agreed-on disciplinary procedures.

Organizations will also examine their own policies and practices for possible causes of ineffective performance. When organizations terminate employees for ineffective performance, they will make sure that it is the employee, not the organization, who is in fact at fault. If it is the organization, strategies to motivate, rather than terminate, will be designed.

There will be big rewards for personnel who can devise ways to motivate others.

Motivating Employee Behavior. As employee rights increase, it becomes more difficult to terminate employees. Additionally organizations would rather not terminate employees. But with the productivity crisis, organizations can ill afford poor performers. Consequently personnel will have to devise ways of motivating employees to engage in desired behaviors. This will not be easy, but it is most critical to organizations. One way may be using the compensation system more effectively, more fairly.

Compensating Employee Behavior

With society's concern focusing on equal opportunity and equal pay, it is only natural for it to extend to the concern for equal pay for jobs of comparable worth. Because this issue has such significant and far-reaching economic implications, personnel managers will be devoting time in understanding it and how their organizations can respond or act on it. This applies equally to direct compensation and indirect compensation.

Total Compensation. There are several major trends in compensating employees. First is a change in the basis on which compensation is decided. Generally organizations fix the pay for jobs according to an evaluation of the job content and characteristics. In accordance with nondiscriminatory pay policies, people with the same jobs (or jobs of equal evaluation) receive equal pay. However, women still tend to earn less than men because the jobs they have traditionally held have been determined through job evaluation to be less valuable or of less worth to the organization. Some people argue that the jobs many women perform are just as important to the organization as those men perform. In other words, the job evaluation system has biased job worth in favor of traditional men's jobs. In the 1980s, then, there may well be a move to determine the pay of jobs by their intrinsic (true) worth to the organization. This is the essence of comparable worth discussed in Chapter 11. The result could be substantial increases in compensation costs if many jobs are upgraded rather than downgraded to achieve equal pay for jobs of equal worth.

Comparable worth could have a significant impact on compensation.

Another trend in compensation is **salary compression.** Leveling pressures in our economy are decreasing the spread in pay between various positions in an organization. Unions have done much to raise wages at the lower end, and salaries for middle-level jobs have remained about the same due to stable profits, low productivity, and the progressive nature of the tax and social security system.

However, the 1980 steelworkers negotiations redressed some of this potential compression situation by granting relatively small across-the-board increases (twenty-five, twenty, and fifteen cents per hour over the three-year life of the contract) and included a skill differential clause. This skill differential provides for an increase of one cent times an employee's pay grade during each year of the contract. Since there are thirty pay grades, top-graded employees receive thirty, sixty, and ninety cents per hour additions in each of the three years. Nevertheless, it appears that salary compression will increase during the 1980s, making promotion to middle-level jobs less attractive. Consequently promotions to middle-level management may become less attractive. Thus it may be harder for organizations to recruit the most qualified people for management unless salary compression is reduced throughout the organization. Some of this compression could be reduced through indirect compensation.

Indirect Compensation.   Bigger and better benefits are due in the 1980s. By 1985 benefits are expected to average nearly 50 percent of total payroll costs.[4] Benefits that are likely to become more predominant include

- Preretirement counseling and retirement planning programs. Rising inflation has helped reverse the trend toward early retirement. This in turn has heightened awareness in U.S. corporations of the importance of retirement planning and education programs. This has also increased the degree to which corporations perceive they are in part responsible for an employee's retirement plans.

- Career development and support programs. With the traditional fast tracks to promotion and success being jammed because of the glut of twenty-five to fifty-four-year-old employees, the same employees will demand alternate career paths and alternative job experience, such as are provided through job enrichment and even sabbaticals.[5]

- Personal counseling and assistance services. Employee counseling services now include advice and information regarding legal concerns, tax matters, and more personal problems such as drinking and absenteeism. These will continue to expand. Discussion and recognition, especially of personal problems, will be combined with action-oriented programs to help employees deal with problems they

B^-

have. As a matter of fact, the establishment of these programs is a recognition that an employee's problem is also the organization's problem, whether or not the organization caused the employee's problem. This recognition is due in part to two views: the employee is a valuable resource to the organization, and organizations have a social responsibility to assist their employees in dealing with problems related to their performance.

■ Lump-sum pensions withdrawals. Instead of merely providing monthly pension payment plans to employees, organizations will increasingly offer employees the choice of taking all their pension money at once. Some companies are now offering this alternative and from one-quarter (at Great Northern Nekoosa Corporation) to nearly all (at Hewlett Packard Company) employees are taking the lump-sum option. Arthur Young, benefits manager at Hewlett Packard, explains: "Our corporate philosophy is to place a great deal of responsibility on the individual. Giving the lump-sum option is consistent with that philosophy".[6]

■ Payments for adoptions. Currently most organizations provide maternity benefits; however, only a few provide adoption benefits. American Can Company recently adopted a plan that pays up to $2,000 for each adoption of a child under eighteen. Some companies, however, have been providing adoption benefits for years. These companies include S. C. Johnson & Son Inc.; Foote, Cone & Belding Communications Inc, and IBM.[7]

Training and Career Development

In the future, organizations will provide training and development to prevent employee obsolescence. The training and development will be done less on a one-shot basis and more as part of a package of career development opportunities. This shift toward career management will demand that employees take greater responsibility for their own career development.

Second careers, reeducation, consultation, and part-time work are becoming common activities for our older population. Currently about 20 percent of the adult population is between forty-five and sixty-four years of age. By the year 2000, when that figure will reach 38 percent, incentives for retirement and the indexing of benefits will be very important.[8] Already, organizational preretirement programs are steadily improving.

The number of stress management programs that organizations offer will increase by a significant number. There will be greater concern for potential stress due to job assignments, travel, management practices, and a general lack of match between employee ability and job demands and between employee needs and job rewards. As one consequence, organizations will offer more physical exercise programs and even time and room for meditation. Another consequence is that organizations will place an even greater emphasis on the quality of work life in addition to the needed emphasis on productivity.

Improving the Work Environment

For society, organizations, and employees, seeking ways to improve the work environment will be a major concern. Personnel managers will be able to gain increased importance and visibility in organizations by developing and implementing ways to improve the physical and psychological work environments.

Improving Productivity and Quality of Work Life.   Eaton Corporation chairman E. M. DeWindt had this to say about the quality of work life and reasons why it will continue to be important in the 1980s:

> About ten years ago, Eaton launched a massive expansion program, a long-range project involving the building of nearly a score of new plants around the nation. We knew that each plant design would incorporate the most modern methods and machinery for productivity. And, realizing that productivity is really a function of people, we decided that our employee relations practices and policies should get as much streamlining as the plants and equipment. When we looked at our traditional practices, it was obvious that they weren't designed for rushing into the 21st century. These practices were born of mistrust, agitation and negotiation. This was apparent in the paraphernalia and terminology that went along with them. We had the tyrannical time clocks and mindless bells and buzzers. We had probationary periods, posted work rules, disciplinary proceedings and restrictive holiday-eligibility rules for production workers that stamped them as second-class members of the total team.
>
> The building of so many new plants gave us a unique opportunity to start from scratch, and our employee relations people were challenged to break away from tradition and develop a program built on mutual trust.
>
> They responded with vigor and enthusiasm, and today nearly 20 Eaton plants operate under the new philosophy. There are no time clocks in these plants, no bells or buzzers or whistles to remind people that Big Daddy is watching them. All employees of these plants—management, office and production—are salaried, and all participate in major decisions concerning the operation. There are no paycheck penalties for casual absences or tardiness, no segregated parking lots.
>
> The results have been dramatic and productive. Absenteeism averages 2% in these plants and turnover is almost zero. Productivity ranges from 30 to 40% higher than in traditional plants. There is a genuine feeling of involvement and belonging throughout the plants. The program has passed the tests of good and bad times, and many of its elements are working their way into older, organized plants.
>
> While it is true that such sweeping changes could only be made in new and unorganized plants, this is not a program to combat the unions, but rather to combat the climate of mistrust that so often and so easily pervades a manufacturing operation. It has helped bring about productive negotiations in unionized plants, and we are convinced that both management and labor will pursue the course of mutual trust at a greater degree than ever before. . . .[9]

Many organizations are adopting QWL programs. Flextime and job-sharing arrangements, participatory management, management-by-objectives projects and more work redesign projects will all become more commonplace in the 1980s. Consistent with these trends is the trend toward greater union-management cooperation.

Union-Management Relations

Two major trends in union-management relations are likely to be renewed interest in organizing and increased union-management cooperation.

Organizing. Although the proportion of the work force that is unionized has been leveling off in recent years, this trend is expected to reverse:

> Over the next few years we expect the percent in unions to increase again to over 30 percent, perhaps to an historic high, primarily as a result of organization in the public sector. Compared to approximately 30 percent today, we expect that fully 75 percent of public employees will be organized by 1985, representing 40 percent of all organized labor.[10]

The two fastest-growing unions in the United States today are the American Federation of State and Municipal Employees and the United Food and Commercial Workers Union. They will continue this growth into the 1980s.

There are indications that the U.S. Congress may change the entire process of organizing. A controversial labor law (H.R. 8410–S. 2467) was presented to Congress in 1978. Although it did not pass, several of its provisions indicate the possible direction of labor law in the 1980s:

■ The National Labor Relations Board (NLRB) would increase in size from five to seven members, with a high probability that the additional members would be prolabor.

■ Cases before the NLRB would be reviewed and affirmed by a two-person panel. As a result, the board could "rubber stamp" decisions of administrative-law judges instead of providing proper review.

■ The NLRB would be required to rewrite some of its own criteria for decision making, possibly ignoring carefully established precedents in the process.

■ Unions would be allowed to organize on company time on company property. Each time an employer used company time to respond to union literature, union representatives would be allowed the same forum. Unions, but not employers, would be able to contact employees at home, by phone, or in person—and, of course, at union meetings.

■ Unions would be able to call elections with only fifteen days' notice to employers or to postpone elections up to seventy-five days. Employers would have no control at all over these activities.

■ Court review of NLRB decisions would be narrowly limited.

■ The NLRB would be able to assess punitive damages to employers who attempt to fight union representation by disallowing them access to federal contracts for three years.

■ Employers exercising their right to court review of NLRB decisions could be forced to forfeit their rights to collective bargaining.

■ The NLRB would be required to seek a court injunction against any employer who fired someone during an organizing campaign, even if the employer acted in good faith.[11]

Labor-Management Cooperation. Because of the need for improved productivity, international competition, workers' rights, and industrial democracy, the European labor-relations model will become increasingly popular. Codetermination, work councils, and union-controlled funds are all ideas that are transferable to the United States. Multinational companies have been gaining experience with the European model for several years. Chrysler, for instance, already has a union representative on its board of directors. Ideas for implementing other personnel practices will also come from other countries, especially Japan.

PERSONNEL PRACTICES IN OTHER COUNTRIES

Personnel managers in the United States can learn valuable lessons by looking at what other nations are doing. Although many comparisons are possible, only those with Japan are made here since many Japanese examples have already been provided. The focus is on the most significant differences and, in some cases, on practices that might be adopted in the United States.

Japan

Although the Japanese may be more highly motivated, they do not necessarily work any harder than Americans. There are, however, several important differences affecting the management of human resources in Japan and in the United States, as described by Masaya Hattori, a Japanese businessperson working for the World Bank in Washington, D.C.:

> Japanese are often characterized as workaholics, both in the Tokyo newspapers and in the international press. . . .
>
> Is it true that Japanese work harder than others? I think not. . . .
>
> The Japanese practice of working a half day on Saturday makes little sense (in the United States). Since most employees commute long distances, spending two hours traveling in order to put in three hours at the office is a total waste of time.
>
> But the five-day workweek is not as commonly adhered to in Western countries as many Japanese think it is. Of the 250 people in my department, at least a third put in regular overtime without pay. Senior officials work both Saturdays and Sundays at least once a month. A "9-to-5 man" is someone who is considered lazy and refuses to do more than the minimum.
>
> In American companies, it is the top executives, those who make the innovative, risk-taking decisions, who put in the longest hours. Lower-level employees, those who perform routine tasks, are rarely required to work late.
>
> In a Japanese company, heavy demands are placed on lower-level staff, and they often are given responsibilities which would be handled by a top executive in the United States. All workers are expected to be flexible enough to perform any task the department has before it, and for this reason junior staff must put in long hours.
>
> In my opinion, younger employees in Japan are much more capable than their counterparts elsewhere. They are given responsibility much earlier in their careers because complex tasks are delegated to a much lower level. . . .
>
> Just the opposite of Western companies, the proportion of competent people declines with seniority.
>
> The cause of this curious reversal is the unique seniority system in Japan, which more often than not causes a retrogression of talent. Because of guaranteed lifetime employment, the less able are not weeded out through selective advancement. Quite frankly, few Japanese executives over the age of 45 would be able to handle the duties of an equivalent post in Europe or the United States.
>
> Another difference between Japanese and Western organizations is the place of

continuing education. A common Japanese misconception is that the American employee leaves his worries at the office and spends his free time in pursuit of leisure entertainment.

Nothing is further from the truth. The most able executives go to school or study on their own in order to continually upgrade their professional and technical skills.

In the Japanese lifetime employment system, a worker may undergo training during business hours at corporate expense. In the Western firm, 100% of the time on the job is devoted to work. If the employee wishes to improve his skills, he does it on his own time.[12]

Employee Socialization and Development. The Japanese also differ substantially in how they train today's college graduate to become tomorrow's manager.[13] There are two major aspects of this training: preemployment education, or socialization and training given before the first day on the job, and initial managerial education. This training has five general aims:

- To educate new graduates as members of the company, emphasizing self-discipline and the transition from student life to company life
- To teach professionalism and the significance and meaning of work
- To provide background information about the company and to familiarize employees with distinctive management trends
- To familiarize employees with basic company procedures and fundamental business rules and etiquette
- To cultivate a spirit of harmony and teamwork among employees[14]

Preemployment education consists of communications between the company and the future employees, who are still in school. Some companies recommend to future employees what they should read before starting work. Future employees are frequently sent a directory of all new recruits, an employee handbook, a booklet on health and nutrition, and even words of encouragement from senior employees. Many companies also hold meetings that provide an opportunity for future employees to get to know one another.

> [These meetings] afford an opportunity for the future employees to learn the company song, to meet senior employees who are graduates of the same university, to visit the factories and see exhibitions of the company's products and to become familiar with the company's various departments and divisions.[15]

Initial managerial education has three parts: orientation, work experience, and residency. The program of work experience involves real grass-roots exposure, especially in the area of production. For example, the current president of Matsushita Electric Works spent his first six months carrying and shifting goods in the company's storage area. Most of the present executives of Japan's major companies have also passed through similar on-the-job training programs.

During orientation and the work experience program, new employees live together in company residences. Here they learn social rules, etiquette, human relations, and punctuality, all considered necessary for an effective manager.

An important aspect of this training and development is the evaluation of how well the new employees have done. Mitsubishi Corporation and Isetan Department Stores, for example, administer a quiz, which the recruits must pass, on the essential knowledge for handling the companies' products. Immediate supervisors of these new employees also file reports, which are later used in identifying the work areas new employees should be placed in and the jobs they should be rotated through.

Now that we have examined several trends likely to occur in how personnel activities will be implemented in the 1980s, it is appropriate to examine the trends in how these activities are likely to be evaluated.

EVALUATING PERSONNEL MANAGEMENT IN THE 1980s

In Chapter 1, three major sets of indicators or criteria against which to measure the effectiveness of personnel management are discussed. The sets and their components include:

Personnel must prove its worth.

- Productivity
    - Employee performance
    - Employee absenteeism
    - Employee turnover
- Quality of Work Life
    - Employee job involvement
    - Employee satisfaction
    - Employee stress
    - Employee accidents and health
- Legal Compliance
    - Costs of fines for law and regulation violation
    - Costs of lost contracts for not adhering to laws and regulations
    - Community goodwill and general reputation in the community

These indicators are and will continue throughout the 1980s to be the way that personnel can prove that it is worth its salt. Without these indicators, personnel effectiveness cannot be determined and it ends up with the traditional image of not being very useful to an organization.

The time is appropriate, however, for personnel to use these indicators and show its effectiveness. This, will require more attention to data gathering, for example, measures taken before and after personnel activities are implemented and more attention to evaluation design and data analysis to help determine the size and direction of the change due to the personnel activities. This analysis will also enable personnel to improve and make future activities even more effective. Remember: "if you can't measure it, it probably doesn't exist," and "if it doesn't exist, it can't be worth much."

FACING THE CRITICAL ISSUES OF PERSONNEL MANAGEMENT IN THE 1980s

After our discussion of the trends of personnel management in the 1980s and a comparison with Japan, it is appropriate to address the Critical Issues presented at the start of this chapter. Only the highlights of responses to those Issues are presented here. You, however, should be more thorough in developing your responses to them.

Issue: *How can personnel manage the impending promotion squeeze? What will it take to satisfy employees?*

Good personnel planning is certainly essential here. It's important to know exactly how many people you'll need and where and when you'll need them. You'll also need to know their needs and preferences. After this is done, you can do several things to manage the promotion squeeze:

1. Offer long-term incentives.
2. Provide larger raises for really outstanding performers.
3. Provide more flexible benefits that are attractive to your employees.
4. Provide mentoring relationships.
5. Engage in job enrichment and job rotation (lateral promotions).
6. Offer training and career development programs.
7. Select employees less likely to be motivated by promotion.

Issue: *What will be the likely events happening in each of the personnel management activities?*

Some of the major issues for the 1980s are likely to be comparable worth, sexual harassment, labor-management cooperation, QWL, quality circles, salary compression, lateral promotions, more flexible benefits, employee communications and employee rights. Within employee rights, the topic of informing employees of plant closings and relocations will be critical. Of course, job security and the right to a job will also be critical if the economy continues to grow at a slower pace than in the 1960s and 1970s.

Issue: *How can personnel show it is worth its salt and doing worthwhile things for the organization?*

Showing that personnel is worth its salt is the essence of effective personnel management. You, the personnel manager, must demonstrate to the rest of the organization, that personnel activities can: (1) improve employee performance and reduce undesired absenteeism and turnover; (2) increase employee satisfaction, and job involvement and reduce employee stress; and (3) minimize legal costs potentially associated with the inappropriate (illegal) management of human resources.

Thus showing that personnel is worthwhile generally means having the numbers that can be translated in dollar and cents benefits at minimal costs. It also means showing that people and society are better off because of the way the organization utilizes its human resources.

Issue: *Do the Japanese really work harder? Are they really better workers?*

Many people in both countries work very hard, above and beyond what's required. Many other people in both countries just do the work that is required and no more. If the Japanese are found to be harder or better workers it is likely they work in organizations with effective personnel practices. This is supported by the fact that when the Japanese take over a plant in the United States, worker motivation and company profitability often result. So it's often not the differences between Japanese and Americans that may explain why the Japanese work harder and better than Americans; it's the quality of the management in managing its human resources. You are now at a point to jump into organizations and reverse any advantage the Japanese or others may have in utilizing human resources. Good luck!

SUMMARY

This final chapter has presented trends that are likely to occur in personnel work in the 1980s. Many of these trends are based on declining productivity, substantial demographic shifts, changing work force expectations, government regulation, new technologies, and economic conditions. Not only do these forces shape the trends in personnel management, they also increase its importance.

Effective personnel management is considered by many organizations to be vital to organizational growth and increased productivity. The effective use of human resources requires that organizations be concerned with the needs of their employees. Consequently, the drive to increase effectiveness should benefit employees as well as organizations. Because it is likely that this drive will be made within legal constraints and equal employment legislation, society should also benefit.

Thus personnel managers will have a vital role in serving the organization, its employees, and society. Playing this role will be both difficult and challenging.

KEY CONCEPTS

downward transfer
performance contract
salary compression

DISCUSSION QUESTIONS

1. What changes in the labor force will affect personnel activities? How will these changes affect personnel functions?
2. List some important personnel considerations between Japan and the United States that affect the management of human resources.
3. How might job evaluation be changed in the 1980s?
4. What employee socialization and development strategies does Japan use for its employees?
5. What trends are there in store for compensating employee behavior?
6. In what ways will the courts continue to have a bearing on recruiting and selection policies for organizations?
7. Why will personnel management continue to be important to organizations?

FOR YOUR CAREER

- There is probably no better time for you to get involved in personnel management than now. The present and future for personnel are really exciting and challenging.
- It pays to be aware of how other companies and countries handle and manage their human resources. We can always learn from others.
- You'll be much better off if you can show the value of what you do. Document your effectiveness.
- In your career seize every opportunity you can to do well and contribute to the organization.
- Be prepared to move from or change situations that you know are not in your best interests. This, of course, requires that you stay on top of knowing what your best interests are.
- Remember, organizations are basically people. Consequently, they may make mistakes but also may provide enormous benefits.

ENDNOTES

1. M. R. Schiavoni, "Employee Relations: Where Will It Be in 1985?" *Personnel Administrator,* March 1978, p. 28.
2. Reprinted by permission of the *Harvard Business Review.* Excerpt from "Human Resources in the 1980's" by D. Q. Mills (July/August 1979), p. 160. Copyright © 1979 by the President and Fellows of Harvard College; all rights reserved.
3. R. D. Arvey, *Fairness in Selecting Employees* (Reading, Mass.: Addison-Wesley, 1979), pp, 228–232.
4. "Compensation Currents," *Compensation Review,* 1981, pp. 4–10.
5. Gerrie Maloof, "Remarks," *Personnel Journal,* November 1981, pp. 844–846.
6. "Pensions: Taking It All at Once," *New York Times,* April 5, 1981.
7. "When Companies Help Pay for Adoption," *Business Week,* November 2, 1981, p. 56.
8. B. S. Murphy, "The Past Is Prologue: Building Better Industrial Relations in the '80s." *Personnel Journal,* January 1980, p. 35.
9. J. C. Toedtman, "A Decade of Rapid Change: The Outlook for Human Resources Management in the '80s." *Personnel Journal,* January 1980, p. 31. Reprinted with the permission of *Personnel Journal,* Costa Mesa, Calif.: all rights reserved.
10. Schiavoni, p. 27.
11. L. A. Wangler, "The Intensification of the Personnel Role," *Personnel Journal,* February 1979, p. 115.
12. M. Hattori, "Japanese Don't Work Harder," *Cleveland Plain Dealer,* 29 December 1979, p. 13–A. © *The Plain Dealer.* Reprinted with permission.

13. H. Tanaka, ''The Japanese Method of Preparing Today's Graduate to Become Tomorrow's Manager,'' *Personnel Journal,* February 1980, pp. 109–112.

Ibid., pp. 109–110.

14. Ibid., p. 110.

15. Ibid., p. 111.

Legislation and Court Decisions Affecting Effective Personnel Management

EMPLOYMENT LEGISLATION

Act	Jurisdiction	Basic Provisions
Fair Labor Standards Act (1938) and subsequent amendments—FLSA	Most interstate employers; certain types of employees are exempt from overtime provisions—executive, administrative, and professional employees and outside salespeople	Establishes a minimum wage; controls hours through premium pay for overtime; controls working hours for children
Minimum Wage Law (1977)	Small businesses	Sets graduated increases in minimum wage rates
Equal Pay Act (1963 amendment to the FLSA)	Same as FLSA except no employees are exempt	Prohibits unequal pay for males and females with equal skills, effort, and responsibility working under similar working conditions
Civil Rights Act (1964) (Amended by EEOA 1972)	Employers with twenty-five or more employees, employment agencies, and labor unions	Prevents discrimination on the basis of race, color, religion, sex, or national origin; establishes EEOC
Equal Employment Opportunity Act (1972)—EEOA	Adds employees of state and local government and educational institutions; reduces number of employees required to fifteen	Amends Title VII; increases enforcement powers of EEOC
Executive Order 11246 (1965) as amended by Executive Order 11375 (1966)	Federal contractors and subcontractors with contracts over $50,000 and fifty or more employees	Prevents discrimination on the basis of race, color, religion, sex or national origin; establishes Office of Federal Contract Compliance (OFCC)
Revised Order Number 4 (1971)	Federal contractors	Defines acceptable affirmative action program

Act	Jurisdiction	Basic Provisions
Executive Order 11478 (1969)	Federal agencies	Prevents discrimination on the basis of race, color, religion, sex, or national origin
Age Discrimination in Employment Act (1967)	Employers with more than twenty-five employees	Prevents discrimination against persons forty to sixty-five years of age
Revised 1978		Revises discrimination protection from sixty-five to seventy and states compulsory retirement for some workers
Rehabilitation Act (1973)	Government contractors and federal agencies	Prevents discrimination against persons with physical and/or mental handicaps
Prevailing wage laws—1. Davis-Bacon Act (1931) and 2. Walsh-Healey Act (1935)	Employers with government construction projects of $2,000 (Davis-Bacon) and government contracts of $10,000 or more	Guarantees prevailing wages to employees of government contractors
Legally required fringe benefits— 1. OASDHI (1935 and amendments)—	Virtually all employers	Provides income and health care to retired employees and income to the survivors of employees who have died
2. Unemployment compensation (1935)	Virtually all employers	Provides income to employees who are laid off or fired
3. Worker's compensation (dates differ from state to state)	Virtually all employers	Provides benefits to employees who are injured on the job and to the survivors of employees who are killed on the job
Occupational Safety and Health Act (1970)—OSHA	Most interstate employers	Assures as far as possible every working man and woman in the nation safe and healthful working conditions and to preserve our human resources
Employee Retirement Income Security Act (1974)—ERISA	Most interstate employers with pension plans (no employer is required to have such a plan)	Protects employees covered by a pension plan from losses in benefits due to ▪ mismanagement ▪ plant closings and bankruptcies ▪ job changes
Freedom of Information Act	Federal agencies only	Allows individuals to see all the material used in a decision made about them
The Pregnancy Discrimination Act of 1978 (1978 Civil Rights Act Amendment to Title VII)	Same as Civil Rights Act (1964)	Pregnancy is a disability and, furthermore, must receive the same benefits as any other disability
Privacy Act of 1974 (Public Law 93–579)	Federal agencies only	Allows individuals to review employer's records on them and bring civil damages

Act	*Jurisdiction*	*Basic Provisions*
	EMPLOYMENT GUIDELINES	
Uniform Guidelines (1978)	Same as EEOA (1972)	Updates EEOC 1970 guidelines to more clearly define adverse unpaid and test validation*
Guidelines on Sexual Harassment (1980)	Same as EEOA (1972)	Defines standards for what constitutes harassment

*SOME WAYS TO DEMONSTRATE ADVERSE IMPACT (DISCRIMINATION) THUS CAUSING NEED TO DEFEND SELECTION OR EMPLOYMENT PRACTICES

1. Individual evidence (*McDonnell Douglas Corporation* v. *Green* [1973]) showing (by plaintiff):
   a. she or he belongs to a racial minority;
   b. she or he applied for job for which employer was seeking applicants;
   c. That despite qualifications, she or he was rejected; and
   d. After this rejection, employer kept looking for people with applicant's qualifications

2. Statistical evidence including:
   a. Whether members of protected class as a whole (or in given area) are disqualified at a disproportionately high rate by the employment practice (essentially the 80/20 rule);
   b. Comparison of the percentage of minority applicants with the percentage of other job applicants excluded by the practice; and
   c. Examination of whether the percentage of the protected class employed by defendent is equivalent to that in relevant geographic area

SOME WAYS TO DEFEND ADVERSE IMPACT CHARGES

1. Business necessity
2. Validation of the employment practice and with finding no alternative procedures producing less adverse impact. Validate by
   a. Empirical studies
   b. Construct
   c. Content
   d. Differentiation
3. Bona fide Occupational Qualifications (BFOQ).
4. Voluntary, yet formal, transient affirmative action program without substantial harm to the innocent party and with evidence of correcting past discrimination
5. Bona fide seniority systems without intent to discriminate and having been established without that intent

LABOR RELATIONS LEGISLATION: PRIVATE SECTOR

Act	*Jurisdiction*	*Basic Provisions*
Railway Labor Act (1926)—RLA	Railroad workers and airline employees	Provides right to organize; provides majority choice of representatives; prohibits "yellow dog" contracts; outlines dispute settlement procedures
Norris-LaGuardia Act (1932)	All employers and labor organizations	No yellow dog contracts; no injunction for nonviolent activity of unions (strikes, picketing and boycotts); Limited union liability
National Labor Relations Act (1935)—Wagner Act	Nonmanagerial employees in private industry not covered by Railway Labor Act (RLA)	Provides right to organize; provides for collective bargaining; requires employers to bargain; unions must represent all members equally
Labor-Management Relations Act (1947)—Taft-Hartley	Nonmanagerial employees in private industry not covered by RLA	Prohibits unfair labor practices of unions; outlaws closed shop; prohibits strikes in national emergencies; requires both parties to bargain in good faith
Labor Management Reporting and Disclosure Act (1959)—Landrum-Griffin	Labor organizations	Outlines procedures for redressing internal union problems
Amendments to Taft-Hartley Act (1974)	Labor organizations	Specifies illegal activities within union

LABOR RELATIONS LEGISLATION: PUBLIC SECTOR

Executive Order 10988 (1962)	Federal employees	Recognizes employees' right to join unions and bargain collectively; prohibits strikes. Requires agency to meet and confer with union on policy practices and working conditions
Executive Order 11491 (1969)	Federal employees	Created a Labor Relations Council and Federal Services Impasses Panel
Executive Orders 11616 (1971) 11838 (1975)	Federal employees	Expand EO 11491 to cover labor-management relations; cover disputes of bargaining rights; order elections; consolidate units; limit scope of grievance and arbitration procedures
Civil Service Reform Act Title VII (1978)	Federal employees	Defines grievance procedure and requirements for goal-type performance appraisals; establishes Senior Executive Service (SES)

COURT DECISIONS/BASIC PROVISIONS

Title/Date

Griggs v. *Duke Power* (1971)
Test for hiring cannot be used unless job-related. Organization must show evidence of job relatedness. Not necessary to establish intent to discriminate.

Albermarle v. *Moody* (1975)
Need to establish evidence that test related to content of job. Could use job analysis to do so, but not evidence from global performance ratings made by supervisors.

Washington v. *Davis* (1976)
When a test procedure is challenged under *constitutional law*, intent to discriminate must be established. No need to establish intent if file under Title VII, just show effects. Could use communication test to select applicants for police force.

Dothard v. *Rawlinson* (1977)
Height requirements not valid, therefore constitutes discriminatory practice.

Bakke v. *Regents of The University of California* (1978)
Reverse discrimination not allowed. Race, however, can be used in selection decisions. Affirmative Action programs permissible when prior discrimination established.

Brito v. *Zia Company* (1973)
Zia violated Title VII because they laid off a disproportionate number of a protected group on the basis of low performance scores on measures that were not validated.

Marshall v. *Barlow's Inc.* (1979)
Employers are not required to let OSHA inspectors enter their premises unless they have search warrants.

Marshall v. *Whirlpool* (1980)
Employees have right to refuse job assignment if constitutes clear and present danger to life or limb. Employer, however, not required to pay if, as a result, employee sent home because of no work.

Wade v. *Mississippi Cooperative Extension Service* (1976)
Performance scores used to decide promotions and salary issues not valid because no job analysis.

James v. *Stockman Valves and Fittings Company* (1977)
Applicants to apprenticeship program selected by white supervisors without formal guidelines is discriminatory. Need more discrete performance appraisal.

Patterson v. *American Tobacco Company* (1976, 1978)

Sledge v. *J. P. Stevens & Company* (1978)

Title/Date

Donaldson v. Pillsbury Company (1977)
All of these three require clear establishment and communication of job requirements and performance standards.

Rowe v. General Motors Corporation (1972)

Robinson v. Union Carbide Corporation (1976)
These two require written standards for promotion to help prevent discrimination.

Watkins v. Scott Paper Company (1976)
Performance data to validate tests that are derived from graphic scales are too vague and easily subject to discrimination.

Gilmore v. Kansas City Terminal Railway Company (1975)

Meyer v. Missouri State Highway Commission (1977)

United States v. City of Chicago (1978)
These three require in promotion cases specific promotion criteria that are related to the job to which being promoted.

Spurlock v. United Airlines (1972)
Use of college degree as a selection criterion valid because job-related, even though no performance data provided.

Hodgson v. Greyhound Lines, Inc (1974)
Could discriminate without empirical evidence on basis of age. Good faith used to show older people would make less safe drivers.

Richardson v. Hotel Corporation of America (1972)
Dismissal on grounds on conviction record resulted in adverse impact. But since conviction record argued (not shown) to be related to business necessity (not job performance) dismissal is okay.

Northwest Airlines, Inc. v. Transport Workers (1981)
An employer found guilty of job discrimination cannot force an employee's union to contribute to the damages, even though the union may have negotiated the unequal terms.

Texas Department of Community Affairs v. Joyce Ann Burdine (1981)
A defendant in a job discrimination case need only provide a legitimate, non-discriminatory explanation for not hiring or promoting a woman or minority, and need not prove that the white man hired was better qualified. The burden of proving intentional discrimination rests with the plaintiff.

Fernandez v. Wynn Oil Company (1981)
Title VII does not permit employers to use stereotypic impressions of male and female

Title/Date

roles as a BFOQ defense to sex discrimination. Employer can't use customer preferences for working with male employees as a defense of discrimination.

EEOC v. Sandia Corporation (1980)
Discrimination against employees protected by ADEA in regards to a decision on work force reduction required by budget restraints. Used a subjective (ranking) evaluation form for their scientists, engineers and technical employees. Statistical impact and informal comments indicated bias.

Weahkee v. Perry (1978) and *Weahkee v. Norton* (1980)
Use of quotas in performance evaluation not objectively used or enforced so not justified in using if discrimination results. Weahkee was reinstated but no finding of discrimination.

Flowers v. Crouch-Walter Corporation (1977)
Plaintiff established *prima facie* evidence that a discharge was discriminatory and not based on performance.

Diaz v. Pan American World Airways, Inc. (1971)
The primary function of an airline is to transport passengers safely from one point to another. Therefore, not hiring males for flight attendants is discriminatory. *Business necessity* is established.

Harper v. Trans World Airlines, Inc. (1975)

Smith v. Mutual Benefit Life Insurance Company (1976)

Tuck v. McGraw-Hill, Inc. (1976)

Yukas v. Libbey-Owens-Ford (1977)
All of these against nepotism, especially close relatives and spouses, are non-discriminatory, especially in some department and/or as in supervisor-subordinate relationship.

Smith v. Mutual Benefit Life Insurance Company (1976)
Employer is not discriminating if refusing to hire male appearing to be effeminate.

United Air Lines, Inc. v. McMann (1977)
Employer can force retirement before age of sixty-five if has bona fide retirement plan; since AEDA (1978), can't force retirement before seventy.

Lehman v. Yellow Freight System (1981)
Informal affirmative action not permissible although formal voluntary one like *Weber* is okay.

Fullilove v. Klutznick (1980)
Congress can impose racial quotas in handing out Federal money (10 percent) to federal contractors who are minority owned (51 percent).

Title/Date

International Brotherhood of Teamsters v. *United States* (1977)
Bona fide seniority systems maintained without discriminatory intent are exempt from Title VII liability if established before 1964.

American Tobacco v. *Patterson* (1982)
Bona fide seniority systems without discriminating intent are exempt from Title VII liability.

United States v. *Trucking Management, Inc.* (1981)
Same as in above Teamsters case, but adds exemption from EO 11246 also.

County of Washington, Oregon v. *Gunther* (1981)
It can be illegal (under Title VII and EPA 1963) to pay women unfairly low wages even if not doing same work as men (not a comparable worth case).

First National Maintenance, v. *NLRB* (1981)
Management does not have to negotiate with unions in advance over closing plants or dropping lines.

American Textile Manufacturers Institute v. *Donovan* (1981)
OSHA need not do cost benefit analyses before issuing working health standards.

Los Angeles Department of Water v. *Manhart* (1978)
Employer is required to provide equal benefits to employees under both Title VII and EPA.

Tomkins v. *Public Service Electric and Gas Company et al.* (1977)

Heelen v. *Johns-Manville Corporation* (1978)

William v. *Saxbe* (1976)

Barnes v. *Costle* (1977)
All of these state that sexual harassment is a form of sex discrimination under Title VII, Section 703, and employer is responsible if takes no action on learning of events.

Tooley v. *Martin-Marietta Corporation* (1981)
Must be religious accommodation for employee who object to union membership or support (as long as no undue hardship on union).

McDonnell Douglas Corporation v. *Green* (1973)
Employer's test device constitutes *prima facie* case of racial discrimination under four different criteria.

Rogers v. *International Paper Company* (1975)
Subjective criteria are not to be condemned as unlawful per se because some decisions about hiring and promotions in supervisory and managerial jobs cannot be made

Title/Date

using objective standards alone. This opinion, however, is somewhat contrary to those in *Albemarle Paper Company* v. *Moody* (1973); *Baxter* v. *Savannah Sugar Refining Corporation* (1974); *Rowe* v. *General Motors* (1972); and *United States* v. *Bethlehem Steel Corporation.*

Stringfellow v. *Monsanto Corporation* (1970)
Established the precedent for giving credit to the employer for making performance appraisal-based decisions on the basis of evidence that the appraisal uses definite identificable criteria based on the quality and quantity of an employee's work.

Mastie v. *Great Lakes Steel Corporation* (1976)
As with *Stringfellow,* the court said that the objectivity of evaluation can be established by demonstrating that the company performed and relied on a thorough evaluation process intended to be used fairly and accurately.

Oshiver v. *Court of Common Pleas* (1979)
Without objective or extrinsic documented evidence of poor performance or evidence not hastily developed, an employment decision is suspect if based on the notion of "poor performance."

Mistretta v. *Sandia Corporation* (1977)
Employment decisions suspect when based on evaluations that reflect only best judgments and opinions of evaluators rather than identifiable criteria based on quality or quantity of work or specific performances that are supported by some kind of record.

Clayton v. *United Auto Workers* (1981)
When a union member feels unfairly represented and only the employer can grant the relief requested, the employee need not exhaust internal union remedies before suing the employer.

NLRB v. *Wright Line, Inc* (1981)
In cases where an employee is fired for what may appear to be union-related activities, the employer must show (to be vindicated in the dismissal) that the discipline imposed is the same as in other cases where union activity was not an issue.

Connecticut v. *Teal* (1982)
Employers must defend each part of a selection process against adverse impact and not just the end result of the entire process (the bottom-line).

Activities Handled by Personnel Departments

ACTIVITY

Personnel records/reports
Personnel research
Insurance benefits administration
Unemployment compensation administration
EEO compliance/affirmative action
Wage/salary administration
Workers' compensation administration
Tuition aid/scholarships
Job evaluation
Health/medical services
Retirement preparation programs
Pre-employment testing
Vacation/leave processing
Induction/orientation
Promotion/transfer/separation processing
Counseling/employee assistance programs
Pension/profit-sharing plan administration
College recruiting
Recreation/social/recognition programs
Recruiting/interviewing/hiring
Attitude surveys
Union/labor relations
Complaint/disciplinary procedures
Relocation services administration

Supervisory training
Employee communications/publications
Executive compensation administration
Human resource planning
Safety programs/OSHA compliance
Management development
Food services
Performance evaluation, nonmanagement
Community relations/fund drives
Suggestion systems
Thrift/savings plan administration
Security/plant protection
Organization development
Management appraisal/MBO
Stock plan administration
Skill training, nonmanagement
Public relations
Administrative services (mail, PBX, phone, messengers, etc.)
Payroll processing
Travel/transportation services administration
Library
Maintenance/janitorial services

From *Bulletin to Management*, May 21, 1981, p. 2.

Jobs and Career Paths in Personnel Management

Numerous jobs are available in the field of personnel and human resource management. As suggested in Chapter 1, people seeking a career in the field may enter directly or indirectly through an operations line job. Depending upon experience and education, new personnel employees can be specialists or generalists, managers or nonmanagers. A typical first job for someone fresh out of college and without much experience would be as a nonmanagerial specialist, say in compensation analysis or employment counseling.

Career paths in personnel depend on the company. Since most large organizations undertake all of the personnel functions discussed in this book, they often have groups or units that specialize. These groups or units are all part of the company's office, division, or department of personnel and human resources management. One could spend an entire career working in just one unit or could work in several different units. However, the health and safety group or the medical unit is less likely than the others to encourage cross-fertilization.

In large companies, the way to make it to the top of the personnel department is by coming up through just one unit or functional area or by working in another part of the organization and then coming in at a managerial level. It is common for a person on the way up to leave an area of specialty and become a generalist. Thus the trip to the top often involves a tour of duty as manager of all the personnel functions in a regional office or plant of the parent company. One may be a specialist in either the parent company (headquarters) or at the plant or regional office, then become manager in a specialty, then become manager of all personnel functions in a plant or office, and then return to headquarters. Back at headquarters, one may become a director of an entire unit (in charge of one or several functions). The next step is to become vice president of personnel for the entire company.

Here are some typical job titles found in personnel departments:

- Personnel interviewer
- Employment assistant
- Claims examiner
- Employment counselor
- Senior employee benefits counselor
- Nurse
- Training services coordinator
- Personnel administration analyst
- Senior employment supervisor
- Personnel administration senior analyst
- Personnel counselor

- Compensation analyst
- Senior compensation analyst
- Personnel compensation specialist
- Personnel development specialist
- Personnel administration specialist
- Employment and placement manager
- Junior analyst
- Regional personnel manager
- Plant personnel manager
- Physician
- Assistant medical director
- Health services coordinator
- Director of employment placement
- Vice president of personnel
- Human resource planning specialist
- Recruiter
- Job analyst
- Wage and salary specialist
- Safety specialist
- Labor relations specialist
- Director of labor relations
- Manager of affirmative action

Exhibit 1.3 (in Chapter 1) shows some other personnel job titles at Xerox Corporation.

Journals in Personnel and Human Resource Management

RESEARCH AND ACADEMIC JOURNALS

Administrative Science Quarterly, Graduate School of Business and Public Administration, Cornell University, Ithaca, New York. Broad coverage of management opinion and research reports, with a continuing emphasis on theory and philosophy; book reviews and abstracts.

American Journal of Sociology, published for the American Sociological Association by the University of Chicago Press, 5750 Ellis Avenue, Chicago, Illinois. Increasing attention to the broad area of industrial sociology, with frequent reports on studies of work and organizational theory.

American Management Association Research Reports, American Management Association, 1515 Broadway, New York, New York. Reports of company philosophy, policy, and practice in all phases of management.

Behavioral Sciences, Mental Health Research Institute, University of Michigan, Ann Arbor, Michigan. Articles on general theories of behavior and on empirical research.

Bulletin of Industrial Psychology and Personnel Practice, Department of Labor and National Service, Melbourne, Australia. Reports of research in Australia and abroad, book reviews, and abstracts of articles from numerous other foreign and domestic publications.

Ergonomics, Taylor and Francis, Ltd., Red Lion Court, Fleet Street, London, England. Emphasizes human engineering; combines approaches of human biology, anatomy, physiology, and psychology with mechanical engineering.

Harvard Business Review, Graduate School of Business Administration, Harvard University, Soldier's Field, Boston, Massachusetts. A review of the general field of business, with frequent articles on industrial relations.

Human Organizations, Society for Applied Anthropology, New York State School of Industrial and Labor Relations, Cornell University, Ithaca, New York. Intercultural approach to problems of human relations, including industrial relations.

Industrial and Labor Relations Review, New York State School of Labor and Industrial Relations, Cornell University, Ithaca, New York. Opinions and reports of studies on labor legislation, collective bargaining, and related subjects.

Industrial Medicine and Surgery, Industrial Medicine Publishing Company, 605 North Michigan Avenue, Chicago, Illinois. Emphasizes health programs in industry, with reports on health hazards, occupational diseases, handicapped workers, medical services, and related subjects.

Industrial Relations, Institute of Industrial Relations, University of California, Berkeley and Los Angeles, California. Ideas and opinions as well as reports of research.

Industrial Training Abstracts, Wayne State University Press, Detroit, Michigan. Abstracts articles dealing with apprentice, foreman, and supervisory safety and related types of training in industry.

Journal of Applied Psychology, American Psychological Association, 1313 Sixteenth Street N.W., Washington D.C. All phases of applied psychology, with numerous reports of personnel research.

Labor Law Journal, Commerce Clearing House, Inc., 214 N. Michigan Avenue, Chicago, Illinois. Generally presents nonlegalistic discussions of legal phases of industrial relations.

Monthly Labor Review, Bureau of Labor Statistics, U.S. Department of Labor, Washington D.C. Summaries of staff studies on industrial relations; statistical sections include continuing series on industrial disputes, employment, payrolls, and cost of living.

TRADE JOURNALS

Advanced Management, Society for the Advancement of Management, 74 Fifth Avenue, New York, New York. Successor to *The Society for the Advancement of Management Journal, and Bulletin of the Taylor Society,* and *Modern Management;* reports on managerial developments and viewpoints in all phases of management.

Fair Employment Practices and **Bulletin to Management,** published by the Bureau of National Affairs, 1231 25th St. N.W., Washington, D.C. 20037.

Fair Employment Report, published by Business Publishers, Inc., 951 Pershing Drive, Silver Spring, MD 20910.

FEP Guidelines, published by the Bureau of Business Practices, 24 Rope Ferry Road, Waterford, CT 06386.

Journal of Personnel Administration and Industrial Relations, Personnel Research Publishers, Washington D.C. Reports original studies and theoretical analyses in all phases of industrial relations.

Journal of the American Society of Training Directors, official publication of the American Society of Training Directors, 2020 University Avenue, Madison, Wisconsin. Broad coverage of the personnel field, with a special emphasis on training problems.

Management Record, The Conference Board, 247 Park Avenue, New York, New York. Numerous reports of both experience and research, surveys conducted by the NICB staff, and digests of symposia.

Management Review, American Management Association, 330 West Forty-second Street, New York, New York. General coverage of all phases of management.

Personnel, American Management Association, 330 West Forty-second Street, New York, New York. Broad interest in entire field of industrial relations, with numerous reports of surveys, studies, and experience.

Personnel Journal, published at *Personnel Journal,* 866 West Eighteenth Street, Costa Mesa, California. Covers a broad spectrum of topics in personnel and labor relations.

Personnel Management, formerly the *Journal of the Institute of Personnel Management,* Institute of Personnel Management, Management House, 80 Fetter Lane, London, England. Theory and practice in both personnel management and labor relations.

Personnel Management Abstracts, Bureau of Industrial Relations, University of Michigan, Ann Arbor, Michigan. Abstracts of books and articles in both personnel management and labor relations.

Personnel Psychology, PO Box 6965, College Station, Durham, North Carolina. Emphasizes reports on research in psychological aspects of personnel and industrial relations.

Public Personnel Quarterly, published by the International Personnel Management Association, 1859 K Street N.W., Washington D.C.

The Personnel Administrator, published by the American Society for Personnel Administration/ASPA, 30 Park Drive, Berea, Ohio. Information on taking the ASPA's examinations for the purpose of becoming a certified personnel administrator can be obtained by writing to the ASPA.

Studies in Personnel Policy, National Industrial Conference Board, 247 Park Avenue, New York, New York. Mainly compares experience and evaluations of programs, with frequent surveys of policy and practice.

How to Prepare a Resume

The best advice is to make your resume clear, concise, easy to read, and easy to understand.

Make your resume one page—or two pages at the most. Remember, when a company needs people, it receives many resumes. Neither the technical directors nor the personnel director have time to read long, involved descriptions. Also, the general procedure is that one copy remains with personnel and a photocopy is prepared for routing. Thus you may want to send two copies.

A time-tested sequence for the contents of your resume:

- *Your name, address, and telephone number*
- *Summary, highlights, or synopsis:* Whatever it's called, employers like it. In the advertising industry, the first lesson a writer learns is that the first ten words are the most important. This is where you win or lose your audience.
- *Education:* List your most recent degree first, the date, your major(s), and the university. List your thesis title if it's relevant to the type of job you seek. Many employers also like to see a GPA. If you're proud of it, put it in.
- *Experience:* List your title, the company, the dates, and your responsibilities chronologically, with your present position first. The description of your duties or responsibilities should highlight your accomplishments and contributions. Don't waste space describing the functions of your company, division, or project. The reader wants to know what you did.
- *Publications:* If space permits, list only those you authored and especially those that may be relevant to the type of job you seek.
- *Personal information:* At the bottom, describe your marital status, number of children, present salary, and asking salary. Your date of birth is optional, but most employers appreciate it.

Exhibit D.1 provides an example using this format.

Prepared by Eva M. June, president, Ability Search, Inc., 1629 K Street N.W., Washington D.C. 20006. Presented at the 41st National Operations Research Society of America Meeting, New Orleans, Louisiana, April 1972. Reprinted with permission.

Exhibit D.1
Sample Resume

RICHARD L. GOODE
141 East 15th Avenue
Columbus, Ohio 43201
Telephone: (614) 291-7371

OBJECTIVE:	A challenging college internship or entry-level position offering on-the-job training in the field of accounting, finance, or economics
EDUCATION:	The Ohio State University, Columbus, Ohio Candidate for BS in Business Administration, December 1980. Major: Finance GPA: 2.8 GPA in Major: 3.5
	Oxford University, Oxford, England Summer Study Program, 1979, Curriculum: Eighteenth-Century Art, Literature, and History
	Hanover High School, Hanover, New Hampshire Graduated 1976
COLLEGE ACTIVITIES:	Phi Kappa Tau Fraternity Treasurer, 1979: Managed financial affairs of fraternity under a $90,000 annual budget; made a significant contribution in eliminating a $4,000 deficit
	Vice President of Rush, 1978: Organized and coordinated the recruitment program, which was highlighted by "formal rush" involving 500 rushees
	Scarlet Representative to Interfraternity Council, 1978: Acted as liaison between fraternity presidents and executive board
JOB EXPERIENCE:	April–June 1979 T.G.I. Friday's, 4540 Kenny Rd., Columbus, Ohio 43220 Fulltime waiter on day shift
	Summer 1977 and 1978 Chieftain Motel, Lyme Rd., Hanover, New Hampshire 03755 Manager on evening shift
	November 1973-September 1976 Mary Hitchcock Memorial Hospital, Manor St., Hanover, New Hampshire 03755 Worked in transportation department as an orderly, fulltime summers and parttime during the school year
PERSONAL:	Age: 23 Height: 5'8" Weight: 145 lbs. Health: Excellent Marital Status: Single
REFERENCES:	Available on request

The biggest problem people have in preparing a resume is writing a synopsis and being concise. Before you even try to write a synopsis, build a resume in the sequence I recommend. Type up a rough draft, then abstract the highlights from your resume. It is easier to synopsize once everything is on paper.

To be concise, you should review the resume and see if you can cut it down. If you are like most people, you will find repetitions and ways to make some of your sentences say more with fewer words. Be your own editor!

As long as you've come this far, you might consider preparing two versions of your resume, each highlighting a different significant experience. You might also play with the layout to make sure your presentation is as clear as possible.

Now there is only one thing left to do—have a final type. If you have followed these procedures, you will have an eye-catching resume packed with factual data, but most importantly a resume that will be easy and inviting to read.

Measuring the Costs of Absenteeism

Let's assume your curiosity has been aroused to the point where you would like to estimate the cost of absenteeism to your organization for a one-year period—1978, for example. As in most research projects, the first step involves gathering information. Assuming your organization regularly computes traditional absence statistics and labor cost data, much of the information you will need should not be too burdensome or time-consuming to gather. Some estimates will involve discussions with other staff and management personnel, but the overall time you spend on this project should be well worth the effort.

As an aid in computing estimates for your organization, we'll provide examples at each step along the way. Using the hypothetical firm Acme International, a medium-sized steel manufacturer employing 1,200 people, our examples will hopefully provide a realistic portrayal of the problems and costs related to employee absenteeism. The data you'll need to collect and compute are outlined below.

1. *The organization's total man-hours lost to absenteeism for the period for all employees—blue-collar, clerical, management and professional.* Include time lost for all reasons except organizationally-sanctioned time off such as vacations, holidays, official "bad weather" days, etc. Be sure to include both whole-day and part-day absences in computing the total hours lost. Include, for example, absences resulting from illness, accidents, funerals, jury duty, emergencies, personal time off and doctor's appointments, whether "excused" or "unexcused."

In our example, let's assume Acme International's personnel records show 9,792 days, or 78,336 total man-hours lost to employee absenteeism for all reasons except vacations and holidays in 1978. This figure represents an absence rate of 3.4 percent for the year—about average for manufacturing firms.

A great deal of confusion exists concerning the computation of absence rates, as a number of different formulas have reportedly been published and used. The formula used here is recommended by the U.S. Department of Labor and also used by the majority of firms responding to absenteeism surveys conducted by the Bureau of

This material is graciously provided by Frank E. Kuzmits and is reprinted with permission from the June 1979 issue of the *Personnel Administrator*, copyright 1979. The American Society for Personnel Administration, 30 Park Drive, Berea, OH 44017.

National Affairs (see "Employee Absenteeism and Turnover," *Personnel Policies Forum,* Survey No. 106, Washington D.C., Bureau of National Affairs, Inc., 1974). The formula is illustrated below:

$$\text{Absenteeism rate} = \frac{\begin{array}{c}\text{Number of man-days lost through job}\\ \text{absence during the period}\end{array}}{\text{Average number of employees} \times \text{number of work days}} \times 100$$

This computation may not be quite as straightforward as it appears. Often, wage earners are not covered under a sick leave plan while salaried employees are. Look closely at your organization's employee benefits program to determine if your estimates should reflect differential absenteeism costs for employee groups who receive sick pay and those who do not. In addition, some organizations have policies which define the kinds of absences for which employees are not paid ("unauthorized" or "unexcused"). Should this be the case in your organization, you will need to segregate absences by "paid" vs. "unpaid" and apply the appropriate costs to each category.

2. *The weighted average hourly wage/salary level for the various occupational groups that claimed absenteeism during the period.* Note: If your organization *does not pay* absent workers, *skip this step* and go directly to step three.

For Acme International, let's assume about 85 percent of all absentees were blue collar, 13 percent clerical, and two percent management and professional. And, to keep our example simple, we'll also assume all employees were paid for sick days taken under the company's employee benefits program. The average hourly wage rate per absentee is computed by applying the appropriate percentages to the average hourly rate for each major occupational regrouping. The following illustration reflects how this figure is computed:

Occupational Class	Approximate Percent of Total Absenteeism	Average Hourly Wage	Weighted Average Hourly Wage
Blue collar	85	$4.25	$3.61
Clerical	13	3.95	.51
Management and professional	2	9.85	.20
			$4.32 Total

3. *The cost of employee benefits per hour per employee.* For most organizations, employee benefits (profit-sharing, pensions, health and life insurance, paid vacations and holidays, etc.) represent a sizable portion of total employee compensation—often as much as one-quarter to one-third. One method for computing the cost of employee benefits per hour per employee is to divide the total cost of benefits per employee per week by the number of hours worked per week.

We'll assume Acme International's cost of benefits per employee is $76.00 per week. Using this figure, Acme's cost for this item is computed as follows:

$$\text{Cost of benefits/hour/employee} = \frac{\text{Cost of benefits/week/employee}}{\text{Hours worked/week}} = \frac{\$76.00}{40} = \$1.90$$

4. *The estimated total number of supervisory hours lost to employee absenteeism for the period.* This estimate will be more difficult to make compared to wage and benefits estimates, as existing records seldom provide the information necessary to compute this figure. First, estimate the average number of supervisory hours spent *per day* rectifying the myriad of problems resulting from employee absenteeism. Examples of such problems include time spent solving production problems, instructing replacement employees, checking on the performance of replacements and counseling and disciplining absentees. Perhaps the most accurate way to develop this estimate is through discussions with a sampling of supervisors. In estimating your average, be sure to take into account typically high-absence days (Monday, Friday, days before and after holidays, day after pay day). After estimating this figure, compute the total number of supervisory hours lost to your organization by multiplying three figures: the estimated average number of hours lost per supervisor per day times the total number of supervisors who deal with problems of absenteeism times the number of working days for the period. Include all shifts and weekend work, if any, in your estimate.

In our example, let's assume Acme International's data in these areas are:

- Estimated number of supervisory hours lost per day: ½ hour
- Total number of supervisors who deal with absence problems: 32
- Total number of working days for the year: 240

Acme International's total supervisory hours lost to absenteeism for the year is estimated by multiplying . . . one-half hour per day per supervisor × 32 supervisors × 240 working days = 3,840 total supervisory hours lost to employee absenteeism.

5. *The average hourly wage rate for supervisors, including benefits.* In your estimate, include only the salaries of supervisors who normally deal with problems of absenteeism. Usually the first level of supervision within the manufacturing and clerical areas bears the lion's share of absenteeism problems.

We'll estimate Acme International's cost for the figure as follows:

Average hourly supervisory salary:	$7.25
Cost of benefits per hour per employee:	1.90
Total compensation per hour per supervisor:	$9.15

6. *The last estimate is a catchall—a conglomerate of costs unique to your organization that were not included in the above estimates.* Such costs may include temporary help, labor pools for absent workers, overtime premiums, production losses, machine downtime, quality problems and inefficient materials usage. Like the previous figure, the estimates will be difficult to generate and should be based on discussions with a number of management and staff personnel.

We'll assume Acme International incurred overtime premiums, production losses and inefficient materials usage problems as a result of absenteeism and these problems resulted in an estimated financial loss of $38,500 for the year. Having computed all the necessary estimates, the total cost of employee absenteeism is determined by summing the individual cost figures pertaining to wages and salaries, benefits, supervisory salaries and other costs incidental to absenteeism.

Space has been provided [in Exhibit A] for your figures and we'll also put Acme International's estimates next to your estimates for illustrative purposes. (Remember that Acme International is a hypothetical firm—don't pass judgment on your figures by comparing them to Acme's!)

Are Acme's costs too high? "About right?" And more importantly, what about *your* estimates? Just what do they say about the absenteeism problem your organization may be facing? Having computed the costs of absenteeism for your organization, the next step is to evaluate the figures against some pre-determined cost standard or financial measure of performance. A comparison of the absence costs of your organization to an industry average would provide valuable information in determining whether an "absenteeism problem" does in fact exist or how significant the problem may be.

Unfortunately, absenteeism cost data are not published on a regular or periodic basis. Unlike traditional cost, revenue and profit data, where regularly published financial ratios and composite income statements and balance sheets enable one to accurately gauge the financial soundness of an individual organization, very little data are available for passing judgment upon the level of dollars and cents lost to employee absenteeism. While the costs of absenteeism to individual organizations occasionally appear in the literature, these estimates normally result from case studies of individual firms rather than surveys of specific industries.

Without a sound basis for comparing the costs of absenteeism by industry category or other relevant organizational criteria, is it worth the time and effort to undertake a cost analysis of the individual organization? Yes—and at least two compelling reasons exist for doing so. Perhaps the principal reason for computing the economic costs of employee absenteeism is to call management's attention to the severity of the problem. Translating behavioral acts into dollars and cents enables managers to readily grasp the burdens of absenteeism, particularly in a firm suffering from extraordinary absence problems. The spark recognition of a five, six, or even seven figure outlay for absenteeism will likely result in a concentrated effort to combat the problem.

A second reason for computing the cost of employee absenteeism is to create meaningful criteria for evaluating the effectiveness of absence control programs. Comparing the quarterly, semi-annual and annual costs of absenteeism across various departments and supervisory work units provides a valid and reliable information system for measuring the success—or lack of success—of methods and techniques designed to reduce the problem. Organizations with computerized absence reporting systems should find this additional information relatively easy and inexpensive to generate.

Exhibit A
Total Estimated Cost of Employee Absenteeism

Item	Acme International	Your Organization
1. Total man-hours lost to employee absenteeism for the period	78,336	
2. Weighted average wage salary per hour per employee	$4.32	
3. Cost of employee benefits per hour per employee	$1.90	
4. Total compensation lost per hour per absent employee A. If absent workers are paid (wage salary plus benefits)	$6.22	
B. If absent workers are not paid (benefits only)		
5. Total compensation lost to absent employees (total man-hours lost × 4.A or 4.B, whichever applicable)	$487,250	
6. Total supervisory hours lost on employee absenteeism	3,840	
7. Average hourly supervisory wage, including benefits	$9.15	
8. Total supervisory salaries lost to managing problems of absenteeism (hours lost × average hourly supervisory wage—item 6 × item 7)	$35,136	
9. All other costs incidental to absenteeism not included in the above items	$38,500	
10. Total estimated cost of absenteeism—summation of items, 5, 8, and 9	$560,887	
11. Total estimated cost of absenteeism per employee (Total estimated costs)	$560,886	=
(Total number of employees)	1200 $467.41 per employee	

From Frank E. Kuzmits, "How Much is Absenteeism Costing Your Organization?" p. 31. Reprinted with permission from the June 1979 issue of the *Personnel Administrator* copyright 1979, The American Society for Personnel Administration, 30 Park Drive, Berea, OH 44017.

Absolute Standards this approach allows superiors to evaluate each subordinates' performance independent of the other subordinates and often on several dimensions of performance.

Actual costs those costs actually incurred in hiring applicants.

Adversarial System a view of labor and management which depicts each of the two parties in conflict over achieving incompatible goals.

Affirmative action programs (AAP) programs that are designed to ensure proportional representation of employees on the basis of race, color, religion, or sex. AAPs are required by the federal government of companies that have federal contracts exceeding $50,000. They can also be established on a voluntary basis or as part of a consent decree.

AFL-CIO a major umbrella for national unions; also called the American Federation of Labor and Congress of Industrial Organizations that represents about 77 percent of the union members in the United States.

Alternative Ranking a comparative approach in which the superior alternates between ranking the best and the worst until all subordinates are ranked.

Apprentice Training is a training format based on learning while doing for a long time before being recognized as competent to be a full fledged employee.

Arbitration a procedure in which a central third party studies the bargaining situation, listening to both parties and gathering information, and then reaches a decision which is usually binding for the parties.

Assessment Center Method an extensive procedure using several evaluators (assessors) who evaluate how well employees in an assessment center exercise perform.

Attitudinal Structuring the relationships between labor and management during collective bargaining that results in shaping of attitudes toward one another.

Authorization card after initial contact between unions and employees, the union may begin to get the signatures of employees; if it gets 30 percent it can petition the NLRB for a certification election.

Autonomy the degree to which the job provides substantial freedom, independence and discretion to the worker in performing the job.

Avoidance behavior undesirable actions including leaving for lunch early, returning late, and playing practical jokes. Also includes alcohol and drug use during working hours.

Band Width is the maximum length of work day from which an employee can choose the hours he or she will work.

Bargaining Unit the heart of labor-management relationship. A group of employees certified by the NLRB to be able to be included in the union.

Base rate the rate at which job applicants chosen for the job would do well based on random assignment.

Behavior-Outcome Expectancy one critical expectancy in the expectancy model of motivation that describes the individual's perception of the probability that a behavior will lead to outcomes.

Behavioral Anchored Rating Scale a quantitative absolute form which expands upon the conventional rating form by more extensively specifying the anchors on behavioral dimensions used to evaluate the subordinate.

Benchmark jobs jobs against which the worth of other jobs is determined by an analysis of the compensable factors and their dollar values in the benchmark jobs and the extent factors exist in the other jobs.

Bonus units this is a cash award given to a manager and often accompanies the performance shares.

Bottom-Line Criterion is the 80% rule whereby

adverse impact is demonstrated if the hiring rate (after an applicant goes through all the selection procedures) of the minority or female applicant is less than 80% of the hiring rate for white males.

Boulewarism a bargaining practice occurring when management reaches a contract offer to a union and holds fast to that agreement. Modifications in the contract may result only when additional "facts" are presented which contribute to a clearer view of relevant issues for negotiation.

BSG a term referring to a category of learning involved with the acquisition of grammar, math, safety, reading, listening and writing skills.

BST a term referring to a category of learning involved with the acquisition of technical skills required to do a specific job.

Cafeteria approach an approach to compensation that gives individuals a chance to choose what types of compensation they prefer as opposed to the organization, just handing them a fixed compensation package.

Candidate Profiles a major component of a job matching system that contains the descriptions of the candidates that are available for jobs.

Career Balance Sheet a technique where one systematically lists the advantages and disadvantages of each job and compares them to help make a decision among more than one choice.

Career Management Programs concerted efforts in career planning and development aimed at satisfying a dual match between employee ability and job demands and employee needs and job rewards.

Career Pathing two major activities of identifying employee abilities, values, goals, strengths and weaknesses (career planning) and providing a set of job experiences that aid the employee in satisfying those attributes (job progression).

Career Planning is offered by the organization to help individuals identify strengths, weaknesses, specific goals and jobs they would like to attain.

Case Discussion a training method where individuals analyze and discuss cases of companies and their not-so-apparent problems.

Cash plans are a type of profit sharing plan that provide for payment of profit shares at regular intervals.

Centralization a term applied to organizations where essential decision making and policy formulation is done at one location (i.e., headquarters).

Certification election an election conducted by the NLRB to determine if a majority of the employees in a bargaining unit want the union to represent them all.

CIS a term referring to a learning category involved with the acquisition of integrative skills such as strategic and operational planning or organizational design and policy skills.

Collective bargaining bargaining or joint discussion over wages, hours and conditions of employment between management and a formal representative of the employees.

Commissions individual incentive pay plans for sales people.

Comparable worth the notion grounded in the belief that men's jobs are not necessarily inherently of more value than women's jobs. Advocates of this concept believe compensation, among other important aspects of employment, is largely a subjective and discriminatory practice favoring traditionally male held positions in the workforce.

Comparative Approach in this approach to performance evaluation, subordinates are all compared against each other to determine their relative performance.

Compensable factor yardsticks or factors against which to compare or measure jobs in order to determine their relative worth.

Compressed Work Weeks work weeks of fewer than the traditional five days yet equal in time to those five days.

Confirmation approach when a manager "loads the deck" to favor a particular candidate by selecting several candidates for final decision who have far less qualifications.

Consent Decree a specific statement by an organization indicating the affirmative action steps it will take.

Conspiracy Doctrine a major legal tool for employers during the 19th century to combat and prosecute workers' organizations as illegal attempts to restrain trade.

Contemporary Organizational Form describes an organization where supervisors loosely watch employees, jobs are complex and non-routine and where challenge, responsibility and meaningfulness are used to motivate. This form is the essence of Match 2.

Content validity estimates or judges the relevance of a predictor variable for a specific performance criteria without actually collecting the performance information.

Continuous Bargaining when unions and management representatives meet on a regularly scheduled basis to review contract issues of common interest.

Contrast Effect a good person looks even better when placed next to a bad person and a good person looks not as good when placed next to a great person.

Contract Plan an informal agreement written by each participant in training specifying one aspect of the training that will be most beneficial when back on the job and agreeing to effect that aspect once back on the job. An important dimension of the contract is selecting a "buddy" to follow-up or check on the trainee's success in implementing that aspect of the training.

Contributory programs a type of retirement plan in which both the employee and the organization contribute for benefits to be obtained at retirement.

Control systems include such things as production and quality control reports, scrap report and attendance reports to help monitor (control) the workers in the organization.

Conventional Rating a quantitative absolute form in which a superior evaluates subordinates by checking how well they are doing on a form with several dimensions (traits) and numbers.

Cooperative System a view of labor and management which depicts each of the two parties engaging in reciprocal problem solving, information sharing and integration of goals.

Coordinated bargaining when several unions bargain jointly with a single employer.

Core Time is the time in which everyone must work, there is no choice about this time.

Corporate citizenship a concept denoting the quality of loyalty to an organization's policies and rules.

Cost of living adjustments (COLAS) salary or compensation variation which is related to economic conditions (cost of living changes) rather than performance.

Criteria these are the measures or indicators (e.g., performance appraisal results) that indicate how well an employee is doing.

Critical Incidents Format an absolute form in which the superior records the critical or important events exhibited by a subordinate on a predetermined list of critical incidents.

Criticism is negative information without any constructive or useful insights to allow an employee to improve his or her performance. Criticism is evaluative not descriptive.

Cross-functional or cross-departmental transfer a method of moving an employee from one type of job activity to another so that he/she may be prepared to advance to the next level of management.

Decentralization a term applied to organizations where essential decision making and policy formulation is done at several locations (i.e., in the divisions or departments of the organization).

Decentification election an election conducted by the NLRB to remove a union from representation if the employees currently represented by the union vote to do so.

Delphi technique a number of experts take turns at presenting a forecast statement. As the process continues, the forecast is subject to other members' revisions until a viable forecast emerges.

Demographics characteristics of a population (e.g., ages, sex, race)

Dictionary of Occupational Titles source for obtaining the job descriptions for almost 30,000 different jobs.

Differential validity discriminates between applicants who will perform well in a particular job and those who will not.

Direct compensation the basic wage and performance based pay including merit and incentive pay.

Direct Indexes this approach tends to be more objective because such things as units sold, scrap rate, absenteeism and units produced are used to evaluate performance.

Distributive Bargaining a type of collective bargaining where both labor and management try to attain goals that would result in a gain for one party but a loss for the other.

Downward Transfer a relatively new concept applied to an employee job change resulting from obsolescence or demotion.

Duties the specific activities that comprise a job are called duties. Duties form the essence of the jobs.

Earned Time a positive behavioral control strategy to reduce absenteeism through a "no-fault" approach which provides employees potential days off they use as (if) needed.

Economic Supplements a type of compensation for employees including things like pensions, vacations, paid holidays, sick leave, health and insurance, and supplemental unemployment benefits.

Effective personnel management the recognition of the importance of an organization's workforce as vital human resources and the efficient and fair use of several function and activities to ensure that the individual, the organization and the society benefit from them.

Effective Personnel Planning is the first step in any effective personnel program. It predicts or estimates future human resource needs and establishes personnel activities to enable the organization to meet the future needs.

Effectiveness Indicators measures personnel departments use to demonstrate their effectiveness in the areas of productivity, quality of work life and legal compliance. They can be one of two types: general or specific.

Effort-Behavior Expectancy the other critical expectancy in the expectancy model of motivation that describes the individual's perception of the probability that exerting a given level of energy will result in a successful behavior.

Employee assistance programs (EAPs) programs specifically designed to assist employees with chronic personal problems (for example, marital dysfunctions, alcohol abuse) that hinder their job performance, attendance, and corporate citizenship.

Employee association a formal group of individuals that represents them as employees before the employer in many ways similar to a union except that an association often is involved in fewer functions than a union.

Employee contract this is a formal and frequently written agreement between employer and employee specifying the wages, hours and type of work conditions.

Employee pacing condition in which the pace or rate at which the employee works is determined by the employee and not the machine as under machine pacing.

Employee prerequisites & services a form of indirect compensation which varies depending on employee type and organization to offset the problems associated with working (e.g., day care) or used to symbolize a status differential (e.g., company paid memberships to country, athletic and social clubs).

Employee Referral Programs (ERPs) are essentially word of mouth advertising involving current employees recruiting (informally) potentially qualified job applicants.

Employee training and development any attempt to improve current or future employee performance by increasing, through learning, an employee's ability to perform, especially by changing an employee's attitudes and increasing his or her skills and knowledge.

Equity the fairness which exists in the administration of rewards and punishments in relationship to the employees' contributions to the organization and what they bring to the organization.

Ergonomic approach an approach to job design concerned with designing and shaping jobs to fit the physical abilities and characteristics of individual workers.

ERISA (Employees' Retirement Income Security Act) passed to protect employees against their company's retirement fund from going broke.

Essay Method a performance evaluation method in which the superior describes in writing (essay form) the performance of the subordinates.

Essentiality the amount of power a job holder (any employee) has which is determined by how critical the job is to the organization and by exclusivity.

Evaluation Designs methods by which training programs can be evaluated to determine how effective (how much change is made) the training programs are.

Exempt jobs in which the incumbents are not paid overtime for working overtime; they are exempt from the wage–hour laws requiring overtime pay.

Exclusivity the difficulty in replacing a job holder.

Expectancy Model of Motivation a model explaining and predicting how much energy or effort an individual is likely to exert based upon his/her perceptions of expectancies and outcomes.

Extension of bargaining where the arbitrator attempts to reach a rational and equitable decision acceptable to both parties in arbitration.

External source a set of recruitment locations that are places of obtaining potentially qualified applicants outside of the organization. Examples include public and private employment agencies.

Extrinsic Outcomes one set of outcomes an individual can receive are from others, the supervisor, the organization and the co-workers such as pay, promotion, recognition and friendship.

Factor comparison method similar to point rating in that it has compensable factors but in factor comparison the factors have dollar not point values.

Federal Labor Relations Authority (FLRA) modelled after and similar to the NLRB but intended to serve to remedy unfair labor practices in the federal government.

Feedback the degree to which the job itself provides the worker with information about how well the job is being performed.

FICA is the Federal Insurance Contribution Act passed to establish a way to fund the social security system with payments from employee and employer.

Field review a technique in performance evaluation where the superior of the superior rating the subordinates is brought in to evaluate the same subordinates.

Final offer arbitration a type of arbitration where the arbitrator chooses between the final offers of either union or management.

Flextime is the time a worker can choose to work within the band width yet outside of the core time.

Follow-up once a person leaves a training program, it is important (in order to evaluate the effectiveness of the training program) to find out how well the person is doing once back on the job.

Forced Choice an absolute form in which the superior evaluate the subordinate by choosing which item in a pair of items better describes the subordinate.

Forced Distribution a comparative approach in which the superiors are forced to place subordinates in ranks which represent groups or percentage clusters.

Formal Course Method is an off-the-job training program that includes self training and formal classroom and lectures.

Frequency Rate a formula to determine amount of accidents and diseases similar to the incidence rate except that it is calculated using the number of hours worked rather than on a per annum basis.

Functional job analysis a description of the nature of jobs, job summaries, job descriptions and employee specifications.

Fundamental Knowledge a level of skill learning where the trainee passively learns aspects of what is being taught (e.g. reading).

Goals and Quotas these are parts of Affirmative Action Programs that specify what the organization will do in terms of staffing its organization with women, minorities and handicapped individuals.

Goals a basis against which to evaluate how well employees are performing, especially managers.

Goal Setting people learn quickly and perform better when specific, hard and clear objectives are set such as in goal setting.

Grievance procedure the most common method of resolving disputes between union and management over application and interpretation of the agreement or contract.

Handicap an impairment that substantially limits one or more of a person's major life activities.

Hay plan a structured procedure for analyzing jobs which is systematically tied into a job evaluation and compensation system. The Hay plan includes information about the nature and scope of a position as well as how to reward that position.

High performance obtaining a superior quality evaluation, regardless of the method used.

HMOs are health maintenance organizations including hospitals, clinics, doctors, nurses and technicians that came about as a result of the Health Maintenance Organization Act of 1973.

Hot Stove Principles include: provide ample and clear warning; administer discipline quickly; administer discipline same for all for same offense and administer it impersonally.

Human Resource Information System (HRIS) is a method that allows more rapid and frequent data collection to back up a forecast of personnel needs.

Identity the degree to which a job requires completion of a "whole" and identifiable piece of work.

Incentive pay plans methods of monetary and nonmonetary compensation related to direct indexes of performance for the individual group, or organization and generally represents a substantial proportion of an individual's direct compensation.

Incidence Rate an explicit formula for determining the amount of accidents and diseases per year by the number of employee exposure levels. Required by OSHA.

Indirect compensation those rewards or benefits provided by the organization to employees for their memberships or participation (attendance) in the organization. Also known as fringe benefits or supplemental compensation.

Individual Contemporary a major classification of approaches to job design that focus on the individual worker–job design interface (or relationships).

Industrywide bargaining where employers bargain as a group with the union at the national level.

Initial demand point an asked for (by the union) or demand for a wage settlement that is higher than what is expected to be granted.

Initial offer made by the management to represent what wages and conditions it will grant to the union.

IPS a term referring to a category of learning involved with the acquisition interpersonal skills including communications, human relations, decision making, and leadership and labor relations.

Integrative Bargaining a type of collective bargaining where labor and management work to solve contractual problems to the benefit of both.

Internal source a set of recruitment locations that are places of obtaining potentially qualified applicants that are within the organization. Examples are promotions and transfers.

Internships are training programs often part of an agreement between schools, colleges and universities and organizations where an individual may work full time but only for a short while.

Intraorganizational Bargaining the process of negotiating teams influencing their constituents over changes in bargaining positions.

Intrinsic Outcomes one set of outcomes an individual receives from his or her own experiences on the job, such as feelings of accomplishment, responsibility, meaningfulness.

Job analysis the process of describing or recording the purposes, task characteristics and task duties of a job is a given organization setting to determine a match for individual skill, experience, knowledge and needs.

Job Banks places where listings of jobs and their characteristics are maintained. These banks are generally associated with public employment agencies.

Job Burnout a specific set of symptoms brought on by severe or chronic stress directly related to the career rather than personal difficulties. Related symptoms are chronic fatigue, low energy, irritability and negative attitude toward job and self.

Job classes this is used interchangeably with job families.

Job classification method similar to ranking except that classes or grades are established and then the jobs are placed into the classes.

Job description a detailed statement of the duties, purposes, and conditions under which a job is to be performed (cf. job analysis).

Job Design Characteristics there are seven critical jobs design characteristics. They are skill variety, significance identity, feedback, autonomy, overload and underload. These characteristics help determine how a worker will psychologically feel about the jobs.

Job enlargement an approach to job design that loads a job horizontally, that is, that adds more of the same types of duties requiring the same skills.

Job enrichment an approach to job design that loads a job vertically, that is, that increases the number of skills needed and the sense of significance.

Job evaluation comparison of jobs by the use of formal and systematic procedures to determine their relative worth within the organization.

Job families means grouping together all jobs of nearly the same difficulty for the purpose of establishing a wage structure that reflects internal equity.

Job Instruction Training (JIT) a systematic technique for on-the-job training consisting of four steps: 1) careful selection and preparation of trainer and trainee for the learning experience to follow; 2) full explanation and demonstration by the trainer; 3) a trial on-the-job performance by the trainee; and 4) a thorough feedback session high-lighting job performance and job requirements.

Job matching an essential function in effective recruiting that entails fitting the needs of people to the requirements of the job.

Job Needs Analysis an examination of the organization which provides information on the tasks to be performed on each job, the skills necessary to perform those tasks and the minimum acceptable standards of performance.

Job Posting a procedure of posting within the organization, a list of what jobs are available.

Job Profile a major component of a job matching system that contains the descriptions of jobs that are available.

Job Progression Program a systematic effort by companies to tie individual career needs to the practical needs of the organization by identifying what individuals want and what organizations need and can offer.

Job Rotation an approach to job design that does not change the design of a job, but rather rotates the worker from job to job.

Job sex-typing classifying a job according to a male or female suffix (e.g., male-foreman; female-seamstress) generally reflecting a traditional sex-role bias.

Job Sharing arrangements for two people or more to share (split) the hours of one job, e.g., two people will take one job and each will work four hours.

Job specification a detailed statement of the skills, knowledge, and abilities required by a given job (cf. job analysis).

Knowledge of Results an important reinforcement is the knowledge of how well a task was done or having the knowledge of results.

Labor force dichotomy a term used to indicate a distinction between highly educated managers and professionals and less educated/unskilled workers.

Labor-Management Cooperation Act a law passed by the 95th Congress which encourages joint labor and management efforts to promote innovation, cooperation and communications supplemental to the traditional adversarial relationship between these two parties.

Labor Relations System a conceptual paradigm used to help elucidate the interrelationships between management, union, and employees.

Lack of Control a feeling an individual has of not being able to influence what happens or what can be done to change things as they are.

Landrum-Griffin Act passed in 1959 and also known as the Labor-Management Reporting and Disclosure Act to regulate the internal affairs of unions.

Lockout a refusal of management to allow workers to work.

Low quality of work life a sociopsychological work environment component characterized by one-way communications, lack of respect for employee rights, poor personnel and policies that produce unfavorable psychological conditions and outcomes.

Machine pacing a condition under which the machine determines how fast the work must be done, therefore, the pace at which the employee works is determined by the machine.

Management by Objectives this approach evaluates the performance of managers (typically) on the basis of how well they have attained their predetermined goals or objectives.

Manager the person who directs and is responsible for other employees who are either supervisors or managers.

Managerial Incentive Plans are plans used to reward managerial employees.

Mandatory issue issues of wages, hours and other terms and conditions of employment over which management must bargain according to the NLRA.

Marginal performance obtaining a less than average evaluation, regardless of the method used.

Marshall v Barlow's, Inc. An important Supreme Court case resulting in limiting the conditions under which OSHA could inspect work environments.

Match 1: A match or fit between worker skills and abilities and organizational/job demands. The traditional organizational form is most concerned about this. Match 1 should (but it doesn't always) lead to high productivity.

Match 2: A match or fit between worker needs and values and organizational characteristics. For example, providing employees with jobs that have flexible working hours, allow participation and involvement for those individuals who have those needs. Matches 1 and 2 are often served by the contemporary organizational form so that both productivity and QWL are served.

Measured day work an incentive pay plan where production standards are established, although not as precisely as in piecework plans, and employees are paid according to those standards.

Mediation a procedure in which a central third party assist union and management negotiators in reaching a voluntary agreement.

Merit pay plans methods of monetary compensation generally related to subjectively evaluated performance which represents only a small percentage increment in an employee's direct compensation.

Method analysis the use of individual activity units to describe the way a job is to be performed and evaluated. Also known as motion study. Best application is to nonmanagerial jobs.

MPPAA (Multiemployer Pension Plan Amendment Act) passed to enable pension plans to be funded across several employers.

Multiemployer bargaining where employers bargain as a group with the union at the local level.

Multilateral Bargaining a type of collective negotiating wherein more than two parties are involved in the negotiating and there is no clear union-management dichotomy.

Multiple Management Programs are training programs for managers where lower and middle level managers get an opportunity to work with top level managers.

Multiple regression an extension of simple linear regression where several independent variables (X_s) are used to more accurately predict or forecast future events. For example,

$$X_1 \searrow$$
$$X_2 \rightarrow Y, \text{ or}$$
$$X_3 \nearrow$$

$$\text{absenteeism } (X_1) \searrow$$
$$\text{turnover } \quad (X_2) \rightarrow \text{productivity } (Y)$$
$$\text{waste } \qquad (X_3) \nearrow$$

Mutual recruitment refers to the reciprocal relationships among parties to the recruitment process. Especially important are the relationships between personnel staff and line managers (cf. job analysis and job design) and between the organization and the job applicant (cf. job matching and realistic interview).

National Institute of Occupational Safety and Health (NIOSH) a Federal agency conceived to aid in the research, dissemination and education of health and safety issues and provide expertise to organizations in need of such services.

National Labor Relations Board (NLRB) was established by the Wagner Act to administer the National Labor Relations Act.

National Union a basic unit of labor unions that organizes, charters, and controls member union locals and develops general policies and procedures by which locals operate.

Negative settlement range when there is no overlap between union demands and management's concessions thus resulting in no ground for settlement.

Negative behavioral control strategy involves controls used to discourage unwanted behavior by either punishing or ignoring undesired behavior.

Network a collection of friends, acquaintances, and colleagues, both inside and outside one's workplace, that can be summoned to provide some kind of help or support.

No-Risk Standard An enforcement tool used by OSHA which would require organizations to make their work environments absolutely free of any risks from employee exposure.

Nominal grouping a technique in which several individuals list and identify their ideas (cf., brain storming). All ideas are considered by all members and action is decided upon by using the best approach.

Non-exempt jobs in which the incumbents are paid overtime for working overtime; they are not exempt from the wage—hour laws not requiring overtime pay.

Noncontributory programs a type of retirement plan in which the employee is the sole contributor for benefits to be obtained at retirement.

Nonverbal cues behavior that does not involve words or speech. Examples include body movement, gestures, handshake, eye contact, and physical appearance.

Occupational accidents accidents such as loss of limb, loss of hearing or even loss of life as a consequence of the physical environment of an organization.

Occupational diseases diseases or illnesses such as cancer and leukemia that result from aspects of the physical work environment.

Occupational Safety and Health physical/physiological and sociopsychological conditions of an organization's work force.

Occupational Safety and Health Administration (OSHA) A Federal agency vested with the power and responsibility for establishing and enforcing occupational safety and health standards and for inspecting and issuing citations to organizations in violation of such standards. Created by the Occupational Safety and Health Act, 1970.

Off-the-Job Programs (OFFJT) training programs that are taught outside the work organization.

On-the-Job Programs (OJT) a whole set of training programs that are conducted on the job or where the people are working.

Operational Efficiency a level of skill learning where the trainee uses and benefits from what is being learned (e.g. "hands-on" experience in an organizational role).

Organizational Needs Analysis an examination of short- and long-term objectives of the organization, human resource needs, efficiency indexes and organizational climate as they relate to the training and development needs of the organization.

Organizational stress a sociopsychological work environment component characterized by organizational changes, work overload, poor supervision, unfair salaries, job insecurity and physical insecurity all producing uncertainty.

Outcome Attractiveness the value an individual attaches to the outcomes or rewards which may be attached to various behaviors the individual can exhibit.

Outplacement the removal of ineffective or unnecessary performers by helping them find a new job, which produces minimal disruption to the organization and maximum benefit to the individual.

Overload quantitative overload refers to having too many tasks to do in a given time period and qualitative overload refers to tasks which require skills exceeding those possessed by the worker.

Paired Comparison a comparative approach in which the superior compares each subordinate with every other subordinate in order to evaluate the subordinates.

PAPPs performance appraisal processes and procedures comprise many activities and forms in the total performance appraisal and evaluation system. All of these activities and forms are essential in a good evaluation system.

Pay equity ensuring that what employees are paid is in relationship to what they and others give to the organization.

Pay for time not worked a form of indirect compensation received by an employee for time not spent working. Two categories: *off-the-job,* e.g., vacations, sick leave, holidays, personal days, comprising the major portion of costs of indirect benefits, and *on-the-job,* e.g., lunch & rest periods, physical fitness facilities.

Pay level the absolute pay or wage that employees receive.

Pay secrecy the issue of whether employees should or should not have access to the organizations compensation schedule.

Performance based pay systems pay systems that relate pay to performance including incentive pay plans and merit pay plans.

Performance Contracts an employment agreement with clearly specified objectives for a given period of time and the appropriate rewards or disciplinary action of meeting or failing to meet agreed upon goals.

Performance shares under this managerial incentive plan, managers receive shares or stocks in a company as a performance reward based upon how well the company is doing.

Permanent Part-Time fixed arrangements to work fewer than five days per week or forty hours per week.

Permissive issue are those issues over which it is not mandatory to bargain but are not specifically illegal.

Person Needs Analysis an examination of the deficiencies between an employee's actual performance and the desired performance or between an employee's proficiency on critical job dimensions and the desired proficiency required on the job dimensions.

Personal Appraisal identifying your abilities, value and goals across several life dimensions that are important to you. Strengths and weaknesses are also noted.

Personality Inventory tests that tap individual traits or characteristics, for example, California Psychological Inventory, Minnesota Multiphasic Personality Inventory.

Personal competence a test designed to measure whether individuals know how to make appropriate and timely decisions for themselves and whether they put forth the effort to do so.

Personnel generalist personnel staff with moderate experience of the language, needs and requirements of the line. Generally found in organizations characterized by centralization.

Personnel manager a person or position heading up the personnel department.

Personnel practices refers to all the ways, techniques and philosophies utilized in treating the organization's human resources. Included here are all the personnel functions and activities discussed in this text.

Personnel Roles functions of the personnel department that improve the organization's productivity, enhance the quality of working life, or maintain compliance with legal codes.

Personnel specialist personnel staff with specific skills related to a particular area or department of the organization. Generally found in organizations characterized by decentralization.

Piecework plan is the most common type of incentive pay plan. Under this plan employees get a standard pay rate for each unit of output.

Physical work environment is composed of the building, chairs, equipment, machines, lights, noise, heat, chemicals, toxics and the like which are associated with occupational accidents and diseases.

Placement an activity concerned with ensuring that job demands are filled and that individual needs and preferences are met.

Point rating method or point factor a job evaluation strategy which assigns point values to previously determined compensable factors and adds them to arrive at a total score used to determine wage levels.

Position Analysis Questionnaire (PAQ) a structured procedure used in job analysis which describes jobs in terms of worker activities. PAQ is based on person-oriented trait system that allows it to be applied across a number of jobs and organizations without modification. A salient disadvantage is its length.

Positive behavioral control strategy involves efforts to encourage desirable behavior by establishing behavior standards and setting up reward systems that are contingent upon successful (desired) behaviors.

Positive discipline an approach where a supervisor discusses an employee problem with the employee in a calm, nonaccusatory fashion and eventually asks the employee to make a choice between specific options.

Positive settlement range overlap area between management's resistance point and the union's resistance point that facilitates an acceptable settlement.

Potential costs those costs that might be incurred if the wrong selection decision is made.

Pre-election Campaign preliminary efforts by management and labor to persuade employees to vote for or against union certification.

Pre-retirement counseling this is counseling given to employees before retiring in order to facilitate their transition from work to non-work. This may result in early retirement decisions but it need not always.

Predictor rate this rate at which job applicants chosen for the job would do well according to predictors and criteria derived from job analysis.

Predictors these are the tests, the pieces of information used by personnel departments to predict how well an applicant is likely to do if hired.

Predictive validity similar to concurrent validity except that the predictor variable is measured some time *before* the performance variable (cf. empirical validity).

Prices or wage rates the actual rates of pay to be attached to a particular job, e.g., benchmark jobs.

Private employment agencies an external recruiting source that caters primarily to two types of job applicants: professional and managerial workers and unskilled workers. These agencies supply service for all ages of job applicants and charge a fee for setting up connections between applicants and employers.

Proactive Training is any training done prior to the time it is needed because a situation has gone wrong or as a response to a negative situation.

Productivity the outputs of an individual, group, or organization divided by the inputs needed by the individual, group or organization for the creation of outputs.

Productivity Bargaining a special form of integrative bargaining where labor agrees to scrap old work habits for new and more effective ones desired by management. In exchange, management offers labor the gain of modernization and increased efficiency to labor in the form of work incentives.

Programmed Instruction (PI) a systematic and stepwise presentation of skills and tasks broken down into "frames" where each "frame" must be successfully completed before going into the next. Feedback concerning the correctness of response for each "frame" is provided immediately and allows individuals to pace themselves.

Prohibited issue issues about which it is illegal for unions and employers to bargain.

Protection programs indirect compensation designed to protect the employee and family if and when the employee's income (direct compensation) is terminated and to protect the employee and family against the burden of health care expenses in the event of disability.

Psychological contract this is an informal and unwritten understanding between employees and employer about what is reasonable to expect to get from an employee in exchange for what's in the employment contract.

Psychomotor tests aptitude tests that combine mental and physical aspects of individual ability, for example, Mac Quarrie Test for Mechanical Ability, Tweeser Dexterity Tests.

Public employment agencies an external recruiting source coordinated with the U.S. Training and Employment Service. Such agencies at the state level provide counseling, testing, and placement for everyone. These agencies also have access to a nationwide network of job information and applicant information.

Purposes these are the reason for the creation and existence of a job.

Quality Circles an innovative management concept which helps contribute to an organization's growth and well being and based on the philosophy that a company's work force participation is its most valuable resource because they are often the most qualified to identify and solve work-related problems.

Quality of Work Life a process by which all members of the organization, through appropriate channels of communication set up for this purpose, have some say about the design of their jobs in particular and the work environment in general to satisfy their needs.

Railway Labor Act (RLA) was passed by Congress in 1926 to prevent serious economic consequences in the railway industry from labor unrest.

Ranking method a hierarchy or ladder of jobs constructed from the job analysis to reflect the relative value of the jobs.

Rates of absenteeism a percentage of unscheduled (random) absences or working days lost over a period of time divided by the number of workers, times the number of working days, multiplied by 100.

Realistic job interview a recruitment interview where the potential applicant is made aware of the positive and negative aspects of the organization.

An applicant is encouraged to approach current employees and the line manager and to ask questions about the appropriate fit between his or her needs and the organization's needs.

Reality Shock this is the career disappointment from having higher expectations of jobs than what jobs can really fulfill.

Recognition tests examples of past behavior or performance that indicate the quality of an individual's work, for example, portfolios.

Recruitment the set of activities and processes used to legally obtain a sufficient number of the right people at the right place and time so that the people and the organization can select in their own best short-run and long-run interests.

Redundancy planning developing alternative strategies for obsolete employees to acquire skills necessary for other types of work. Planning includes counselling, training and part-time employment.

Reference verification a method for validating information provided by the application, for example, using school records & transcripts, calling previous employers.

Reinforcement essentially means giving people immediate follow-up on their performance based on the premise people will do what's rewarded and avoid doing what is punished.

Resistance point the lowest acceptable level that the union can take on behalf of its members or the highest acceptable level for management.

Right to Work Law a provision which does not require employees to join a union to work even if a union exists.

Role Playing is off-the-job training where a realistic situation is created and individuals learn by playing roles in the situation.

Salary Compression a term connoting a decrease in the range of pay between various positions (levels) in the organization.

Sales incentive plans are those administered for individuals engaged in selling and are generally called commissions plans.

Scanlon plan a type of company wide incentive program emphasizing management-employee relations, especially employee participation, and underscores efficient operations through cooperation. In effect, employees share in organization profits as a result of contributing and cooperating to attain higher productivity.

Scheduled Absenteeism planned absenteeism which allows the organization to predict and control which employees and how many will be absent.

Scientific approach an approach to designing jobs that minimize the skills needed by the worker to perform the job. The result is often a job that is simple and repetitive.

Selection the process of gathering information for the purposes of evaluating and deciding who should be hired, under legal guidelines, for the short- and long-term interests of the individual and the organization.

Selection ratio the proportion of individuals actually hired to those who applied and did not get the job.

Semiautonomous Work Groups a collection of individuals who work interdependently in the production of a good or service and who make important decisions concerning employment, discipline and salary.

Sensitivity Training is an unstructured learning situation focusing upon the here-and-now rather than the there-and-then.

Severity Rate reflects the hours actually lost due to injury or illness by differentially weighting for categories of injuries and illnesses.

Sex-role stereotyping when roles in society become defined as being or having a sex type, e.g., traditionally the role of a housekeeper was defined as being female and the job of bread-winner as being male.

Significance the degree to which the job has a substantial impact on the lives of other people.

Significant Risks an enforcement tool superseding the no risk standard as a result of a court decision in the *Industrial Union Department, AFI-CIO v. American Petroleum Institute, 1980*. This standard implied that OSHA cannot demand compliance with the no-risk standard if the organization in question can show its existing exposure level to harmful agents to be below a threshold assessment as determined by OSHA (cf. benzene standard and lead or cotton standard).

Simple linear regression a quantitative formula or equation used to predict or forecast future events given certain variables. For example, $x \rightarrow y$ or demand (x) influences (predicts) sales (y).

Simulation a training program that presents individuals with situations that are similar to actual job conditions and that are off the job.

Skill based evaluation a job evaluation strategy where the organization compensates the employee by paying the person for skills and experience relative to the organizations mission.

Skill Development a level of skill learning where the trainee actually learns by doing some of the things being discussed (e.g., performance of a role).

Skill Variety the degree to which a job requires a number of different skills to perform it correctly.

Sociopsychological work environment the non-physical parts of the work environment including such things as relationships with supervisors, company policies, structure of the organization, organizational changes, uncertainty, conflicts and relationships with co-workers.

Sociotechnical Approach a productivity program under the heading of task redesign which is based on the notion that jobs are man-made inventions related to a number of technical and social systems that are themselves constantly changing. The concept reflects a sensitivity to bridging technical and social systems in such a way as to be optimally productive.

Standard hour plan this second most widely used incentive pay plan pays on the basis of time per unit of output rather than the quantity of output.

Standard Resume an organized chronological documentation of work and educational experience relating to one's career and qualifications. Generally prepared by an applicant for a position.

Steward an employee elected by the work unit to act as the union representative on the work site and to respond to company actions against employees that violate the labor agreement.

Stock options is a managerial incentive plan where the manager is given an opportunity to buy stocks of the company at a later date but at a price established at the time the option is given.

Straight Ranking a comparative approach in which the superior lists the subordinates from best to worst usually on the basis of overall performance.

Strike a refusal of employees to work at the company.

Structured job analysis the use of a standard format for job descriptions so that all organizations can use the same job categories.

Style of communication refers to what, how, and when the supervisor communicates to employees that influences their level of role awareness, satisfaction, and performance.

SUB (Supplemental Unemployment Benefits) benefits received by employees, who are on layoff, from their company until returning to work or until the benefits expire (e.g. after 26 weeks).

Subordinate for Chapter 9, this term is used to

denote the person whose performance is being appraised.

Suggestion systems a form of incentive compensation paid to employees who are responsible for money-saving or money producing ideas for the organization.

Superior for Chapter 9, this term is used to denote the person doing the appraising of another's performance.

Supervisor the person who directs and is responsible for other employees who are non-supervisors and non-managers.

Supervisory Assistance an informal method of training often being discussions between a supervisor and his or her employee.

Taft-Hartley Act enacted by Congress in 1947 to restore the balance between labor and management and respond to the pro-union bias alleged to have been a part of the Wagner Act.

Target point a realistic assessment of what wage and conditions of employment the union is likely to get from management.

Team Contemporary a major classification of approaches to job design that focus on the group–job design interface (or relationships).

Technological System refers to the machines, methods and materials that are used to produce the organization's output.

Theory A a management theory which is characterized by short term employment, specialized career paths, rapid evaluations and promotions and individual decision making and responsibility.

Theory J a management theory which is characterized by long term employment, non specialized careers, slow evaluations and promotions and collective responsibility.

Theory Z a current management philosophy modifying some of the more traditional American management concerns (Theory A) and integrating some of the ideas from conventional Japanese management (Theory J).

Time study/work measurement the determination of standard times for all units of work activity in any task. Includes the assessment of "actual effort" exerted and the "real effort" required to accomplish a task. (cf. methods analysis)

Title VII of the Civil Service Reform Act passed in 1978 and also known as the Federal Service Labor-Management Relations Statute, has been referred to as the most significant change in federal personnel administration since the passage of the Civil Service Act of 1883.

Total compensation the activity by which organizations evaluate the contributions of employees in order to fairly distribute direct and indirect monetary and nonmonetary rewards, within the organization's ability to pay and legal regulations.

Traditional Organizational Form describes an organization where supervisors closely watch employees, jobs are simple and routine and where economic inventives and job security are used to motivate. In total this form is the essence of Match 1.

Turnover the permanent departure (voluntary or involuntary) of individuals from an organization.

Uncertainty a lack of predictability or an inability to tell what things are or will be like, a state of unpredictability.

Underload quantitative underload refer to having too few tasks to do and qualitative underload refers to tasks which require fewer skills than those possessed by the worker.

Unfair representation breach of duty by a union to fairly represent all employees covered by the union-management contract.

Union an organization with the legal authority to negotiate with the employer on behalf of the employees and to administer the ensuing agreement.

Unionizing the effort by employees and outside agencies (unions and associations) to ban together and act as single unit when dealing with management over issues related to their work.

Union locals the grass-roots unit of the labor organization that represents the employees who are in the same union unit at a given work site.

Union Shop a provision (in about 30 states) that says that employees must join the union (if the company has one) after a set number of days from initial employment.

Unscheduled Absenteeism casual absenteeism that cannot be predicted, as such the organization must hire additional workers for the times (unpredictable) when other workers will be absent.

Vested rights pertains to qualifications required to become eligible for an organization's pension benefits.

Wage dividend plans are a special type of cash plan where the percentage of profits paid to employees is determined by the amount of dividends paid to stockholders.

Wage-loss a concept implying that worker compensation as a result of injury is paid in accordance with the actual amount of pay that would have been gained during the time the employee was displaced from their job due to the injury.

Wagner Act was the major comprehensive labor code in 1935 with the intent by Congress to restore equality of bargaining power between labor and management. This is also known as the National Labor Relations Act.

Weighted Check List identical to a critical incidents format but with various points to differentiate the varying importance of different incidents.

Wellness Tests Health assessments of employees which include measures of blood pressure, blood cholesterol, high density cholesterol, skin fold evaluation of diet, life change events, smoking, drinking and family history of CHD.

Wildcat strike a strike that is not legal because the contract forbids it, yet the union strikes anyway.

Wilderness Training an off-the job training program designed to help trainees learn their own potentials and limitations by confronting them with immediate, physical tasks which require cooperation decision making.

Worker compensation insurance is a health insurance program offered by an employer to cover (compensate for) worker sickness and disability.

Worker–job interface also referred to as the worker–machine interface, refers to where the worker meets the job and is concerned with whether or not the needs of the worker are met by the nature of the job.

Work Sample Test this is a sample of the actual work given to a job applicant to determine how well he or she performs.

Work sampling the process of taking instantaneous samples of the work activities of individuals or groups of individuals. Activities are then timed and classified according to predetermined categories. The result is a description of the activities by classification of a job and the percentage of time for each activity (cf. methods analysis).

Work Standards a type of goal oriented form of evaluation, similar to management by objectives, except that the predetermined goals are dictated by management and often established by work measurement.

Name Index

Anderson, D. Kent, 366
Anderson, Kenneth, 114
Aplander, Guvene G., 43
Aslanjan, Carol B., 415
Athos, Anthony, 497
Auchter, Thorne G., 518, 520

Baird, John E., Jr., 214
Beihoffer, Dale, 167
Bennett, Roy F., 489
Berg, Norbert R., 419–420
Bishop, Jerry E., 452
Blackmun, Justice Harry A., 576
Blount, W. Frank, 414
Bognano, Mario, 615
Bolle, Mary Jane, 518–519
Brennan, Justice William J., Jr., 576
Bricknell, Henry M., 415
Brown, Charles L., 488
Burck, Charles, 6
Burger, Chief Justice Warren E., 576

Calore, Raymond, 490
Caprio, Marcia, 616
Carroll, Steve, 278
Carter, Jimmy, 561
Carter, Judge Robert, 186, 187
Chamberlain, Joyce, 116
Churm, Peter, 137
Cianci, Vincent S., Jr., 616
Clem, Steve, 605
Cook, Daniel D., 553
Corman, Charles, 227
Corn, Morton, 539
Craig, Robert, 415
Curtis, Carol E., 397–398

Danforth, Douglas D., 8
Daniell, James, 226–227
DeBernardo, M. A., 519
Deitsch, C. R., 300
Dewar, Dan, 493
DeWindt, H. M., 639
Dilts, D. A., 300
Donahue, Thomas, 491
Druckner, Peter, 384, 385
Dunn, Frederica, 245

Farish, Phil, 482, 518–520
Finley, Ruth C., 502–504
Fischer, Ben, 597
Flanagan, Joseph E., 414
Foltz, Roy G., 214
Ford, Gerald, 157
Franklin, Ben A., 530
Fraser, Douglas, 604
Froinds, Dr. John, 530

Gallese, Liz Roman, 85–86
Getmaa, Julius G., 253
Gibson, Robert E., 330
Gilchrist, Bruce, 62–63
Gompers, Samuel, 570
Graham, Thomas, 499
Gray, Harry, 360
Gundvaldson, Gundy, 486–487

Hage, Dave, 482, 483
Hanley, Edward, 361
Harman, Sidney, 488–489
Hattori, Masaya, 641–642
Hayes, Thomas C., 591
Henderson, James, 21
Houser, Carrol D., 420–421
Hubert, Paul, 482

Iacocca, Lee A., 360
Ingrassia, Lawrence, 615–616

Jackson, Tom, 461
Johnson, Lyndon, B., 157
Jonas, Gary, 272–273

Kayser, Paul W., 127
Kennedy, James H., 128
Kennedy, John F., 157, 560
Kermit, Francis, 615
Kerns, David T., 488
Kiddoo, K. R., 127–128
King, Kelly, 519
Kirkland, Lane, 361, 571
Koch, Edward, 186
Korn, Lester B., 127
Kovach, Kenneth A., 552
Kraft, Donald C., 98
Krigman, Ruben, 10
Kuzmits, Frank E., 313

Lafley, Alan F., 127–128, 425
Lakhein, Alan, 461
Langley, M., 152
Lannamann, Richard S., 128
Licata, Corinne S., 503, 504
Liebers, Donald, 86
Lincoln, Carrie, 415
Livingston, Sterling, 272
Loeser, Edward A., 499
Lublin, Joann S., 578–579
Lundine, Stanley, 488

McCafrey, William T., 452
McCardell, Archie R., 360
McDonnell, Lynda, 498
McGregor, Douglas R., 591
McKeown, Anthony F., 552–553
Macky, Craig B., 42
Makower, Joel, 531
Mallof, Gerries, 385
Manoogian, John, 86
Marks, Nancy, 452
Marshall, Justice Thurgood, 576
Martin, Wallace, 214–215
Matteis, Richard, 62
Mayleas, Davidyne, 461
Meany, George, 491
Menk, Carl W., 128
Miller, Christopher S., 273–274
Miller, Saul, 604
Moroney, Lott, 414
Murphy, B. S., 632

Nelson, David, 167

O'Connor, Justice Sandra D., 576
O'Connor, Mary S., 361
Oreskes, Michael, 483
Ouchi, William, 488

Pascale, Richard Tanner, 496, 497–498
Paul, Robert, 227
Pearson, Gaylene, 114
Pestillo, Peter J., 118
Peters, Thomas J., 6
Petersen, Donald J., 109
Powell, Justice Lewis F., 576

Quie, Albert, 616

Raferty, Frank, 530
Randolph, Deborah, 400
Reagan, Ronald, 398, 518, 615, 619
Reder, Melvin W., 603, 604, 605
Rehnquist, Justice William H., 576

Renier, James, 497
Ricklefs, Roger, 128
Ris, Cindy, 227
Robinson, Jim, 504
Rochlin, Jay, 114
Ryerson, Diane, 452

Sachs, Judge Howard, 116
Salamon, Julie, 366
Sanger, David E., 428
Schaumburger, Joan, 366
Scher, Paul, 114
Schneier, Craig, 278
Schrank, Robert, 300
Schuler, Randall, S., 272
Schuster, Michael H., 273–274
Schwartz, Allen, 186
Seaberry, Jane, 576
Shapiro, Kenneth P., 632
Shenkin, Arliaana, 62–63
Smith, Gerald H., 366
Snook, Stover, 86
Springer, Joseph, 98
Staub, Rusty, 361
Steiner, Robert E., 590
Stevens, Justice John Paul, 576
Stevens, Whitney, 575
Stiehl, Christian, 86
Sturgeon, W. R., 98

Taft, Robert, 559
Thurow, Lester C., 108
Tidwell, Gary L., 249
Tortoriello, Thomas R., 441
Tucker, Howie, 167
Tulkoff, Joseph, 504

Ulrich, Max, 127

Vatalaro, Ralph, 615
Vogt, Tom, 167

Walters, Roy W., 75
Weatherman, Mary, 576
Weber, Brian, 118
Westin, Alan, 245
White, Justice Bryon R., 576
Wiencek, Dr. Robert, 86
Willette, David, 519–520
Williams, Winston, 605
Winfield, Dave, 360, 361

Young, Arthur, 638
Young, E. James, 137
Youngblood, S. A., 249

Subject Index

Ability of the employee, 308, 310, 314
Absenteeism, 300–301, 312, 315
  costs of, 305, 671, 675
  policy for, 313–314
  rates of, 303–304
  scheduled, 303
  unscheduled, 303
Absolute standards approach, 280
Academic journals, list of, 663–664
Accreditation, 28
Achievement communication behavior, 233
Achievement tests, 174–175
Active listening, 228
Adoption benefits, 638
Adversarial system, 593–594
Adverse impact, 158–159, 192
  defending, 651
  demonstrating, 651
Advertising, recruitment by, 129–130
Affirmative action programs (AAPs), 114–121
Age, labor force distribution by, 57
Age Discrimination in Employment Act (1967), 64, 156, 157, 202, 244, 255, 336, 388, 421
Air-traffic controllers strike, 615, 619
Albermarle Paper Company v. Moody (1975), 75, 277
Alcoholism, 304
  costs of, 305–306
Aliens, recruitment of, 125, 129
Allied Bancshares Inc., 365–366
Allied Corporation, 466
Alternative procedures requirements, 161–162
Alternative ranking approach, 280
Amalgamated Clothing and Textile Workers Union, 574–575
AMAX Copper Company, 199
American Can Company, 398, 399, 638
American Compensation Association, 28
American Express Company, 502–504
American Federation of Labor (AFL), 570
American Federation of Labor and Congress of Industrial Organizations (AFL-CIO), 567, 570–571, 572, 577, 578, 604, 605
American Federation of State and Municipal Employees, 640
American Hospital Supply Corporation, 260
American Management Association, 482
American Society for Personnel Administration (ASPA), 28
American Society for Training & Development, 415
American Standard Inc., 127
American Telephone & Telegraph (AT&T) Company, 85, 86, 114, 117, 414, 488, 501, 605

Ameritrust Company, 470
Anti-Kickback Law (1948), 336
Application blanks, 177–178
Appraisal forms, 276–284
Apprenticeship training, 432
Aptitude tests, 173–174
Arbitration, 591, 609
Armour & Company, 603
Arthritis Foundation, 539
ASPA Accreditation Institute (AAI), 28
Assessment center method, 189, 284, 434
Assessment phase of objectives, 422–423
Assistance services, 637–638
Assistantships, 432
Associated General Contractors (AGC), 415
Attitudinal structuring, 598
Auditor role, the, 19, 20
Austria, 531
Authorization cards, 574
Automation, 61–62, 504–505
Autonomy, 80
Avoidance behavior, 304

B. F. Goodrich Company, 371
Backus v. Baptist Medical Center, 162
Bakke v. Regents of The University of California, 118, 119
BancOhio National Bank, 199
Band width, 135
Bargaining, *see* Collective bargaining
Bargaining units, 575
Barnes v. Castle, 257
Base rates, 196–197
Basic skills of a technical nature (BST), 424
Basic skills of grammar (BSG), 424
Baxter v. Savannah Sugar Refinery Corp., 277
Behavioral control strategy, 315–316
Behavior anchored rating scale (BARS), 281, 283
Behavior-outcome expectancy, 307
Belgium, 330
Bell Telephone Company, 64
Benchmark jobs, 344
Benefits, *see* types of benefits
Benefits package, 397–400
Bethlehem Steel Corporation, 394, 492, 494
Blacks, discrimination against, 152–153, 257–258
Blue Cross/Blue Shield, 248, 393
Board of Regents of State Colleges v. Roth, 251
Boeing Company, 64, 360, 492, 497–498

Bona fide occupational qualification (BFOQ), 129, 159, 160, 162
Bonuses, 360, 370, 373
  defined, 370
Bonus units, 368
Booz-Allen & Hamilton, 505
Bottom-line criterion, 158
Boulwarism, 599
Boyden Associates, 128
Boyer v. Western Union Tel. Co., 249
Breaks, 607
Brito v. Zia Company (1973), 73, 276
Buckley Amendment, 255
Bunker Ramo Corporation, 97–98
Burlington Industries, 539
Business necessity, 161
Business Roundtable, 415
Business Week, 401

Cafeteria approach, 348
California Agricultural Relations Act (1975), 574
California Brewers Association v. Bryant, 562
Canada, 223, 330
Candidate profiles, 111
Career balance sheets, 467
Career management, 45, 334
Career pathing, 458
Career planning and development, 451–476
  activities of, 455, 461–469
  careers and, 457, 463, 474
  case study, 472–473
  critical issues in, 453, 470–471
  evaluating, 469–470
  importance of, 454–455
  organization and, 458–461
  programs for, 454–455, 458–461
  purposes of, 454–455
  relationships of, 455–457
Career stress, 459–461
Case discussion, 434
Cash plans, 370
Centralization vs. decentralization, 22–24
Central tendency, error of, 288
Certification, professional, 28
Certification elections, 573, 577
Chamber of Commerce v. OSHA, 525
Change, pace and complexity of, 10–11
Chase Manhattan Bank, 127–128, 414, 425
Checkoffs, 607
Chief executive officers (CEOs), 360
  quality of work life and, 488–489
Childcare assistance, 133
Chrisner v. Complete Auto Transit, 186–187
Chrysler Corporation, 54, 88, 360, 601, 603, 604, 605, 606, 641
Citibank, 62, 111, 132, 200, 330, 503
Citizens & Southern National Bank, 500
Civilian labor force
  defined, 58
  occupational makeup of, 59
Civil rights, 114–122, 152–153, 157–158
  See also Discrimination
Civil Rights Act (1866), 115
Civil Rights Act (1964), 75, 159, 259, 336
  on compensation, 331

  on employee rights, 244, 250, 255, 259
  on performance appraisal, 276
  on recruitment, 115, 118–119
  on religious discrimination, 559
  on staffing, 152–153, 156, 157, 162, 186, 200, 202
  on training, 421
  on union-management relations, 562, 593
Civil Service Act (1883), 560
Civil Service Reform Act (1978), 560–561, 614, 617
Cleanup time, 607
Coaching, 289–290
Collective bargaining, 561, 588–627
  careers and, 624
  case study, 622–624
  compensation and, 603
  critical issues in, 592, 618–620
  management strategies in, 598–599
  model of the process of, 595–598
  public-sector, 614–617
  union-management relationships in, 593–595
  union-management strategies in, 600–601
  union strategies in, 599–600
Commissions, 368
Communicating with employees, 212–241
  careers and, 224, 239
  case study, 238–239
  content of, 223
  critical issues in, 215, 236–237
  evaluating, 235–236
  importance of, 216–217
  information and, 216
  issues in, 219–224
  job assignments and, 222–223
  methods of, 229–235
  in the 1980s, 635
  the organization and, 220–223, 225
  productivity and, 214, 215, 235
  purposes of, 216–217
  quality of work life and, 235–236
  relationships of, 218–219
  skills in, 217, 225–229
  supervisors and, 225–226, 232–235
  unionization of employees and, 556
  union-management relations and, 218–219
  value of, 223–224
Communication, 214
  barriers to, 225–226
  defined, 216
  downward, 223
  of expectations, 253
  formal, 216
  informal, 216
  of performance criteria and standards, 278
  principles of, 227–228
  of prohibitions, 253
  safety and health and, 524
  upward, 223, 225
Communication behavior, 233–234
Communications Workers of America, 605
Comparable worth, 330–331, 336–337
Comparative approach to performance appraisal, 279–280
Compensating employee behavior, 14, 17
  in the 1980s, 636–638

Compensation, 26–27, 79, 327–408
  collective bargaining and, 603
  communicating with employees and, 219
  cutting, 603–605
  direct, 332
  environmental impact on, 334–338, 387, 388
  indirect, 332
  individual determination of, 346
  job evaluation and, 338–344
  the market and, 337–338
  minimum wages, 330, 335
  satisfaction with, 349
  training and development and, 418–420
  unionization of employees and, 557
  See also Indirect compensation; Performance-based pay; Total
    compensation
Compensation benefits, 392
Compressed work weeks, 136
Computers, 6, 504–505, 531
  impact on employment, 62–63
Computer simulations, 48, 49–51
Conceptual integrative skills (CIS), 425, 431
Concurrent validity, 193
Conference Board Inc., 414
Confirmation approach, 201
Conflict resolutions, 588–627
  arbitration, 591, 609
  careers and, 624
  case study, 622–624
  critical issues in, 592, 618–620
  lockouts, 608–609
  mediation, 609
  strikes, 607, 608–609
    in the public sector, 614–618, 619
    wildcat, 611, 613
Congress of Industrial Organizations (CIO), 570
Connecticut General Life Insurance Company, 414
Connecticut v. Teal, 188
Conrail, 603
Consent decree, 115
Consistency, 346
Constructs, 194
Construct validity, 194
Consultants, 578–579
Contaminated appraisal forms, 279
Contemporary organizational form, 53–54
Content validity, 193–194
Continental Bank, 414
Contingent approval communication behavior, 233
Contingent disapproval communication behavior, 233–234
Contingent rewards, 430
Continuous bargaining, 600–601
Contract administration, 588–627
  careers and, 624
  case study, 622–624
  critical issues in, 592, 618–620
  grievance issues, 611–613
  grievance procedures, 608, 610–611
    effectiveness of, 617–618
  management procedures, 613
  union procedures, 613–614
Contract plan, 430
Contrast effects, 170

Contributory programs, 391
Control Data Corporation, 114, 167, 417, 419–420, 492
Conventional rating method, 281
Cooperative acceptance, 255, 256–257
Cooperative systems, 594–595
Coordinated bargaining, 602
Copeland Act (1934), 336
Core time, 135
Corning Glass Works, 505–506
Corporate citizenship, 304
Correlation coefficient, 191
Cosmic search, 162
Cost-of-living adjustments (COLAs), 366–367
Criterion validity, 192
Critical incidents format, 280
Criticism, 286
Cross-functional (cross-departmental) transfer, 459
Cummins Engine Company, 21

Davis-Bacon Act (1931), 335
Decentralization vs. centralization, 22–24
Decertification elections, 577
Decertification of unions, 553
Defensibility, 346
Deficient appraisal forms, 279
Delaware & Hudson Railroad, 605
Delegator role, 19–20
Delphi technique, 48
Delta Airlines, 6, 506–507
Denmark, 330
Depth interviews, 168
Design stage participation, 371–372
Detroit Edison Company, 163
Development, *see* Training and development
Diaz vs. Pan American World Airways, Inc., 161
Dictionary of Occupational Titles (DOT), 92
Differential validity, 194
Direct index approach, 284
Directive communication behavior, 234
Disability benefits, 392
Disability insurance, 393
Discharge, 607
Discipline, 607
Discrimination, 114–122, 152–153, 156–162, 186
  demonstrating, 651
  rights of employees and, 244
  See also names of cases; types of discrimination
Dismissal pay, 606
Distributive bargaining, 595–596
Doe v. Syracuse School District, 178
Donaldson v. Pillsbury Co., 219
Donald T. Regan School of Advanced Financial Management, 415
Downward communication, 223
Downward transfer, 635
Due process, 253
DuPont de Nemours, E. I. & Company, 519, 527
Duration of the agreement, 608

Earned time, 315
Earnings per share (EPS), 368
Eaton Corporation, 350, 639
Ebling v. Masco Corporation, 251
Economic Recovery Tax Act (1981), 389

Economic supplements, 605–606
Economic Tax Act (1981), 385
Economy, the, trends in, 60–62
Education, 10, 28, 59
Effective personnel management (EPM), 3–37
 activities of, 14–18
 careers in, 12, 24–25, 33–34, 646
 case study, 32–33
 critical issues in, 7–8, 30–31, 633, 643–645
 defined, 8
 determining, 11–14
 function of, 14–18
 importance of, 9–14
 list of journals for, 663–665
 list of legislation and court decisions affecting, 649–657
 in the 1980s, 629–647
  appraising employee behavior, 636
  compensating employee behavior, 636 638
  evaluating, 643
  improving work environment, 638–639
  in Japan, 641–643
  motivating employee behavior, 636
  planning for, 633–634
  relationships in, 635–636
  staffing in, 634–635
  training and development in, 638
  trends in, 633–641
  union-management relations in, 639–641
 in the organization, 18–20
 plan of the book, 29–30
 purposes of, 8
 responsibility for, 24
Effective personnel planning (EPP), 40–71
 careers and, 45, 48, 52, 53, 58–59, 69, 456
 case study, 68
 compensation and, 334
 critical issues in, 43, 65–66
 defined, 44
 developing strategies for, 46–52
 evaluating activity in, 65
 four phases in, 46–52
 importance of, 44
 in the 1980s, 56–65, 634
  changes in social values in, 62–64
  the government in, 64–65
  labor force characteristics in, 57–60
  population characteristics in, 57–60
  trends in the economy in, 60–62
 programs for, 52–56
 purposes of, 44
 quality of work life and, 489
 recruitment and, 112–113
 relationships of, 45, 56
 responsibility for, 45–46
 staffing and, 45
Effort-behavior expectancy, 307–308
Ego deflation communication behavior, 233
80 percent rule, 158
Elections of unions, 572–577
Empirical validity, 192–193
Employed, defined, 58
Employee assistance programs (EAPs), 317
Employee associations, 554

Employee pacing, 533
Employee referral programs (ERPs), 123, 125
Employee Relocation Council, 64
Employee services and perquisites, 396
Employees' Retirement Income Security Act (ERISA), 388–389, 404
Employment agencies, 125–127
Employment contract, 562
Employment legislation, list of, 649–651
Environment, see Work environment
Environmental impact on compensation, 334–338, 387, 388
Environmental Protection Agency (EPA), 384, 385
Equal Employment Act (1972), 157
Equal employment opportunity (EEO), 120–121, 220
 promotion and, 152
 selection and placement and, 152, 157
Equal Employment Opportunity Act, 252
Equal Employment Opportunity Commission (EEOC), 13
 on compensation, 384
 on recruitment, 115–118, 120–121
 on selection and placement, 157–159, 162, 166, 203
 on sexual harassment, 257, 258–259
Equal Pay Act (1963), 156, 157, 202, 336, 338–339, 384, 385, 389, 421
Equitable Life Insurance Company, 137
Equity, 309, 349
Ergonomic approach in job design, 83, 84–86
Essay method, 284
Essentiality, 564
Ethics, code of, 27–28
Evaluation designs, 439–440
Exclusivity, 564
Executive Order (EO)
 10925, 157
 10988, 560
 11246, 115, 157
 11491, 560
 11616, 559
 11838, 560
Exempt employees, 281, 283, 336
Expectancy model of motivation, 307–308
Expert forecasts, 48–49
Extension of bargaining, 609
Extrinsic outcomes, 308

Face validity, 194
Factor-comparison method, 344
Factory automation, 504
Fair Credit and Reporting Act, 255
Fair Labor Standards Act (FLSA-1938), 335–336
Family Education Rights and Privacy Act, 255
Federal Insurance Contribution Act (FICA), 390
Federal Labor Relations Authority (FLRA), 561
Federal Mediation and Conciliation Service, 611
Federal Services Impasses Panel, 560
Federal Society of Journeymen Cordwainers, 566, 567
Federal Wage Garnishment Law (1970), 336
Feedback, 80, 229, 310, 314
 in performance appraisal, 285–287
Field review technique, 289
Final-offer arbitration, 609
Firestone Tire & Rubber Company, 603, 604, 605
Firing, 244, 317
First Federal Saving and Loan Bank, 414

First National Maintenance v. NLRB, 255–256, 561
Flexible time, 135
Flextime schedules, 135–136
Fluorocarbon Company, 136–137
Follow-up, 430
Foote, Cone & Belding Communications Inc., 638
Forced choice, 281
Forced distribution method, 280
Ford Motor Company, 13, 85–86, 88, 117–118, 394, 489, 492, 601, 604
Ford Motor Co. v. Huffman, 562
Forecasting techniques, 48–51
Formal communications, 216
Formal course method, 433
Formulator role, 19
France, 330
Freedom of Information Act, 255
Frequency rate, 536
Friedman-Jacobs Company, 372
Fringe benefits, 384, 385
Fulltime workers, defined, 59
Functional job analysis (FJA), 91, 92, 94
Functional Standards Committees, 28
Fundamental knowledge, 428

GAF Corporation, 466
General Electric Company (GE), 49, 64, 200, 245, 286, 420–421, 492, 599
General Foods Corporation, 495
Generalists, 25–26, 28
General Motors Corporation (GM), 86, 88, 284, 300, 305, 316, 397–398, 590–591, 595, 601, 604
   assessment program of, 189–190
   safety and health at, 539, 540–541
   work environment at, 484, 486, 488, 490, 493, 494, 495, 498
General Tire & Rubber Company, 136
Georgia-Pacific Railroad, 64
Getty Oil Company, 424
Goals, 115, 279
   characteristics of, 310, 314
Goal setting, 115, 430
Good-cause compromise, 252–253
Government
   in the 1980s, 64–65
   terms used in labor studies by, 58–59
Grandfather clause, 162
Great Britain, 602
Grievance issues, 611–613
Grievance procedures, 253, 608, 610–611
   effectiveness of, 617–618
Griggs v. Duke Power, 158
Group gain sharing, 84
Group-level incentive plans, 368–370
Gunther v. County of Washington, 331

Halo effect, 169, 288
Handbook for Analyzing Jobs, 111
Handicapped, discrimination against, 119–120
Harman International Industries, Inc., 488
Harris Corporation, 42–43
Hay plan, 91, 93–94, 343–344, 456, 458
Head hunters, 126
Health, *see* Safety and health

Health insurance, 393, 606
Health Maintenance Organization Act (1973), 392
Health maintenance organizations (HMOs), 392
Heidrick & Struggles, Inc., 9–10
Hewlett Packard Company, 6, 638
High performance, 303
Hines v. Anchor Motor Freight Co., 562
Historical records in performance appraisal, 279
Hodgson v. Greyhound Lines, Inc., 161
Holidays, paid, 606
Honeywell Inc., 167, 484, 492, 495, 497
Horizontal loading, 84
Hospital benefits, 392
Hot stove principles, 315–316
Hughes Aircraft Company, 492
Human resource analysis, 423
Human resource costs, 9–10
Human resource information system (HRIS), 51
Human resource management
   list of journals in, 663–665
   planning for, 14–15

In-basket exercise, 175
Incentive pay plans, 362, 364–365
   types of, 367–371
Incentive plans, organizational-level, 370–371
Incidence rate, 536
Indirect compensation, 382–408
   administrative issues in, 396–400
   careers and, 391, 406
   case study, 405
   critical issues in, 385, 401–403
   defined, 386
   environmental impact on, 387, 388
   evaluating, 400–401
   importance of, 386–387
   the law and, 387–389, 393–394
   in the 1980s, 637–638
   pay for time not worked, 395–396
   perquisites and, 396
   protection programs, 389–395
      private, 392–395
      public, 389–392
   purposes of, 386–387
   safety and health and, 523–524
   services and, 396
Individual contemporary approaches, 83–84, 85
Individual-level incentive plans, 367–368
Individual Retirement Accounts (IRAs), 389
Industrial Union Department, AFL-CIO v. American Petroleum Institute, 625
Industrywide bargaining, 602
Inflation, 60–61
Informal communications, 216
Information, defined, 216
Initial demand point, 596
Initial offer, 596
Inland Steel v. National Labor Relations Board, 388
Innovator role, 19, 20
Insurance, 392–393, 606
   See also types of insurance
Integrative bargaining, 598
Intel Corporation, 500

Interest tests, 176
International Association of Machinists (IAM), 553
International Brotherhood of Electrical Workers, 599
International Brotherhood of Painters and Allied Trades, 530
International Brotherhood of Teamsters & Chauffeurs, 251, 562, 570, 571, 573–574
International Brotherhood of Teamsters v. United States, 562
International Business Machines Corporation (IBM), 6, 49, 64, 114, 199, 201, 350, 497–498, 638
  career planning and development at, 456, 470
  training and development at, 414–415
International Harvester Company, 360, 603, 604
International Ladies Garment Workers Union (ILGWU), 571
International Longshoremen's Association, 607
International Telephone and Telegraph Company (ITT), 132–133, 497–498
International Typographical Union (ITU), 579
International Woodworkers of America, 486
Internships, 432
Interpersonal competence tests, 174
Interpersonal skills (IPS), 424, 431
Interviews, 111, 131, 165–173, 466–467
Intraorganizational bargaining, 598
Intrinsic outcomes, 308
Isetan Department Stores, 642–643

J. C. Penney Company, 200, 470
J. P. Stevens Company, 574–575
Japan, 10, 214, 330, 492, 497–498, 504, 572
  motivation in, 632
  in the 1980s, 641–643
  profit sharing in, 360
  Theory J management, 496
  unions in, 571
Japanese Federation of Electrical Machine Workers Union, 571
Job analysis, 72–79, 90–103
  activities of, 76–79
   evaluating, 98
  careers and, 101–102, 456
  case study, 101
  compensation and, 79, 334
  critical issues in, 76, 98–99
  defined, 76
  importance of, 77–79
  information for, 90–91
   collecting, 96–98
  the law and, 75, 77
  methods analysis in, 94–96
  in the 1980s, 634
  purposes of, 77–78
  quality of work life and, 79, 489
  recruitment and, 113–114
  relationships of, 77, 78–79
  selection and placement and, 155–156
  structured procedures for, 91–94
  training and development and, 417
  in validation studies, 192
Job applicants
  increasing pool of, 131–138
   alternative work arrangements in, 133–138
   expanding opportunities in, 131–133
   realistic job previews, 131

  information about, 163–164
  methods of obtaining, 122–130
   external, 129–130
   internal, 123–125
  organization relationships, 111
  sources of, 122–130
   external, 125–129
   internal, 122–123
Job assignments, 222–223
Job banks, 126
Job burnout, 452, 460
Job classes, 345
Job classification method, 340–341
Job description, 76–77, 90–91
Job design, 72–90, 98–103
  activities of, 76–79, 80–82
   evaluating, 98
  approaches to, 83–86
  careers and, 101–102
  case study, 101
  characteristics of, 80
  critical issues in, 76, 98–99
  defined, 76
  duties in, 80–82
  importance of, 77–78
  in the 1980s, 634
  productivity and, 78, 79
  purposes of, 77–78, 80
  qualities of, 80
  quality of work life and, 78, 79
  recruitment and, 113–114
  relationships of, 77, 78–79
  selecting, 87–89
Job enlargement, 84
Job enrichment, 84, 501
Job evaluation
  compensation and, 338–344
  quality of work life and, 489
  steps in, 339–340
Job families, 345
Job feedback, 80
Job instruction training (JIT), 432
Job loss, dealing with, 54–55
Job matching, 111
Job needs analysis, 423
Job posting, 123–125
Job preferences, 60
Job preview, realistic, 131
Job profiles, 111
Job progression programs, 458–459
Job qualities, information about, 163
Job redesign
  determining need for, 88
  implementing, 89–90
  time for, 87, 88
Job relatedness, 158, 160–161, 166
Job rotation, 83–84, 317, 432
Job sample tests, 193
Job security, 607
  rights of employees to, 246, 250–254
Job sharing, 138
Job specifications, 76–77, 91

Johns-Manville Products Corporation, 394, 539
Jones & Laughlin Steel Corporation, 499
Journals in personnel and human resource management, 663–665

Kaiser Aluminum Company, 118
Knowledge
    employee, 87
    fundamental, 428
Korn-Ferry International, 127

Labor force, characteristics of, 57–60
Labor force dichotomy, 59
Labor Management Cooperation Act, 590, 591
Labor-Management Relations Act (1947), 128, 558–559, 602
Labor-Management Reporting and Disclosure Act (1959), 219, 559, 593
Labor Relations Council, 560
Labor relations legislation, list of, 652
Labor relations system, 593, 594
Labor studies by the government, terms used, 58–59
Landrum-Griffin Act, *see* Labor-Management Reporting and Disclosure Act (1959)
Last chance agreement, 254
Law, the
    employment legislation, list of, 649–651
    indirect compensation and, 387–389, 393–394
    job analysis and, 75, 77
    labor relations legislation, list of, 652
    motivating employees and, 306–307
    performance appraisal and, 276–278
    recruitment and, 114–122
    rights of employees and, 250–256
    safety and health and, 524–526
    selection and placement and, 152–153, 156–162
    total compensation and, 334–337
    training and development and, 421–422
    unionization of employees and, 557–562
Legal compliance, 9
    indicators of, 13–14
Lehman v. Yellow Freight System, 119
Leniency, error of, 288
Levi Strauss & Company, 114
Lewis v. Minnesota Mutual Life Insurance Company, 249
Liberty Mutual Insurance Company, 86
Lie detector tests, 177
Life insurance, 392–393, 606
Lincoln National Life Insurance Company, 489
Linear regressions, 49
Listening efficiently, 228
Loading, 84
Lockheed Corporation, 127–128, 227, 492
Lockouts, 608–609
Long-term level, 19
Los Angeles Department of Water v. Manhart, 384, 389
Low quality of work life, 522, 531–532
Lump sum salary increases, 371

McDonald's Hamburger University, 415
McDonnell Douglas Corporation v. Green, 158–159
Machine pacing, 533
Management by objectives (MBO), 281–284
    motivation and, 289
Management position description questionnaire (MPDQ), 91, 93, 94

Managerial incentive plans, 368
Managerial level, 19
Managerial prerogatives, 607
Mandatory issues, 602–603
MANPLAN, 49
Manufacturer's Life Insurance Company, 495
Marginal performance, 303
Marshall v. Barlow's, Inc., 525
Marshall v. Georgia Southwestern College, 339
Martin Marietta Corporation, 284, 435, 484, 492
MASCO Corporation, 248
Mastie v. Great Lakes Steel Corp., 278
Match 1, 53, 54
Match 2, 53–54, 165
Measured day work plans, 367
Mediation, 609
Medical benefits, 392
Medicare, 392
Medium-term level, 19
Merit pay plans, 362, 364, 365–367
Merrill Lynch, Pierce, Fenner & Smith, Inc., 415
Methods analysis, 94–96
Metropolitan Life Insurance Company, 414
Miller v. Bank of America, 257–258
Milstead v. Teamsters Local 957, 562
Minimum wage, 330, 335
Minimum Wage Law (1977), 335
Mistretta v. Sandia Corp., 273–274
Mitsubishi Corporation, 642–643
Mobility, 62, 64, 452
Modeling techniques, 48, 49–51
Morge v. Beeke Rubber Co., 251
Motivating employees, 14, 16, 298–324
    careers and, 311, 322
    case study, 321–322
    critical issues in, 302, 318–319
    defined, 302
    desired behaviors, 302–304
    importance of, 304–306
    in Japan, 632
    the law and, 306–307
    management by objectives and, 289
    in the 1980s, 636
    policies and, 311–314
    purposes of, 304–306
    rules and, 311–314
    strategies for, 311–318
        evaluating, 318
    understanding employees and, 307–311
    undesired behaviors, 302–304, 311, 316–317
Motivation-behavior-satisfaction relationships, 309
Motivation tests, 175
Multiemployer bargaining, 602
Multiemployer Pension Plan Amendment Act (1980), 385, 389
Multilateral bargaining, 615
Multiple linear regression, 49
Multiple-management programs, 432–433
Multiple predictors approach, 188–189
Mutual recruitment, 110–111

National Association of Suggestion Systems (NASS), 368
National Distillers & Chemical Corporation, 226

National Education Association (NEA), 554, 568
National Institute for Occupational Safety and Health (NIOSH), 84, 525, 526
National Labor Relations Act (NLRA-1935), 250, 252, 255, 388, 558, 559–560, 576, 593
National Labor Relations Board (NLRB), 250, 252, 255, 558, 561–562, 599, 614
  major function of, 572–573
  in the 1980s, 640
  in union elections, 572–577
National Mediation Board, 557–558
National Railway Adjustment Board, 558
National Safety Council, 519
National unions, 570
Nationwide Insurance Company, 163, 199, 456
Needs, employee, 87
Negative behavioral control strategy, 315–316
Negative settlement range, 596
Negotiating, 588–627
  careers and, 624
  case study, 622–624
  committees for, 601
  critical issues in, 592, 618–620
  effectiveness of, 617
  issues for, 602–608
  structure for, 601–602
Netherlands, the, 330
Networks, 468
New Breed, the, 53, 63–64
New York Times, The, 129
New York Typographical Union, 55
Nominal grouping technique (NGT), 48–49
Non-contributory program, 391
Nonexempt employees, 281, 282, 336
Nonverbal cues, 171
No-risk standards, 526
Northrop Corporation, 466
Northwest Airlines, Inc., 506
Northwestern National Bank, 167
Norton Company, 64
Not in civilian labor force, defined, 58
Nucor Corporation, 369–370

Obesity, discrimination due to, 152
Objective appraisal forms, 277–278
Occupational accidents, 521–522, 536–538
  factors affecting, 527–528
Occupational Classification System, 61
Occupational diseases, 522, 538–539
  categories of, 528
  factors affecting, 528–531
Occupational groups at risk, 530
Occupational safety and health, *see* Safety and health
Occupational Safety and Health Act (1970), 18, 250, 252, 524–526
Occupational Safety and Health Administration (OSHA), 518–519, 520, 522, 525–526, 528, 534–541, 607
Office automation, 505
Office design, 505–506
Office Hazards: How Your Job Can Make Sick (Makower), 531
Office of Federal Contract Compliance Programs (OFCCP), 109, 115, 118, 120, 157
Off-the-job payments, 395
Off-the-job training programs (OFFJT), 433, 436

One-shot syndrome, 361
On-the-job payments, 395
On-the-job training programs (OJT), 431–432, 436
Operational efficiency, 429
Operational level, 19
Order effects, 170
Organizational change, 532–533
Organizational climate analysis, 423
Organizational context, information about, 163–164
Organizational forms, 52–54
Organizational needs analysis, 422–423
Organizational restyling, 495–498
Organizational stress, 522, 532, 540
Organizational surveys, 229–232
Organizational-level incentive plans, 370–371
Orientation programs, 220–222
  handbooks for, 220, 221
Oshiver v. Court of Common Pleas, 277
Outcome attractiveness, 307
Outward Bound, 428, 431, 435
Owens-Illinois Company, 163

Painters & Allied Trades Union, 397
Paired comparison method, 280
Panel interviews, 168
Paper-and-pencil achievement tests, 175
Parke, Davis and Company, 167
Participative communication behavior, 234
Parttime workers, defined, 59
PATCO, 615, 619
Patterned interviews, 168
Patterson v. American Tobacco, 162
Pay, *see* Compensation
Pay administration practices, 349–350
Pay equity, 349
Pay for time not worked, 395–396
Pay level, 349
Payne v. Western & A.R.R. Co., 249
Pay secrecy, 349
Pay structure, basic, 338–346
Peer appraisal, 285
Pensions, 388–389, 606, 638
PepsiCo Inc., 399
Perfectly negative validity, 191
Perfectly positive validity, 191
Performance appraisal and evaluation, 270–297
  careers and, 275, 278, 295, 457
  case study, 294
  communicating with employees and, 219
  compensation and, 334
  critical issues in, 274, 292–292
  defined, 275
  importance of, 275–276
  the law and, 276–278
  in the 1980s, 636
  purposes of, 275–276
  rights of employees and, 250
  selection and placement and, 156
  as a set of processes and procedures, 278–290
  training and development and, 417
Performance appraisal forms, 276–284
Performance appraisal processes and procedures (PAPPs), 290–291

Performance-based pay, 358–380
  administrative issues in, 371–372
  careers and, 378
  case study, 377–378
  critical issues in, 361–362, 394–395
  effectiveness of plans, 373
  evaluating, 372–374
  importance of, 363–364
  incentive pay plans, 362, 364–365
    types of, 367–371
  merit pay plans, 362, 364, 365–367
  systems of, 362–365
Performance contracts, 636
Performance criteria, 279
Performance shares, 368
Performance standards, 279
Permanent part-time (PPT), 137–138
Permissive issues, 602
Perry v. Sindermann, 251
Personal appraisal, 457
Personal competence test, 174
Personality inventories, 175–176
Person needs analysis, 423–424
Personnel department, 21–26
  budgets of, 26
  career paths in, list of, 660–661
  certification and, 28
  hierarchy in, 21–22
  jobs in, 26–28
    list of, 660–661
  list of activities of, 659
  manager relationship, 111
  organizing, 21–24
  professionalism in, 27–28
  qualities of the staff, 25–26
  roles in, 19–20
  staffing, 14, 15–16, 25–26
Personnel files, 253
Personnel management, see Effective personnel management (EPM)
Personnel planning, see Effective personnel planning (EPP)
Petermann v. International Brotherhood of Teamsters, 251
Physical fitness benefits, 395–396
Piecework plans, 367
Placement, see Selection and placement
Planning, see Effective personnel planning (EPP)
Plant closing notification, 255–256, 259–260
Point rating method, 341–343
Polaroid Corporation, 86, 414
Population, characteristics in the 1980s, 57–60
Position analysis questionnaire (PAQ), 91, 92, 94
Positive behavioral control strategy, 315
Positive settlement range, 596
Pratt & Whitney, 360
Predictive validity, 193
Predictor approaches, 187–189
Predictor rates, 191, 196–197
Predictors, 164
Preelection campaigns, 575–577
Preference tests, 176
Pregnancy Discrimination Act (1978), 389
Preretirement counseling, 51, 55–56, 637
Preventive strategies, 316–317
Price rates, 344

Primacy effects, 170
Privacy Act (1974), 254–255
Privacy rights, 254–255, 256
Private employment agencies, 126–127
Private protection programs, 392–395
Proactive training, 435
Proctor & Gamble Company, 470
Production standards, 607
Productivity, 7, 8, 74, 480–514
  careers and, 512
  case study, 510–512
  communicating with employees and, 214, 215, 235
  crisis in, 10
  critical issues in, 484, 508–509
  defined, 485
  evaluating programs for, 507–508
  importance of, 485–487
  indicators of, 12
  job design and, 78, 79
  in the 1980s, 639
  performance-based pay and, 363
  programs for, 499–507
  purposes of, 485–487
  quality of work life and, 218
  relationships of, 488–491
  statistics on, 330
  unionization of employees and, 557
Productivity, 6
Productivity bargaining, 600
Professional certification, 28
Profit sharing, 360–361, 370
  in Japan, 360
Programed instruction (PI), 433–434
Progressive discipline procedures, 254
Prohibited issues, 602
  communicating, 253
Promotions, 122
  decision for, 199–201
  equal employment opportunity and, 152
  the impending squeeze in, 632
  success without, 459
  tips on, 468
  types of, 200
Protection programs, 389–395
  private, 392–395
  public, 389–392
Provident National Bank, 424
Provider role, the, 19–20
Prudential Life Insurance Company, 399–400
Psychological contract, 562
Psychological Corporation, The, 28
Psychomotor tests, 173–174
Public employment agencies, 125–126
Public protection programs, 389–392
Public sector
  collective bargaining in, 614–618
  strikes in, 614–618, 619
Pygmalion effect, 223

Qualitative overload, 80
Qualitative underload, 80
Quality circles (QCs), 18, 229, 492–494

Quality of work life (QWL), 8–9, 18, 78, 480–514
  careers and, 512
  case studies, 498–499, 510–512
  communicating with employees and, 235–236
  critical issues in, 484, 508–509
  defined, 485
  evaluating programs for, 507–508
  in the future, 64
  importance of, 485–487
  indicators of, 12–13
  job analysis and, 79, 489
  job design and, 78, 79
  job evaluation and, 489
  low, 522, 531–532
  in the 1980s, 639
  performance-based pay and, 363
  productivity and, 218
  programs for, 491–499
  purposes of, 485–487
  relationships of, 488–491
  safety and health and, 490, 524, 526
  unionization of employees and, 557
Quantitative overload, 80
Quantitative underload, 80
Questionnaires
  management position description, 91, 93, 94
  position analysis, 91, 92, 94
  surveys by, 231–232
Quotas for recruitment, 115–116

Race, labor force distribution by, 58
Racial discrimination, 114–122, 152–153, 157–158, 186, 253, 257–258
Radio, recruitment and, 129, 130
Railway Labor Act (1926), 557–558
Range of validity, 191
Ranking method, 279–280, 340
RCA Corporation, 492
Reality shock, 465
Recency-of-events error, 170, 288
Recognition tests, 175
Recruitment, 106–148
  activities of, 110–122
  careers and, 130–133, 144
  case study, 141–144
  compensation and, 334
  critical issues in, 100, 139–140
  defined, 110
  evaluating, 138–139
  goals of, 115
  importance of, 111–112
  the law and, 114–122
  mutual, 110–111
  in the 1980s, 634–635
  purposes of, 111–112
  quotas for, 115–116
  relationships of, 112–114
  training and development and, 417–418
  See also Job applicants
Redundancy planning, 55
Redundant workers, 51
Reference verification, 178
Regressions, linear, 49

Rehabilitation Act (1973), 156–157, 178, 202, 244, 255
Reinforcement, 429–430
Reliability of tests, 195–196
Religious discrimination, 249, 559
Relocation, 101, 132–133
Replacement charts, 49–50
Research, 29–30, 290
Research journals, list of, 663–664
Resistance point, 596
Résumé, preparing, 466, 667–669
Retaliation, 259
Retirement, 62, 64, 388–391, 638
  preretirement counseling, 51, 55–56, 637
Retirement benefits, 392
Rights of employees, 242–267
  careers and, 247, 265–266
  case study, 264–265
  critical issues in, 245–246, 261–262
  evaluating, 260–261
  importance of, 246–248
  on the job, 246, 254–260
  to job security, 246, 250–254
  the law and, 250–256
  in the 1980s, 635–636
  purposes of, 246–248
  relationships of, 248–250
  unionization of employees and, 556–557
  union-management relations and, 248
Right-to-work, 556, 561
RMI Company, 226–227
Robinson v. Union Carbide Corporation, 200
Robots, 6, 61–62
Rockwell International Corporation, 499
Roger v. International Paper Co., 277
Role playing, 434
Rowe v. General Motors, 75, 200, 277

S. C. Johnson & Son Inc., 638
Safety and health, 516–547
  benefits of, 521–522
  careers and, 545
  case study, 544–545
  communicating with employees and, 218
  costs of, 521–522
  critical issues in, 520, 542–543
  evaluating, 540–541
  importance of, 521–522
  the law and, 524–526
  model of, 522
  physiological/physical conditions, 521
  preventable aspect of, 522
  psychological conditions, 521
  quality of work life and, 490, 524, 526
  rates of, 534–536
  relationships of, 522–524
  sources of, 526–534
  strategies for improvement in, 534–540
  union-management relations and, 607
Salaries, *see* Compensation
Salary compression, 637
Salary surveys, 345–346
Sales incentive plans, 367–368
Samsonite Company, 539

Satisfaction, employee, 87
Scanlon plan, 370–371
Schools, recruitment and, 125, 129
Scientific approach in job design, 83, 85
Scott Paper Company, 424
Sears, Roebuck & Company, 114, 200, 456, 458, 470
Security Pacific Bank, 466
Selection and placement, 150–208
    application blanks for, 177–178
    assessment center approach, 189
    benefits of, 198
    careers and, 158–159, 160, 162, 171, 178, 181, 195, 198, 206
    case studies, 180, 205–206
    costs of, 198
    criteria for evaluation, 164, 190–198
    critical issues in, 153, 202–203
    decision for, 198–201
    defined, 154
    evaluating procedures of, 202
    importance of, 154
    information for, 162–178
        obtaining, 164–178
    interviews, 165–173
    the law and, 152–153, 156–162
    multiple predictors approach, 188–189
    in the 1980s, 635
    purposes of, 154
    relationships of, 154–156
    single predictor approach, 187–188
    tests for, 160–161, 173–177
        reliability of, 195–196
Selection ratios, 191, 197–198
Self-appraisal, 285
Semiautonomous work groups, 494–495
Seniority, 607
Sensitivity, increased, 228
Sensitivity training, 434–435
Sentry Insurance Company, 539
Settlement range, 596
Severance pay, 606
Severity rate, 536
Sex, labor force distribution by, 58, 59
Sex-typing, 59, 60, 61, 132
Sexual discrimination, 114–122, 157, 160, 186, 247, 253, 339
Sexual harassment, 157, 249, 256–259
Short-term level, 19
Short-time compensation (STC), 55
Sick leave, 606
Sickness insurance, 393
Significant risks, 526
Simple linear regression, 49
Simulation tests, 175
Single predictor approach, 187–188
Skill based evaluation, 344
Skills, 59, 87, 431, 437
    basic, 414–416
    categories of, 424–425
    in communicating with employees, 217, 255–229
    development of, 428–429
Skill variety, 80
Social Security Act (1935), 388–391
Social values in the 1980s, 62–64
Society, changes in, 10–11

Sociopsychological work environment, 522, 523, 539–540
    strategies for, 541
Sociotechnical approach, 501
Solar Turbine Company, 492
Southern California Edison Company, 466
Specialists
    accreditation of, 28
    qualities of, 26
Specifications, job, 76–77, 91
Spurlock v. United Airlines, 161
Staffing, 105–208
    effective personnel planning and, 45
    in the 1980s, 634–635
    productivity and, 488
    quality of work life and, 488
    rights of employees and, 249
    safety and health and, 523
    unionization of employees and, 556
    See also types of staffing
Standard hour plans, 367
Standard Oil of Ohio, 200, 470
Standard résumé, 466
State Street Bank and Trust Company, 414
Statistical projections, 48, 49
Stereotyping, sex-role, 59, 60, 61, 132
Stewards, 571
Stimulation, 434
Stock options, 368
Straight ranking approach, 279–280
Strategic level, 19
Stress
    career, 459–461
    organizational, 522, 532, 540
Stress interviews, 168
Strictness, error of, 288
Strikes, 607, 608–609
    in the public sector, 614–618, 619
    wildcat, 611, 613
Stringfellow v. Monsanto Corp., 276
Structured interviews, 168
Subjective appraisal forms, 277
Subordinates
    appraisal by, 285
    defined, 275
    problems with, 288
Suggestion systems, 368
Superiors
    defined, 275
    performance appraisal by, 285
    problems with, 287–288
Supervisory assistance, 433
Supplemental unemployment benefits (SUB), 395, 606
Supportive communication behavior, 234–235
Supportive environment, 596
Sweden, 88, 330, 495, 531, 594–595
Switzerland, 330
Systems Research Institute, 414

Taft-Hartley Act, see Labor-Management Relations Act (1947)
Target point, 596
Tarrytown project, 498–499, 507
Task
    changes in, 500–504

Task (cont.)
conflict, 310
identity, 80
overload, 80
significance, 80
uncertainty, 310
underload, 80
Team contemporary approach in job design, 83, 84, 85
Teamsters v. United States, 162
Technologies, 61–62, 74, 75, 88
Television, recruitment and, 129, 130
Temporary help agencies, 125, 127
Tenneco Company, 15
Termination-at-will rule, 248, 249
Termination for good cause, 251
Termination for just cause, 251
Tests, 160–161, 173–177, 195–196
See also types of tests
Texas Department of Community Affairs v. Joyce Ann Burdine, 160
Textile Workers Union v. Lincoln Mills, 561
Theory, 29–30
Theory A management, 496
Theory J management, 496
Theory Z (Ouchi), 488
Theory Z management, 495, 496
Time studies, 95
Timex Company, 371
Tooley v. Martin-Marietta Corp., 559
Total compensation, 329–356
basic pay structure, 338–346
careers and, 354–355
case study, 353–354
critical issues in, 332, 351–352
wage and salary administration, 347–350
defined, 332
environmental impact on, 334–338
evaluating, 350–351
importance of, 333
the law and, 334–337
in the 1980s, 636–637
purposes of, 333
relationships of, 334
Toussaint v. Blue Cross/Blue Shield, 251
Trade associations, recruitment and, 125, 128, 129
Trade journals
list of, 664–665
recruitment and, 130
Traditional organization form, 53, 54
Training and development, 412–449, 637
careers and, 445, 456
case study, 444–445
critical issues in, 416, 441–442
determining needs and targets, 422–425
evaluating programs, 427–441
implementing programs, 425–437
importance of, 417
the law and, 421–422
in the 1980s, 638
purpose of, 417
quality of work life and, 489–490
relationships of, 417–421
rights of employees and, 249
safety and health and, 524

Transfers, 122, 123, 635
decision for, 199–201
types of, 200
True worth, 337
TRW Inc., 398, 482, 540
Turnovers, 304, 312
costs of, 305, 306
rate of, 304

Underload, task, 80
Unemployed, defined, 58
Unemployment compensation, 391
Unemployment rate, defined, 59
Unfair representation, 561–562, 614
Uniform Guidelines, 160–162, 192, 194, 195–196
Uniform Guidelines on Employee Selection Procedures, 157, 158, 159
Union Carbide Corporation, 10, 132–133
Unionization of employees, 550–586
attraction of, 562–566
careers and, 564–566, 570–571, 579, 584
case study, 583
communicating with employers and, 556
critical issues in, 554, 580–581
defined, 554
development of, 566–572
evaluating, 580
importance of, 554–555
the law and, 557–562
the organizing campaign, 572–579
purposes of, 554–555
relationships of, 556–557
rights of employees and, 556–557
state of, 566–572
structure of, 570–571
Unionizing, defined, 554
Union locals, 570
Union-management relations, 549–627
in collective bargaining, 593–595
strategies in, 600–601
communicating with employees and, 218–219
compensation and, 334
evaluating, 617–618
in job design, 89
managing, 14, 18
in the 1980s, 639–641
quality of work life and, 490–491
rights of employees and, 248
safety and health and, 524
Unions, 244, 346, 397–398, 570
background data on, 566–569
civil rights and, 118
compensation and, 337
decertification of, 553
decision to join, 562–565
decision not to join, 565–566
defined, 554
discrimination and, 162
elections of, 572–577
in Japan, 571
membership in, 567–569
need for, 552
in the 1980s, 640

operations of, 572
procedures in contract
 administration, 613–614
quality circles and, 493
recruitment and, 125, 128
redundancy planning and, 55
strategies in collective bargaining, 599–600
women in, 571
Union security, 606
Union shop, 556
Uniroyal Inc., 394, 603, 604
United Automobile Workers (UAW), 300, 316, 398, 490, 498, 570, 571, 572, 573, 601, 604, 606
United Farm Workers, 573–574
United Food and Commercial Workers Union, 640
United Mine Workers, 559
United Rubber Workers, 605
U.S. Bureau of Labor, 364
U.S. Bureau of Labor Statistics, 330
U.S. Chamber of Commerce, 9, 415, 525
U.S. Constitution, 115, 121, 157
U.S. Defense Department, 49
U.S. Immigration and Naturalization Service, 129
U.S. Internal Revenue Service (IRS), 398
U.S. Justice Department, 115, 157, 562
U.S. Labor Department, 10, 59, 60, 108, 111, 115, 129, 157, 219, 422, 432
U.S.A. v. City of Chicago (1978), 75, 200, 276
U.S. State Department, 49, 129
U.S. Steel Corporation, 226
U.S. Supreme Court, 255–256, 561–562, 576, 602
 on civil rights, 118, 119, 158, 162
 on compensation, 335, 337, 384, 388, 389
 list of decisions by, 653–657
 on safety and health, 525–526
 See also names of cases
U.S. Training and Employment Service (USTES), 126
United Steelworkers of American, 118, 484, 526
United Steelworkers of America, AFL-CIO v. Marshall, 526
United Technologies Corporation, 360
United Transportation Union, 605
University of Michigan Survey Research Center, 555
University Research Corporation, 272
Upward communication, 223, 225
Upward mobility, 452

Vacations, paid, 606
Validity, 191–194
Valid predictors, 187
Vangas Inc., 393–394
Vertical loading, 84
Vested rights, 388
Vietnam Era Veterans Readjustment Act (1974), 157, 255
Vocational Rehabilitation Act (1973), 119–120

W. R. Grace & Company, 128
W. W. Cross v. National Labor Relations Board, 388
Wage and salary administration, 347–350
Wage-dividend plans, 370
Wage rates, 344
Wages, *see* Compensation
Wage surveys, 337–338, 345–346
Wagner Act, *see* National Labor Relations Act (NLRA-1935)
Wall Street Journal, 129
Walsh-Healey Public Contract Act (1936), 335
Walt Disney Productions, 6
Ward Howell International, 127
Weahkee v. Perry, 219
Weber case, 118, 119, 562
Weighted check list, 280–281
Wellness tests, 540
Western Electric Company, 424, 539
West Germany, 10, 330, 504, 531, 594–595
Westinghouse Electric Corporation, 8, 371, 492
Whirlpool Corp. v. Marshall, 250
Wildcat strikes, 611, 613
Wilderness training, 435
Women
 blue-collar, 85–86
 discrimination against, 114–122, 157, 160, 186, 247, 253, 339
 harassment of, 157, 249, 256–259
 special programs for, 435
 in unions, 571
Work, values toward, 63–64
Work arrangements, alternative, 133–138
Work environment
 improving, 14, 18
 in the 1980s, 638–639
 physical, 522, 523
 strategies for, 541
 sociopsychological, 522, 523, 539–540
 strategies for, 541
Worker compensation insurance, 393
Worker-job interface, 75
Workers' Compensation Act (1911), 393
Workers' Compensation Institute, 394
Work flow, 502
Working relationships, 14, 16
Work measurement, 95
Work overload, 534
Work pace, 533
Work sample tests, 175
Work sampling, 95–96
Work schedules, standard, 134–135
Work standards approach, 284
Work weeks, compressed, 136
Worth, comparable, 330–331, 336–337

Xerox Corporation, 22–24, 199, 414, 456, 488, 540

Yugoslavia, 594–595